F. R. LaMacchia

READINGS IN POLITICAL
PHILOSOPHY

THE MACMILLAN COMPANY
NEW YORK · BOSTON · CHICAGO · DALLAS
ATLANTA · SAN FRANCISCO

MACMILLAN AND CO., Limited
LONDON · BOMBAY · CALCUTTA · MADRAS
MELBOURNE

THE MACMILLAN COMPANY
OF CANADA, Limited
TORONTO

READINGS

in

POLITICAL PHILOSOPHY

By

FRANCIS WILLIAM COKER

Alfred Cowles Professor of Government, Yale University

REVISED AND ENLARGED EDITION

New York

THE MACMILLAN COMPANY

PREFACE TO REVISED EDITION

This enlargement and revision consists of the following items: the addition of selections from Cicero's *Republic* and *Laws*, St. Augustine's *City of God*, John of Salisbury's *Policraticus*, Nicholas of Cusa's *De concordantia catholica*, and Martin Luther's *Concerning Good Works, Open Letter to the Christian Nobility of the German Nation*, and *Concerning Secular Authority;* an extension of the selections from Aristotle and Locke, to include their discussions of private property; a revision of the translation of Marsiglio of Padua's *Defensor pacis;* and a revision of the introductions and bibliographical lists. As with the selections in the original edition, so with these, the space allotments for the several authors cannot be taken as a measure of the relative importance of the authors. The translation from the *De concordantia catholica* would have been impossible without the guidance and correction generously supplied by my colleagues, Professors Edmund T. Silk, and Roland H. Bainton; by Mrs. Anne-Marie Holborn; and by Mr. LeRoy A. Campbell, Martin Kellogg Fellow in Classical Languages, Yale University.

I am indebted to the Ohio State University Press and to Professors George H. Sabine and Stanley B. Smith for permission to use their translation of Cicero's *Republic*, and to the Harvard University Press for the selections from Professor Clinton Walker Keyes' translation of the *Laws;* to Charles Scribner's Sons for the selections from Rev. Marcus Dods' translation of the *City of God;* to F. S. Crofts & Co. for the selections from Dr. John Dickinson's translation of the *Policraticus;* to the A. J. Holman Co. for the selections from the *Works of Martin Luther;* and to the Cambridge University Press for permission to make the translation from the text of the *Defensor pacis* edited by Professor C. W. Previté-Orton. I am also indebted to Mrs. Marion S. MacKay for her careful assistance in the preparation of manuscript for the printer.

NEW HAVEN, CONN.   F. W. C.
February, 1938.

v

PREFACE TO FIRST EDITION

In guiding college classes in the study of political theories the writer has found that the interest of students is manifested more naturally and fruitfully when they read directly from original works than when they rely solely upon historical and expository treatises. For many important works this reading at first-hand is not generally practicable, because they are not in libraries accessible to most readers, or because they are not available in satisfactory translations. The aim of this volume is to furnish a handy collection of readings from foremost political philosophers. In furtherance of this design it has seemed wise to include substantial parts of a few preëminent works rather than to cover a wide range of writings with brief passages from each. It is believed that reading according to the former, rather than the latter, plan will give the student the more realistic impression, and the more effective command, of fundamental political ideas, and will lead him to a more coherent, if less detailed, view of the evolution of political thought. In order to confine the matter within a single volume writers later than Bentham have been omitted; in this period, speaking generally, philosophical discussions of politics either are exhaustive disquisitions upon fragments of the subject (e.g. Thomas Hill Green) or they form subordinate parts of comprehensive systems of thought (e.g. Auguste Comte); for a volume of readings from works of the nineteenth century, a plan of selection somewhat different from that followed in this work would be necessary.

The primary purpose of this work will be fulfilled if it supplies helpful illustrations for such general histories of political philosophy as those by Dunning, Pollock, Janet, Willoughby and Bluntschli. These and other general treatises, besides special works of exposition and criticism, are cited in references appended to each selection. The lists of references are obviously not exhaustive. They are intended to guide the reader to the particular works to which he may most profitably go for full discussions; so that for each selection he may obtain a setting and interpretation more satisfactory than is provided by the slight introductions of this volume.   The topics in the table of contents are headings supplied by the writer for his subdivisions of each selection.

For the purpose of this volume entirely original translations were required only for the selections from St. Thomas Aquinas, Marsiglio of Padua, and the *Vindiciæ contra Tyrannos*.   The translations from Bodin and Grotius are in part original.   The passages from Bodin's *De Republica* were translated with constant assistance from the Knolles translation of Bodin's French version of the work.   For the *De Jure Belli ac Pacis* of Grotius the Latin text was carefully worked over in order to revise the translation by Whewell.   For all other selections the translations or editions cited were followed faithfully, with minor changes in a few instances.

The writer desires to make grateful acknowledgment for assistance that has been received in the preparation of this volume. Professor William A. Dunning, of Columbia University, has generously supplied expert advice and criticism in all parts of the work, especially in the translations.   Professor Edward G. Elliott, of Princeton University, contributed valuable counsel as to the general plan and scope of the work.

The writer is indebted to Messrs. G. P. Putnam's Sons for the privilege of using the passages from Conway's edition of *The Writings of Thomas Paine,* and to the Delegates of the Clarendon Press for the selections from Montague's edition of Bentham's *Fragment on Government* and from Church's edition of Book I of Hooker's *Ecclesiastical Polity.*

June 26, 1914.

CONTENTS

ix

INTRODUCTION

Dominant interest in the study of political questions is usually in practical or technical aspects of the study. Many practical and technical political problems require for their solution, however, reasoning in terms of general theory. Whatever our formal laws and precedents may be, and however fully and precisely we may record, systematize, and compare our observations of experience, we cannot speak intelligently of the success or failure of this or that governmental device, or of the justification of the state's entrance into some new sphere of action, until we attain somewhat clear ideas as to what in general we expect to accomplish through the agency of civil government. This is a plea not for merely abstract speculation, but rather for a neglected side of practical reflection concerning our expectations from political action. Discussions of practical questions of government are generally impractical unless the argument proceeds from and tends toward general propositions as to the character and province of government.

Why do we have political government? What in our present condition do we owe to it? What future advantages may we properly expect from it? What are its best forms? Who should control it? What is its proper relation to the ideas and sentiments of the people? What spheres of individual and social life is it incompetent to enter beneficially? Numerous writers have sought to answer these questions in abstract terms. In other words, their answers, although in many instances strongly influenced by an interest in special cases within their view, have been intended as statements of general truth, conceived apart from such cases.

The study of the reasoning on such questions is the study of political philosophy. Obviously, advocates of this study should not rest its claims for attention upon any pretension that it can alone supply the key to the solution of political problems of our time. As with other historical and philosophical studies, its objects are chiefly intellectual, not technical. A review of the political thought of the past can not provide us with a complete and definite political creed for the present. Such a study, however, has practical value in so far as it helps to form habits of more thorough and candid examination of the meaning and tendency of our political undertakings.

Political philosophy is as old as organized political society. Even among primitive peoples the wielders of political power usually have to depend on some kind of general justification or explanation of the demands they make upon the allegiance of their subjects. The extant documents from the literature of the most ancient civilizations contain occasional discussions of the duties of political rulers, the obligations of subjects, and the criteria by which governmental forms and methods should be appraised. In writings prior to those of the Greeks of fourth-century Athens, however, theoretical reflection on such matters usually holds only a very limited place. The discussion sometimes appears as a brief addition to some record or description of actual laws and regulations, or as incidental to some more general ethical or philosophical inquiry. Ancient oriental writers commonly assumed that existing forms and policies of government were sufficiently sanctioned by religion or tradition; when they discussed political topics, they were usually more concerned with the personal virtues or vices of rulers than with the general nature of government.[1]

The Greeks looked more philosophically on man's social life. The active intercommunication between a number of small city-states, and the frequent transformations passed through by each, supplied from experience a stimulus to comparative and critical analysis of political institutions and practices. In the vigorous cultural and political life of the classical period of Greek history,

---

[1] For illustrations of political discussion in ancient oriental writings, see C. F. Horne, ed., *Sacred Books and Early Literature of the East*, 14 vols. (1917), Vols. I–III, V, VII, IX, XI; James Legge, ed., *The Chinese Classics*, 5 vols. in 8 (1861–72), Vols. I, II. See also Kuo-Cheng Wu, *Ancient Chinese Political Theories* (1928); Elbert D. Thomas, *Chinese Political Thought* (1927); William S. A. Pott, *Chinese Political Philosophy* (1925); Narendra N. Law, *Aspects of Ancient Indian Polity* (1921); B. K. Sarkar, *Political Institutions and Theories of the Hindus* (1922); Upandranath Ghoshal, *History of Hindu Political Theories* (1923); Beni Prasad, *Theory of Government in Ancient India* (Allahabad, 1927); Raymond G. Gettell, *History of Political Thought* (1924), ch. 2; Westel W. Willoughby, *Political Theories of the Ancient World* (1903), chs. 2–3; Paul Janet, *Histoire de la science politique dans ses relations avec la morale*, 2 vols. (fifth ed., 1925), Vol. I, pp. 1–51.

great philosophers of Athens elaborately explored political questions that we still consider basically significant, and in terms that we still widely accept.[1] The study of the historical background of our own political thought may very properly begin with Plato. Since Plato's time there have appeared, in every philosophic age of the western world, significant discussions of the general justification of political organization, the relative merits of different governmental forms and policies, and the appropriate position and privileges of individual man as subject, member, or master of a political society.

The purpose of this volume is to make more accessible, for reading at first-hand, significant parts of some of the greater writings in political philosophy. By supplying illustrative materials the volume may serve to supplement, and at points vivify, general works in the history and exposition of political theory. The space allotted to the several writers could not, for obvious reasons, be measured by their relative importance. In a brief introduction preceding each selection an attempt is made to indicate important points of the writer's contribution to the development of political thought; and following each selection there is a list of works in which the writer's doctrines are authoritatively interpreted.

[1] On the beginnings of political philosophy in Greece, see Charles H. McIlwain, *Growth of Political Thought in the West* (1932), ch. 1; George H. Sabine, *History of Political Theory* (1937), chs. 1-2; Ernest Barker, *Plato and His Predecessors* (2d ed., 1925), chs. 1, 3, 4; Thomas I. Cook, *History of Political Philosophy* (1936), ch. 2; Westel W. Willoughby, *Political Theories of the Ancient World* (1903), ch. 4; William A. Dunning, *Political Theories, Ancient and Mediæval* (1902), ch. 2, §1.

GENERAL HISTORIES OF POLITICAL THOUGHT

Carlyle, R. W. and A. J., *A History of Mediæval Political Theory in the West*, 6 vols. (Edinburgh and London, 1908–36).
Cook, Thomas I., *A History of Political Philosophy from Plato to Burke* (New York, 1936).
Dunning, William A., *Political Theories, Ancient and Mediæval* (New York, 1902).
Dunning, William A., *Political Theories, from Luther to Montesquieu* (New York, 1905).
Dunning, William A., *Political Theories, from Rousseau to Spencer* (New York, 1920).
Gettell, Raymond G., *A History of Political Thought* (New York, 1924).
Gierke, Otto, *Political Theories of the Middle Ages*, translated by F. W. Maitland (Cambridge, 1900).
Hearnshaw, F. J. C., ed., *The Social and Political Ideas of Some Great Mediæval Thinkers* (London, 1923); *The Social and Political Ideas of Some Great Thinkers of the Renaissance and Reformation* (London, 1925); *The Social and Political Ideas of Some Great Thinkers of the Sixteenth and Seventeenth Centuries* (London, 1926); *The Social and Political Ideas of Some Great English Thinkers of the Augustan Age, A.D. 1650–1750* (London, 1928); *The Social and Political Ideas of Some Great French Thinkers of the Age of Reason* (London, 1930); *Social and Political Ideas of the Revolutionary Era* (London, 1931); *Social and Political Ideas of the Victorian Age* (London, 1933).
McIlwain, Charles H., *The Growth of Political Thought in the West from the Greeks to the End of the Middle Ages* (London, 1932).
Pollock, Sir Frederick, *An Introduction to the History of the Science of Politics* (revised ed., London, 1911).
Sabine, George H., *A History of Political Theory* (New York, 1937).
Willoughby, Westel W., *The Political Theories of the Ancient World* (New York, 1903).

Bluntschli, Johann Kaspar, *Geschichte der neueren Statswissenschaft, allgemeines Statsrechts und Politik* (third ed., Munich and Leipsic, 1881).
Gumplowicz, Ludwig, *Geschichte der Staatstheorien* (Innsbrück, 1905).
Janet, Paul, *Histoire de la science politique dans ses rapports avec la morale*, 2 vols. (fifth ed., Paris, 1925).
Mohl, Robert von, *Die Geschichte und Literatur der Staatswissenschaften*, 3 vols. (Erlangen, 1855–58).
Rehm, Hermann, *Geschichte der Staatsrechtswissenschaft* (Freiburg and Leipsic, 1896), in Heinrich von Marquardsen and Max von Seydel, eds., *Handbuch von Oeffentlichen Rechts der Gegenwart*, Vols. I–II.

PLATO

I. PLATO (B.C. 427-347)

INTRODUCTION

The life of Plato is not known in great detail. Born of an aristocratic Athenian family, he lived during an era of political turbulence and degeneration in Athens: it was the period of the Peloponnesian War, the ensuing wars in northern Greece, and the beginning of the Macedonian invasion. He was a disciple and friend of Socrates, whose trial and death occurred during Plato's early manhood and whose doctrines are known to us principally through Plato's writings. Throughout the last fifty years of his life Plato was lecturer and teacher to a small group of pupils, who met at a pleasure-grove, called "Academe," in the vicinity of Athens. The school there originated was perpetuated by his disciples as a permanent "philosophical school for lectures, study, and friendly meetings of studious men;" [1] whence the philosophic successors of Plato are called "Academicians" or, collectively, the "Greek Academy."

The basis of Plato's philosophical system is Socrates' doctrine of reality. According to this doctrine, reality inheres only in the ideas of things—that is, in the perfect, permanent, immutable, self-existent entities which underlie the changing and imperfect objects of perception; the latter are merely the superficial appearances of things. Plato interpreted and developed this theory and its ethical application in the identification of virtue with knowledge of absolute reality. All of his writings are in the form of "dialogues": critical and argumentative conversations which are represented as having taken place between a principal speaker, who is Socrates in most of the dialogues, and other associates and friends of Plato.

The state constitutes a cardinal concept in Plato's general philosophy. To him, political theory was an essential part of

[1] George Grote, *Plato and the Other Companions of Socrates* (second ed., 1867), Vol. I, p. 133.

1

general philosophy: knowledge of the perfect life for man under ideal conditions was a characteristic aim of all philosophical inquiry; and an understanding of such a life could be attained only through an understanding of the relations that develop naturally among men, in the life of a political community.

Incidental discussions of questions we consider distinctively political appear in many of Plato's works.   Three of the dialogues are devoted mainly to the subject: the *Republic*, the *Statesman*, and the *Laws*.   The *Republic* is universally regarded as one of the greatest works of all times.   In this dialogue particularly the conception of the state is closely involved in a general philosophical, ethical, and social theory.   Plato is describing what a community must be if man within it is to realize fully his highest capacities. Thus the dialogue is concerned with projecting an ideal condition of society, and it is listed among the political "utopias"; but it is concerned also with criticism of an actual condition of society, and it is a work of great practical insight.   The *Statesman* and the *Laws*, probably written several decades after the *Republic*, present ideas which appear to be, in some important respects, sharply in contrast with the theory of the earlier work.   But there is no essential inconsistency.   The *Statesman* is concerned chiefly with the qualities of the true ruler, who must be an all-wise philosopher; and with his duties, which are primarily those of education and character-building.   Plato here concedes that no such perfect statesman is really available, and that in actual states there is no guaranty of good rule save in the supremacy of "the law" — embodied in the traditional public customs of the people.   This principle of the necessary subjection of government to law supplies the key to Plato's discrimination between good and bad forms of government.   In the *Laws*, Plato describes, at great length, a general constitutional scheme and detailed rules for the social, economic, and administrative arrangements of an actual community designed to approach as nearly as possible to the ideal set forth in the *Republic*.

The selections below are from the *Republic*.   The principal persons of the dialogue are Socrates (the narrator); Glaucon and Adeimantus, brothers of Plato; and Thrasymachus, a sophist philosopher of the time.   Adeimantus is speaking in the opening paragraph of the selection, and Socrates in the second.

READINGS FROM THE REPUBLIC [1]

1. *The Origin of the State* [2]

Let others praise justice and censure injustice, magnifying the rewards and honors of the one and abusing the other; that is a manner of arguing which, coming from them, I am ready to tolerate, but from you who have spent your whole life in the consideration of this question, unless I hear the contrary from your own lips, I expect something better. And therefore, I say, not only prove to us that justice is better than injustice, but show what they either of them do to the possessor of them, which makes the one to be a good and the other an evil, whether seen or unseen by gods and men.

I had always admired the genius of Glaucon and Adeimantus, but on hearing these words I was quite delighted, and said : Sons of an illustrious father, that was not a bad beginning of the Elegiac verses which the admirer of Glaucon made in honor of you after you had distinguished yourselves at the battle of Megara :

"Sons of Ariston," he sang, "divine offspring of an illustrious hero."

The epithet is very appropriate, for there is something truly divine in being able to argue as you have done for the superiority of injustice, and remaining unconvinced by your own arguments. And I do believe that you are not convinced — this I infer from your general character, for had I judged only from your speeches I should have mistrusted you. But now, the greater my confidence in you, the greater is my difficulty in knowing what to say. For I am in a strait between two ; on the one hand I feel that I am unequal to the task ; and my inability is brought home to me by the fact that you were not satisfied with the answer which I made to Thrasymachus, proving, as I thought, the superiority which justice has over injustice. And yet I cannot refuse to help, while breath and speech remain to me ; I am afraid that there would be an impiety in being present when justice is evil spoken of and not lifting up a hand in her defence. And therefore I had best give such help as I can.

Glaucon and the rest entreated me by all means not to let the question drop, but to proceed in the investigation. They wanted

[1] The selections are taken from *The Republic of Plato, translated into English*, by Benjamin Jowett, third edition, Oxford, 1888. Published by the Clarendon Press.

[2] II, 367–374. Jowett, pp. 47–56.

to arrive at the truth, first, about the nature of justice and injustice, and secondly, about their relative advantages. I told them, what I really thought, that the inquiry would be of a serious nature, and would require very good eyes. Seeing then, I said, that we are no great wits, I think that we had better adopt a method which I may illustrate thus: suppose that a short-sighted person had been asked by some one to read small letters from a distance; and it occurred to some one else that they might be found in another place which was larger and in which the letters were larger—if they were the same and he could read the larger letters first, and then proceed to the lesser—this would have been thought a rare piece of good fortune.

Very true, said Adeimantus; but how does the illustration apply to our inquiry?

I will tell you, I replied; justice, which is the subject of our inquiry, is, as you know, sometimes spoken of as the virtue of an individual, and sometimes as the virtue of a state.

True, he replied.

And is not a state larger than an individual?

It is.

Then in the larger the quantity of justice is likely to be larger and more easily discernible. I propose therefore that we inquire into the nature of justice and injustice, first as they appear in the state, and secondly in the individual, proceeding from the greater to the lesser and comparing them.

That, he said, is an excellent proposal.

And if we imagine the state in process of creation, we shall see the justice and injustice of the state in process of creation also.

I dare say.

When the state is completed there may be a hope that the object of our search will be more easily discovered.

Yes, far more easily.

But ought we to attempt to construct one? I said; for to do so, as I am inclined to think, will be a very serious task. Reflect therefore.

I have reflected, said Adeimantus, and am anxious that you should proceed.

A state, I said, arises, as I conceive, out of the needs of mankind; no one is self-sufficing, but all of us have many wants. Can any other origin of a state be imagined?

There can be no other.

Then, as we have many wants, and many persons are needed to supply them, one takes a helper for one purpose and another for another; and when these partners and helpers are gathered together in one habitation the body of inhabitants is termed a state.

True, he said.

And they exchange with one another, and one gives, and another receives, under the idea that the exchange will be for their good.

Very true.

Then, I said, let us begin and create in idea a state; and yet the true creator is necessity, who is the mother of our invention.

Of course, he replied.

Now the first and greatest of necessities is food, which is the condition of life and existence.

Certainly.

The second is a dwelling and the third clothing and the like.

True.

And now let us see how our city will be able to supply this great demand: We may suppose that one man is a husbandman, another a builder, some one else a weaver—shall we add to them a shoemaker, or perhaps some other purveyor to our bodily wants?

Quite right.

The barest notion of a state must include four or five men.

Clearly.

And how will they proceed? Will each bring the result of his labors into a common stock?—the individual husbandman, for example, producing for four, and laboring four times as long and as much as he need in the provision of food with which he supplies others as well as himself; or will he have nothing to do with others and not be at the trouble of producing for them, but provide for himself alone a fourth of the food in a fourth of the time, and in the remaining three-fourths of his time be employed in making a house or a coat or a pair of shoes, having no partnership with others, but supplying himself all his own wants?

Adeimantus thought that he should aim at producing food only and not at producing everything.

Probably, I replied, that would be the better way; and when I hear you say this, I am myself reminded that we are not all alike; there are diversities of natures among us which are adapted to different occupations.

Very true.

And will you have a work better done when the workman has many occupations, or when he has only one?

When he has only one.

Further, there can be no doubt that a work is spoiled when not done at the right time?

No doubt.

For business is not disposed to wait until the doer of the business is at leisure; but the doer must follow up what he is doing, and make the business his first object.

He must.

And if so, we must infer that all things are produced more plentifully and easily and of a better quality when one man does one thing which is natural to him and does it at the right time, and leaves other things.

Undoubtedly.

Then more than four citizens will be required; for the husbandman will not make his own plough or mattock, or other implements of agriculture, if they are to be good for anything. Neither will the builder make his tools—and he too needs many; and in like manner the weaver and shoemaker.

True.

Then carpenters, and smiths, and many other artisans, will be sharers in our little state, which is already beginning to grow?

True.

Yet even if we add neatherds, shepherds, and other herdsmen, in order that our husbandmen may have oxen to plough with, and builders as well as husbandmen may have draught cattle, and curriers and weavers fleeces and hides,—still our state will not be very large.

That is true; yet neither will it be a very small state which contains all these.

Then, again, there is the situation of the city—to find a place where nothing need be imported is well nigh impossible.

Impossible.

Then there must be another class of citizens who will bring the required supply from another city?

There must.

But if the trader goes empty-handed, having nothing which they require who would supply his need, he will come back empty-handed.

That is certain.

And therefore what they produce at home must be not only enough for themselves, but such both in quantity and quality as to accommodate those from whom their wants are supplied.

Very true.

Then more husbandmen and more artisans will be required?

They will.

Not to mention the importers and exporters, who are called merchants?

Yes.

Then we shall want merchants?

We shall.

And if merchandise is to be carried over the sea, skilful sailors will also be needed, and in considerable numbers?

Yes, in considerable numbers.

Then, again, within the city, how will they exchange their productions? To secure such an exchange was, as you will remember, one of our principal objects when we formed them into a society and constituted a state.

Clearly they will buy and sell.

Then they will need a market-place, and a money-token for purposes of exchange.

Certainly.

Suppose now that a husbandman, or an artisan, brings some production to market, and he comes at a time when there is no one to exchange with him,—is he to leave his calling and sit idle in the market-place?

Not at all; he will find people there who, seeing the want, undertake the office of salesmen. In well-ordered states they are commonly those who are the weakest in bodily strength, and therefore of little use for any other purpose; their duty is to be in the market, and to give money in exchange for goods to those who desire to sell and to take money from those who desire to buy.

This want, then, creates a class of retail-traders in our state. Is not "retailer" the term which is applied to those who sit in the market-place engaged in buying and selling, while those who wander from one city to another are called merchants?

Yes, he said.

And there is another class of servants, who are intellectually hardly on the level of companionship; still they have plenty of bodily strength for labor, which accordingly they sell, and are called, if I do not mistake, hirelings, hire being the name which is given to the price of their labor.

True.

Then hirelings will help to make up our population?

Yes.

And now, Adeimantus, is our state matured and perfected?

I think so.

Where, then, is justice, and where is injustice, and in what part of the state did they spring up?

Probably in the dealings of these citizens with one another. I cannot imagine that they are more likely to be found anywhere else.

I dare say that you are right in your suggestion, I said; we had better think the matter out, and not shrink from the inquiry.

Let us then consider, first of all, what will be their way of life, now that we have thus established them. Will they not produce corn, and wine, and clothes, and shoes, and build houses for themselves? And when they are housed, they will work, in summer, commonly, stripped and barefoot, but in winter substantially clothed and shod. They will feed on barley-meal and flour of wheat, baking and kneading them, making noble cakes and loaves; these they will serve up on a mat of reeds or on clean leaves, themselves reclining the while upon beds strewn with yew or myrtle. And they and their children will feast, drinking of the wine which they have made, wearing garlands on their heads, and hymning the praises of the gods, in happy converse with one another. And they will take care that their families do not exceed their means; having an eye to poverty or war.

But, said Glaucon, interposing, you have not given them a relish to their meal.

True, I replied, I had forgotten; of course they must have a relish—salt, and olives, and cheese, and they will boil roots and herbs such as country people prepare; for a dessert we shall give them figs, and peas, and beans; and they will roast myrtle-berries and acorns at the fire, drinking in moderation. And with such a diet they may be expected to live in peace and health to a good old age, and bequeath a similar life to their children after them.

Yes, Socrates, he said, and if you were providing for a city of pigs, how else would you feed the beasts?

But what would you have, Glaucon? I replied.

Why, he said, you should give them the ordinary conveniences of life. People who are to be comfortable are accustomed to lie on sofas, and dine off tables, and they should have sauces and sweets in the modern style.

Yes, I said, now I understand: the question which you would have me consider is, not only how a state, but how a luxurious state is created; and possibly there is no harm in this, for in such a state we shall be more likely to see how justice and injustice originate. In my opinion the true and healthy constitution of the state is the one which I have described. But if you wish also to

see a state at fever-heat, I have no objection. For I suspect
that many will not be satisfied with the simpler way of life. They
will be for adding sofas, and tables, and other furniture; also
dainties, and perfumes, and incense, and courtesans, and cakes,
all these not of one sort only, but in every variety; we must go
beyond the necessaries of which I was at first speaking, such as
houses, and clothes, and shoes: the arts of the painter and the
embroiderer will have to be set in motion, and gold and ivory and
all sorts of materials must be procured.

True, he said.

Then we must enlarge our borders; for the original healthy
state is no longer sufficient. Now will the city have to fill and
swell with a multitude of callings which are not required by any
natural want; such as the whole tribe of hunters and actors, of
whom one large class have to do with forms and colors; another
will be the votaries of music—poets and their attendant train of
rhapsodists, players, dancers, contractors; also makers of divers
kinds of articles, including women's dresses. And we shall want
more servants. Will not tutors be also in request, and nurses
wet and dry, tirewomen and barbers, as well as confectioners and
cooks; and swineherds, too, who were not needed and therefore
had no place in the former edition of our state, but are needed now?
They must not be forgotten: and there will be animals of many
other kinds, if people eat them.

Certainly.

And living in this way we shall have much greater need of physicians than before?

Much greater.

And the country which was enough to support the original
inhabitants will be too small now, and not enough?

Quite true.

Then a slice of our neighbor's land will be wanted by us for
pasture and tillage, and they will want a slice of ours, if, like ourselves, they exceed the limit of necessity, and give themselves up
to the unlimited accumulation of wealth?

That, Socrates, will be inevitable.

And so we shall go to war, Glaucon. Shall we not?

Most certainly, he replied.

Then, without determining as yet whether war does good or harm,
thus much we may affirm, that now we have discovered war to be
derived from causes which are also the causes of almost all the
evils in states, private as well as public.

Undoubtedly.

And our state must once more enlarge; and this time the enlargement will be nothing short of a whole army, which will have to go out and fight with the invaders for all that we have, as well as for the things and persons whom we were describing above.

Why? he said; are they not capable of defending themselves?

No, I said; not if we were right in the principle which was acknowledged by all of us when we were framing the state: the principle, as you will remember, was that one man cannot practise many arts with success.

Very true, he said.

But is not war an art?

Certainly.

And an art requiring as much attention as shoemaking?

Quite true.

And the shoemaker was not allowed by us to be a husbandman, or a weaver, or a builder—in order that we might have our shoes well made; but to him and to every other worker was assigned one work for which he was by nature fitted, and at that he was to continue working all his life long and at no other; he was not to let opportunities slip, and then he would become a good workman. Now nothing can be more important than that the work of a soldier should be well done. But is war an art so easily acquired that a man may be a warrior who is also a husbandman, or shoemaker, or other artisan; although no one in the world would be a good dice or draught player who merely took up the game as a recreation, and had not from his earliest years devoted himself to this and nothing else? No tools will make a man a skilled workman, or master of defence, nor be of any use to him who has not learned how to handle them, and has never bestowed any attention upon them. How then will he who takes up a shield or other implement of war become a good fighter all in a day, whether with heavy-armed or any other kind of troops?

Yes, he said, the tools which would teach men their own use would be beyond price.

And the higher the duties of the guardian, I said, the more time, and skill, and art, and application will be needed by him?

No doubt, he replied.

Will he not also require natural aptitude for his calling?

Certainly.

Then it will be our duty to select, if we can, natures which are fitted for the task of guarding the city?

It will.

2. *The Governors and Protectors of the State* [1]

There can be no doubt that the elder must rule the younger.

Clearly.

And that the best of these must rule.

That is also clear.

Now, are not the best husbandmen those who are most devoted to husbandry?

Yes.

And as we are to have the best of guardians for our city, must they not be those who have most the character of guardians?

Yes.

And to this end they ought to be wise and efficient, and to have a special care of the state?

True.

And a man will be most likely to care about that which he loves?

To be sure.

And he will be most likely to love that which he regards as having the same interests with himself, and that of which the good or evil fortune is supposed by him at any time most to affect his own?

Very true, he replied.

Then there must be a selection. Let us note among the guardians those who in their whole life show the greatest eagerness to do what is for the good of their country, and the greatest repugnance to do what is against her interests.

Those are the right men.

And they will have to be watched at every age, in order that we may see whether they preserve their resolution, and never, under the influence either of force or enchantment, forget or cast off their sense of duty to the state.

How cast off? he said.

I will explain to you, I replied. A resolution may go out of a man's mind either with his will or against his will; with his will when he gets rid of a falsehood and learns better, against his will whenever he is deprived of a truth.

I understand, he said, the willing loss of a resolution; the meaning of the unwilling I have yet to learn.

Why, I said, do you not see that men are unwillingly deprived of good, and willingly of evil? Is not to have lost the truth an evil, and to possess the truth a good? and you would agree that to conceive things as they are is to possess the truth?

[1] III, 412 to IV, 421. Jowett, pp. 100–109.

Yes, he replied; I agree with you in thinking that mankind are deprived of truth against their will.

And is not this involuntary deprivation caused either by theft, or force, or enchantment?

Still, he replied, I do not understand you.

I fear that I must have been talking darkly, like the tragedians. I only mean that some men are changed by persuasion and that others forget; argument steals away the hearts of one class, and time of the other; and this I call theft. Now you understand me?

Yes.

Those again who are forced, are those whom the violence of some pain or grief compels to change their opinion.

I understand, he said, and you are quite right.

And you would also acknowledge that the enchanted are those who change their minds either under the softer influence of pleasure, or the sterner influence of fear?

Yes, he said; everything that deceives may be said to enchant.

Therefore, as I was just now saying, we must inquire who are the best guardians of their own conviction that what they think the interest of the state is to be the rule of their lives. We must watch them from their youth upwards, and make them perform actions in which they are most likely to forget or to be deceived, and he who remembers and is not deceived is to be selected, and he who fails in the trial is to be rejected.   That will be the way?

Yes.

And there should also be toils and pains and conflicts prescribed for them, in which they will be made to give further proof of the same qualities.

Very right, he replied.

And then, I said, we must try them with enchantments—that is the third sort of test—and see what will be their behavior: like those who take colts amid noise and tumult to see if they are of a timid nature, so must we take our youth amid terrors of some kind, and again pass them into pleasures, and prove them more thoroughly than gold is proved in the furnace, that we may discover whether they are armed against all enchantments, and of a noble bearing always, good guardians of themselves and of the music which they have learned, and retaining under all circumstances a rhythmical and harmonious nature, such as will be most serviceable to the individual and to the state.   And he who at every age, as boy and youth and in mature life, has come out of the trial victorious and pure, shall be appointed a ruler and guardian of the state; he shall be honored in life and death, and shall receive sepulture and other memorials of honor, the greatest that we have to give. But him who fails, we must reject. I am inclined to think that this is the sort of way in which our rulers and guardians should be chosen and appointed. I speak generally and not with any pretension to exactness.

And, speaking generally, I agree with you, he said.

And perhaps the word "guardian" in the fullest sense ought to be applied to this higher class only who preserve us against foreign enemies and maintain peace among our citizens at home, that the one may not have the will, or the others the power, to harm us. The young men whom we before called guardians may be more properly designated auxiliaries and supporters of the principles of the rulers.

I agree with you, he said.

How then may we devise one of those needful falsehoods of which we lately spoke—just one royal lie which may deceive the rulers, if that be possible, and at any rate the rest of the city?

What sort of lie? he said.

Nothing new, I replied; only an old Phœnician tale of what has often occurred before now in other places (as the poets say, and have made the world believe), though not in our time, and I do not know whether such an event could ever happen again, or could now even be made probable, if it did.

How your words seem to hesitate on your lips!

You will not wonder, I replied, at my hesitation when you have heard.

Speak, he said, and fear not.

Well then, I will speak, although I really know not how to look you in the face, or in what words to utter the audacious fiction, which I propose to communicate gradually, first to the rulers, then to the soldiers, and lastly to the people. They are to be told that their youth was a dream, and the education and training which they received from us, an appearance only; in reality during all that time they were being formed and fed in the womb of the earth, where they themselves and their arms and appurtenances were manufactured; when they were completed, the earth, their mother, sent them up; and so their country being their mother and also their nurse, they are bound to advise for her good, and to defend her against attacks, and her citizens they are to regard as children of the earth and their own brothers.

You had good reason, he said, to be ashamed of the lie which you were going to tell.

True, I replied, but there is more coming; I have only told you half. Citizens, we shall say to them in our tale, you are brothers, yet God has framed you differently. Some of you have the power of command, and in the composition of these he has mingled gold, wherefore also they have the greatest honor; others he has made of silver, to be auxiliaries; others again who are to be husbandmen and craftsmen he has composed of brass and iron; and the species will generally be preserved in the children. But as all are of the same original stock, a golden parent will sometimes have a silver son, or a silver parent a golden son. And God proclaims as a first principle to the rulers, and above all else, that there is nothing which they should so anxiously guard, or of which they are to be such good guardians, as of the purity of the race. They should observe what elements mingle in their offspring; for if the son of a golden or silver parent has an admixture of brass and iron, then nature orders a transposition of ranks, and the eye of the ruler must not be pitiful towards the child because he has to descend in the scale and become a husbandman or artisan, just as there may be sons of artisans who having an admixture of gold or silver in them are raised to honor, and become guardians or auxiliaries. For an oracle says that when a man of brass or iron guards the state, it will be destroyed. Such is the tale; is there any possibility of making our citizens believe in it?

Not in the present generation, he replied; there is no way of accomplishing this; but their sons may be made to believe in the tale, and their sons' sons, and posterity after them.

I see the difficulty, I replied; yet the fostering of such a belief will make them care more for the city and for one another. Enough, however, of the fiction, which may now fly abroad upon the wings of rumor, while we arm our earth-born heroes, and lead them forth under the command of their rulers. Let them look round and select a spot whence they can best suppress insurrection, if any prove refractory within, and also defend themselves against enemies, who like wolves may come down on the fold from without; there let them encamp, and when they have encamped, let them sacrifice to the proper Gods and prepare their dwellings.

Just so, he said.

And their dwellings must be such as will shield them against the cold of winter and the heat of summer.

I suppose that you mean houses, he replied.

Yes, I said; but they must be the houses of soldiers, and not of shop-keepers.

What is the difference? he said.

That I will endeavor to explain, I replied. To keep watch-dogs, who, from want of discipline or hunger, or some evil habit or other, would turn upon the sheep and worry them, and behave not like dogs but wolves, would be a foul and monstrous thing in a shepherd?

Truly monstrous, he said.

And therefore every care must be taken that our auxiliaries, being stronger than our citizens, may not grow to be too much for them and become savage tyrants instead of friends and allies?

Yes, great care should be taken.

And would not a really good education furnish the best safeguard?

But they are well-educated already, he replied.

I cannot be so confident, my dear Glaucon, I said; I am much more certain that they ought to be, and that true education, whatever that may be, will have the greatest tendency to civilize and humanize them in their relations to one another, and to those who are under their protection.

Very true, he replied.

And not only their education, but their habitations, and all that belongs to them, should be such as will neither impair their virtue as guardians, nor tempt them to prey upon the other citizens. Any man of sense must acknowledge that.

He must.

Then now let us consider what will be their way of life, if they are to realize our idea of them. In the first place, none of them should have any property of his own beyond what is absolutely necessary; neither should they have a private house or store closed against any one who has a mind to enter; their provisions should be only such as are required by trained warriors, who are men of temperance and courage; they should agree to receive from the citizens a fixed rate of pay, enough to meet the expenses of the year and no more; and they will go to mess and live together like soldiers in a camp. Gold and silver we will tell them that they have from God; the diviner metal is within them, and they have therefore no need of the dross which is current among men, and ought not to pollute the divine by any such earthly admixture; for that commoner metal has been the source of many unholy deeds, but their own is undefiled. And they alone of all the citizens may not touch or handle silver or gold, or be under the same roof with them, or wear them, or drink from them. And this will be their salvation, and they will be the saviours of the state. But should they ever acquire homes or lands or moneys of their own, they will become housekeepers and husbandmen instead of guardians, enemies and tyrants instead of allies of the other citizens; hating and being hated, plotting and being plotted against, they will pass their whole life in much greater terror of internal than of external enemies, and the hour of ruin, both to themselves and to the rest of the state, will be at hand.   For all which reasons may we not say that thus shall our state be ordered, and that these shall be the regulations appointed by us for our guardians concerning their houses and all other matters?

Yes, said Glaucon.

Here Adeimantus interposed a question: How would you answer, Socrates, said he, if a person were to say that you are making these people miserable, and that they are the cause of their own unhappiness; the city in fact belongs to them, but they are none the better for it; whereas other men acquire lands, and build large and handsome houses, and have everything handsome about them, offering sacrifices to the gods on their own account, and practising hospitality; moreover, as you were saying just now, they have gold and silver, and all that is usual among the favorites of fortune; but our poor citizens are no better than mercenaries who are quartered in the city and are always mounting guard?

Yes, I said; and you may add that they are only fed, and not paid in addition to their food, like other men; and therefore they cannot, if they would, take a journey of pleasure; they have no money to spend on a mistress or any other luxurious fancy, which, as the world goes, is thought to be happiness; and many other accusations of the same nature might be added.

But, said he, let us suppose all this to be included in the charge.

You mean to ask, I said, what will be our answer?

Yes.

If we proceed along the old path, my belief, I said, is that we shall find the answer.   And our answer will be that, even as they are, our guardians may very likely be the happiest of men; but that our aim in founding the state was not the disproportionate happiness of any one class, but the greatest happiness of the whole; we thought that in a state which is ordered with a view to the good of the whole we should be most likely to find justice, and in the ill-ordered state injustice: and, having found them, we might then decide which of the two is the happier.   At present, I take it, we are fashioning the happy state, not piecemeal, or with a view of making a few happy citizens, but as a whole; and by-and-by we will proceed to view the opposite kind of state.   Suppose that we were painting a statue, and some one came up to us and said,

Why do you not put the most beautiful colors on the most beautiful parts of the body—the eyes ought to be purple, but you have made them black—to him we might fairly answer, Sir, you would not surely have us beautify the eyes to such a degree that they are no longer eyes; consider rather whether, by giving this and the other features their due proportion, we make the whole beautiful. And so I say to you, do not compel us to assign to the guardians a sort of happiness which will make them anything but guardians; for we too can clothe our husbandmen in royal apparel, and set crowns of gold on their heads, and bid them till the ground as much as they like, and no more. Our potters also might be allowed to repose on couches, and feast by the fireside, passing round the winecup, while their wheel is conveniently at hand, and working at pottery only as much as they like; in this way we might make every class happy—and then, as you imagine, the whole state would be happy. But do not put this idea into our heads; for, if we listen to you, the husbandman will be no longer a husbandman, the potter will cease to be a potter, and no one will have the character of any distinct class in the state. Now this is not of much consequence where the corruption of society, and pretension to be what you are not, is confined to cobblers; but when the guardians of the laws and of the government are only seeming and not real guardians, then see how they turn the state upside down; and on the other hand they alone have the power of giving order and happiness to the state. We mean our guardians to be true saviours and not the destroyers of the state, whereas our opponent is thinking of peasants at a festival, who are enjoying a life of revelry, not of citizens who are doing their duty to the state. But, if so, we mean different things, and he is speaking of something which is not a state. And therefore we must consider whether in appointing our guardians we would look to their greatest happiness individually, or whether this principle of happiness does not rather reside in the state as a whole. But if the latter be the truth, then the guardians and auxiliaries, and all others equally with them, must be compelled or induced to do their own work in the best way. And thus the whole state will grow up in a noble order, and the several classes will receive the proportion of happiness which nature assigns to them.

3. The Three Classes of the State [1]

But where, amid all this, is justice? son of Ariston, tell me where. Now that our city has been made habitable, light a candle and search, and get your brother and Polemarchus and the rest of our friends to help, and let us see where in it we can discover justice and where injustice, and in what they differ from one another, and which of them the man who would be happy should have for his portion, whether seen or unseen by gods and men.

Nonsense, said Glaucon: did you not promise to search your-self, saying that for you not to help justice in her need would be an impiety?

I do not deny that I said so; and as you remind me, I will be as good as my word; but you must join.

We will, he replied.

Well, then, I hope to make the discovery in this way: I mean to begin with the assumption that our state, if rightly ordered, is perfect.

That is most certain.

And being perfect, is therefore wise and valiant and temperate and just.

That is likewise clear.

And whichever of these qualities we find in the state, the one which is not found will be the residue?

Very good.

If there were four things, and we were searching for one of them, wherever it might be, the one sought for might be known to us from the first, and there would be no further trouble; or we might know the other three first, and then the fourth would clearly be the one left.

Very true, he said.

And is not a similar method to be pursued about the virtues, which are also four in number?

Clearly.

First among the virtues found in the state, wisdom comes into view, and in this I detect a certain peculiarity.

What is that?

The state which we have been describing is said to be wise as being good in counsel?

Very true.

And good counsel is clearly a kind of knowledge, for not by ignorance, but by knowledge, do men counsel well?

[1] IV, 427–434. Jowett, pp. 116–125.

Clearly.

And the kinds of knowledge in a state are many and diverse?

Of course.

There is the knowledge of the carpenter; but is that the sort of knowledge which gives a city the title of wise and good in counsel?

Certainly not; that would only give a city the reputation of skill in carpentering.

Then a city is not to be called wise because possessing a knowledge which counsels for the best about wooden implements?

Certainly not.

Nor by reason of a knowledge which advises about brazen pots, he said, nor as possessing any other similar knowledge?

Not by reason of any of them, he said.

Nor yet by reason of a knowledge which cultivates the earth; that would give the city the name of agricultural?

Yes.

Well, I said, and is there any knowledge in our recently-founded state among any of the citizens which advises, not about any particular thing in the state, but about the whole, and considers how a state can best deal with itself and with other states?

There certainly is.

And what is this knowledge, and among whom is it found? I asked.

It is the knowledge of the guardians, he replied, and is found among those whom we were just now describing as perfect guardians.

And what is the name which the city derives from the possession of this sort of knowledge?

The name of good in counsel and truly wise.

And will there be in our city more of these true guardians or more smiths?

The smiths, he replied, will be far more numerous.

Will not the guardians be the smallest of all the classes who receive a name from the profession of some kind of knowledge?

Much the smallest.

And so by reason of the smallest part or class, and of the knowledge which resides in this presiding and ruling part of itself, the whole state, being thus constituted according to nature, will be wise; and this, which has the only knowledge worthy to be called wisdom, has been ordained by nature to be of all classes the least.

Most true.

Thus, then, I said, the nature and place in the state of one of the four virtues has somehow or other been discovered.

And, in my humble opinion, very satisfactorily discovered, he replied.

Again, I said, there is no difficulty in seeing the nature of courage, and in what part that quality resides which gives the name of courageous to the state.

How do you mean?

Why, I said, every one who calls any state courageous or cowardly, will be thinking of the part which fights and goes out to war on the state's behalf.

No one, he replied, would ever think of any other.

The rest of the citizens may be courageous or may be cowardly, but their courage or cowardice will not, as I conceive, have the effect of making the city either the one or the other.

Certainly not.

The city will be courageous in virtue of a portion of herself which preserves under all circumstances that opinion about the nature of things to be feared and not to be feared in which our legislator educated them; and this is what you term courage.

I should like to hear what you are saying once more, for I do not think that I perfectly understand you.

I mean that courage is a kind of salvation.

Salvation of what?

Of the opinion respecting things to be feared, what they are and of what nature, which the law implants through education; and I mean by the words "under all circumstances" to intimate that in pleasure or in pain, or under the influence of desire or fear, a man preserves, and does not lose this opinion. Shall I give you an illustration?

If you please.

You know, I said, that dyers, when they want to dye wool for making the true sea-purple, begin by selecting their white color first; this they prepare and dress with much care and pains, in order that the white ground may take the purple hue in full perfection. The dyeing then proceeds; and whatever is dyed in this manner becomes a fast color, and no washing either with lyes or without them can take away the bloom. But, when the ground has not been duly prepared, you will have noticed how poor is the look either of purple or of any other color.

Yes, he said; I know that they have a washed-out and ridiculous appearance.

Then now, I said, you will understand what our object was in selecting our soldiers, and educating them in music and gymnastic; we were contriving influences which would prepare them to take the dye of the laws in perfection, and the color of their opinion about dangers and of every other opinion was to be indelibly fixed by their nurture and training, not to be washed away by such potent lyes as pleasure—mightier agent far in washing the soul than any soda or lye; or by sorrow, fear, and desire, the mightiest of all other solvents. And this sort of universal saving power of true opinion in conformity with law about real and false dangers I call and maintain to be courage, unless you disagree.

But I agree, he replied; for I suppose that you mean to exclude mere uninstructed courage, such as that of a wild beast or of a slave—this, in your opinion, is not the courage which the law ordains, and ought to have another name.

Most certainly.

Then I may infer courage to be such as you describe?

Why, yes, said I, you may, and if you add the words "of a citizen," you will not be far wrong;—hereafter, if you like, we will carry the examination further, but at present we are seeking not for courage but justice; and for the purpose of our inquiry we have said enough.

You are right, he replied.

Two virtues remain to be discovered in the state—first temperance, and then justice which is the end of our search.

Very true.

Now, can we find justice without troubling ourselves about temperance?

I do not know how that can be accomplished, he said, nor do I desire that justice should be brought to light and temperance lost sight of; and therefore I wish that you would do me the favor of considering temperance first.

Certainly, I replied, I should not be justified in refusing your request.

Then consider, he said.

Yes, I replied; I will; and as far as I can at present see, the virtue of temperance has more of the nature of harmony and symphony than the preceding.

How so? he asked.

Temperance, I replied, is the ordering or controlling of certain pleasures and desires; this is curiously enough implied in the saying of "a man being his own master;" and other traces of the same notion may be found in language.

No doubt, he said.

There is something ridiculous in the expression "master of himself;" for the master is also the servant and the servant the master, and in all these modes of speaking the same person is denoted.

Certainly.

The meaning is, I believe, that in the human soul there is a better and also a worse principle; and when the better has the worse under control, then a man is said to be master of himself; and this is a term of praise: but when, owing to evil education or association, the better principle, which is also the smaller, is overwhelmed by the greater mass of the worse—in this case he is blamed and is called the slave of self and unprincipled.

Yes, there is reason in that.

And now, I said, look at our newly-created state, and there you will find one of these two conditions realized; for the state, as you will acknowledge, may be justly called master of itself, if the words "temperance" and "self-mastery" truly express the rule of the better part over the worse.

Yes, he said, I see that what you say is true.

Let me further note that the manifold and complex pleasures and desires and pains are generally found in children and women and servants, and in the freemen so called who are of the lowest and more numerous class.

Certainly, he said.

Whereas the simple and moderate desires which follow reason, and are under the guidance of mind and true opinion, are to be found only in a few, and those the best born and best educated.

Very true.

These two, as you may perceive, have a place in our state; and the meaner desires of the many are held down by the virtuous desires and wisdom of the few.

That I perceive, he said.

Then if there be any city which may be described as master of its own pleasures and desires, and master of itself, ours may claim such a designation?

Certainly, he replied.

It may also be called temperate, and for the same reasons?

Yes.

And if there be any state in which rulers and subjects will be agreed as to the question who are to rule, that again will be our state?

Undoubtedly.

And the citizens being thus agreed among themselves, in which class will temperance be found—in the rulers or in the subjects?

In both, as I should imagine, he replied.

Do you observe that we were not far wrong in our guess that temperance was a sort of harmony?

Why so?

Why, because temperance is unlike courage and wisdom, each of which resides in a part only, the one making the state wise and the other valiant; not so temperance, which extends to the whole, and runs through all the notes of the scale, and produces a harmony of the weaker and the stronger and the middle class, whether you suppose them to be stronger or weaker in wisdom or power or numbers or wealth, or anything else. Most truly then may we deem temperance to be the agreement of the naturally superior and inferior, as to the right to rule of either, both in states and individuals.

I entirely agree with you.

And so, I said, we may consider three out of the four virtues to have been discovered in our state. The last of those qualities which make a state virtuous must be justice, if we only knew what that was.

The inference is obvious.

The time then has arrived, Glaucon, when, like huntsmen, we should surround the cover, and look sharp that justice does not steal away, and pass out of sight and escape us; for beyond a doubt she is somewhere in this country: watch therefore and strive to catch a sight of her, and if you see her first, let me know.

Would that I could! but you should regard me rather as a follower who has just eyes enough to see what you show him—that is about as much as I am good for.

Offer up a prayer with me and follow.

I will, but you must show me the way.

Here is no path, I said, and the wood is dark and perplexing; still we must push on.

Let us push on.

Here I saw something: Halloo! I said, I begin to perceive a track, and I believe that the quarry will not escape.

Good news, he said.

Truly, I said, we are stupid fellows.

Why so?

Why, my good sir, at the beginning of our inquiry, ages ago, there was justice tumbling out at our feet, and we never saw her; nothing could be more ridiculous. Like people who go about looking for what they have in their hands—that was the way with us—we looked not at what we were seeking, but at what was far off in the distance; and therefore, I suppose, we missed her.

What do you mean?

I mean to say that in reality for a long time past we have been talking of justice, and have failed to recognize her.

I grow impatient at the length of your exordium.

Well then, tell me, I said, whether I am right or not: You remember the original principle which we were always laying down at the foundation of the state, that one man should practise one thing only, the thing to which his nature was best adapted:— now justice is this principle or a part of it.

Yes, we often said that one man should do one thing only.

Further, we affirmed that justice was doing one's own business, and not being a busybody; we said so again and again, and many others have said the same to us.

Yes, we said so.

Then to do one's own business in a certain way may be assumed to be justice.   Can you tell me whence I derive this inference?

I cannot, but I should like to be told.

Because I think that this is the only virtue which remains in the state when the other virtues of temperance and courage and wisdom are abstracted; and, that this is the ultimate cause and condition of the existence of all of them, and while remaining in them is also their preservative; and we were saying that if the three were discovered by us, justice would be the fourth or remaining one.

That follows of necessity.

If we are asked to determine which of these four qualities by its presence contributes most to the excellence of the state, whether the agreement of rulers and subjects, or the preservation in the soldiers of the opinion which the law ordains about the true nature of dangers, or wisdom and watchfulness in the rulers, or whether this other which I am mentioning, and which is found in children and women, slave and freeman, artisan, ruler, subject,—the quality I mean, of every one doing his own work, and not being a busybody, would claim the palm—the question is not so easily answered.

Certainly, he replied, there would be a difficulty in saying which.

Then the power of each individual in the state to do his own work appears to compete with the other political virtues, wisdom, temperance, courage.

Yes, he said.

And the virtue which enters into this competition is justice?

Exactly.

Let us look at the question from another point of view: Are not the rulers in a state those to whom you would intrust the office of determining suits at law?

Certainly.

And are suits decided on any other ground but that a man may neither take what is another's, nor be deprived of what is his own?

Yes; that is their principle.

Which is a just principle?

Yes.

Then on this view also justice will be admitted to be the having and doing what is a man's own, and belongs to him?

Very true.

Think, now, and say whether you agree with me or not. Suppose a carpenter to be doing the business of a cobbler, or a cobbler of a carpenter; and suppose them to exchange their implements or their duties, or the same person to be doing the work of both, or whatever be the change; do you think that any great harm would result to the state?

Not much.

But when the cobbler or any other man whom nature designed to be a trader, having his heart lifted up by wealth or strength or the number of his followers, or any like advantage, attempts to force his way into the class of warriors, or a warrior into that of legislators and guardians, for which he is unfitted, and either to take the implements or the duties of the other; or when one man is trader, legislator, and warrior all in one, then I think you will agree with me in saying that this interchange and this meddling of one with another is the ruin of the state.

Most true.

Seeing then, I said, that there are three distinct classes, any meddling of one with another, or the change of one into another, is the greatest harm to the state, and may be most justly termed evil-doing?

Precisely.

And the greatest degree of evil-doing to one's own city would be termed by you injustice?

Certainly.

This then is injustice; and on the other hand when the trader, the auxiliary, and the guardian each do their own business, that is justice, and will make the city just.

4. Communism [1]

I do not think, I said, that there can be any dispute about the very great utility of having wives and children in common; the possibility is quite another matter, and will be very much disputed.

I think that a good many doubts may be raised about both.

You imply that the two questions must be combined, I replied. Now I meant that you should admit the utility; and in this way, as I thought, I should escape from one of them, and then there would remain only the possibility.

But that little attempt is detected, and therefore you will please to give a defence of both.

Well, I said, I submit to my fate. Yet grant me a little favor: let me feast my mind with the dream as day dreamers are in the habit of feasting themselves when they are walking alone; for before they have discovered any means of effecting their wishes— that is a matter which never troubles them—they would rather not tire themselves by thinking about possibilities; but assuming that what they desire is already granted to them, they proceed with their plan, and delight in detailing what they mean to do when their wish has come true—that is a way which they have of not doing much good to a capacity which was never good for much. Now I myself am beginning to lose heart, and I should like, with your permission, to pass over the question of possibility at present. Assuming therefore the possibility of the proposal, I shall now proceed to inquire how the rulers will carry out these arrangements, and I shall demonstrate that our plan, if executed, will be of the greatest benefit to the state and to the guardians. First of all, then, if you have no objection, I will endeavor with your help to consider the advantages of the measure; and hereafter the question of possibility.

I have no objections; proceed.

First, I think that if our rulers and their auxiliaries are to be worthy of the name which they bear, there must be willingness to obey in the one and the power of command in the other; the guardians must themselves obey the laws, and they must also imitate the spirit of them in any details which are intrusted to their care.

That is right, he said.

[1] V, 457–465. Jowett, pp. 150–160.

You, I said, who are their legislator, having selected the men, will now select the women and give them to them;—they must be as far as possible of like natures with them; and they must live in common houses and meet at common meals. None of them will have anything specially his or her own; they will be together, and will be brought up together, and will associate at gymnastic exercises. And so they will be drawn by a necessity of their natures to have intercourse with each other—necessity is not too strong a word, I think?

Yes, he said; necessity, not geometrical, but another sort of necessity which lovers know, and which is far more convincing and constraining to the mass of mankind.

True, I said; and this, Glaucon, like all the rest, must proceed after an orderly fashion; in a city of the blessed, licentiousness is an unholy thing which the rulers will forbid.

Yes, he said, and it ought not to be permitted.

Then clearly the next thing will be to make matrimony sacred in the highest degree, and what is most beneficial will be deemed sacred?

Exactly.

And how can marriages be made most beneficial?—that is a question which I put to you, because I see in your house dogs for hunting, and of the nobler sort of birds not a few. Now, I beseech you, do tell me, have you ever attended to their pairing and breeding?

In what particulars?

Why, in the first place, although they are all of a good sort, are not some better than others?

True.

And do you breed from them all indifferently, or do you take care to breed from the best only?

From the best.

And do you take the oldest or the youngest, or only those of ripe age?

I choose only those of ripe age.

And if care was not taken in the breeding, your dogs and birds would greatly deteriorate?

Certainly.

And the same of horses and of animals in general?

Undoubtedly.

Good heavens! my dear friend, I said, what consummate skill will our rulers need if the same principle holds of the human species!

Certainly, the same principle holds; but why does this involve any particular skill?

Because, I said, our rulers will often have to practise upon the body corporate with medicines. Now you know that when patients do not require medicines, but have only to be put under a regimen, the inferior sort of practitioner is deemed to be good enough; but when medicine has to be given, then the doctor should be more of a man.

That is quite true, he said; but to what are you alluding?

I mean, I replied, that our rulers will find a considerable dose of falsehood and deceit necessary for the good of their subjects: we were saying that the use of all these things regarded as medicines might be of advantage.

And we were very right.

And this lawful use of them seems likely to be often needed in the regulations of marriages and births.

How so?

Why, I said, the principle has been already laid down that the best of either sex should be united with the best as often, and the inferior with the inferior as seldom, as possible; and that they should rear the offspring of the one sort of union, but not of the other, if the flock is to be maintained in first-rate condition. Now these goings on must be a secret which the rulers only know, or there will be a further danger of our herd, as the guardians may be termed, breaking out into rebellion.

Very true.

Had we not better appoint certain festivals at which we will bring together the brides and bridegrooms, and sacrifices will be offered and suitable hymeneal songs composed by our poets: the number of weddings is a matter which must be left to the discretion of the rulers, whose aim will be to preserve the average of population? There are many other things which they will have to consider, such as the effects of wars and diseases and any similar agencies, in order as far as this is possible to prevent the state from becoming either too large or too small.

Certainly, he replied.

We shall have to invent some ingenious kind of lots which the less worthy may draw on each occasion of our bringing them together, and then they will accuse their own ill-luck and not the rulers.

To be sure, he said.

And I think that our braver and better youth, besides their other honors and rewards, might have greater facilities of intercourse with women given them; their bravery will be a reason, and such fathers ought to have as many sons as possible.

True.

And the proper officers, whether male or female or both, for offices are to be held by women as well as by men—

Yes—

The proper officers will take the offspring of the good parents to the pen or fold, and there they will deposit them with certain nurses who dwell in a separate quarter; but the offspring of the inferior, or of the better when they chance to be deformed, will be put away in some mysterious, unknown place, as they should be.

Yes, he said, that must be done if the breed of the guardians is to be kept pure.

Advocates exposure of weak, inferior children

They will provide for their nurture, and will bring the mothers to the fold when they are full of milk, taking the greatest possible care that no mother recognizes her own child; and other wet-nurses may be engaged if more are required. Care will also be taken that the process of suckling shall not be protracted too long; and the mothers will have no getting up at night or other trouble, but will hand over all this sort of thing to the nurses and attendants.

You suppose the wives of our guardians to have a fine easy time of it when they are having children.

child-bearing for the state.

Why, said I, and so they ought. Let us, however, proceed with our scheme. We were saying that the parents should be in the prime of life?

Very true.

And what is the prime of life? May it not be defined as a period of about twenty years in a woman's life, and thirty in a man's?

Which years do you mean to include?

A woman, I said, at twenty years of age may begin to bear children to the state, and continue to bear them until forty; a man may begin at five-and-twenty, when he has passed the point at which the pulse of life beats quickest, and continue to beget children until he be fifty-five.

Certainly, he said, both in men and women those years are the prime of physical as well as of intellectual vigor.

Any one above or below the prescribed ages who takes part in the public hymeneals shall be said to have done an unholy and unrighteous thing; the child of which he is the father, if it steals into life, will have been conceived under auspices very unlike the sacrifices and prayers, which at each hymeneal priestesses and priests and the whole city will offer, that the new generation may

be better and more useful than their good and useful parents,
whereas his child will be the offspring of darkness and strange lust.

Very true, he replied.

And the same law will apply to any one of those within the prescribed age who forms a connection with any woman in the prime
of life without the sanction of the rulers; for we shall say that he is
raising up a bastard to the state, uncertified and unconsecrated.

Very true, he replied.

This applies, however, only to those who are within the specified age: after that we allow them to range at will, except that
a man may not marry his daughter or his daughter's daughter,
or his mother or his mother's mother; and women, on the other
hand, are prohibited from marrying their sons or fathers, or son's
son or father's father, and so on in either direction.   And we grant
all this, accompanying the permission with strict orders to prevent
any embryo which may come into being from seeing the light; and
if any force a way to the birth, the parents must understand that
the offspring of such a union cannot be maintained, and arrange
accordingly.

That also, he said, is a reasonable proposition.   But how will
they know who are fathers and daughters, and so on?

They will never know.   The way will be this:—dating from the
day of the hymeneal, the bridegroom who was then married
will call all the male children who are born in the seventh and the
tenth month afterwards his sons, and the female children his
daughters, and they will call him father, and he will call their
children his grandchildren, and they will call the elder generation
grandfathers and grandmothers.   All who were begotten at the
time when their fathers and mothers came together will be called
their brothers and sisters, and these, as I was saying, will be forbidden to inter-marry.   This, however, is not to be understood
as an absolute prohibition of the marriage of brothers and sisters;
if the lot favors them, and they receive the sanction of the Pythian
oracle, the law will allow them.

Quite right, he replied.

Such is the scheme, Glaucon, according to which the guardians
of our state are to have their wives and families in common.   And
now you would have the argument show that this community is
consistent with the rest of our polity, and also that nothing can
be better—would you not?

Yes, certainly.

Shall we try to find a common basis by asking of ourselves what
ought to be the chief aim of the legislator in making laws and in

the organization of a state,—what is the greatest good, and what is the greatest evil, and then consider whether our previous description has the stamp of the good or of the evil?

By all means.

Can there be any greater evil than discord and distraction and plurality where unity ought to reign? or any greater good than the bond of unity?

There cannot.

And there is unity where there is community of pleasures and pains—where all the citizens are glad or grieved on the same occasions of joy and sorrow?

No doubt.

Yes; and where there is no common but only private feeling a state is disorganized—when you have one-half of the world triumphing and the other plunged in grief at the same events happening to the city or the citizens?

Certainly.

Such differences commonly originate in a disagreement about the use of the terms "mine" and "not mine," "his" and "not his."

Exactly so.

And is not that the best-ordered state in which the greatest number of persons apply the terms "mine" and "not mine" in the same way to the same thing?

Quite true.

Or that again which most nearly approaches to the condition of the individual—as in the body, when but a finger of one of us is hurt, the whole frame, drawn towards the soul as a centre and forming one kingdom under the ruling power therein, feels the hurt and sympathizes all together with the part affected, and we say that the man has a pain in his finger; and the same expression is used about any other part of the ¦body, which has a sensation of pain at suffering or of pleasure at the alleviation of suffering.

Very true, he replied; and I agree with you that in the best-ordered state there is the nearest approach to this common feeling which you describe.

Then when any one of the citizens experiences any good or evil, the whole state will make his case their own, and will either rejoice or sorrow with him?

Yes, he said, that is what will happen in a well-ordered state.

It will now be time, I said, for us to return to our state and see whether this or some other form is most in accordance with these fundamental principles.

Very good.

Our state like every other has rulers and subjects?

True.

All of whom will call one another citizens?

Of course.

But is there not another name which people give to their rulers in other states?

Generally they call them masters, but in democratic states they simply call them rulers.

And in our state what other name besides that of citizens do the people give the rulers?

They are called saviours and helpers, he replied.

And what do the rulers call the people?

Their maintainers and foster-fathers.

And what do they call them in other states?

Slaves.

And what do the rulers call one another in other states?

Fellow-rulers.

And what in ours?

Fellow-guardians.

Did you ever know an example in any other state of a ruler who would speak of one of his colleagues as his friend and of another as not being his friend?

Yes, very often.

And the friend he regards and describes as one in whom he has an interest, and the other as a stranger in whom he has no interest?

Exactly.

But would any of your guardians think or speak of any other guardian as a stranger?

Certainly he would not; for every one whom they meet will be regarded by them either as a brother or sister, or father or mother, or son or daughter, or as the child or parent of those who are thus connected with him.

Capital, I said; but let me ask you once more: Shall they be a family in name only; or shall they in all their actions be true to the name? For example, in the use of the word "father," would the care of a father be implied and the filial reverence and duty and obedience to him which the law commands; and is the violator of these duties to be re-garded as an impious and unrighteous person who is not likely to receive much good either at the hands of God or of man? Are these to be or not to be the strains which the children will hear repeated in their ears by all the citizens about those who are intimated to them to be their parents and the rest of their kinsfolk?

These, he said, and none other; for what can be more ridiculous than for them to utter the names of family ties with the lips only and not to act in the spirit of them?

Then in our city the language of harmony and concord will be more often heard than in any other. As I was describing before, when any one is well or ill, the universal word will be "with me it is well" or "it is ill."

Most true.

And agreeably to this mode of thinking and speaking, were we not saying that they will have their pleasures and pains in common?

Yes, and so they will.

And they will have a common interest in the same thing which they will alike call "my own," and having this common interest they will have a common feeling of pleasure and pain?

Yes, far more so than in other states.

And the reason of this, over and above the general constitution of the state, will be that the guardians will have a community of women and children?

That will be the chief reason.

And this unity of feeling we admitted to be the greatest good, as was implied in our own comparison of a well-ordered state to the relation of the body and the members, when affected by pleasure or pain?

That we acknowledged, and very rightly.

Then the community of wives and children among our citizens is clearly the source of the greatest good to the state?

Certainly.

And this agrees with the other principle which we were affirming,—that the guardians were not to have houses or lands or any other property; their pay was to be their food, which they were to receive from the other citizens, and they were to have no private expenses; for we intended them to preserve their true character of guardians.

Right, he replied.

Both the community of property and the community of families, as I am saying, tend to make them more truly guardians; they will not tear the city in pieces by differing about "mine" and "not mine"; each man dragging any acquisition which he has made into a separate house of his own, where he has a separate wife and children and private pleasures and pains; but all will be affected as far as

may be by the same pleasures and pains because they are all of
one opinion about what is near and dear to them, and therefore
they all tend towards a common end.

Certainly, he replied.

And as they have nothing but their persons which they can call
their own, suits and complaints will have no existence among them;
they will be delivered from all those quarrels of which money or
children or relations are the occasion.

Of course they will.

Neither will trials for assault or insult ever be likely to occur
among them. For that equals should defend themselves against
equals we shall maintain to be honorable and right; we shall make
the protection of the person a matter of necessity.

That is good, he said.

Yes; and there is a further good in the law; viz. that if a man has
a quarrel with another he will satisfy his resentment then and there,
and not proceed to more dangerous lengths.

Certainly.

To the elder shall be assigned the duty of ruling and chastising
the younger.

Clearly.

Nor can there be a doubt that the younger will not strike or
do any other violence to an elder, unless the magistrates
command him; nor will he slight him in any way. For there
are two guardians, shame and fear, mighty to prevent him:
shame, which makes men refrain from laying hands on those
who are to them in the relation of parents; fear, that the injured
one will be succored by the others who are his brothers, sons,
fathers.

That is true, he replied.

Then in every way the laws will help the citizens to keep the
peace with one another?

Yes, there will be no want of peace.

And as the guardians will never quarrel among themselves
there will be no danger of the rest of the city being divided either
against them or against one another.

None whatever.

I hardly like even to mention the little meannesses of which
they will be rid, for they are beneath notice: such, for example, as
the flattery of the rich by the poor, and all the pains and pangs
which men experience in bringing up a family, and in finding money
to buy necessaries for their household, borrowing and then repu-
diating, getting how they can, and giving the money into the hands

of women and slaves to keep—the many evils of so many kinds
which people suffer in this way are mean enough and obvious
enough, and not worth speaking of.[1]

5. Government by Philosophers [2]

We were inquiring into the nature of absolute justice and into
the character of the perfectly just, and into injustice and the
perfectly unjust, that we might have an ideal. We were to look
at these in order that we might judge of our own happiness and
unhappiness according to the standard which they exhibited and
the degree in which we resembled them, but not with any view of
showing that they could exist in fact.

True, he said.

Would a painter be any the worse because, after having de-
lineated with consummate art an ideal of a perfectly beautiful
man, he was unable to show that any such man could ever have
existed?

He would be none the worse.

Well, and were we not creating an ideal of a perfect state?

To be sure.

And is our theory a worse theory because we are unable to
prove the possibility of a city being ordered in the manner described?

Surely not, he replied.

That is the truth, I said. But if, at your request, I am to try
and show how and under what conditions the possibility is highest,
I must ask you, having this in view, to repeat your former admissions.

What admissions?

I want to know whether ideals are ever fully realized in language?
Does not the word express more than the fact, and must not the
actual, whatever a man may think, always, in the nature of things,
fall short of the truth? What do you say?

I agree.

Then you must not insist on my proving that the actual state
will in every respect coincide with the ideal: if we are only
able to discover how a city may be governed nearly as we proposed,
you will admit that we have discovered the possibility which you

[1] V, 457–465. Jowett, pp. 150–160.
[2] V, 472–473; VI, 484–490, 502–504; VII, 520–521, 536–537, 540–541.
Jowett. pp. 169–171, 180–188, 202–203, 220–222, 240–241, 244–246.

demand; and will be contented.   I am sure that I should be contented—will not you?

Yes, I will.

Let me next endeavor to show what is that fault in states which is the cause of their present maladministration, and what is the least change which will enable a state to pass into the truer form; and let the change, if possible, be of one thing only, or, if not, of two; at any rate, let the changes be as few and slight as possible.

Certainly, he replied.

I think, I said, that there might be a reform of the state if only one change were made, which is not a slight or easy though still a possible one.

What is it? he said.

Now then, I said, I go to meet that which I liken to the greatest of the waves; yet shall the word be spoken, even though the wave break and drown me in laughter and dishonor; and do you mark my words.

Proceed.

I said: *Until philosophers are kings, or the kings and princes of this world have the spirit and power of philosophy, and political greatness and wisdom meet in one, and those commoner natures who pursue either to the exclusion of the other are compelled to stand aside, cities will never have rest from their evils,—no, nor the human race, as I believe,—and then only will this our state have a possibility of life and behold the light of day.*   Such was the thought, my dear Glaucon, which I would fain have uttered if it had not seemed too extravagant; for to be convinced that in no other state can there be happiness private or public is indeed a hard thing.[1]

And thus, Glaucon, after the argument has gone a weary way, the true and the false philosophers have at length appeared in view.

I do not think, he said, that the way could have been shortened.

I suppose not, I said; and yet I believe that we might have had a better view of both of them if the discussion could have been confined to this one subject and if there were not many other questions awaiting us, which he who desires to see in what respect the life of the just differs from that of the unjust must consider.

And what is the next question? he asked.

Surely, I said, the one which follows next in order.   Inasmuch as philosophers only are able to grasp the eternal and unchangeable, and those who wander in the region of the many and variable are

[1] V, 472–473. Jowett, pp. 169–171.

not philosophers, I must ask you which of the two classes should be the rulers of our state?

And how can we rightly answer that question?

Whichever of the two are best able to guard the laws and institutions of our state—let them be our guardians.

Very good.

Neither, I said, can there be any question that the guardian who is to keep anything should have eyes rather than no eyes?

There can be no question of that.

And are not those who are verily and indeed wanting in the knowledge of the true being of each thing, and who have in their souls no clear pattern, and are unable as with a painter's eye to look at the absolute truth and to that original to repair, and having perfect vision of the other world to order the laws about beauty, goodness, justice in this, if not already ordered, and to guard and preserve the order of them—are not such persons, I ask, simply blind?

Truly, he replied, they are much in that condition.

And shall they be our guardians when there are others who, besides being their equals in experience and falling short of them in no particular of virtue, also know the very truth of each thing?

There can be no reason, he said, for rejecting those who have this greatest of all great qualities; they must always have the first place unless they fail in some other respect.

Suppose then, I said, that we determine how far they can unite this and the other excellences.

By all means.

In the first place, as we began by observing, the nature of the philosopher has to be ascertained. We must come to an understanding about him, and, when we have done so, then, if I am not mistaken, we shall also acknowledge that such a union of qualities is possible, and that those in whom they are united, and those only, should be rulers in the state.

What do you mean?

Let us suppose that philosophical minds always love knowledge of a sort which shows them the eternal nature not varying from generation and corruption.

Agreed.

And further, I said, let us agree that they are lovers of all true being; there is no part whether greater or less, or more or less honorable, which they are willing to renounce; as we said before of the lover and the man of ambition.

True.

And if they are to be what we were describing, is there not another quality which they should also possess?

What quality?

Truthfulness: they will never intentionally receive into their mind falsehood, which is their detestation, and they will love the truth.

Yes, that may be safely affirmed of them.

"May be," my friend, I replied, is not the word; say rather, "must be affirmed": for he whose nature is amorous of anything cannot help loving all that belongs or is akin to the object of his affections.

Right, he said.

And is there anything more akin to wisdom than truth?

How can there be?

Can the same nature be a lover of wisdom and a lover of falsehood?

Never.

The true lover of learning then must from his earliest youth, as far as in him lies, desire all truth?

Assuredly.

But then again, as we know by experience, he whose desires are strong in one direction will have them weaker in others; they will be like a stream which has been drawn off into another channel.

True.

He whose desires are drawn towards knowledge in every form will be absorbed in the pleasures of the soul, and will hardly feel bodily pleasure—I mean, if he be a true philosopher and not a sham one.

That is most certain.

Such a one is sure to be temperate and the reverse of covetous; for the motives which make another man desirous of having and spending, have no place in his character.

Very true.

Another criterion of the philosophical nature has also to be considered.

What is that?

There should be no secret corner of illiberality; nothing can be more antagonistic than meanness to a soul which is ever longing after the whole of things both divine and human.

Most true, he replied.

Then how can he who has magnificence of mind and is the spectator of all time and all existence, think much of human life?

He cannot.

Or can such a one account death fearful?

No indeed.

Then the cowardly and mean nature has no part in true philosophy?

Certainly not.

Or again: can he who is harmoniously constituted, who is not covetous or mean, or a boaster, or a coward—can he, I say, ever be unjust or hard in his dealings?

Impossible.

Then you will soon observe whether a man is just and gentle, or rude and unsociable; these are the signs which distinguish even in youth the philosophical nature from the unphilosophical.

True.

There is another point which should be remarked.

What point?

Whether he has or has not a pleasure in learning; for no one will love that which gives him pain, and in which after much toil he makes little progress.

Certainly not.

And again, if he is forgetful and retains nothing of what he learns, will he not be an empty vessel?

That is certain.

Laboring in vain, he must end in hating himself and his fruitless occupation?

Yes.

Then a soul which forgets cannot be ranked among genuine philosophic natures; we must insist that the philosopher should have a good memory?

Certainly.

And once more, the inharmonious and unseemly nature can only tend to disproportion?

Undoubtedly.

And do you consider truth to be akin to proportion or to disproportion?

To proportion.

Then, besides other qualities, we must try to find a naturally well-proportioned and gracious mind, which will move spontaneously towards the true being of everything.

Certainly.

Well, and do not all these qualities, which we have been enumerating, go together, and are they not, in a manner, necessary to a soul, which is to have a full and perfect participation of being?

They are absolutely necessary, he replied.

And must not that be a blameless study which he only can pursue who has the gift of a good memory, and is quick to learn,— noble, gracious, the friend of truth, justice, courage, temperance, who are his kindred?

The god of jealousy himself, he said, could find no fault with such a study.

And to men like him, I said, when perfected by years and education, and to these only you will intrust the state.

Here Adeimantus interposed and said: To these statements, Socrates, no one can offer a reply; but when you talk in this way, a strange feeling passes over the minds of your hearers: They fancy that they are led astray a little at each step in the argument, owing to their own want of skill in asking and answering questions; these littles accumulate, and at the end of the discussion they are found to have sustained a mighty overthrow and all their former notions appear to be turned upside down. And as unskilful players of draughts are at last shut up by their more skilful adversaries and have no piece to move, so they too find themselves shut up at last; for they have nothing to say in this new game of which words are the counters; and yet all the time they are in the right. The observation is suggested to me by what is now occurring. For any one of us might say, that although in words he is not able to meet you at at each step of the argument, he sees as a fact that the votaries of philosophy, when they carry on the study, not only in youth as a part of education, but as the pursuit of their maturer years, most of them become strange monsters, not to say utter rogues, and that those who may be considered the best of them are made useless to the world by the very study which you extol.

Well, and do you think that those who say so are wrong?

I cannot tell, he replied; but I should like to know what is your opinion.

Hear my answer; I am of opinion that they are quite right.

Then how can you be justified in saying that cities will not cease from evil until philosophers rule in them, when philosophers are acknowledged by us to be of no use to them?

You ask a question, I said, to which a reply can only be given in a parable.

Yes, Socrates; and that is a way of speaking to which you are not at all accustomed, I suppose.

I perceive, I said, that you are vastly amused at having plunged me into such a hopeless discussion; but now hear the parable, and then you will be still more amused at the meagerness of my imagination: for the manner in which the best men are treated in their own states is so grievous that no single thing on earth is comparable to it; and therefore, if I am to plead their cause, I must have recourse to fiction, and put together a figure made up of many things, like the fabulous unions of goats and stags which are found in pictures. Imagine then a fleet or a ship in which there is a captain who is taller and stronger than any of the crew, but he is a little deaf and has a similar infirmity in sight, and his knowledge of navigation is not much better. The sailors are quarreling with one another about the steering—every one is of opinion that he has a right to steer, though he has never learned the art of navigation and cannot tell who taught him or when he learned, and will further assert that it cannot be taught, and they are ready to cut in pieces any one who says the contrary. They throng about the captain, begging and praying him to commit the helm to them; and if at any time they do not prevail, but others are preferred to them, they kill the others or throw them overboard, and having first chained up the noble captain's senses with drink or some narcotic drug, they mutiny and take possession of the ship and make free with the stores; thus, eating and drinking, they proceed on their voyage in such manner as might be expected of them. Him who is their partisan and cleverly aids them in their plot for getting the ship out of the captain's hands into their own whether by force or persuasion, they compliment with the name of sailor, pilot, able seaman, and abuse the other sort of man, whom they call a good-for-nothing; but that the true pilot must pay attention to the year and seasons and sky and stars and winds, and whatever else belongs to his art, if he intends to be really qualified for the command of a ship, and that he must and will be the steerer, whether other people like or not—the possibility of this union of authority with the steerer's art has never seriously entered into their thoughts or been made part of their calling. Now in vessels which are in a state of mutiny and by sailors who are mutineers, how will the true pilot be regarded? Will he not be called by them a prater, a star-gazer, a good-for-nothing?

Of course, said Adeimantus.

Then you will hardly need, I said, to hear the interpretation of the figure, which describes the true philosopher in his relation to the state; for you understand already.

Certainly.

Then suppose you now take this parable to the gentleman who is surprised at finding that philosophers have no honor in their cities; explain it to him and try to convince him that their having honor would be far more extraordinary.

I will.

Say to him, that, in deeming the best votaries of philosophy to be useless to the rest of the world, he is right; but also tell him to attribute their uselessness to the fault of those who will not use them, and not to themselves. The pilot should not humbly beg the sailors to be commanded by him—that is not the order of nature; neither are "the wise to go to the doors of the rich"—the ingenious author of this saying told a lie—but the truth is, that, when a man is ill, whether he be rich or poor, to the physician he must go, and he who wants to be governed, to him who is able to govern. The ruler who is good for anything ought not to beg his subjects to be ruled by him; although the present governors of mankind are of a different stamp; they may be justly compared to the mutinous sailors, and the true helmsmen to those who are called by them good-for-nothings and star-gazers.

Precisely so, he said.

For these reasons, and among men like these, philosophy, the noblest pursuit of all, is not likely to be much esteemed by those of the opposite faction; not that the greatest and most lasting injury is done to her by her opponents, but by her own professing followers, the same of whom you suppose the accuser to say, that the greater number of them are arrant rogues, and the best are useless; in which opinion I agreed.

Yes.

And the reason why the good are useless has now been explained?

True.

Then shall we proceed to show that the corruption of the majority is also unavoidable, and that this is not to be laid to the charge of philosophy any more than the other?

By all means.

And let us ask and answer in turn, first going back to the description of the gentle and noble nature. Truth, as you will remember, was his leader, whom he followed always and in all things; failing in this, he was an impostor, and had no part or lot in true philosophy.

Yes, that was said.

Well, and is not this one quality, to mention no others, greatly at variance with present notions of him?

Certainly, he said.

And have we not a right to say in his defence, that the true lover of knowledge is always striving after being—that is his nature; he will not rest in the mutiplicity of individuals which is an appearance only, but will go on—the keen edge will not be blunted, nor the force of his desire abate until he have attained the knowledge of the true nature of every essence by a sympathetic and kindred power in the soul, and by that power drawing near and mingling and becoming incorporate with very being, having begotten mind and truth, he will have knowledge and will live and grow truly, and then, and not till then, will he cease from his travail.

Nothing, he said, can be more just than such a description of him.

And will the love of a lie be any part of a philosopher's nature? Will he not utterly hate a lie?

He will.

And when truth is the captain, we cannot suspect any evil of the band which he leads?

Impossible.

Justice and health of mind will be of the company, and temperance will follow after?

True, he replied.[1]

I omitted the troublesome business of the possession of women, and the procreation of children, and the appointment of the rulers, because I knew that the perfect state would be eyed with jealousy and was difficult of attainment; but that piece of cleverness was not of much service to me, for I had to discuss them all the same. The women and children are now disposed of, but the other question of the rulers must be investigated from the very beginning. We were saying, as you will remember, that they were to be lovers of their country, tried by the test of pleasures and pains, and neither in hardships, nor in dangers, nor at any other critical moment were to lose their patriotism—he was to be rejected who failed, but he who always came forth pure, like gold tried in the refiner's fire, was to be made a ruler, and to receive honors and rewards in life and after death. This was the sort of thing which was being said, and then the argument turned aside and veiled her face; not liking to stir the question which has now arisen.

I perfectly remember, he said.

Yes, my friend, I said, and I then shrank from hazarding the bold word; but now let me dare to say—that the perfect guardian must be a philosopher.

Yes, he said, let that be affirmed.

And do not suppose that there will be many of them; for the gifts which were deemed by us to be essential rarely grow together; they are mostly found in shreds and patches.

What do you mean? he said.

[1] VI, 484–490. Jowett, pp. 180–188.

You are aware, I replied, that quick intelligence, memory, sagacity, cleverness, and similar qualities, do not often grow together, and that persons who possess them and are at the same time high-spirited and magnanimous are not so constituted by nature as to live orderly and in a peaceful and settled manner; they are driven any way by their impulses, and all solid principle goes out of them.

Very true, he said.

On the other hand, those steadfast natures which can better be depended upon, which in a battle are impregnable to fear and immovable, are equally immovable when there is anything to be learned; they are always in a torpid state, and are apt to yawn and go to sleep over any intellectual toil.

Quite true.

And yet we were saying that both qualities were necessary in those to whom the higher education is to be imparted, and who are to share in any office or command.

Certainly, he said.

And will they be a class which is rarely found?

Yes, indeed.

Then the aspirant must not only be tested in those labors and dangers and pleasures which we mentioned before, but there is another kind of probation which we did not mention—he must be exercised also in many kinds of knowledge, to see whether the soul will be able to endure the highest of all, or will faint under them as in any other studies and exercises.[1]

Observe, Glaucon, that there will be no injustice in compelling our philosophers to have a care and providence of others; we shall explain to them that in other states, men of their class are not obliged to share in the toils of politics: and this is reasonable, for they grow up at their own sweet will, and the government would rather not have them. Being self-taught, they cannot be expected to show any gratitude for a culture which they have never received. But we have brought you into the world to be rulers of the hive, kings of yourselves and of the other citizens, and have educated you far better and more perfectly than they have been educated, and you are better able to share in the double duty. Wherefore each of you, when his turn comes, must go down to the general underground abode, and get the habit of seeing in the dark. When you have acquired the habit, you will see ten thousand times better than the inhabitants of the den, and you will

---

[1] VI, 502–504. Jowett, pp. 202–203.

know what the several images are, and what they represent, because you have seen the beautiful and just and good in their truth. And thus our state, which is also yours, will be a reality, and not a dream only, and will be administered in a spirit unlike that of other states, in which men fight with one another about shadows only and are distracted in the struggle for power, which in their eyes is a great good. Whereas the truth is that the state in which the rulers are most reluctant to govern is always the best and most quietly governed, and the state in which they are most eager, the worst.

Quite true, he replied.

And will our pupils, when they hear this, refuse to take their turn at the toils of state, when they are allowed to spend the greater part of their time with one another in the heavenly light?

Impossible, he answered; for they are just men, and the commands which we impose upon them are just; there can be no doubt that every one of them will take office as a stern necessity, and not after the fashion of our present rulers of state.

Yes, my friend, I said; and there lies the point. You must contrive for your future rulers another and a better life than that of a ruler, and then you may have a well-ordered state; for only in the state which offers this, will they rule who are truly rich, not in silver and gold, but in virtue and wisdom, which are the true blessings of life. Whereas if they go to the administration of public affairs, poor and hungering after their own private advantage, thinking that hence they are to snatch the chief good, order there can never be; for they will be fighting about office, and the civil and domestic broils which thus arise will be the ruin of the rulers themselves and of the whole state.

Most true, he replied.

And the only life which looks down upon the life of political ambition is that of true philosophy. Do you know of any other?

Indeed, I do not, he said.

And those who govern ought not to be lovers of the task? For, if they are, there will be rival lovers, and they will fight.

No question.

Who then are those whom we shall compel to be guardians? Surely they will be the men who are wisest about affairs of state, and by whom the state is administered, and who at the same time have other honors and another and better life than that of politics?

They are the men, and I will choose them, he replied.[1]

[1] VII, 520–521. Jowett, pp. 220–222.

And now let me remind you that, although in our former selection we chose old men, we must not do so in this. Solon was under a delusion when he said that a man when he grows old may learn many things—for he can no more learn much than he can run much; youth is the time for any extraordinary toil.

Of course.

And, therefore, calculation and geometry and all the other elements of instruction, which are a preparation for dialectic, should be presented to the mind in childhood; not, however, under any notion of forcing our system of education.

Why not?

Because a freeman ought not to be a slave in the acquisition of knowledge of any kind. Bodily exercise, when compulsory, does no harm to the body; but knowledge which is acquired under compulsion obtains no hold on the mind.

Very true.

Then, my good friend, I said, do not use compulsion, but let early education be a sort of amusement; you will then be better able to find out the natural bent.

That is a very rational notion, he said.

Do you remember that the children, too, were to be taken to see the battle on horseback; and that if there were no danger they were to be brought close up and, like young hounds, have a taste of blood given them?

Yes, I remember.

The same practice may be followed, I said, in all these things—labors, lessons, dangers—and he who is most at home in all of them ought to be enrolled in a select number.

At what age?

At the age when the necessary gymnastics are over: the period whether of two or three years which passes in this sort of training is useless for any other purpose; for sleep and exercise are unpropitious to learning; and the trial of who is first in gymnastic exercises is one of the most important tests to which our youth are subjected.

Certainly, he replied.

After that time those who are selected from the class of twenty years old will be promoted to higher honor, and the sciences which they learned without any order in their early education will now be brought together, and they will be able to see the natural relationship of them to one another and to true being.

Yes, he said, that is the only kind of knowledge which takes lasting root.

Yes, I said; and the capacity for such knowledge is the great criterion of dialectical talent: the comprehensive mind is always the dialectical.

I agree with you, he said.

These, I said, are the points which you must consider; and those who have most of this comprehension, and who are most steadfast in their learning, and in their military and other appointed duties, when they have arrived at the age of thirty will have to be chosen by you out of the select class, and elevated to higher honor; and you will have to prove them by the help of dialectic, in order to learn which of them is able to give up the use of sight and the other senses, and in company with truth to attain absolute being.[1]

Suppose, I said, the study of philosophy to take the place of gymnastics and to be continued diligently and earnestly and exclusively for twice the number of years which were passed in bodily exercise—will that be enough?

Would you say six or four years? he asked.

Say five years, I replied; at the end of the time they must be sent down again into the den and compelled to hold any military or other office which young men are qualified to hold: in this way they will get their experience of life, and there will be an opportunity of trying whether, when they are drawn all manner of ways by temptation, they will stand firm or flinch.

And how long is this stage of their lives to last?

Fifteen years, I answered; and when they have reached fifty years of age, then let those who still survive and have distinguished themselves in every action of their lives and in every branch of knowledge come at last to their consummation: the time has now arrived at which they must raise the eye of the soul to the universal light which lightens all things, and behold the absolute good; for that is the pattern according to which they are to order the state and the lives of individuals, and the remainder of their own lives also; making philosophy their chief pursuit, but, when their turn comes, toiling also at politics and ruling for the public good, not as though they were performing some heroic action, but simply as a matter of duty; and when they have brought up in each generation others like themselves and left them in their place to be governors of the state, then they will depart to the Islands of the Blest and dwell there; and the city will give them public memorials and sacrifices and honor them,

[1] VII, 536–537. Jowett, pp. 240–241.

if the Pythian oracle consent, as demigods, but if not, as in any case blessed and divine.

You are a sculptor, Socrates, and have made statues of our governors faultless in beauty.

Yes, I said, Glaucon, and of our governesses too; for you must not suppose that what I have been saying applies to men only and not to women as far as their natures can go.

There you are right, he said, since we have made them to share in all things like the men.

Well, I said, and you would agree (would you not?) that what has been said about the state and the government is not a mere dream, and although difficult not impossible, but only possible in the way which has been supposed; that is to say, when the true philosopher kings are born in a state, one or more of them, despising the honors of this present world which they deem mean and worthless, esteeming above all things right and the honor that springs from right, and regarding justice as the greatest and most necessary of all things, whose ministers they are, and whose principles will be exalted by them when they set in order their own city?

How will they proceed?

They will begin by sending out into the country all the inhabitants of the city who are more than ten years old, and will take possession of their children, who will be unaffected by the habits of their parents; these they will train in their own habits and laws, I mean in the laws which we have given them: and in this way the state and constitution of which we were speaking will soonest and most easily attain happiness, and the nation which has such a constitution will gain most.

Yes, that will be the best way. And I think, Socrates, that you have very well described how, if ever, such a constitution might come into being.

Enough then of the perfect state, and of the man who bears its image—there is no difficulty in seeing how we shall describe him.

There is no difficulty, he replied; and I agree with you in thinking that nothing more need be said.[1]

---

[1] VII, 540–541. Jowett, pp. 244–246.

SELECTED BIBLIOGRAPHY

Sabine, George H., *A History of Political Theory*, chs. 2–4.
Cook, Thomas I., *History of Political Philosophy from Plato to Burke*, chs. 2, 3.
McIlwain, Charles H., *The Growth of Political Thought in the West: from the Greeks to the End of the Middle Ages*, chs. 1, 2.
Dunning, William A., *A History of Political Theories, Ancient and Mediæval*, chs. 1, 2.
Nettleship, Richard L., *Lectures on the Republic of Plato* (second ed., London, 1901).
Dickinson, G. Lowes, *Plato and His Dialogues* (London, 1931), chs. 4, 5.
Barker, Ernest, "Greek Political Thought and Theory in the Fourth Century," in *Cambridge Ancient History* (Cambridge, 1927), Vol. VI, ch. 16.
Barker, Ernest, *Greek Political Theory: Plato and His Predecessors* (second ed., London, 1925), chs. 6–17.
Taylor, A. E., *Plato: the Man and His Work* (third ed., New York, 1929), chs. 1, 2, 11, 15, 18.
Burns, C. Delisle, *Greek Ideals: a Study of Social Life* (second ed., London, 1919), chs. 6, 10–15.
Cornford, F. M., "The Athenian Philosophical Schools," in *Cambridge Ancient History*, Vol. VI, ch. 11.
Zeller, Eduard Gottlob, *Plato and the Older Academy*, translated by Sarah Frances Alleyne and Alfred Goodwin (London, 1876), chs. 10–13.
Grote, George, *Plato and the Other Companions of Socrates*, 3 vols. (second ed., London, 1867), Vol. I, chs. 3, 6; Vol. II, chs. 27–28; Vol. III, chs. 34–37.
Gomperz, Theodor, *Greek Thinkers*, Vol. II, translated by G. G. Berry (New York, 1905), bk. v, chs. 13, 17, 20.

Chance, Roger, *Until Philosophers Are Kings: a Study of the Political Theory of Plato and Aristotle in Relation to the Modern State* (London, 1928).

ARISTOTLE

II. ARISTOTLE (364–322 B.C.)

INTRODUCTION

Aristotle is commonly called the father, or maker, of political science. The title is justified both by the scope and style of his political writing and by the great influence of his ideas upon later political reflection. The range of his discussion is comprehensive; his analysis is systematic; his exposition is thorough and is fully illustrated from his relatively wide historical knowledge and extensive observation of contemporary governments. The influence of his ideas and methods in political theory became particularly manifest after the revival of the study of his works in the thirteenth century.

Aristotle was a younger contemporary of Plato. He was born at Stagira, in Thrace. His father was physician to Amyntas II, king of Macedonia. Aristotle came to Athens in his youth and was one of Plato's pupils for about twenty years. He next spent a few years at the court of Hermias, prince of Atarneas, in Asia Minor; he fled from that country when the brief tyranny of Hermias was terminated by revolution. He was then invited to the Macedonian court by King Philip, who made him tutor to the young Alexander. Some time after the accession of Alexander to the Macedonian throne Aristotle returned to Athens, where he conducted a school at the gymnasium called the Lyceum. The system of thought there founded came to be known as the "Peripatetic;" this is, as some say, because Aristotle would meet his students in one of the walks of the Lyceum, or, as others say, because of his habit of strolling about while giving his lectures.

Aristotle, like Plato, lived through anarchy and war in the Greek states, and witnessed the failure of any of them to establish lasting supremacy over the others. On the other hand, he saw the accomplishment of Macedonian expansion and lived under the protection of the great wielder of the strong-man power in that expansion.

53

This latter experience, however, had little influence on his political ideas; for he continued to think only in terms of small political communities.

Aristotle's writings cover a wide field: logic and metaphysics; mathematics and physics; the natural sciences; rhetoric and poetry; ethics and politics. There is not complete agreement among historians of philosophy as to the extent to which the metaphysical basis of Aristotle's system accords with that of his teacher, Plato. Aristotle criticised Plato's ascription of exclusive and independent reality to abstract and general qualities; and he argued that these general elements are real only as attributes attached to concrete objects, which are the only completely real things. This philosophical point of view is a basis for inductive reasoning; and whether or not the general theories of Plato and Aristotle are reconcilable, there are very evident differences in their methods. These differences are especially manifest in their political works: Aristotle's discussion is somewhat more practical and precise, and it is based more on history and observation, with relatively slight allegorical and poetical embellishment. Moreover, politics with Aristotle is more nearly a distinct discipline, separate from philosophy and ethics.

Most of the writings of Aristotle that have come down to us are in fragmentary and disarranged form, suggesting that the earliest manuscripts may have been compiled from lecture notes of teacher or pupil. There is much repetition in *The Politics*, as in other works of Aristotle. None of the arrangements that have been made of the books of *The Politics* is such as to present his thought in clear logical sequence. The selections below embody his ideas on fundamental subjects of political theory, as follows: the nature, origin and end of the state; the justification of slavery; the definition of citizenship; the location of supreme political power; forms of state; the departments of government; the relative advantages of common and individual ownership of property and the question of limiting the size of individual ownership; physical conditions of a good state; the causes of fundamental changes in the form of government and the means of securing stability. In following this order it is necessary at a few places to depart from the order in which the passages appear in the translation from which the selections are taken.

READINGS FROM THE POLITICS[1]

1. The Nature, End, and Origin of the State[2]

Every state is a community of some kind, and every community is established with a view to some good; for mankind always act in order to obtain that which they think good. But, if all communities aim at some good, the state or political community, which is the highest of all, and which embraces all the rest, aims, and in a greater degree than any other, at the highest good.

Now there is an erroneous opinion that a statesman, king, householder, and master are the same, and that they differ, not in kind, but only in the number of their subjects. For example, the ruler over a few is called a master; over more, the manager of a household; over a still larger number, a statesman or king, as if there were no difference between a great household and a small state. The distinction which is made between the king and the statesman is as follows: When the government is personal, the ruler is a king; when, according to the principles of the political science, the citizens rule and are ruled in turn, then he is called a statesman.

But all this is a mistake; for governments differ in kind, as will be evident to any one who considers the matter according to the method which has hitherto guided us. As in other departments of science, so in politics, the compound should always be resolved into the simple elements or least parts of the whole. We must therefore look at the elements of which the state is composed, in order that we may see in what they differ from one another, and whether any scientific distinction can be drawn between the different kinds of rule.

He who thus considers things in their first growth and origin, whether a state or anything else, will obtain the clearest view of them. In the first place (1) there must be a union of those who cannot exist without each other; for example, of male and female, that the race may continue; and this is a union which is formed, not of deliberate purpose, but because, in common with other animals and with plants, mankind have a natural desire to leave behind them an image of themselves. And (2) there must be a union of natural ruler and subject, that both may be preserved. For he who can foresee with his mind is by nature intended to be lord

[1] The selections are taken from *The Politics of Aristotle, translated into English,* by Benjamin Jowett, two volumes, Oxford, 1885. Published by the Clarendon Press.

[2] I, i, ii, iii (in part), v; III, ix. Jowett, pp. 1–5, 7–9, 82–84.

and master, and he who can work with his body is a subject, and by nature a slave; hence master and slave have the same interest. Nature, however, has distinguished between the female and the slave. For she is not niggardly, like the smith who fashions the Delphian knife for many uses; she makes each thing for a single use, and every instrument is best made when intended for one and not for many uses. But among barbarians no distinction is made between women and slaves, because there is no natural ruler among them: they are a community of slaves, male and female. Wherefore the poets say,—

It is meet that Hellenes should rule over barbarians;

as if they thought that the barbarian and the slave were by nature one.

Out of these two relationships between man and woman, master and slave, the family first arises, and Hesiod is right when he says,—

First house and wife and an ox for the plough,

for the ox is the poor man's slave. The family is the association established by nature for the supply of men's everyday wants, and the members of it are called by Charondas "companions of the cupboard" and by Epimenides the Cretan, "companions of the manger." But when several families are united, and the association aims at something more than the supply of daily needs, then comes into existence the village. And the most natural form of the village appears to be that of a colony from the family, composed of the children and grandchildren, who are said to be "suckled with the same milk." And this is the reason why Hellenic states were originally governed by kings; because the Hellenes were under royal rule before they came together, as the barbarians still are. Every family is ruled by the eldest, and therefore in the colonies of the family the kingly form of government prevailed because they were of the same blood. As Homer says [of the Cyclopes]:—

Each one gives law to his children and to his wives.

For they lived dispersedly, as was the manner in ancient times. Wherefore men say that the gods have a king, because they themselves either are or were in ancient times under the rule of a king. For they imagine, not only the forms of the gods, but their ways of life to be like their own.

When several villages are united in a single community, perfect and large enough to be nearly or quite self-sufficing, the state comes into existence, originating in the bare needs of life, and continuing in existence for the sake of a good life. And therefore, if the earlier forms of society are natural, so is the state, for it is the end of them, and the [completed] nature is the end. For what each thing is when fully developed, we call its nature, whether we are speaking of a man, a horse, or a family. Besides, the final cause and end of a thing is the best, and to be self-sufficing is the end and the best.

Hence it is evident that the state is a creation of nature, and that man is by nature a political animal. And he who by nature and not by mere accident is without a state, is either above humanity, or below it; he is the

Tribeless, lawless, heartless one,

whom Homer denounces—the outcast who is a lover of war; he may be compared to a bird which flies alone.

Now the reason why man is more of a political animal than bees or any other gregarious animals is evident. Nature, as we often say, makes nothing in vain, and man is the only animal whom she has endowed with the gift of speech. And whereas mere sound is but an indication of pleasure or pain, and is therefore found in other animals (for their nature attains to the perception of pleasure and pain and the intimation of them to one another, and no further), the power of speech is intended to set forth the expedient and inexpedient, and likewise the just and the unjust. And it is a characteristic of man that he alone has any sense of good and evil, of just and unjust, and the association of living beings who have this sense makes a family and a state.

Thus the state is by nature clearly prior to the family and to the individual, since the whole is of necessity prior to the part; for example, if the whole body be destroyed, there will be no foot or hand, except in an equivocal sense, as we might speak of a stone hand; for when destroyed the hand will be no better. But things are defined by their working and power; and we ought not to say that they are the same when they are no longer the same, but only that they have the same name. The proof that the state is a creation of nature and prior to the individual is that the individual, when isolated, is not self-sufficing; and therefore he is like a part in relation to the whole. But he who is unable to live in society, or who has no need because he is sufficient for himself, must be either a beast or a god: he is no part of a state. A social instinct is implanted in all men by nature, and yet he who first founded the state was the greatest of benefactors. For man, when perfected, is the best of animals, but, when separated from law and justice, he is the worst of all; since armed injustice is the more dangerous, and he is equipped at birth with the arms of intelligence and with moral qualities which he may use for the worst ends. Wherefore, if he have not virtue, he is the most unholy and the most savage of animals, and the most full of lust and gluttony. But justice is the bond of men in states, and the administration of justice, which is the determination of what is just, is the principle of order in political society.

Seeing then that the state is made up of households, before speaking of the state, we must speak of the management of the household. The parts of the household are the persons who compose it, and a complete household consists of slaves and freemen. Now we should begin by examining everything in its least elements; and the first and least parts of a family are master and slave, husband and wife, father and children. We have therefore to consider what each of these three relations is and ought to be: I mean the relation of master and servant, of husband and wife, and thirdly of parent and child. And there is another element of a household, the so-called art of money-making, which, according to some, is identical with household management, according to others, a principal part of it; the nature of this art will also have to be considered by us.

He who is by nature not his own but another's and yet a man, is by nature a slave; and he may be said to belong to another who, being a human being, is also a possession. And a possession may be defined as an instrument of action, separable from the possessor. But is there any one thus intended by nature to be a slave, and for whom such a condition is expedient and right, or rather is not all slavery a violation of nature?

There is no difficulty in answering this question, on grounds both of reason and of fact. For that some should rule, and others be ruled is a thing, not only necessary, but expedient; from the hour of their birth, some are marked out for subjection, others for rule.

And whereas there are many kinds both of rulers and subjects, that rule is the better which is exercised over better subjects— for example, to rule over men is better than to rule over wild beasts. The work is better which is executed by better workmen; and where one man rules and another is ruled, they may be said to have a work. In all things which form a composite whole and which are made up of parts, whether continuous or discrete, a distinction between the ruling and the subject element comes to light. Such a duality exists in living creatures, but not in them only; it originates in the constitution of the universe; even in things which have no life, there is a ruling principle, as in musical harmony. But we are wandering from the subject. We will, therefore, restrict ourselves to the living creature which, in the first place, consists of soul and body: and of these two, the one is by nature the ruler, and the other the subject. But then we must look for the intentions of nature in things which retain their nature, and not in things which are corrupted. And therefore we must study the man who is in the most perfect state both of body and soul, for in him we shall see the true relation of the two; although in bad or corrupted natures the body will often appear to rule over the soul, because they are in an evil and unnatural condition. First then we may observe in living creatures both a despotical and a constitutional rule; for the soul rules the body with a despotical rule, whereas the intellect rules the appetites with a constitutional and royal rule. And it is clear that the rule of the soul over the body, and of the mind and the rational element over the passionate is natural and expedient; whereas the equality of the two or the rule of the inferior is always hurtful. The same holds good of animals as well as of men; for tame animals have a better nature than wild, and all tame animals are better off when they are ruled by man; for then they are preserved. Again, the male is by nature superior, and the female inferior; and the one rules, and the other is ruled; this principle, of necessity, extends to all mankind. Where then there is such a difference as that between soul and body, or between men and animals (as in the case of those whose business is to use their body, and who can do nothing better), the lower sort are by nature slaves, and it is better for them as for all inferiors that they should be under the rule of a master. For he who can be, and therefore is another's, and he who participates in reason enough to apprehend, but not to have, reason, is a slave by nature. Whereas the lower animals cannot even apprehend reason; they obey their instincts. And indeed the use made of slaves and of tame animals is not very different; for both with their bodies minister to the needs of life. Nature would like to distinguish between the bodies of freemen and slaves, making the one strong for servile labor, the other upright, and although useless for such services, useful for political life in the arts both of war and peace. But this does not hold universally: for some slaves have the souls and others have the bodies of freemen. And doubtless if men differed from one another in the mere forms of their bodies as much as the statues of the gods do from men, all would acknowledge that the inferior class should be slaves of the superior. And if there is a difference in the body, how much more in the soul? but the beauty of the body is seen, whereas the beauty of the soul is not seen. It is clear, then, that some men are by nature free, and others slaves, and that for these latter slavery is both expedient and right.

But a state exists for the sake of a good life, and not for the sake of life only: if life only were the object, slaves and brute animals might form a state, but they cannot, for they have no share in happiness or in a life of free choice. Nor does a state exist for the sake of alliance and security from injustice, nor yet for the sake of exchange and mutual intercourse; for then the Tyrrhenians and the Carthagenians, and all who have commercial treaties with one another, would be the citizens of one state. True, they have arrangements about imports, and engagements that they will do no wrong to one another, and written articles of alliance. But there are no magistracies common to the contracting parties who will enforce their engagements; different states have each their own magistracies. Nor does one state take care that the citizens of the other are such as they ought to be, nor see that those who come under the terms of the treaty do no wrong or wickedness at all, but only that they do no injustice to one another. Whereas, those who care for good government take into consideration [the larger question of] virtue and vice in states. Whence it may be further inferred that virtue must be the serious care of a state which truly deserves the name: for [without this ethical end] the community becomes a mere alliance which differs only in place from alliances of which the members live apart; and law is only a convention, "a surety to one another of justice," as the sophist Lycophron says, and has no real power to make the citizens good and just.

This is obvious; for suppose distinct places, such as Corinth and Megara, to be united by a wall, still they would not be one city, not even if the citizens had the right to intermarry, which is one of the rights peculiarly characteristic of states. Again, if men dwelt at a distance from one another, but not so far off as to have no intercourse, and there were laws among them that they should not wrong each other in their exchanges, neither would this be a state. Let us suppose that one man is a carpenter, another a husbandman, another a shoemaker, and so on, and that their number is ten thousand: nevertheless, if they have nothing in common but exchange, alliance, and the like, that would not constitute a state. Why is this? Surely not because they are at a distance from one another: for even supposing that such a community were to meet in one place, and that each man had a house of his own, which was in a manner his state, and that they made alliance with one another, but only against evil-doers; still an accurate thinker would not deem this to be a state, if their intercourse with one another was of the same character after as before their union. It is clear then that a state is not a mere society, having a common place, established for the prevention of crime and for the sake of exchange. These are conditions without which a state cannot exist; but all of them together do not constitute a state, which is a community of well-being in families and aggregations of families, for the sake of a perfect and self-sufficing life. Such a community can only be established among those who live in the same place and intermarry. Hence arise in cities family connections, brotherhoods, common sacrifices, amusements which draw men together. They are created by friendship, for friendship is the motive of society. The end is the good life, and these are the means towards it. And the state is the union of families and villages having for an end a perfect and self-sufficing life, by which we mean a happy and honorable life.

Our conclusion, then, is that political society exists for the sake of noble actions, and not of mere companionship. And they who contribute most to such a society have a greater share in it than those who have the same or a greater freedom or nobility of birth but are inferior to them in political virtue; or than those who exceed them in wealth but are surpassed by them in virtue.

2. The Definition of Citizenship [1]

He who would inquire into the nature and various kinds of government must first of all determine "What is a state?" At present this is a disputed question. Some say that the state has done a certain act; others, no, not the state, but the oligarchy or the tyrant. And the legislator or statesman is concerned entirely with the state; a constitution or government being an arrangement of the inhabitants of a state. But a state is composite, and, like any other whole, made up of many parts;— these are the citizens, who compose it. It is evident, therefore, that we must begin by asking, Who is the citizen, and what is the meaning of the term? For here again there may be a difference of opinion. He who is a citizen in a democracy will often not be a citizen in an oligarchy. Leaving out of consideration those who have been made citizens, or who have obtained the name of

[1] III, i, v (in part). Jowett, pp. 67–69, 75–76.

citizen in any other accidental manner, we may say, first, that a citizen is not a citizen because he lives in a certain place, for resident aliens and slaves share in the place; nor is he a citizen who has no legal right except that of suing and being sued; for this right may be enjoyed under the provisions of a treaty. Even resident aliens in many places possess such rights, although in an imperfect form; for they are obliged to have a patron. Hence they do but imperfectly participate in citizenship, and we call them citizens only in a qualified sense, as we might apply the term to children who are too young to be on the register, or to old men who have been relieved from state duties. Of these we do not say simply that they are citizens, but add in the one case that they are not of age, and in the other, that they are past the age, or something of that sort; the precise expression is immaterial, for our meaning is clear. Similar difficulties to those which I have mentioned may be raised and answered about deprived citizens and about exiles. But the citizen, whom we are seeking to define, is a citizen in the strictest sense, against whom no such exception can be taken, and his special characteristic is that he shares in the administration of justice, and in offices. Now of offices some have a limit of time, and the same persons are not allowed to hold them twice, or can only hold them after a fixed interval; others have no limit of time, —for example, the office of dicast or ecclesiast.[1] It may, indeed, be argued that these are not magistrates at all, and that their functions give them no share in the government. But surely it is ridiculous to say that those who have the supreme power do not govern. Not to dwell further upon this, which is a purely verbal question, what we want is a common term including both dicast and ecclesiast. Let us, for the sake of distinction, call it "indefinite office," and we will assume that those who share in such office are citizens. This is the most comprehensive definition of a citizen, and best suits all those who are generally so called.

But we must not forget that things of which the underlying notions differ in kind, one of them being first, another second, another third, have, when regarded in this relation, nothing, or hardly anything, worth mentioning in common. Now we see that governments differ in kind, and that some of them are prior and that others are posterior; those which are faulty or perverted are necessarily posterior to those which are perfect. (What we mean by perversion will be hereafter explained). The citizen then of necessity differs under each form of government; and our defini-

[1] "Dicast" = juryman and judge in one: "ecclesiast" = member of the ecclesia or assembly of the citizens.—J.

tion is best adapted to the citizen of a democracy; but not necessarily to other states. For in some states the people are not acknowledged, nor have they any regular assembly, but only extraordinary ones; and suits are distributed in turn among the magistrates. At Lacedæmon, for instance, the Ephors determine suits about contracts, which they distribute among themselves, while the elders are judges of homicide, and other causes are decided by other magistrates. A similar principle prevails at Carthage; there certain magistrates decide all causes. We may, indeed, modify our definition of the citizens so as to include these states. In other states it is the holder of a definite, not of an indefinite office, who legislates and judges, and to some or all such holders of definite offices is reserved the right of deliberating or judging about some things or about all things. The conception of the citizen now begins to clear up.

He who has the power to take part in the deliberative or judicial administration of any state is said by us to be a citizen of that state; and speaking generally, a state is a body of citizens sufficing for the purposes of life.

There still remains one more question about the citizen: Is he only a true citizen who has a share of office, or is the mechanic to be included? If they who hold no office are to be deemed citizens, not every citizen can have this virtue of ruling and obeying which makes a citizen. And if none of the lower class are citizens, in which part of the state are they to be placed? For they are not resident aliens, and they are not foreigners. To this objection may we not reply, that there is no more absurdity in excluding them than in excluding slaves and freedmen from any of the above-mentioned classes? It must be admitted that we cannot consider all those to be citizens who are necessary to the existence of the state; for example, children are not citizens equally with grown-up men, who are citizens absolutely, but children, not being grown up, are only citizens in a qualified sense. Doubtless in ancient times, and among some nations, the artisan class were slaves or foreigners, and therefore the majority of them are so now. The best form of state will not admit them to citizenship; but if they are admitted, then our definition of the virtue of a citizen will apply to some citizens and freemen only, and not to those who work for their living. The latter class, to whom toil is a necessity, are either slaves who minister to the wants of individuals, or mechanics and laborers who are the servants of the community.

3. The Location of Supreme Political Power [1]

A parallel question is raised respecting the state whether a certain act is or is not an act of the state; for example, in the transition from an oligarchy or a tyranny to a democracy. In such cases persons refuse to fulfil their contracts or any other obligations, on the ground that the tyrant, and not the state, contracted them; they argue that some constitutions are established by force, and not for the sake of the common good. But this would apply equally to democracies, for they too may be founded on violence, and then the acts of the democracy will be neither more nor less legitimate than those of an oligarchy or of a tyranny. This question runs up into another:—when shall we say that the state is the same, and when different? It would be a very superficial view which considered only the place and the inhabitants; for the soil and the population may be separated, and some of the inhabitants may live in one place and some in another. This, however, is not a very serious difficulty; we need only remark that the word "state" is ambiguous, meaning both state and city.

It is further asked: When are men, living in the same place, to be regarded as a single city—what is the limit? Certainly not the wall of the city, for you might surround all Peloponnesus with a wall. But a city, having such vast circuit, would contain a nation rather than a state, like Babylon, which, as they say, had been taken for three days before some part of the inhabitants became aware of the fact. This difficulty may, however, with advantage be deferred to another occasion; the statesman has to consider the size of the state, and whether it should consist of more than one nation or not.

Again, shall we say that while the race of inhabitants, as well as their place of abode, remain the same, the city is also the same, although the citizens are always dying and being born, as we call rivers and fountains the same, although the water is always flowing away and coming again? Or shall we say that the generations of men, like the rivers, are the same, but that the state changes? For, since the state is a community and a community is made up of citizens, when the form of the government changes and becomes different, then it may be supposed that the state is no longer the same, just as a tragic differs from a comic chorus, although the members of both may be identical. And in this manner we speak of every union or composition of elements, when the form of their composition alters; for example, harmony of the same sounds

[1] III, iii, x–xii, xiii (in part). Jowett, pp. 70–72, 84–93.

is said to be different, accordingly as the Dorian or the Phrygian mode is employed. And if this is true it is evident that the sameness of the state consists chiefly in the sameness of the constitution, and may be called or not called by the same name, whether the inhabitants are the same or entirely different. It is quite another question, whether a state ought or ought not to fulfil engagements when the form of government changes.

There is also a doubt as to what is to be the supreme power in the state:—Is it the multitude? Or the wealthy? Or the good? Or the one best man? Or a tyrant? Any of these alternatives seems to involve disagreeable consequences. If the poor, for example, because they are more in number, divide among themselves the property of the rich,—is not this unjust? No, by heaven (will be the reply), for the lawful authority willed it. But if this is not injustice, pray what is? Again, when [in the first division] all has been taken, and the majority divide anew the property of the minority, is it not evident, if this goes on, that they will ruin the state? Yet surely, virtue is not the ruin of those who possess her, nor is justice destructive of a state; and therefore this law of confiscation clearly cannot be just. If it were, all the acts of a tyrant must of necessity be just; for he only coerces other men by superior power, just as the multitude coerce the rich. But is it just then that the few and the wealthy should be the rulers? And what if they, in like manner, rob and plunder the people,— is this just? If so, the other case [i.e. the case of the majority plundering the minority] will likewise be just. But there can be no doubt that all these things are wrong and unjust. Then ought the good to rule and have supreme power? But in that case everybody else, being excluded from power, will be dishonored. For the offices of a state are posts of honor; and if one set of men always hold them, the rest must be deprived of them. Then will it be well that the one best man should rule? Nay, that is still more oligarchical, for the number of those who are dishonored is thereby increased. Some one may say that it is bad for a man, subject as he is to all the accidents of human passion, to have the supreme power, rather than the law. But what if the law itself be democratical or oligarchical, how will that help us out of our difficulties? Not at all; the same consequences will follow.

Most of these questions may be reserved for another occasion. The principle that the multitude ought to be supreme rather than the few best is capable of a satisfactory explanation, and, though not free from difficulty, yet seems to contain an element of truth. For the many, of whom each individual is but an ordinary person, when they meet together may very likely be better than the few good, if regarded not individually but collectively, just as a feast to which many contribute is better than a dinner provided out of a single purse. For each individual among the many has a share of virtue and prudence, and when they meet together they become in a manner one man, who has many feet, and hands, and senses; that is a figure of their mind and disposition. Hence the many are better judges than a single man of music and poetry; for some understand one part, and some another, and among them, they understand the whole. There is a similar combination of qualities in good men, who differ from any individual of the many, as the beautiful are said to differ from those who are not beautiful, and works of art from realities, because in them the scattered elements are combined, although, if taken separately, the eye of one person or some other feature in another person would be fairer than in the picture. Whether this principle can apply to every democracy, and to all bodies of men, is not clear. Or rather, by heaven, in some cases it is impossible of application; for the argument would equally hold about brutes; and wherein, it will be asked, do some men differ from brutes? But there may be bodies of men about whom our statement is nevertheless true. And if so, the difficulty which has been already raised, and also another which is akin to it—viz. what power should be assigned to the mass of freemen and citizens, who are not rich and have no personal merit—are both solved. There is still a danger in allowing them to share the great offices of state, for their folly will lead them into error, and their dishonesty into crime. But there is a danger also in not letting them share, for a state in which many poor men are excluded from office will necessarily be full of enemies. The only way of escape is to assign to them some deliberative and judicial functions. For this reason Solon and certain other legislators give them the power of electing to offices, and of calling the magistrates to account, but they do not allow them to hold office singly. When they meet together their perceptions are quite good enough, and combined with the better class they are useful to the state (just as impure food when mixed with what is pure sometimes makes the entire mass more wholesome than a small quantity of the pure would be), but each individual, left to himself, forms an imperfect judgment. On the other hand, the popular form of government involves certain difficulties. In the first place, it might be objected that he who can judge of the healing of a sick man would be one

who could himself heal his disease, and make him whole—that
is, in other words, the physician; and so in all professions and arts.
As, then, the physician ought to be called to account by physicians,
so ought men in general to be called to account by their peers.
But physicians are of three kinds:—there is the apothecary, and
there is the physician of the higher class, and thirdly the intelligent
man who has studied the art: in all arts there is such a class;
and we attribute the power of judging to them quite as much as
to professors of the art.   Now, does not the same principle apply
to elections?   For a right election can only be made by those who
have knowledge; a geometrician, for example, will choose rightly
in matters of geometry, or a pilot in matters of steering; and,
even if there be some occupations and arts with which private
persons are familiar, they certainly cannot judge better than those
who know.   So that, according to this argument, neither the election of magistrates, nor the calling of them to account, should be
intrusted to the many.   Yet possibly these objections are to a
great extent met by our old answer, that if the people are not utterly degraded, although individually they may be worse judges than
those who have special knowledge—as a body they are as good or
better.   Moreover, there are some artists whose works are judged
of solely, or in the best manner, not by themselves, but by those
who do not possess the art; for example, the knowledge of the
house is not limited to the builder only; the user, or, in other words,
the master, of the house will even be a better judge than the builder, just as the pilot will judge better of a rudder than the carpenter, and the guest will judge better of a feast than the cook.
This difficulty seems now to be sufficiently answered, but
there is another akin to it.   That inferior persons should have
authority in greater matters than the good would appear to be a
strange thing, yet the election and calling to account of the magistrates is the greatest of all.   And these, as I was saying, are
functions which in some states are assigned to the people, for the
assembly is supreme in all such matters.   Yet persons of any age,
and having but a small property qualification, sit in the assembly
and deliberate and judge, although for the great officers of state,
such as controllers and generals, a high qualification is required.
This difficulty may be solved in the same manner as the preceding,
and the present practice of democracies may be really defensible.
For the power does not reside in the dicast, or senator, or ecclesiast,
but in the court and the senate, and the assembly, of which individual senators, or ecclesiasts, or dicasts, are only parts or members,
and for this reason the many may claim to have a higher authority

than the few; for the people, and the senate, and the courts consist of many persons, and their property collectively is greater than the property of one or of a few individuals holding great offices. But enough of this.

The discussion of the first question shows nothing so clearly as that laws, when good, should be supreme; and that the magistrate or magistrates should regulate those matters only on which the laws are unable to speak with precision owing to the difficulty of any general principle embracing all particulars. But what are good laws has not yet been clearly explained; the old difficulty remains. The goodness or badness, justice or injustice, of laws is of necessity relative to the constitutions of states. But if so, true forms of government will of necessity have just laws, and perverted forms of government will have unjust laws.

In all sciences and arts the end is a good, and especially and above all in the highest of all—this is the political science of which the good is justice, in other words, the common interest. All men think justice to be a sort of equality; and to a certain extent they agree in the philosophical distinctions which have been laid down by us about Ethics. For they admit that justice is a thing having relation to persons, and that equals ought to have equality. But there still remains a question; equality or inequality of what? here is a difficulty which the political philosopher has to resolve. For very likely some persons will say that offices of state ought to be unequally distributed according to superior excellence, in whatever respect, of the citizen, although there is no other difference between him and the rest of the community; for that those who differ in any one respect have different rights and claims. But, surely, if this is true, the complexion or height of a man, or any other advantage, will be a reason for his obtaining a greater share of political rights. The error here lies upon the surface, and may be illustrated from the other arts and sciences. When a number of flute-players are equal in their art, there is no reason why those of them who are better born should have better flutes given to them; for they will not play any better on the flute, and the superior instrument should be reserved for him who is the superior artist. If what I am saying is still obscure, it will be made clearer as we proceed. For if there were a superior flute-player who was far inferior in birth and beauty, although either of these may be a greater good than the art of flute-playing, and persons gifted with these qualities may excel the flute-player in a greater ratio than he excels them in his art, still he ought to have the best flutes given to him, unless the advantages of wealth and birth contribute

to excellence in flute-playing, which they do not. Moreover upon
this principle any good may be compared with any other. For
if a given height, then height in general may be measured either
against height or against freedom. Thus if A excels in height more
than B in virtue, and height in general is more excellent than virtue, all things will be commensurable [which is absurd]; for if a
certain magnitude is greater than some other, it is clear that some
other will be equal. But since no such comparison can be made,
it is evident that there is good reason why in politics men do not
ground their claim to office on every sort of inequality any more
than in the arts. For if some be slow, and others swift, that is
no reason why the one should have little and the others much; it
is in gymnastic contests that such excellence is rewarded. Whereas the rival claims of candidates for office can only be based on
the possession of elements which enter into the composition of
a state. And therefore the noble, or free-born, or rich, may
with good reason claim office; for holders of offices must be freemen and tax-payers: a state can be no more composed entirely of
poor men than entirely of slaves. But if wealth and freedom
are necessary elements, justice and valor are equally so; for without
the former a state cannot exist at all, without the latter not well.

If the existence of the state is alone to be considered, then it
would seem that all, or some at least, of these claims are just;
but, if we take into account a good life, as I have already said,
education and virtue have superior claims. As, however, those
who are equal in one thing ought not to be equal in all, nor those
who are unequal in one thing to be unequal in all, it is certain that
all forms of government which rest on either of these principles
are perversions. All men have a claim in a certain sense, as I
have already admitted, but they have not an absolute claim. The
rich claim because they have a greater share in the land, and land
is the common element of the state; also they are generally more
trustworthy in contracts. The free claim under the same title
as the noble; for they are nearly akin. And the noble are citizens
in a truer sense than the ignoble, since good birth is always valued
in a man's own home and country. Another reason is, that those
who are sprung from better ancestors are likely to be better men,
for nobility is excellence of race. Virtue, too, may be truly said to
have a claim, for justice has been acknowledged by us to be a social
virtue, and it implies all others. Again, the many may urge their
claim against the few; for, when taken collectively, and compared
with the few, they are stronger and richer and better. But, what
if the good, the rich, the noble and the other classes who make up

a state, are all living together in the same city, will there, or will there not, be any doubt who shall rule?—No doubt at all in determining who ought to rule in each of the above-mentioned forms of government. For states are characterized by differences in their governing bodies—one of them has a government of the rich, another of the virtuous, and so on. But a difficulty arises when all these elements coexist. How are we to decide? Suppose the virtuous to be very few in number: may we consider their numbers in relation to their duties, and ask whether they are enough to administer the state, or must they be so many as will make up a state? Objections may be urged against all the aspirants to political power. For those who found their claims on wealth or family have no basis of justice; on this principle, if any one person were richer than all the rest, it is clear that he ought to be the ruler of them. In like manner he who is very distinguished by his birth ought to have the superiority over all those who claim on the ground that they are freeborn. In an aristocracy, or government of the best, a like difficulty occurs about virtue; for if one citizen be better than the other members of the government, however good they may be, he too, upon the same principle of justice, should rule over them. And if the people are to be supreme because they are stronger than the few, then if one man, or more than one, but not a majority, is stronger than the many, they ought to rule, and not the many.

All these considerations appear to show that none of the principles on which men claim to rule, and hold all other men in subjection to them, are strictly right. To those who claim to be masters of the state on the ground of their virtue or their wealth, the many might fairly answer that they themselves are often better and richer than the few—I do not say individually, but collectively. And another ingenious objection which is sometimes put forward may be met in a similar manner. Some persons doubt whether the legislator who desires to make the justest laws ought to legislate with a view to the good of the higher classes or of the many, when the case which we have mentioned occurs [i.e. when all the elements coexist]. Now what is just or right is to be interpreted in the sense of "what is equal"; and that which is right in the sense of being equal is to be considered with reference to the advantage of the state, and the common good of the citizens. And a citizen is one who shares in governing and being governed. He differs under different forms of government, but in the best state he is one who is able and willing to be governed and to govern with a view to the life of virtue.

If, however, there be some one person, or more than one, although not enough to make up the full complement of a state, whose virtue is so preëminent that the virtues or the political power of all the rest admit of no comparison with his or theirs, he or they can be no longer regarded as part of a state; for justice will not be done to the superior, if he is reckoned only as the equal of those who are so far inferior to him in virtue and in political power. Such a one may truly be deemed a god among men. Hence we see that legislation is necessarily concerned only with those who are equal in birth and in power; and that for men of preeminent virtue there is no law—they are themselves a law. Any one would be ridiculous who attempted to make laws for them: they would probably retort what, in the fable of Antisthenes, the lions said to the hares ["where are your claws?"], when in the council of the beasts the latter began haranguing and claiming equality for all. And for this reason democratic states have instituted ostracism; equality is above all things their aim, and therefore they ostracise and banish from the city for a time those who seem to predominate too much through their wealth, or the number of their friends, or through any other political influence.

4. Forms of State [1]

Having determined these questions, we have next to consider whether there is only one form of government or many, and if many, what they are, and how many, and what are the differences between them.

A constitution is the arrangement of magistracies in a state, especially of the highest of all. The government is everywhere sovereign in the state, and the constitution is in fact the government. For example, in democracies the people are supreme, but in oligarchies, the few; and, therefore, we say that these two forms of government are different: and so in other cases.

First, let us consider what is the purpose of a state, and how many forms of government there are by which human society is regulated. We have already said, in the former part of this treatise, when drawing a distinction between household-management and the rule of a master, that man is by nature a political animal. And therefore, men, even when they do not require one another's help, desire to live together all the same, and are in fact brought

[1] III, vi–viii, xiv–xv (in part), xvi–xvii; IV, i, vii–viii, ix (in part), xi, xii (in part); VI, ii–iii. Jowett, pp. 77–81, 95, 97–100, 101–105, 107–109, 120–124, 126–131, 189–193.

together by their common interests in proportion as they severally attain to any measure of well-being. This is certainly the chief end, both of individuals and of states. And also for the sake of mere life (in which there is possibly some noble element) mankind meet together and maintain the political community, so long as the evils of existence do not greatly overbalance the good. And we all see that men cling to life even in the midst of misfortune, seeming to find in it a natural sweetness and happiness.

There is no difficulty in distinguishing the various kinds of authority; they have been often defined already in popular works. The rule of a master, although the slave by nature and the master by nature have in reality the same interests, is nevertheless exercised primarily with a view to the interest of the master, but accidentally considers the slave, since, if the slave perish, the rule of the master perishes with him. On the other hand, the government of a wife and children and of a household, which we have called household-management, is exercised in the first instance for the good of the governed or for the common good of both parties, but essentially for the good of the governed, as we see to be the case in medicine, gymnastics, and the arts in general, which are only accidentally concerned with the good of the artists themselves. (For there is no reason why the trainer may not sometimes practise gymnastics, and the pilot is always one of the crew). The trainer or the pilot considers the good of those committed to his care. But, when he is one of the persons taken care of, he accidentally participates in the advantage, for the pilot is also a sailor, and the trainer becomes one of those in training. And so in politics: when the state is framed upon the principle of equality and likeness, the citizens think that they ought to hold office by turns. In the order of nature every one would take his turn of service; and then again, somebody else would look after his interest, just as he, while in office, had looked after theirs. But nowadays, for the sake of the advantage which is to be gained from the public revenues and from office, men want to be always in office. One might imagine that the rulers, being sickly, were only kept in health while they continued in office; in that case we may be sure that they would be hunting after places. The conclusion is evident: that governments, which have a regard to the common interest, are constituted in accordance with strict principles of justice, and are therefore true forms; but those which regard only the interest of the rulers are all defective and perverted forms, for they are despotic, whereas a state is a community of freemen.

Having determined these points, we have next to consider how many forms of government there are, and what they are; and in the first place what are the true forms, for when they are determined the perversions of them will at once be apparent. The words constitution and government have the same meaning, and the government, which is the supreme authority in states, must be in the hands of one, or of a few, or of many. The true forms of government, therefore, are those in which the one, or the few, or the many, govern with a view to the common interest; but governments which rule with a view to the private interest, whether of the one, or of the few, or of the many, are perversions. For citizens, if they are truly citizens, ought to participate in the advantages of a state. Of forms of government in which one rules, we call that which regards the common interests, kingship or royalty; that in which more than one, but not many, rule, aristocracy, and it is so called, either because the rulers are the best men, or because they have at heart the best interests of the state and of the citizens. But when the citizens at large administer the state for the common interest, the government is called by the generic name,—a constitution [πολιτεία]. And there is a reason for this use of language. One man or a few may excel in virtue; but of virtue there are many kinds: and as the number increases it becomes more difficult for them to attain perfection in every kind, though they may in military virtue, for this is found in the masses. Hence, in a constitutional government the fighting-men have the supreme power, and those who possess arms are the citizens.

Of the above-mentioned forms, the perversions are as follows:— of royalty, tyranny; of aristocracy, oligarchy; of constitutional government, democracy. For tyranny is a kind of monarchy which has in view the interest of the monarch only; oligarchy has in view the interest of the wealthy; democracy, of the needy: none of them the common good of all.

But there are difficulties about these forms of government, and it will therefore be necessary to state a little more at length the nature of each of them. For he who would make a philosophical study of the various sciences, and does not regard practice only, ought not to overlook or omit anything, but to set forth the truth in every particular. Tyranny, as I was saying, is monarchy exercising the rule of a master over political society; oligarchy is when men of property have the government in their hands; democracy, the opposite, when the indigent, and not the men of property, are the rulers. And here arises the first of our difficulties, and it relates to the definition just given. For democracy is said to be the government of the many. But what if the many are men of property and have the power in their hands? In like manner oligarchy is said to be the government of the few; but what if the poor are fewer than the rich, and have the power in their hands because they are stronger? In these cases the distinction which we have drawn between these different forms of government would no longer hold good.

Suppose, once more, that we add wealth to the few and poverty to the many, and name the governments accordingly—an oligarchy is said to be that in which the few and the wealthy, and a democracy that in which the many and the poor are the rulers—there will still be a difficulty. For, if the only forms of government are the ones already mentioned, how shall we describe those other governments also just mentioned by us, in which the rich are the more numerous and the poor are the fewer, and both govern in their respective states?

The argument seems to show that, whether in oligarchies or in democracies, the number of the governing body, whether the greater number, as in a democracy, or the smaller number, as in an oligarchy, is an accident due to the fact that the rich everywhere are few, and the poor numerous. But if so, there is a misapprehension of the causes of the difference between them. For the real difference between democracy and oligarchy is poverty and wealth. Wherever men rule by reason of their wealth, whether they be few or many, that is an oligarchy, and where the poor rule, that is a democracy. But as a fact the rich are few and the poor many: for few are well-to-do, whereas freedom is enjoyed by all, and wealth and freedom are the grounds on which the oligarchical and democratical parties respectively claim power in the state.

Let us see whether in order to be well governed a state or country should be under the rule of a king or under some other form of government; and whether monarchy, although good for some, may not be bad for others. But first we must determine whether there is one species of royalty or many. It is easy to see that there are many, and that the manner of government is not the same in all of them.

These, then, are the four kinds of royalty. First the monarchy of the heroic ages; this was exercised over voluntary subjects, but limited to certain functions; the king was a general and a judge, and had the control of religion. The second is that of the barbarians, which is an hereditary despotic government in accordance with law. A third is the power of the so-called Æsymnete or Dictator; this is an elective tyranny. The fourth is the Lacedæmonian, which is in fact a generalship, hereditary and perpetual. These four forms differ from one another in the manner which I have described.

There is a fifth form of kingly rule in which one has the disposal of all, just as each tribe or each state has the disposal of the public property; this form corresponds to the control of a household. For as household management is the kingly rule of a house, so kingly rule is the household management of a city, or of a nation, or of many nations.

Of these forms we need only consider two, the Lacedæmonian and the absolute royalty; for most of the others lie in a region between them, having less power than the last, and more than the first. Thus the inquiry is reduced to two points: first, is it advantageous to the state that there should be a perpetual general, and if so, should the office be confined to one family, or open to the citizens in turn? Secondly, is it well that a single man should have the supreme power in all things? The first question falls under the head of laws rather than of constitutions; for perpetual generalship might equally exist under any form of government, so that this matter may be dismissed for the present. The other kind of royalty is a sort of constitution; this we have now to consider, and briefly to run over the difficulties involved in it. We will begin by inquiring whether it is more advantageous to be ruled by the best man or by the best laws.

The advocates of royalty maintain that the laws speak only in general terms, and cannot provide for circumstances; and that for any science to abide by written rules is absurd. Even in Egypt the physician is allowed to alter his treatment after the fourth day, but if sooner, he takes the risk. Hence it is argued that a government acting according to written laws is plainly not the best. Yet surely the ruler cannot dispense with the general principle which exists in law; and he is a better ruler who is free from passion than he who is passionate. Whereas the law is passionless, passion must ever sway the heart of man.

Yes, some one will answer, but then on the other hand an individual will be better able to advise in particular cases. [To whom we in turn make reply:] A king must legislate, and laws must be passed, but these laws will have no authority when they miss the mark, though in all other cases retaining their authority. When the law cannot determine a point at all, or not well, should the one best man or should all decide? According to our present practice assemblies meet, sit in judgment, deliberate and decide, and their judgments all relate to individual cases. Now any member of the assembly, taken separately, is certainly inferior to the wise man. But the state is made up of many individuals. And as a feast to which all the guests contribute is better than a banquet furnished by a single man, so a multitude is a better judge of many things than any individual.

Again, the many are more incorruptible than the few; they are like the greater quantity of water which is less easily corrupted than a little. The individual is liable to be overcome by anger or by some other passion, and then his judgment is necessarily perverted; but it is hardly to be supposed that a great number of persons would all get into a passion and go wrong at the same moment. Let us assume that they are freemen, never acting in violation of the law, but filling up the gaps which the law is obliged to leave. Or, if such virtue is scarcely attainable by the multitude, we need only suppose that the majority are good men and good citizens, and ask which will be the more incorruptible, the one good ruler, or the many who are all good? Will not the many? But, you will say, there may be parties among them, whereas the one man is not divided against himself. To which we may answer that their character is as good as his. If we call the rule of many men, who are all of them good, aristocracy, and the rule of one man royalty, then aristocracy will be better for states than royalty, whether the government is supported by force or not, provided only that a number of men equal in virtue can be found.

At this place in the discussion naturally follows the inquiry respecting the king who acts solely according to his own will; he has now to be considered. The so-called limited monarchy, or kingship according to law, as I have already remarked, is not a distinct form of government, for under all governments, as, for example, in a democracy or aristocracy, there may be a general holding office for life, and one person is often made supreme over the administration of a state. A magistracy of this kind exists at Epidamnus, and also at Opus, but in the latter city has a more limited power. Now, absolute monarchy, or the arbitrary rule of a sovereign over all the citizens, in a city which consists of equals, is thought by some to be quite contrary to nature; it is argued that those who are by nature equals must have the same natural right and worth, and that for unequals to have

an equal share, or for equals to have an unequal share, in the offices of state, is as bad as for different bodily constitutions to have the same food and clothing or the same different. Wherefore it is thought to be just that among equals every one be ruled as well as rule, and that all should have their turn. We thus arrive at law; for an order of succession implies law. And the rule of the law is preferable to that of any individual. On the same principle, even if it be better for certain individuals to govern, they should be made only guardians and ministers of the law. For magistrates there must be,—this is admitted; but then men say that to give authority to any one man when all are equal is unjust. There may indeed be cases which the law seems unable to determine, but in such cases can a man? Nay, it will be replied, the law trains officers for this express purpose, and appoints them to determine matters which are left undecided by it to the best of their judgment. Further it permits them to make any amendment of the existing laws which experience suggests. [But still they are only the ministers of the law.] He who bids the law rule, may be deemed to bid God and Reason alone rule, but he who bids man rule adds an element of the beast; for desire is a wild beast, and passion perverts the minds of rulers, even when they are the best of men. The law is reason unaffected by desire. We are told | Law
that a patient should call in a physician; he will not get better if he is doctored out of a book. But the parallel of the arts is clearly not in point; for the physician does nothing contrary to reason from motives of friendship; he only cures a patient and takes a fee; whereas magistrates do many things from spite and partiality. And, indeed, if a man suspected the physician of being in league with his enemies to destroy him for a bribe, he would rather have recourse to the book. Even physicians when they are sick, call in other physicians, and training-masters when they are in training, other training-masters, as if they could not judge truly about their own case and might be influenced by their feelings. Hence it is evident that in seeking for justice men seek for the mean or neutral, and the law is the mean. Again, customary laws have more weight, and relate to more important matters, than written laws, and a man may be a safer ruler than the written law, but not safer than the customary law.

Again, it is by no means easy for one man to superintend many things; he will have to appoint a number of subordinates, and what difference does it make whether these subordinates always existed or were appointed by him because he needed them? If, as I said before, the good man has a right to rule because he is

better, then two good men are better than one: this is the old saying,—

two going together;

and the prayer of Agamemnon,—

would that I had ten such counsellors!

And at this day there are some magistrates, for example judges,
who have authority to decide matters which the law is unable to
determine, since no one doubts that the law would command and
decide in the best manner whatever it could. But some things
can, and other things cannot, be comprehended under the law,
and this is the origin of the vexed question whether the best law
or the best man should rule. For matters of detail about which
men deliberate cannot be included in legislation. Nor does any
one deny that the decision of such matters must be left to man,
but it is argued that there should be many judges, and not ône
only. For every ruler who has been trained by the law judges
well; and it would surely seem strange that a person should see
better with two eyes, or hear better with two ears, or act better
with two hands or feet, than many with many; indeed, it is already
the practice of kings to make to themselves many eyes and ears
and hands and feet. For they make colleagues of those who are
the friends of themselves and their governments. They must
be friends of the monarch and of his government; if not his friends,
they will not do what he wants; but friendship implies likeness
and equality; and, therefore, if he thinks that friends ought to
rule, he must think that those who are equal to himself and like
himself ought to rule. These are the principal controversies
relating to monarchy.

But may not all this be true in some cases and not in others?
for there is a natural justice and expediency in the relation of a
master to his servants, or, again, of a king to his subjects, as also
in the relation of free citizens to one another; whereas there is no
such justice or expediency in a tyranny, or in any other perverted
form of government, which comes into being contrary to nature.
Now, from what has been said, it is manifest that, where men are
alike and equal, it is neither expedient nor just that one man should
be lord of all, whether there are laws, or whether there are no laws,
but he himself is in the place of law. Neither should a good man
be lord over good men, or a bad man over bad; nor, even if he
excels in virtue, should he have a right to rule, unless in a particular case, which I have already mentioned, and to which I will
once more recur. But first of all, I must determine what natures

are suited for royalties, and what for an aristocracy, and what for a constitutional government.

A people who are by nature capable of producing a race superior in virtue and political talent are fitted for kingly government; and a people submitting to be ruled as freemen by men whose virtue renders them capable of political command are adapted for an aristocracy: while the people who are suited for constitutional freedom, are those among whom there naturally exists a warlike multitude able to rule and to obey in turn by a law which gives office to the well-to-do according to their desert. But when a whole family, or some individual, happens to be so preëminent in virtue as to surpass all others, then it is just that they should be the royal family and supreme over all, or that this one citizen should be king of the whole nation. For, as I said before, to give them authority is not only agreeable to that ground of right which the founders of all states, whether aristocratical, or oligarchical, or again democratical, are accustomed to put forward; (for these all recognize the claim of excellence, although not the same excellence), but accords with the principle already laid down. For it would not be right to kill, or ostracise, or exile such a person, or require that he should take his turn in being governed. The whole is naturally superior to the part, and he who has this preeminence is in the relation of a whole to a part. But if so, the only alternative is that he should have the supreme power, and that mankind should obey him, not in turn, but always. These are the conclusions at which we arrive respecting royalty and its various forms, and this is the answer to the question, whether it is or is not advantageous to states, and to whom, and how.

In all arts and sciences which embrace the whole of any subject, and are not restricted to a part only, it is the province of a single art or science to consider all that appertains to a single subject. For example, the art of gymnastic considers not only the suitableness of different modes of training to different bodies (2), but what sort is absolutely the best (1); (for the absolutely best must suit that which is by nature best and best furnished with the means of life), and also what common form of training is adapted to the great majority of men (4). And if a man does not desire the best habit of body or the greatest skill in gymnastics, which might be attained by him, still the trainer or the teacher of gymnastic should be able to impart any lower degree of either (3). The same principle equally holds in medicine and ship-building, and the making of clothes, and in the arts generally.

Hence it is obvious that government, too, is the subject of a single science, which has to consider what kind of government would be best and most in accordance with our aspirations, if there were no external impediment, and also what kind of government is adapted to particular states. For the best is often unattainable, and therefore the true legislator and statesman ought to be acquainted, not only with (1) that which is best in the abstract, but also with (2) that which is best relatively to circumstances. We should be able further to say how a state may be constituted under any given conditions (3); both how it is originally formed and, when formed, how it may be longest preserved; the supposed state being so far from the very best that it is unprovided even with the conditions necessary for the very best; neither is it the best under the circumstances, but of an inferior type.

He ought, moreover, to know (4) the form of government which is best suited to states in general; for political writers, although they have excellent ideas, are often unpractical. We should consider, not only what form of government is best, but also what is possible and what is easily attainable by all. There are some who would have none but the most perfect; for this many natural advantages are required. Others, again, speak of a more attainable form, and, although they reject the constitution under which they are living, they extol some one in particular, for example the Lacedæmonian. Any change of government which has to be introduced should be one which men will be both willing and able to adopt, since there is quite as much trouble in the reformation of an old constitution as in the establishment of a new one, just as to unlearn is as hard as to learn. And therefore, in addition to the qualifications of the statesman already mentioned, he should be able to find remedies for the defects of existing constitutions. This he cannot do unless he knows how many forms of a government there are. It is often supposed that there is only one kind of democracy and one of oligarchy. But this is a mistake; and, in order to avoid such mistakes, we must ascertain what differences there are in the constitutions of states, and in how many ways they are combined. The same political insight will enable a man to know which laws are the best, and which are suited to different constitutions; for the laws are, and ought to be, relative to the constitution, and not the constitution to the laws. A constitution is the organization of offices in a state, and determines what is to be the governing body, and what is the end of each community. But laws are not to be confounded with the principles of the constitution: they are the rules according to which the magistrates should administer the state, and proceed against offenders. So that we must know the number and varieties of the several forms of government, if only with a view to making laws. For the same laws cannot be equally suited to all oligarchies and to all democracies, and there is certainly more than one form both of democracy and of oligarchy.

There are still two forms besides democracy and oligarchy; one of them is universally recognized and included among the four principal forms of government which are said to be (1) monarchy, (2) oligarchy, (3) democracy, and (4) the so-called aristocracy or government of the best. But there is also a fifth, which retains the generic name of polity or constitutional government; this is not common, and therefore has not been noticed by writers who attempt to enumerate the different kinds of government; like Plato in his books about the state, they recognize four only. The term "aristocracy" is rightly applied to the form of government which is described in the first part of our treatise; for that only can be rightly called aristocracy [the government of the best] which is a government formed of the best men absolutely, and not merely of men who are good when tried by any given standard. In the perfect state the good man is absolutely the same as the good citizen; whereas in other states the good citizen is only good relatively to his own form of government. But there are some states differing from oligarchies and also differing from the so-called polity or constitutional government; these are termed aristocracies, and in them magistrates are certainly chosen, both according to their wealth and according to their merit. Such a form of government is not the same with the two just now mentioned, and is termed an aristocracy. For indeed in states which do not make virtue the aim of the community, men of merit and reputation for virtue may be found. And so where a government has regard to wealth, virtue, and numbers, as at Carthage, that is aristocracy; and also where it has regard only to two out of the three, as at Lacedæmon, to virtue and numbers, and the two principles of democracy and virtue temper each other. There are these two forms of aristocracy in addition to the first and perfect state, and there is a third form, viz. the polities which incline towards oligarchy.

I have yet to speak of the co-called polity and of tyranny. I put them in this order, not because a polity or constitutional government is to be regarded as a perversion any more than the above-mentioned aristocracies. The truth is, that they all fall

short of the most perfect form of government, and so they are
reckoned among perversions, and other forms (sc. the really
perverted forms) are perversions of these, as I said before. Last
of all I will speak of tyranny, which I place last in the series because
I am inquiring into the constitutions of states, and this is the very
reverse of a constitution.

Having explained why I have adopted this order, I will proceed
to consider constitutional government; of which the nature will
be clearer now that oligarchy and democracy have been defined.
For polity or constitutional government may be described generally as a fusion of oligarchy and democracy; but the term is usually
applied to those forms of government which incline towards
democracy, and the term aristocracy to those which incline towards
oligarchy, because birth and education are commonly the accom-
paniments of wealth. Moreover, the rich already possess the
external advantages the want of which is a temptation to crime,
and hence they are called noblemen and gentlemen. And inasmuch as aristocracy seeks to give predominance to the best of
the citizens, people say also of oligarchies that they are composed
of noblemen and gentlemen. Now it appears to be an impossible
thing that the state which is governed by the best citizens should
be ill-governed, and equally impossible that the state which is ill-
governed should be governed by the best. But we must remember that good laws, if they are not obeyed, do not constitute good
government. For there are two parts of good government; one
is the actual obedience of citizens to the laws, the other part is the
goodness of the laws which they obey; they may obey bad laws
as well as good. And there may be a further subdivision; they
may obey either the best laws which are attainable to them, or the
best absolutely.

The distribution of offices according to merit is a special characteristic of aristocracy, for the principle of an aristocracy is virtue,
as wealth is of an oligarchy, and freedom of a democracy. In all
of them there of course exists the right of the majority, and whatever seems good to the majority of those who share in the government has authority. Generally, however, a state of this kind is
called a constitutional government, for the fusion goes no further
than the attempt to unite the freedom of the poor and the wealth
of the rich, who commonly take the place of the noble. And
as there are three grounds on which men claim an equal share
in the government, freedom, wealth, and virtue (for the fourth or
good birth is the result of the two last, being only ancient wealth
and virtue), it is clear that the admixture of the two elements,

that is to say, of the rich and poor, is to be called a polity or constitutional government; and the union of the three is to be called aristocracy or the government of the best, and more than any other form of government, except the true and ideal, has a right to this name.

Thus far I have described the different forms of states which exist besides monarchy, democracy, and oligarchy, and what they are, and in what aristocracies differ from one another, and polities from aristocracies—that the two latter are not very unlike is obvious.

Next we have to consider how by the side of oligarchy and democracy the so-called polity or constitutional government springs up, and how it should be organized. The nature of it will be at once understood from a comparison of oligarchy and democracy; we must ascertain their different characteristics, and taking a portion from each, put the two together, like the parts of an indenture. Now there are three modes in which fusions of government may be effected. The nature of the fusion will be made intelligible by an example of the manner in which different governments legislate, say concerning the administration of justice. In oligarchies they impose a fine on the rich if they do not serve as judges, and to the poor they give no pay; but in democracies they give pay to the poor and do not fine the rich. Now (1) the union of these two modes is a common or middle term between them, and is therefore characteristic of a constitutional government, for it is a combination of both. This is one mode of uniting the two elements. Or (2) a mean may be taken between the enactments of the two: thus democracies require no property qualification, or only a small one, from members of the assembly, oligarchies a high one; here neither of these is the common term, but a mean between them. (3) There is a third mode, in which something is borrowed from the oligarchical and something from the democratical principle. For example, the appointment of magistrates by lot is democratical, and the election of them oligarchical; democratical again when there is no property qualification, oligarchical when there is. In the aristocratical or constitutional state, one element will be taken from each—from oligarchy the mode of electing to offices, from democracy the disregard of qualification. Such are the various modes of combination.

We have now to inquire what is the best constitution for most states, and the best life for most men, neither assuming a standard of virtue which is above ordinary persons, nor an edu-

cation which is exceptionally favored by nature and circumstances, nor yet an ideal state which is an aspiration only, but
having regard to the life in which the majority are able to share,
and to the form of government which states in general can attain.
As to those aristocracies, as they are called, of which we were just
now speaking, they either lie beyond the possibilities of the greater
number of states, or they approximate to the so-called constitutional government, and therefore need no separate discussion.
And in fact the conclusion at which we arrive respecting all these
forms rests upon the same grounds. For if it has been truly
said in the *Ethics* that the happy life is the life according to un-
impeded virtue, and that virtue is a mean, then the life which is
in a mean, and in a mean attainable by every one, must be the
best. And the same principles of virtue and vice are characteristic of cities and of constitutions; for the constitution is in a figure
the life of the city.

Now in all states there are three elements; one class is very
rich, another very poor, and a third in a mean. It is admitted
that moderation and the mean are best, and therefore it will
clearly be best to possess the gifts of fortune in moderation; for
in that condition of life men are most ready to listen to reason.
But he who greatly excels in beauty, strength, birth or wealth, or
on the other hand who is very poor, or very weak, or very much
disgraced, finds it difficult to follow reason. Of these two the
one sort grow into violent and great criminals, the others into
rogues and petty rascals. And two sorts of offences correspond
to them, the one committed from violence, the other from roguery.
The petty rogues are disinclined to hold office, whether military
or civil, and their aversion to these two duties is as great an injury
to the state as their tendency to crime. Again, those who have
too much of the goods of fortune, strength, wealth, friends, and
the like, are neither willing nor able to submit to authority. The
evil begins at home: for when they are boys, by reason of the luxury
in which they are brought up, they never learn, even at school
the habit of obedience. On the other hand, the very poor, who are
in the opposite extreme, are too degraded. So that the one class
cannot obey, and can only rule despotically; the other knows not
how to command and must be ruled like slaves. Thus arises a
city, not of freemen, but of masters and slaves, the one despising,
the other envying; and nothing can be more fatal to friendship
and good fellowship in states than this: for good fellowship tends
to friendship; when men are at enmity with one another, they
would rather not even share the same path. But a city ought to

be composed, as far as possible, of equals and similars; and these are generally the middle classes. Wherefore the city which is composed of middle-class citizens is necessarily best governed; they are, as we say, the natural elements of a state. And this is the class of citizens which is most secure in a state, for they do not, like the poor, covet their neighbors' goods; nor do others covet theirs, as the poor covet the goods of the rich; and as they neither plot against others, nor are themselves plotted against, they pass through life safely. Wisely then did Phocylides pray,—

Many things are best in the mean ; I desire to be of a middle condition in my city.

Thus it is manifest that the best political community is formed by citizens of the middle class, and that those states are likely to be well-administered, in which the middle class is large, and larger if possible than both the other classes, or at any rate than either singly; for the addition of the middle class turns the scale, and prevents either of the extremes from being dominant. Great then is the good fortune of a state in which the citizens have a moderate and sufficient property; for where some possess much, and the others nothing, there may arise an extreme democracy, or a pure oligarchy; or a tyranny may grow out of either extreme,— either out of the most rampant democracy, or out of an oligarchy; but it is not so likely to arise out of a middle and nearly equal condition. I will explain the reason of this hereafter, when I speak of the revolutions of states. The mean condition of states is clearly best, for no other is free from faction; and where the middle class is large, there are least likely to be factions and dissensions. For a similar reason large states are less liable to faction than small ones, because in them the middle class is large; whereas in small states it is easy to divide all the citizens into two classes who are either rich or poor, and to leave nothing in the middle. And democracies are safer and more permanent than oligarchies, because they have a middle class which is more numerous and has a greater share in the government; for when there is no middle class, and the poor greatly exceed in number, troubles arise, and the state soon comes to an end. A proof of the superiority of the middle class is that the best legislators have been of a middle condition; for example, Solon, as his own verses testify; and Lycurgus, for he was not a king; and Charondas, and almost all legislators.

These considerations will help us to understand why most governments are either democratical or oligarchical. The reason is that the middle class is seldom numerous in them, and which-

ever party, whether the rich or the common people, transgresses
the mean and predominates, draws the government to itself, and
thus arises either oligarchy or democracy.   There is another reason—the poor and the rich quarrel with one another, and whichever side gets the better, instead of establishing a just or popular
government, regards political supremacy as the prize of victory,
and the one party sets up a democracy and the other an oligarchy.
Both the parties which had the supremacy in Hellas looked only
to the interest of their own form of government, and established
in states, the one, democracies, and the other, oligarchies; they
thought of their own advantage, of the public not at all.   For
these reasons the middle form of government has rarely, if ever,
existed, and among a very few only.   One man alone of all who ever
ruled in Hellas was induced to give this middle constitution to
states.   But it has now become a habit among the citizens of
states, not even to care about equality; all men are seeking for
dominion, or, if conquered, are willing to submit.

What then is the best form of government, and what makes it
the best is evident; and of other states, since we say that there
are many kinds of democracy and many of oligarchy, it is not
difficult to see which has the first and which the second or any
other place in the order of excellence, now that we have determined which is the best.   For that which is nearest to the best must
of necessity be better, and that which is furthest from it worse,
if we are judging absolutely and not relatively to given conditions:
I say "relatively to given conditions," since a particular government may be preferable for some, but another form may be better
for others.

We have now to consider what and what kind of government is
suitable to what and what kind of men.   I may begin by assuming, as a general principle common to all governments, that the
portion of the state which desires permanence ought to be stronger
than that which desires the reverse.   Now every city is composed
of quality and quantity.   By quality I mean freedom, wealth,
education, good birth, and by quantity, superiority of numbers.
Quality may exist in one of the classes which make up the state,
and quantity in the other.   For example, the meanly-born may
be more in number than the well-born, or the poor than the
rich, yet they may not so much exceed in quantity as they fall
short in quality; and therefore there must be a comparison of
quantity and quality.   Where the number of the poor is more than
proportioned to the wealth of the rich, there will naturally be a
democracy, varying in form with the sort of people who compose

it in each case. If, for example, the husbandmen exceed in number, the first form of democracy will then arise; if the artisans and laboring class, the last; and so with the intermediate forms. But where the rich and the notables exceed in quality more than they fall short in quantity, there oligarchy arises, similarly assuming various forms according to the kind of superiority possessed by the oligarchs.

The legislator should always include the middle class in his government; if he makes his laws oligarchical, to the middle class let him look; if he makes them democratical, he should equally by his laws try to attach this class to the state. There only can the government ever be stable where the middle class exceeds one or both of the others, and in that case there will be no fear that the rich will unite with the poor against the rulers. For neither of them will ever be willing to serve the other, and if they look for some form of government more suitable to both, they will find none better than this, for the rich and the poor will never consent to rule in turn, because they mistrust one another. The arbiter is always the one trusted, and he who is in the middle is an arbiter. The more perfect the admixture of the political elements, the more lasting will be the state. Many even of those who desire to form aristocratical governments make a mistake, not only in giving too much power to the rich, but in attempting to over-reach the people. There comes a time when out of a false good there arises a true evil, since the encroachments of the rich are more destructive to the state than those of the people.

The basis of a democratic state is liberty; which, according to the common opinion of men, can only be enjoyed in such a state;— this they affirm to be the great end of every democracy. One principle of liberty is for all to rule and be ruled in turn,and indeed democratic justice is the application of numerical not proportionate equality; whence it follows that the majority must be supreme, and that whatever the majority approve must be the end and the just. Every citizen, it is said, must have equality, and therefore in a democracy the poor have more power than the rich, because there are more of them, and the will of the majority is supreme. This, then, is one note of liberty which all democrats affirm to be the principle of their state. Another is that a man should live as he likes. This, they say, is the privilege of a freeman, and, on the other hand, not to live as a man likes is the mark of a slave. This is the second characteristic of democracy, whence has arisen the claim of men to be ruled by none, if possible, or, if this is impossible,

to rule and be ruled in turns; and so it coincides with the freedom
based upon equality [which was the first characteristic].

Such being our foundation and such the nature of democracy,
its characteristics are as follows:—the election of officers by all
out of all; and that all should rule over each, and each in his turn
over all; that the appointment to all offices, or to all but those
which require experience and skill, should be made by lot; that
no property qualification should be required for offices, or only a
very low one; that no one should hold the same office twice, or
not often, except in the case of military offices; that the tenure
of all offices, or of as many as possible, should be brief; that all
men should sit in judgment, or that judges selected out of all
should judge in all matters, or in most, or in the greatest and most
important,—such as the scrutiny of accounts, the constitution,
and private contracts; that the assembly should be supreme over
all causes, or at any rate over the most important, and the magistrates over none or only over a very few. Of all institutions, a
council is the most democratic when there is not the means of
paying all the citizens, but when they are paid even this is robbed
of its power; for the people then draw all cases to themselves, as
I said in the previous discussion. The next characteristic of
democracy is payment for services; assembly, law-courts, magistrates, everybody receives pay, when it is to be had; or when it
is not to be had for all, then it is given to the law-courts and to the
stated assemblies, to the council and to the magistrates, or at least
to any of them who are compelled to have their meals together.
And whereas oligarchy is characterized by birth, wealth, and
education, the notes of democracy appear to be the opposite
of these,—low birth, poverty, mean employment. Another note
is that no magistracy is perpetual, but if any such have survived
some ancient change in the constitution it should be stripped of
its power, and the holders should be elected by lot and no longer
by vote. These are points common to all democracies; but democracy and demos in their truest form are based upon the recognized
principle of democratic justice, that all should count equally;
for equality implies that the rich should have no more share in
the government than the poor, and should not be the only rulers,
but that all should rule equally according to their numbers. And
in this way men think that they will secure equality and freedom
in their state.

Next comes the question, how is this equality to be obtained?
Is the qualification to be so distributed that five hundred rich
shall be equal to a thousand poor? and shall we give the thousand

a power equal to that of the five hundred? or, if this is not to be the mode, ought we, still retaining the same ratio, to take equal numbers from each and give them the control of the elections and of the courts?—Which, according to the democratical notion, is the juster form of the constitution,—this or one based on numbers only? Democrats say that justice is that to which the majority agree, oligarchs that to which the wealthier class; in their opinion the decision should be given according to the amount of property. In both principles there is some inequality and injustice. For if justice is the will of the few, any one person who has more wealth than all the rest of his class put together, ought, upon the oligarchical principle, to have the sole power—but this would be tyranny; or if justice is the will of the majority, as I was before saying, they will unjustly confiscate the property of the wealthy minority. To find a principle of equality in which they both agree we must inquire into their respective ideas of justice.

Now they agree in saying that whatever is decided by the majority of the citizens is to be deemed law. Granted:—but not without some reserve; since there are two classes out of which a state is composed,—the poor and the rich,—that is to be deemed law, on which both or the greater part of both agree; and if they disagree, that which is approved by the greater number, and by those who have the high qualification. For example, suppose that there are ten rich and twenty poor, and some measure is approved by six of the rich and is disapproved by fifteen of the poor, and the remaining four of the rich join with the part of the poor, and the remaining five of the poor with that of the rich; in such a case the will of those whose qualifications, when both sides are added up, are the greatest, should prevail. If they turn out to be equal, there is no greater difficulty than at present, when, if the assembly or the courts are divided, recourse is had to the lot, or to some similar expedient. But, although it may be difficult in theory to know what is just and equal, the practical difficulty of inducing those to forbear who can, if they like, encroach, is far greater, for the weaker are always asking for equality and justice, but the stronger care for none of these things.

5. *The Organs of Government* [1]

All states have three elements, and the good law-giver has to regard what is expedient for each state. When they are well-ordered, the state is well-ordered, and as they differ from one an-

---
[1] IV, xiv, xv–xvi (in part). Jowett, pp. 133–136, 139–141, 142–143.

other, constitutions differ. What is the element first (1) which deliberates about public affairs; secondly (2) which is concerned with the magistrates and determines what they should be, over whom they should exercise authority, and what should be the mode of electing them; and thirdly (3) which has judicial power?

The deliberative element has authority in matters of war and peace, in making and unmaking alliances; it passes laws, inflicts death, exile, confiscation, audits the accounts of magistrates. All these powers must be assigned either to all the citizens or to some of them, for example, to one or more magistracies; or different causes to different magistracies, or some of them to all, and others of them only to some. That all things should be decided by all is characteristic of democracy; this is the sort of equality which the people desire. But there are various ways in which all may share in the government; they may deliberate, not all in one body, but by turns, as in the constitution of Telecles the Milesian. There are other states in which the boards of magistrates meet and deliberate, but come into office by turns, and are elected out of the tribes and the very smallest divisions of the state, until every one has obtained office in his turn. The citizens, on the other hand, are assembled only for the purposes of legislation, and to consult about the constitution, and to hear the edicts of the magistrates. In another variety of democracy the citizens form one assembly, but meet only to elect magistrates, to pass laws, to advise about war and peace, and to make scrutinies. Other matters are referred severally to special magistrates, who are elected by vote or by lot out of all the citizens. Or again, the citizens meet about election to offices and about scrutinies, and deliberate concerning war or alliances, while other matters are administered by the magistrates, who, as far as is possible, are elected by vote. I am speaking of those magistracies in which special knowledge is required. A fourth form of democracy is when all the citizens meet to deliberate about everything, and the magistrates decide nothing, but only make the preliminary inquiries; and that is the way in which the last and worst form of democracy, corresponding, as we maintain, to the close family oligarchy and to tyranny, is at present administered. All these modes are democratical.

On the other hand, that some should deliberate about all is oligarchical. This again is a mode which, like the democratical, has many forms. When the deliberative class being elected out of those who have a moderate qualification are numerous and they respect and obey the law without altering it, and any one who has the required qualification shares in the government, then, just because of this moderation, the oligarchy inclines toward polity. But when only selected individuals and not the whole people share in the deliberations of the state, then, although, as in the former case, they observe the law, the government is a pure oligarchy. Or, again, when those who have the power of deliberation are self-elected, and son succeeds father, and they and not the laws are supreme—the government is of necessity oligarchical. Where, again, particular persons have authority in particular matters;—for example, when the whole people decide about peace and war and hold scrutinies, but the magistrates regulate everything else, and they are elected either by vote or by lot—there the form of government is an aristocracy or polity. And if some questions are decided by magistrates elected by vote, and others by magistrates elected by lot, either absolutely or out of select candidates, or elected both by vote and by lot— these practices are partly characteristic of an aristocratical government, and partly of a pure constitutional government.

These are the various forms of the deliberative body; they correspond to the various forms of government. And the government of each state is administered according to one or other of the principles which have been laid down. Now it is for the interest of democracy, according to the most prevalent notion of it (I am speaking of that extreme form of democracy, in which the people are supreme even over the laws), with a view to better deliberation to adopt the custom of oligarchies respecting courts of law. For in oligarchies the rich who are wanted to be judges are compelled to attend under pain of fine, whereas in democracies the poor are paid to attend. And this practice of oligarchies should be adopted by democracies in their public assemblies, for they will advise better if they all deliberate together,—the people with the notables and the notables with the people. It is also a good plan that those who deliberate should be elected by vote or by lot in equal numbers out of the different classes; and that if the people greatly exceed in number those who have political training, pay should not be given to all, but only to as many as would balance the number of the notables, or that the number in excess should be eliminated by lot. But in oligarchies either certain persons should be chosen out of the mass, or a class of officers should be appointed such as exist in some states, who are termed probuli and guardians of the law; and the citizens should occupy themselves exclusively with matters on which these have previously deliberated; for so the people will have a share in the deliberations of the state, but will not be able to disturb the principles of the constitution. Again, in oligarchies either the people ought to accept the measures of the government, or not to pass anything contrary to them; or, if all are allowed to share in counsel, the decision should rest with the magistrates. The opposite of what is done in constitutional governments should be the rule in oligarchies; the veto of the majority should be final, their assent not final, but the proposal should be referred back to the magistrates. Whereas in constitutional governments they take the contrary course; the few have the negative not the affirmative power; the affirmation of everything rests with the multitude.

These, then, are our conclusions respecting the deliberative, that is, the supreme element in states.

I will now inquire into the appointment of offices. There are three questions to be answered, and the combinations of answers give all possible differences: first, who appoints? secondly, from whom? and thirdly, how? Each of these three may further differ in three ways: (1) All the citizens, or only some, appoint; (2) either the magistrates are chosen out of all or out of some who are distinguished either by property qualification, or by birth, or merit, or for some special reason, as at Megara only those were eligible who had returned from exile and fought together against the democracy; (3) they may be appointed either by vote or by lot. Again, these several modes may be combined: I mean that some officers may be elected by some, others by all, and some again out of some, and others out of all, and some by vote and others by lot. Each of these differences admits of four variations. (1) Either all may elect out of all by vote, or all out of all by lot; and either out of all collectively or by sections, as, for example, by tribes, and wards, and phratries, until all the citizens have been gone through; or the citizens may be in all cases eligible indiscriminately, and in some cases they may be elected by vote, and in some by lot. Again (2), if only some appoint, they may appoint out of all by vote, or out of all by lot; or out of some by vote, out of some by lot, and some offices may be appointed in one way and some in another, I mean if they are appointed by all they may be appointed partly by vote and partly by lot. Thus there will be twelve forms of appointment without including the two combinations in the mode of election. Of these varieties two are democratic forms, namely, when the choice is made by all the people out of all by vote or by lot, or by both, that is to say, some by lot and some by vote. The cases in which they do not all appoint at one time, but some appoint out of all or out of some by vote or by lot or by both (I mean some by lot and some by vote), or some out of all and others out of some both by lot and vote, are characteristic of a polity or constitutional government. That some should be appointed out of all by vote or by lot or by both, is oligarchical, and still more oligarchical when some are elected from all and some from some. That some should be elected out of all and some out of some, or again some by vote and others by lot, is characteristic of a constitutional government, which inclines to an aristocracy. That some should be chosen out of some, and some taken by lot out of some, is oligarchical though not equally oligarchical; oligarchical, too, is the appointment of some out of some in both ways, and of some out of all. But that all should elect by vote out of some is aristocratical.

These are the different ways of constituting magistrates, and in this manner officers correspond to different forms of government:—which are proper to which, or how they ought to be established, will be evident when we determine the nature of their powers. By powers I mean such power as a magistrate exercises over the revenue or in defence of the country; for there are various kinds of power: the power of the general, for example, is not the same with that which regulates contracts in the market.

Of the three parts of government, the judicial remains to be considered, and this we shall divide on the same principle. There are three points on which the varieties of law-courts depend:— the persons from whom they are appointed, the matters with which they are concerned, and the manner of their appointment. I mean, (1) are the judges taken from all, or from some only? (2) how many kinds of law-courts are there? (3) are the judges chosen by vote or by lot?

Now if all the citizens judge, in all the different cases which I have distinguished, they may be appointed by vote or by lot, or sometimes by lot and sometimes by vote. Or when a certain class of causes are tried, the judges who decide them may be appointed, some by vote, and some by lot. These then are the four modes of appointing judges from the whole people, and there will be likewise four modes, if they are elected from a part only; for they may be appointed from some by vote and judge in all causes; or they may be appointed from some by lot and judge in all causes; or they may be elected in some cases by vote, and in some cases taken by lot, or some courts, even when judging the same causes, may be composed of members some appointed by vote and some by lot. These then are the ways in which the aforesaid judges may be appointed.

Once more, the modes of appointment may be combined; I mean, that some may be chosen out of the whole people, others out of some, some out of both; for example, the same tribunal may be composed of some who were elected out of all, and of others who were elected out of some, either by vote or by lot or by both.

In how many forms law-courts can be established has now been considered. The first form, viz. that in which the judges are taken from all the citizens, and in which all causes are tried, is democratical; the second, which is composed of a few only who try all causes, oligarchical; the third, in which some courts are taken from all classes, and some from certain classes only, aristocratical and constitutional.

6. Whether Property Should Be Held in Common [1]

Next let us consider what should be our arrangements about property : should the citizens of the perfect state have their possessions in common or not? This question may be discussed separately from the enactments about women and children. Even supposing that the women and children belong to individuals, according to the custom which is at present universal, may there not be an advantage in having and using possessions in common? Three cases are possible : (1) the soil may be appropriated, but the produce may be thrown for consumption into the common stock; and this is the practice of some nations. Or (2), the soil may be common, and may be cultivated in common, but the produce divided among individuals for their private use; this is a form of common property which is said to exist among certain barbarians. Or (3), the soil and the produce may be alike common.

When the husbandmen are not the owners, the case will be different and easier to deal with; but when they till the ground themselves the question of ownership will give a world of trouble. If they do not share equally in enjoyments and toils, those who labour much and get little will necessarily complain of those who labour little and receive or consume much. There is always a difficulty in men living together and having things in common, but especially in their having common property. The partnerships of fellow-travellers are an example to the point; for they generally fall out by the way and quarrel about any trifle which turns up.

[1] II, v, vi (in part), vii. Jowett, pp. 33-38, 39-40, 42-46.

So with servants : we are most liable to take offence at those with whom we most frequently come into contact in daily life.

These are only some of the disadvantages which attend the community of property; the present arrangement, if improved as it might be by good customs and laws, would be far better, and would have the advantages of both systems. Property should be in a certain sense common, but, as a general rule, private; for, when every one has a distinct interest, men will not complain of one another, and they will make more progress, because every one will be attending to his own business. And yet among the good, and in respect of use, "Friends," as the proverb says, "will have all things common." Even now there are traces of such a principle, showing that it is not impracticable, but, in well-ordered states, exists already to a certain extent and may be carried further. For, although every man has his own property, some things he will place at the disposal of his friends, while of others he shares the use with them. The Lacedaemonians, for example, use one another's slaves, and horses, and dogs, as if they were their own; and when they happen to be in the country, they appropriate in the fields whatever provisions they want. It is clearly better that property should be private, but the use of it common; and the special business of the legislator is to create in men this benevolent disposition. Again, how immeasurably greater is the pleasure, when a man feels a thing to be his own; for the love of self is a feeling implanted by nature and not given in vain, although selfishness is rightly censured; this, however, is not the mere love of self, but the love of self in excess, like the miser's love of money; for all, or almost all, men love money, and other such objects in a measure. And further, there is the greatest pleasure in doing a kindness or service to friends or guests or companions, which can only be rendered when a man has private property. The advantage is lost by the excessive unification of the state. Two virtues are annihilated in such a state : first, temperance towards women (for it is an honourable action to abstain from another's wife for temperance sake); secondly, liberality in the matter of property. No one, when men have all things in common, will any longer set an example of liberality or do any liberal action; for liberality consists in the use which is made of property.

Such legislation may have a specious appearance of benevolence; men readily listen to it, and are easily induced to believe that in some wonderful manner everybody will become everybody's friend, especially when some one is heard denouncing the evils now existing in states, suits about contracts, convictions for perjury, flatteries of rich men and the like, which are said to arise out of the possession of private property. These evils, however, are due to a very different cause — the wickedness of human nature. Indeed, we see that there is much more quarrelling among those who have all things in common, though there are not many of them when compared with the vast numbers who have private property.

Again, we ought to reckon, not only the evils from which the citizens will be saved, but also the advantages which they will lose. The life which they are to lead appears to be quite impracticable. The error of Socrates must be attributed to the false notion of unity from which he starts. Unity there should be, both of the family and of the state, but in some respects only. For there is a point at which a state may attain such a degree of unity as to be no longer a state, or at which, without actually ceasing to exist, it will become an inferior state, like harmony passing into unison, or rhythm which has been reduced to a single foot. The state, as I was saying, is a plurality, which should be united and made into a community by education; and it is strange that the author of a system of education which he thinks will make the state virtuous, should expect to improve his citizens by regulations of this sort, and not by philosophy or by customs and laws, like those which prevail at Sparta and Crete respecting common meals, whereby the legislator has [to a certain degree] made property common. Let us remember that we should not disregard the experience of ages; in the multitude of years these things, if they were good, would certainly not have been unknown; for almost everything has been found out, although sometimes they are not put together; in other cases men do not use the knowledge which they have. Great light would be thrown on this subject if we could see such a form of government in the actual process of construction; for the legislator could not form a state at all without distributing and dividing the citizens into associations for common meals, and into phratries and tribes. But all this legislation ends only in forbidding agriculture to the guardians, a prohibition which the Lacedaemonians try to enforce already.

Again, Socrates has not said, nor is it easy to decide, what in such a community will be the general form of the state. The citizens who are not guardians are the majority, and about them nothing has been determined: are the husbandmen, too, to have their property in common? Or, besides the common land which he tills, is each individual to have his own? and are their wives and children to be individual or common? If, like the guardians, they are to have all things in common, in what do they differ from them, or what will they gain by submitting to their government? Or, upon what principle would they submit, unless indeed the government class adopt the ingenious policy of the Cretans, who give their slaves the same institutions as their own, but forbid them gymnastic exercises and the possession of arms. If, on the other hand, the inferior classes are to be like other cities in respect of marriage and property, what will be the form of the community? Must it not contain two states in one, each hostile to the other? One class will consist of the guardians, who are a sort of watchmen; another, of the husbandmen, and there will be the artisans and the other citizens. But [if so] the suits and quarrels, and all the evils which Socrates affirms to exist in other states, will exist equally among them. He says indeed that, having so good an education, the citizens will not need many laws, for example laws about the city or about the markets; but then he confines his education to the guardians. Again, he makes the husbandmen owners of the land upon condition of their paying a tribute. But in that case they are likely to be much more unmanageable and conceited than the Helots, or Penestae, or slaves in general. And whether community of wives and property be necessary for the lower equally with the higher class or not, and the questions akin to this, what will be the education, form of government, laws of the lower class, Socrates has nowhere determined: neither is it easy, though very important, to discover what should be the character of the inferior classes, if the common life of the guardians is to be maintained.

Again, if Socrates makes the women common, and retains private property, the men will see to the fields, but who will see to the house? And what will happen if the agricultural class have both their property and their wives in common? Once more; it is absurd to argue, from the analogy of the animals, that men and women should follow the same pursuits; for animals have not to manage a household. The government, too, as constituted by Socrates, contains elements of danger; for he makes the same persons always rule. And if this is often a cause of disturbance among the meaner sort, how much more among high-spirited warriors? But that the persons whom he makes rulers must be the same is evident; for the gold which the God mingles in the souls of men is not at one time given to one, at another time to another, but always to the same: as he says, "God mingles gold in some, and silver in others, from their very birth; but brass and iron in those who are meant to be artisans and husbandmen." Again, he deprives the guardians of happiness, and says that the legislator ought to make the whole state happy. But the whole cannot be happy unless most, or all, or some of its parts enjoy happiness. In this respect happiness is not like the even principle in numbers, which may exist only in the whole, but in none of the parts ; not so happiness. And if the guardians are not happy, who are ? Surely not the artisans, or the common people. The Republic of which Socrates discourses has all these difficulties, and others quite as great.

. . . There is another point : Should not the amount of property be defined in some clearer way ? For Socrates says that a man should have so much property as will enable him to live temperately, which is only a way of saying " to live well ; " this would be the higher or more general conception. But a man may live temperately and yet miserably. A better definition would be that a man must have so much property as will enable him to live not only temperately but liberally ; if the two are parted, liberality will combine with luxury ; toil will be associated with temperance. For liberality and temperance are the only virtues which have to do with the use of property. A man cannot use property with mildness or courage, but temperately and liberally he may ; and therefore the practice of these virtues is inseparable from property. There is an inconsistency, too, in equalizing the property and not regulating the number of the citizens ; the population is to remain unlimited, and he thinks that it will be sufficiently equalized by a certain number of marriages being unfruitful, however many are born to others, because he finds this to be the case in existing states. But [in Plato's imaginary state] greater care will be required than now ; for among ourselves, whatever may be the number of citizens, the property is always distributed among them, and therefore no one is in want ; but, if the property were incapable of division [as in the Laws], the supernumeraries, whether few or many, would get nothing. One would have thought that it was even more necessary to limit population than property ; and that the limit should be fixed by calculating the chances of mortality in the children, and of sterility in married persons. The neglect of this subject, which in existing states is so common, is a never-failing cause of poverty among the citizens ; and poverty is the parent of revolution and crime. Pheidon the Corinthian, who was one of the most ancient legislators, thought that the families and the number of citizens ought to remain the same, although originally all the lots may have been of different sizes ; but in the Laws, the opposite principle is maintained. What in our opinion is the right arrangement will have to be explained hereafter. . . .

. . . Other constitutions have been proposed ; some by private persons, others by philosophers and statesmen, which all come nearer to established or existing ones than either of Plato's. No one else has introduced such novelties as the community of women and children, or public tables for women : other legislators begin with what is necessary. In the opinion of some, the regulation of property is the chief point of all, that being the question upon which all revolutions turn. This danger was recognized by Phaleas of Chalcedon, who was the first to affirm that the citizens of a state ought to have equal possessions. He thought that in a new colony the equalization might be accomplished without difficulty, not so easily when a state was already established ; and that then the shortest way of compassing the desired end would be for the rich to give and not to receive marriage portions, and for the poor not to give but to receive them.

Plato in the Laws was of opinion that, to a certain extent, accumulation should be allowed, forbidding, as I have already observed, any citizen to possess more than five times the minimum qualification. But those who make such laws should remember what they are apt to forget, — that the legislator who fixes the amount of property should also fix the number of children ; for, if the children are too many for the property, the law must be broken. And, besides the violation of the law, it is a bad thing that many from being rich should become poor ; for men of ruined fortunes are sure to stir up revolutions. That the equalization of property exercises an influence on political society was clearly understood even by some of the old legislators. Laws were made by Solon and others prohibiting an individual from possessing as much land as he pleased ; and there are other laws in states which forbid the sale of property : among the Locrians, for example, there is a law that a man is not to sell his property unless he can prove unmistakably that some misfortune has befallen him. Again, there have been laws which enjoin the preservation of the original lots. Such a law existed in the island of Leucas, and the abrogation of it made the constitution too democratic, for the rulers no longer had the prescribed qualification. Again, where there is equality of property, the amount may be either too large or too small, and the possessor may be living either in luxury or penury. Clearly, then, the legislator ought not only to aim at the equalization of properties, but at moderation in their amount. And yet, if he prescribe this moderate amount equally to all, he will be no nearer the mark ; for it is not the possessions but the desires of mankind which require to be equalized, and this is impossible, unless a sufficient education is provided by the state.

But Phaleas will probably reply that this is precisely what he means; and that, in his opinion, there ought to be in states, not only equal property, but equal education. Still he should tell us what will be the character of his education; there is no use in having one and the same for all, if it is of a sort that predisposes men to avarice, or ambition, or both. Moreover, civil troubles arise, not only out of the inequality of property, but out of the inequality of honour, though in opposite ways. For the common people quarrel about the inequality of property, the higher class about the equality of honour; as the poet says, —

> The bad and good alike in honour share.

There are crimes of which the motive is want; and for these Phaleas expects to find a cure in the equalization of property, which will take away from a man the temptation to be a highwayman, because he is hungry or cold. But want is not the sole incentive to crime; men desire to gratify some passion which preys upon them, or they are eager to enjoy the pleasures which are unaccompanied with pain, and therefore they commit crimes. Now what is the cure of these three disorders? Of the first, moderate possessions and occupation; of the second, habits of temperance; as to the third, if any desire pleasures which depend on themselves, they will find the satisfaction of their desires nowhere but in philosophy; for all other pleasures we are dependent on others. The fact is that the greatest crimes are caused by excess and not by necessity. Men do not become tyrants in order that they may not suffer cold; and hence great is the honour bestowed, not on him who kills a thief, but on him who kills a tyrant. Thus we see that the institutions of Phaleas avail only against petty crimes.

There is another objection to them. They are chiefly designed to promote the internal welfare of the state. But the legislator should consider also its relation to neighbouring nations, and to all who are outside of it. The government must be organized with a view to military strength; and of this he has said not a word. And so with respect to property: there should not only be enough to supply the internal wants of the state, but also to meet dangers coming from without. The property of the state should not be so large that more powerful neighbours may be tempted by it, while the owners are unable to repel the invaders; nor yet so small that the state is unable to maintain a war even against states of equal power, and of the same character. Phaleas has not laid down any rule; and we should bear in mind that a certain amount of wealth is an advantage. The best limit will probably be, not so much as will tempt a more powerful neighbour, or make it his interest to go to war with you. There is a story that Eubulus, when Autophradates was going to besiege Atarneus, told him to consider how long the operation would take, and then reckon up the cost which would be incurred in the time. " For," said he, " I am willing for a smaller sum than that to leave Atarneus at once." These words of Eubulus made an impression on Autophradates, and he desisted from the siege.

One advantage gained by the equalization of property is that it prevents the citizens from quarrelling. Not that the gain in this direction is very great. For the nobles will be dissatisfied because they do not receive the honours which they think their due ; and this is often found to be a cause of sedition and revolution. And the avarice of mankind is insatiable ; at one time two obols was pay enough ; but now, when this sum has become customary, men always want more and more without end ; for it is of the nature of desire not to be satisfied, and most men live only for the gratification of it. The beginning of reform is not so much to equalize property as to train the nobler sort of natures not to desire more, and to prevent the lower from getting more ; that is to say, they must be kept down, but not ill-treated. Besides, the equalization proposed by Phaleas is imperfect ; for he only equalizes land, whereas a man may be rich also in slaves, and cattle, and money, and in the abundance of what are called his moveables. Now either all these things must be equalized, or some limit must be imposed on them, or they must all be let alone. It would appear that Phaleas is legislating for a small city only, if, as he supposes, all the artisans are to be public slaves and not to form a part of the population of the city. But if there is a law that artisans are to be public slaves, it should only apply to those engaged on public works, as at Epidamnus, or at Athens on the plan which Diophantus once introduced.

From these observations any one may judge how far Phaleas was wrong or right in his ideas. . . .

7. *Material Conditions of the Ideal State* [1]

In what has preceded I have discussed other forms of government ; in what remains the first point to be considered is what should be the conditions of the ideal or perfect state ; for the perfect state cannot exist without a due supply of the means of life.

[1] VII, iv–v. Jowett, pp. 213–216.

And therefore we must pre-suppose many purely imaginary conditions, but nothing impossible. There will be a certain number
of citizens, a country in which to place them, and the like. As the
weaver or shipbuilder or any other artisan must have the material
proper for his work (and in proportion as this is better prepared,
so will the result of his art be nobler), so the statesman or legislator
must also have the materials suited to him.

First among the materials required by the statesman is population: he will consider what should be the number and character
of the citizens, and then what should be the size and character
of the country. Most persons think that a state in order to be
happy ought to be large; but even if they are right, they have no
idea what is a large and what a small state. For they judge of
the size of the city by the number of the inhabitants; whereas they
ought to regard, not their number, but their power. A city, too,
like an individual, has a work to do; and that city which is best
adapted to the fulfilment of its work is to be deemed greatest, in
the same sense of the word great in which Hippocrates might be
called greater, not as a man, but as a physician, than some one
else who was taller. And even if we reckon greatness by numbers,
we ought not to include everybody, for there must always be in
cities a multitude of slaves and sojourners and foreigners; but we
should include those only who are members of the state, and who
form an essential part of it. The number of the latter is a proof
of the greatness of a city; but a city which produces numerous
artisans and comparatively few soldiers cannot be great, for a
great city is not to be confounded with a populous one. Moreover, experience shows that a very populous city can rarely, if ever,
be well governed; since all cities which have a reputation for good
government have a limit of population. We may argue on grounds
of reason, and the same result will follow. For law is order, and
good law is good order; but a very great multitude cannot be orderly: to introduce order into the unlimited is the work of a divine
power—of such a power as holds together the universe. Beauty
is realized in number and magnitude, and the state which combines
magnitude with good order must necessarily be the most beautiful. To the size of states there is a limit, as there is to other things,
plants, animals, implements; for none of these retain their natural
power when they are too large or too small, but they either wholly
lose their nature, or are spoiled. For example, a ship which is
only a span long will not be a ship at all, nor a ship a quarter of a
mile long; yet there may be a ship of a certain size, either too large
or too small, which will still be a ship, but bad for sailing. In like

manner a state when composed of too few is not as a state ought to be, self-sufficing; when of too many, though self-sufficing in all mere necessaries, it is a nation and not a state, being almost incapable of constitutional government. For who can be the general of such a vast multitude, or who the herald, unless he have the voice of a Stentor?

A state then only begins to exist when it has attained a population sufficient for a good life in the political community: it may indeed somewhat exceed this number. But, as I was saying, there must be a limit. What should be the limit will be easily ascertained by experience. For both governors and governed have duties to perform; the special functions of a governor are to command and to judge. But if the citizens of a state are to judge and to distribute offices according to merit, then they must know each other's characters; where they do not possess this knowledge, both the election to offices and the decision of lawsuits will go wrong. When the population is very large they are manifestly settled at haphazard, which clearly ought not to be. Besides, in an overpopulous state foreigners and metics will readily acquire the rights of citizens, for who will find them out? Clearly then the best limit of the population of a state is the largest number which suffices for the purposes of life, and can be taken in at a single view. Enough concerning the size of a city.

Much the same principle will apply to the territory of the state: every one would agree in praising the state which is most entirely self-sufficing; and that must be the state which is all-producing, for to have all things and to want nothing is sufficiency. In size and extent it should be such as may enable the inhabitants to live temperately and liberally in the enjoyment of leisure. Whether we are right or wrong in laying down this limit we will inquire more precisely hereafter, when we have occasion to consider what is the right use of property and wealth; a matter which is much disputed, because men are inclined to rush into one of two extremes, some into meanness, others into luxury.

It is not difficult to determine the general character of the territory which is required; there are, however, some points on which military authorities should be heard; they tell us that it should be difficult of access to the enemy, and easy of egress to the inhabitants. Further, we require that the land as well as the inhabitants of whom we were just now speaking should be taken in at a single view, for a country which is easily seen can be easily protected. As to the position of the city, if we could have what we wish, it should be well-situated in regard both to sea or land. This then is one principle, that it should be a convenient center for the protection of the whole country: the other is, that it should be suitable for receiving the fruits of the soil, and also for the bringing in of timber and any other products.

8. *The Cause and Prevention of Revolution* [1]

Next in order follow the causes of revolution in states, how many, and of what nature they are; what elements work ruin in particular states, and out of what, and into what they mostly change; also what are the elements of preservation in states generally, or in a particular state, and by what means each state may be best preserved: these questions remain to be considered.

In the first place we must assume as our starting-point that in the many forms of government which have sprung up there has always been an acknowledgment of justice and proportionate equality, although mankind fail in attaining them, as indeed I have already explained. Democracy, for example, arises out of the notion that those who are equal in any respect are equal in all respects; because men are equally free, they claim to be absolutely equal. Oligarchy is based on the notion that those who are unequal in one respect are in all respects unequal; being unequal, that is, in property, they suppose themselves to be unequal absolutely. The democrats think that as they are equal they ought to be equal in all things; while the oligarchs, under the idea that they are unequal, claim too much, which is one form of inequality. All these forms of government have a kind of justice, but, tried by an absolute standard, they are faulty; and, therefore, both parties, whenever their share in the government does not accord with their preconceived ideas, stir up revolution. Those who excel in virtue have the best right of all to rebel (for they alone can with reason be deemed absolutely unequal), but then they are of all men the least inclined to do so. There is also a superiority which is claimed by men of rank; for they are thought noble because they spring from wealthy and virtuous ancestors. Here then, so to speak, are opened the very springs and fountains of revolution; and hence arise two sorts of changes in governments; the one affecting the constitution, when men seek to change from an existing form into some other, for example, from democracy into oligarchy, and from oligarchy into democracy, or from either of them into constitutional government or aristocracy, and con-

[1] V, i (in part), ii, iii (in part), viii–ix (in part).   Jowett, pp. 144–145, 147–148, 162–165, 168–169.

versely; the other not affecting the constitution, when, without disturbing the form of government, whether oligarchy, or monarchy, or any other, they try to get the administration into their own hands. Further, there is a question of degree; an oligarchy, for example, may become more or less oligarchical, and a democracy more or less democratical; and in like manner the characteristics of the other forms of government may be more or less strictly maintained. Or, the revolution may be directed against a portion of the constitution only, e.g. the establishment or overthrow of a particular office: as at Sparta it is said that Lysander attempted to overthrow the monarchy, and king Pausanias, the ephoralty.

In considering how dissensions and political revolutions arise, we must first of all ascertain the beginnings and causes of them which affect constitutions generally. They may be said to be three in number; and we have now to give an outline of each. We want to know (1) what is the feeling? and (2) what are the motives of those who make them? (3) whence arise political disturbances and quarrels? The universal and chief cause of this revolutionary feeling has been already mentioned; viz. the desire of equality, when men think that they are equal to others who have more than themselves; or, again, the desire of inequality and superiority, when conceiving themselves to be superior they think that they have not more but the same or less than their inferiors; pretensions which may and may not be just. Inferiors revolt in order that they may be equal, and equals that they may be superior. Such is the state of mind which creates revolutions. The motives for making them are the desire of gain and honor, or the fear of dishonor and loss; the authors of them want to divert punishment or dishonor from themselves or their friends. The causes and reasons of these motives and dispositions which are excited in men, about the things which I have mentioned, viewed in one way, may be regarded as seven, and in another as more than seven. Two of them have been already noticed; but they act in a different manner, for men are excited against one another by the love of gain and honor — not, as in the case which I have just supposed, in order to obtain them for themselves, but at seeing others, justly or unjustly, engrossing them. Other causes are insolence, fear, love of superiority, contempt, disproportionate increase in some part of the state; causes of another sort are election intrigues, carelessness, neglect about trifles, dissimilarity of elements.

What share insolence and avarice have in creating revolutions, and how they work, is plain enough. When the magistrates are insolent and grasping they conspire against one another and also against the constitution from which they derive their power, making their gains either at the expense of individuals or of the public. It is evident, again, what an influence honor exerts and how it is a cause of revolution. Men who are themselves dishonored and who see others obtaining honors rise in rebellion; the honor or dishonor when undeserved is unjust; and just when awarded according to merit. Again, superiority is a cause of revolution when one or more persons have a power which is too much for the state and the power of the government; this is a condition of affairs out of which there arises a monarchy, or a family oligarchy. And, therefore, in some places, as at Athens and Argos, they have recourse to ostracism. But how much better to provide from the first that there should be no such preëminent individuals instead of letting them come into existence and then finding a remedy.

Another cause of revolution is fear. Either men have committed wrong, and are afraid of punishment, or they are expecting to suffer wrong and are desirous of anticipating their enemy. Thus at Rhodes the notables conspired against the people through fear of the suits that were brought against them. Contempt is also a cause of insurrection and revolution; for example, in oligarchies— when those who have no share in the state are the majority, they revolt, because they think that they are the stronger. Or, again, in democracies, the rich despise the disorder and anarchy of the state; at Thebes, for example, where, after the battle of Œnophyta, the bad administration of the democracy led to its ruin.[1]

We have next to consider what means there are of preserving states in general, and also in particular cases. In the first place it is evident that if we know the causes which destroy states, we shall also know the causes which preserve them; for opposites produce opposites, and destruction is the opposite of preservation. In all well-attempered governments there is nothing which should be more jealously maintained than the spirit of obedience to law, more especially in small matters; for transgression creeps in unperceived and at last ruins the state, just as the constant recurrence of small expenses in time eats up a fortune. The change does not take place all at once, and therefore is not observed; the mind is deceived, as in the fallacy which says that "if each part is little, then the whole is little." And this is true in one way, but not in another, for the whole and the all are not little, although they are made up of littles.

[1] Aristotle continues with the analysis of the five other causes of revolutions.

In the first place, then, men should guard against the beginning of change, and in the second place they should not rely upon the political devices of which I have already spoken, invented only to deceive the people, for they are proved by experience to be useless. Further we note that oligarchies as well as aristocracies may last, not from any inherent stability in such forms of government, but because the rulers are on good terms both with the unenfranchised and with the governing classes, not maltreating any who are excluded from the government, but introducing into it the leading spirits among them. They should never wrong the ambitious in a matter of honor, or the common people in a matter of money; and they should treat one another and their fellow-citizens in a spirit of equality. The equality which the friends of democracy seek to establish for the multitude is not only just but likewise expedient among equals. Hence, if the governing class are numerous, many democratic institutions are useful; for example, the restriction of the tenure of offices to six months, that all those who are of equal rank may share in them. Indeed, equals or peers when they are numerous become a kind of democracy, and therefore demagogues are very likely to arise among them, as I have already remarked. The short tenure of office prevents oligarchies and aristocracies from falling into the hands of families; it is not easy for a person to do any great harm when his tenure of office is short, whereas long possession begets tyranny in oligarchies and democracies. For the aspirants to tyranny are either the principal men of the state, who in democracies are demagogues and in oligarchies members of ruling houses, or those who hold great offices, and have a long tenure of them.

States are preserved when their destroyers are at a distance, and sometimes also because they are near, for the fear of them makes the government keep in hand the state. Wherefore the ruler who has a care of the state should invent terrors, and bring distant dangers near, in order that the citizens may be on their guard, and, like sentinels in a night-watch, never relax their attention. He should endeavor, too, by help of the laws to control the contentions and quarrels of the notables, and to prevent those who have not hitherto taken part in them from being drawn in. No ordinary man can discern the beginning of evil, but only the true statesman.

As to the change produced in oligarchies and constitutional governments by the alteration of the qualification, when this arises, not out of any variation in the census but only out of the increase of money, it is well to compare the general valuation of

property with that of past years, annually in those cities in which
the census is taken annually, and in larger cities every third or
fifth year. If the whole is many times greater or many times less
than when the rates were fixed at the previous census, there should
be power given by law to raise or lower the qualification as the
amount is greater or less. Where in the absence of any such
provision the standard is raised, a constitutional government
passes into an oligarchy, and an oligarchy is narrowed to a rule of
families; where the standard is lowered, constitutional government
becomes democracy, and oligarchy either constitutional government or democracy.

It is a principle common to democracy, oligarchy, and every
other form of government not to allow the disproportionate increase of any citizen, but to give moderate honor for a long time
rather than great honor for a short time. For men are easily
spoiled; not every one can bear prosperity. But if this rule is
not observed, at any rate the honors which are given all at once
should be taken away by degrees and not all at once. Especially
should the laws provide against any one having too much power,
whether derived from friends or money; if he has, he and his followers should be sent out of the country. And since innovations
creep in through the private life of individuals, there ought to be
a magistracy which will have an eye to those whose life is not in
harmony with the government, whether oligarchy or democracy
or any other. And for a like reason an increase of prosperity in
any part of the state should be carefully watched. The proper
remedy for this evil is always to give the management of affairs
and offices of state to opposite elements; such opposites are the
virtuous and the many, or the rich and the poor. Another way
is to combine the poor and the rich in one body, or to increase the
middle class: thus an end will be put to the revolutions which arise
from inequality.

But above all every state should be so administered and so
regulated by law that its magistrates cannot possibly make
money. In oligarchies special precautions should be used against
this evil. For the people do not take any great offence at being
kept out of the government—indeed they are rather pleased than
otherwise at having leisure for their private business—but what
irritates them is to think that their rulers are stealing the public
money; then they are doubly annoyed; for they lose both honor
and profit. If office brought no profit, then and then only could
democracy and aristocracy be combined; for both notables and
people might have their wishes gratified. All would be able to

hold office, which is the aim of democracy, and the notables would be magistrates, which is the aim of aristocracy. And this result may be accomplished when there is no possibility of making money out of the offices; for the poor will not want to have them when there is nothing to be gained from them—they would rather be attending to their own concerns; and the rich, who do not want money from the public treasury, will be able to take them; and so the poor will keep to their work and grow rich, and the notables will not be governed by the lower class.

But of all the things which I have mentioned that which most contributes to the permanence of constitutions is the adaptation of education to the form of government, and yet in our own day this principle is universally neglected. The best laws, though sanctioned by every citizen of the state, will be of no avail unless the young are trained by habit and education in the spirit of the constitution, if the laws are democratical, democratically, or oligarchically, if the laws are oligarchical. For there may be a want of self-discipline in states as well as in individuals. Now, to have been educated in the spirit of the constitution is not to perform the actions in which oligarchs or democrats delight, but those by which the existence of an oligarchy or of a democracy is made possible. Whereas among ourselves the sons of the ruling class in an oligarchy live in luxury, but the sons of the poor are hardened by exercise and toil, and hence they are both more inclined and better able to make a revolution. And in democracies of the more extreme type there has arisen a false idea of freedom which is contradictory to the true interests of the state. For two principles are characteristic of democracy, the government of the majority and freedom. Men think that what is just is equal; and that equality is the supremacy of the popular will; and that freedom and equality mean the doing what a man likes. In such democracies every one lives as he pleases, or in the words of Euripides, "according to his fancy." But this is all wrong; men should not think it slavery to live according to the rule of the constitution; for it is their salvation.

SELECTED BIBLIOGRAPHY

McIlwain, Charles H., *The Growth of Political Thought in the West*, ch. 3.
Sabine, George H., *A History of Political Theory*, chs. 5 and 6.
Cook, Thomas I., *A History of Political Philosophy*, ch. 4.
Dunning, William A., *Political Theories, Ancient and Mediæval*, ch. 3.

Bradley, A. C., "Aristotle's Conception of the State," in Evelyn Abbott, ed., *Hellenica: a Collection of Essays on Greek Poetry, Philosophy, History and Religion* (second ed., London, 1898), pp. 181–243.
Burns, C. Delisle, *Greek Ideals: a Study of Social Life* (second ed., London, 1919), ch. 16.
Ross, W. D., *Aristotle* (New York, 1924), ch. 8.
Zeller, Eduard Gottlob, *Aristotle and the Earlier Peripatetics*, translated by B. F. C. Costelloe and J. H. Muirhead, 2 vols. (London, 1897), Vol. I, chs. 1 and 4; Vol. II, chs. 12 and 13.
Gomperz, Theodor, *Greek Thinkers*, Vol. IV, translated by G. G. Berry (New York, 1912), Bk. vi, chs. 26–34.
Rehm, Hermann, *Geschichte der Staatsrechtswissenschaft* (Freiberg and Leipsic, 1896), pt. iv, chs. 1, 2.
Newman, William L., *The Politics of Aristotle*, 4 vols. (Oxford, 1887–1902), Vol. I.
Oncken, Wilhelm, *Die Staatslehre des Aristoteles in historische-politischen Umrissen.*   2 vols. in one (Leipsic, 1870, 1875).
Wilamowitz-Moellendorff, Ulrich von, *Aristoteles und Athen*, 2 vols. (Berlin, 1893).

POLYBIUS

III. POLYBIUS (204-122 B.C.)

INTRODUCTION

The fame of Polybius, a Greek author, rests upon his history of Rome; his theoretical discussion of government is incidental to his analysis of the Roman constitution. He was born in Megalopolis, in Arcadia, leading state of the Achæan League. He became one of a group of statesmen who directed the policy of the league during the Roman invasion which ended Macedonian power and brought Greece under Roman dominion. In that period he was of the moderate party, which sought primarily to maintain for the league a negative attitude towards Rome. With the accomplishment of the Roman conquest the eminent men of that party, suffering under false charges made by the radical pro-Roman leaders of the league, were taken as hostages to Rome; here they lived rather as distinguished visitors than as prisoners.

In Italy the experience and ability of Polybius were recognized and utilized. He was sent to Greece on a mission of mediation between Rome and the Achæans. Though this mission was fruitless he was subsequently representative of the Roman government in the reconstruction of Greece. Most of his later life, however, he spent in scholarly leisure, enjoying the friendship and patronage of Roman statesmen—particularly of Scipio Africanus, the younger. These facilities he put to good purpose by devoting them to travel, observation, and the collection of materials for a history of Rome.

The motive of his *History* was to explain the greatness of Rome, to trace the steps—from the second Punic War to the conquest of Macedonia—through which Rome became the ruling power of the world, and to describe the manner in which her control over this vast dominion had been exercised. Of this work there are extant the first five books entire and the other thirty-five books in fragments. In the part of the sixth book that is preserved the author sets forth certain principles of government, with a view to

113

indicating what elements of the governmental organization of Rome had enabled it to acquire and maintain its extensive sway.[1] He there presents a theory of the origin of political society and an interpretation of its periodic revolution through a cycle of six forms, in alternate succession of good and bad forms. Upon this basis he analyzes the constitution of the Roman Republic in such a way as to show that through its combination of elements of each of the three good forms—in other words, through its system of checks and balances, it furnishes a type of mixed constitution which is secure against the decay natural to any one of the simple types.

READINGS FROM THE HISTORIES [2]

1. The Forms of Government and the Cycle of Constitutional Revolution [3]

I am aware that some will be at a loss to account for my interrupting the course of my narrative for the sake of entering upon the following disquisition on the Roman constitution. But I think that I have already in many passages made it fully evident that this particular branch of my work was one of the necessities imposed on me by the nature of my original design; and I pointed this out with special clearness in the preface which explained the scope of my history. I there stated that the feature of my work which was at once the best in itself, and the most instructive to the students of it, was that it would enable them to know and fully realize in what manner, and under what kind of constitution, it came about that nearly the whole world fell under the power of Rome in somewhat less than fifty-three years,—an event certainly without precedent. This being my settled purpose, I could see no more fitting period than the present for making a pause, and examining the truth of the remarks about to be made on this constitution. In private life if you wish to satisfy yourself as to the badness or goodness of particular persons, you would not, if you wish to get a genuine test, examine their conduct at a time of uneventful repose, but in the hour of brilliant success or conspicuous reverse. For the true test of a perfect man is the power of

---

[1] Cf. James L. Strachan-Davidson, Polybius (in Evelyn Abbott's Hellenica), p. 411.
[2] The selections are taken from the translation by Evelyn S. Schuckburgh; London and New York, 1889. Macmillan and Company.
[3] Bk. VI, §§ 1–9. Schuckburgh, Vol. I, pp. 458–466.

bearing with spirit and dignity violent changes of fortune. An examination of a constitution should be conducted in the same way: and therefore being unable to find in our day a more rapid or more signal change than that which has happened to Rome, I reserved my disquisition for this place. . . .

What is really educational and beneficial to students of history is the clear view of the causes of events, and the consequent power of choosing the better policy in a particular case. Now in every practical undertaking by a state we must regard as the most powerful agent for success or failure the form of its constitution; for from this as from a fountain-head all conceptions and plans of action not only proceed, but attain their consummation. . . .

Of the Greek Republics, which have again and again risen to greatness and fallen into insignificance, it is not difficult to speak, whether we recount their past history or venture an opinion on their future. For to report what is already known is an easy task, nor is it hard to guess what is to come from our knowledge of what has been. But in regard to the Romans it is neither an easy matter to describe their present state, owing to the complexity of their constitution; nor to speak with confidence of their future, from our inadequate acquaintance with their peculiar institutions in the past whether affecting their public or their private life. It will require, then, no ordinary attention and study to get a clear and comprehensive conception of the distinctive features of this constitution.

Now, it is undoubtedly the case that most of those who profess to give us authoritative instruction on this subject distinguish three kinds of constitutions, which they designate *kingship, aristocracy, democracy*. But in my opinion the question might fairly be put to them, whether they name these as being the *only* ones, or as the *best*. In either case I think they are wrong. For it is plain that we must regard as the best constitution that which partakes of all these three elements. And this is no mere assertion, but has been proved by the example of Lycurgus, who was the first to construct a constitution—that of Sparta—on this principle. Nor can we admit that these are the only forms; for we have had before now examples of absolute and tyrannical forms of government, which, while differing as widely as possible from kingship, yet appear to have some points of resemblance to it; on which account all absolute rulers falsely assume and use, as far as they can, the title of king. Again there have been many instances of oligarchical governments having in appearance some analogy to aristocracies, which are, if I may say so, as different from them as it is possible to be.   The same also holds good about democracy.

I will illustrate the truth of what I say.   We cannot hold every absolute government to be a kingship, but only that which is accepted voluntarily, and is directed by an appeal to reason rather than to fear and force.   Nor again is every oligarchy to be regarded as an aristocracy; the latter exists only where the power is wielded by the justest and wisest men selected on their merits. Similarly, it is not enough to constitute a democracy that the whole crowd of citizens should have the right to do whatever they wish or propose.   But where reverence to the gods, succor of parents, respect to elders, obedience to laws, are traditional and habitual, in such communities if the will of the majority prevail, we may speak of the form of government as a democracy.   So then we enumerate six forms of government,—the three commonly spoken of which I have just mentioned, and three more allied forms, I mean *despotism, oligarchy* and *mob-rule.*   The first of these arises without artificial aid and in the natural order of events.   Next to this, and produced from it by the aid of art and adjustment, comes *kingship:* which degenerating into the evil form allied to it, by which I mean *tyranny,* both are once more destroyed and *aristocracy* produced.   Again the latter being in the course of nature perverted to *oligarchy,* and the people passionately avenging the unjust acts of their rulers, *democracy* comes into existence; which again by its violence and contempt of law becomes sheer *mob-rule.*   No clearer proof of the truth of what I say could be obtained than by a careful observation of the natural origin, genesis, and decadence of these several forms of government. For it is only by seeing distinctly how each of them is produced that a distinct view can also be obtained of its growth, zenith, and decadence, and the time, circumstance, and place in which each of these may be expected to recur.   This method I have assumed to be especially applicable to the Roman constitution, because its origin and growth have from the first followed natural causes.

Now the natural laws which regulate the merging of one form of government into another are perhaps discussed with greater accuracy by Plato and some other philosophers.   But their treatment, from its intricacy and exhaustiveness, is only within the capacity of a few.   I will therefore endeavor to give a summary of the subject, just so far as I suppose it to fall within the scope of a practical history and the intelligence of ordinary people.   For if my exposition appear in any way inadequate, owing

to the general terms in which it is expressed, the details contained
in what is immediately to follow will amply atone for what is
left for the present unsolved.

What is the origin then of a constitution, and whence is it produced? Suppose that from floods, pestilences, failure of crops,
or some such causes the race of man is reduced almost to extinc-
tion. Such things we are told have happened, and it is reasonable
to think will happen again. Suppose accordingly all knowledge
of social habits and arts to have been lost. Suppose that from the
survivors, as from seeds, the race of man to have again multiplied.
In that case I presume they would, like the animals, herd together;
for it is but reasonable to suppose that bodily weakness would
induce them to seek those of their own kind to herd with. And in
that case, too, as with the animals, he who was superior to the rest
in strength of body or courage of soul would lead and rule them.
For what we see happen in the case of animals that are without the
faculty of reason, such as bulls, goats, and cocks,—among whom
there can be no dispute that the strongest take the lead,—that
we must regard as in the truest sense the teaching of nature.
Originally then it is probable that the condition of life among men
was this,—herding together like animals and following the strongest and bravest as leaders. The limit of this authority would be
physical strength, and the name we should give it would be despotism. But as soon as the idea of family ties and social relation has
arisen amongst such agglomerations of men, then is born also the
idea of kingship, and then for the first time mankind conceives
the notion of goodness and justice and their reverse.

The way in which such conceptions originate and come into
existence is this: The intercourse of the sexes is an instinct of
nature, and the result is the birth of children. Now, if any one
of these children who have been brought up, when arrived at
maturity, is ungrateful and makes no return to those by whom he
was nurtured, but on the contrary presumes to injure them by word
and deed, it is plain that he will probably offend and annoy such
as are present, and have seen the care and trouble bestowed by
the parents on the nurture and bringing up of their children. For
seeing that men differ from the other animals in being the only
creatures possessed of reasoning powers, it is clear that such a
difference of conduct is not likely to escape their observation;
but that they will remark it when it occurs, and express their
displeasure on the spot: because they will have an eye to the future,
and will reason on the likelihood of the same occurring to each of
themselves. Again, if a man has been rescued or helped in an hour

of danger, and, instead of showing gratitude to his preserver,
seeks to do him harm, it is clearly probable that the rest will be
displeased and offended with him, when they know it: sympathiz-
ing with their neighbor and imagining themselves in his case.
Hence arises a notion in every breast of the meaning and theory of
duty, which is in fact the beginning and end of justice.   Similarly,
again, when any one man stands out as the champion of all in a
time of danger, and braves with firm courage the onslaught of
the most powerful wild beasts, it is probable that such a man would
meet with marks of favor and preëminence from the common
people; while he who acted in a contrary way would fall under their
contempt and dislike.   From this, once more, it is reasonable to
suppose that there would arise in the minds of the multitude
a theory of the disgraceful and the honorable, and of the difference
between them; and that one should be sought and imitated for
its advantages, the other shunned.   When, therefore, the leading
and most powerful man among his people ever encourages such
persons in accordance with the popular sentiment, and thereby
assumes in the eyes of his subjects the appearance of being the dis-
tributor to each man according to his deserts, they no longer obey
him and support his rule from fear of violence, but rather from
conviction of its utility, however old he may be, rallying round
him with one heart and soul, and fighting against all who form
designs against his government.   In this way be becomes a *king*
instead of a *despot* by imperceptible degrees, reason having ousted
brute courage and bodily strength from their supremacy.

This then is the natural process of formation among mankind of the notion of goodness and justice, and their opposites;
and this is the origin and genesis of genuine kingship: for people do
not only keep up the government of such men personally, but for
their descendants also for many generations; from the conviction
that those who are born from and educated by men of this kind
will have principles also like theirs.   But if they subsequently
become displeased with their descendants, they do not any longer
decide their choice of rulers and kings by their physical strength
or brute courage; but by the differences of their intellectual and
reasoning faculties, from practical experience of the decisive importance of such a distinction.   In old times, then, those who
were once thus selected, and obtained this office, grew old in their
royal functions, making magnificent strongholds and surrounding
them with walls and extending their frontiers, partly for the
security of their subjects, and partly to provide them with abundance of the necessaries of life; and while engaged in these works

they were exempt from all vituperation or jealousy; because they did not make their distinctive dress, food, or drink, at all conspicuous, but lived very much like the rest, and joined in the everyday employments of the common people. But when their royal power became hereditary in their family, and they found every necessary for security ready to their hands, as well as more than was necessary for their personal support, then they gave the rein to their appetites; imagined that rulers must needs wear different clothes from those of subjects, have different and elaborate luxuries of the table, and must even seek sensual indulgence, however unlawful the source, without fear of denial. These things having given rise in the one case to jealousy and offence, in the other to outburst of hatred and passionate resentment, the kingship became a tyranny: the first step in disintegration was taken; and plots began to be formed against the government, which did not now proceed from the worst men but from the noblest, most high-minded, and most courageous, because these are the men who can least submit to the tyrannical acts of their rulers.

But as soon as the people got leaders, they co-operated with them against the dynasty for the reasons I have mentioned; and then *kingship* and *despotism* were alike entirely abolished, and *aristocracy* once more began to revive and start afresh. For in their immediate gratitude to those who had deposed the despots, the people employed them as leaders, and intrusted their interests to them; who, looking upon this charge at first as a great privilege, made the public advantage their chief concern, and conducted all kinds of business, public or private, with diligence and caution. But when the sons of those men received the same position of authority from their fathers,—having had no experience of misfortunes, and none at all of civil equality and freedom of speech, but having been bred up from the first under the shadow of their fathers' authority and lofty position,—some of them gave themselves up with passion to avarice and unscrupulous love of money, others to drinking and the boundless debaucheries which accompany it, and others to the violation of women or the forcible appropriation of boys; and so they turned an *aristocracy* into an *oligarchy*. But it was not long before they roused in the minds of the people the same feelings as before; and their fall therefore was very like the disaster which befel the tyrants.

For no sooner had the knowledge of the jealousy and hatred existing in the citizens against them emboldened some one to oppose the government by word or deed, than he was sure to find

the whole people ready and prepared to take his side.   Having
then got rid of these rulers by assassination or exile, they do not
venture to set up a king again, being still in terror of the injustice
to which this led before; nor dare they intrust the common interests again to more than one, considering the recent example
of their misconduct: and therefore, as the only sound hope left
them is that which depends upon themselves, they are driven to
take refuge in that; and so changed the constitution from an oligarchy to a *democracy*, and took upon themselves the superintend-
ence and charge of the state.   And as long as any survive who
have had experience of oligarchical supremacy and domination,
they regard their present constitution as a blessing, and hold
equality and freedom as of the utmost value.   But as soon as a
new generation has arisen, and the democracy has descended
to their children's children, long association weakens their value
for equality and freedom, and some seek to become more powerful than the ordinary citizens; and the most liable to this temptation are the rich.   So when they begin to be fond of office, and
find themselves unable to obtain it by their own unassisted efforts
and their own merits, they ruin their estates, while enticing and
corrupting the common people in every possible way.   By which
means when, in their senseless mania for reputation, they have
made the populace ready and greedy to receive bribes, the virtue
of democracy is destroyed, and it is transformed into a government
of violence and the strong hand.   For the mob, habituated to
feed at the expense of others, and to have its hopes of a livelihood
in the property of its neighbors, as soon as it has got a leader
sufficiently ambitious and daring, being excluded by poverty from
the sweets of civil honors, produces a reign of mere violence.   Then
come tumultuous assemblies, massacres, banishments, redivisions
of land; until, after losing all trace of civilization, it has once more
found a master and a despot.

This is the regular cycle of constitutional revolutions, and the
natural order in which constitutions change, are transformed, and
return again to their original stage.   If a man have a clear grasp of
these principles he may perhaps make a mistake as to the dates at
which this or that will happen to a particular constitution; but
he will rarely be entirely mistaken as to the stage of growth or
decay at which it has arrived, or as to the point at which it will
undergo some revolutionary change.   However, it is in the case
of the Roman constitution that this method of inquiry will most
fully teach us its formation, its growth, and zenith, as well as the
changes awaiting it in the future; for this, if any constitution ever

did, owed, as I said just now, its original foundation and growth
to natural causes, and to natural causes will owe its decay. My
subsequent narrative will be the best illustration of what I say.

2. *The System of Checks and Balances* [1]

As for the Roman constitution, it had three elements, each of
them possessing sovereign powers; and their respective share of
power in the whole state had been regulated with such a scrupu-
lous regard to equality and equilibrium, that no one could say
for certain, not even a native, whether the constitution as a whole
were an aristocracy or democracy or despotism. And no wonder:
for if we confine our observation to the power of the consuls we
should be inclined to regard it as despotic; if that of the senate,
as aristocratic; and if finally one looks at the power possessed by
the people it would seem a clear case of democracy. What the
exact powers of these several parts were, and still, with slight
modifications, are, I will now state.

The consuls, before leading out the legions, remain in Rome
and are supreme masters of the administration. All other magistrates, except the tribunes, are under them and take their orders.
They introduce foreign ambassadors to the senate; bring matters
requiring deliberation before it; and see to the execution of its
decrees. If, again, there are any matters of state which require
the authorization of the people, it is their business to see to them,
to summon the popular meetings, to bring the proposals before
them, and to carry out the decrees of the majority. In the preparations for war also, and in a word, in the entire administration
of a campaign, they have all but absolute power. It is competent
to them to impose on the allies such levies as they think good, to
appoint the military tribunes, to make up the roll for soldiers,
and select those that are suitable. Besides they have absolute
power of inflicting punishment on all who are under their command
while on active service: and they have authority to expend as much
of the public money as they choose, being accompanied by a
quæstor who is entirely at their orders. A survey of these powers
would in fact justify our describing the constitution as despotic,—
a clear case of royal government. Nor will it affect the truth
of my description, if any of the institutions I have described are
changed in our time, or in that of our posterity: and the same
remarks apply to what follows.

The senate has first of all the control of the treasury, and

[1] Bk. VI, §§ 11-18. Schuckburgh, Vol. I, pp. 468-474.

regulates the receipts and disbursements alike. For the quæstors cannot issue any public money for the various departments of the state without a decree of the senate, except for the service of the consuls. The senate controls also what is by far the largest and most important expenditure, that, namely, which is made by the censors every *lustrum* for the repair or construction of public buildings; this money cannot be obtained by the censors except by the grant of the senate. Similarly all crimes committed in Italy requiring a public investigation, such as treason, conspiracy, poisoning, or wilful murder, are in the hands of the senate. Besides, if any individual or state among the Italian allies requires a controversy to be settled, a penalty to be assessed, help or protection to be afforded,—all this is the province of the senate. Or again, outside Italy, if it is necessary to send an embassy to reconcile warring communities, or to remind them of their duty, or sometimes to impose requisitions upon them, or to receive their submission, or finally to proclaim war against them,—this too is the business of the senate. In like manner the reception to be given to foreign ambassadors in Rome, and the answers to be returned to them, are decided by the senate. With such business the people have nothing to do. Consequently, if one were staying at Rome when the consuls were not in town, one would imagine the constitution to be a complete aristocracy: and this has been the idea entertained by many Greeks, and by many kings as well, from the fact that nearly all the business they had with Rome was settled by the senate.

After this one would naturally be inclined to ask what part is left for the people in the constitution, when the senate has these various functions, especially the control of the receipts and expenditure of the exchequer; and when the consuls, again, have absolute power over the details of military preparation, and an absolute authority in the field? There is, however, a part left the people, and it is a most important one. For the people is the sole fountain of honor and of punishment; and it is by these two things and these alone that dynasties and constitutions and, in a word, human society are held together: for where the distinction between them is not sharply drawn both in theory and practice, there no undertaking can be properly administered,—as indeed we might expect when good and bad are held in exactly the same honor. The people then are the only court to decide matters of life and death; and even in the cases where the penalty is money, if the sum to be assessed is sufficiently serious, and especially when the accused have held the high magistracies. And in regard to this arrangement there is one point deserving especial commendation and record. Men who are on trial for their lives at Rome, while sentence is in process of being voted,—if even only one of the tribes whose votes are needed to ratify sentence has not voted,- —have the privilege at Rome of openly departing and condemning themselves to a voluntary exile. Such men are safe at Naples or Præneste or at Tibur and at other towns with which this arrangement has been duly ratified on oath.

Again, it is the people who bestow offices on the deserving, which are the most honorable rewards of virtue. It has also the absolute power of passing or repealing laws; and, most important of all, it is the people who deliberate on the question of peace or war. And when provisional terms are made for alliance, suspension of hostilities, or treaties, it is the people who ratify them or the reverse.

These considerations again would lead one to say that the chief power in the state was the people's, and that the constitution was a democracy.

Such then is the distribution of power between the several parts of the state. I must now show how each of these several parts can, when they choose, oppose or support each other.

The consul, then, when he has started on an expedition with the powers I have described, is to all appearance absolute in the administration of the business in hand; still he has need of the support both of people and senate, and without them, is quite unable to bring the matter to a successful conclusion. For it is plain that he must have supplies sent to his legions from time to time; but without a decree of the senate they can be supplied neither with corn, nor clothes, nor pay, so that all the plans of a commander must be futile, if the senate is resolved either to shrink from danger or hamper his plans. And again, whether a consul shall bring any undertaking to a conclusion or not depends entirely upon the senate: for it has absolute authority at the end of a year to send another consul to supersede him, or to continue the existing one in his command. Again, even to the successes of the generals the senate has the power to add distinction and glory, and on the other hand to obscure their merits and lower their credit. For these high achievements are brought in tangible form before the eyes of the citizens by what are called "triumphs." But these triumphs the commanders cannot celebrate with proper pomp, or in some cases celebrate at all, unless the senate concurs and grants the necessary money. As for the people, the consuls are preeminently obliged to court their favor, however distant from home may be the field of their operations; for it is the people, as

I have said before, that ratifies, or refuses to ratify, terms of peace and treaties; but most of all because when laying down their office they have to give an account of their administration before it. Therefore in no case is it safe for the consuls to neglect either the senate or the good-will of the people.

As for the senate, which possesses the immense power I have described, in the first place it is obliged in public affairs to take the multitude into account, and respect the wishes of the people; and it cannot put into execution the penalty for offences against the republic, which are punishable with death, unless the people first ratify its decrees. Similarly even in matters which directly affect the senators,—for instance, in the case of a law diminishing the senate's traditional authority, or depriving senators of certain dignities and offices, or even actually cutting down their property,—even in such cases the people have the sole power of passing or rejecting the law. But most important of all is the fact that, if the tribunes interpose their veto, the senate not only are unable to pass a decree, but cannot even hold a meeting at all, whether formal or informal. Now, the tribunes are always bound to carry out the decree of the people, and above all things to have regard to their wishes: therefore, for all these reasons the senate stands in awe of the multitude, and cannot neglect the feelings of the people.

In like manner the people on its part is far from being independent of the senate, and is bound to take its wishes into account both collectively and individually. For contracts, too numerous to count, are given out by the censors in all parts of Italy for the repairs or construction of public buildings; there is also the collection of revenue from many rivers, harbors, gardens, mines, and land—everything, in a word, that comes under the control of the Roman government: and in all these the people at large are engaged; so that there is scarcely a man, so to speak, who is not interested either as a contractor or as being employed in the works. For some purchase the contracts from the censors for themselves; and others go partners with them; while others again go security for these contractors, or actually pledge their property to the treasury for them. Now over all these transactions the senate has absolute control. It can grant an extension of time; and in case of unforeseen accident can relieve the contractors from a portion of their obligation, or release them from it altogether, if they are absolutely unable to fulfil it. And there are many details in which the senate can inflict great hardships, or, on the other hand, grant great indulgences to the contractors: for in every case the appeal is to it. But the most important point of all is that the judges are taken from its members in the majority of trials, whether public or private, in which the charges are heavy. Consequently, all citizens are much at its mercy; and being alarmed at the uncertainty as to when they may need its aid, are cautious about resisting or actively opposing its will. And for a similar reason men do not rashly resist the wishes of the consuls, because one and all may become subject to their absolute authority on a campaign.

The result of this power of the several estates for mutual help or harm is a union sufficiently firm for all emergencies, and a constitution than which it is impossible to find a better. For whenever any danger from without compels them to unite and work together, the strength which is developed by the state is so extraordinary, that everything required is unfailingly carried out by the eager rivalry shown by all classes to devote their whole minds to the need of the hour, and to secure that any determination come to should not fail for want of promptitude; while each individual works, privately and publicly alike, for the accomplishment of the business in hand. Accordingly, the peculiar constitution of the state makes it irresistible, and certain of obtaining whatever it determines to attempt. Nay, even when these external alarms are past, and the people are enjoying their good fortune and the fruits of their victories, and, as usually happens, growing corrupted by flattery and idleness, show a tendency to violence and arrogance,—it is in these circumstances, more than ever, that the constitution is seen to possess within itself the power of correcting abuses. For when any one of the three classes becomes puffed up, and manifests an inclination to be contentious and unduly encroaching, the mutual interdependency of all the three, and the possibility of the pretensions of any one being checked and thwarted by the others, must plainly check this tendency: and so the proper equilibrium is maintained by the impulsiveness of the one part being checked by its fear of the other. . . .

SELECTED BIBLIOGRAPHY

Dunning, William A., *Political Theories, Ancient and Mediæval*, ch. 4, §4.
Willoughby, Westel Woodbury, *The Political Theories of the Ancient World*, ch. 18.
Strachan-Davidson, James L., *Polybius*, in Evelyn Abbott, ed., *Hellenica: a Collection of Essays on Greek Poetry, Philosophy, History and Religion* (second ed., New York, 1898), pp. 353–387.
Glover, T. R., "Polybius," in *Cambridge Ancient History*, Vol. VIII (Cambridge, 1930), ch. 1.
Fustel de Coulanges, Numa Denis, "Polybe ou la Grèce conquise par les romains": pp. 119–211 of his *Questions historiques* (Paris, 1893).
Laqueur, R. A., *Polybius* (Leipsic, 1913).

MARCUS TULLIUS CICERO

IV. MARCUS TULLIUS CICERO (106–43 B.C.)

INTRODUCTION

Roman literature furnishes no original contribution to political thought. Jurists and essayists of the Republic and the Empire supplied valuable expositions of the logical and practical phases of the great systems of Roman law and administration; but in their more philosophical writings on governmental structure and policy they copied in the main the speculations of the Greeks. Particularly under the influence of the Greek Stoics, Roman writers wove principles of "natural law" into the principles of Roman jurisprudence and thereby put into clear and concrete form ideas of fundamental significance for later political theory.[1]

The only native Roman who wrote extensively on questions of political theory was Cicero. He is generally called the greatest of Roman prose writers; he was also one of the most successful lawyers of his day, as well as an able political orator, and an influential statesman and politician. He held many of the most important public offices in Rome, was an active leader in the bitter party politics, spent several years in political exile, and was killed in the course of a violent political struggle. His writings are in various fields—rhetoric, oratory, ethics and political philosophy. In his theoretical writings his primary object was, not to create a new philosophy, but rather to make better known and understood by his fellow-countrymen the ideas of the classical and Stoic writers of Greece, and to show how those ideas could be practically applied in Rome. Two political works survive, in part: the *Republic* (*De republica*) published in 51 B.C., and the *Laws* (*De legibus*) published posthumously.

---

[1] On political ideas in the Hellenistic period of Greece, see George H. Sabine, *History of Political Theory*, ch. 7; Cyril Bailey, *The Greek Atomists and Epicurus* (1928); Eduard Zeller, *The Stoics, Epicureans and Sceptics* (1892).

For reviews of political thought in ancient Rome, see Charles H. McIlwain, *Growth of Political Thought in the West*, ch. 4; George H. Sabine, *op. cit.*, chs. 8–10; Thomas I. Cook, *History of Political Philosophy*, ch. 5; William A. Dunning, *Political Theories, Ancient and Mediæval*, ch. 4.

A specific and immediate object of Cicero's political writings was to show how the great Roman tradition of devoted public service could be established on the solid foundation of universal social and political truths, as expounded by the Greeks, and to point out the exalted place of the state in the realization of those truths. His general method was to describe the structure of a perfect state and to argue that the Roman Republic had moved slowly toward that model throughout most of its history. He took from Polybius, as well as from Plato and Aristotle, the idea that a mixed constitution was ordinarily the best form for actual states; and he followed Polybius in maintaining that the Roman government had, in its best days, exhibited generally the essential principles of such a constitution. Usually he was less definite than Polybius in identifying the particular institutions through which those principles were realized; although in the *Laws* he proposed certain new devices for rectifying and completing the mixed constitution of Rome.

In his historical and theoretical analysis of the Roman constitution (always in reference to the perfect state) Cicero set forth, with exceptional clarity and eloquence, the Stoic doctrine of natural law and from that doctrine drew striking conclusions concerning the ethical aims of the state, the ultimate supremacy of the people in a true political community, and the essential legal equality of the individual members of such a community. It is in his presentation of these juristic and socio-ethical ideas that his special contribution to the evolution of political ideas is to be found. His works were extensively read and quoted throughout the Middle Ages, where they were, without much difficulty, merged with basic social doctrines of the Christian Church.

READINGS FROM THE REPUBLIC AND THE LAWS [1]

1. *The Qualifications and Duties of Statesmanship* [2]

I. [Without a sense of public duty, Manius Curius, Gaius Fabricius, and Tiberius Coruncanius] would not have freed [Italy] from the attack [of Pyrrhus.] Without this feeling Gaius Duelius,

[1] The selections from the *Republic* are taken from *On the Commonwealth: Marcus Tullius Cicero*, translated, with Notes and Introduction, by George H.

[2] *Republic*, Bk. I, chs. 1-2, 5-7, 20.

Aulus Atilius, and Lucius Metellus would not have banished the fear of Carthage.[1] Without it, the two Scipios would not have quenched with their own blood the rising fire of the Second Punic War; nor, when fresh fuel had been added to the flames, would Quintus Maximus have stayed its violence, nor Marcus Marcellus have stamped it out. Without it, Publius Scipio Africanus would not have snatched the brand of war from before the city's gates, and hurled it within the enemy's walls.

Now take the case of Marcus Cato,[2] who serves as the model of an active and virtuous life for all of us whose interests, like his, are political. Unknown and without an inherited tradition of public service, he might surely have enjoyed himself in quiet repose at Tusculum, a healthful and convenient place. But he was a fool, as your philosophical friends believe, because he chose to ride the storms and tempests of public life until advanced age, rather than to live a life of ease amid the calm and restfulness of Tusculum.

I pass by countless men who have individually contributed their share to the safety of the state; and others, whose lives are too nearly contemporaneous, I do not mention for fear that someone may complain that he or one of his family has been slighted. I content myself with this one assertion: The need and love for noble actions, which nature has given to men that they may defend the common weal, are so compelling that they have overcome all the enticements of pleasure and of ease.

II. But merely to possess virtue as you would an art is not

Sabine and Stanley B. Smith (Columbus, Ohio, 1929). By courtesy of the Ohio State University Press. The selections from the *Laws* are taken from *Cicero: de re publica, de legibus*, with an English translation by Clinton Walker Keyes (London and New York, 1928). By courtesy of the Harvard University Press.

Both works are in dialogue form. In the *Republic* the speakers are Scipio Africanus the Younger, celebrated Roman general and statesman; Laelius, a prominent political and literary figure; and several friends of these two men. The conversation is represented as having taken place in Scipio's garden, in the latter part of the second century B.C. Scholars estimate that the extant fragments constitute about one third of the work as originally written by Cicero. In the *Laws*, the speakers are Cicero himself, his brother Quintus, and Atticus—Cicero's friend and adviser. The translators have at a few places supplied their own words, enclosed in brackets, to indicate a conjectural meaning where a fragmentary passage leaves Cicero's meaning incompletely stated.

Footnotes appearing in the following pages of the *Republic* are selected from the translators' footnotes.

[1] These were generals in the First Punic War.

[2] Marcus Porcius Cato the Censor (234–149 B.C.), the famous model of ancient Roman austerity and the persistent foe of Greek learning and manners, was for some thirty-five years the most influential man in Rome. He also composed the earliest history of Rome in Latin, the *Origines*, cited by Cicero (*de rep*. 2. 1, below).

enough, unless you apply it. For an art, even if unused, can still be retained in the form of theoretical knowledge, but virtue depends entirely upon its use. And its highest use is the government of a state and the actual performance, not the mere discussion, of those deeds which your philosophers rehearse in their secluded retreats. For, even when philosophers express just and sincere sentiments about these matters, they merely state in words what has been actually realized and put into effect by those statesmen who have given states their laws. From whom, we may ask, comes our sense of moral obligation and our reverence toward the gods? From whom do we derive that law which is common to all peoples, or that to which we apply the term civil? From whom comes our feeling for justice, for honor, for fair dealing? Whence our sense of shame, our self-control, our avoidance of what is base, our craving for a name and reputation? From whom is derived our courage in the face of toil and danger? Assuredly, from those statesmen who have developed these qualities by education and have embedded some of them in custom and have enforced others by the provisions of their laws. Xenocrates,[1] one of the most distinguished of philosophers, was once asked, so the story goes, what his pupils gained from his instruction. He replied that of their own free will they would perform the duties they would be forced to do by the laws.

A statesman, therefore, who by his authority and by the punishments which his laws impose obliges all men to adopt that course which only a mere handful can be persuaded to adopt by the arguments of philosophers, should be held in even greater esteem than the teachers who make these virtues the subject of their discussions. For what argument of your philosophers is so carefully wrought out that it should be preferred to a state firmly established under public law and custom? Cities "mighty and imperial," to quote Ennius,[2] ought, in my opinion, to be considered superior to hamlets and outposts. Similarly, those who by their advice and influence rule such cities must, I feel, be assigned a far higher place in respect to wisdom itself than those who take no part in any public duty. Since, therefore, we are powerfully moved to increase the resources of the human race, since we desire through our planning and toiling to render life safer and richer, and since we are spurred on to this agreeable task by nature herself, let us persevere in that

[1] Xenocrates of Chalcedon was the head of the Academy second after Plato, i.e., from 339 to 314 B.C.
[2] Ennius (239–169 B.C.) was the first important figure in Latin literature and the friend of Cato the Censor and Scipio Africanus the Elder.

course which has ever been chosen by the best of men, and let us not heed the trumpets which sound retreat and would recall even the soldiers who have already advanced.

V. To the evasions by which men would fain excuse themselves from public duties, in order to enjoy retirement the more comfortably, we must by no means give ear. It is asserted, for example, that political life attracts in general only utterly worthless men, to be compared with whom is disgusting, and to contend with whom, especially when the mob is aroused, is deplorable and dangerous. Therefore, it is said, a wise man does not grasp the reins of government, since he cannot restrain the mad lunges of the untamed rabble, nor does a free man strive against vile and savage opponents, or submit to the lash of insult, or suffer injuries that a wise man should not bear. As if a good and brave and high-minded man could find a more honorable reason for entering public life than the desire to avoid the rule of scoundrels or to prevent them from rending the commonwealth, while he himself, though eager to aid, looks impotently on!

VI. And who, moreover, can approve of the exception that they make when they say that the wise man will not assume a rôle in political life except under the compulsion of circumstances? As if a greater compulsion could come to any man than came to me! And yet what could I have done in that emergency had I not then been consul? And how could I have been consul if I had not from early youth persisted in that course of life by which, though born in the equestrian order, I finally attained the highest position in the state?[1] You cannot aid the state at a moment's notice or when you wish, although she is faced with great danger, unless you are in a position to do so. It has always seemed especially strange to me in the discourses of the learned, that men who admit that they cannot pilot the ship when the sea is calm, because they have never learned how nor troubled about such knowledge, nevertheless declare that they will take the helm when the waves are highest. Your philosophers, indeed, assert openly—and they even pride themselves not a little upon it—that they have not learned, nor do they teach, anything about the principles either of founding or preserving the state. According to them, such knowledge should be the province, not of scholars and philosophers, but of

---

[1] The higher offices in Rome were limited in practice, though not in theory, to the *nobiles*, that is, members of families whose ancestors had held such offices. Cicero was a *novus homo*, one of the exceptional men who attained high office without being born in the privileged class.

practical politicians. How, then, is it becoming for them to proffer their aid to the commonwealth only under the pressure of necessity, although they do not know how to perform the far easier task of ruling the state when no emergency confronts it ? But even if we grant that the philosopher of his own accord does not generally condescend to deal with affairs of state, though he does not refuse the duty if circumstances make it necessary, nevertheless I should feel that the philosopher ought by no means to neglect the science of politics, since he should be forearmed with all the weapons which he may sometime be obliged to use.

VII. I have spoken thus at length because in the present work I have projected and undertaken a discussion of the commonwealth. That it might not be in vain, I had first to banish the reluctance that is felt toward entering politics. But if there still are any who are influenced by the prestige of philosophers, I would have them give earnest attention for a moment to thinkers whose influence and renown have great weight with the learned. These thinkers, even though not actually holding public office, have investigated and treated many problems of the state ; and I accordingly feel that they have performed some public function. I notice that nearly all of those whom the Greeks called the Seven Sages [1] passed their lives in the midst of public affairs. There is, indeed, nothing in which human excellence can more nearly approximate the divine than in the foundation of new states or in the preservation of states already founded.

XX. MUCIUS : What studies do you think we should master, Laelius, in order to bring about the end that you desire ?

LAELIUS : Assuredly, such subjects as would make us useful to the state. For service to the state I consider the most glorious function of the wise and the chief mark or duty of the good. Accordingly, in order that we may spend this holiday in discussions conducive to the highest interests of our country, let us request Scipio to explain what he regards as the best form of constitution for the state. After that we shall conduct other inquiries. When these are answered, I hope that we shall immediately arrive at the discussion of our present political situation, and explain the meaning of the perils that are now upon us.

---

[1] The Seven Sages lived in the sixth century B.C. and, as the list is generally given, included Solon of Athens, Periander of Corinth, Chilon of Sparta, Pittacus of Mitylene, Bias of Priene, Thales of Miletus, and Cleobulus of Lindus. See Bury : *History of Greece* (1916), p. 321 ; Beloch : *Gr. Gesch.* I. 1 (1924), p. 427 ; I. 2 (1913), pp. 352 ff.

2. The Nature of a Commonwealth and of the Different Forms of Government [1]

XXV. SCIPIO: The commonwealth, then, is the people's affair; and the people is not every group of men, associated in any manner, but is the coming together of a considerable number of men who are united by a common agreement about law and rights and by the desire to participate in mutual advantages. The original cause of this coming together is not so much weakness as a kind of social instinct natural to man. For the human kind is not solitary, nor do its members live lives of isolated roving; but it is so constituted that, even if it possessed the greatest plenty of material comforts, [it would nevertheless be impelled by its nature to live in social groups..........]

XXVI. SCIPIO: ....[These gregarious impulses] are, so to speak, the seeds [of social virtues]; nor can any other source be found for the remaining virtues or, indeed, for the commonwealth itself. Such groups, therefore, brought into being for the reason I have mentioned, first settled themselves in a fixed abode that they might have dwellings. And when they had fortified this abode, either by taking advantage of the natural features of the land or by building artificial works, they called such a group of buildings, with the places set aside for shrines and for common use, either a town or a city. Consequently, every people, which is a number of men united in the way I have explained, every state, which is an organization of the people, every commonwealth, which, as I have said, is the people's affair, needs to be ruled by some sort of deliberating authority in order that it may endure. This authority, in the first place, must always be relative to the peculiar grounds which have brought the particular state into being. It must, in the second place, be delegated either to a single man, or to certain selected persons, or it must be retained by all the members of the group.

When, therefore, the supreme power is in the hands of one man, we call that man a king and that form of government a monarchy. When it is in the hands of certain selected persons, the state is said to be ruled by the will of an aristocracy. And a state is democratic—for that is the term used—when all authority is in the hands of the people themselves. Any one of these three forms of government, while not, of course, perfect nor in my judgment the best, is nevertheless a passable form of government, if the bond holds which originally united its members in the social order of the com-

[1] *Republic*, Bk. I, chs. 25 (in part), 26–35.

monwealth; and one may be better than another.[1] For either a just and wise king, or an aristocracy of leading citizens, or even the people themselves—though this last is the least desirable form of the three—appears capable of carrying on a stable government so long as injustice and greed have not crept into the state.

XXVII. Nevertheless, in a monarchy all except the king are too much excluded from the protection of the law and from participation in deliberative functions, though these rights belong to the whole people. In a government dominated by an aristocracy the mass of the people have hardly any share in freedom, since they have no part in common deliberative and executive powers. And when the state is governed by the people, even though they be just and self-disciplined, yet their very equality is inequitable in that it does not recognize degrees of merit.[2] Therefore, even if Cyrus the Persian was a perfectly just and wise king, nevertheless the condition of the commons—that is, the commonwealth, as I have said above—does not seem to have been one which we should particularly covet, since it was subject to the caprice of a single man. Similarly, even if our clients, the Massilians, are governed with the greatest justice by their oligarchy of nobles, still in a people so situated there exists something like slavery. And even if the Athenians at certain periods after the fall of the Areopagus conducted all public business through enactments and decrees of the people, still their state did not preserve its glory, since it failed to regard differences of worth.[3]

XXVIII. I am speaking of the three types of government, not as they are when they have become disordered and deranged, but as they are when they maintain their true character. In this condition, each type is subject, first, to the defects which I have mentioned, and in addition has other faults likely to be fatal to its permanence. For each of these types of commonwealth has a tendency to slip headlong into that form of evil government which is most closely related to it. Take, for example, a king at his best,

---

[1] The Latin text of this last clause is corrupt.

[2] A reference to proportional as against absolute equality. The distinction depends on Plato's definition of justice as the performance of function (*Republic*, 433 b), and the principle is clearly stated in the *Laws*, 757 a ff. See also Isocrates (3.14): "The essence of justice is . . . that unequals should not receive equal treatment, but that individuals should both act and be honored in accordance with their merits." . . . When developed as a legal conception, proportional justice becomes the Roman principle *ius suum cuique tribuere*.

[3] In 462-1 B.C. the democratic party, under the leadership of Ephialtes and Pericles, took from the Areopagus all its significant powers. The aristocratic tradition of Athenian history represents the epoch before the fall of the Areopagus as the golden age of Athens.

a Cyrus, who was an endurable or, if you like, even a lovable ruler. Nevertheless, his character may change, for there lurks in him the utterly inhuman Phalaris into whose likeness arbitrary power in the hands of one man readily and easily degenerates.[1] Furthermore, the government of the Massilian state by a few chief men is closely approximated by the oligarchical conspiracy of the Thirty Tyrants which once ruled Athens.[2] And finally, at Athens the Athenians themselves—to seek no other [authority—admit] that the absolute power of the people degenerated into the irresponsible madness of a mob.........

XXIX. Scipio: .... a veritable scoundrel [comes to the front;] and from this condition of the state there may arise an aristocracy or a tyrannical government by a party or a monarchy or, quite frequently, even a democracy.[3] And likewise it often happens that from this last type there grows up one of those forms of state which I have noted before. For there is a remarkable rotation and, if I may say so, cycle of changes in the life of states. It is the business of a philosopher to understand the order in which these changes occur; but to foresee impending modifications, and at the same time to pilot the state, to direct its course, and to keep it under control, is the part of a great statesman and a man of all but godlike powers. There is, accordingly, a fourth kind of commonwealth which, in my opinion, should receive the highest approval, since it is formed by the combination, in due measure, of the three forms of state which I described as original.

XXX. Laelius: I know, Africanus, that you prefer this composite type of state, for I have often heard you say so. But still, if there is no objection, I should like to know which of the three unmixed kinds of state you consider the best. For it will be of some use to know.........

XXXI. Scipio: .... and every state varies according to the character and inclination of its sovereign. Consequently, no state except one in which the people have supreme power provides a habitation for liberty, than which surely nothing can be sweeter. But if liberty is not equally enjoyed by all the

---

[1] Phalaris, the tyrant of Agrigentum (sixth century B.C.), was noted in antiquity as the inventor of a hollow bronze bull into which his enemies were put and roasted to death.

[2] The régime of the Thirty Tyrants and of the Ten Commissioners who followed them occurred in 404-3 B.C., and was set up by Lysander.

[3] The lacuna which precedes this sentence prevents us from understanding with certainty the relation which the sentence bears to Cicero's theory of constitutional cycles. It would appear that the "scoundrel" (*taeterrimus*) refers to the tyrant; and that the "tyrannical government by a party" refers to the Thirty Tyrants mentioned at the end of the preceding chapter.

citizens, it is not liberty at all. And yet, how can all citizens have an equal share in liberty—I pass over the citizens in a monarchy, for there, of course, the subjection of the people is neither concealed nor questionable—but even in those states in which all men are nominally free? They do, of course, cast their votes; they elect the civil and military officials; their suffrages are solicited for purposes of election and legislation. Nevertheless, the powers which they bestow they would have to bestow, even against their will; and they do not possess the powers which others seek to obtain from them. For they have no share in military commands, or in advisory councils, or in special jury panels.[1] These offices are in fact reserved to men of ancient family or to men of wealth. But in a free people, as at Rhodes or at Athens, there is no citizen who [is not eligible to all the offices of state][2] . . . .

XXXII. Scipio: [The advocates of democracy] affirm that, [when] one man or a few men become wealthier and more powerful than the other citizens, their pride and arrogance give rise [to special privileges], because the inactive and the weak give way and submit to the pretensions of the rich. So long, however, as the people actually retain their power, these thinkers hold that no form of government is better, more liberal, or more prosperous, since the people have control over legislation, the administration of justice, the making of war and peace, the concluding of treaties, and over the civil status and property of each individual citizen. This, according to their view, is the only form of government which can properly be called a commonwealth, that is, the people's affair; and therefore, while there are many instances where the people's affair is freed from the yoke of kings and patricians, there is none of a free people's demanding a king or an aristocratic form of government. They assert, moreover, that it is not right for democracy in general to be condemned because an uncontrolled populace has defects; that, so long as a people is harmonious and subordinates everything to its safety and freedom, there is no form of government less subject to revolution or more stable; and that the kind of state in which harmony is most easily attained is one in which the interests of all the citizens are the same. Dissension, as they hold, arises from diversity of interests, whenever the well-being of some is contrary to the well-being of others. Conse-

---

[1] Cicero apparently refers to the fact that at Rome the possession of *nobilitas* was usually necessary if a man aspired to important political offices or to a military career.
[2] If our reconstruction of the meaning of the sentence be correct, Cicero's statement is accurate, generally speaking, for Athens, though there were some exceptions.

quently, when the government was in the hands of aristocrats, the form of the state has never remained stable. Still less has this been the case with monarchies, for, in Ennius' words,

In a kingdom there is no sacred fellowship or trust.

Since, then, law is the bond that holds political society together, and since equality of rights is a part of law, by what principle of right can an association of citizens be held together, when the status of these citizens is not equal? For, if it is not thought desirable that property should be equally distributed, and if the natural capacities of all men cannot possibly be equal, yet certainly all who are citizens of the same commonwealth ought to enjoy equal rights in their mutual relations. What, indeed, is a state, if it is not an association of citizens united by law?[1].........

XXXIII. SCIPIO : .... in fact, [the advocates of democracy] do not think that the other forms of government deserve even the names by which they would be called. Why, indeed, should I apply the word king—a name which belongs properly to Jupiter the Most High—to a human being who is greedy for lordship and exclusive dominion and who is the slave-driver of an oppressed people? Should I not rather call him a tyrant? For mercy is as possible in a tyrant as cruelty in a king. Accordingly, the only concern of the people is whether they are the slaves of a kindly or of a harsh master, since under this form of government they are inevitably the slaves of someone. Moreover, how was it that, at the time when Spartan political institutions were supposedly at their best, this famous people contrived to have only good and just kings, although they had to take as king anyone who happened to be born of the royal family? And as for aristocrats, who can tolerate those who have assumed this title, not as the result of popular grant but as the result of their own election? What, I ask, is the criterion by which your aristocrat is judged? Is it learning, or culture, or scholarly tastes, as I hear? When....

XXXIV. SCIPIO : .... if a state [chooses its rulers] at haphazard, it will be overthrown as quickly as a ship will founder if its pilot is chosen by lot from among the passengers.[2]

[1] Since a lacuna immediately follows the word *civium*, it is impossible to tell whether the sentence ends with that word; and indeed *civium* may belong to the following sentence which has been lost.

[2] In the lacuna Cicero passes to the arguments for aristocracy. The reference in the first sentence following the lacuna is to election by lot and to Socrates' criticism of it. This criticism, which is mentioned in Xenophon (*Mem.* I. 2. 9), was probably one of the grounds for the prosecution of Socrates. Until the end of the fourth century B.C., all Athenian magistrates were chosen by this method, with the exception of military commanders, certain financial officials, and a few others.

But if a free people chooses those to whose guidance it will submit itself, and if it chooses for this purpose all its best citizens—provided, of course, that the people wish to be secure—surely, then, the safety of the state has been founded upon the wisdom of its ablest members. This is particularly true since nature has contrived to make the men who are superior in courage and ability rule over the weak, and the weak willing to submit themselves to the best. This perfect relationship between men has been overthrown, according to the partizans of aristocracy, by the false notions that prevail about human excellence. For, as few men possess excellence, so few are able to recognize and judge it. Thus, being ignorant of its nature, the masses suppose that men of wealth, influence, and important family connections are the best. When, as a result of this error on the part of the commons, the wealth rather than the excellence of a few men has come to control the state, these leaders cling stubbornly to the title of aristocrats, utterly lacking though they may be in the substance of excellence. For riches and reputation and power, if devoid of wisdom and of moderation in conduct and in the exercise of authority, are characterized by shamelessness and insufferable arrogance. There is, indeed, no uglier kind of state than one in which the richest men are thought to be the best.

On the other hand, when excellence governs the commonwealth, what can be more glorious? For then he who rules over others is not himself the slave of any base desire; the requirements which he lays upon his fellow-citizens he has fulfilled himself; he does not impose upon the people laws which he does not himself obey; he holds up his own life before his fellow-citizens as the law by which they may guide their lives. If one such man were able to accomplish effectively all the business of the state, there would be no need for others; and if the body of citizens could always discover this perfect ruler and agree in regard to him, no one would demand specially chosen leaders. The difficulty of determining policy wisely has caused the transfer of authority from the king to several persons; and, conversely, the ignorance and recklessness of the commons have caused it to pass from the many to the few. Thus, between the weakness inherent in a single ruler and the recklessness inherent in the many, aristocracy has come to hold a middle place. Nothing, in fact, can be more perfectly balanced; and as long as an aristocracy guards the state, the people are necessarily in the happiest condition, since they are free from all care and anxiety. Their ease has been put into the safe-keeping of others, who must protect it and take care that nothing arises to make the people believe that their interests are being neglected by their leaders.

Now the equal rights of which democracies are so fond cannot be maintained. Indeed, no matter how free and untrammeled popular governments may be, they are still exceptionally prone to confer many favors on many men, and show decided preferences in the matter of individuals and in the matter of high rank. And what is called equality is, in reality, extremely unequal. For when the same importance is attached to the high and the low—and in every community these two classes necessarily exist—that very equality is most unequal. Such a condition cannot arise in states that are governed by aristocracies.

Arguments of much this character, Laelius, and others of the same kind, are usually put forward by those who praise most highly the aristocratic form of government.

XXXV. LAELIUS: But of the three simple forms of state, Scipio, which do you especially approve?

SCIPIO: You frame your question well when you ask, "Which of the three" I especially approve, because I do not approve any one of them considered separately and by itself. I prefer rather the mixed form, which is a combination of all three, to any one taken by itself. Still, if I had to express preference for one of the unmixed forms, I should choose monarchy [1 and accord it first place. In this kind of state] we find that the king is described as if he were a father, planning for his subjects as if they were his children, and zealously protecting them [but never reducing them to subjection. Thus it is much better for the weak and ignorant] to be guarded by the care of one man, who is at once the strongest and the best man in the state. There are, to be sure, the aristocrats, who claim that they do this better than the king, and assert that there would be greater wisdom in a number of men than in one, and withal the same justice and good faith. Finally, the people themselves declare loudly that they do not wish to obey either one man or several. Nothing, they say, is sweeter than freedom, even to wild beasts; and no citizen possesses freedom when he is subject either to a king or to an aristocracy.

Thus I prefer monarchy for the love which the king bears to his subjects; aristocracy for its wisdom in counsel; and democracy for its freedom. When I compare them, I find it hard to decide which feature we desire the most.

LAELIUS: I suppose so, but the rest of the subject can hardly be developed if you leave this point unsettled.

1 The Vatican manuscript is mutilated at this point.

3. The Cycle of Governments [1]

XLII. SCIPIO: After I have set forth my views about the form of state that I consider the best, I must certainly discuss with considerable care the revolutions that occur in governments, though I do not think that my favorite type of mixed government will readily be subject to them.

In a kingdom, however, the first and most certain change is that which occurred under Tarquinius: when the king ceases to rule justly, the royal form of government is straightway destroyed. The king becomes a tyrant; and tyranny, though closest to the best type, is the worst of all states. If, as is usually the case, the tyrant is crushed by the leading citizens, the commonwealth enjoys the second of the three forms of government I mentioned. For there is a certain regal or paternal element in the council of chief men who study to serve well the people's needs. If, on the other hand, the people themselves have slain or driven out the tyrant, they govern with considerable restraint so long as they are prudent and wise. Taking pride in their achievement, they are willing to guard the commonwealth which they have established. But let us suppose that the people have revolted against a just king or have deprived such a ruler of his royal power, or again let us suppose—what more frequently happens—that they have even tasted the blood of the foremost citizens and have made the whole state subserve their lust. If this happens—and, believe me, there is no sea so hard to calm and no fire so hard to check as the vengeance of the unrestrained mob—then that condition exists which Plato vividly describes. I wish that I could render it adequately into Latin. It is hard to do, but I shall try it.

XLIII. "Once the insatiable gullet of the people is parched with a thirst for freedom [2] and once the thirsty populace has been led by its bad servants to drain draughts, not of decently blended, but of undiluted freedom, they are continually censuring and accusing and incriminating their magistrates and leaders; and unless the latter supinely yield and grant freedom in generous measure, the people call them masters, kings, and tyrants." I feel sure that you are familiar with this passage.

LAELIUS: Perfectly familiar.

SCIPIO: Then Plato continues: "Those who obey their leaders are harassed by such a democracy and reproached with being willing slaves. Magistrates who are willing to perform their

[1] *Republic*, Bk. I, chs. 42–45.
[2] This passage, which purports to be a translation, is really a paraphrase of Plato: *Republic*, 562 ff.

public duties as if they were merely private citizens, and those private citizens who would do away with all distinctions which mark off the magistrates, are extolled to the skies and rewarded with honors. Thus, it inevitably comes about that under such a government everything is full of liberty. No authority is exercised in any private home, and the evil extends even to the dumb animals, until finally the father fears his son, the son slights his father, and every feeling of respect is gone. Thus men are indeed free. There is no distinction between citizen and foreigner; teachers fear their pupils and flatter them; pupils scorn their teachers; the young affect the gravity of age; and old men revert to youthful pranks in order not to be tiresome and displeasing to the young. Even slaves conduct themselves with undue freedom; and wives enjoy the same rights as their husbands. And even the dogs and the horses and the asses live in such an atmosphere of freedom that they run on us and make us give them the right of way. From this boundless license," Plato continues, "the following result inevitably follows: so sensitive and effeminate do the feelings of the citizens become that, if the least restraint is applied to them, they are enraged and cannot endure it. Then they begin to ignore the laws also, and so are completely without any master."

XLIV. LAELIUS: You have exactly rendered Plato's words.

SCIPIO: This extreme of license, which is their only idea of freedom—to return now to Plato [1]—is a sort of root from which the tyrant springs and, if I may say so, is born. Even as the extreme power of the aristocracy brings about the downfall of the aristocracy, so freedom itself punishes with slavery a people whose freedom has no bounds. Thus, every extreme—in climate, in fertility, or in health—which has been too pleasant, passes generally into the opposite extreme. This happens especially in the case of states, where the extreme of freedom becomes, both for peoples and for individuals, the extreme of slavery. Thus, from perfect freedom arises the tyrant, bringing with him arbitrary and oppressive subjection. Out of the untamed, or better still, the bestial populace, there is generally chosen a champion to guide them against their former leaders, who by this time have been overwhelmed and driven from their positions of authority. Overreaching and vicious, such a champion wantonly assails men who have often carned the gratitude of the state. He curries favor with the people by giving them the property of others as well as his own. Because he is still a private citizen, and because the insecurity of his position

[1] In the following paragraph Cicero paraphrases several sentences from Plato: *Republic*, 563 e–566 b.

makes him afraid, great powers are granted him and are never resigned; and, as happened with Peisistratus at Athens, his person is protected even by armed guards. The final stage is reached when the tyrant tyrannizes over the very citizens who have elevated him to his tyranny.

If the tyrant is overthrown by citizens with aristocratic leanings, as often happens, constitutional government is revived. If, on the other hand, political adventurers cause his downfall, there develops that turbulent oligarchy which is merely another form of tyranny. This kind of oligarchical state often arises also from the good form of aristocracy, when some lack of rectitude has corrupted the leaders themselves. The government is thus bandied about like a ball: tyrants receive it from kings; from tyrants it passes either to aristocrats or to the people; and from the people to oligarchs or tyrants. The same form of government is never long retained.

XLV. In view of these facts, monarchy is, in my judgment, far the best of the three simple types of state. But even monarchy will be excelled by the kind of state that is formed by an equal balancing and blending of the three unmixed types. For I hold it desirable, first, that there should be a dominant and royal element in the commonwealth; second, that some powers should be granted and assigned to the influence of the aristocracy; and third, that certain matters should be reserved to the people for decision and judgment. Such a government insures at once an element of equality, without which the people can hardly be free, and an element of strength. For, whereas the three forms of simple state which we mentioned first readily lapse into the perverted forms opposed to their respective virtues—tyranny arising from monarchy, oligarchy from aristocracy, and turbulent ochlocracy from democracy—and whereas the types themselves are often discarded for new ones, this instability can hardly occur in the mixed and judiciously blended form of state, unless its leaders fall into exceptional degradation. There is, indeed, no cause for change when each individual is firmly set in his proper place, and when there is no inferior position into which he may rapidly decline.

4. The Nature of Law [1]

. . . IV. *M*.[2] My opinions? Well then, I believe that there have been most eminent men in our state whose customary func-

[1] *Laws*, Bk. I, chs. 4–11 (in part); Bk. III, ch. 1; *Republic*, Bk. III, ch. 22.
[2] *M* is Cicero.

tion it was to interpret the law to the people and answer questions in regard to it, but that these men, though they have made great claims, have spent their time on unimportant details. What subject indeed is so vast as the law of the state? But what is so trivial as the task of those who give legal advice? It is, however, necessary for the people. But, while I do not consider that those who have applied themselves to this profession have lacked a conception of universal law, yet they have carried their studies of this civil law, as it is called, only far enough to accomplish their purpose of being useful to the people. Now all this amounts to little so far as learning is concerned, though for practical purposes it is indispensable. What subject is it, then, that you are asking me to expound? To what task are you urging me? Do you want me to write a treatise on the law of eaves and house-walls? Or to compose formulas for contracts and court procedure? These subjects have been carefully treated by many writers, and are of a humbler character, I believe, than what is expected of me.

V. A.[1] Yet if you ask what I expect of you, I consider it a logical thing that, since you have already written a treatise on the constitution of the ideal state, you should also write one on its laws. For I note that this was done by your beloved Plato, whom you admire, revere above all others, and love above all others.

. . . M. But in our present investigation we intend to cover the whole range of universal justice and law in such a way that our own civil law, as it is called, will be confined to a small and narrow corner. For we must explain the nature of justice, and this must be sought for in the nature of man; we must also consider the laws by which states ought to be governed; then we must deal with the enactments and decrees of nations which are already formulated and put in writing; and among these the civil law, as it is called, of the Roman people will not fail to find a place.

VI. Q.[2] You probe deep, and see, as you should, the very fountain-head, to find what we are after, brother. And those who teach the civil law in any other way are teaching not so much the path of justice as of litigation.

M. There you are mistaken, Quintus, for it is rather ignorance of the law than knowledge of it that leads to litigation. But that will come later; now let us investigate the origins of justice.

Well, then, the most learned men have determined to begin with law, and it would seem that they are right, if, according to their definition, law is the highest reason, implanted in Nature, which

[1] A is Atticus.
[2] Q is Quintus.

commands what ought to be done and forbids the opposite. This reason, when firmly fixed and fully developed in the human mind, is law. And so they believe that law is intelligence, whose natural function it is to command right conduct and forbid wrong-doing. They think that this quality has derived its name in Greek from the idea of granting to every man his own, and in our language I believe it has been named from the idea of choosing.[1] For as they have attributed the idea of fairness to the word law, so we have given it that of selection, though both ideas properly belong to law. Now if this is correct, as I think it to be in general, then the origin of justice is to be found in law, for law is a natural force; it is the mind and reason of the intelligent man, the standard by which justice and injustice are measured. But since our whole dis-cussion has to do with the reasoning of the populace, it will some-times be necessary to speak in the popular manner, and give the name of law to that which in written form decrees whatever it wishes, either by command or prohibition. For such is the crowd's definition of law. But in determining what justice is, let us begin with that supreme law which had its origin ages before any written law existed or any state had been established.

Q. Indeed that will be preferable and more suitable to the character of the conversation we have begun.

M. Well, then, shall we seek the origin of justice itself at its fountain-head? For when that is discovered we shall undoubtedly have a standard by which the things we are seeking may be tested.

Q. I think that is certainly what we must do.

A. Put me down also as agreeing with your brother's opinion.

M. Since, then, we must retain and preserve that constitution of the state which Scipio proved to be the best in the six books[2] devoted to the subject, and all our laws must be fitted to that type of state, and since we must also inculcate good morals, and not prescribe everything in writing, I shall seek the root of justice in Nature, under whose guidance our whole discussion must be con-ducted.

. . . VII. *M.* I will not make the argument long. Your admission leads us to this : that animal which we call man, endowed with foresight and quick intelligence, complex, keen, possessing memory, full of reason and prudence, has been given a certain distinguished status by the supreme God who created him; for he is the only one among so many different kinds and varieties of

---

[1] Νόμος is derived by Cicero from νέμω, "to distribute," *lex* from *lego*, "to choose." (Translator's note.)
[2] Cicero's *De republica*.

living beings who has a share in reason and thought, while all the rest are deprived of it. But what is more divine, I will not say in man only, but in all heaven and earth, than reason? And reason, when it is full grown and perfected, is rightly called wisdom. Therefore, since there is nothing better than reason, and since it exists both in man and God, the first common possession of man and God is reason. But those who have reason in common must also have right reason in common. And since right reason is law, we must believe that men have law also in common with the gods. Further, those who share law must also share justice; and those who share these are to be regarded as members of the same commonwealth. If indeed they obey the same authorities and powers, this is true in a far greater degree; but as a matter of fact they do obey this celestial system, the divine mind, and the God of transcendent power. Hence we must now conceive of this whole universe as one commonwealth of which both gods and men are members.

And just as in states distinctions in legal status are made on account of the blood relationships of families, according to a system which I shall take up in its proper place so in the universe the same thing holds true, but on a scale much vaster and more splendid, so that men are grouped with Gods on the basis of blood relationship and descent.

VIII. For when the nature of man is examined, the theory is usually advanced (and in all probability it is correct) that through constant changes and revolutions in the heavens, a time came which was suitable for sowing the seed of the human race. And when this seed was scattered and sown over the earth, it was granted the divine gift of the soul. For while the other elements of which man consists were derived from what is mortal, and are therefore fragile and perishable, the soul was generated in us by God. Hence we are justified in saying that there is a blood relationship between ourselves and the celestial beings; or we may call it a common ancestry or origin. Therefore among all the varieties of living beings, there is no creature except man which has any knowledge of God, and among men themselves there is no race either so highly civilized or so savage as not to know that it must believe in a god, even if it does not know in what sort of god it ought to believe. Thus it is clear that man recognizes God because, in a way, he remembers and recognizes the source from which he sprang.

Moreover, virtue exists in man and God alike, but in no other creature besides; virtue, however, is nothing else than Nature perfected and developed to its highest point; therefore there is a

likeness between man and God. As this is true, what relationship
could be closer or clearer than this one? For this reason, Nature
has lavishly yielded such a wealth of things adapted to man's convenience and use that what she produces seems intended as a gift
to us, and not brought forth by chance; and this is true, not only
of what the fertile earth bountifully bestows in the form of grain
and fruit, but also of the animals; for it is clear that some of them
have been created to be man's slaves, some to supply him with their
products, and others to serve as his food. Moreover innumerable
arts have been discovered through the teachings of Nature; for
it is by a skilful imitation of her that reason has acquired the
necessities of life.

IX. Nature has likewise not only equipped man himself with
nimbleness of thought, but has also given him the senses, to be, as
it were, his attendants and messengers; she has laid bare the
obscure and none too [obvious] meanings of a great many things,
to serve as the foundations of knowledge, as we may call them;
and she has granted us a bodily form which is convenient and well
suited to the human mind. For while she has bent the other
creatures down toward their food, she has made man alone erect,
and has challenged him to look up toward heaven, as being, so to
speak, akin to him, and his first home. In addition, she has so
formed his features as to portray therein the character that lies
hidden deep within him; for not only do the eyes declare with
exceeding clearness the innermost feelings of our hearts, but also
the countenance, as we Romans call it, which can be found in no
living thing save man, reveals the character. (The Greeks are
familiar with the meaning which this word "countenance" conveys,
though they have no name for it.) I will pass over the special
faculties and aptitudes of the other parts of the body, such as the
varying tones of the voice and the power of speech, which is the
most effective promoter of human intercourse; for all these things
are not in keeping with our present discussion or the time at our
disposal; and besides, this topic has been adequately treated, as
it seems to me, by Scipio in the books which you have read.[1] But,
whereas God has begotten and equipped man, desiring him to be
the chief of all created things, it should now be evident, without
going into all the details, that Nature, alone and unaided, goes a
step farther; for, with no guide to point the way, she starts with
those things whose character she has learned through the rudimentary beginnings of intelligence, and, alone and unaided,
strengthens and perfects the faculty of reason.

[1] The *De republica*.

X. *A.* Ye immortal gods, how far back you go to find the origins of justice! And you discourse so eloquently that I not only have no desire to hasten on to the consideration of the civil law, concerning which I was expecting you to speak, but I should have no objection to your spending even the entire day on your present topic; for the matters which you have taken up, no doubt, merely as preparatory to another subject, are of greater import than the subject itself to which they form an introduction.

M. The points which are now being briefly touched upon are certainly important; but out of all the material of the philosophers' discussions, surely there comes nothing more valuable than the full realization that we are born for justice, and that right is based, not upon men's opinions, but upon Nature. This fact will immediately be plain if you once get a clear conception of man's fellowship and union with his fellow-men. For no single thing is so like another, so exactly its counterpart, as all of us are to one another. Nay, if bad habits and false beliefs did not twist the weaker minds and turn them in whatever direction they are inclined, no one would be so like his own self as all men would be like all others. And so, however we may define man, a single definition will apply to all. This is a sufficient proof that there is no difference in kind between man and man; for if there were, one definition could not be applicable to all men; and indeed reason, which alone raises us above the level of the beasts and enables us to draw inferences, to prove and disprove, to discuss and solve problems, and to come to conclusions, is certainly common to us all, and, though varying in what it learns, at least in the capacity to learn it is invariable. For the same things are invariably perceived by the senses, and those things which stimulate the senses, stimulate them in the same way in all men; and those rudimentary beginnings of intelligence to which I have referred, which are imprinted on our minds, are imprinted on all minds alike; and speech, the mind's interpreter, though differing in the choice of words, agrees in the sentiments expressed. In fact, there is no human being of any race who, if he finds a guide, cannot attain to virtue.

XI. The similarity of the human race is clearly marked in its evil tendencies as well as in its goodness. For pleasure also attracts all men; and even though it is an enticement to vice, yet it has some likeness to what is naturally good. For it delights us by its lightness and agreeableness; and for this reason, by an error of thought, it is embraced as something wholesome. It is through a similar misconception that we shun death as though it were a dissolution of nature, and cling to life because it keeps us in the

sphere in which we were born; and that we look upon pain as one
of the greatest of evils, not only because of its cruelty, but also
because it seems to lead to the destruction of nature. In the same
way, on account of the similarity between moral worth and renown,
those who are publicly honored are considered happy, while those
who do not attain fame are thought miserable. Troubles, joys,
desires, and fears haunt the minds of all men without distinction,
and even if different men have different beliefs, that does not prove,
for example, that it is not the same quality of superstition that
besets those races which worship dogs and cats as gods, as that
which torments other races. But what nation does not love
courtesy, kindliness, gratitude, and remembrance of favors bestowed? What people does not hate and despise the haughty,
the wicked, the cruel, and the ungrateful? Inasmuch as these
considerations prove to us that the whole human race is bound
together in unity, it follows, finally, that knowledge of the
principles of right living is what makes men better.

I.[1]   *M.*   I will follow again, then, as I did before, the example
of that divine personage, whom I praise oftener, perhaps, than I
should, such is the admiration I feel for him.
    A.   Of course you mean Plato.
    M.   None other, Atticus.
    A.   Surely you can never praise him too highly or too often;
for even those friends of ours who object to the praise of anyone
outside their own company allow me to be as fond of him as I like.
    M.   And .they are certainly right in that. For what could be
more appropriate to the good taste of a man like yourself, who in
both his life and his language has achieved, in my opinion, that
most difficult combination of dignity and refinement?
    A.   I am very glad indeed that I interrupted you, since you have
given me so fine a proof of your good opinion. But go on as you
have begun.
    M.   First, then, let us commend the law itself with words of
praise which are both merited and appropriate to its character.
    A.   By all means, just as you did in the case of the law of
religion.
    M.   You understand, then, that the function of a magistrate
is to govern, and to give commands which are just and beneficial
and in conformity with the law. For as the laws govern the
magistrate, so the magistrate governs the people, and it can truly
be said that the magistrate is a speaking law, and the law a silent

[1] Laws, Bk. III.

magistrate. Nothing, moreover, is so completely in accordance with the principles of justice and the demands of Nature (and when I use these expressions, I wish it understood that I mean law) as is government, without which existence is impossible for a household, a city, a nation, the human race, physical nature, and the universe itself. For the universe obeys God; seas and lands obey the universe, and human life is subject to the decrees of supreme law.

XXII.[1] LAELIUS: There is in fact a true law—namely, right reason—which is in accordance with nature, applies to all men, and is unchangeable and eternal. By its commands this law summons men to the performance of their duties; by its prohibitions it restrains them from doing wrong. Its commands and prohibitions always influence good men, but are without effect upon the bad. To invalidate this law by human legislation is never morally right, nor is it permissible ever to restrict its operation, and to annul it wholly is impossible. Neither the senate [2] nor the people can absolve us from our obligation to obey this law, and it requires no Sextus Aelius [3] to expound and interpret it. It will not lay down one rule at Rome and another at Athens, nor will it be one rule today and another tomorrow. But there will be one law, eternal and unchangeable, binding at all times upon all peoples; and there will be, as it were, one common master and ruler of men, namely God, who is the author of this law, its interpreter, and its sponsor. The man who will not obey it will abandon his better self, and, in denying the true nature of a man, will thereby suffer the severest of penalties, though he has escaped all the other consequences which men call punishment.

[1] From the *Republic*, Bk. III.
[2] While the Roman senate did not possess the right of legislation, it had the power to exempt persons from the operation of the law. During the last century B.C. an attempt was made to deprive the senate of this right and to confer it solely upon the people. As a result of the agitation it was enacted that, when the senate granted such an exemption, there must be present at least two hundred senators.
[3] Sextus Aelius Paetus Catus, consul in 198 B.C. and censor in 194, was a jurisconsult and the author of a work on the law of the Twelve Tables. The book was generally known as the *ius Aelianum*.

SELECTED BIBLIOGRAPHY

McIlwain, Charles H., *The Growth of Political Thought in the West*, pp. 106–118.
Sabine, George H., *A History of Political Theory*, pp. 159–167.
Cook, Thomas I., *History of Political Philosophy*, pp. 143–149.
Dunning, William A., *Political Theories, Ancient and Mediæval*, ch. 4, § 5.

Sabine, George H., and Stanley B. Smith, *On the Commonwealth: Marcus Tullius Cicero*, translated with notes and Introduction (Columbus, Ohio, 1929), pp. 1–102.
Carlyle, R. W. and A. J., *A History of Mediæval Political Theory in the West*, 6 vols. (Edinburgh and London, 1903–36), Vol. I, ch. 1.
Keyes, C. W., "Original Elements in Cicero's Ideal Constitution," *American Journal of Philology*, Vol. 42 (1921), pp. 309–323.
Cauer, F., *Ciceros politisches Denken* (Berlin, 1903).

AUGUSTINE

V. AUGUSTINE (354-430 A.D.)

INTRODUCTION

Throughout most of the Middle Ages, the state played a smaller part than the Church in controlling or guiding man's social life; and we find in this period relatively few profound and comprehensive discussions of the origin and nature of political society. Conflicting claims of political and ecclesiastical rulers often gave rise to debates concerning the proper scope and form of political rule. The disputants usually argued in terms of an appeal to authority: each side acknowledging the same authorities—the Bible, the Church Fathers, and the pronouncements of Popes and ecclesiastical councils; and each side citing precedents from the history of the Christian Church. Medieval political thought was not, however, wholly subordinated to doctrines of the Bible and the Church. In interpreting and showing the application of these doctrines, the Christian writers often brought into the discussion ideas inherited from pagan writers of Greece and Rome. Medieval political theory carries forward, in application to new cultural conditions, some of the most fundamental ideas of ancient political theory. Moreover, some of the Christian doctrines had, on their own part, important implications for the appraisal of political action. Thus the Middle Ages is by no means a barren period in the evolution of political theory.[1]

The writings of St. Augustine were one of the most important mediums for the transmission of ancient ideas into the medieval Christian world. Augustine, generally called "greatest of the Fathers" of the Church, was born in Numidia, Africa, of a pagan father and a Christian mother. Although educated as a Christian, he aligned himself in his youth with the Manichæan sect, one of

[1] By far the most extensive history of political ideas in this period is the six-volume work of R. W. and A. J. Carlyle, *A History of Mediæval Theory in the West* (1908–1936). Shorter reviews may be found in the histories, listed on p. xvi, *supra*, by Sabine, McIlwain, Gierke, Cook, Hearnshaw, and Gettell; and in more specialized works by John Neville Figgis and Reginald Lane Poole, listed on pp. 253, 273, *infra*.

the stronger rivals to Christianity. His conversion to Christianity
came about in his early thirties, influenced both by his mother's
example and persuasion and by the eloquent writing and preaching
of another of the four great Church Fathers—Ambrose, Bishop
of Milan. Augustine rose rapidly in the Church. He was made
Bishop of Hippo (in Africa) in his forty-second year and remained
in this office until his death forty-five years later.

Aside from the celebrated *Confessions* and a few early treatises on
general philosophical questions, Augustine's writing was devoted
mainly to an interpretation and defense of the Christian religion.
He wrote works in criticism of other religious sects of his day (Mani-
chæans, Donatists, Pelagians) ; commentaries on several Books of
the Bible ; and, most important, the *City of God*. This last work
occupied him for over a dozen years ; the particular occasion for it
was the sack of Rome by the Visigoths under Alaric, in 410. A
century earlier Rome had adopted Christianity as its official
religion. Now, pagan writers said, the vast and powerful Roman
empire—built up through a thousand years of pagan rule—had
"perished in the Christian days." Augustine devoted the first
ten books of the *City of God* to a refutation of that charge. In the
other twelve books he set forth more positively and comprehen-
sively his own conceptions of man and society. Man, because
his nature is two-fold—bodily, worldly, and spiritual, other-worldly
—is a citizen of two cities : an earthly city and the Heavenly City.
He is a citizen of either city in so far as he acts in accord with either
side of his nature. Neither of the two cities can be completely
identified with any actual community that has yet appeared ; yet
the explanation of all human history is to be found in the inter-
mingling and conflict between the two cities. The Assyrian and
Roman empires, representative of the earthly city, fell, as all
pagan empires must fall. Only the Heavenly City endures ; and
the Christian Church, aided by a Christianized empire, will even-
tually bring about the union of all believers under the leadership of the Church. The Heavenly City will then be realized on
earth.

In the elaboration and illustration of the main themes of the
City of God, Augustine blended certain basic ideas of Greek and
Roman authors (particularly Plato and Cicero) with the emerging
Christian ideas on the essential nature and functions of a political

community. The book exercised a profound influence over later medieval discussion of questions concerning the origin of political society; the relations of civil government to divine law, natural law, and justice; the qualities of a just ruler and of his opposite—the tyrant; and the Christian attitude towards slavery and private property.

READINGS FROM THE CITY OF GOD [1]

1. The Two Cities [2]

Ch. 3. *Whether the Great Extent of the Empire, which has been Acquired only by Wars, is to be Reckoned among the Good Things either of the Wise or the Happy.*

Now, therefore, let us see how it is that they dare to ascribe the very great extent and duration of the Roman empire to those gods whom they contend that they worship honorably, even by the obsequies of vile games and the ministry of vile men: although I should like first to inquire for a little what reason, what prudence, there is in wishing to glory in the greatness and extent of the empire, when you cannot point out the happiness of men who are always rolling, with dark fear and cruel lust, in warlike slaughters and in blood, which, whether shed in civil or foreign war, is still human blood; so that their joy may be compared to glass in its fragile splendor, of which one is horribly afraid lest it should be suddenly broken in pieces. That this may be more easily discerned, let us not come to nought by being carried away with empty boasting, or blunt the edge of our attention by loud-sounding names of things, when we hear of peoples, kingdoms, provinces. But let us suppose a case of two men; for each individual man, like one letter in a language, is as it were the element of a city or kingdom, however far-spreading in its occupation of the earth. Of these two men let us suppose that one is poor, or rather of middling circumstances; the other very rich. But the rich man is anxious with fears, pining with discontent, burning with covetousness, never secure, always uneasy, panting from the perpetual strife of his enemies, adding to his patrimony indeed by these miseries to an immense degree, and by these additions also heaping up most bitter cares. But that other man of moderate wealth is contented with a small and com-

[1] The selections are taken from the translation by Rev. Marcus Dods, printed in Vol. II (1887) of *A Select Library of the Nicene and Post-Nicene Fathers of the Christian Church*, edited by Philip Schaff, 14 vols. (Buffalo and New York, 1886–1890). By courtesy of Charles Scribner's Sons.

[2] Bk. iv, chs. 3–4; bk. xiv, ch. 28; bk. xv, chs. 1, 4.

pact estate, most dear to his own family, enjoying the sweetest peace with his kindred neighbors and friends, in piety religious, benignant in mind, healthy in body, in life frugal, in manners chaste, in conscience secure. I know not whether any one can be such a fool, that he dare hesitate which to prefer. As, therefore, in the case of these two men, so in two families, in two nations, in two kingdoms, this test of tranquillity holds good ; and if we apply it vigilantly and without prejudice, we shall quite easily see where the mere show of happiness dwells, and where real felicity. Wherefore if the true God is worshipped, and if He is served with genuine rites and true virtue, it is advantageous that good men should long reign both far and wide. Nor is this advantageous so much to themselves, as to those over whom they reign. For, so far as concerns themselves, their piety and probity, which are great gifts of God, suffice to give them true felicity, enabling them to live well the life that now is, and afterwards to receive that which is eternal. In this world, therefore, the dominion of good men is profitable, not so much for themselves as for human affairs. But the dominion of bad men is hurtful chiefly to themselves who rule, for they destroy their own souls by greater license in wickedness ; while those who are put under them in service are not hurt except by their own iniquity. For to the just all the evils imposed on them by unjust rulers are not the punishment of crime, but the test of virtue. Therefore the good man, although he is a slave, is free ; but the bad man, even if he reigns, is a slave, and that not of one man, but, what is far more grievous, of as many masters as he has vices ; of which vices when the divine Scripture treats, it says, "For of whom any man is overcome, to the same he is also the bond-slave."[1]

Ch. 4. *How Like Kingdoms without Justice are to Robberies.*

Justice being taken away, then, what are kingdoms but great robberies ? For what are robberies themselves, but little kingdoms ? The band itself is made up of men ; it is ruled by the authority of a prince, it is knit together by the pact of the confederacy ; the booty is divided by the law agreed on. If, by the admittance of abandoned men, this evil increases to such a degree that it holds places, fixes abodes, takes possession of cities, and subdues peoples, it assumes the more plainly the name of a kingdom, because the reality is now manifestly conferred on it, not by the removal of covetousness, but by the addition of impunity. Indeed, that was an apt and true reply which was given to Alexander the

[1] 2 Pet. ii. 19.

Great by a pirate who had been seized. For when that king had asked the man what he meant by keeping hostile possession of the sea, he answered with bold pride, "What thou meanest by seizing the whole earth; but because I do it with a petty ship, I am called a robber, whilst thou who dost it with a great fleet art styled emperor."

Bk. XIV, Ch. 28. *Of the Nature of the Two Cities, the Earthly and the Heavenly.*

Accordingly, two cities have been formed by two loves: the earthly by the love of self, even to the contempt of God; the heavenly by the love of God, even to the contempt of self. The former, in a word, glories in itself, the latter in the Lord. For the one seeks glory from men; but the greatest glory of the other is God, the witness of conscience. The one lifts up its head in its own glory, the other says to its God, "Thou art my glory; and the lifter up of mine head." [1] In the one, the princes and the nations it subdues are ruled by the love of ruling; in the other, the princes and the subjects serve one another in love, the latter obeying, while the former take thought for all. The one delights in its own strength, represented in the persons of its rulers; the other says to its God, "I will love Thee, O Lord, my strength." [2] And therefore the wise men of the one city, living according to man, have sought for profit to their own bodies or souls, or both, and those who have known God "glorified Him not as God, neither were thankful, but became vain in their imaginations, and their foolish heart was darkened; professing themselves to be wise,"—that is, glorying in their own wisdom, and being possessed by pride,—"they became fools, and changed the glory of the incorruptible God into an image made like to corruptible man, and to birds, and to four-footed beasts, and creeping things." For they were either leaders or followers of the people in adoring images, "and worshipped and served the creature more than the Creator, who is blessed for ever." [3] But in the other city there is no human wisdom, but only godliness, which offers due worship to the true God, and looks for its reward in the society of the saints, of holy angels as well as holy men, "that God may be all in all." [4]

Bk. XV, Ch. 1. *Of the Two Lines of the Human Race which from First to Last Divide It.*

Of the bliss of Paradise, of Paradise itself, and of the life of our first parents there, and of their sin and punishment, many have

[1] Ps. iii. 3.   [2] Ps. xviii. 1.   [3] Rom. i. 21-25.   [4] 1 Cor. xv. 28.

thought much, spoken much, written much. We ourselves, too, have spoken of these things in the foregoing books, and have written either what we read in the Holy Scriptures, or what we could reasonably deduce from them. And were we to enter into a more detailed investigation of these matters, an endless number of endless questions would arise, which would involve us in a larger work than the present occasion admits. We cannot be expected to find room for replying to every question that may be started by unoccupied and captious men, who are ever more ready to ask questions than capable of understanding the answer. Yet I trust we have already done justice to these great and difficult questions regarding the beginning of the world, or of the soul, or of the human race itself. This race we have distributed into two parts, the one consisting of those who live according to man, the other of those who live according to God. And these we also mystically call the two cities, or the two communities of men, of which the one is predestined to reign eternally with God, and the other to suffer eternal punishment with the devil. This, however, is their end, and of it we are to speak afterwards. At present, as we have said enough about their origin, whether among the angels, whose numbers we know not, or in the two first human beings, it seems suitable to attempt an account of their career, from the time when our two first parents began to propagate the race until all human generation shall cease. For this whole time or world-age, in which the dying give place and those who are born succeed, is the career of these two cities concerning which we treat.

Of these two first parents of the human race, then, Cain was the first-born, and he belonged to the city of men; after him was born Abel, who belonged to the city of God. For as in the individual the truth of the apostle's statement is discerned, "that is not first which is spiritual, but that which is natural, and afterward that which is spiritual,"[1] whence it comes to pass that each man, being derived from a condemned stock, is first of all born of Adam evil and carnal, and becomes good and spiritual only afterwards, when he is grafted into Christ by regeneration : so was it in the human race as a whole. When these two cities began to run their course by a series of deaths and births, the citizen of this world was the first-born, and after him the stranger in this world, the citizen of the city of God, predestinated by grace, elected by grace, by grace a stranger below, and by grace a citizen above. By grace,—for so far as regards himself he is sprung from the same mass, all of which is condemned in its origin : but God, like a potter (for this com-

[1] 1 Cor. xv. 46.

parison is introduced by the apostle judiciously, and not without thought), of the same lump made one vessel to honor, another to dishonor.[1] But first the vessel to dishonor was made, and after it another to honor. For in each individual, as I have already said, there is first of all that which is reprobate, that from which we must begin, but in which we need not necessarily remain; afterwards is that which is well-approved, to which we may by advancing attain, and in which, when we have reached it, we may abide. Not, indeed, that every wicked man shall be good, but that no one will be good who was not first of all wicked; but the sooner any one becomes a good man, the more speedily does he receive this title, and abolish the old name in the new. Accordingly, it is recorded of Cain that he built a city,[2] but Abel, being a sojourner, built none. For the city of the saints is above, although here below it begets citizens, in whom it sojourns till the time of its reign arrives, when it shall gather together all in the day of the resurrection; and then shall the promised kingdom be given to them, in which they shall reign with their Prince, the King of the ages, time without end.

Ch. 4. *Of the Conflict and Peace of the Earthly City.*
But the earthly city, which shall not be everlasting (for it will no longer be a city when it has been committed to the extreme penalty), has its good in this world, and rejoices in it with such joy as such things can afford. But as this is not a good which can discharge its devotees of all distresses, this city is often divided against itself by litigations, wars, quarrels, and such victories as are either life-destroying or short-lived. For each part of it that arms against another part of it seeks to triumph over the nations through itself in bondage to vice. If, when it has conquered, it is inflated with pride, its victory is life-destroying; but if it turns its thoughts upon the common casualties of our mortal condition, and is rather anxious concerning the disasters that may befall it than elated with the successes already achieved, this victory, though of a higher kind, is still only short-lived; for it cannot abidingly rule over those whom it has victoriously subjugated. But the things which this city desires cannot justly be said to be evil, for it is itself, in its own kind, better than all other human good. For it desires earthly peace for the sake of enjoying earthly goods, and it makes war in order to attain to this peace; since, if it has conquered, and there remains no one to resist it, it enjoys a peace which it had not while there were opposing parties who contested for the enjoyment of those things which were too small to satisfy both.

[1] Rom. ix. 21. [2] Gen. iv. 17.

This peace is purchased by toilsome wars; it is obtained by what they style a glorious victory. Now, when victory remains with the party which had the juster cause, who hesitates to congratulate the victor, and style it a desirable peace? These things, then, are good things, and without doubt the gifts of God. But if they neglect the better things of the heavenly city, which are secured by eternal victory and peace never-ending, and so inordinately covet these present good things that they believe them to be the only desirable things, or love them better than those things which are believed to be better,—if this be so, then it is necessary that misery follow and ever increase.

2. The Nature of Earthly Rule [1]

Ch. 5. *Of the Social Life, which, though Most Desirable, is Frequently Disturbed by Many Distresses.*

We give a much more unlimited approval to their idea that the life of the wise man must be social. For how could the city of God (concerning which we are already writing no less than the nineteenth book of this work) either take a beginning or be developed, or attain its proper destiny, if the life of the saints were not a social life? But who can enumerate all the great grievances with which human society abounds in the misery of this mortal state? Who can weigh them? Hear how one of their comic writers makes one of his characters express the common feelings of all men in this matter: "I am married; this is one misery. Children are born to me; they are additional cares." [2] What shall I say of the miseries of love which Terence also recounts—"slights, suspicions, quarrels, war to-day, peace to-morrow?" [3] Is not human life full of such things? Do they not often occur even in honorable friendships? On all hands we experience these slights, suspicions, quarrels, war, all of which are undoubted evils; while, on the other hand, peace is a doubtful good, because we do not know the heart of our friend, and though we did know it to-day, we should be as ignorant of what it might be to-morrow. Who ought to be, or who are more friendly than those who live in the same family? And yet who can rely even upon this friendship, seeing that secret treachery has often broken it up, and produced enmity as bitter as the amity was sweet, or seemed sweet by the most perfect dissimulation? It is on this account that the words of Cicero so move the heart of every one, and provoke a sigh: "There are no snares more danger-

[1] Bk. xix, chs. 5, 12, 14–17, 21, 24, 27.   [2] Terent. *Adelph.* v. 4.
[3] *Eunuch,* i. I.

ous than those which lurk under the guise of duty or the name of
relationship. For the man who is your declared foe you can
easily baffle by precaution; but this hidden, intestine, and domestic
danger not merely exists, but overwhelms you before you can foresee and examine it." [1] It is also to this that allusion is made by
the divine saying, "A man's foes are those of his own household" [2]
—words which one cannot hear without pain; for though a man
have sufficient fortitude to endure it with equanimity, and sufficient
sagacity to baffle the malice of a pretended friend, yet if he himself
is a good man, he cannot but be greatly pained at the discovery of
the perfidy of wicked men, whether they have always been wicked
and merely feigned goodness, or have fallen from a better to a
malicious disposition. If, then, home, the natural refuge from the
ills of life, is itself not safe, what shall we say of the city, which, as
it is larger, is so much the more filled with lawsuits civil and criminal, and is never free from the fear, if sometimes from the actual
outbreak, of disturbing and bloody insurrections and civil wars?

Ch. 12. *That even the Fierceness of War and all the Disquietude
of Men Make towards this One End of Peace, which Every Nature
Desires.*

Whoever gives even moderate attention to human affairs and to
our common nature, will recognize that if there is no man who does
not wish to be joyful, neither is there any one who does not wish
to have peace. For even they who make war desire nothing but
victory,—desire, that is to say, to attain to peace with glory. For
what else is victory than the conquest of those who resist us? and
when this is done there is peace. It is therefore with the desire for
peace that wars are waged, even by those who take pleasure in
exercising their warlike nature in command and battle. And
hence it is obvious that peace is the end sought for by war. For
every man seeks peace by waging war, but no man seeks war by
making peace. For even they who intentionally interrupt the
peace in which they are living have no hatred of peace, but only
wish it changed into a peace that suits them better. They do not,
therefore, wish to have no peace, but only one more to their mind.
And in the case of sedition, when men have separated themselves
from the community, they yet do not effect what they wish, unless
they maintain some kind of peace with their fellow-conspirators.
And therefore even robbers take care to maintain peace with their
comrades, that they may with greater effect and greater safety invade the peace of other men. And if an individual happen to be of

[1] *In Verrem*, ii. 1. 15.   [2] Matt. x. 36.

such unrivalled strength, and to be so jealous of partnership, that he
trusts himself with no comrades, but makes his own plots, and commits depredations and murders on his own account, yet he maintains some shadow of peace with such persons as he is unable to kill,
and from whom he wishes to conceal his deeds.   In his own home,
too, he makes it his aim to be at peace with his wife and children,
and any other members of his household; for unquestionably their
prompt obedience to his every look is a source of pleasure to him.
And if this be not rendered, he is angry, he chides and punishes; and
even by this storm he secures the calm peace of his own home, as
occasion demands.   For he sees that peace cannot be maintained
unless all the members of the same domestic circle be subject to
one head, such as he himself is in his own house.   And therefore
if a city or nation offered to submit itself to him, to serve him in
the same style as he had made his household serve him, he would
no longer lurk in a brigand's hiding-places, but lift his head in open
day as a king, though the same covetousness and wickedness
should remain in him.   And thus all men desire to have peace with
their own circle whom they wish to govern as suits themselves.
For even those whom they make war against they wish to make
their own, and impose on them the laws of their own peace.

But let us suppose a man such as poetry and mythology speak
of,—a man so insociable and savage as to be called rather a semi-
man than a man.[1]   Although, then, his kingdom was the solitude
of a dreary cave, and he himself was so singularly bad-hearted that
he was named Κακός, which is the Greek word for *bad;* though he
had no wife to soothe him with endearing talk, no children to play
with, no sons to do his bidding, no friend to enliven him with
intercourse, not even his father Vulcan (though in one respect he
was happier than his father, not having begotten a monster like
himself); although he gave to no man, but took as he wished whatever he could; from whomsoever he could, when he could; yet in
that solitary den, the floor of which, as Virgil[2] says, was always
reeking with recent slaughter, there was nothing else than peace
sought, a peace in which no one should molest him, or disquiet him
with any assault or alarm.   With his own body he desired to be at
peace, and he was satisfied only in proportion as he had this peace.
For he ruled his members, and they obeyed him; and for the sake
of pacifying his mortal nature, which rebelled when it needed
anything, and of allaying the sedition of hunger which threatened
to banish the soul from the body, he made forays, slew, and
devoured, but used the ferocity and savageness he displayed in

---

[1] He refers to the giant Cacus.   [2] *Æneid*, viii. 195.

these actions only for the preservation of his own life's peace. So
that, had he been willing to make with other men the same peace
which he made with himself in his own cave, he would neither have
been called bad, nor a monster, nor a semi-man. Or if the appearance of his body and his vomiting smoky fires frightened men from
having any dealings with him, perhaps his fierce ways arose not
from a desire to do mischief, but from the necessity of finding a
living. But he may have had no existence, or, at least, he was not
such as the poets fancifully describe him, for they had to exalt
Hercules, and did so at the expense of Cacus. It is better, then,
to believe that such a man or semi-man never existed, and that
this, in common with many other fancies of the poets, is mere
fiction. For the most savage animals (and he is said to have been
almost a wild beast) encompass their own species with a ring of
protecting peace. They cohabit, beget, produce, suckle, and bring
up their young, though very many of them are not gregarious, but
solitary,—not like sheep, deer, pigeons, starlings, bees, but such
as lions, foxes, eagles, bats. For what tigress does not gently purr
over her cubs, and lay aside her ferocity to fondle them? What
kite, solitary as he is when circling over his prey, does not seek a
mate, build a nest, hatch the eggs, bring up the young birds, and
maintain with the mother of his family as peaceful a domestic
alliance as he can? How much more powerfully do the laws of
man's nature move him to hold fellowship and maintain peace with
all men so far as in him lies, since even wicked men wage war to
maintain the peace of their own circle, and wish that, if possible,
all men belonged to them, that all men and things might serve but
one head, and might, either through love or fear, yield themselves
to peace with him! It is thus that pride in its perversity apes God.
It abhors equality with other men under Him; but, instead of His
rule, it seeks to impose a rule of its own upon its equals. It abhors,
that is to say, the just peace of God, and loves its own unjust peace;
but it cannot help loving peace of one kind or other. For there
is no vice so clean contrary to nature that it obliterates even the
faintest traces of nature.

He, then, who prefers what is right to what is wrong, and what
is well-ordered to what is perverted, sees that the peace of unjust
men is not worthy to be called peace in comparison with the peace
of the just. And yet even what is perverted must of necessity be
in harmony with, and in dependence on, and in some part of the
order of things, for otherwise it would have no existence at all.
Suppose a man hangs with his head downwards, this is certainly
a perverted attitude of body and arrangement of its members;

for that which nature requires to be above is beneath, and *vice versa*. This perversity disturbs the peace of the body, and is therefore painful. Nevertheless the spirit is at peace with its body, and labors for its preservation, and hence the suffering; but if it is banished from the body by its pains, then, so long as the bodily framework holds together, there is in the remains a kind of peace among the members, and hence the body remains suspended. And inasmuch as the earthly body tends towards the earth, and rests on the bond by which it is suspended, it tends thus to its natural peace, and the voice of its own weight demands a place for it to rest; and though now lifeless and without feeling, it does not fall from the peace that is natural to its place in creation, whether it already has it, or is tending towards it. For if you apply embalming preparations to prevent the bodily frame from mouldering and dissolving, a kind of peace still unites part to part, and keeps the whole body in a suitable place on the earth,—in other words, in a place that is at peace with the body. If, on the other hand, the body receive no such care, but be left to the natural course, it is disturbed by exhalations that do not harmonize with one another, and that offend our senses; for it is this which is perceived in putrefaction until it is assimilated to the elements of the world, and particle by particle enters into peace with them. Yet throughout the process the laws of the most high Creator and Governor are strictly observed, for it is by Him the peace of the universe is administered. For although minute animals are produced from the carcass of a larger animal, all these little atoms, by the law of the same Creator, serve the animals they belong to in peace. And although the flesh of dead animals be eaten by others, no matter where it be carried, nor what it be brought into contact with, nor what it be converted and changed into, it still is ruled by the same laws which pervade all things for the conservation of every mortal race, and which bring things that fit one another into harmony.

Ch. 14. *Of the Order and Law which Obtain in Heaven and Earth, whereby it Comes to Pass that Human Society is Served by those who Rule it.*

The whole use, then, of things temporal has a reference to this result of earthly peace in the earthly community, while in the city of God it is connected with eternal peace. And therefore, if we were irrational animals, we should desire nothing beyond the proper arrangement of the parts of the body and the satisfaction of the appetites,—nothing, therefore, but bodily comfort and abundance of pleasures, that the peace of the body might contribute to the peace of the soul. For if bodily peace be awanting, a bar is put to the peace even of the irrational soul, since it cannot obtain the gratification of its appetites. And these two together help out the mutual peace of soul and body, the peace of harmonious life and health. For as animals, by shunning pain, show that they love bodily peace, and, by pursuing pleasure to gratify their appetites, show that they love peace of soul, so their shrinking from death is a sufficient indication of their intense love of that peace which binds soul and body in close alliance. But, as man has a rational soul, he subordinates all this which he has in common with the beasts to the peace of his rational soul, that his intellect may have free play and may regulate his actions, and that he may thus enjoy the well-ordered harmony of knowledge and action which constitutes, as we have said, the peace of the rational soul. And for this purpose he must desire to be neither molested by pain, nor disturbed by desire, nor extinguished by death, that he may arrive at some useful knowledge by which he may regulate his life and manners. But, owing to the liability of the human mind to fall into mistakes, this very pursuit of knowledge may be a snare to him unless he has a divine Master, whom he may obey without misgiving, and who may at the same time give him such help as to preserve his own freedom. And because, so long as he is in this mortal body, he is a stranger to God, he walks by faith, not by sight; and he therefore refers all peace, bodily or spiritual or both, to that peace which mortal man has with the immortal God, so that he exhibits the well-ordered obedience of faith to eternal law. But as this divine Master inculcates two precepts,—the love of God and the love of our neighbor,—and as in these precepts a man finds three things he has to love,—God, himself, and his neighbor, —and that he who loves God loves himself thereby, it follows that he must endeavor to get his neighbor to love God, since he is ordered to love his neighbor as himself. He ought to make this endeavor in behalf of his wife, his children, his household, all within his reach, even as he would wish his neighbor to do the same for him if he needed it; and consequently he will be at peace, or in well-ordered concord, with all men, as far as in him lies. And this is the order of this concord, that a man, in the first place, injure no one, and in the second, do good to every one he can reach. Primarily, therefore, his own household are his care, for the law of nature and of society gives him readier access to them and greater opportunity of serving them. And hence the apostle says, "Now, if any provide not for his own, and specially for those of his own

house, he hath denied the faith, and is worse than an infidel." [1]
This is the origin of domestic peace, or the well-ordered concord
of those in the family who rule and those who obey.   For they who
care for the rest rule,—the husband the wife, the parents the children, the masters the servants ; and they who are cared for obey,—
the women their husbands, the children their parents, the servants
their masters.   But in the family of the just man who lives by faith
and is as yet a pilgrim journeying on to the celestial city, even those
who rule serve those whom they seem to command ; for they rule
not from a love of power, but from a sense of the duty they owe to
others—not because they are proud of authority, but because they
love mercy.

Ch. 15.   *Of the Liberty Proper to Man's Nature, and the Servitude
Introduced by Sin,—a Servitude in which the Man whose Will is
Wicked is the Slave of his own Lust, though he is Free so far as Regards
other Men.*

This is prescribed by the order of nature : it is thus that God has
created man.   For "let them," He says, "have dominion over the
fish of the sea, and over the fowl of the air, and over every creeping
thing which creepeth on the earth." [2]   He did not intend that
His rational creature, who was made in His image, should have
dominion over anything but the irrational creation,—not man over
man, but man over the beasts.   And hence the righteous men in
primitive times were made shepherds of cattle rather than kings
of men, God intending thus to teach us what the relative position
of the creatures is, and what the desert of sin ; for it is with justice,
we believe, that the condition of slavery is the result of sin.   And
this is why we do not find the word "slave" in any part of Scripture
until righteous Noah branded the sin of his son with this name.
It is a name, therefore, introduced by sin and not by nature.   The
origin of the Latin word for slave is supposed to be found in the
circumstance that those who by the law of war were liable to be
killed were sometimes preserved by their victors, and were hence
called servants. [3]   And these circumstances could never have
arisen save through sin.   For even when we wage a just war, our
adversaries must be sinning ; and every victory, even though
gained by wicked men, is a result of the first judgment of God, who
humbles the vanquished either for the sake of removing or of
punishing their sins.   Witness that man of God, Daniel, who, when
he was in captivity, confessed to God his own sins and the sins of

[1] 1 Tim. v. 8.   [2] Gen. i. 26.
[3] *Servus*, "a slave," from *servare*, "to preserve."

his people, and declares with pious grief that these were the cause of the captivity.[1] The prime cause, then, of slavery is sin, which brings man under the dominion of his fellow,—that which does not happen save by the judgment of God, with whom is no unrighteousness, and who knows how to award fit punishments to every variety of offence. But our Master in heaven says, "Every one who doeth sin is the servant of sin." [2] And thus there are many wicked masters who have religious men as their slaves, and who are yet themselves in bondage; "for of whom a man is overcome, of the same is he brought in bondage." [3] And beyond question it is a happier thing to be the slave of a man than of a lust; for even this very lust of ruling, to mention no others, lays waste men's hearts with the most ruthless dominion. Moreover, when men are subjected to one another in a peaceful order, the lowly position does as much good to the servant as the proud position does harm to the master. But by nature, as God first created us, no one is the slave either of man or of sin. This servitude is, however, penal, and is appointed by that law which enjoins the preservation of the natural order and forbids its disturbance; for if nothing had been done in violation of that law, there would have been nothing to restrain by penal servitude. And therefore the apostle admonishes slaves to be subject to their masters, and to serve them heartily and with good will, so that, if they cannot be freed by their masters, they may themselves make their slavery in some sort free, by serving not in crafty fear, but in faithful love, until all unrighteousness pass away, and all principality and every human power be brought to nothing, and God be all in all.

Ch. 16. *Of Equitable Rule.*

And therefore, although our righteous fathers [4] had slaves, and administered their domestic affairs so as to distinguish between the condition of slaves and the heirship of sons in regard to the blessings of this life, yet in regard to the worship of God, in whom we hope for eternal blessings, they took an equally loving oversight of all the members of their household. And this is so much in accordance with the natural order, that the head of the household was called *pater-familias;* and this name has been so generally accepted, that even those whose rule is unrighteous are glad to apply it to themselves. But those who are true fathers of their households desire and endeavor that all the members of their household, equally with their own children, should worship and win God, and should

---

[1] Dan. ix.   [2] John viii. 34.
[3] 2 Pet. ii. 19.   [4] The patriarchs.

come to that heavenly home in which the duty of ruling men
is no longer necessary, because the duty of caring for their everlasting happiness has also ceased ; but, until they reach that home,
masters ought to feel their position of authority a greater burden
than servants their service. And if any member of the family
interrupts the domestic peace by disobedience, he is corrected
either by word or blow, or some kind of just and legitimate punishment, such as society permits, that he may himself be the
better for it, and be readjusted to the family harmony from which
he had dislocated himself. For as it is not benevolent to give a man
help at the expense of some greater benefit he might receive, so it
is not innocent to spare a man at the risk of his falling into graver
sin. To be innocent, we must not only do harm to no man, but
also restrain him from sin or punish his sin, so that either the man
himself who is punished may profit by his experience, or others be
warned by his example. Since, then, the house ought to be the
beginning or element of the city, and every beginning bears
reference to some end of its own kind, and every element to the
integrity of the whole of which it is an element, it follows plainly
enough that domestic peace has a relation to civic peace,—in other
words, that the well-ordered concord of domestic obedience and
domestic rule has a relation to the well-ordered concord of civic
obedience and civic rule. And therefore it follows, further, that
the father of the family ought to frame his domestic rule in accordance with the law of the city, so that the household may be
in harmony with the civic order.

Ch. 17. *What Produces Peace, and what Discord, between the
Heavenly and Earthly Cities.*

But the families which do not live by faith seek their peace in the
earthly advantages of this life ; while the families which live by
faith look for those eternal blessings which are promised, and use
as pilgrims such advantages of time and of earth as do not fascinate
and divert them from God, but rather aid them to endure with
greater ease, and to keep down the number of those burdens of the
corruptible body which weigh upon the soul. Thus the things
necessary for this mortal life are used by both kinds of men and
families alike, but each has its own peculiar and widely different
aim in using them. The earthly city, which does not live by faith,
seeks an earthly peace, and the end it proposes, in the well-ordered
concord of civic obedience and rule, is the combination of men's
wills to attain the things which are helpful to this life. The
heavenly city, or rather the part of it which sojourns on earth and

lives by faith, makes use of this peace only because it must, until this mortal condition which necessitates it shall pass away. Consequently, so long as it lives like a captive and a stranger in the earthly city, though it has already received the promise of redemption, and the gift of the Spirit as the earnest of it, it makes no scruple to obey the laws of the earthly city, whereby the things necessary for the maintenance of this mortal life are administered; and thus, as this life is common to both cities, so there is a harmony between them in regard to what belongs to it. But, as the earthly city has had some philosophers whose doctrine is condemned by the divine teaching, and who, being deceived either by their own conjectures or by demons, supposed that many gods must be invited to take an interest in human affairs, and assigned to each a separate function and a separate department,—to one the body, to another the soul; and in the body itself, to one the head, to another the neck, and each of the other members to one of the gods; and in like manner, in the soul, to one god the natural capacity was assigned, to another education, to another anger, to another lust; and so the various affairs of life were assigned,— cattle to one, corn to another, wine to another, oil to another, the woods to another, money to another, navigation to another, wars and victories to another, marriages to another, births and fecundity to another, and other things to other gods: and as the celestial city, on the other hand, knew that one God only was to be worshipped, and that to Him alone was due that service which the Greeks call λατρεία, and which can be given only to a god, it has come to pass that the two cities could not have common laws of religion, and that the heavenly city has been compelled in this matter to dissent, and to become obnoxious to those who think differently, and to stand the brunt of their anger and hatred and persecutions, except in so far as the minds of their enemies have been alarmed by the multitude of the Christians and quelled by the manifest protection of God accorded to them. This heavenly city, then, while it sojourns on earth, calls citizens out of all nations, and gathers together a society of pilgrims of all languages, not scrupling about diversities in the manners, laws, and institutions whereby earthly peace is secured and maintained, but recognizing that, however various these are, they all tend to one and the same end of earthly peace. It therefore is so far from rescinding and abolishing these diversities, that it even preserves and adopts them, so long only as no hindrance to the worship of the one supreme and true God is thus introduced. Even the heavenly city, therefore, while in its state of pilgrimage, avails itself of the peace of earth, and, so

far as it can without injuring faith and godliness, desires and maintains a common agreement among men regarding the acquisition
of the necessaries of life, and makes this earthly peace bear upon
the peace of heaven ; for this alone can be truly called and esteemed
the peace of the reasonable creatures, consisting as it does in the
perfectly ordered and harmonious enjoyment of God and of one
another in God.   When we shall have reached that peace, this
mortal life shall give place to one that is eternal, and our body shall
be no more this animal body which by its corruption weighs down
the soul, but a spiritual body feeling no want, and in all its members
subjected to the will.   In its pilgrim state the heavenly city
possesses this peace by faith ; and by this faith it lives righteously
when it refers to the attainment of that peace every good action
towards God and man ; for the life of the city is a social life.

Ch. 21.   *Whether there ever was a Roman Republic Answering to
the Definitions of Scipio in Cicero's Dialogue.*
  This, then, is the place where I should fulfill the promise given in
the second book of this work, and explain, as briefly and clearly as
possible, that if we are to accept the definitions laid down by
Scipio in Cicero's *De Republica*, there never was a Roman republic ;
for he briefly defines a republic as the weal of the people.   And if
this definition be true, there never was a Roman republic, for the
people's weal was never attained among the Romans.   For the
people, according to his definition, is an assemblage associated by
a common acknowledgment of right and by a community of interests.   And what he means by a common acknowledgment of right
he explains at large, showing that a republic cannot be administered
without justice.   Where, therefore, there is no true justice there
can be no right.   For that which is done by right is justly done,
and what is unjustly done cannot be done by right.   For the unjust
inventions of men are neither to be considered nor spoken of as
rights ; for even they themselves say that right is that which
flows from the fountain of justice, and deny the definition which is
commonly given by those who misconceive the matter, that right
is that which is useful to the stronger party.   Thus, where there
is not true justice there can be no assemblage of men associated by
a common acknowledgment of right, and therefore there can be no
people, as defined by Scipio or Cicero ; and if no people, then no
weal of the people, but only of some promiscuous multitude
unworthy of the name of people.   Consequently, if the republic
is the weal of the people, and there is no people if it be not associated
by a common acknowledgment of right, and if there is no right

where there is no justice, then most certainly it follows that there is no republic where there is no justice. Further, justice is that virtue which gives every one his due. Where, then, is the justice of man, when he deserts the true God and yields himself to impure demons? Is this to give every one his due? Or is it he who keeps back a piece of ground from the purchaser, and gives it to a man who has no right to it, unjust, while he who keeps back himself from the God who made him, and serves wicked spirits, is just?

This same book, *De Republica*, advocates the cause of justice against injustice with great force and keenness. The pleading for injustice against justice was first heard, and it was asserted that without injustice a republic could neither increase nor even subsist, for it was laid down as an absolutely unassailable position that it is unjust for some men to rule and some to serve ; and yet the imperial city to which the republic belongs cannot rule her provinces without having recourse to this injustice. It was replied in behalf of justice, that this ruling of the provinces is just, because servitude may be advantageous to the provincials, and is so when rightly administered,—that is to say, when lawless men are prevented from doing harm. And further, as they became worse and worse so long as they were free, they will improve by subjection. To confirm this reasoning, there is added an eminent example drawn from nature : for "why," it is asked, "does God rule man, the soul the body, the reason the passions and other vicious parts of the soul?" This example leaves no doubt that, to some, servitude is useful ; and, indeed, to serve God is useful to all. And it is when the soul serves God that it exercises a right control over the body ; and in the soul itself the reason must be subject to God if it is to govern as it ought the passions and other vices. Hence, when a man does not serve God, what justice can we ascribe to him, since in this case his soul cannot exercise a just control over the body, nor his reason over his vices? And if there is no justice in such an individual, certainly there can be none in a community composed of such persons. Here, therefore, there is not that common acknowledgment of right which makes an assemblage of men a people whose affairs we call a republic. And why need I speak of the advantageousness, the common participation in which, according to the definition, makes a people? For although, if you choose to regard the matter attentively, you will see that there is nothing advantageous to those who live godlessly, as every one lives who does not serve God but demons, whose wickedness you may measure by their desire to receive the worship of men though they are most impure spirits, yet what I have said of the common acknowledgment of right is enough to demonstrate that, according to the above definition, there can be no people, and therefore no republic, where there is no justice. For if they assert that in their republic the Romans did not serve unclean spirits, but good and holy gods, must we therefore again reply to this evasion, though already we have said enough, and more than enough, to expose it ? He must be an uncommonly stupid, or a shamelessly contentious, person, who has read through the foregoing books to this point, and can yet question whether the Romans served wicked and impure demons. But, not to speak of their character, it is written in the law of the true God, "He that sacrificeth unto any god save unto the Lord only, he shall be utterly destroyed." [1] He, therefore, who uttered so menacing a commandment decreed that no worship should be given either to good or bad gods.

Ch. 24. *The Definition which must be Given of a People and a Republic, in order to Vindicate the Assumption of these Titles by the Romans and by other Kingdoms.*

But if we discard this definition of a people, and, assuming another, say that a people is an assemblage of reasonable beings bound together by a common agreement as to the objects of their love, then, in order to discover the character of any people, we have only to observe what they love. Yet whatever it loves, if only it is an assemblage of reasonable beings and not of beasts, and is bound together by an agreement as to the objects of love, it is reasonably called a people ; and it will be a superior people in proportion as it is bound together by higher interests, inferior in proportion as it is bound together by lower. According to this definition of ours, the Roman people is a people, and its weal is without doubt a commonwealth or republic. But what its tastes were in its early and subsequent days, and how it declined into sanguinary seditions and then to social and civil wars, and so burst asunder or rotted off the bond of concord in which the health of a people consists, history shows, and in the preceding books I have related at large. And yet I would not on this account say either that it was not a people, or that its administration was not a republic, so long as there remains an assemblage of reasonable beings bound together by a common agreement as to the objects of love. But what I say of this people and of this republic I must be understood to think and say of the Athenians or any Greek state, of the Egyptians, of the early Assyrian Babylon, and of every other nation, great or small, which had a public government. For, in

[1] Ex. xxii. 20.

general, the city of the ungodly, which did not obey the command of God that it should offer no sacrifice save to Him alone, and which, therefore, could not give to the soul its proper command over the body, nor to the reason its just authority over the vices, is void of true justice.

Ch. 27. *That the Peace of those who Serve God cannot in this Mortal Life be Apprehended in its Perfection.*

But the peace which is peculiar to ourselves we enjoy now with God by faith, and shall hereafter enjoy eternally with Him by sight. But the peace which we enjoy in this life, whether common to all or peculiar to ourselves, is rather the solace of our misery than the positive enjoyment of felicity. Our very righteousness, too, though true in so far as it has respect to the true good, is yet in this life of such a kind that it consists rather in the remission of sins than in the perfecting of virtues. Witness the prayer of the whole city of God in its pilgrim state, for it cries to God by the mouth of all its members, "Forgive us our debts as we forgive our debtors." [1] And this prayer is efficacious not for those whose faith is "without works and dead," [2] but for those whose faith "worketh by love." [3] For as reason, though subjected to God, is yet "pressed down by the corruptible body," [4] so long as it is in this mortal condition, it has not perfect authority over vice, and therefore this prayer is needed by the righteous. For though it exercises authority, the vices do not submit without a struggle.

For however well one maintains the conflict, and however thoroughly he has subdued these enemies, there steals in some evil thing, which, if it do not find ready expression in act, slips out by the lips, or insinuates itself into the thought; and therefore his peace is not full so long as he is at war with his vices. For it is a doubtful conflict he wages with those that resist, and his victory over those that are defeated is not secure, but full of anxiety and effort. Amidst these temptations, therefore, of all which it has been summarily said in the divine oracles, "Is not human life upon earth a temptation?" [5] who but a proud man can presume that he so lives that he has no need to say to God, "Forgive us our debts?" And such a man is not great, but swollen and puffed up with vanity, and is justly resisted by Him who abundantly gives grace to the humble. Whence it is said, "God resisteth the proud, but giveth grace to the humble." [6] In this, then, consists the righteousness

[1] Matt. vi. 12.
[3] Gal. v. 6.
[5] Job vii. 1.

[2] Jas. ii. 17.
[4] Wisdom ix. 15.
[6] Jas. iv. 6; 1 Pet. v. 5.

of a man, that he submit himself to God, his body to his soul, and his vices, even when they rebel, to his reason, which either defeats or at least resists them; and also that he beg from God grace to do his duty,[1] and the pardon of his sins, and that he render to God thanks for all the blessings he receives. But, in that final peace to which all our righteousness has reference, and for the sake of which it is maintained, as our nature shall enjoy a sound immortality, and incorruption, and shall have no more vices, and as we shall experience no resistance either from ourselves or from others, it will not be necessary that reason should rule vices which no longer exist, but God shall rule the man, and the soul shall rule the body, with a sweetness and facility suitable to the felicity of a life which is done with bondage. And this condition shall there be eternal, and we shall be assured of its eternity; and thus the peace of this blessedness and the blessedness of this peace shall be the supreme good.

SELECTED BIBLIOGRAPHY

Cook, Thomas I., *History of Political Philosophy*, pp. 196–212.
McIlwain, Charles H., *Growth of Political Thought in the West*, pp. 154–160.
Sabine, George H., *A History of Political Theory*, pp. 187–193.
Dunning, William A., *Political Theories, Ancient and Mediæval*, ch. 6, § 2.

Figgis, John Neville, *The Political Aspects of St. Augustine's City of God* (London, 1921).
Carlyle, A. J., "St. Augustine and the City of God," in F. J. C. Hearnshaw, ed., *The Social and Political Ideas of Some Great Mediæval Thinkers* (London and New York, 1923), ch. 2.
Baynes, Norman H., *The Political Ideas of St. Augustine's De Civitate Dei*. Historical Association Pamphlet, No. 104 (London, 1936).
Gilson, Etienne, *Introduction à l'étude de Saint Augustin* (Paris, 1931), ch. 4.
Leisegang, Hans, "Der Ursprung der Lehre Augustins von der Civitas Dei," in *Archiv für Kulturgeschichte*, vol. 16 (1925), pp. 127–158.

Combès, Gustave, *La Doctrine politique de Saint Augustin* (Paris, 1927).
Salin, Edgar, *Civitas Dei* (Tübingen, 1926).
Schilling, Otto, *Die Staats- und Soziallehre des hl. Augustinus* (Freiburg i. B., 1910).
Seidel, "Die Lehre vom Staat beim heiligen Augustinus," in M. Sdralek, ed., *Kirchengeschichtliche Abhandlungen* (Breslau, 1909), vol. 9, pt. i.

[1] Gratia meritorum.

JOHN OF SALISBURY

VI. JOHN OF SALISBURY (C. 1120–1180)

INTRODUCTION

Ecclesiastical controversy determined much of the content and form of political discussion in the later Middle Ages. A few less polemical, more systematic, writings appeared from time to time, however, particularly in the period between the middle of the twelfth and the end of the thirteenth centuries; the most important of these are the writings of John of Salisbury and St. Thomas Aquinas.

John of Salisbury represents at its best the earlier period of the later Middle Ages. He was a polished writer and a learned ecclesiastical and theological scholar. He acquired his literary and philosophical training in France, under leading teachers of the day, including Abélard and two of the disciples of the great classical scholar, Bernard of Chartres. He was also a man of some experience in practical ecclesiastical and civic affairs. He was an adviser and agent of Theobald, Archbishop of Canterbury, when Theobald was one of the most powerful figures in the political life of England; and he was intimately associated with Theobald's successor, Thomas Becket, during the period when Becket was engaged in his significant and tragic dispute with King Henry II. In these and other affairs John was a close observer, and sometimes a victim, of the oppressive acts of political rulers.

John's published writings include lives of St. Anselm and of St. Thomas of Canterbury; a long elegiac poem; his letters; and two theoretical works—the *Metalogicus* (containing, besides an account of his student years, a discussion of traditional medieval conceptions of Aristotle's principles of logic) and the *Policraticus* (1159). We are not certain as to the meaning of the word "Policraticus"; it was probably invented by John and it is generally rendered as "Statesman's Book." The work is the most comprehensive medieval writing in political theory, prior to the introduction of Aristotle's ideas into political discussion. It is chiefly an exposition and discussion of the principles of civil government;

179

but it sets forth these principles in their relation to all important phases of the intellectual, religious, and social life of John's time. It contains somewhat typical examples of traditional medieval ideas on the qualities and duties of a true civil ruler—the "king" or "prince" as opposed to a "tyrant"—and on the right relations of such a ruler to his subjects, to the "law," and to the Church. John was perhaps the first to maintain explicitly the superior and direct authority of the Pope and his agents in temporal affairs; there are some ambiguities in his discussion of the specific implications of this ecclesiastical supremacy.

John of Salisbury has been often characterized as notable chiefly for his philosophical summarizing of the thought of the Middle Ages up to his time; but his own ideas were of considerable influence on later medieval discussions. He was probably the first medieval writer to employ a detailed organismic analogy in an explanation of the nature of a political community. He gave the clearest analysis of the characteristics of a tyrant and he stated the case for the right of tyrannicide more emphatically than any other writer before the sixteenth century.

READINGS FROM THE POLICRATICUS [1]

1. The Character of the True Prince as Opposed to a Tyrant. [2]

Ch. I. *Of the difference between a prince and a tyrant and of what is meant by a prince.*

Between a tyrant and a prince there is this single or chief difference, that the latter obeys the law and rules the people by its dictates, accounting himself as but their servant. It is by virtue of the law that he makes good his claim to the foremost and chief place in the management of the affairs of the commonwealth and in the bearing of its burdens; and his elevation over others consists in this, that whereas private men are held responsible only for their private affairs, on the prince fall the burdens of the whole community. Wherefore deservedly there is conferred on him, and gathered together in his hands, the power of all his subjects, to the end that he may be sufficient unto himself in seeking and

[1] The selections are taken from *The Statesman's Book of John of Salisbury: Being the Fourth, Fifth, and Sixth Books, and Selections from the Seventh and Eighth Books of the Policraticus,* translated with an Introduction by John Dickinson (New York, 1927). By permission of F. S. Crofts & Co.

[2] Bk. iv, chs. 1, 2, 3 (in part), 8 (in part); bk. v, ch. 2 (in part).

bringing about the advantage of each individually, and of all; and to the end that the state of the human commonwealth may be ordered in the best possible manner, seeing that each and all are members one of another. Wherein we indeed but follow nature, the best guide of life; for nature has gathered together all the senses of her microcosm or little world, which is man, into the head, and has subjected all the members in obedience to it in such wise that they will all function properly so long as they follow the guidance of the head, and the head remains sane. Therefore the prince stands on a pinnacle which is exalted and made splendid with all the great and high privileges which he deems necessary for himself. And rightly so, because nothing is more advantageous to the people than that the needs of the prince should be fully satisfied; since it is impossible that his will should be found opposed to justice. Therefore, according to the usual definition, the prince is the public power, and a kind of likeness on earth of the divine majesty. Beyond doubt a large share of the divine power is shown to be in princes by the fact that at their nod men bow their necks and for the most part offer up their heads to the axe to be struck off, and, as by a divine impulse, the prince is feared by each of those over whom he is set as an object of fear. And this I do not think could be, except as a result of the will of God. For all power is from the Lord God, and has been with Him always, and is from everlasting. The power which the prince has is therefore from God, for the power of God is never lost, nor severed from Him, but He merely exercises it through a subordinate hand, making all things teach His mercy or justice. "Who, therefore, resists the ruling power, resists the ordinance of God," [1] in whose hand is the authority of conferring that power, and when He so desires, of withdrawing it again, or diminishing it. For it is not the ruler's own act when his will is turned to cruelty against his subjects, but it is rather the dispensation of God for His good pleasure to punish or chasten them. Thus during the Hunnish persecution, Attila, on being asked by the reverend bishop of a certain city who he was, replied, "I am Attila, the scourge of God." Whereupon it is written that the bishop adored him as representing the divine majesty. "Welcome," he said, "is the minister of God," and "Blessed is he that cometh in the name of the Lord," and with sighs and groans he unfastened the barred doors of the church, and admitted the persecutor through whom he attained straightway to the palm of martyrdom. For he dared not shut out the scourge of God, knowing that His beloved Son was scourged, and

[1] Rom. xiii. 2.

that the power of this scourge which had come upon himself was as nought except it came from God. If good men thus regard power as worthy of veneration even when it comes as a plague upon the elect, who should not venerate that power which is instituted by God for the punishment of evil-doers and for the reward of good men, and which is promptest in devotion and obedience to the laws? To quote the words of the Emperor, "it is indeed a saying worthy of the majesty of royalty that the prince acknowledges himself bound by the Laws."[1] For the authority of the prince depends upon the authority of justice and law; and truly it is a greater thing than imperial power for the prince to place his government under the laws, so as to deem himself entitled to do nought which is at variance with the equity of justice.

Ch. II. *What the law is; and that although the prince is not bound by the law, he is nevertheless the servant of the law and of equity, and bears the public person, and sheds blood blamelessly.*

Princes should not deem that it detracts from their princely dignity to believe that the enactments of their own justice are not to be preferred to the justice of God, whose justice is an everlasting justice, and His law is equity. Now equity, as the learned jurists define it, is a certain fitness of things which compares all things rationally, and seeks to apply like rules of right and wrong to like cases, being impartially disposed toward all persons, and allotting to each that which belongs to him. Of this equity the interpreter is the law, to which the will and intention of equity and justice are known. Therefore Chrysippus asserted that the power of the law extends over all things, both divine and human, and that it accordingly presides over all goods and ills, and is the ruler and guide of material things as well as of human beings. To which Papinian, a man most learned in the law, and Demosthenes, the great orator, seem to assent, subjecting all men to its obedience because all law is, as it were, a discovery, and a gift from God, a precept of wise men, the corrector of excesses of the will, the bond which knits together the fabric of the state, and the banisher of crime;[2] and it is therefore fitting that all men should live according to it who lead their lives in a corporate political body. All are accordingly bound by the necessity of keeping the law, unless perchance there is any who can be thought to have been given the license of wrong-doing. However, it is said that the prince is absolved from the obligations of the law; but this is not true in the sense that it is lawful for him to do unjust acts, but only in the sense that his character should be

---

[1] Justin., Cod., I, 14, § 4.   [2] Dig., I, 3, §§ 1-2.

such as to cause him to practice equity not through fear of the penalties of the law but through love of justice; and should also be such as to cause him from the same motive to promote the advantage of the commonwealth, and in all things to prefer the good of others before his own private will. Who, indeed, in respect of public matters can properly speak of the will of the prince at all, since therein he may not lawfully have any will of his own apart from that which the law or equity enjoins, or the calculation of the common interest requires? For in these matters his will is to have the force of a judgment; and most properly that which pleases him therein has the force of law, because his decision may not be at variance with the intention of equity. "From thy countenance," says the Lord, "let my judgment go forth, let thine eyes look upon equity";[1] for the uncorrupted judge is one whose decision, from assiduous contemplation of equity, is the very likeness thereof. The prince accordingly is the minister of the common interest and the bondservant of equity, and he bears the public person in the sense that he punishes the wrongs and injuries of all, and all crimes, with even-handed equity. His rod and staff also, administered with wise moderation, restore irregularities and false departures to the straight path of equity, so that deservedly may the Spirit congratulate the power of the prince with the words, "Thy rod and thy staff, they have comforted me."[2] His shield, too, is strong, but it is a shield for the protection of the weak, and one which wards off powerfully the darts of the wicked from the innocent. Those who derive the greatest advantage from his performance of the duties of his office are those who can do least for themselves, and his power is chiefly exercised against those who desire to do harm. Therefore not without reason he bears a sword, wherewith he sheds blood blamelessly, without becoming thereby a man of blood, and frequently puts men to death without incurring the name or guilt of homicide. For if we believe the great Augustine, David was called a man of blood not because of his wars, but because of Uria. And Samuel is nowhere described as a man of blood or a homicide, although he slew Agag, the fat king of Amalech. Truly the sword of princely power is as the sword of a dove, which contends without gall, smites without wrath, and when it fights, yet conceives no bitterness at all. For as the law pursues guilt without any hatred of persons, so the prince most justly punishes offenders from no motive of wrath but at the behest, and in accordance with the decision, of the passionless law. For although we see that the prince has lictors of his own, we must yet think of him as in reality

[1] Ps. xvii. 2.   [2] Ps. xxiii. 4.

himself the sole or chief lictor, to whom is granted by the law the privilege of striking by a subordinate hand. If we adopt the opinion of the Stoics, who diligently trace down the reason for particular words, "lictor" means "legis ictor," or "hammer of the law," because the duty of his office is to strike those who the law adjudges shall be struck. Wherefore anciently, when the sword hung over the head of the convicted criminal, the command was wont to be given to the officials by whose hand the judge punishes evil-doers, "Execute the sentence of the law," or "Obey the law," to the end that the misery of the victim might be mitigated by the calm reasonableness of the words.

Ch. III. *That the prince is the minister of the priests and inferior to them; and of what amounts to faithful performance of the prince's ministry.*

This sword, then, the prince receives from the hand of the Church, although she herself has no sword of blood at all. Nevertheless she has this sword, but she uses it by the hand of the prince, upon whom she confers the power of bodily coercion, retaining to herself authority over spiritual things in the person of the pontiffs. The prince is, then, as it were, a minister of the priestly power, and one who exercises that side of the sacred offices which seems unworthy of the hands of the priesthood. For every office existing under, and concerned with the execution of, the sacred laws is really a religious office, but that is inferior which consists in punishing crimes, and which therefore seems to be typified in the person of the hangman. Wherefore Constantine, most faithful emperor of the Romans, when he had convoked the council of priests at Nicaea, neither dared to take the chief place for himself nor even to sit among the presbyters, but chose the hindmost seat. Moreover, the decrees which he heard approved by them he reverenced as if he had seen them emanate from the judgment-seat of the divine majesty. Even the rolls of petitions containing accusations against priests which they brought to him in a steady stream he took and placed in his bosom without opening them. And after recalling them to charity and harmony, he said that it was not permissible for him, as a man, and one who was subject to the judgment of priests, to examine cases touching gods, who cannot be judged save by God alone. And the petitions which he had received he put into the fire without even looking at them, fearing to give publicity to accusations and censures against the fathers, and thereby incur the curse of Cham, the undutiful son, who did not hide his father's shame. Wherefore he said, as is narrated in the writings of Nicholas the Roman pontiff, "Verily if with mine own eyes I had seen a priest of God, or any of those who wear the monastic garb, sinning, I would spread my cloak and hide him, that he might not be seen of any." Also Theodosius, the great emperor, for a merited fault, though not so grave a one, was suspended by the priest of Milan from the exercise of his regal powers and from the insignia of his imperial office, and patiently and solemnly he performed the penance for homicide which was laid upon him. Again, according to the testimony of the teacher of the gentiles, greater is he who blesses man than he who is blessed; [1] and so he in whose hands is the authority to confer a dignity excels in honor and the privileges of honor him upon whom the dignity itself is conferred. Further, by the reasoning of the law it is his right to refuse who has the power to grant, and he who can lawfully bestow can lawfully take away.[2] Did not Samuel pass sentence of deposition against Saul by reason of his disobedience, and supersede him on the pinnacle of kingly rule with the lowly son of Ysai?[3] But if one who has been appointed prince has performed duly and faithfully the ministry which he has undertaken, as great honor and reverence are to be shown to him as the head excels in honor all the members of the body. Now he performs his ministry faithfully when he is mindful of his true status, and remembers that he bears the person of the *universitas* of those subject to him; and when he is fully conscious that he owes his life not to himself and his own private ends, but to others, and allots it to them accordingly, with duly ordered charity and affection. Therefore he owes the whole of himself to God, most of himself to his country, much to his relatives and friends, very little to foreigners, but still somewhat. He has duties to the very wise and the very foolish, to little children and to the aged. Supervision over these classes of persons is common to all in authority, both those who have care over spiritual things and those who exercise temporal jurisdiction. Wherefore Melchisedech, the earliest whom the Scripture introduces as both king and priest (to say nought at present concerning the mystery wherein he prefigures Christ, who was born in heaven without a mother and on earth without a father); of him, I say, we read that he had neither father nor mother, not because he was in fact without either, but because in the eyes of reason the kingly power and the priestly power are not born of flesh and blood, since in bestowing either, regard for ancestry ought not to prevail over merits and virtues, but only the wholesome wishes (*vota*) of faithful subjects should prevail; and

---

[1] Heb. vii. 7. [2] Dig., I, 17, § 3. [3] i. e., Jesse.

when anyone has ascended to the supreme exercise of either power, he ought wholly to forget the affections of flesh and blood, and do only that which is demanded by the safety and welfare of his subjects. And so let him be both father and husband to his subjects, or, if he has known some affection more tender still, let him employ that; let him desire to be loved rather than feared, and show himself to them as such a man that they will out of devotion prefer his life to their own, and regard his preservation and safety as a kind of public life; and then all things will prosper well for him, and a small bodyguard will, in case of need, prevail by their loyalty against innumerable adversaries. For love is strong as death; and the wedge [1] which is held together by strands of love is not easily broken. . . .

Ch. VIII. *That the prince should effect a reconciliation of justice with mercy, and should so temper and combine the two as to promote the advantage of the commonwealth.*

It should hold true of the prince, as it should hold true of all men, that no one should seek his own interest but that of others. Yet the measure of the affection with which he should embrace his subjects like brethren in the arms of charity must be kept within the bounds of moderation. For his love of his brethren should not prevent him from correcting their errors with proper medicine; he acknowledges the ties of flesh and blood to the end that he may subdue these to the rule of the spirit. It is the practice of physicians when they cannot heal a disease with poultices and mild medicines to apply stronger remedies such as fire or steel. But they never employ these unless they despair of restoring health by milder means, and so the ruling power when it cannot avail by mild measures to heal the vices of its subjects, rightly resorts, though with grief, to the infliction of sharp punishments, and with pious cruelty vents its rage against wrong-doers to the end that good men may be preserved uninjured. But who was ever strong enough to amputate the members of his own body without grief and pain? Therefore the prince grieves when called upon to inflict the punishment which guilt demands, and yet administers it with reluctant right hand. For the prince has no left hand, and in subjecting to pain the members of the body of which he is the head, he obeys the law in sadness and with groans. Philip once heard that a certain Phicias, who was a good fighting man, had become alienated from him because in his poverty he found difficulty in supporting his three daughters and yet received

[1] i. e., a military formation.

no aid from the king. When his friends advised him accordingly
to beware of the man, "What," said Philip, "if a part of my body
were sick, would I cut it off rather than seek to heal it?" Then
he sought out this Phicias privately in a friendly way, and provided him with sufficient money which he accepted for the necessities of his private difficulties. And thereby the king made
this man better disposed toward him and more faithful than he
had been before he supposed himself offended. Accordingly,
as Lucius says: "A prince should have an old man's habit of
mind, who follows moderate counsels, and should play the part
of a physician, who heals diseases sometimes by reducing the diet
of the overfed, and again by increasing that of the under-nourished,
who allays pain at times by cautery, and at other times by poultices." In addition, he should be affable of speech, and generous
in conferring benefits, and in his manners he should preserve the
dignity of his authority unimpaired. A pleasant address and a
gracious tongue will win for him the reputation of benignity.
Kindness will compel the most faithful and constant love from
even the sternest, and will increase and confirm the love which
it has produced. And the reverence of subjects is the fit reward
of dignity of manners.

Excellently did Trajan, the best of the pagan emperors, answer his friends when they reproached him with making himself too common toward all men and more so, they thought, than
was becoming for an emperor; for he said that he desired to be
toward private citizens such an emperor as he had desired to
have over him when he was a private citizen himself. And in
accordance with this principle, acting on the report of the younger
Pliny who at that time with other judges was designated to per-
secute the Church, he recalled the sword of persecution from the
slaughter of the martyrs and moderated his edict. And perchance he would have dealt more gently still with the faithful,
had not the laws and examples of his predecessors, and the advice
of men who were considered wise counsellors, and the authority
of his judges, all urged him to destroy a sect regarded by public
opinion (*opinio publica*) as superstitious, and as enemies of true
religion. I do not unreservedly and in all respects commend the
judgment of a man who knew not Christ, yet I do extenuate the
fault of him who broke loose from the pressure of others and
followed the instinct of his own natural piety toward kindness
and pity, a man whose nature it was to be merciful toward all,
though stern toward the few whom it would be sinful to spare;
so that in the course of his whole reign only one of the senators

or nobles of the city was condemned, although a great number could have been found who had offended grievously against him. And this man was condemned by the senate without the knowledge of Trajan himself. For it was his habit to say that a man is insane who, having inflamed eyes, prefers to dig them out rather than to cure them. So again he said that the nails, if they are too sharp, should be trimmed and not plucked out. For if a cithern player and other performers on stringed instruments can by diligence find a way to correct the fault of a string which is out of tune and bring it again into accord with the other strings, and so out of discord make the sweetest harmony, not by breaking the strings but by making them tense or slack in due proportions; with how much care should the prince moderate his acts, now with the strictness of justice, and now with the leniency of mercy, to the end that he may make his subjects all be of one mind in one house, and thus as it were out of discordant dispositions bring to pass one great perfect harmony in the service of peace and in the works of charity? This, however, is certain, that it is safer for the cords to be relaxed than to be stretched too tautly. For the tension of slack cords can be corrected by the skill of the artificer so that they will again give forth the proper sweetness of tone; but a string that has once been broken, no artificer can repair. Further, if a sound is asked of them which they do not have, they are stretched in vain, and more often come speedily to nought than to what is improperly asked. As the ethical writer says:

> The true prince is slow to punish, swift to reward,
> And grieves whenever he is compelled to be severe.[1]

For while justice is one thing and godliness another, still both are so necessary to the prince that whoever without them attains, not necessarily to princely power, but even to any magistracy whatever, mocks himself in vain but will surely provoke against himself the mockery and scorn and hatred of others. "Let not kindness and truth," saith the Lord, "forsake thee, bind them about thy neck, and write them on the tablet of thy heart; so shalt thou find favor and obedience in the sight of God and men."[2] For kindness deserves favor, justice deserves obedience. The favor and love of one's subjects, which are brought to pass by divine favor, are the most effective instrument of all accomplishments. But love without obedience is of no avail, because when the spur of justice ceases, then the people relax into unlaw-

[1] Ovid, *Pont.*, i, 2, lines 123–24.   [2] Proverbs iii. 3, 4.

ful courses. Therefore he must ceaselessly meditate wisdom, that by its aid he may do justice, without the law of mercy being ever absent from his tongue; and so temper mercy with the strictness of justice that his tongue speaks nought save judgment. For his office transmutes his justice into judgment continually and of necessity because he may never lawfully repose therefrom without thereby divesting himself of the honor that has been conferred on him. For the honor of a king delights in judgment and represses the faults of offenders with tranquil moderation of mind. . . .

Bk. V, Ch. II. *What a commonwealth is, according to Plutarch, and what fills therein the place of the soul and the members.*

. . . A commonwealth, according to Plutarch, is a certain body which is endowed with life by the benefit of divine favor, which acts at the prompting of the highest equity, and is ruled by what may be called the moderating power of reason. Those things which establish and implant in us the practice of religion, and transmit to us the worship of God (here I do not follow Plutarch, who says "of the Gods") fill the place of the soul in the body of the commonwealth. And therefore those who preside over the practice of religion should be looked up to and venerated as the soul of the body. For who doubts that the ministers of God's holiness are His representatives? Furthermore, since the soul is, as it were, the prince of the body, and has rulership over the whole thereof, so those whom our author calls the prefects of religion preside over the entire body. Augustus Cæsar was to such a degree subject to the priestly power of the pontiffs that in order to set himself free from this subjection and have no one at all over him, he caused himself to be created a pontiff of Vesta, and thereafter had himself promoted to be one of the gods during his own life-time. The place of the head in the body of the commonwealth is filled by the prince, who is subject only to God and to those who exercise His office and represent Him on earth, even as in the human body the head is quickened and governed by the soul. The place of the heart is filled by the Senate, from which proceeds the initiation of good works and ill. The duties of eyes, ears, and tongue are claimed by the judges and the governors of provinces. Officials and soldiers correspond to the hands. Those who always attend upon the prince are likened to the sides. Financial officers and keepers (I speak now not of those who are in charge of the prisons, but of those who are keepers of the privy chest) may be compared with the stomach and intestines, which, if they become congested through excessive avidity, and retain too tenaciously their accumulations, generate innumerable and incurable diseases, so that through their ailment the whole body is threatened with destruction. The husbandmen correspond to the feet, which always cleave to the soil, and need the more especially the care and foresight of the head, since while they walk upon the earth doing service with their bodies, they meet the more often with stones of stumbling, and therefore deserve aid and protection all the more justly since it is they who raise, sustain, and move forward the weight of the entire body. Take away the support of the feet from the strongest body, and it cannot move forward by its own power, but must creep painfully and shamefully on its hands, or else be moved by means of brute animals. . . .

2. The Rights of Subjects against Tyrants [1]

Bk. VI, Ch. XXV. *Of the cohesion and mutual dependence of the head and members of the commonwealth; and that the prince is as it were the likeness of deity; and of the crime of lèse majesté, and of the obligations of fealty.*

For myself, I am satisfied and persuaded that loyal shoulders should uphold the power of the ruler; and not only do I submit to his power patiently, but with pleasure, so long as it is exercised in subjection to God and follows His ordinances. But on the other hand if it resists and opposes the divine commandments, and wishes to make me share in its war against God; then with unrestrained voice I answer back that God must be preferred before any man on earth. Therefore inferiors should cleave and cohere to their superiors, and all the limbs should be in subjection to the head; but always and only on condition that religion is kept inviolate. We read that Socrates framed a polity for a commonwealth and laid down precepts therefor which are said to flow from the purity of wisdom as from a natural fountain. And this one thing he emphasized above all else, that the more humble elements of the commonwealth should receive proportionately greater care and attention from those in higher station as part of their public duty. Read diligently again the "Instruction of Trajan," of which mention has been made above, and you will find these things discussed there at large.

Let it suffice at present to have said so much concerning the

[1] Bk. vi, ch. 25; bk. vii, chs. 17, 20, and 25 (in part); bk. viii, chs. 17, 20, 21 (in part).

unity of head and members, adding only what we have already premised, namely that an injury to the head, as we have said above, is brought home to all the members, and that a wound unjustly inflicted on any member tends to the injury of the head. Furthermore whatsoever is attempted foully and with malice against the head, or corporate community, of the members, is a crime of the greatest gravity and nearest to sacrilege; for as the latter is an attempt against God, so the former is an attack upon the prince, who is admitted to be as it were the likeness of deity upon earth. And therefore it is called the crime of lèse majesté, for the reason that it is aimed against the likeness of Him who alone, as the famous Count Robert of Leicester, a man who modestly discharged the office of proconsul in the British lands, was wont to say, wears the truth of true and native majesty,—to wit if any one undertakes aught against the security of the prince or of the people, either directly or through another. In the punishment of such a man, all are treated as of equal rank and in like case; and generally it comes to pass that such men, with whom none have any commerce in life, are not even released by the kindness of death; but if they are convicted, then after death their memory is condemned and their goods are forfeited by their heirs. For where the wickedness of an offender lies as here in having taken most wicked counsel, for such an offence he is punished as it were in mind. And when once a man has committed such a crime, it is settled that he can neither legally alienate nor manumit, nor can his debtor lawfully discharge his debt to him.[1] Because of the greatness of this crime, even infamous persons who in other cases do not have the right of bringing accusations are here permitted to do so without any impediment, as well as soldiers, who may not maintain other actions. For those who are on guard to defend the peace are all the more properly admitted to bring this charge. Also slaves may lawfully inform against their masters and freedmen against their patrons. Nevertheless this accusation is not to be dealt with by judges as an opportunity for displaying their subservience to the prince's majesty, but solely on the basis of the truth. The person of the accused must be looked to, as to whether he could have done the act, and whether he actually did it, or whether he devised it, and whether, before he presumed so far, he was of sane mind. Nor ought a mere slip of the tongue to be drawn readily on to punishment; for although the foolhardy are deserving of punishment, still even such men should be spared if their

[1] Justin., Cod., ix, 8, 4–6.

offence is not one which flows directly from the letter of the law or which must be punished in accordance with the analogy of the law.[1] Women also are heard on a question of lèse majesté; for the conspiracy of Sergius Cathelina was disclosed by a woman, a certain Julia, who supplied Marcus Tully with information in proceeding against him.[2] Also, if necessity or utility recommends, torture is to be applied to those who are thought to be guilty of this crime, as well as to those by whose counsel and instigation they appear to have undertaken the alleged criminal act, so that the prescribed penalty may be brought home to all who were concerned or had knowledge therein.[3]

The acts are many which constitute the crime of lèse majesté, as for example if one conceives the death of the prince or magistrates, or has borne arms against his country, or, forsaking his prince, has deserted in a public war, or has incited or solicited the people to rebel against the commonwealth; or if by the act or criminal intent of any, the enemies of the people and commonwealth are aided with supplies, armor, weapons, money, or any thing else whatsoever, or if, from being friends, they are turned into enemies of the commonwealth; or if by the criminal intent or act of any, it comes to pass that pledges or money are given against the commonwealth, or the people of a foreign country are perverted from their obedience to the commonwealth; likewise he commits the crime who effects the escape of one who after confessing his guilt in court has on this account been thrown into chains; and many other acts of this nature, which it would be too long or impossible to enumerate.[4]

But because the formula of fidelity or fealty ought herein above all else to be kept, there is language in the oath from which we can most conveniently learn a few of the acts which are not permitted. For a thing which is the opposite of something that is necessary is impossible, and by the same process of reasoning a thing which ought to be done is contradicted only by something that is not permitted. The formula of fealty, then, exacts the things which are inserted therein as being the necessary elements of loyalty, and expresses the latter by the words "sound," "safe," "honorable," "advantageous," "easy," "possible." If therefore, we are bound by fealty to anyone, we must not harm his soundness of body, or take from him the military resources upon which his safety depends, or presume to commit any act whereby his honor or advantage is diminished; neither is it

---

[1] Dig. xviii. 4, 7.
[2] Dig. xlviii. 4, 8.
[3] Justin., Cod., ix, 8, 4–6.
[4] Dig. xlviii. 4, 1–4.

lawful that that which is easy for him should be made difficult, or that which is possible impossible. Besides, one who holds a benefice from him whose liege man he is, owes to him aid and counsel in his undertakings; from which fact it is clearer than the sun how much is owed to the God of all, if so much is owed even to those to whom we are bound only by fealty.

As to the punishment of this crime, it is so severe that I cannot easily suppose that anything more severe could be devised even by those lords of the isles who too frequently put on the tyrant. And lest the severity of the penalty be thought to have had its origin in the cruelty of tyrants, I will set forth in part the language of the dispassionate law itself. It says: "Whoever with soldiers or private men or barbarians has entered into any wicked conspiracy, or has taken or given any guilty oath, or has conceived the death (for the laws desire that the will to commit a crime shall be punished with the same severity as the completed act) of the illustrious men who participate in our counsels or cabinet, or of any of the senators (for they too are a part of our body), or finally of any who are in our service as soldiers, let such a man be put to the sword, as guilty of a crime against our majesty and let all his goods be forfeited to our fisc. And let his sons, whose life we spare by the special grace of our imperial clemency,—for rightly they should perish by the same punishment as their fathers, to the end that fear may be inspired by the warning example of a crime which is hereditary,—let his sons be held excluded from the inheritance and succession of their mother and grandfather and of all their other relatives as well, and let them be permitted to take nothing by will from strangers. Let them forever be propertyless and paupers, and let their father's infamy attend them always. Let them never attain to any honors nor be permitted to take any oath. Finally let them be forever in such poverty and squalor that death will be a comfort to them and life a torture. And we command also that whoever shall be so rash as to intercede with us in their favor shall be infamous and without pardon. As to the daughters of such criminals, however numerous they may be, our will is that they shall receive only the Falcidian proportion of the goods of their mother, whether she dies testate or intestate, to the end that they may rather have the moderate means of a young girl than the full portion and rights of an heir. For with regard to them greater mildness ought to be shown than to the sons, since we trust that because of the weakness of their sex they will be less audacious. And as to the wives of the aforesaid, let them

recover their dower, and then, if they are in the position that
what they have received from their husbands by title of gift
must revert to their children at the termination of their own
life-estate, let them know that they must leave to our fisc all
the property which was thus lawfully owing to their children;
and from it let only the Falcidian proportion be assigned to the
daughters, but nothing at all to the sons. We decree that the
provisions concerning the aforesaid and their children shall also
apply to all their accomplices, abettors, and servants, and to
the children of all the latter with like severity. With reason,
however, if any of these at the outset and commencement of a
conspiracy is inspired by the desire of true praise to give information of the same, he shall receive from us reward and honor.
But one who has actually participated in a conspiracy, and then
while its secret counsels are still undisclosed reveals them, shall
be considered as meriting only pardon and indulgence." [1]

Bk. VII, Ch. XVII. *Of ambition; and that cupidity is the companion of folly: and of the origin of tyranny: and of the diverse ways
of the ambitious.*

. . . Now there is none who can help taking joy in liberty,
or who does not desire the strength wherewith to preserve it;
there is nought which would not be given in exchange therefor
if need arose. For slavery is as it were the image of death, and
liberty is the assured certainty of life. Therefore it is that wealth
is poured out in wooing power; and the more a man lusts after
power, the more lavishly he spends for the sake of it. But when
such a man does attain to power, he exalts himself into a tyrant,
and, spurning equity, does not scruple in the sight of God Himself to oppress and humiliate the equals of his rank and nature.
And though it is not given to all men to seize princely or royal
power, yet the man who is wholly untainted by tyranny is rare
or non-existent. In common speech the tyrant is one who oppresses a whole people by rulership based on force; and yet
it is not only over a people as a whole that a man can play the
tyrant, but he can do so if he will in even the meanest station.
For if not over the whole body of the people, still each man will
lord it as far as his power extends. I am not here speaking
of men whose hearts are wholly cleansed and who rejoice in
continual subjection, declining to be set over any in this life;
my task is rather to analyze the life of men in the political state.
And whom will you name me among them who does not desire

[1] Justin., Cod., ix, 8, 5.

in point of power to be set ahead of at least one other? Who is there who does not wish to have authority over some one? Who is there who treats those subject to him as he would wish to be treated if he were himself a subject? And so when ambition takes root, equity is trampled under foot and injustice advances apace and, giving rise to tyranny, pursues all the means by which the latter grows. He who does not prevail by his own powers, strives to make use of the power of others. It is plain to the sight how many hunters after power, wooers of honors, cleave to the side of the powerful, meddle in the public concerns of the commonwealth, trying to find some way whereby they can lift themselves aloft on one side or the other, whereby they can become more powerful than others, or at least seem more powerful by reason of those with whom they associate. They pour out their patrimony, they set about and perform immense labors; they do not scruple to press with their services and worry with their flatteries those whom they seek to captivate. And so no office is gratuitous, no duke or judge, no centurion or captain of ten, nay, not even a crier or publican is appointed save for a price.

Ch. XX. *Of the laws of secular princes whereby courtiers and officials are excluded from ecclesiastical honors; and by what examples the Dathanites and Abironites strive to prevail.*
. . . These are the precepts of secular princes. I cite them because, although the doctors of the Church enlarge upon this subject at length, nevertheless since the standard which they set seems too lofty to maintain in practice, what they say tends accordingly to be held of small account. But he who does not heed even the secular enactments is more blind than Hipseas,[1] and more deaf than the Dulichian oarsman,[2] and deserves to be struck down and hurled into the deepest deep by the angel whom he despises. You have heard how Nadab and Abiu[3] were consumed by their own fire and carried forth from the Tabernacle by the command of the Lord; but these men strive to burst into the temple of the Lord and into the very Holy of Holies against the prohibition of Moses, that is to say against the prohibition of the law of the Lord. They are followed by a numerous progeny which fills the courtyard of the Lord's House, and kindles an alien fire. They attempt to burn the forbidden incense, and contracting an alliance with the Datanites and

---

[1] Hor., *Sat.*, I, 2, 91.   [2] i.e., Ulysses.   [3] Lev. x. I ff.

Abironites,[1] they rise up against Moses, dividing the Church, throwing the priestly power into confusion, and stirring up sedition among the people, unless they are permitted to assume the priestly power themselves. For having won for themselves the favor of the secular powers, they assert that all things are opened to them of right, because (as they say) the prince is not subject to the laws, and what pleases the prince has the force of law. Since the people have conferred upon him and concentrated in him all their authority, it is the crime of lèse majesté, and a manifest subversion of government, to oppose him. Indeed it is the same thing as sacrilege to doubt whether one whom the prince has chosen is worthy to be chosen; and a man does not escape the stigma, and indeed it is lucky for him if he escapes the penalty, of his temerity, who for any reason whatsoever undertakes to nullify the will of the prince. They believe that no laws are superior in authority to the civil laws.

Anacarsis Cithica[2] has compared the latter to the webs of the spider, which catch flies and gnats but let birds and larger insects through; in the same manner the civil laws restrain the wills of people of the humbler sort but give way at once to the more powerful. For they do not exact of the latter the lawful penalty of transgression or disobedience, but without even putting them to the question pass them by with studied neglect. Those who support the view that all things are lawful for rulers also search out and bring forward the examples of tyrants to sustain their thesis. Yet for the most part you will find that they were rulers of places where ancient custom prevails, even though contrary to reason or to the law. They recount how one tyrant thrust his servant or crony into this or that church without election, how another by menaces and confiscation compelled the election of some unknown or unworthy clerk, how another sold the Church of God openly, how still another compelled an Archbishop to consecrate a reprobate, how one drove bishops or monks into exile or forced them to remain in banishment after they had been driven out by others, how another burdened the Church and its property with base services, or tortured men of religion with shameful cruelty, or humiliated and persecuted the clergy, or introduced the justice of wild beasts into the provinces, or stamped out the laws and canons from his territories, or imposed silence on the bishops so that he might commit all the worst outrages with impunity and without any

---

[1] Num. xvi. 1 ff.   [2] See Val. Max. vii. 2. ext. 14.

reproof, or long and obstinately vaunted himself in pride against the Church of Rome, or guided his whole conduct not so much by any law of his own as by a perversion of all law, or in short was wont to identify law with his own good pleasure.

The more fertile a man is in remembering such precedents and the more mischievous in executing iniquity, the more sincere is supposed to be his loyalty and the more effective his industry. But whoever in behalf of the truth of the faith or in defence of the purity of morals says aught concerning the divine law, will be at once branded as either superstitious or envious, or, what is the capital crime, hostile to the prince. If you should say that the fire which through seventy years of the Babylonish captivity had remained alive beneath the water, was at last quenched when Antiochus sold to Jason the office of high priest; [1] or (upon the testimony of blessed Gregory) that pestilences and famines, upheavals of nations, clashes between kingdoms, and countless adversities come upon countries from the fact that ecclesiastical honors are bestowed for a price or by reason of human favor upon undeserving persons; if you should say that Oza was struck down by God because he presumed to put forth his hand upon the ark when it was shaken; [2] if you say that Esias was silent during the reign of Ozia, the leprous king, and after the death of the latter saw God sitting exalted upon the throne; [3] if you say that the weight of the tabernacle rested solely on the shoulders and wagons of the Levites, or any other such things which are found in the law of God, it will be fortunate for you if you are not mutilated and thrust into prison, or banished into exile. A shout of fury will go up against you from all sides, and both the ambitious and their supporters will not scruple to pass against you the severest sentence of condemnation. But one solace God will provide for you, namely that the conscience of every wise and God-fearing man is in agreement with your words. Thence it follows that by the authority of God these men's judgment upon you will not prevail forever. For if they are to be believed, you will be adjudged a public enemy, as guilty of lèse majesté. It will be said that you are bringing to nought the judgments of the public authority, and while you are exalting ecclesiastical liberty as a zealot for your own profession, you are subverting the wisdom of princes and scheming to make them appear foolish and contemptible. Better would it be by far that the diadem were torn from the head of

[1] Grat., *Decret.*, I, i, I, c. 29 (Friedberg, i, 371).
[2] 2 Sam. vi. 6, 7.   [3] 2 Chron. xxvi. 16; Isa. vi. I.

the prince than that the good order of the chief and best part
of the commonwealth, which is the part that is concerned with
religion, should be destroyed at his pleasure. . . .

Ch. XXV. *Of the love and pursuit of liberty; and of those of old
time who patiently bore with free speaking; and of the difference
between a gibe and a taunt.*

Liberty means judging everything freely in accordance with
one's individual judgment, and does not hesitate to reprove what
it sees opposed to good morals. Nothing but virtue is more
splendid than liberty, if indeed liberty can ever properly be
severed from virtue. For to all right-thinking men it is clear
that true liberty issues from no other source. Wherefore, since
all agree that virtue is the highest good in life, and that it alone
can strike off the heavy and hateful yoke of slavery, it has
been the opinion of philosophers that men should die, if need
arose, for the sake of virtue, which is the only reason for living.
But virtue can never be fully attained without liberty, and the
absence of liberty proves that virtue in its full perfection is
wanting.   Therefore a man is free in proportion to the measure
of his virtues, and the extent to which he is free determines
what his virtues can accomplish; while, on the other hand, it is
the vices alone which bring about slavery, and subject a man to
persons and things in unmeet obedience; and though slavery
of the person may seem at times the more to be pitied, in reality
slavery to the vices is ever far the more wretched. And so what
is more lovely than liberty? And what more agreeable to a man
who has any reverence for virtue? We read that it has been
the impelling motive of all good princes; and that none ever trod
liberty under foot save the open foes of virtue. The jurists
know what good laws were introduced for the sake of liberty,
and the testimony of historians has made famous the great
deeds done for love of it. Cato drank poison, pierced himself
with his sword, and that no delay might prolong life on terms
which he deemed ignoble, he thrust in his hand to widen the
wound, and poured out his noble blood, that he might not see
Cæsar reigning.   Brutus set on foot civil wars to save the city
from slavery; and that seat of empire preferred rather to bear
the wretched afflictions of perpetual war than to endure a lord,
though of the mildest character. . I pass on to the weaker sex.
The wives of the Teutons, because of the value they set upon
their chastity, besought Marius after his victory that they might
be presented as a gift to the Vestal Virgins, promising that they

would abstain from all unchastity; and when their prayers were not heeded, on the following night they ended their lives by strangling themselves in order not to become slaves or suffer loss of their chastity. If I wished to recall individual instances of this kind, time would run out before the examples were exhausted. The practice of liberty is a notable thing and displeasing only to those who have the character of slaves.

Things which are done or spoken freely avoid the fault of timidity on the one hand and of rashness on the other, and so long as the straight and narrow path is followed, merit praise and win affection. But when under the pretext of liberty rashness unleashes the violence of its spirit, it properly incurs reproach, although, as a thing more pleasing in the ears of the vulgar than convincing to the mind of the wise man, it often finds in the indulgence of others the safety which it does not owe to its own prudence. Nevertheless, it is the part of a good and wise man to give a free rein to the liberty of others and to accept with patience the words of free speaking, whatever they may be. Nor does he oppose himself to its works so long as these do not involve the casting away of virtue. For since each virtue shines by its own proper light, the merit of tolerance is resplendent with a very special glory.

Once a certain man of Privernum, when asked how the captives from his city would keep the peace if they were granted amnesty, replied to the Roman consul: "If you grant them an advantageous peace, they will keep it forever; if a disadvantageous one, they will not keep it long." By these bold words, freely spoken, it came to pass that the citizens of Privernum obtained not only pardon for their rebellion, but the benefits of Roman citizenship besides, because one man of them had dared to speak out thus boldly in the Senate. On another occasion a certain Philip used his liberty to speak against the senatorial order, and before the rostrum he censured their inactivity, saying that for his part he thought that another Senate was needed; but not even by this could the gravity of the senators be shaken, nor the presence of mind of the consul Philip be disturbed, when the accused, upon whom he bade one of his lictors to lay hands, replied to him: "Philip, to me you are not comporting yourself like a consul, since in your eyes I am not a senator." . . .

Bk. VIII, Ch. XVII. *Wherein consists the difference between a tyrant and a true prince; and of the tyranny of priests; and wherein a shepherd, a thief and a hireling differ from one another.*

Wherein the prince differs from the tyrant has already been set forth above when we were reviewing Plutarch's "Instruction of Trajan"; and the duties of the prince and of the different members of the commonwealth were also carefully explained at that point. Wherefore it will be easier to make known here, and in fewer words, the opposite characteristics of the tyrant. A tyrant, then, as the philosophers have described him, is one who oppresses the people by rulership based upon force, while he who rules in accordance with the laws is a prince. Law is the gift of god, the model of equity, a standard of justice, a likeness of the divine will, the guardian of well-being, a bond of union and solidarity between peoples, a rule defining duties, a barrier against the vices and the destroyer thereof, a punishment of violence and all wrong-doing. The law is assailed by force or by fraud, and, as it were, either wrecked by the fury of the lion or undermined by the wiles of the serpent. In whatever way this comes to pass, it is plain that it is the grace of God which is being assailed, and that it is God himself who in a sense is challenged to battle. The prince fights for the laws and the liberty of the people; the tyrant thinks nothing done unless he brings the laws to nought and reduces the people to slavery. Hence the prince is a kind of likeness of divinity; and the tyrant, on the contrary, a likeness of the boldness of the Adversary, even of the wickedness of Lucifer, imitating him that sought to build his throne to the north and make himself like unto the Most High,[1] with the exception of His goodness. For had he desired to be like unto Him in goodness, he would never have striven to tear from Him the glory of His power and wisdom. What he more likely did aspire to was to be equal with him in authority to dispense rewards. The prince, as the likeness of the Deity, is to be loved, worshipped and cherished; the tyrant, the likeness of wickedness, is generally to be even killed. The origin of tyranny is iniquity, and springing from a poisonous root, it is a tree which grows and sprouts into a baleful pestilent growth, and to which the axe must by all means be laid. For if iniquity and injustice, banishing charity, had not brought about tyranny, firm concord and perpetual peace would have possessed the peoples of the earth forever, and no one would think of enlarging his boundaries. Then kingdoms would be as friendly and peaceful, according to the authority of the great father Augustine,[2] and would enjoy as undisturbed

[1] Isa. xiv. 12–14.   [2] Aug., *De Civ. Dei.* iv, 15.

repose, as the separate families in a well-ordered state, or as different persons in the same family; or perhaps, which is even more credible, there would be no kingdoms at all, since it is clear from the ancient historians that in the beginning these were founded by iniquity as presumptuous encroachments against the Lord, or else were extorted from Him. . . .

Ch. XX. *That by the authority of the divine page it is a lawful and glorious act to slay public tyrants, provided that the slayer is not bound by fealty to the tyrant, or does not for some other reason sacrifice justice and honor thereby.*

It would be a long and tedious task if I wished to bring down to our own times the series of gentile tyrants; a man with only one life will hardly be able to recall the list, for it eludes the mind and overpowers the tongue. My opinions on the subject of tyrants are, however, set forth more fully in my little work entitled "Of the Ends of Tyrants," [1] a brief manual wherein I have carefully sought to avoid the tedium of prolixity and the obscurity of too great compression. But lest the authority of Roman history be held in small account because it has for the most part been written by infidels concerning infidels, let its lesson be confirmed by examples drawn from sacred and Christian history. For it is everywhere obvious that, in the words of Valerius, only that power is secure in the long run which places bounds to its own exercise. And surely nought is so splendid or so magnificent that it does not need to be tempered by moderation. The earliest tyrant whom the divine page brings before us is Nembroth, the mighty hunter before the Lord (who is also called Ninus in some histories, although this does not agree with the proper reckoning of dates); and I have already said above that he was a reprobate. For verily he desired to be lord in his own right and not under God, and it was in his time that the attempt to raise a tower to Heaven was made by frail mortality, destined in their blindness to be overthrown and scattered in confusion. Let us, therefore, advance to him who was set over the people by the divine choice, which deserted him when he gave himself up to a wicked desire of ruling rather than of reigning, and in the end he was so utterly overthrown that in the anguish of his suffering he was compelled to put an end to himself. For a right and wholesome assumption of the royal office is of no avail, or only of very little, if the later life of the ruler is at variance therewith, nor does a judge look wholly to the origin of things, but makes his judgment to depend upon their outcome and ending.

[1] This work of John of Salisbury is not known to be extant.

. . . The histories teach, however, that none should undertake the death of a tyrant who is bound to him by an oath or by the obligation of fealty. For we read that Sedechias, because he disregarded the sacred obligation of fealty, was led into captivity; and that in the case of another of the kings of Juda whose name escapes my memory, his eyes were plucked out because, falling into faithlessness, he did not keep before his sight God, to whom the oath is taken; since sureties for good behavior are justly given even to a tyrant.

But as for the use of poison, although I see it sometimes wrongfully adopted by infidels, I do not read that it is ever permitted by any law. Not that I do not believe that tyrants ought to be removed from our midst, but it should be done without loss of religion and honor. For David, the best of all kings that I have read of, and who, save in the incident of Urias Etheus, walked blamelessly in all things, although he had to endure the most grievous tyrant, and although he often had an opportunity of destroying him, yet preferred to spare him, trusting in the mercy of God, within whose power it was to set him free without sin. He therefore determined to abide in patience until the tyrant should either suffer a change of heart and be visited by God with return of charity, or else should fall in battle, or otherwise meet his end by the just judgment of God. How great was his patience can be discerned from the fact that when he had cut off the edge of Saul's robe in the cave, and again when, having entered the camp by night, he rebuked the negligence of the sentinels, in both cases he compelled the king to confess that David was acting the juster part. And surely the method of destroying tyrants which is the most useful and the safest, is for those who are oppressed to take refuge humbly in the protection of God's mercy, and lifting up undefiled hands to the Lord, to pray devoutly that the scourge wherewith they are afflicted may be turned aside from them. For the sins of transgressors are the strength of tyrants. Wherefore Achior, the captain of all the children of Amon, gave this most wholesome counsel to Holofernes: "Inquire diligently, my lord," said he, "whether there be any iniquity of the people in the sight of their God, and then let us go up to them, because their God will abandon them and deliver them to thee, and they shall be subdued beneath the yoke of thy power. But if there be no offence of this people in the sight of their God, we shall not be able to withstand them, because their God will defend them, and we shall be exposed to the reproach and scorn of all the earth." [1]

[1] Judith v. 5, 24–25.

Ch. XXI. *That all tyrants come to a bad end; and that God will punish them if the hand of man should fail, and that this is shown in the case of Julian the Apostate and many examples from the sacred Scriptures.*
Thus the end of tyrants is confusion, leading to destruction if they persist in malice, to pardon if they return into the way of righteousness. For there is prepared a great fire wherewith to consume the scourge after the Father has employed it for the correction of His children. And it is written, "Acab has humbled himself before my face ; therefore will I not bring evil in his days." [1] But Jezebel, who persisted in cruelty, paid the penalty therefor in the merited cruelty of her end, giving her blood to be lapped up by dogs in the place where dogs had lapped up the blood of innocent Naboth. But if the blood of innocent Naboth was thus required at her hands, will not the blood of so many other innocent victims also be required ? Her unrighteousness coveted the vineyard of a just man, and as the price thereof she lost her rights to a whole kingdom. Thus wickedness is always punished by the Lord ; but sometimes it is His own, and at others it is a human hand, which He employs as a weapon wherewith to administer punishment to the unrighteous. . . .

SELECTED BIBLIOGRAPHY

McIlwain, Charles H., *Growth of Political Thought in the West*, pp. 228–230, 319–324.
Cook, Thomas I., *History of Political Philosophy*, pp. 212–216.
Dickinson, John, "The Place of the Policraticus in the Development of Political Thought," in his translation of *The Statesman's Book of John of Salisbury*, pp. xvii–lxxxii.
Jacob, E. F., "John of Salisbury and the 'Policraticus,'" in F. J. C. Hearnshaw, ed., *Social and Political Ideas of Some Great Mediæval Thinkers* (New York, 1923), ch. 3.
Webb, Clement C. J., *John of Salisbury* (London, 1932), chs. 1, 2.
Carlyle, R. W. and A. J., *History of Mediæval Political Theory in the West*, 6 vols. (Edinburgh and London, 1903–1936), Vol. III, pp. 136–146; Vol. IV, pt. iv, ch. 2.
Gennrich, Paul, *Die Staats- und Kirchenlehre Johanns von Salisbury* (Gotha, 1894).
Schubert, Ernst A. W., *Die Staatslehre Johanns von Salisbury* (Berlin, 1897).

[1] I Kings xxi. 29.

ST. THOMAS AQUINAS

VII. ST. THOMAS AQUINAS (C. 1226-1274)

INTRODUCTION

The prevailing system of later medieval thought is known as "Scholasticism." It is characterized chiefly by its attempt to effect a conciliation between Christian dogma and rational thought, to procure a scientific form for the doctrines of the Church. All scholastics assumed that the creed of the Church was absolutely true; but all desired to show that the revealed truths of that creed were comprehensible to human reason. The greater scholastics— such as Peter Lombard in the twelfth century and Albertus Magnus, Thomas Aquinas, and Dun Scotus in the thirteenth century— erected comprehensive and elaborately symmetrical systems for the discussion of metaphysical, epistemological, theological, and practical ethical and social questions. The scholastic method was formal and deductive—a systematic application of the syllogism to all questions, a balancing of authorities, a definition and discrimination of words. Scholasticism reached its zenith in the later thirteenth century after the recovery and translation of Aristotle's scientific, ethical, and political works. Aristotle's writings were more compendious and analytical than any writings hitherto known to the medieval mind. A characteristic aim of the thirteenth-century scholastics was to interweave the higher tenets of human reason as set forth by Aristotle (called "the philosopher") with the doctrines of Christian theology as revealed in the Bible and the tradition of the Church. Where the two elements appeared incompatible, the former was adjusted to the latter.[1]

The greatest of the scholastics was Thomas Aquinas. His writings were in general too closely governed by dogmatic theology to have comprised any consistently worked-out scheme of political theory; but his definition and classification of laws were of notable influence upon important juristic treatises by theologians and others of later periods; and the discussion of the limits of

[1] *Cf.* Ueberweg, *History of Philosophy*, Vol. I, pp. 355-356.

government, in his *Rule of Princes* (*De Regimine Principum*, 1266),
shows independent thinking in advance of his school.

Aquinas was born in the early part of the thirteenth century,
in the kingdom of Naples, of a family of noble descent. He was a
devoted student of philosophy and theology, and was a lecturer
and teacher in these subjects at Paris, Naples, Rome, and other
places. He was active and influential in the service of the church
and of the Dominican order of friars, which he joined in his youth.
From his teachings and writings he ranks with St. Augustine as
one of the two most influential theologians of the Roman Catholic
church. His analysis of law forms a part of his *Summa Theologica*,
a work which was designed to cover the whole field of learning
defined and interpreted according to the philosophy of Aristotle
and the doctrines of the church. The *Rule of Princes* was intended
as a distinctly political treatise; it was not completed at the
author's death; the parts which he wrote deal with the origin
and basis of civil government, the best form of state, and the sphere
of government.[1] This study is dominated by the prevailing assumption of the superiority of the monarchical to other forms of
government; and it reflects in the main the church's view as to
the supremacy of ecclesiastical over temporal authority. However, the examination of the limits of government is set forth with
skill and originality, and at points conclusions are reached which
accord pretty closely with ideas commonly considered to be distinctively modern.

The high position that Aquinas still holds in the thought of the
Catholic church is shown impressively in an Encyclical of Pope
Leo XIII (August 4, 1879), which directs that Aquinas' teaching
be accepted as the basis of theology. For political thought generally, Aquinas' discussion of law is perhaps his greatest contribution. He distinguishes four forms of law : Eternal (the reason of
God), Natural (the reflection of divine reason in all creation),
Divine (the direct revelation of the reason of God, as in the code
of laws He gave the Jews), and Human (the more specific application, by human reason, of natural law to particular circumstances
of man's earthly life). The forms are essentially connected :
Human law is derivative from Natural law, which is a reflection

---

[1] These subjects are treated in the first book and in the first part of the second
book. The remainder of the work was written by another author.

of Eternal law; and Divine law supplements the limitations of human reason. Each form exhibits every essential characteristic of law in general. Present-day writers have vigorously argued the question as to whether certain rules of social conduct are to be recognized as laws because, on the one hand, they have issued, in proper form, from some formally qualified governing office; or because, on the other hand, they are intrinsically reasonable rules, directed to the welfare of the community. Aquinas showed greater perspicacity in his general analysis of law: he recognized the essential importance both of the source and of the substance and end of law. Despite his formalistic method, his definition of law is singularly comprehensive, reasonable, and realistic.

READINGS FROM ST. THOMAS AQUINAS [1]

1. The Definition of Law [2]

Article I. *Whether law is a thing of the reason.*[3]

We proceed thus to the first article. 1. It seems that law is not a thing of the reason. For the Apostle says, *I see another law in my members.* But nothing pertaining to the reason exists in the members of the body; for reason does not employ corporeal organs. Therefore, law is not a thing of the reason.

2. Furthermore, in reason we find only power, mode and performance. Law is clearly not the power of reason; likewise, law is not a mode of the reason, for the modes of reason constitute intellectual faculties; nor is law a performance of reason, for in such case when reason ceased to act, law would cease. Therefore, law is not a thing of the reason.

3. Moreover, law impels those who are subject to it to right conduct. But to impel to action pertains, properly speaking, to the will, not to the reason; thus the jurist says, *quod placuit principi, legis habet vigorem.*

On the other hand, it is the function of law to command and forbid. But command issues from the reason, as we have shown. Therefore, law is a thing of the reason.

Conclusion : <u>Since law is a rule and standard</u> (*regula et mensura*) <u>of human action, it is necessarily related to</u> reason.

To the objections I answer that law is a rule and standard of

---

[1] The translations are made from a Paris edition (1871–1880) of his *Opera Omnia,* 34 vols. *Summa Theologica* is in Vols. I–VI; *De Regimine Principum* is in Vol. XXVII (opusc. 16).

[2] *Summa Theologica,* Vol. II, ch. i, question xc : *De Lege.*

[3] *Utrum lex sit aliquid rationis.*

conduct, according to which one is induced to act or to be restrained from acting. The word *lex* is said to be derived from the word *ligando*, because it binds one to action. Moreover, the rule and standard of human acts is reason, which is the first principle of human conduct. For it is the function of reason to direct anything towards an end; and that, according to the Philosopher,[1] is the first impulse of action. Again, in a thing of any class that which is its first principle is the standard and rule of that species; as unity, in the category, number, or first motion, in the category, motion. Whence it follows that law is something pertaining to the reason.

To the first argument above it should be replied that, since law is a rule and standard, it may be said to exist in a two-fold manner in anything. In one sense it exists in the subject which governs and regulates; this being the property of reason, law, in this sense, is in the reason alone. In another aspect law is a part of the object which is governed and regulated; thus law exists in anything which is inclined in a certain direction by law; an inclination proceeding from a law may be said to be, not essentially law, but law by participation. In this sense, the propensity of bodily members towards concupiscence is called a *law of the members*.

To the second argument it should be replied that, just as in external acts it is necessary to consider both the operation and the thing produced—for example, the process of construction and the completed building—so, in the works of the reason, we consider, on the one hand, the action of reason—that is, the comprehension and ratiocination—and, on the other hand, what is accomplished through the action of reason, which, in speculative reason includes the definition, the proposition, and the syllogism, or argumentation. And since even the practical reason makes use of the syllogism in ethics, we find in the practical reason that which is related to actions as the proposition, in speculative reason, is related to conclusions. These universal propositions of the practical reason, which relate to acts, have the nature of law. Reason examines these propositions individually; moreover, it conserves them collectively, as customs.

To the third argument it is to be replied that reason derives its moving force from the will. For when one wills a certain end, reason prescribes the means to that end. But since the will, with respect to the things which it commands with some end in view, has the nature of law, it should be regulated by law. It is

---

[1] "The Philosopher" was a common title for Aristotle in the thirteenth and following centuries.

in this sense that the principle—"the will of the prince has the force of law," should be understood; otherwise the will of the prince would be injustice rather than law.

Article II. *Whether law is always ordained for the common good.*[1]

We proceed thus to the second article. 1. It seems that law is not always ordained for the common good as its end. For it pertains to law to command and forbid. But commands are ordained for certain particular goods. Therefore, the end of law is not always the common good.

2. Again, law directs man to action. But human conduct is made up of particular acts. Therefore, law is ordained for some particular good.

3. Furthermore, Isidore says, "if law is made of the reason, law will be everything that is constituted of reason."[2] But reason consists not only of that which has as its end the common good, but also of that which is ordained to the private good of an individual. Therefore, *etc.*

On the other hand, Isidore says that "law is made for the private advantage of no one, but for the common benefit of all the citizens."

Conclusion: Since law is the rule of human conduct, the ultimate end of which is happiness, and, indeed, the common happiness, it is necessarily always ordained for the common good.

To the objections I answer that law relates to the principle of human action, since it is a standard and rule. Moreover, as reason is the principle of human conduct, so in reason itself there is something which is the principle with respect to everything else in reason; wherefore it is to this principle of reason that law should fundamentally and especially pertain. The first principle of acts governed by the practical reason is the final end; the final end of human life is happiness, or blessedness; whence it is necessary that law should have special regard for the condition of happiness. Again, since every part is ordained for the whole, as the imperfect for the perfect (and as one man is a part of the perfect community), it is necessary that law should have in view the common happiness. Wherefore, the Philosopher, in defining legal things, speaks of felicity and the political community; he says, "we call just those laws which produce and conserve the happiness of the state, and of the individuals, by virtue of their

---

[1] *Utrum lex ordinetur semper ad bonum commune.*
[2] "*Si ratione lex constat, lex erit omne quod ratione constiterit.*"

political association." The perfect community is the state, as he also says. But in any generic thing, that which is named particularly is the principle of the other qualities, which are said to pertain to the principal quality. Thus fire, which is hot above all things else, is the cause of heat in bodies partly hot, which are said to be hot in so far as they partake of fire. Whence it follows necessarily that, since law has regard especially for the common good, every precept concerning a particular deed should have the character of law only in so far as it looks to the common good. Thus every law is ordained for the common good.

To the first argument above it should be replied that a precept implies the application of a law to those things which are governed by the law. An order, however, which relates to the common good and which pertains to law, is thus applicable to individual ends; accordingly, there are precepts concerning particular acts.

To the second argument it is to be replied that performances indeed consist in particular acts; but these particular acts can relate to the common good, not through community of kind, but through community of final purpose; accordingly, the common good is said to be the common end.

To the third argument it may be replied that just as nothing is firmly established by speculative reason, save through resolution into first, undemonstrable principles, so nothing is firmly established by practical reason save through relating it to the final end, which is the common good. It is in this sense that what is established by reason has the nature of law.

Article III.   *Whether everyone's reason makes law.*[1]

We proceed thus to the third article.   1. It would seem that the reason of anyone might produce law. For the Apostle says, *For when the Gentiles, which have not the law, do by nature the things contained in the law, these are a law unto themselves.* But this is commonly said of everybody. Therefore anyone may make law for himself.

2.   Furthermore, the Philosopher says, "the aim of the law-maker is to lead man to virtue." But anyone can lead another to virtue. Therefore, the reason of any man may produce law.

3.   Again, as a prince of a state is governor of that state, so a father of a family is governor of his home. But the prince of a state can make law in that state. Therefore, any father of a family can make law in his own home.

On the other hand, Isidore says, what we also read in the canon

[1] *Utrum ratio cujuslibet sit factiva legis.*

law, "Law is that which has been established by the people and in accordance with which the elders have, with the concurrence of the multitude, decreed this or that thing." Therefore, it is not the function of everyone to make law.

Conclusion: Since law ordains the common good, law can be created by the reason, not of any individual, but of the multitude, or of the prince acting for the multitude.

To the objections I answer that law, properly understood, has regard primarily and principally to the common good. To ordain anything for the common good is the province either of the entire multitude or of some one acting for the entire multitude. Therefore, to create law pertains either to the entire multitude or to the public person who is charged with the interests of the multitude; for in every undertaking it is the function of him who has the care of the end to ordain the means to that end.

To the first argument above it should, therefore, be answered that law not only emanates from the subject which governs but is a part also of the object which is governed. In this sense anyone is a law unto himself in so far as he takes to himself the order of him who rules. Wherefore, the Apostle adds, *which shew the work of the law written in their hearts.*

To the second argument it should be replied that a private person cannot effectually lead anyone to virtue; he can only admonish; if his admonition is rejected he lacks the compulsive force which law must have in order to lead actually to virtue. This compulsive force, however, inheres in the multitude, or in the public person to whom it pertains to impose penalties; thus it is his function to make law.

To the third argument it should be replied that as a man is part of a household, so the household is part of the state; the state, however, is the perfect community. Therefore, just as the good of a single man is not an ultimate end, but his good is itself ordained for the common good, so the good of a single household is ordained for the good of the state, which is the perfect community. Consequently, though he who governs a family may issue certain precepts or statutes, his commands do not have the character of law.

Article IV. *Whether promulgation is essential to law.*[1]

We proceed thus to the fourth article. 1. It seems that promulgation is not of the essence of law. For natural law has pre-eminently the essence of law. But natural law does not require

1 *Utrum promulgatio sit de ratione legis.*

promulgation.   Therefore, it is not of the essence of law that it should be promulgated.

2.   Moreover, law obliges one to do or to abstain from doing something.   But not only those in whose presence the law is promulgated are bound to obey the law, but others as well.   Therefore, promulgation is not essential to law.

3.   Furthermore, the obligation of law extends to the future, for "laws place constraint upon future transactions," as the civil law says.   But promulgation is addressed to those of the present.   Therefore, promulgation is not a requirement of law.

On the contrary, it is said in the canon law that "laws are instituted when they are promulgated."

Conclusion: Since law is established as a rule which is to be applied to those upon whom it is imposed, it is necessary, in order that it may have obligatory force, that it should be promulgated and brought to the notice of those who are subject to the law.

I answer, then, that, as we have shown, law is imposed upon men as a rule and standard.   A rule or standard is imposed by virtue of being applied to that which is governed or regulated. Wherefore, in order that law may obtain binding power, which is the proper character of law, it must be applied to those persons who are to be ruled by it.   Such application is made by bringing it to their knowledge through promulgation.   Thus promulgation is necessary in order for law to have its peculiar virtue.

From the four foregoing propositions we may now derive the definition of law, which is nothing but an ordinance of reason for the common good, promulgated by him who has the care of the community.[1]

To the first argument above, therefore, it should be answered that promulgation of natural law exists by virtue of the fact that God has implanted that law in the minds of men in such manner that they apprehend it naturally.

To the second argument it should be replied that those in whose presence the law is not promulgated are bound to its observance in so far as it has come, or can come, into their knowledge through others, after it has been promulgated.

To the third argument it is to be responded that promulgation in the present extends into the future through the permanence of writing, which in a way promulgates it forever.   Wherefore, Isidore says, "the word 'law' is said to be derived from 'reading' (*legendo*), because it is written."

[1] "Quædam rationis ordinatio ad bonum commune, et ab eo qui curam communitatis habet, promulgata."

2. The Nature and Duties of Royal Authority [1]

Ch. i. *What is meant by the name, king.* [2]

Our plan must begin with an explanation of what is to be understood by the word "king." In all pursuits which are directed toward some end and in which it is possible to proceed in more than one way, there is need of some controlling force by which one may arrive by a straight course at the appointed goal. A ship, driven in various directions by the impulse of varying winds, would never reach her destination were she not guided to the port by the diligence of the helmsman. But for a man there is an end toward which his whole life and action are directed; for he acts by virtue of the intellect, whose property is to act purposefully. Moreover, it happens that men proceed through various ways toward the proper destination of mankind; this is revealed in the diversity of human interests and actions. Man, therefore, needs something to guide him toward his goal. There dwells naturally within every man the light of reason, by which he in his actions is directed toward his proposed end. If it suited man to live singly, as many animals do, he would need no one else to guide him to his end; every man would be his own king, under God—the supreme king; by the light of reason, divinely given, he would direct himself in all his acts. But it is the nature of man to be a social and political animal, living in a multitude,—more so than other animals, as natural necessity makes manifest. For other animals nature has prepared food, coverings of hair, and means of defence—such as teeth, horns, and claws; or, at least, they have speed for flight. Man was created with none of these things prepared for him by nature; in place of them all reason was given him by which he might provide them for himself with the work of his hands. But to obtain such things one man is not sufficient; for one man alone could not live an adequate life. [3] It is, therefore, natural to man to live in the society of many.

Furthermore, in other animals there exists a natural instinct (*industria*) with regard to all things which are beneficial or harmful to them; for example, the sheep naturally considers the wolf his enemy; animals also by natural instinct know that some herbs are necessary to their lives and that others are medicinal. But only in a community does man have natural knowledge

[1] *De Regimine Principum*, Bk. I, chs. i, ii, and xv.
[2] *Quid significetur nomine regis.*
[3] "Nam unus homo per se sufficienter vitam transigere non posset."

of those things which are necessary to his life, as if having power through reason to obtain from general principles the knowledge of the simple things which are necessary to human life. It is not possible, however, for one man by his own reason to accomplish all of this. It is, therefore, necessary for men to live in multitudes, so that one may be helped by another and different ones may be occupied in discovering different things, through reason; thus one is engaged in medicine, another in this pursuit, another in that. This system is made very manifest in the fact that it is a characteristic of man to use speech, by means of which he is able to set completely forth his conceptions to his fellows. Other animals express their passions to each other in various ways, as dogs indicate their anger by barking. But man is more disposed to communication than any other gregarious animal, such as the crane, the ant, or the bee. Regarding this matter Solomon says (Eccl. iv. 9), *Two are better than one, because they have the reward of mutual society.*

If it is natural to man to live in a numerous society it is necessary that there should be provision for ruling such a society. Where there are many men and each seeks that which is agreeable to himself, the group will soon fall apart, unless there be some one who cares for those things which concern the good of the aggregate; just as the body of a man (or any other animal) would be destroyed if there were no controlling force in the body working for the common benefit of all the members. Thus Solomon says (Prov. xi. 14), *Where no counsel is, the people will fall.* And this is reasonable; for what is individual (*proprium*) is not the same as that which is common; in private matters men differ, in common affairs they are united. Moreover, the interests of different people are diverse. It is, therefore, right that in addition to that which works to the private advantage of each there should be something which acts for the common good of the many; for in all things which are organized into a unity one is found to rule the others. In the universe of bodies, the first—that is, the astral, body rules all the others, according to the plan of divine providence; and all bodies are ruled by the rational creature. In a man, moreover, the soul rules the body, and within the soul the irascible and sensual parts are controlled by the reason. Among the members of the body one is chief—the heart, or the head, which rules the others. Thus there must be within every multitude a ruling power.

In some pursuits directed toward an end it is possible to proceed rightly or wrongly. There is a right and a wrong way in the government of a multitude. Anything is rightly directed when it is brought to its proper goal, and wrongly when it is guided to an unfitting end. The appropriate goal for a multitude of freemen is different from that for a multitude of slaves. He is free who lives for his own sake; he is a slave who exists for another. If a multitude of freemen is governed by a ruler for their common good, the government is right and just, and appropriate for free men. If the government is directed not to the common good, but to the private good of the ruler, then it is unjust and perverted. The Lord threatens such a ruler, saying (Ezek. xxxiv. 2), *Woe be to the shepherds that do feed themselves! should not the shepherds feed the flocks?* Shepherds should seek the good of the flock, and every ruler the good of the multitude subject to him.

If an unjust government should be established by one man who in governing seeks his own benefit, and not that of the multitude committed to him, such a ruler is called a tyrant, a name derived from might (*fortitudine*), because he coerces with force, instead of ruling with justice; thus among the ancients some powerful persons were called tyrants. When an unjust government is founded, not by one, but by a few, it is called an *oligarchy*, which is the rule of a few who, for the sake of riches, oppress the people; it differs from a tyranny only in number. If the evil government be conducted by the many, it is called a *democracy*, which is the rule of the common people who through force of numbers overwhelm the wealthy; the whole people here are as one tyrant. Just governments should be distinguished in the same manner. If just government is controlled by a multitude it is called by the general name of *polity*, as when a multitude of warriors rule within a state or province. If it is conducted by a few who are virtuous, it is called an *aristocracy*—which is the best dominion, or the government of the best, who are thus called *optimates*. If the just power belongs to one alone, he is properly called king; wherefore the Lord says (Ezek. xxxvii. 24), *Daniel my servant shall be king over them; and they all shall have one shepherd.* Thus it is clearly manifest that from the nature of a king he is one who is set above,[1] and that he should be a shepherd seeking the common good of the multitude and not his own.

Since it is fitting for man to live in a multitude because he is not sufficient unto himself with regard to the necessaries of life, the society of the multitude ought to be as much more perfect than life in isolation as it is in itself more sufficient in the necessaries of life. There is indeed a certain sufficiency for life in

---

[1] "Ex quo manifeste ostenditur quod de ratione regis est quod sit unus qui præsit," *etc.*

the family of one household, as much, that is, as is needed for natural acts of nutrition, reproduction of offspring, and other similar purposes. There is a sufficiency in one village, so far as the things belonging to one craft go. But in a city (*civitate*), which is a perfect community, there is everything that is required for all the necessaries of life; and still more sufficient is a province, when there is need for mutual assistance in fighting against common enemies. Therefore, the one who rules a perfect community— that is, a city or a province, is called by the title of king. The one who rules a house is called not king but *paterfamilias;* but he has a certain likeness to a king; so kings are sometimes called fathers of their people.

It appears, then, from what has been said, that a king is one who rules the multitude of a city or province, and rules it for the public good; wherefore Solomon says (Eccl. v. 8), *The king reigneth over all the land subject to him.*

Ch. ii. *Whether it is better for a city or province to be governed by several rulers or by one.*[1]

Having made these introductory remarks we ought now to inquire which is more advantageous to a province or city, to be ruled by several or by one. This can be answered from a considera- tion of the actual purpose of government.

The aim of any ruler ought to be to secure the safety of that which he has undertaken to rule. Thus it is the duty of the pilot, by preserving his ship against the perils of the sea, to bring it uninjured to a port of safety. Now the good and safety of an associated multitude consist in the preservation of its unity, which is peace; if this be lost the advantages of social life vanish; nay more, the multitude in disagreement becomes a burden to itself. It is for this, therefore, that the ruler of a multitude ought especially to strive, that he may obtain the unity of peace. Nor is it right for him to debate whether he will maintain peace in the multitude subject to him, as it is not right for a physician to con- sider whether he will cure a patient intrusted to his care. For one ought to debate not concerning the end which it is his duty to seek but concerning the means to that end. Wherefore, the Apostle, commanding the unity of the faithful, says (Ephes. iv. 3), *Be solicitous to keep the unity of the Spirit in the bond of peace.* The more efficacious is the government in preserving the unity of peace, the more useful will it be. For we regard that as more useful which leads more directly to a proposed end. And it is

---

[1] *Quid plus expediat civitati vel provinciæ pluribus aut uno regi rectore.*

clear that unity can be more readily created by that which is one in itself than by a multiple agent, just as heat is produced most effectively by a body which is in itself hot or a source of heat. Therefore, the rule of one is more beneficial than the rule of many.

Moreover, where several rulers disagree completely they cannot control the multitude. Among any number a certain union is necessary if they are to rule at all. Many cannot propel a ship in one direction unless they are joined together in some way. But a number of things are united in so far as they approach to one thing. . . .

Furthermore, those things which follow nature are best, for in every instance nature operates best. But all natural government is by one. Among the numerous members of the human body, there is one member, the heart, which controls all the others; and in the parts of the soul, one force rules supreme, namely, the reason. There is one king among bees; in the universe there is one God, the creator and ruler of all things. And this is reasonable. For every multitude is derived from one. Wherefore, if things of art imitate things of nature, and a work of art is by so much the better as it achieves similitude to what is in nature, then necessarily a human multitude is best governed by one. Experience proves the same thing. Those provinces and cities which are not ruled by one are beset with dissension and are buffeted about without any peace; thus here appears to be fulfilled the complaint of the Lord, who said, through His prophet (Jer. xii. 10), *Many pastors have destroyed my vineyard.* On the other hand, the provinces and states which are ruled by one king enjoy peace, are strong in justice, and rejoice in affluence. Wherefore, the Lord, through His prophets, promised His people, as a great reward, that He would place over them one head, and that there should be one prince among them.

Ch. xv. *That a kingdom ought to be governed primarily with a view to creating happiness.*[1]

Just as the life which men live well here is ordered with a view to a happy life in heaven, for which we hope as the end of this life, so whatever special benefits are sought by men here— wealth, health, eloquence, or learning—are ordained for the good of the multitude. If he who has care of the final end should preside over and direct those who have care of the means to that end, then the king, on the one hand, subject to the dominion and gov-

---

[1] *Quod regnum ordinari debet ad beatitudinem consequendam principaliter.* Several other chapters treat of the duties of a king.

ernment administered by the priest, should, on the other hand, guide and control all human tasks. Whoever finds it his duty to perform a task which is directed towards some further purpose ought to strive to make his work appropriate to that purpose; as the smith makes the sword suitable for war, and the builder arranges the house so that it will be fitted for a dwelling.

Since the end of the life which we live well at present is heavenly happiness, it pertains to the duty of the king to make the life of the multitude good, in accordance with what is suitable for that heavenly happiness; he must command those things which lead to heavenly happiness and forbid their opposites, as far as possible. The way to true happiness and the obstructions on the way are revealed in the divine law, the teaching of which is the duty of priests. . . . The king, having learned the divine law, ought to study especially how the multitude subject to him may live well. This study has three parts: first, how a king may institute a good life among the subject multitude; secondly, how he may preserve what has been instituted; thirdly, how he may advance what he has preserved to a better condition.

For the good life of an individual two things are needed: one thing, which is fundamental, is action according to virtue (for virtue is that by which one lives well); the other, which is secondary and instrumental, is a sufficiency of material goods, the use of which is necessary to virtuous action. The unity of an individual man is produced by nature; the unity of a multitude, which is called peace, must be obtained through the efforts of the ruler. Therefore, to establish good life for a multitude three things are required: first, that the multitude should be brought into the unity of peace; secondly, that the multitude, having been united by the bond of peace, should be directed to good action; for as a man can do nothing well unless the unity of his parts be first established, so a multitude of men, lacking the unity of peace and fighting itself, is prevented from acting well; thirdly, that through the care of the ruler there should be provided a sufficient supply of the necessaries for good living. When, therefore, good life is established in a multitude by the services of the king, he should next work for the conservation of that life.

There are three things which prevent the public good from enduring. One of them comes from nature. For the good of the multitude ought to be established not for one time but for all time. But since men are mortal they cannot live forever; nor while they live are they always equally vigorous, because human life is subject to variations and men are not fitted to perform the same duties throughout their lives. Another hindrance to the maintenance of the public good comes from within and depends upon the perversity of wills, which are either too weak to achieve those things which common welfare requires, or are hostile to the peace of the multitude and, despising justice, disturb the tranquillity of others. The third impediment to the preservation of the state arises from without, when peace is upset by the encroachments of enemies which sometimes altogether destroy a kingdom or a city. A three-fold responsibility, therefore, rests upon the king. First, for the succession of men in the various offices, since by divine law in things corruptible they cannot always remain the same, he must see that others are born to take the places left vacant; thus the integrity of the whole and the good of the subject multitude are preserved by the care of the king. Secondly, by his laws and commands he must keep his subjects from wickedness and lead them into works of virtue, taking his example from God, who has given laws to men and returns rewards to those who keep the laws, and punishments to those who transgress. Thirdly, it rests with the king to keep the multitude subject to him safe from enemies. For it would avail them nothing to escape the inner perils if they be not also defended from those without.

Finally, for the good government of a multitude there remains a third thing which pertains to the duty of the king; it is that he take care for their advancement. This he does when in each of the matters mentioned above he corrects whatever is wrong, supplies whatever is lacking, and strives to perfect whatever can be improved. Wherefore, the Apostle warns the faithful always to covet earnestly the *better gifts*.

These then are the things which pertain to the duty of a king; each should be considered carefully and in detail.

SELECTED BIBLIOGRAPHY

McIlwain, Charles H., *Growth of Political Thought in the West*, pp. 324-338.
Sabine, George H., *A History of Political Theory*, pp. 247-257.
Cook, Thomas I., *History of Political Philosophy*, pp. 216-227.
Dunning, William A., *Political Theories, Ancient and Mediæval*, ch. 8.

Aveling, F., "St. Thomas Aquinas and the Papal Monarchy," in F. J. C. Hearnshaw, ed., *The Social and Political Ideas of Some Great Mediæval Thinkers* (New York and London, 1923), ch. 4.
Carlyle, R. W. and A. J., *History of Mediæval Political Theory in the West* (Edinburgh and London, 1903-1936), Vol. V, pp. 9-24, 31-44, 67-70, 89-97, 348-354.
"Encyclical Letter of . . . Pope Leo XIII on The Restoration of Christian Philosophy, According to the Mind of St. Thomas Aquinas, the Angelic Doctor": pp. ix-xxxiii in part I, First Number, of *The Summa Theologica of St. Thomas Aquinas*, literally translated by Fathers of the English Dominican Province. 20 vols. (London, New York, etc., 1911-35). "The Scholastic Philosophy": *Ibid.*, pp. xxxvii-lx.
Jarrett, Bede, *Social Theories of the Middle Ages* (Boston, 1926), *passim*.
Vaughn, Roger W. B., *The Life and Labours of Saint Thomas of Aquin* (second ed., abridged and edited by David Jerome Vaughn, London and New York, 1890), chs. 15-21.
Wulf, Maurice de, *Mediæval Philosophy Illustrated from the System of Thomas Aquinas* (Cambridge, 1924), ch. 15: "Group Life and the State."
Franck, Adolphe, *Réformateurs et publicistes de l'Europe. Moyen-âge—Renaissance* (Paris, 1864), pp. 39-69.

Murphy, Edward Francis, *St. Thomas' Political Doctrine and Democracy* (Washington, 1921).
Roland-Gosselin, Bernard, *La doctrine politique de Saint Thomas d'Aquin* (Paris, 1928).
Schilling, Otto, *Die Staats- und Soziallehre des heiligen Thomas von Aquin* (Paderborn, 1923).
Zeiller, J., *L'idée de l'état dans Saint Thomas d'Aquin* (Paris, 1910).
Baumann, J. J., *Die Staatslehre des h. Thomas von Aquino* (Leipsic, 1873; 1909).
Feugueray, H. R., *Essai sur les doctrines politiques de Saint Thomas d'Aquin* (Paris, 1857).

DANTE

VIII. DANTE (1265-1321)

INTRODUCTION

Dante has been called the first learned layman of the middle ages. His renown rests chiefly upon his literary productions. But the experiences of his life led him into careful and original thinking upon certain questions of civil government. The habitual antagonism between imperial and papal authority had assumed a special phase in Italian politics in the twelfth and thirteenth centuries. The German Emperor claimed political supremacy over the Italian cities; the broader conflict thus became involved in Italy with the resistance offered by these cities, and their defenders, to the Emperor's designs. Furthermore, family feuds and rivalries among political factions divided upon local issues, were common in Italy in that period; and these local strifes became entangled in the more far-reaching combat.

Dante was born in Florence at the time when these contentions were at their worst; and throughout his life he was implicated in the many-sided conflict. His family was of the Guelf or anti-imperial party. After the decisive triumph of this party over the Ghibelline, or pro-imperial, party, in 1289, Dante served several times in the councils of Florence. He subsequently aligned himself with a new faction, which, though an offshoot from the Guelf party, was, nevertheless, inclined to Ghibelline opinions. The defeat of this branch by the dominant Guelfs brought about the banishment of Dante from Florence. In exile he wrote his political work—the De Monarchia (c. 1311).

Dante believed that the success of the efforts of the Emperor, Henry VII., to bring the Italian cities under his sway was essential to peace in Italy; and the inspiration of the De Monarchia was the author's desire to find a power that would be competent to secure for Italy permanent deliverance from the rivalries and strifes among communities, classes, and families. He established his plea for peace upon a broad foundation. He held that for the

225

complete development of man's characteristic faculties a life of repose was indispensable, and that lasting peace could be maintained
only under a universal empire. By universal empire he meant
the rule of a single head controlling the whole human race in all
temporal relations and interests. He developed this main thesis
from *a priori* principles; but he drew confirmation for his conclusions from analogies in nature, from scriptural parallels, and from
the history of Rome. The argument is in three stages, which
form the subjects, respectively, of the three books of the volume.
The first proposition is that universal monarchy is essential to
human welfare; the direct action of this common sovereignty is
to be principally as mediator and as preserver of peace, national
autonomy and individual liberty being maintained in so far as
compatible with the primary end of the universal state. Secondly,
the preëminent historical type of the universal state is the Roman
Empire, which attained its extensive sway with divine sanction—
evidenced in the continued success accorded by divine justice
to Roman arms. Thirdly, imperial authority comes directly from
God, and not through any vicar; in other words, the imperial power
is independent of the papal power in all secular affairs.

The Holy Roman Empire had lost its hegemony of Europe, and
never regained it. Accordingly, the *De Monarchia* has been characterized as "an epitaph, instead of a prophecy." However, Dante
was one of the first medieval writers to maintain that the possession
of temporal power is incompatible with the nature of the church.

READINGS FROM THE DE MONARCHIA [1]

1. *The End of Civil Order.   The State* [2]

I. It very greatly concerns all men on whom a higher nature
has impressed the love of truth, that, as they have been enriched
by the labor of those before them, so they also should labor
for those that are to come after them, to the end that posterity
may receive from them an addition to its wealth. For he is far
astray from his duty—let him not doubt it—who, having been
trained in the lessons of public business, cares not himself to
contribute aught to the public good. He is no "tree planted by

---

[1] The selections are taken from the *De Monarchia*, translated by F. J. Church.
London, 1879.   (Bound with *Dante, an Essay*, by R. W. Church.)   The Macmillan Co.   A few of the translator's notes are reproduced.
[2] Bk. I, i–v.

the water-side, that bringeth forth his fruit in due season." He is rather the devouring whirlpool, ever engulfing, but restoring nothing. Pondering, therefore, often on these things, lest some day I should have to answer the charge of the talent buried in the earth, I desire not only to show the budding promise, but also to bear fruit for the general good, and to set forth truths by others unattempted. For what fruit can he be said to bear who should go about to demonstrate again some theorem of Euclid? or when Aristotle has shown us what happiness is, should show it to us once more? or when Cicero has been the apologist of old age, should a second time undertake its defence? Such squandering of labor would only engender weariness and not profit.

But seeing that among other truths, ill-understood yet profitable, the knowledge touching temporal monarchy is at once most profitable and most obscure, and that because it has no immediate reference to worldly gain it is left unexplored by all, therefore it is my purpose to draw it forth from its hiding-places, as well that I may spend my toil for the benefit of the world, as that I may be the first to win the prize of so great an achievement to my own glory. The work indeed is difficult, and I am attempting what is beyond my strength; but I trust not in my own powers, but in the light of that Bountiful Giver, "Who giveth to all men liberally, and upbraideth not."

II. First, therefore, we must see what is it that is called Temporal Monarchy, in its idea, so to speak, and according to its purpose. Temporal Monarchy, then, or, as men call it, the Empire, is the government of one prince above all men in time, or in those things and over those things which are measured by time. Three great questions are asked concerning it. First, there is the doubt and the question, is it necessary for the welfare of the world? Secondly, did the Roman people take to itself by right the office of Monarchy? And thirdly, does the authority of Monarchy come from God directly, or only from some other minister or vicar of God?

Now, since every truth, which is not itself a first principle, becomes manifest from the truth of some first principle, it is therefore necessary in every inquiry to have a knowledge of the first principle involved, to which by analysis we may go back for the certainty of all the propositions which are afterwards accepted. And since this treatise is an inquiry, we must begin by examining the first principle on the strength of which deductions are to rest. It must be understood then that there are certain things which, since they are not subject to our power, are matters of speculation, but not of action: such are Mathematics and Physics, and things divine. But there are some things which, since they are subject to our power, are matters of action as well as of speculation, and in them we do not act for the sake of speculation, but contrariwise: for in such things action is the end. Now, since the matter which we have in hand has to do with states, nay, with the very origin and principle of good forms of government, and since all that concerns states is subject to our power, it is manifest that our subject is not in the first place speculation, but action. And again, since in matters of action the end sought is the first principle and cause of all (for that it is which first moves the agent to act), it follows that all our method concerning the means which are set to gain the end must be taken from the end. For there will be one way of cutting wood to build a house, and another to build a ship. That therefore, if it exists, which is the ultimate end for the universal civil order of mankind, will be the first principle from which all the truth of our future deductions will be sufficiently manifest. But it is folly to think that there is an end for this and for that particular civil order, and yet not one end for all.

III. Now, therefore, we must see what is the end of the whole civil order of men; and when we have found this, then, as the Philosopher says in his book of Nicomachus, the half of our labor will have been accomplished. And to render the question clearer, we must observe that as there is a certain end for which nature makes the thumb, and another, different from this, for which she makes the whole hand, and again another for which she makes the arm, and another different from all for which she makes the whole man; so there is one end for which she orders the individual man, and another for which she orders the family, and another end for the city, and another for the kingdom, and finally an ultimate one for which the Everlasting God, by His art which is nature, brings into being the whole human race. And this is what we seek as a first principle to guide our whole inquiry.

Let it then be understood that God and nature make nothing to be idle. Whatever comes into being, exists for some operation or working. For no created essence is an ultimate end in the creator's purpose, so far as he is a creator, but rather the proper operation of that essence. Therefore it follows that the operation does not exist for the sake of the essence, but the essence for the sake of the operation.

There is therefore a certain proper operation of the whole body of human kind, for which this whole body of men in all its multitudes is ordered and constituted, but to which no one man, nor single family, nor single neighborhood, nor single city, nor particular kingdom can attain. What this is will be manifest, if we can find what is the final and characteristic capacity of humanity as a whole. I say then that no quality which is shared by different species of things is the distinguishing capacity of any one of them. For were it so, since this capacity is that which makes each species what it is, it would follow that one essence would be specifically distributed to many species, which is impossible. Therefore the ultimate quality of men is not existence, taken simply; for the elements share therein. Nor is it existence under certain conditions;[1] for we find this in minerals too. Nor is it existence with life; for plants too have life. Nor is it percipient existence; for brutes share in this power. It is to be percipient [2] with the possibility of understanding, for this quality falls to the lot of none but man, either above or below him. For though there are other beings which with him have understanding, yet this understanding is not as man's, capable of development. For such beings are only certain intellectual natures, and not anything besides, and their being is nothing other than to understand; which is without interruption, otherwise they would not be eternal. It is plain, therefore, that <u>the distinguishing quality of humanity is the faculty or the power of understanding.</u>

And because this faculty cannot be realized in act in its entirety at one time by a single man, nor by any of the individual societies which we have marked, therefore there must be multitude in the human race, in order to realize it: just as it is necessary that there should be a multitude of things which can be brought into being, so that the capacity of the primal matter for being acted on may be ever open to what acts on it. For if this were not so, we could speak of a capacity apart from its substance, which is impossible. And with this opinion Averroes, in his comment on [Aristotle's] treatise on the Soul, agrees. For the capacity for understanding, of which I speak, is concerned not only with universal forms or species, but also, by a kind of extension, with particular ones. Therefore it is commonly said that the speculative understanding becomes practical by extension; and then its end is to do and to make. This I say in reference to things which may be *done*, which are regulated by political wisdom, and in reference to things which may be *made*, which are regulated by art; all which things wait as handmaidens on the speculative

[1] "*Esse complexionatum.*"—Ch.
[2] "*Apprehensivum per intellectum possibilem.*"—Ch.

intellect, as on that best good, for which the Primal Goodness created the human race. Hence the saying of _The Politics_ that those who are strong in understanding are the natural rulers of others.

IV. It has thus been sufficiently set forth that the proper work of the human race, taken as a whole, is to set in action the whole capacity of that understanding which is capable of development: first in the way of speculation, and then, by its extension, in the way of action. And seeing that what is true of a part is true also of the whole, and that it is by rest and quiet that the individual man becomes perfect in wisdom and prudence; so the human race, by living in the calm and tranquillity of peace, applies itself most freely and easily to its proper work; a work which according to the saying, "Thou hast made him a little lower than the angels," is almost divine. Whence it is manifest that of all things that are ordered to secure blessings to men, peace is the best. And hence the word which sounded to the shepherds from above was not riches, nor pleasure, nor honor, nor length of life, nor health, nor strength, nor beauty; but peace. For the heavenly host said: "Glory to God in the highest, and on earth, peace to men of goodwill." Therefore also, "Peace be with you," was the salutation of the Saviour of mankind. For it behoved Him, who was the greatest of saviours, to utter in His greeting the greatest of saving blessings. And this custom His disciples, too, chose to preserve; and Paul also did the same in his greetings, as may appear manifest to all.

Now that we have declared these matters, it is plain what is the better, nay the best, way in which mankind may attain to do its proper work. And consequently we have seen the readiest means by which to arrive at the point, for which all our works are ordered, as their ultimate end; namely, the universal peace, which is to be assumed as the first principle for our deductions. As we said, this assumption was necessary, for it is as a sign-post to us, that into it we may resolve all that has to be proved, as into a most manifest truth.

V. As therefore we have already said, there are three doubts, and these doubts suggest three questions, concerning Temporal Monarchy, which in more common speech is called the Empire; and our purpose is, as we explained, to inquire concerning these questions in their given order, and starting from the first principle which we have just laid down. The first question, then, is whether Temporal Monarchy is necessary for the welfare of the world; and that it is necessary can, I think, be shown by the strongest and most manifest arguments; for nothing, either of reason or of authority, opposes me. Let us first take the authority of the Philosopher in his *Politics*. There, on his venerable authority, it is said that where a number of things are arranged to attain an end, it behoves one of them to regulate or govern the others, and the others to submit. And it is not only the authority of his illustrious name which makes this worthy of belief, but also reason, instancing particulars.

If we take the case of a single man, we shall see the same rule manifested in him: all his powers are ordered to gain happiness; but his understanding is what regulates and governs all the others; and otherwise he would never attain to happiness. Again, take a single household: its end is to fit the members thereof to live well; but there must be one to regulate and rule it, who is called the father of the family, or, it may be, one who holds his office. As the Philosopher says: "Every house is ruled by the oldest." And, as Homer says, it is his duty to make rules and laws for the rest. Hence the proverbial curse: "Mayst thou have an equal at home." Take a single village: its end is suitable assistance as regards persons and goods, but one in it must be the ruler of the rest, either set over them by another, or with their consent, the head man amongst them. If it be not so, not only do its inhabitants fail of this mutual assistance, but the whole neighborhood is sometimes wholly ruined by the ambition of many, who each of them wish to rule. If, again, we take a single city: its end is to secure a good and sufficient life to the citizens; but one man must be ruler in imperfect as well as in good forms of the state. If it is otherwise, not only is the end of civil life lost, but the city too ceases to be what it was. Lastly, if we take any one kingdom, of which the end is the same as that of a city, only with greater security for its tranquillity, there must be one king to rule and govern. For if this is not so, not only do his subjects miss their end, but the kingdom itself falls to destruction, according to that word of the infallible truth: "Every kingdom divided against itself shall be brought to desolation." If then this holds good in these cases, and in each individual thing which is ordered to one certain end, what we have laid down is true.

Now it is plain that the whole human race is ordered to gain some end, as has been before shown. There must, therefore, be one to guide and govern, and the proper title for this office is Monarch or Emperor. And so it is plain that Monarchy or the Empire is necessary for the welfare of the world.

2. Universal Empire [1]

X. Wherever there is controversy, there ought to be judgment, otherwise there would be imperfection without its proper remedy,[2] which is impossible; for God and Nature, in things necessary, do not fail in their provisions. But it is manifest that there may be controversy between any two princes, where the one is not subject to the other, either from the fault of themselves or even of their subjects. Therefore between them there should be means of judgment. And since, when one is not subject to the other, he cannot be judged by the other (for there is no rule of equals over equals), there must be a third prince of wider jurisdiction, within the circle of whose laws both may come. Either he will or he will not be a Monarch. If he is, we have what we sought; if not, then this one again will have an equal, who is not subject to his jurisdiction, and then again we have need of a third. And so we must either go on to infinity, which is impossible, or we must come to that judge who is first and highest; by whose judgment all controversies shall be either directly or indirectly decided; and he will be Monarch or Emperor. Monarchy is therefore necessary to the world, and this the Philosopher saw when he said: "The world is not intended to be disposed in evil order; 'in a multitude of rulers there is evil, therefore let there be one prince.'"

XII. Again, the human race is ordered best when it is most free. This will be manifest if we see what is the principle of freedom. It must be understood that the first principle of our freedom is freedom of will, which many have in their mouth, but few understand. For they come so far as to say that freedom of the will means a free judgment concerning will. And this is true. But what is meant by the words is far from them: and they do just as our logicians do all day long with certain propositions which are set as examples in the books of logic, as that, "the three angles of a triangle are equal to two right angles."

Therefore I say that Judgment is between Apprehension and Appetite. First, a man apprehends a thing; then he judges it to be good or bad; then he pursues or avoids it accordingly. If therefore the Judgment guides the Appetite wholly, and in no way is forestalled by the Appetite, then is the Judgment free. But if the Appetite in any way at all forestalls the Judgment and

---

[1] Bk. I, x, xii, xv–xvi.
[2] "Sine proprio perfectivo."—Ch.

guides it, then the Judgment cannot be free: it is not its own: it is captive to another power. Therefore the brute beasts cannot have freedom of Judgment; for in them the Appetite always forestalls the Judgment. Therefore, too, it is that intellectual beings whose wills are unchangeable, and souls which are separate from the body, which have gone hence in peace, do not lose the freedom of their wills, because their wishes cannot change; nay, it is in full strength and completeness that their wills are free.

It is therefore again manifest that this liberty, or this principle of all our liberty, is the greatest gift bestowed by God on mankind: by it alone we gain happiness as men: by it alone we gain happiness elsewhere as gods. But if this is so, who will say that humankind is not in its best state, when it can most use this principle? But he who lives under a Monarchy is most free. Therefore let it be understood that he is free who exists not for another's sake but for his own, as the Philosopher, in his Treatise of simple Being, thought. For everything which exists for the sake of some other thing is necessitated by that other thing, as a road has run to its ordained end. Men exist for themselves, and not at the pleasure of others, only if a Monarch rules; for then only are the perverted forms of government set right, while democracies, oligarchies, and tyrannies, drive mankind into slavery, as is obvious to any who goes about among them all; and public power is in the hands of kings and aristocracies, which they call the rule of the best, and champions of popular liberty. And because the Monarch loves his subjects much, as we have seen, he wishes all men to be good, which cannot be the case in perverted forms of government: therefore the Philosopher says, in his *Politics:* "In the bad state the good man is a bad citizen, but in the good state the two coincide." Good states in this way aim at liberty, that in them men may live for themselves. The citizens exist not for the good of consuls, nor the nation for the good of its king; but the consuls for the good of the citizens, and the king for the good of his nation. For as the laws are made to suit the state, and not the state to suit the laws, so those who live under the laws are not ordered for the legislator, but he for them; as also the Philosopher holds, in what he has left us on the present subject. Hence, too, it is clear that although the king or the consul rule over the other citizens in respect of the means of government, yet in respect of the end of government they are the servants of the citizens, and especially the Monarch, who, without doubt, must be held the servant of all. Thus it becomes clear that the Monarch is bound by the end appointed to himself in making his laws. Therefore mankind is best off under a Monarchy, and hence it follows that Monarchy is necessary for the welfare of the world.

XV. I say also that Being, and Unity, and the Good come in order after the fifth mode of priority.[1] For Being comes by nature before Unity, and Unity before Good. Where Being is most, there Unity is greatest; and where Unity is greatest, there Good is also greatest; and in proportion as anything is far from Being in its highest form, is it far from Unity, and therefore from Good. Therefore in every kind of things, that which is most one is best, as the Philosopher holds in the treatise about simple Being. Therefore it appears that to be one is the root of Good, and to be many the root of Evil. Therefore, Pythagoras in his parallel tables placed the one, or Unity, under the line of good, and the many under the line of Evil; as appears from the first book of the *Metaphysics*. Hence we may see that to sin is nothing else than to pass on from the one which we despise and to seek many things, as the Psalmist saw when he said: "By the fruit of their corn and wine and oil, are they multiplied."

Hence it is plain that whatever is good, is good for this reason, that it consists in unity. And because concord is a good thing in so far as it is concord, it is manifest that it consists in a certain unity, as its proper root, the nature of which will appear if we find the real nature of concord. Concord then is the uniform motion of many wills; and hence it appears that a unity of wills, by which is meant their uniform motion, is the root of concord, nay, concord itself. For as we should say that many clods of earth are concordant, because that they all gravitate together towards the center; and that many flames are concordant because that they all ascend together towards the circumference, if they did this of their own free will, so we say that many men are in concord because that they are all moved together, as regards their willing, to one thing, which one thing is formally in their wills just as there is one quality formally in the clods of earth, that is gravity, and one in the flame of fire, that is lightness. For the force of willing is a certain power; but the quality of good which it apprehends is its form; which form, like as others, being one is multiplied in itself, according to the multiplication of the matters which receive it, as the soul, and numbers, and other forms which belong to what is compound.

[1] Arist. *Categ.*, e. g.: Priority is said in five ways. 1. First in *time*. 2. First in *pre-supposition*. 3. First in *order*. 4. First in *excellence*. 5. First in *logical sequence*.—Ch.

To explain our assumption as we proposed, let us argue thus: All concord depends on unity which is in wills; the human race, when it is at its best, is a kind of concord; for as one man at his best is a kind of concord, and as the like is true of the family, the city, and the kingdom; so is it of the whole human race. Therefore the human race at its best depends on the unity which is in will. But this cannot be unless there be one will to be the single mistress and regulating influence of all the rest. For the wills of men, on account of the blandishments of youth, require one to direct them, as Aristotle shows in the tenth book of his *Ethics*. And this cannot be unless there is one prince over all, whose will shall be the mistress and regulating influence of all the others. But if all these conclusions be true, as they are, it is necessary for the highest welfare of the human race that there should be a Monarch in the world; and therefore Monarchy is necessary for the good of the world.

XVI. To all these reasons alleged above a memorable experience adds its confirmation. I mean that condition of mankind which the Son of God, when, for the salvation of man, He was about to put on man, either waited for, or, at the moment when He willed, Himself so ordered. For if, from the fall of our first parents, which was the turning point at which all our going astray began, we carry our thoughts over the distribution of the human race and the order of its times, we shall find that never but under the divine Augustus, who was sole ruler, and under whom a perfect Monarchy existed, was the world everywhere quiet. And that then the human race was happy in the tranquillity of universal peace, this is the witness of all writers of history; this is the witness of famous poets; this, too, he who wrote the story of the "meekness and gentleness of Christ" has thought fit to attest. And last of all, Paul has called that most blessed condition "the fulness of the times." For then, indeed, time was full, and all the things of time; because no office belonging to our felicity wanted its minister. But how the world has fared since that "seamless robe" has suffered rending by the talons of ambition, we may read in books; would that we might not see it with our eyes. Oh, race of mankind! what storms must toss thee, what losses must thou endure, what shipwrecks must buffet thee, as long as thou, a beast of many heads, strivest after contrary things! Thou art sick in both thy faculties of understanding; thou art sick in thine affections. Unanswerable reasons fail to heal thy higher understanding; the very sight of experience convinces not thy lower understanding; not even the sweetness of divine persuasion charms thy affections, when it breathes into thee through the music of the Holy Ghost: "Behold, how good and how pleasant a thing it is, brethren, to dwell together in unity." [1]

3. *The Divine Basis of Temporal Authority* [2]

I. "He hath shut the lions' mouths and they have not hurt me, forasmuch as before Him justice was found in me." [3] At the beginning of this work I proposed to examine into three questions, according as the subject-matter would permit me. Concerning the two first questions our inquiry, as I think, has been sufficiently accomplished in the preceding books. It remains to treat of the third question; and, perchance, it may arouse a certain amount of indignation against me, for the truth of it cannot appear without causing shame to certain men. But seeing that truth from its changeless throne appeals to me—that Solomon, too, entering on the forest of his proverbs, teaches me in his own person "to meditate on truth, to hate the wicked;" [4] seeing that the Philosopher, my instructor in morals, bids me, for the sake of truth, to put aside what is dearest; I will, therefore, take confidence from the words of Daniel in which the power of God, the shield of the defenders of truth, is set forth, and, according to the exhortation of St. Paul, "putting on the breast-plate of faith," and in the heat of that coal which one of the seraphim had taken from off the altar, and laid on the lips of Isaiah, I will enter on the present contest, and, by the arm of Him who delivered us by His blood from the powers of darkness, drive out from the lists the wicked and the liar, in the sight of all the world. Why should I fear, when the Spirit, which is co-eternal with the Father and the Son, saith by the mouth of David: "The righteous shall be had in everlasting remembrance, he shall not be afraid of evil tidings"? [5]

The present question, then, concerning which we have to inquire, is between two great luminaries, the Roman Pontiff and the Roman Prince: and the question is, does the authority of the Roman Monarch, who, as we have proved in the second book, is the monarch of the world, depend immediately on God, or on some minister or vicar of God; by whom I understand the successor of Peter, who truly has the keys of the kingdom of heaven?

[1] Ps. cxxxiii. 1.
[3] Dan. vi. 22. Vulg.
[5] Ps. cxii. 7.

[2] Bk. III, i, iii, xvi.
[4] Prov. vii. 7. Vulg.

III. At the outset we must note in reference to this third question, that the truth of the first question had to be made manifest rather to remove ignorance than to end a dispute. In the second question we sought equally to remove ignorance and to end a dispute. For there are many things of which we are ignorant, but concerning which we do not quarrel. In geometry we know not how to square the circle, but we do not quarrel on that point. The theologian does not know the number of the angels, but he does not quarrel about the number. The Egyptian is ignorant of the political system of the Scythians, but he does not therefore quarrel concerning it. But the truth in this third question provokes so much quarreling that, whereas in other matters ignorance is commonly the cause of quarreling, here quarreling is the cause of ignorance. For this always happens where men are hurried by their wishes past what they see by their reason; in this evil bias they lay aside the light of reason, and being dragged on blindly by their desires, they obstinately deny that they are blind. And, therefore, it often follows not only that falsehood has its own inheritance, but that many men issue forth from their own bounds and stray through the foreign camp, where they understand nothing, and no man understands them; and so they provoke some to anger, and some to scorn, and not a few to laughter.

Now three classes of men chiefly strive against the truth which we are trying to prove.

First, the Chief Pontiff, Vicar of our Lord Jesus Christ and the successor of Peter, to whom we owe, not indeed all that we owe to Christ, but all that we owe to Peter, contradicts this truth, urged it may be by zeal for the keys; and also other pastors of the Christian sheepfolds, and others whom I believe to be only led by zeal for our mother, the Church. These all, perchance from zeal and not from pride, withstand the truth which I am about to prove.

But there are certain others in whom obstinate greed has extinguished the light of reason, who are of their father the devil, and yet pretend to be sons of the Church. They not only stir up quarrels in this question, but they hate the name of the most sacred office of Prince, and would shamelessly deny the principles which we have laid down for this and the previous questions.

There is also a third class called Decretalists, utterly without knowledge or skill in philosophy or theology, who, relying entirely on their Decretals (which doubtless, I think, should be venerated), and hoping, I believe, that these Decretals will prevail, disparage

the power of the Empire. And no wonder, for I have heard of
them, speaking of these Decretals, assert shamelessly that the
traditions of the Church are the foundation of the faith. May
this wickedness be taken away from the thoughts of men by those
who antecedently to the traditions of the Church, have believed
in Christ the Son of God, whether to come, or present, or as
having already suffered; and who from their faith have hoped,
and from their hope have kindled into love, and who, burning with love, will, the world doubts not, be made co-heirs with
Him.

And that such arguers may be excluded once for all from the
present debate, it must be noted that part of the Scripture was
before the Church, that part of it came *with* the Church, and part
after the Church.

Before the Church were the Old and the New Testament—the
covenant which the Psalmist says was "commanded for ever,"
of which the Church speaks to her Bridegroom, saying: "Draw
me after thee." [1]

With the Church came those venerable chief Councils, with
which no faithful Christian doubts but that Christ was present.
For we have his own words to His disciples when He was about to
ascend into heaven: "Lo, I am with you always, even unto the
end of the world," to which Matthew testifies. There are also
the writings of the doctors, Augustine and others, of whom, if
any doubt that they were aided by the Holy Spirit, either he has
never beheld their fruit, or if he has beheld, he has never tasted
thereof.

After the Church are the traditions which they call Decretals,
which, although they are to be venerated for their apostolical
authority, yet we must not doubt that they are to be held inferior
to fundamental Scripture, seeing that Christ rebuked the Pharisees
for this very thing; for when they had asked: "Why do thy
disciples transgress the tradition of the elders?" (for they neglected
the washing of hands), He answered them as Matthew testifies:
"Why do ye also transgress the commandment of God by your
tradition?" Thus He intimates plainly that tradition was to
have a lower place.

But if the traditions of the Church are *after* the Church, it
follows that the Church had not its authority from traditions,
but rather traditions from the Church; and, therefore, the men of
whom we speak, seeing that they have nought but traditions, must
be excluded from the debate. For those who seek after this

[1] Ps. cxi. 9. Cant. i. 3.

truth must proceed in their inquiry from those things from which flows the authority of the Church.

Further, we must exclude others who boast themselves to be white sheep in the flock of the Lord, when they have the plumage of crows. These are the children of wickedness, who, that they may be able to follow their evil ways, put shame on their mother, drive out their brethren, and when they have done all will allow none to judge them. Why should we seek to reason with these, when they are led astray by their evil desires, and so cannot see even our first principle?

Therefore there remains the controversy only with the other sort of men who are influenced by a certain kind of zeal for their mother the Church, and yet know not the truth which is sought for. With these men, therefore—strong in the reverence which a dutiful son owes to his father, which a duitful son owes to his mother, dutiful to Christ, dutiful to the Church, dutiful to the Chief Shepherd, dutiful to all who profess the religion of Christ —I begin in this book the contest for the maintenance of the truth.

XVI. Although it has been proved in the preceding chapter that the authority of the Empire has not its cause in the authority of the Supreme Pontiff; for we have shown that this argument led to absurd results; yet it has not been entirely shown that the authority of the Empire depends directly upon God, except as a result from our argument. For it is a consequence that, if the authority comes not from the vicar of God, it must come from God Himself. And therefore, for the complete determination of the question proposed, we have to prove directly that the emperor or monarch of the world stands in an immediate relation to the King of the universe, who is God.

For the better comprehending of this, it must be recognized that man alone, of all created things, holds a position midway between things corruptible and things incorruptible; and therefore philosophers rightly liken him to a dividing line between two hemispheres. For man consists of two essential parts, namely, the soul and the body. If he be considered in relation to his body only, he is corruptible; but if he be considered in relation to his soul only, he is incorruptible. And therefore the Philosopher spoke well concerning the incorruptible soul when he said in the second book "of the Soul:" "It is this alone which may be separated, as being eternal, from the corruptible."

If, therefore, man holds this position midway between the corruptible and the incorruptible, since every middle nature partakes of both extremes, man must share something of each nature. And since every nature is ordained to gain some final end, it follows that for man there is a double end. For as he alone of all beings participates both in the corruptible and the incorruptible, so he alone of all beings is ordained to gain two ends, whereby one is his end in so far as he is corruptible, and the other in so far as he is incorruptible.

Two ends, therefore, have been laid down by the ineffable providence of God for man to aim at: the blessedness of this life, which consists in the exercise of his natural powers, and which is prefigured in the earthly Paradise; and next, the blessedness of the life eternal, which consists in the fruition of the sight of God's countenance, and to which man by his own natural powers cannot rise, if he be not aided by the divine light; and this blessedness is understood by the heavenly Paradise.

But to these different kinds of blessedness, as to different conclusions, we must come by different means. For at the first we may arrive by the lessons of philosophy, if only we will follow them, by acting in accordance with the moral and intellectual virtues. But at the second we can only arrive by spiritual lessons, transcending human reason, so that we follow them in accordance with the theological virtues, faith, hope, and charity. The truth of the first of these conclusions and of these means is made manifest by human reason, which by the philosophers has been all laid open to us. The other conclusions and means are made manifest by the Holy Spirit, who by the mouth of the Prophets and holy writers, and by Jesus Christ, the co-eternal Son of God, and His disciples, has revealed to us supernatural truth of which we have great need. Nevertheless human passion would cast them all behind its back, if it were not that men, going astray like the beasts that perish, were restrained in their course by bit and bridle, like horses and mules.

Therefore man had need of two guides for his life, as he had a twofold end in life; whereof one is the Supreme Pontiff, to lead mankind to eternal life, according to the things revealed to us; and the other is the Emperor, to guide mankind to happiness in this world, in accordance with the teaching of philosophy. And since none, or but a few only, and even they with sore difficulty, could arrive at this harbor of happiness, unless the waves and blandishments of human desires were set at rest, and the human race were free to live in peace and quiet, this therefore is the mark at which he who is to care for the world, and whom we call the Roman Prince, must most chiefly aim at: I mean, that in this little plot of earth belonging to mortal men, life may pass in freedom and with peace. And since the order of this world follows the order of the heavens, as they run their course, it is necessary, to the end that the learning which brings liberty and peace may be duly applied by this guardian of the world in fitting season and place, that this power should be dispensed by Him who is ever present to behold the whole order of the heavens. And this is He who alone has preordained this, that by it in His providence He might bind all things together, each in their own order.

But if this is so, God alone elects, God alone confirms: for there is none higher than God. And hence there is the further conclusion, that neither those who now are, nor any others who may, in whatsoever way, have been called "Electors," ought to have that name; rather they are to be held as declarers and announcers of the providence of God. And, therefore, it is that they to whom is granted the privilege of announcing God's will sometimes fall into disagreement; because that, all of them or some of them have been blinded by their evil desires, and have not discerned the face of God's appointment.

It is therefore clear that the authority of temporal Monarchy comes down, with no intermediate will, from the fountain of universal authority; and this fountain, one in its unity, flows through many channels out of the abundance of the goodness of God.

And now, methinks, I have reached the goal which I set before me. I have unravelled the truth of the question which I asked: whether the office of Monarchy was necessary to the welfare of the world; whether it was by right that the Roman people assumed to themselves the office of Monarchy; and, further, that last question, whether the authority of the Monarch springs immediately from God, or from some other. Yet the truth of this latter question must not be received so narrowly as to deny that in certain matters the Roman Prince is subject to the Roman Pontiff. For that happiness, which is subject to mortality, in a sense is ordered with a view to the happiness which shall not taste of death. Let, therefore, Cæsar be reverent to Peter, as the first-born son should be reverent to his father, that he may be illuminated with the light of his father's grace, and so may be stronger to lighten the world over which he has been placed by Him alone, who is the ruler of all things spiritual as well as temporal.

SELECTED BIBLIOGRAPHY

Sabine, George, *A History of Political Theory*, pp. 257–262.
Dunning, William A., *Political Theories, Ancient and Mediæval*, ch. 9, § 4.

Smith, E. Sharwood, "Dante and World-Empire," in F. J. C. Hearnshaw, ed., *The Social and Political Ideas of Some Great Mediæval Thinkers* (London and New York, 1923), ch. 5.

Carlyle, R. W. and A. J., *History of Mediæval Political Theory in the West*, Vol. VI (Edinburgh and London, 1936), pt. i, ch. 7.

Church, R. W., *Dante: an Essay* (London, 1879), pp. 13–48, 84–97.

Reade, W. H. V., "The Political Theory of Dante," in Edward Moore, ed., *Dante, De Monarchia* (Oxford, 1916): "Introduction."

Witte, Karl, "Dante and United Italy," in *Essays on Dante*, translated by C. M. Lawrence and P. H. Wicksteed (London, 1898).

Franck, Adolphe, *Réformateurs et publicistes de l'Europe. Moyen-âge—Renaissance* (Paris, 1864), pp. 103–134.

Gilbert, A. H., *Dante's Conception of Justice* (Duke University Publications: Durham, N. C., 1925).

Rolbiecki, John J., *The Political Philosophy of Dante Alighieri* (Washington, 1921).

Kelsen, Hans, *Die Staatslehre des Dante Alighieri* (Vienna, 1905).

MARSIGLIO

IX. MARSIGLIO OF PADUA (C. 1274–C. 1343)

INTRODUCTION

One of the most prolonged of the many contests between secular and ecclesiastical authorities in the middle ages was the dispute between Lewis of Bavaria and Pope John XXII, in the fourteenth century. This conflict originated in a contention for the German crown, between Lewis and a cousin. The Pope, instigated by the King of France, refused to recognize either claimant and put forward a third candidate. There then reappeared the controversy over the Pope's claim of right—through absolving subjects from their oaths of allegiance—to withhold sanction to the accession of a secular ruler. As in other such controversies a multitude of polemical tracts were put forth, arguing the old questions of ultimate supremacy as between the two authorities, and of the functions and powers appropriate to either. A dispute within the church brought additional support to Lewis; the dispute arose from the decree of Pope John attacking the doctrine of poverty held by the Franciscan order of friars. This action of the Pope evoked general antagonism to him on the part of the Franciscans; and among the leading defenders of the imperial claims in the contest between Lewis and the Pope were partisans of the Franciscans; the ablest of these was the Italian, Marsiglio of Padua.

Marsiglio was a member of the secular clergy; he seems also to have followed other callings, including the practice of medicine; and he was for a few months rector of the University of Paris. His *Defensor Pacis* (1324), [1] written in support of imperial authority and of its freedom from rightful control by the church, has been called "the greatest and most original political treatise of the middle ages." [2] It brings forward, early in the fourteenth century,

[1] The work was apparently written by Marsiglio in collaboration with John of Jandun, a professor at the University of Paris and the author of several commentaries on Aristotle. Some writers have attributed the chief authorship of Book I, from which the selections below are made, to the latter author; but most special students of the *Defensor* attribute the major authorship of all parts to Marsiglio.

[2] Reginald Lane Poole, *Illustrations of the History of Mediæval Thought* (1884), p. 265.

ideas which did not receive wide expression until the time of ecclesiastical reconstruction in the sixteenth century and the periods of political revolution in the seventeenth and eighteenth centuries.

Marsiglio enunciated far-reaching principles concerning the popular basis of government in state and in church, and the subordination of church to state. The end of political society, he held, is the good of the people; the maker of law is the whole body of citizens, or, at least, the "weightier part"[1] of them; the administration of government is in the hands of persons selected by the people and responsible to them, the sanction of this responsibility lying in the right of the people to discipline their governors for acting in disobedience to law or in excess of authority, and to depose them in case of flagrant dereliction of duty. Highest authority in the church, he further maintained, rests in a general council of believers summoned by the Emperor; the Pope should be chosen by the people, represented through secular rulers or through the general council; and the latter have authority to correct or depose the Pope.

Marsiglio drew freely from the ideas of Aristotle; he made somewhat less use of scriptural quotations than did his contemporaries. It is difficult in translating to escape the diffuseness and occasional obscurity of his style. However, the passages given below will reveal his advanced ideas in politics.

READINGS FROM THE DEFENSOR PACIS[2]

1. The Purpose of the State[3]

The state, according to Aristotle, is a perfect community, comprising every element of sufficiency in itself, and instituted

---

[1] Professor Charles H. McIlwain contends (in his *Growth of Political Thought in the West*, pp. 301 ff.) that most of the commentators on the *Defensor Pacis* have misinterpreted the words *valentior pars;* he argues that the author meant "dominant part" of the community, and not a majority or any large part of the people. However, the author frequently refers to the "number" (*quantitas*) as well as *qualitas* in indicating the proper source of law-making authority in the community. Moreover, it is difficult to understand the author's statement of his reasons for regarding law-making authority as vested in the community or in its *valentior pars*, unless he is understood to have had in mind substantial numbers of the members of the community.

[2] The translation is made from the text (based on the manuscripts) edited by C. W. Previté-Orton and published in 1928. By courtesy of the Cambridge University Press. Marsiglio's quotations from Aristotle are generally omitted.

[3] *Defensor Pacis*, Bk. I, ch. iv.

for the sake not merely of living, but of living well. The latter part of this definition indicates the ultimate purpose of the state; for they who live politically not only live—beasts and slaves do that; they live well, even though they may be wanting in the liberalizing products of civilization and enlightenment. As the object of the state is that men may live and live well, we must first treat of living, and of its modes; for the state is instituted for this and is necessary for everything done by men who live together as a community. We may enunciate the following first principle as a postulate held naturally by everyone: all men, if not bereft of reason or otherwise perverted, strive naturally for a complete and satisfying life; they also repel or shun that which is harmful, as every kind of animal does.

To live and live well—that is, as is befitting for man—has been customarily regarded under two aspects—the temporal or mundane, and the eternal or celestial. What eternal life is, the whole company of philosophers have not been able to show; nor is it among the things which are manifest in themselves; therefore, the philosophers have not concerned themselves with teaching the things which pertain to that sort of life. But concerning living and living well, in the mundane sense of the good life, and concerning the things which are essential to that life, renowned philosophers have given an almost complete demonstration. They have reached the conclusion that for fulfilling that life a civil community is necessary; for a sufficient life cannot be attained otherwise. Although observation and experience may teach us this truth, nevertheless we wish to point out more distinctly its cause, showing that, since man is innately composed of contrary elements, something of his substance is being continually wasted because of the conflicting actions and passions of these elements. Moreover, since man is born naked and unprotected from disturbances of the weather and the other elements, and is thus liable to suffering and destruction, he needs arts of diverse sorts whereby he may ward off noxious things. And since such arts cannot be employed save by a number of men, nor preserved save through their communication from age to age, it is necessary for men to congregate in order to acquire what is useful and escape what is injurious.

Among men thus congregated contention and strife arise naturally, which, if not regulated by the rule of justice, lead to division and conflict, and finally to the dissolution of the community. It is, therefore, necessary to introduce into the community the rule of justice and to set up a guardian, or protector.

Since it is the function of the guardian to restrain dangerous
transgressors and others who are agitators or who seek to harass
the community from within or without, the state must have
within itself the means of repression.   Moreover, the community
needs other conveniences, improvements, and arrangements
for safeguarding certain common matters—certain things in
time of peace, others in time of war ; it is, therefore, necessary
that there shall be in the community those who will provide
these things, in order that the common demands can be supplied
whenever expedient or necessary.

Besides the things mentioned above, which administer solely
to the needs of this life, there is something else which those who
live together civilly need : it relates to the affairs of the future
life promised to mankind through supernatural revelation from
God, though it is useful also for the affairs of the present life ; we
mean the worship and honor of God, and the giving of thanks
to Him for the benefits received in this world, as well as for those
to be received in the future world.   For instructing and guiding
men in these things the state must provide teachers.

We may then summarize what we have said.   Men are associated together for the sake of living sufficiently—that is, to obtain
the things which are necessary to themselves and to transmit such
things from generation to generation.   This congregation in its
perfected form, containing the limit of sufficiency in itself, is
called the state.   The various things needed by those desiring
to live well cannot be procured by men of a single rank or office.
It is necessary that there be diverse ranks or offices among the
members of the community, each rank or office contributing
something which man needs for the sufficiency of life.   These
various orders or offices of men constitute the multiplicity and
diversity of the parts of the state.

2.   The "People" as Legislator [1]

We now propose to point out the effective cause of law ; and
this we can demonstrate in plain terms.   Concerning the ordinances created directly by act or declaration of God without
the participation of human will, and concerning the institution
of the Mosaic law, we have not here to do—not even with the
political precepts which such laws provide for the affairs of this
life.   We are now concerned solely with the institution of law
and authority that proceed directly from the arbitrament of

[1] *Defensor Pacis*, Bk. I, ch. xii (in part).

the human mind. Law in its secular signification, or, in other words, the science of civil justice and expediency, can be discovered by any citizen; though such an exposition can be derived more properly from the observations of men who have opportunities for leisure, who are older and experienced in active affairs, and who are thus called "wise," than from the opinions of mechanics, whose energies are absorbed in obtaining the necessaries of physical life. But the knowledge and true discovery of the just and the expedient, and of their opposites, does not bring us to law in the ultimate and proper signification—as a standard for human civil acts—unless from that discovery a compulsive command has issued, set forth in the form of a command from one by whose authority transgressors ought to be and can be restrained. It is in order now, therefore, to determine who have the authority to make such a command and to restrain its transgressors: this is to inquire as to the originator, or maker, of law.

We declare, according to truth and the opinion of Aristotle, the *legislator*, or the prime and proper effective cause of law, to be the people or the whole body of citizens or its weightier part, commanding or deciding by its own choice or will, expressed verbally in a general assemblage of the citizens, that something be done or omitted concerning the civil actions of men, under a temporal punishment or penalty. I say weightier part, taking into consideration both the number of persons and their quality in the community for which the law is enacted.[1] The whole body of citizens, or its weightier part, either makes law directly or commits this duty to some one or few; the latter do not, and cannot, constitute the legislator in the strict sense of the term; they act only in such matters and for such periods as are covered by the authorization from the primary legislator. Laws, and anything else established through election, require the approbation of no other authority, and need no ceremonies or solemnities that are not demanded by the electors or that are not necessary to a valid election. Through the same process should be undertaken the expansion, elimination, or modification of laws, or their interpretation and suspension, as such may be required

[1] "Nos autem dicamus secundam veritatem atque consilium Aristotelis III *Politicae*, capitulo 6, *legislatorem* seu causam legis effectivam primam et propriam esse populum seu civium universitatem, aut eius valentiorem partem per suam electionem seu voluntatem in generali civium congregatione per sermonem expressam, praecipientem seu determinantem aliquid fieri vel omitti circa civiles actus humanos sub poena vel supplicio temporali: valentiorem inquam partem considerata quantitate personarum et qualitate in communitate illa super quam lex fertur."

for the common interest by the exigencies of time, place, or other circumstance. By the same authority likewise must laws be promulgated or proclaimed after their enactment, lest any citizen or stranger, delinquent in them, should be excused through ignorance. Following Aristotle, I call citizen him who participates in the civil community with either deliberative or judicial authority, according to his rank. By this definition boys, slaves, aliens, and women are distinguished, though in different respects, from citizens. For example, the sons of citizens are potential citizens, lacking citizenship solely through defect of age. . . .

Having thus defined citizen and the weightier multitude of citizens, we may return to the proposed task—namely, to demonstrate that human legislative authority pertains solely to the whole body of citizens or to its weightier part. . . . It is not easy, or even possible, for all persons to come to one opinion; for the nature of some is depraved, or divergent from the common opinion on account of malice or ignorance; the common deliberations ought not to be impeded or omitted because of the unreasonable complaints or disputes of these. Therefore, it is only to the whole body of citizens, or to its weightier part, that the authority of making or instituting law pertains. . . . Only out of the deliberation and will of the whole multitude is the best law produced; as Aristotle says: the best law is that which relates to the common advantage of the citizens, and right (in law, that is) is to be considered with reference to the advantage of the state and the common good of the citizens. . . . A majority can, more readily than any of its parts, discern the defect in a law proposed for enactment; for an entire body is greater in power and worth than any of its separate parts; and general utility is more apt to be found in law issuing from the whole multitude, since no one knowingly injures himself. Under such conditions, moreover, anyone can observe whether a proposed law tends to the advantage rather of a certain one or few than of others or of the community, and can protest; this is not possible where law is made by a single person or by a few who may seek their own rather than the common good. . . .

Let us return to our principal conclusion—namely, that the sole legislative authority is that authority from whom the best laws will proceed and whose laws will be most readily observed. This is the whole body of citizens; it has the authority to legislate. . . . A law is useless if it is not obeyed. The second proposition may be demonstrated as follows: since that law is better observed by any one of the citizens, which he seems to have imposed upon himself, the best law is made by the deliberation and command of the whole multitude of citizens. The first proposition seems almost axiomatic, since the state is a community of free men. . . . This cannot be if a single man or a few make law by their own authority over the whole body of citizens, for those making the law would be despots over the others. In such case the remainder of the citizens, perhaps the majority, would endure such a law, however good, with impatience, or not at all, and bearing contempt toward the law would contend that not having been invited to share in its creation they would in no wise observe it. On the other hand, any citizen will endure and obey a law, however irksome, that is made from the deliberation and consent of the whole multitude, because he himself seems to have imposed it upon himself and, therefore, cannot complain against it, but must suffer its penalties with an even mind. . . .

Most of this demonstration falls among those things approximately known in themselves, and among the permanent truths which are set forth in an earlier chapter. Men have come together into civil association for the sake of convenience and the resulting sufficiency of life, and in order to escape the opposite conditions. The things, therefore, which can effect the advantage or disadvantage of all ought to be known and heard by all, so that they may be able to seek the beneficial and repel the injurious. Thus we get laws; for in the proper adjustment of laws a great part of general human well-being consists. Under unjust laws, oppression, servitude, and intolerable miseries of the citizens arise, resulting finally in the dissolution of the polity. . . .

The authority for making laws pertains solely to the whole body of citizens, or to a single one or to the few. It cannot pertain to one man . . . for he, looking rather to his own than to the common interest, can, through ignorance or malice, produce a bad law, whence a tyranny will arise. For the same reason it cannot pertain to the few; they likewise in making law plan for a particular interest and not for the common good; we see this in oligarchies. For the opposite reasons, lawmaking pertains to the whole body of citizens or to its weightier part. For all citizens must be duly regulated by law, and no man knowingly does injury or injustice to himself; therefore, all, or at least most, desire a law adapted to the common good of the citizens.

Through the same process of reasoning it can be shown that the ratification, interpretation, and suspension of law pertain also to the authority of the sole legislator. This is true with respect to everything established through election. The right of approval or disapproval must pertain to those who have the authority of election, or to whomever they may endow with that function. The part would be greater than, or at least equal to, the whole, if that which is decreed by the whole can be nullified by some particular authority.

3. The Relation between Legislator and Government [1]

It now remains to show the effective cause of the governing function, through which cause the authority of government, established through election, is conferred upon some one or several persons. A prince is set up in authority not through knowledge of the laws or through practical wisdom or moral virtue, although these are the qualities of a perfect governor. For many may have these qualities who, lacking the authority, are not governors, unless perchance they are near to power. The effective power in the institution of a governing body, that is, in election, pertains to the legislator—that is, to the whole body of citizens. The latter likewise have the power of correcting the government, and even the power of deposition, should such become expedient for the common interest. . . . The manner of coming to agreement in election or appointment may vary in different countries. But whatever these differences may be, the election or appointment must always take place by the authority of the legislator, which is, as we have often said, the whole body of citizens or its weightier part. Now this proposition can be maintained by the same proofs by which we concluded that the power to make laws, and to change them, belonged to the whole body of citizens. We change only the lesser term of the conclusion, substituting the word "government" for the word "law."

This proposition can be tested by its own truth. For whoever has the power to create a form has the power to determine its underlying substance, as may be seen in all the productive acts. . . . In all things, both artificial and natural, this is apparent by induction. There is a reason for this; for the forms and their operation are the ends, the materials are the means. Since then it belongs to the whole body of citizens to create the form according to which civil acts are to be regulated—that is, the law—it belongs to the same body to determine the material or subject-matter of this form. . . . From this it seems possible

---

[1] *Defensor Pacis*, Bk. I, ch. xv (in part).

to infer consistently that a ruler who is elected without hereditary succession is greatly to be preferred to rulers who are hereditary. . . .

Thus one part of the state institutes and determines the other parts or offices of the state. The former we call the legislator; the latter we call the instrumental or executive, governing by virtue of the authority conferred upon it by the legislator and according to the form given to it by the same power—that is, according to law, in conformity to which it must always, as far as possible, perform and regulate civil acts. For though the legislator, as the first and proper source of authority, must determine who are to fulfill the various functions of the state, nevertheless, the governing part (*pars principans*) directs, and, under proper conditions, stays the execution of these functions as also of laws in general. For the execution of laws is more conveniently accomplished through such a body than through the entire multitude of citizens, since for this work one ruler or a few will suffice. In such duties the whole community would be vainly engaged and would be diverted from other necessary activities. The whole community is acting when the executive acts, since the latter acts according to the decision of the community—that is, according to law, which is more easily executed by a few or even one. . . .

SELECTED BIBLIOGRAPHY

Sabine, George H., *A History of Political Theory*, pp. 287–304.
McIlwain, Charles H., *Growth of Political Thought in the West*, pp. 297–313.
Cook, Thomas I., *History of Political Philosophy*, pp. 237–242.
Dunning, William A., *Political Theories, Ancient and Mediæval*, ch. 9, §§ 5–8.

Allen, J. W., "Marsilio of Padua and Mediæval Secularism," in F. J. C. Hearnshaw, ed., *The Social and Political Ideas of Some Great Mediæval Thinkers* (New York and London, 1923), ch. 7.
Carlyle, R. W. and A. J., *History of Mediæval Political Theory in the West*, vol. VI (Edinburgh and London, 1936), pt. i, ch. 1, and pp. 40–44.
Brampton, C. Kenneth, "Marsiglio of Padua . . . Life," in *English Historical Review*, vol. 37 (1922), pp. 501–515.
Previté-Orton, C. W., "Marsiglio of Padua . . . Doctrine," in *English Historical Review*, vol. 38 (1923), pp. 1–18.
Previté-Orton, C. W., "Marsilius of Padua": Annual Italian Lecture . . . Proceedings of the British Academy, vol. 21 (1935).
Sullivan, James, "Marsiglio of Padua and William of Ockham," in *American Historical Review*, vol. 2 (1896–97), pp. 409–426, 593–610.
Poole, Reginald Lane, *Illustrations of the History of Mediæval Thought in the Departments of Theology and Ecclesiastical Politics* (London, 1884), pp. 263–277.
Tooley, Marian J., "The Authorship of the *Defensor Pacis*," *Transactions of the Royal Historical Society*, Fourth Series, vol. 9 (London, 1926), pp. 85–106.
Valois, Noël, "Jean de Jandun et Marsile de Padoue, auteurs du Defensor pacis," in *Histoire littéraire de la France*, vol. 23 (1906), pp. 528–623.

Guggenheim, M., "Marsilius von Padua und die Staatslehre des Aristoteles," in *Historische Viertel-Jahresschrift*, vol. 7 (1904), pp. 343–362.

Riezler, Sigmund von, *Die literarischen Widersacher der Päpste zur Zeit Ludwig des Baiers* (Leipsic, 1874), pp. 30–41, 193–240.

Emerton, Ephram, *The Defensor Pacis of Marsiglio of Padua* (Cambridge, Mass., 1920).

Legarde, Georges de, *La naissance de l'esprit laïque au déclin du moyen âge*, 2 vols. (Vienna, 1934), Vol. II : *Marsile de Padoue ou le premier théoricien de l'État laïque*.

Stieglitz, Leopold, *Die Staatstheorie des Marsilius von Padua.*

Beiträge zur Kulturgeschichte des Mittelalters und der Renaissance, vol. 19 (Leipsic, 1914).

NICHOLAS OF CUSA

X. NICHOLAS OF CUSA (1401-1464)

INTRODUCTION

Our final selection for medieval political ideas is from the last of the greater medieval writers: Nicholas, a German prelate and theologian, native of Cues and thereby known as "Cusanus." Born in poverty, he obtained an advanced education only by the aid of his admiring employer. He secured a doctorate in law at the University of Padua, but after a brief and unpromising experience in legal practice he turned to the study of theology and took holy orders. He held high offices in the church, notably as Cardinal, as Bishop of Brixen, and as papal representative on various church missions. For a brief period he was one of the leaders of the "conciliar movement"—an effort to heal the "Great Schism" in the church and repress certain inefficient and corrupt practices in the papacy, through the deliberations of broadly representative councils vested with authority no less than that of the Popes themselves. He played an important part in the first of these councils—the Council of Basel (1431-38); but before the adjournment of this body he abandoned the conciliar party and became thenceforth a strong defender of papal supremacy. He continued to be active in the efforts to check the notorious ecclesiastical abuses, and he is known as one of the foremost of the "Reformers before the Reformation."

Nicholas' influence in the subsequent history of the church has been chiefly in the fields of theology and philosophy. He was among the first to break away from the extreme rationalism of the later scholasticism. In his philosophical works (notably *De docta ignorantia*, *De possest*, and *De conjecturis*), he maintained that God could be apprehended only through intuition, not reason; he insisted upon the limited and conjectural character of human knowledge, and rejected generally the presupposition of scholasticism that scientific demonstration could be applied to matters of revelation.

257

The significance of Nicholas in the history of political thought is derived from the ideas he set forth in a work (*De catholica concordantia*) written for the Council of Basel, in defense of the conciliar idea. Catholic harmony, he there contended, could be restored only through a recognition that the church, like other divinely sanctioned associations of men, is an organic unity; and that in an organic entity, the functionally diverse and interdependent parts can work together only where there is a directing and harmonizing organ so constituted as to be sensitive both to the needs of the parts and to the common interest of the whole. A general council, broadly representative of the faithful, fills this requirement for the church, and a similar body should function as the highest authority in matters of fundamental policy in the empire. Nicholas cited historical examples of the parts that such councils had played in both the church and the empire.

Following these organismic and historical arguments, Nicholas proceeded to a reasoning in terms, for the most part, of a principle of "divine and natural right" according to which the consent of those persons to whom a law applies forms the essential basis of the validity of the law. This approval is shown chiefly through usage and custom; and a body broadly representative of the community in which the law applies can best determine, in case of doubt, what is really the usage and custom. Nicholas is not altogether clear and consistent in showing how the people consent to the law that binds them in church or state. For the church, he repeatedly proclaims the supremacy of a General Council and contends that the Council may depose a corrupt or law-breaking Pope; yet he attributes high prerogatives to the Pope and acknowledges that only he can summon an official General Council. For the empire, he finds expressions of general popular consent in the choice of an Emperor by a few electors and in the approval of laws by small bodies composed chiefly of *ex officio* members. In the statement of his general argument, he expresses ideas that clearly anticipate the modern conceptions of law resting on consent and of consent expressed through a supreme representative body. With Nicholas and the other conciliarists, however, no organ makes the law. A general representative body, not necessarily made up of elected members, expresses the community's consent by stating the community's custom.

READINGS FROM DE CONCORDANTIA CATHOLICA [1]

1. The Basis of Authority in Law and Consent [2]

Bk. II, Ch. XII. Any one who notes the force of custom derived solely from usage easily understands how true it is that the force of a law consists in the voluntary submission to it by those bound by it. Accordingly, we respect that which is derived from custom, even when we do not know whether or not the consent of any ruler having authority to enact laws has intervened; and even though the force of custom should depend in part on the tacit consent of a superior, as in the case of many particular legally enacted customs (the same does not apply to prescribed human laws of general scope), nevertheless the principle of validity derived from usage, with no antecedent consent whatever, is evident in the case where the Holy Council of Nicæa argued from usage in regard to the authority of the patriarchs, adducing that the Roman Church has a like practice—namely, as the Roman pontiff has authority over all his own bishops, so the bishop of Alexandria ought by custom to have such an authority throughout Egypt; for it is decreed that custom be heeded in respect to the authority of the patriarchs. We see how great a degree of submissive obedience the Roman pontiff has acquired today, from usage and custom, beyond the sacred practices of old.

In short, one conclusion can be drawn from the laws, based in part on the endorsement of the signatories and partly on the reasoning in the councils : that the Roman pontiff does not have, in the making of general statutes, the authority which certain flatterers attribute to him—namely, that he alone has the power to legislate while the others merely serve as counsellors. I do not deny that the Pope has always had authority to respond to a consultation, to advise, and to address [the council] in writing; I am talking of statutes that have the force of canons and of decretals that are universally binding in the Church. Whether even today the Pope alone may decree, as universally binding, that which has been transmitted by long usage, I am not at present considering. I do say that even though he has such power it does not contradict our thesis, which holds merely that the authority of enacting canons depends, not on the Pope alone, but on common agreement.

[1] The passages are translated from the 1514, Paris, edition by Jodocus Badius Ascensius (facsimile reprint, Bonn, 1928), and checked with the 1564, Basel, edition.

[2] Bk. II, chs. xii, xiii (in part), xiv (in part); Bk. III, ch. iv.

No rule or custom can prevail against this conclusion any more than against the divine or natural law upon which the conclusion depends. The preëminent power of the Roman pontiff in respect to this matter in a general or universal council is no different from that of a metropolitan in a provincial council; or rather the pontiff's power, in respect to authoritative action, is less in a universal council of the whole catholic church than in a patriarchal council. In the latter, indeed, the Pope is rightly likened to the metropolitan in a provincial council, as we have shown. Accordingly, the Roman pontiff is frequently called "archbishop" by the ancients. Indeed a lesser preëminence is attributable to the Roman pontiff in a universal council of the whole church than to the same pontiff in a patriarchal council or to a metropolitan in a provincial council, as will be shown below.

Ch. XIII.   This will perhaps appear strange to any who have read the writings of Roman pontiffs declaring that plenitude of authority is in the Roman pontiff and that all others may be called by virtue of his favor; as well as to those who have read Gelasius, Sylvester, Nicholas, Symmachus and other Roman pontiffs, maintaining that the Pope passes judgment on other ecclesiastical authorities but that none passes judgment on him: since the authority of the Pope is divine, transmitted to him by God with the words "Whatsoever ye shall bind," and accordingly, the Pope, as vicar of Christ, presides over the universal church; and since he himself holds this supreme authority and is known to have condemned and absolved subjects of any bishops whatsoever even when their own bishops were not negligent; and he may be appealed to without any intermediary. The power of making statutes depends on a power of jurisdiction; therefore [according to this argument] it is absurd to say that something more than his will is necessary to the validity of any statute, since what pleases the prince has the force of law. Furthermore: it can not be doubted that the head of a corporation has authority to exercise jurisdiction, although jurisdiction itself remains ostensibly in the corporation. And no one doubts that the Pope is the "rector" of the ship of St. Peter and of the universal church; wherefore the validity of fundamental laws depends upon him, just as it is impossible to legislate for a corporation without the head. . . .

However, in order to discover the truth of this statement that inferior prelates hold jurisdiction under positive law *papa derivative*—that is derived from the Pope himself, it would be necessary, if that were true, that in the beginning Peter should have received something special from Christ and that the Pope was his successor in this. Yet we know that Peter received from Christ no more authority than the other apostles; for nothing was said to Peter that was not also said to the others. Is it not true that just as it was said to Peter, "Whatsoever thou shalt bind upon the earth," it was also said to the others, "Whomsoever ye shall bind"? And although it was said to Peter, "Thou art Peter and upon this Rock"; nevertheless, by rock we understand Christ, whom Peter confessed. And if by *petra* ("rock"), Peter is to be understood as the foundation stone of the church, then, according to St. Jerome, all the other apostles were similarly foundation stones of the church (concerning which there is a discussion in next to the last chapter of the Apocalypse, wherein by the twelve foundation stones of the city of Jerusalem—that is, the holy church—no one doubts that the apostles are meant). If it was said to Peter, "Feed the sheep," it is nevertheless clear that this feeding is by word and example. So also, according to St. Augustine in his gloss upon the same passage, the same command was given for all. In the verse—"Go ye into all the world" (Matthew and Mark, at the end), it does not appear that anything was said to Peter that implied any supremacy. Therefore, we rightly say that all the apostles are equal in authority to Peter. It should also be remembered that at the beginning of the church there was only one general episcopate, diffused throughout the whole world, without division into dioceses. . . .

Therefore, since the power of binding and loosing, on which all ecclesiastical jurisdiction is founded, is immediately from Christ, and since from this power comes the power of divine jurisdiction, it is evident that all bishops, and perhaps even presbyters, are of equal authority in respect to jurisdiction, although not in respect to the execution, which is confined within certain positive limits. . . .

Ch. XIV. In order that everyone may be better satisfied, I add another consideration, which, if it were practicable, should be set forth at greater length. Seeking to be brief and to please the reader, I shall definitely compress the matter.

Every constitution is founded on natural law (*jure naturali*), and if it contradicts this it cannot be valid. Wherefore, since natural law exists by nature in reason, every law (*lex*) is basically congenital with man. Accordingly, those who are wiser and more excellent than others are chosen as rulers, in order that, endowed with a naturally clear reason and with wisdom and prudence, they may choose just laws and by these govern others and hear cases, so as to preserve the peace; such are the judgments of the wise. Thus those who are strong in reason are by nature masters and rulers of others, yet not by means of coercive laws or of judgments rendered against an unwilling subject.

Since by nature all men are free, all government—whether based on written law or on law embodied in a ruler through whose government the subjects are restrained from evil deeds and their liberty regulated, for a good end, by fear of punishment—arises solely from agreement and consent of the subjects. For if men are by nature powerful and equally free, a valid and ordained authority of any one person, whose power by nature is like that of the rest, cannot be created save by election and consent of the others, just as law is established by consent. . . .

A judge must judge justly, since according to the law (*iure*) itself a sentence is void if it is pronounced contrary to the laws (*leges*) or canons. We read that not even the Apostolic seat has ever judged contrary to the canons. On the contrary, his own judgment is reviewed by a plenary council; this would be in vain if everything the Roman pontiff willed were law (*ius*); for he would then be incapable of pronouncing sentences unlawfully. It is necessary, therefore, that his judgment should be bound by the canons, to which it is subject and by which his sentence is tested as to whether it is lawful. Moreover, the canons have their roots in natural law, against which a ruler has no authority; accordingly, he has no authority against a canon grounded in and supplementary to natural law. Since this is so, how could we say that it is within the authority of a judge to create canons and statutes, since, if this were so and the judge had authority to create canons by himself, a judge could never be charged with giving an unjust (*iniusta*) judgment; for the judgment would be law (*jus*) and, therefore, always just (*justa*). But since a law (*lex*) ought to be reasonable, practicable, and not against the custom of the country, we cannot call that a law which has not actually been accepted by the usage of those employing it in some civil or canonical court. If usage is necessary as a sanctioner of laws, then we cannot justly condemn an accused person under a new law, since he could not have sinned against that which has not yet existed; he must have violated an approved law, accepted through custom and usage.

From the foregoing then it is clear that laws and canons constitute the norms for every judge, and that every law or canon i superior to any judge in rendering judgments. Furthermore, a canon is approved by agreement, usage, and acceptance, then the stability of any constitution rests on acceptance. Accordingly, ecclesiastical canons are rightly decreed by a common council; for the church is a congregation. A single person cannot rightly issue ecclesiastical canons. Wherefore we see that in councils, canons issue from agreement, acceptance, consent, and approval; and that decretals or judicial decisions of the Roman pontiffs, or of contested incumbents in emergencies, have received the strength of stability and justness, not from a merely powerful will, but from the fact that in accordance with the canons it was right that those decisions should be made.

Bk. III, Ch. IV. We must also consider the imperial electors. For every ordained empire or kingdom takes its origin from election (as has been said above) and it is then that it can be conceived of as set up by the providence of God. Wherefore the Emperors Valentinian and Martian wrote as follows to Pope Leo concerning the assembling of the Synod: "The Conquerors Valentinian and Martian, ever the gloriously triumphant Augusti, to Leo, reverend Archbishop of the glorious city of Rome: To this supreme authority through the providence of the true God and through election by the most excellent Senate and the whole army." Thus Henry the First, father of Otto, was by order of Conrad the King, we read, made King through election, although he was already Duke of Saxony and had previously been made king of the Teutons. Otto, his son, indeed received from the synod and from the Roman populace the authority to choose his own successor, and by that arrangement the succession was preserved until Otto the Third; after the latter's death, Henry the Second, son of the brother of Otto the Third, was elected. This Emperor, in the time of Gregory V (German kinsman of an earlier Otto), arranged, with the consent of the nobles and primates of the two estates of clergy and people, the perpetual electors who chose in behalf of all. Wherefore, it can not be conceded that the electors hold their elective authority from the Roman pontiff; for in that case if the pontiff did not consent, they would not have the authority; or if he desired he could take it away from them. Who, I ask, has given the Roman people the power of electing an emperor, if not divine and natural law itself? For by voluntary submission and consent to a chief governing authority harmonious preferential rights have been rightly and sacredly established in every kind of rulership.

All violence is opposed to law; for to submit to rules rests on a universal human convention. Thus at the council of Toledo, in the year of Christ 581 (at the time of King Sysenandus), it was decreed, at the King's death, that the primates of the people, together with the priests, would have to set up a successor in a common council of the kingdom, in order that, with the bond of unity preserved, no division of country and people should arise from the motive of ambition. There is added a provision that he who as a tyrant has wrongly usurped authority may be excommunicated; and terrible anathemas and maledictions are imposed. Thus kings are in Greek called "Basilei," since as *bases* they support the people in a collective harmony; wherefore bases have crowns. "Tyrants" in Greek are the same as "kings" in Latin; for "tyro" means strong, and a tyrant is a strong king. Subsequently it became customary to call tyrants the worst and most dishonorable kings—luxury loving, craving and cruelly exercising dominion over the people. They are called tyrants as usurpers of authority, who are neither invited nor elected.

Observe, if you recall what has been shown above, that every ordered superiority arises from an elective agreement of free submission; and that there is in the people a divine seed, by virtue of the common and equal needs and the equal natural rights of all men; so that every authority that is in the beginning from God may then, like man himself, be recognized as divine, when it arises from the common consent of the subjects. Let one so set up in authority, as if he bore within himself the will of all, live as a father of the people, in order that he, in governing, may be called a public, common person and a father of the several individuals, ruling in a right and regularly established government, without the haughtiness of pride, while recognizing himself as the creature of his subjects collectively. This is that divinely ordained marital state of the spiritual family, founded in the roots of eternal harmony, whereby the commonwealth is guided best toward the goal of eternal bliss in the fulness of peace. Since the roots of this divine and human law have been shown above, I do not repeat the matter here. It is sufficient to know that free election, depending on natural and divine law, does not have its origin in positive law or in any man, in such way that the validity of an election—especially the election of a king or emperor, whose existence and power depend on no one man—should rest in his discretion.

Thus the electors—who were created in the time of Henry the Second by common agreement of all the Germans and other subjects of the empire—have their authority fundamentally from the common consent of all those who could by natural law have created the Emperor, not from the Roman pontiff, who has no authority to give to any region in the world a king or emperor without its consent. Gregory V concurred in the arrangement, but in the rôle of a particular Roman pontiff, who has to participate, according to his rank, in agreeing to the common emperor. So also in general councils, the pontiff's authority rightly concurs by consent, in the first degree, with all others attending the same council. The force of a decree depends, nevertheless, not on the chief pontiff, but on the common consent of himself and the others. The fact that in setting up a king or emperor the consent of priests as well as of laymen must be obtained, is not because the authority of kings is outweighed by the priesthood in matters of government, for we know that the priesthood of the sun and the imperium of the moon are equal, but because the temporal possessions of the church, without which the priesthood cannot survive in this perishable life, are subject to the imperium and its laws. He who is concerned in protecting the existence of the priest has an interest in consenting to the election of the king; and he looks properly to the Roman pontiff, who bears chief responsibility for the priesthood. Thus I truly believe that in the beginning the consent of the Roman pontiff concurred in the arrangement when these electors were set up. The latter elect officers by virtue of a general delegation of authority from all who are under imperial authority, as well as from the entire priesthood and the Roman pontiff. He who is elected surely does everything by virtue of his election, since he receives the submission of all, and thereby the power of commanding, in which consists the essence of the imperium; for the emperors originally derived their title from commanding an army.

The anointing and coronation, which, we read, is accorded to other rulers also, does not prove the supremacy of the Pope in confirming or annulling the election or a superiority to the imperium in temporal affairs; just as nothing of that sort is involved in the anointing of the King of France at Rheims or in the coronation of the Emperor himself by the colonial archbishop of Aachen. This follows, because we read that Otto the First was invested with the kingship of Germany and the French by Hildebert of Mainz, Archbishop of Aachen, at the wish and consent of the rulers and of all the people of Alemannia, Saxony, and Franconia. We also read that at the death of King Conrad anointment and a diadem were accorded to Henry the First by Hergers the Archbishop of Mainz, with the consent of all, and that when he received the diadem he was unwilling to be anointed, since he said he was unworthy.

Thus it is clear that anointment and the diadem in no way add to imperial authority; for these insignia are added to the ceremonies as means of showing, with a visible and material means, the sacred majesty that exists in the imperium, in order that there may be signs proclaiming an authority that is to be revered. We know that similar things are done in the case of the Roman pontiff, and yet before they are done he is Pope—as soon as he is elected. Is anything changed in the Pope's coronation of the Emperor so that he is called King beforehand and Emperor afterwards ? Not in the sense that previously he had less governing power ; and this is well known, for when he has had it in his full power to rule, he has been really Emperor even if he was not publicly so called. However, in order that the ruler may greatly desire the coronation, the title is reserved until this solemn occasion. While the commanders used the title, "imperator," the Senate decreed that this should be the name of Augustus Cæsar alone and that by this name he should be distinguished from other rulers of nations. Accordingly, the emperors (*Cæsares*) have to this day assumed this name for themselves, particularly at the time when they are adorned with a diadem by the pontiff of the Romans, and from them the empire is derived.

Since this matter has been discussed most eloquently by many, it may be sufficient for us to recognize that our imperial electors, when they elect by one common consent of all who are under the empire, do this through an harmonious transfusion of the powers from all to themselves (in which concord the Roman pontiff, Gregory V, was most certainly included). It follows that the Emperor is created by election, without any confirmation whatever. In choosing a Pope, the authority of the church is rightly transferred to the cardinals, through the common consent, tacit or occasionally expressed, of all. For this reason the Pope is elected without any confirmation.

Just as elective authority falls by agreement to certain princes of the two estates, so, since there must be in the same estates an equivalent authority of destroying authority, I do not believe that the authority of the Roman pontiff alone can take the authority from these princes ; but when the consent of both the Roman pontiff and of all others concurs, it is not to be doubted that the authority can be destroyed by them. It is the common opinion of all the learned that the Roman people can take away from the Emperor the authority to make laws, because he derives his authority from the people. Thus we read that when the Roman people, ruled for a long time by kings, could no longer endure their haughtiness, they created annual rulerships and two consuls, and also dictators and other arrangements that seemed to suit their government in accordance with the needs of the times.

2. Representative Councils and the Election of an Emperor [1]

Bk. III, Ch. XII. In sum and substance then, this ought to be understood: the aim of a ruler should be to establish laws by agreement. It is, therefore, fitting that all general matters affecting the commonwealth should be decided and ordered in a council of the two estates of primates and bishops (*primatum et praesulum*). Indeed the king must be the executor of what is enacted by the council, since this very legislation is the rule according to which the subjects desire the authority of the king to be controlled. No one doubts that a universal council has the power to regulate, by agreement of the head and members, the chief governing (*praesidentialem*) authority, for the good of the commonwealth. Although it is true that the king, by the principle of equity, can—in doubtful cases, in the interest of the public good and the furtherance of justice—suspend or interpret a law, even though it has been established as described above, nevertheless this in its own way should be understood as we have already explained in reference to the Roman pontiff and the canons : it is not that the king can without a council abolish a law which has been enacted with a council, but that he has the right merely to declare that the essence of a law does not apply in a particular case.

This is sufficient for understanding how it is the function of the king in synodical councils to endorse, exhort, and enforce ; and also to obey and follow ecclesiastical constitutions concerned with the faith and with divine worship. At the same time, in matters related to the public welfare he must decide and act in the manner correctly stated above in reference to the metropolitan, who is head of his council and can decide nothing affecting the whole province except with the consent of the suffragans. For the king ought to preside in the council in which matters pertaining to the government of the commonwealth are discussed ; and he ought to determine all things in order, by agreement with a council composed of leading men and bishops from among the subjects. For this purpose the ruler ought, of course, to have elected, from all parts of the realm, the best qualified men among his subjects, to be in daily conference with him. These councillors ought indeed to act in behalf of all the inhabitants of the realm, just as it has been set forth above concerning the cardinals who are in attendance upon the Roman pontiff. Such councillors ought constantly to defend the public interest of those whom they represent, giving advice and serving as the appropriate medium through which the king can

[1] Bk. III, chs. xii, xxv (in part), xxxv (in part), xxxvi, xxxvii.

govern and influence his subjects, and the subjects, on proper occasions, react upon him. In this daily conference abides the great strength of the kingdom. The councillors ought certainly to be appointed to this task by agreement in a universal meeting of the kingdom, and they ought to be publicly pledged, by laws and oaths, to plead for the public good. Since St. Thomas, Aegidius Romanus, Sedulius Scotus, and before them, Plato and Cicero (although the books of these last are not at hand) and many others have left large volumes covering the government of the common-wealth, everyone may refer to these works for the rest. . . .

Ch. XXV. . . . We know that the Emperor is head and chief of all ; and from him comes the imperial command for the assem-bling of subordinate kings and princes, while they, as members, have to concur with the head. In this universal council are the heads of the provinces, as representatives of their provinces ; also the rectors and teachers of the great universities ;[1] and those who are of the senatorial rank, which is called the holy diet, since they are illustrious as closest to the ruler and parts of his body ; or they are notable members of the middle group ; or those most distin-guished in the lowest group—beyond which grades none was found among the well-defined grade (*certum*) of the Senators. The first orders are the rulers and electors of the empire and the highest nobles. The second are the dukes, governors, prefects, and others of this sort. The third are the marquises, landgraves and the like. All those who are superior to the rest and who are nearer to the imperial government, compose that imperial body whose head is the Emperor himself ; and when they are met in one complete representative body, the whole imperial authority is brought together.

I have discovered in old books that several imperial general councils have been held in which rulers signed their names, after the Emperor, in their own hand, with a perpetual guarantee, in the manner customary in ecclesiastical synods. I have also read that a council of King Dagobert was held at Cologne, with twenty-four rulers, in which were determined, by agreement of all, many matters essential for preserving the utmost peace and justice. Also a general council examined, arranged, and, as opportunity was presented, revised and added to the laws, of Charlemagne, Hilde-bert and others, which were drawn up in consultations among the faithful, giving definite regulations for the diverse parts of our empire : for the Alemanni, different regulations than for the

---

[1] "universitatum magnarum rectores et magistri." An alternative rendering would be "heads and officials of the great corporations."

Baiovarii (whom we now call Bavarians); for the Riboarians, different than for the Burgundians and Lombardians; and it issued other laws, called *salic*, for the peoples of Saxony and those regions. I have seen all these things collected in order; and I have learned that many of them, especially those preferred in popular usage because of their ancient origin, are retained, with their forms, particularly in the rural courts, rather than in towns and cities where municipal ordinances are probably supplanting them. I read that once or twice every year the ancient kings held such councils, which are called conventicles, in different cities of the empire, for the public good. In these councils the severest penalties were devised against those disturbing the peace or violating the public laws, especially in the case of perjurers and those not keeping their trust; and it was out of fear of these conventicles, to which persons were compelled to come when summoned by the prescribed imperial warrant, that various disturbances, pillagings, and arsons were prevented. No one could escape or reject the judgment of this assembly; and the Emperor, with the assembly, assigned to the military forces the execution of the sentences there imposed upon the disobedient. Important members of this council are those who are called the principal men of the empire, whether bishops, laymen, or abbots. Others were not in the council unless they were especially summoned. At the close of any conventicle, when the business had been taken care of, the time and place for a future meeting was set; it was, however, always within the authority of the Emperor to change the time and place, if reasons for change arose.

There never has been a worthier or more useful device or one more beneficial to the whole church as well as to people merely living under the empire. Legates of the Roman pontiff used to come together for ecclesiastical cases, and legates of other rulers when difficult questions were pending in their kingdoms; and in all public emergencies help was to be had from this useful council. I believe nothing can bring more good to the public order than the introduction of this holy institution; since matters that would have to be so determined in a common council would (as has been the custom) be signed or marked with a certain cross by each party in his own hand, in order to ensure the greatest certainty— this being the law, so that if any one should rashly attempt to violate a rule endorsed or signed in his own hand, he would lose his repute and by the very act be deprived of all honor as one most untrue to himself and his own pledge.

This was the practice of the ancients, which will be readily obvious to those who have delved tirelessly into the deeds of kings and emperors and the statutes decreed in their conventicles. I do not insist on speaking at length concerning the organization of this conventicle; for as to the order of seats for the electors, that was provided for by Charles the Fourth, of most blessed memory, and his golden bull, in the conventicle of Metz. Other rulers know their places, according to rank and age. When, however, the rulers are present, they are called upon to decide, in keeping with their oath of allegiance, in current cases regarding matters best for the empire and the common welfare and according to the dictates of their conscience, all sinister motives set aside; all are to speak openly and freely, without fear. . . .

Ch. XXXV. Let the annual meeting be set for about the feast of Pentecost, in Frankfort, which seems to be the most suitable place from its situation and from other circumstances. To this meeting all the judges and electors of the empire should come in person, without pomp or heavy expense. Let his lordship the Emperor himself preside, if he can be present in person; otherwise, the chief of the electors in the Emperor's name. Let affairs of the empire, and even local affairs that have come before the judges, be dealt with; and let things that need reforming be reformed. If a critical matter of business really demands that a full meeting of all the chief officials take place, there or elsewhere, let whatever is most suitable be done. However, a regular annual council of lords, judges, and electors—in which cases of the princes are to be decided through a common vote—should never be omitted. And since it is useful to introduce any reform on the basis of precedent, I would submit an imperial letter which is credited to Constantine, who ordered a similar meeting of judges to be held at Arles. . . .

Following this form, an annual council should be established in Frankfort (which, by reason of its situation and the converging of merchandise there, may be correctly likened to Arles), to be held for at least one month, in either May or September; and, with those mentioned above, at least one should come from each city and metropolis and from the large imperial towns. The chief electors should bring with them those whom they wish as counsellors. The nobles and all should be bound by oath to contribute counsels for the public good, according to the right verdict of reason. Let provincial customs be there examined, and harmonized as nearly as possible with the common practices; and especially let captious formalities be completely laid aside; for the simple poor are often most unjustly led outside the case (*extra formam*) by the sophistries of lawyers, and so lose their whole case, since he who loses a syllable loses a case, as I have often seen happen in the diocese of Treves. Moreover, those very bad usages that permit an oath against anyone whomsoever and witnesses of whatever number should be abolished. Throughout Germany there are many such bad practices that are against true justice and are also breeders of crimes which no one could enumerate in detail. Wherefore judges of the provinces ought to come together and put the customs of their provinces into writing and lay them out before the council, so that they may be examined.

Ch. XXXVI. Finally, in this holy imperial council of Basel, the greatest care should be taken to see that the electors are given a most rigid code, which is in no respect to be violated and in which they are by oath bound above everything to make their choice with no particular considerations, for no reward, and for no special interest, but purely and simply for the public good and for the preservation and honor of the holy empire, in obedience to God and conscience. If any one should be found acting otherwise, he should be subjected to perpetual infamy and to the penalties for the crime of *lèse majesté*. In view of the perversion of elections, it is highly necessary that the electors should be constrained by the most severe penalties, because of absurd and dishonest practices which, I have read, have occurred in the past, when the electors were looking out for their own interests, forcing an election by many illegitimate devices, as a result of which the public interest was entirely neglected. Because certain electors dwelt in certain towns and forts of the empire, and because of custom houses and other special interests of this sort, shamefully negotiated elections are said to have been brought about by iniquitous bargains. Above all, the differences that give electors fear of losing what they have had for some time and, for that reason, motivate them to act in this way [i.e., tamper with elections] ought to be settled in a general meeting, by genuine and honest discussion, so that each elector may be made firm in the freedom of a clean election. And since he who appears best in the common opinion of all the electors ought to be put in charge of the empire, I shall now describe a certain plan that will be very useful in this matter, as well as in a council of assembly where a common intent is to be elicited from the votes of all.

Ch. XXXVII. The electors of the holy empire, when they wish to proceed to the election of the next emperor, should assemble on an appointed day, in all humility and with the utmost devotion to the divine service, freeing themselves from all sin, in order that Christ the Lord may be in their midst. Having invoked the favor of the Holy Spirit and after a solemn introduction of the order of business, they should consider the many persons who, because of their outer and inner attitude to the empire, may be worthy of so great a dignity. And in order that the election may be carried out without any fear and in complete freedom and secrecy, after sworn oaths at the altar of the Lord concerning the choice of the best man by the just decision of a free conscience, they should cause the names of all whom they are considering to be put down by a notary on ballots precisely alike, with only one name on each ballot; and after that name a series of numbers should be affixed—1, 2, 3, as many as the number of persons that have been mentioned in the discussion as being eligible. Suppose there have been found in Germany ten who appear worthy and from among whom the one most worthy is to be chosen by a combined judgment; let the name of only one [candidate] be placed on the ballot, the numbers one to ten placed under the name, or at its side, and the ten ballots, each containing one of the ten names, given to each elector.

When the ballots have been received by the electors, each should go aside alone and secretly, or with a secretary if he is illiterate; and with all ten ballots placed before him he should read the name of each. Then in the name of God he should ponder, according to his own conscience, which number among them all is appropriate [to a particular candidate] and check with a mark of ink: above this number a simple long mark; after this he should decide which number is suitable for the next candidate and indicate a second number with a simple long mark; and so on until he arrives at the best, in his judgment, and there he will mark the tenth number, or that number which corresponds to the total number of persons. This is a good idea—that all mark with the same ink, pens just alike, and the same simple marks—long or short, whichever is agreed upon—so that the mark of one cannot be distinguished from the others; for this reason, namely, that greater freedom for the electors may be obtained, and peace among all. When these votes have been made, each of the electors should carry his own ballots in hand and throw them with his own hand into an empty sack hanging in the midst of the electors. When the ballots have been deposited in the sack, the priest who has celebrated mass, or some one else, should be called; also an accountant, having a list on which are the names, in order, of the ten, let us say, from whom the choice is to be made. Sitting among the electors, let the priest withdraw the ballots from the sack, in the order in which they come to hand; and let him read the name and the number marked; let the accountant write the number at the side of the name; and so on for all. When this is completed, the accountant should add the numbers for each name ; and he then will be Emperor who has the larger number. By following this procedure, innumerable frauds are avoided. Nothing sinister can happen. It will not be possible to devise a more righteous, just, honest, and free method of election ; and so it will be impossible, if they vote according to conscience, that he should not be put into power who is judged better by a collective verdict. It will not be possible to discover a safer method. Nay, by this method an infallible decision can be obtained, since every sort of comparison of all persons and of all the estimates and arguments likely to be made by each elector would be actually included in the process—which I was not able to devise save with great study. You may well believe that no more perfect method can be found. Still, lest any elector be perverted by self-interest, this precaution should be taken : if one or more from the laity have been listed for general consideration among those to be chosen, the form with his own name should not be given to him, although all the others, with that exception, should be given him ; in order to avoid an occasion for suspicion ; for he could adjudge himself the best of all, indicating the higher number for his own name. With this single exception, the prescribed procedure should be followed completely ; and there will be held an election than which none better can be found.

SELECTED BIBLIOGRAPHY

McIlwain, Charles H., *Growth of Political Thought in the West*, pp. 345–350.
Dunning, William A., *Political Theories, Ancient and Mediæval*, ch. 10, § 4.

Jacob, E. F., "Nicolas of Cusa," in F. J. C. Hearnshaw, ed., *The Social and Political Ideas of Some Great Thinkers of the Renaissance and Reformation* (London, 1925), ch. 2.
Figgis, John Neville, *Studies of Political Thought from Gerson to Grotius* (Cambridge, 1907), No. ii.
Carlyle, R. W. and A. J., *History of Mediæval Political Theory in the West*, Vol. VI (London and Edinburgh, 1936), pt. ii, chs. 1, 3, 6.
Cassirer, Ernst, *Individuum und Kosmos in der Philosophie der Renaissance* (Berlin, 1927), chs. 1 and 2.

Vansteenberghe, E., *Le Cardinal Nicolas de Cues (1401–1464): l'action—la pensée* (Paris, 1920).
Posch, Andreas, *Die "Concordantia catholica" des Nikolaus von Cusa. Görres Gesellschaft, Sektion für Rechts- und Staatswissenschaft, Veröffentlichungen*, vol. 54 (Paderborn, 1930).

MACHIAVELLI

XI. MACHIAVELLI (1469–1527)

INTRODUCTION

Machiavelli's *Prince* is commonly called the first distinctively "modern" work in political theory. The celebrated work is called modern because its conclusions are sustained by references to history and contemporary politics rather than by citation of authority or by derivation from theological dogma and philosophical tradition; and because it examines political questions in thorough isolation from religious, metaphysical, and ethical principles. The *Prince* treats of the means whereby a strong and adroit man may most successfully acquire, increase, and perpetuate political dominion. Questions of right and wrong, considerations of public welfare or of conformity to religious creeds, are introduced only with regard to their bearing upon the success of an autocrat. The completeness with which this detachment of method is pursued in the *Prince*, and the particular type of conclusions of statecraft reached, seem properly to be assigned to no special epoch or school. They seem rather the peculiar product, on the one hand, of the temperament of the author, and, on the other hand, of the character of the political events in Italy and other European states in Machiavelli's time.

Machiavelli was born in Florence. He was in the public service of that city-state from 1494 (the year of the invasion by Charles VIII, the first expulsion of the Medici, and the temporary restoration of the Republic) until the return of the Medici in 1512. Following this he was in exile for nine years. It was during his banishment that he wrote his two important political works—the *Prince*, the *Discourses on the First Ten Books of Livy*, and several historical and dramatic works. Both the *Discourses* and the *Prince* are concerned with the rise and decline of states and with the means of maintaining strong and durable government. The former deals generally with methods for preserving and strengthening republican government, and particularly with the expansion of the Roman

Republic. The latter is concerned with the methods of absolute monarchical government. Machiavelli had held the highest diplomatic office of the Florentine Republic. He was sent on missions to petty principalities and cities of Italy and to the courts of Louis XII of France, Emperor Maximilian and other important heads of state. These missions afforded him opportunity for observing governmental practices under diverse conditions. Of peculiar significance was his mission to the camp of Cæsar Borgia at the time when that skilful and infamous tyrant had attained his summit of success. The career of single-minded cruelty and fraud which Cæsar Borgia followed furnished Machiavelli with many suggestions in practical politics. His experience and observation had provided him a broader field for observing the efficacy of despotism. The principle of direct autocracy was dominant in the governments of the great states of Europe, and in that of the church. Furthermore, recent events in Machiavelli's own city, and the general political condition of Italy, indicated to him the need for analysing the qualities of a successful ruler. From the instability which was chronic within each of the small Italian states, and from the turmoil of continually conflicting claims of territorial jurisdiction, escape appeared to be possible only through the agency of a single powerful and unscrupulous despot. A common "justification" of the *Prince* is the argument that Machiavelli was not subordinating political morality to political expediency, but only subordinating political policy to the sublime moral ideal of an independent, stable, unified community. However, any vision of a farther goal—of a popular welfare to be served by the callous and unscrupulous despotism—does not appear in the *Prince*, except vaguely in an abruptly added peroration.

The *Prince* was completed in 1513. Machiavelli planned to dedicate the work to one of the Medici, hoping thereby to obtain recall from exile and restoration to public office and favor, and also to bring his manual to the attention of one who, by following its doctrines, might accomplish the unification of Italy. He finally dedicated the work to Lorenzo de' Medici (grandson of Lorenzo the Magnificent), who became *de facto* head of the Florentine government in 1516. Machiavelli was subsequently recalled from exile and was employed in the capacity of adviser and diplomatic representative of Medici rulers in Florence and Rome.

READINGS FROM THE PRINCE[1]

The Conduct of a Successful Ruler[2]

Ch. xv. *Of Such Things as Render Men (especially Princes) Worthy of Blame or Applause.*

It remains now that we see in what manner a prince ought to comport with his subjects and friends; and because many have written of this subject before, it may perhaps seem arrogant in me, especially considering that in my discourse I shall deviate from the opinion of other men. But my intention being to write for the benefit and advantage of him who understands, I thought it more convenient to respect the essential verity, rather than an imaginary view, of the subject; for many have framed imaginary commonwealths and governments to themselves which never were seen nor had any real existence. And the present manner of living is so different from the way that ought to be taken, that he who neglects what is done to follow what ought to be done, will sooner learn how to ruin than how to preserve himself; for a tender man, and one that desires to be honest in everything, must needs run a great hazard among so many of a contrary principle. Wherefore it is necessary for a prince who is willing to subsist to harden himself, and learn to be good or otherwise according to the exigence of his affairs. Laying aside, therefore, all imaginary notions of a prince, and discoursing of nothing but what is actually true, I say that all men when they are spoken of, and especially princes, who are in a higher and more eminent station, are remarkable for some quality or other that makes them either honorable or contemptible. Hence it is that some are counted liberal, others miserly; . . . some munificent, others rapacious; some cruel, others merciful; some faithless, others precise; one poor-spirited and effeminate, another fierce and ambitious; one courteous, another haughty; one modest, another libidinous; one sincere, another cunning; one rugged and morose, another accessible and easy; one grave, another giddy; one devout, another an atheist.

No man, I am sure, will deny but that it would be an admirable thing and highly to be commended to have a prince endued with all the good qualities aforesaid; but because it is impossible to

---

[1] The selections are from Henry Morley's edition of *The Prince and Other Pieces*, but many changes, in wording and construction, have been made.
[2] Chs. xv–xix, xxi. Part of ch. xix is omitted.

have, much less to exercise, them all by reason of the frailty and
grossness of our nature, it is convenient that he be so well instructed as to know how to avoid the scandal of those vices which
may deprive him of his state, and be very cautious of the rest,
though their consequence be not so pernicious but that where they
are unavoidable he need trouble himself the less. Again, he is
not to concern himself if he incur the infamy of those vices
without which his dominion is not to be preserved; for if we
consider things impartially we shall find some things are virtuous
in appearance, and yet, if pursued, would bring certain destruction;
while others, seemingly bad, yet, if followed by a prince, procure
his peace and security.

Ch. xvi.   *Of Liberality and Parsimony.*

To begin, then, with the first of the above-mentioned qualities,
I say, it would be advantageous to be accounted liberal; nevertheless, liberality so used as not to render you formidable does
but injure you; for if it be used virtuously as it ought to be it
will not be known, nor secure you from the imputation of its contrary.   To keep up, therefore, the name of liberal amongst men,
it is necessary that no kind of luxury be omitted, so that a
prince of that disposition will consume his revenue in that kind
of expenses, and be obliged at last, if he would preserve that
reputation, to become grievous, and a great exactor upon the
people, and do whatever is practicable for the getting of money,
which will cause him to be hated of his subjects and despised by
everybody else when he once comes to be poor, so that offending
many with his liberality and rewarding but few, he becomes
sensible of the first disaster, and runs great hazard of being ruined
the first time he is in danger; which, when afterward he discovers,
and desires to remedy, he runs into the other extreme, and grows
as odious for his avarice.   So, then, if a prince cannot exercise
this virtue of liberality so as to be publicly known, without
detriment to himself, he ought, if he be wise, not to dread the
imputation of being covetous, for in time he shall be esteemed
liberal when it is discovered that by his parsimony he has increased his revenue to a condition of defending himself against
invasion and of engaging in enterprises upon other people without
oppressing his subjects; so that he shall be accounted noble to all
from whom he takes nothing away, which are an infinite number,
and near and parsimonious only to such few as he gives nothing to.

In our days we have seen no great action done but by those
who were accounted miserly; others have failed always. Pope

Julius II made use of his bounty to get into the Chair, but to enable himself to make war with the King of France he never practised it afterwards, and by his frugality he maintained several wars without any tax or imposition upon the people, his long parsimony having furnished him for his extraordinary expenses. The present King of Spain, if he had affected to be thought liberal, could never have undertaken so many great designs nor obtained so many great victories. A prince, therefore, ought not to be much concerned over being accounted covetous—so long as he is enabled thereby to forbear from burdening his subjects, to defend himself, and to keep himself from becoming poor and despicable; covetousness is one of those vices which fortify his dominion. If any one objects that Cæsar by his liberality made his way to the empire, and many others upon the same score of reputation have made themselves great, I answer: "Either you are actually a prince, or you are in a fair way to be made one. In the first case, liberality is hurtful; in the second, it is necessary; Cæsar aspired to the sovereignty of Rome; when he was arrived at that dignity, if he had lived, and had not retrenched his expenses, he would have ruined that empire." If any one replies that many have been princes, and with their armies performed great matters, who have been reputed liberal, I rejoin that a prince spends either of his own, or his subjects', or other people's. In the first case he is to be frugal; in the second, he may be as profuse as he pleases, and baulk no point of liberality. But that prince whose army is to be maintained with free quarter and plunder and exactions from other people, is obliged to be liberal, or his army will desert him; and well he may be prodigal of what neither belongs to him nor his subjects, as was the case with Cæsar, and Cyrus, and Alexander; for to spend upon another's stock rather adds to than subtracts from his reputation; it is spending of his own that is so mortal and pernicious. Nor is there anything that destroys itself like liberality; for in practising it you lose the means whereby it can be practised, and you become poor and contemptible, or, to avoid that poverty, you make yourself odious and a tyrant; and there is nothing of so much importance to a prince to avoid as to be either contemptible or odious, both of which depend much upon the prudent exercise of your liberality. Upon these considerations it is more wisdom to lie under the scandal of being miserly, which is an imputation rather infamous than odious, than to be thought liberal and run yourself into a necessity of playing the tyrant, which is infamous and odious both.

Ch. xvii.   *Of Cruelty and Clemency, and Whether it is Best for a Prince to be Beloved or Feared.*

To come now to the other qualities proposed, I say every prince is to desire to be esteemed rather merciful than cruel, but with great caution that his mercy be not abused; Cæsar Borgia was counted cruel, yet that cruelty reduced Romagna, united it, settled it in peace, and rendered it faithful: so that if well considered, he will appear much more merciful than the Florentines, who rather than be thought cruel suffered Pistoia to be destroyed. A prince, therefore, is not to regard the reproach of being cruel, if thereby he keeps his subjects in their allegiance and united, seeing that by some few examples of justice he may be more merciful than they who by a universal exercise of pity permit several disorders to follow, which occasion rapine and murder; and the reason is, because that exorbitant mercy has an ill effect upon the whole community, whereas particular executions extend only to particular persons. But among all princes a new prince has the hardest task to avoid the scandal of being cruel by reason of the newness of his government, and the dangers which attend it: hence Virgil in the person of Dido excused the inhospitality of her government.

> *Res dura, et regni novitas, me talia cogunt*
> *Moliri, et late fines Custode tueri.*

> My new dominion and my harder fate
> Constrains me to't, and I must guard my state.

Nevertheless, he is not to be too credulous of reports, too hasty in his motions, nor create fears and jealousies to himself, but so to temper his administrations with prudence and humanity that neither too much confidence may make him careless, nor too much diffidence intolerable. And hence arises a new question, Whether it be better to be beloved than feared, or feared than beloved? It is answered, both would be convenient, but because that is hard to attain, it is better and more secure, if one must be wanting, to be feared than beloved; for in general men are ungrateful, inconstant, hypocritical, fearful of danger, and covetous of gain; while they receive any benefit by you, and the danger is at a distance, they are absolutely yours, and their blood, their estates, their lives and their children, as I said before, are all at your service; but when mischief is at hand, and you have present need of their help, they make no scruple to revolt; and that prince who leaves himself naked of other preparations, and relies wholly upon their professions, is sure to be ruined;

for amity contracted by price, and not by the greatness and generosity of the mind, may seem a good pennyworth; yet when you have occasion to make use of it, you will find no such thing. Moreover, men do with less remorse offend against those who desire to be beloved than against those who are ambitious of being feared; the reason is that love is fastened only by a ligament of obligation, which the ill-nature of man breaks upon every occasion that is presented to his profit; but fear depends upon an apprehension of punishment, which is never to be dispelled. Yet a prince is to render himself awful in such sort that, if he gains not his subjects' love, he may escape their hatred; for to be feared and not hated are compatible enough, and he may be always in that condition if he offers no violence to their estates, nor attempts anything upon the honor of their wives, and when he has occasion to take away any man's life, if he takes his time when the cause is manifest, and he has good matter for his justification; but above all things he is to have a care of intrenching upon their estates, for men do sooner forget the death of their father than the loss of their patrimony; besides, occasions of confiscation never fail, and he that once gives way to that humor of rapine shall never want temptation to ruin his neighbor. But, on the contrary, provocations to blood are more rare, and do sooner evaporate; but when a prince is at the head of his army, and has a multitude of soldiers to govern, then it is absolutely necessary not to value the epithet of cruel, for without that no army can be kept in unity, nor in disposition for any great act.

Among the several instances of Hannibal's great conduct, it is one that, having a vast army constituted out of several nations, and conducted to make war in an enemy's country, there never happened any sedition among them, or any mutiny against their general, either in his adversity or prosperity. This can only be attributed to his great cruelty, which, added to his infinite virtues, rendered him both awful and terrible to his soldiers; without that all his virtues would have signified nothing. Some writers there are, but of little consideration, who admire his great exploits and condemn the true causes of them. But to prove that his other virtues would never have carried him through, let us reflect upon Scipio, a person honorable not only in his own time, but in all history whatever; nevertheless his army mutinied in Spain, and the true cause of it was his too much gentleness and lenity, which gave his soldiers more liberty than was suitable or consistent with military discipline. Fabius Maximus upbraided him for it in the senate, and called him corrupter of the Roman Militia; the inhabitants of Locris having been plundered and destroyed by one of Scipio's lieutenants, they were never redressed, nor the legate's insolence corrected, all proceeding from the mildness of Scipio's nature, which was so eminent in him, that a person undertaking to excuse him in the senate declared that there were many who knew better how to avoid doing ill themselves than to punish it in other people; whioh temper would doubtless in time have eclipsed the glory and reputation of Scipio, had that authority been continued in him; but receiving orders and living under the direction of the senate, that ill quality was not only not discovered in him, but turned to his renown. I conclude, therefore, according to what I have said about being feared or beloved, that forasmuch as men do love at their own discretion, but fear at their prince's, a wise prince is obliged to lay his foundation upon that which is in his own power, not that which depends on other people, but, as I said before, with great caution that he does not make himself odious.

Ch. xviii. *How far a Prince is Obliged by his Promise.*
How honorable it is for a prince to keep his word, and act rather with integrity than collusion, I suppose everybody understands: nevertheless, experience has shown in our times that those princes who have not pinned themselves up to that punctuality and preciseness have done great things, and by their cunning and subtilty have not only circumvented those with whom they had to deal, but have overcome and been too hard for those who have been so superstitiously exact. For further explanation you must understand there are two ways of contending—by law and by force: the first is proper to men; the second to beasts; but because many times the first is insufficient, recourse must be had to the second. It belongs, therefore, to a prince to understand both—when to make use of the rational and when of the brutal way; and this is recommended to princes, though abstrusely, by ancient writers, who tell them how Achilles and several other princes were committed for education to Chiron the Centaur, who was half man and half beast—thus showing how necessary it is for a prince to be acquainted with both natures, for one without the other will be of little duration. Seeing, therefore, it is of such importance to a prince to take upon him the nature and disposition of a beast, of all the whole flock he ought to imitate the lion and the fox; for the lion is in danger of toils and snares, and the fox of the wolf; so that he

must be a fox to find out the snares, and a lion to fight away the wolves, but they who keep wholly to the lion have no true notion of themselves. A prince, therefore, who is wise and prudent, cannot or ought not to keep his word, when the keeping of it is to his prejudice, and the causes for which he promised removed. Were men all good this doctrine would not be taught, but because they are wicked and not likely to be punctual with you, you are not obliged to any such strictness with them; nor was there ever any prince that lacked lawful pretence to justify his breach of promise. I might give many modern examples, and show how many confederations, and peaces, and promises have been broken by the infidelity of princes, and how he that best personated the fox had the better success. Nevertheless, it is of great consequence to disguise your inclination, and to play the hypocrite well; and men are so simple in their temper and so submissive to their present necessities that he that is neat and cleanly in his collusions shall never want people to practise them upon. I cannot forbear one example which is still fresh in our memory. Alexander VI never did, nor thought of, anything but cheating, and never wanted matter to work upon; and though no man promised a thing with greater asseveration, nor confirmed it with more oaths and imprecations, and observed them less, yet understanding the world well he never miscarried.

A prince, therefore, is not obliged to have all the forementioned good qualities in reality, but it is necessary he have them in appearance; nay, I will be bold to affirm that, having them actually, and employing them upon all occasions, they are extremely prejudicial, whereas, having them only in appearance, they turn to better account; it is honorable to seem mild, and merciful, and courteous, and religious, and sincere, and indeed to be so, provided your mind be so rectified and prepared that you can act quite contrary upon occasion. And this must be premised, that a prince, especially if come but lately to the throne, cannot observe all those things exactly which cause men to be esteemed virtuous, being oftentimes necessitated, for the preservation of his state, to do things inhuman, uncharitable, and irreligious; and, therefore, it is convenient for his mind to be at his command, and flexible to all the puffs and variations of fortune; not forbearing to be good while it is in his choice, but knowing how to be evil when there is a necessity. A prince, then, is to have particular care that nothing falls from his mouth but what is full of the five qualities aforesaid, and that to see and hear him he appears all goodness, integrity, humanity, and religion, which last he ought to pretend to more than ordinarily, because more men do judge by the eye than by the touch; for everybody sees but few understand; everybody sees how you appear, but few know what in reality you are, and those few dare not oppose the opinion of the multitude, who have the majesty of their prince to defend them; and in the actions of all men, especially princes, where no man has power to judge, everyone looks to the end.   Let a prince, therefore, do what he can to preserve his life, and continue his supremacy, the means which he uses shall be thought honorable, and be commended by everybody; because the people are always taken with the appearance and event of things, and the greatest part of the world consists of the people; those few who are wise taking place when the multitude has nothing else to rely upon. There is a prince at this time in being (but his name I shall conceal) who has nothing in his mouth but fidelity and peace; and yet had he exercised either the one or the other, they had robbed him before this both of his power and reputation.

Ch. xix.   *That Princes Ought to be Cautious of Becoming either Odious or Contemptible.*

Since in our discourse of the qualifications of a prince we have hitherto spoken only of those which are of greatest importance, we shall now speak briefly of the rest, with the general statements that a prince should make it his business (as is partly hinted before) to avoid such things as may make him odious or contemptible, and that as often as he does that he plays his part very well, and shall meet no danger or inconveniences by the rest of his vices. Nothing, as I said before, makes a prince so insufferably odious as usurping his subjects' estates and debauching their wives, which are two things he ought studiously to forbear; for while the generality of the world live quietly upon their estates and unprejudiced in their honor, they live peaceably enough, and all his contention is only with the pride and ambition of some few persons who can in many ways and with great ease be restrained.

But a prince is contemptible when he is counted effeminate, light, inconstant, pusillanimous, and irresolute; and of this he ought to be as careful as of a rock in the sea; and he should strive that in all his actions there may appear magnanimity, courage, gravity, and fortitude, desiring that in the private affairs of his subjects his sentence and determination may be irrevocable, and that he himself may stand so in their opinion that none may think it possible either to delude or divert him.   The prince who causes himself to be esteemed in that manner shall be highly feared, and if he be feared, people will not easily conspire against him, nor readily invade him, because he is known to be an excellent person and formidable to his subjects; for a prince ought to be terrible in two places— at home to his subjects, and abroad to his equals, from whom he defends himself by good arms and good allies; for, if his power be good, his friends will not be wanting, and while his affairs are fixed at home, there will be no danger from abroad, unless they be disturbed by some former conspiracy; and upon any commotion *ab extra*, if he be composed at home, has lived as I prescribe, and not deserted himself, he will be able to bear up against any attack, according to the example of Nabis the Spartan.

When things are well abroad his affairs at home will be safe enough, unless they be perplexed by some secret conspiracy, against which the prince sufficiently provides if he keeps himself from being hated or despised, and the people remain satisfied of him, which is a thing very necessary, as I have shown at length before. And one of the best remedies a prince can use against conspiracy is to keep himself from being hated or despised by the multitude; for nobody plots but expects by the death of the prince to gratify the people, and the thought of offending them will deter him from any such enterprise, because in conspiracies the difficulties are infinite. By experience we find that many conspiracies have been on foot, but few have succeeded, because no man can conspire alone, nor choose a confederate but out of those who are discontented; and no sooner shall you impart your mind to a malcontent but you give him opportunity to reconcile himself, because there is no advantage which he seeks but what he may hope to gain by betraying you. So that the gain being certain on that side, and hazardous and uncertain on the other, he must be either an extraordinary friend to you or an implacable enemy to the prince if he does not betray you; in short, on the side of the conspirators there is nothing but fear and jealousy, and apprehension of punishment; but, on the prince's side, there is the majesty of the government, the laws, the assistance of his friends and state, which defend him so effectually that, if the affections of the people be added to them, no man can be so rash and precipitate as to conspire; for if, before the execution of his design, the conspirator has reason to be afraid, in this case he has much more afterwards, having offended the people in the execution and left himself no refuge to fly to. Of this many examples may be produced, but I shall content myself with one which happened in the memory of our fathers. Hannibal Bentivoglio, grandfather to this present Hannibal, was Prince of Bologna, and was killed by

the Canneschi who conspired against him, none of his race being
left behind but John, who was then in his cradle; the murder
was no sooner committed but the people took arms and slew all
the Canneschi, which proceeded only from the affection that the
house of the Bentivoglio had at that time among the populace in
Bologna, which was then so great that when Hannibal was dead,
there being none of that family remaining in a capacity for the
government of the state, upon information that at Florence there
was a natural son of the said Bentivoglio's, who till that time
had passed only for the son of a smith, they sent ambassadors for
him, and having conducted him honorably to that city, they
gave him the government, which he executed very well till the
said John came of age.   I conclude, therefore, a prince need not be
much apprehensive of conspiracies while the people are his friends;
but when they are dissatisfied, and have taken prejudice against
him, there is nothing nor no person which he ought not to fear.

It has been the constant care of all wise princes and all
well-governed states not to reduce the nobility to despair nor
the people to discontent, which is one of the most material things
a prince is to prevent.   Among the best-ordered monarchies of
our times France is one, in which there are many good laws and
constitutions tending to the liberty and preservation of the king.
The first of them is the Parliament and the authority wherewith
it is vested; for he who was the founder of that monarchy, was
sensible of the ambition and insolence of the nobles, and judged
it convenient to have them bridled and restrained; he knew,
on the other side, the hatred of the people against the nobility,
and that it proceeded from fear, and he desired to protect the
people; but in order to save himself from the displeasure of the
nobles if he sided with the people, or from the malice of the people
if he inclined to the nobles, he established a third party to be
arbitrator, who, without any reflection upon the king, should
keep the nobility under, and protect the people; nor could there
be a better order, wiser, nor of greater security to the king and the
kingdom, whence we may deduce another observation—That
princes are to leave things of injustice and envy to the ministry
and execution of others, but acts of favor and grace are to be
performed by themselves. . . .

Ch. xxi.   *How a Prince is to Demean Himself to Gain Reputation.*
Nothing recommends a prince so highly to the world as great
enterprises and noble expressions of his own valor and conduct.
We have in our days Ferdinand, King of Aragon—the present

King of Spain—who may, and not improperly, be called a new prince, since from one of the smallest and weakest he has become for fame and renown the greatest monarch in Christendom; and if his exploits be considered you will find them all brave, but some of them extraordinary. In the beginning of his reign he invaded the kingdom of Granada, and that enterprise was the foundation of his grandeur. He began it leisurely, and without suspicion of impediment, holding the barons of Castile employed in that service, and so intent upon that war that they dreamt not of any innovation, while in the meantime, before they were aware, he got reputation and authority over them. He found out a way of maintaining his army at the expense of the church and the people; and by the length of that war he established such order and discipline among his soldiers, that afterwards they gained him many honorable victories. Besides this, to adapt him for greater enterprises (always making religion his pretence), by a kind of devout cruelty he destroyed and exterminated the Moors, than which nothing could be more strange or deplorable. Under the same cloak of religion he invaded Africa, made his expedition into Italy, assaulted France, and began many great things which always kept the minds of his subjects in admiration and suspense, wondering what the event of his machinations would be. And these enterprises had so sudden a spring and result one from the other that they gave no leisure to any man to be at quiet, or to continue anything against him. It is likewise of great advantage to a prince to give some rare example of his own administration at home whenever the actions, good or bad, of someone in civil life give him opportunity to reward or punish such actions in such a way as to make himself much talked of in the world. Above all, a prince is to have a care in all his actions to behave himself so as to give himself the reputation of being excellent as well as great.

A prince is likewise much esteemed when he shows himself a sincere friend or a generous enemy—that is, when without any hesitation he declares himself in favor of one against another, which, as it is more frank and princely, so it is more profitable than to stand neutral; for if two of your potent neighbors be at war, they are either of such condition that you are to be afraid of the victor or not; in either of which cases it will be always more for your benefit to discover yourself freely, and make a fair war. For in the first case, if you do not declare, you shall be a prey to him who overcomes, and it will be a pleasure and satisfaction to him that is conquered to see you his fellow-sufferer; nor will anybody either defend or receive you, and the reason is because the conqueror will never understand them to be his friends who would not assist him in his distress; and he that is worsted will not receive you because you neglected to share his fortune with your arms in your hands. . . . And those princes who are ill-advised to avoid some present danger by following the neutral way are most commonly ruined; but when you pronounce yourself courageously in favor of one party, if he with whom you join overcome, though he be very powerful, and you seem to remain at his discretion, yet he is obliged to you, and must needs have a respect for you; and men are not so wicked with signal and exemplary ingratitude as to oppress you after you have helped them. Besides, victories are never so clear and complete as to leave the conqueror without all sparks of reflection, and especially upon what is just. But if your confederate comes by the worst, you are received by him, and assisted while he is able, and you become a companion of his fortune, which may possibly restore you. In the second place, if they who contend be of such condition that they have no occasion to fear, let which will overcome, you are in prudence to declare yourself the sooner, because by assisting the one you contribute to the ruin of the other, whom, if your confederate had been wise, he ought rather to have preserved; if he whom you help overcomes, he remains wholly in your power, and by your assistance he must of necessity overcome. And here it is to be noted, if he can avoid it, a prince is never to league himself with another more powerful than himself in an offensive war; because in that case if the latter overcomes the former remains at his mercy, and princes ought to be as cautious as possible of falling under the discretion of other people. The Venetians, when there was no necessity for it, associated with France against the Duke of Milan, and that association was the cause of their ruin. But where it is not to be avoided, as happened to the Florentines when the Pope and the Spaniard sent their armies against Lombardy, then a prince is to adhere for the reasons aforesaid. Nor is any prince or government to imagine that in those cases any certain counsel can be taken, because the affairs of this world are so ordered that in avoiding one mischief we fall commonly into another. But a man's wisdom is most conspicuous where he is able to distinguish of dangers and make choice of the least.

Moreover, it is a prince's wisdom to show himself a virtuoso, and honorer of all that is excellent in any art whatsoever. He is likewise to encourage and assure his subjects that they may live quietly in peace, and exercise themselves in their several vocations, whether merchandise, agriculture, or any other employment whatever, to the end that no one may forbear improving or embellishing his estate for fear it should be taken from him, or forbear advancing his trade in apprehension of taxes; but the prince is rather to excite them by propositions of reward and immunities to all such as shall any way amplify his territory or power. He is obliged, likewise, at convenient times in the year to entertain the people by feastings and plays, and spectacles of recreation; and, because all cities are divided into companies or wards, he ought to have respect to those societies, be merry with them sometimes, and give them some instance of his humanity and magnificence, but always retaining the majesty of his degree, which is never to be debased in any case whatever.

SELECTED BIBLIOGRAPHY

Sabine, George H., *History of Political Theory*, ch. 17.

Cook, Thomas I., *History of Political Philosophy*, ch. 10.

Dunning, William A., *Political Theories, Ancient and Mediæval*, ch. 11.

Laski, H. J., *The Dangers of Obedience and Other Essays* (New York, 1930), pp. 238–263; "Machiavelli and the Present Time."

Figgis, John Neville, *Studies of Political Thought from Gerson to Grotius* (Cambridge, 1907), pp. 62–107.

Allen, J. W., *A History of Political Thought in the Sixteenth Century* (London, 1928), pt. iv, ch. 2.

Burd, L. A., "Florence (II): Machiavelli," in *Cambridge Modern History*, Vol. I (1903), ch. 6.

Carlyle, R. W. and A. J., *History of Mediæval Political Theory in the West*, Vol. VI (Edinburgh and London, 1936), pt. iii, ch. 3.

Macaulay, Thomas Babington, "Machiavelli," in Vol. II, pp. 1–37, of his *Critical and Historical Essays*. Newly arranged by A. J. Grieve (Everyman's Library, 2 vols. London, 1907).

Fay, Charles R., "Machiavelli's Political Philosophy," in *Youth and Power* (London, 1931), Appendix.

Meinecke, Friedrich, *Die Idee der Staatsräson* (third ed., Munich, 1929), ch. 1.

Mosca, Gaetano, "Encore quelques mots sur 'Le prince' de Machiavel," in *Revue des science politiques*, vol. 48 (1925), pp. 481–509, and vol. 49 (1926), pp. 5–27.

Morley, John, *Machiavelli* (London, 1897).

Dyer, Louis, *Machiavelli and the Modern State* (Boston, 1904).

Villari, Pasqale, *Niccolò Machiavelli and His Times*, translated by Linda Villari. 2 vols. (revised ed., London, 1892).

Ercole, Francesco, *La politica di Machiavelli*, Politieia, vol. 5 (Rome, 1926).

Schubert, Johannes, *Macchiavelli und die politischen Probleme unserer Zeit* (Berlin, 1927).

Mundt, Theodor, *Niccolò Macchiavelli und das System der modernen Politik* (third ed., Berlin, 1861).

MARTIN LUTHER

XII. MARTIN LUTHER (1483-1546)

INTRODUCTION

Machiavelli has been called the "first modern" political theorist chiefly because of his indifference to the truth of religion and his exclusive appeal to secular experience and human reason. At no time in the history of political thought, however, was greater use made of theological and scriptural arguments than in the half century following the publication of Machiavelli's *Discourses* and *Prince*. Political writing in this period was largely dominated by the ideas and practical consequences of the Protestant Reformation, which marked, in many respects, the beginning of a new era in the history of European culture. The Reformation, as a general movement, was the culmination of various intellectual and practical tendencies that had been under way for over a century : a reaction against the methods of scholasticism, a revival of interest in secular literature, the strivings for national independence, and the efforts of state governments to free themselves from the ecclesiastical hierarchy. The effects of the Reformation were to destroy permanently the ecclesiastical unity of Europe, weaken the force of ecclesiastical tradition as a form of argument, and help expel from political imagination the notion of universal empire. It led to the formation of a number of mutually independent Christian churches. It did not, however, destroy the idea that there should be agreement on religious truth and that organized authority of some sort should see that individual men adhered to the truth ; and it did not put an end to scriptural interpretations as a main form of political argument.

The Reformation began in Germany, in the work of Martin Luther. Born of a poor peasant family, Luther obtained an elementary education as a "charity" student, but he was able to go on to the University of Erfurt—then the best-known of the German universities—when his father became moderately prosperous as operator, under a lease, of a small mine. Preoccupied with a determination to make sure of his personal salvation, Luther became an Augustinian monk and practised fasting, scourging, and other penitential works. When he found no satisfaction in this, he turned to an intensive study of the New Testament and German mystics; under the influence of these readings and the promptings of friends, he reached the conclusion that salvation comes not through "works"—that is, observing the formal prescriptions of the church—but only through faith in Jesus Christ. He was ordained as a priest and entered the newer University of Wittenberg, where, after graduation as Doctor of the Holy Scriptures, he became a professor of theology. About this time he began his sermons and writings against certain practices of the church and in criticism of the prevailing scholastic theology. On the eve of All-Saints day in 1517, he posted on the door of the Castle Church a "Disputation on the Power and Efficacy of Indulgences." This was a comprehensive attack upon the ecclesiastical teaching on indulgences and their relation to the true nature of penance. The "Ninety-five Theses," as the Disputation came to be called, was extensively read and gained for Luther widespread influence, which led to direct conflict with the papal hierarchy. When the papacy tried to silence him, he and his supporters vigorously challenged the right of the papacy to decide on questions of belief and worship. Following his excommunication in 1520, he launched into an extensive attack on the whole historical and theological basis of the papal claims to supremacy in the church and on what he considered to be the doctrinal and ceremonial perversions of the papacy.

Luther's voluminous writings were concerned mainly with theological and ethical questions. Nowhere did he work out any systematic political philosophy. Several of his addresses and brief treatises, however, deal with certain political questions upon which he felt himself required to make definite pronouncements as to the implications of his religious and ethical doctrine. In a booklet entitled *Concerning Good Works*, published in 1519, he replied to the charge that his exaltation of faith over works meant a rejection altogether of works as an element of goodness : by interpretations of the Ten Commandments he attempted to show the relations between faith and works; and in his analysis of the Fifth Commandment he explained his stand on the necessity of civil authority and the duties of civil rulers. In the following year he issued his famous *Open Letter to the Christian Nobility of the German Nation*—his first publication after his full realization of his complete break with the Roman church : in this he demanded a reform of the whole organization and practice of Christianity through the agency of a council of priests and laymen presided over by the Emperor; and in an effort to take advantage of a growing nationalistic sentiment among the Germans, he appealed to the German princes to take the lead in a movement for independence from Italian domination and for the achievement of religious and moral reforms among the German people. In 1523, following the action of the German diet in putting him under the ban of the empire, he issued a treatise entitled *Concerning Secular Authority: to What Extent It Should Be Obeyed.* Here he argued that secular authority is ordained of God and is made necessary because most men are not Christians; that Christians must submit to secular authority, even to the extent of bearing arms in its defense, because of the need for such government by non-Christians; that secular government has to do solely with the kingdom of this world and has no power over matters of belief, in which man is responsible solely and directly to God.

Later experiences led Luther to further statements on the extent of the obligation to obey secular authorities. His teachings concerning the supreme authority of individual conscience had been used by radical leaders, in the peasant uprisings of 1525, as a justification for violent action against oppressive authority in both church and state. Luther, both fearful of serious civil conflict and aware of the dependence of his reform efforts upon support from strong and stable civil government, issued several addresses in condemnation of the extreme demands and aggressive methods of the peasants. He condemned their attempt to secure change by force, challenged their demands for equality ("a worldly kingdom cannot stand unless there is in it an inequality of persons, so that some are free, some imprisoned, some lords, some subjects, etc.") ; reminded them that "the Gospel does not make goods common, except in the case of those who of their own free will do what the apostles and disciples did"; advised them to "keep still, suffer, and make their complaints to God alone"; and urged the princes to pursue a policy of offering "the mad peasants an opportunity to come to terms, even though they are not worthy of it," and "if that does not help, then swiftly grasp the sword." [1] When he was

---

[1] See his *Admonition to Peace: A Reply to the Twelve Articles of the Peasants in Swabia,* in *Works of Martin Luther* (Philadelphia, 1915–34), Vol. IV, pp. 205–244, at pp. 240, 241; and *Against the Robbing and Murdering Hordes of Peasants, ibid.,* pp. 247–254, at pp. 250, 251.

charged with responsibility for the ruthless measures pursued by some of the lords after their decisive victory over the peasants, he issued another address renewing his condemnation of rebellion but offering also a brief warning to "furious, raving, senseless tyrants, who even after the battle cannot get their fill of blood." [1]

Still later, after a sharp cleavage between Protestant princes and the Catholic Emperor, Luther conceded that self-defense against tyranny was the right of Christians and that submission was not due to a ruler who disregarded the laws that rightly bound him. These later views became common among the theoretical champions of dissenting sects in the religious wars of the later sixteenth century; and his doctrine of the supreme authority of individual conscience was of still later influence in establishing another essential idea in the theory of liberal democracy. Luther's own interest in the right of positive action against unlawful authority was limited to his interest in vindicating the rights of Protestant communities against a Catholic empire. His prevailing political views are best represented in the first three works referred to above, in which he set forth in more detail his ideas concerning the distinction in kind between spiritual and secular authority, the duty of passive submission to an established political and social order, and the nature and scope of the duties of secular rulers.

READINGS FROM CONCERNING GOOD WORKS, OPEN LETTER TO THE CHRISTIAN NOBILITY OF THE GERMAN NATION, AND CONCERNING SECULAR AUTHORITY [2]

1. The Duty of Obedience to Secular Authority [3]

The third work of this Commandment [4] is to obey the temporal authority, as Paul teaches, Romans xiii, and Titus iii, and St. Peter, I Peter ii: "Submit yourselves to the king as supreme, and to the princes as his ambassadors, and to all the ordinances

---

[1] *An Open Letter Concerning the Hard Book against the Peasants, op. cit.*, Vol. IV, pp. 257–281, at p. 280.

[2] The selections are taken from *Works of Martin Luther*, a translation of selected treatises, with Introductions and Notes, by Henry E. Jacobs, W. A. Lambert, J. J. Schindel, A. Steimle, A. T. W. Steinhaeuser, C. M. Jacobs, and others, 6 vols. (Philadelphia, 1915–34); to be completed in ten volumes. By courtesy of A. J. Holman Co.

[3] From *A Treatise on Good Works* (translated by W. A. Lambert in *Works of Martin Luther*, Vol. I, pp. 173–285), pp. 262–266.

[4] "Honor thy father and thy mother."

of the worldly power." But it is the work of the temporal power to protect its subjects, and to punish thievery, robbery, and adultery, as St. Paul says, Romans xiii: "It beareth not the sword in vain; it serves God with it, to the terror of evil doers, and to the protection of the good."

Here men sin in two ways. First, if they lie to the government, deceive it, and are disloyal, neither obey nor do as it has ordered and commanded, whether with their bodies or their possessions. For even if the government does injustice, as the King of Babylon did to the people of Israel, yet God would have it obeyed, without treachery and deception. Secondly, when men speak evil of the government and curse it, and when a man cannot revenge himself and abuses the government with grumbling and evil words, publicly or secretly.

In all this we are to regard that which St. Peter bids us regard, namely, that its power, whether it do right or wrong, cannot harm the soul, but only the body and property; unless indeed it should try openly to compel us to do wrong against God or men; as in former days when the magistrates were not yet Christians, and as the Turk is now said to do. For to suffer wrong destroys no one's soul, nay, it improves the soul, although it inflicts loss upon the body and property; but to do wrong, that destroys the soul, although it should gain all the world's wealth.

This also is the reason why there is not such great danger in the temporal power as in the spiritual, when it does wrong. For the temporal power can do no harm, since it has nothing to do with preaching and faith and the first three Commandments. But the spiritual power does harm not only when it does wrong, but also when it neglects its duty and busies itself with other things, even if they were better than the very best works of the temporal power. Therefore, we must resist it when it does not do right, and not resist the temporal power although it does wrong. For the poor people believe and do as they see the spiritual power believing and doing; if they are not set an example and are not taught, then they also believe nothing and do nothing; since this power is instituted for no other reason than to lead the people in faith to God. All this is not found in the temporal power; for it may do and leave undone what it will, my faith to God still goes its way and works its works, because I need not believe what it believes.

Therefore, also, the temporal power is a very small thing in God's sight, and far too slightly regarded by Him, that for its sake, whether it do right or wrong, we should resist, become disobedient and quarrel. On the other hand, the spiritual power is an exceeding great blessing, and far too precious in His eyes, that the very least of Christians should endure and keep silent, if it departs a hair's breadth from its own duty, not to say when it does the very opposite of its duty, as we now see it do every day.

In this power also there is much abuse. First, when it follows the flatterers, which is a common and especially harmful plague of this power, against which no one can sufficiently guard and protect himself. Here it is led by the nose, and oppresses the common people, becomes a government of the like of which a heathen says: "The spider-webs catch the small flies, but the mill-stones roll through." So the laws, ordinances and government of one and the same authority hold the small men, and the great are free ; and where the prince is not himself so wise that he needs nobody's advice, or has such a standing that they fear him, there will and must be (unless God should do a special wonder) a childish government.

For this reason God has considered evil, unfit rulers the greatest of plagues, as He threatens, Isaiah iii, "I will take away from them every man of valor, and will give children to be their princes and babes to rule over them." Four plagues God has named in Scripture, Ezekiel xiv. The first and slightest, which also David chose, is pestilence, the second is famine, the third is war, the fourth is all manner of evil beasts, such as lions, wolves, serpents, dragons ; these are the wicked rulers. For where these are, the land is destroyed, not only in body and property, as in the others, but also in honor, discipline, virtue and the soul's salvation. For pestilence and famine make people good and rich ; but war and wicked rulers bring to naught everything that has to do with temporal and eternal possessions.

A prince must also be very wise and not at all times undertake to enforce his own will, although he may have the authority and the very best cause. For it is a far nobler virtue to endure wrong to one's authority than to risk property and person, if it is advantageous to the subjects ; since worldly rights attach only to temporal goods.

Hence, it is a very foolish saying : I have a right to it, therefore I will take it by storm and keep it, although all sorts of misfortune may come to others thereby. So we read of the Emperor Octavianus, that he did not wish to make war, however just his cause might be, unless there were sure indications of greater benefit than harm, or at least that the harm would not be intolerable, and said : "War is like fishing with a golden net ; the loss risked is always greater than the catch can be." For he who guides a wagon must walk far otherwise than if he were walking alone; when alone he may walk, jump, and do as he will; but when he drives, he must so guide and adapt himself that the wagon and horses can follow him, and regard that more than his own will. So also a prince leads a multitude with him and must not walk and act as he wills, but as the multitude can, considering their need and advantage more than his will and pleasure. For when a prince rules after his own mad will and follows his own opinion, he is like a mad driver, who rushes straight ahead with horse and wagon, through bushes, thorns, ditches, water, up hill and down dale, regardless of roads and bridges; he will not drive long, all will go to smash.

Therefore it would be most profitable for rulers, that they read, or have read to them, from youth on, the histories, both in sacred and in profane books, in which they would find more examples and skill in ruling than in all the books of law; as we read that the kings of Persia did, Esther vi. For examples and histories benefit and teach more than the laws and statutes: there actual experience teaches, here untried and uncertain words.

2. The Relation of Secular to Spiritual Authority [1]

The Romanists, with great adroitness, have built three walls about them, behind which they have hitherto defended themselves in such wise that no one has been able to reform them; and this has been the cause of terrible corruption throughout all Christendom.

First, when pressed by the temporal power, they have made decrees and said that the temporal power has no jurisdiction over them, but, on the other hand, that the spiritual is above the temporal power. Second, when the attempt is made to reprove them out of the Scriptures, they raise the objection that the interpretation of the Scriptures belongs to no one except the pope. Third, if threatened with a council, they answer with the fable that no one can call a council but the pope.

In this wise they have slyly stolen from us our three rods,[2] that they may go unpunished, and have ensconced themselves within the safe stronghold of these three walls, that they may practise all the knavery and wickedness which we now see. Even

---

[1] From *An Open Letter to the Christian Nobility of the German Nation Concerning the Reform of the Christian Estate* (translated by C. M. Jacobs, in *Works of Martin Luther*, Vol. II, pp. 57–164), pp. 65–73.

[2] i. e., the three rods for the punishment of an evil pope.

when they have been compelled to hold a council they have weakened its power in advance by previously binding the princes with an oath to let them remain as they are. Moreover, they have given the pope full authority over all the decisions of the council, so that it is all one whether there are many councils or no councils,—except that they deceive us with puppet-shows and sham-battles. So terribly do they fear for their skin in a really free council! And they have intimidated kings and princes by making them believe it would be an offence against God not to obey them in all these knavish, crafty deceptions.

Now God help us, and give us one of the trumpets with which the walls of Jericho were overthrown, that we may blow down these walls of straw and paper, and may set free the Christian rods for the punishment of sin, bringing to light the craft and deceit of the devil, to the end that through punishment we may reform ourselves, and once more attain God's favor.

Against the first wall we will direct our first attack.

It is pure invention that pope, bishops, priests and monks are to be called the "spiritual estate"; princes, lords, artisans, and farmers the "temporal estate." That is indeed a fine bit of lying and hypocrisy. Yet no one should be frightened by it; and for this reason—viz., that all Christians are truly of the "spiritual estate," and there is among them no difference at all but that of office, as Paul says in I Corinthians xii, We are all one body, yet every member has its own work, whereby it serves every other, all because we have one baptism, one Gospel, one faith, and are all alike Christians; for baptism, Gospel and faith alone make us "spiritual" and a Christian people.

But that a pope or a bishop anoints, confers tonsures, ordains, consecrates, or prescribes dress unlike that of the laity,—this may make hypocrites and graven images, but it never makes a Christian or "spiritual" man. Through baptism all of us are consecrated to the priesthood, as St. Peter says in I Peter ii, "Ye are a royal priesthood, a priestly kingdom," and the book of Revelation says, "Thou hast made us by Thy blood to be priests and kings." For if we had no higher consecration than pope or bishop gives, the consecration by pope or bishop would never make a priest, nor might anyone either say mass or preach a sermon or give absolution. Therefore when the bishop consecrates it is the same thing as if he, in the place and stead of the whole congregation, all of whom have like power, were to take one out of their number and charge him to use this power for the others; just as though ten brothers, all king's sons and equal heirs, were to choose one of themselves to rule the inheritance for them all,—they would all be kings and equal in power, though one of them would be charged with the duty of ruling.

To make it still clearer. If a little group of pious Christian laymen were taken captive and set down in a wilderness, and had among them no priest consecrated by a bishop, and if there in the wilderness they were to agree in choosing one of themselves, married or unmarried, and were to charge him with the office of baptising, saying mass, absolving and preaching, such a man would be as truly a priest as though all bishops and popes had consecrated him. That is why in cases of necessity any one can baptise and give absolution, which would be impossible unless we were all priests. This great grace and power of baptism and of the Christian Estate they have well-nigh destroyed and caused us to forget through the canon law. It was in the manner aforesaid that Christians in olden days chose from their number bishops and priests, who were afterwards confirmed by other bishops, without all the show which now obtains. It was thus that Sts. Augustine, Ambrose and Cyprian became bishops.

Since, then, the temporal authorities are baptised with the same baptism and have the same faith and Gospel as we, we must grant that they are priests and bishops and count their office one which has a proper and a useful place in the Christian community. For whoever comes out of the water of baptism can boast that he is already consecrated priest, bishop and pope, though it is not seemly that every one should exercise the office. Nay, just because we are all in like manner priests, no one must put himself forward and undertake, without our consent and election, to do what is in the power of all of us. For what is common to all, no one dare take upon himself without the will and the command of the community; and should it happen that one chosen for such an office were deposed for malfeasance, he would then be just what he was before he held office. Therefore a priest in Christendom is nothing else than an office-holder. While he is in office, he has precedence; when deposed, he is a peasant or a townsman like the rest. Beyond all doubt, then, a priest is no longer a priest when he is deposed. But now they have invented *characteres indelebiles*, and prate that a deposed priest is nevertheless something different from a mere layman. They even dream that a priest can never become a layman, or be anything else than a priest. All this is mere talk and man-made law.

From all this it follows that there is really no difference between laymen and priests, princes and bishops, "spirituals" and "temporals," as they call them, except that of office and work, but not of "estate"; for they are all of the same estate—true priests, bishops and popes,—though they are not all engaged in the same work, just as all priests and monks have not the same work. This is the teaching of St. Paul in Romans xii and I Corinthians xii, and of St. Peter in I Peter ii, as I have said above, viz., that we are all one body of Christ, the Head, all members one of another. Christ has not two different bodies, one "temporal," the other "spiritual." He is one Head, and He has one body.

Therefore, just as those who are now called "spiritual"— priests, bishops or popes—are neither different from other Christians nor superior to them, except that they are charged with the administration of the Word of God and the sacraments, which is their work and office, so it is with the temporal authorities, —they bear sword and rod with which to punish the evil and to protect the good. A cobbler, a smith, a farmer, each has the work and office of his trade, and yet they are all alike consecrated priests and bishops, and every one by means of his own work or office must benefit and serve every other, that in this way many kinds of work may be done for the bodily and spiritual welfare of the community, even as all the members of the body serve one another.

See, now, how Christian is the decree which says that the temporal power is not above the "spiritual estate" and may not punish it. That is as much as to say that the hand shall lend no aid when the eye is suffering. Is it not unnatural, not to say unchristian, that one member should not help another and prevent its destruction? Verily, the more honorable the member, the more should the others help. I say then, since the temporal power is ordained of God to punish evil-doers and to protect them that do well, it should therefore be left free to perform its office without hindrance through the whole body of Christendom without respect of persons, whether it affect pope, bishops, priests, monks, nuns or anybody else. For if the mere fact that the temporal power has a smaller place among the Christian offices than has the office of preachers or confessors, or of the clergy, then the tailors, cobblers, masons, carpenters, pot-boys, tapsters, farmers, and all the secular tradesmen, should also be prevented from providing pope, bishops, priests and monks with shoes, clothing, houses, meat and drink, and from paying them tribute. But if these laymen are allowed to do their work unhindered, what do the Roman scribes mean by their laws, with which they withdraw themselves from the jurisdiction of the temporal Christian power, only so that they may be free to do evil and to fulfil what St. Peter has said: "There shall be false teachers among you, and through covetousness shall they with feigned words make merchandise of you."

On this account the Christian temporal power should exercise its office without let or hindrance, regardless whether it be pope, bishop or priest whom it affects; whoever is guilty, let him suffer. All that the canon law has said to the contrary is sheer invention of Roman presumption. For thus saith St. Paul to all Christians: "Let every soul (I take that to mean the pope's soul also) be subject unto the higher powers; for they bear not the sword in vain, but are the ministers of God for the punishment of evil-doers, and for the praise of them that do well." St. Peter also says: "Submit yourselves unto every ordinance of man for the Lord's sake, for so is the will of God." He has also prophesied that such men shall come as will despise the temporal authorities; and this has come to pass through the canon law.

So then, I think this first paper-wall is overthrown, since the temporal power has become a member of the body of Christendom, and is of the "spiritual estate," though its work is of a temporal nature. Therefore its work should extend freely and without hindrance to all the members of the whole body; it should punish and use force whenever guilt deserves or necessity demands, without regard to pope, bishops and priests,—let them hurl threats and bans as much as they will.

This is why guilty priests, if they are surrendered to the temporal law, are first deprived of their priestly dignities, which would not be right unless the temporal sword had previously had authority over them by divine right.

Again, it is intolerable that in the canon law so much importance is attached to the freedom, life and property of the clergy, as though the laity were not also as spiritual and as good Christians as they, or did not belong to the Church. Why are your life and limb, your property and honor so free, and mine not? We are all alike Christians, and have baptism, faith, Spirit and all things alike. If a priest is killed, the land is laid under interdict,[1]—

---

[1] The interdict is the prohibition of the administration of the sacraments and of the other rites of the Church within the territory upon which the interdict is laid.

why not when a peasant is killed? Whence comes this great distinction between those who are equally Christians? Only from human laws and inventions!

Moreover, it can be no good spirit who has invented such exceptions and granted to sin such license and impunity. For if we are bound to strive against the works and words of the evil spirit, and to drive him out in whatever way we can, as Christ commands and His Apostles, ought we, then, to suffer it in silence when the pope or his satellites are bent on devilish words and works? Ought we for the sake of men to allow the suppression of divine commandments and truths which we have sworn in baptism to support with life and limb? Of a truth we should then have to answer for all the souls that would thereby be abandoned and led astray.

It must therefore have been the very prince of devils who said what is written in the canon law: "If the pope were so scandalously bad as to lead souls in crowds to the devil, yet he could not be deposed." On this accursed and devilish foundation they build at Rome, and think that we should let all the world go to the devil, rather than resist their knavery. If the fact that one man is set over others were sufficient reason why he should escape punishment, then no Christian could punish another, since Christ commands that every man shall esteem himself the lowliest and the least.

Where sin is, there is no escape from punishment; as St. Gregory also writes that we are indeed all equal, but guilt puts us in subjection one to another. Now we see how they whom God and the Apostles have made subject to the temporal sword deal with Christendom, depriving it of its liberty by their own wickedness, without warrant of Scripture. It is to be feared that this is a game of Anti-christ or a sign that he is close at hand.

3.   The Nature and Scope of Secular Authority [1]

I. We must firmly establish secular law and the sword, that no one may doubt that it is in the world by God's will and ordinance. The passages which establish this are the following: Romans xiii, "Let every soul be subject to power and authority, for there is no power but from God. The power that is everywhere is ordained of God. He then who resists the power re-

---

[1] From *Concerning Secular Authority: To What Extent It Should Be Obeyed* (translated by J. J. Schindel, in *Works of Martin Luther*, Vol. III, pp. 223–273), pp. 231–241, 250–271.

sists God's ordinance. But he who resists God's ordinance, shall bring himself under condemnation." Likewise, I Peter ii, "Be subject to every kind of human ordinance, whether to the king as supreme, or to the governors, as to those sent of Him for the punishing of the evil and for the reward of the good." This penal law existed from the beginning of the world. For when Cain slew his brother he was in such great terror of being in turn killed that God specially forbade it and suspended the sword for his sake,—and no one was to slay him. He would not have had this fear if he had not seen and heard from Adam that murderers should be slain. Moreover God re-established and confirmed it after the Flood in unmistakable terms when He said, "Whoso sheds man's blood, his blood shall be shed again by man." This cannot be understood as a plague and punishment of God upon murderers; for many murderers who repent or are pardoned continue to live, and die by other means than the sword. But it is said of the right of the sword, that a murderer is guilty of death and should in justice be slain by the sword. Though justice be hindered or the sword be tardy, so that the murderer dies a natural death, the Scripture is not on that account false when it says, "Whoso sheddeth man's blood, by man shall his blood be shed." For it is men's fault or merit that this law commanded of God is not carried out; even as other commandments of God are broken.

Afterward it was also confirmed by the law of Moses, Exodus xxi, "If a man presumptuously kill thou shalt take him from My altar that he may die." And again, in the same place, "A life for a life, an eye for an eye, a tooth for a tooth, a foot for a foot, a hand for a hand, a wound for a wound, a bruise for a bruise." Christ also confirms it when He says to Peter in the garden, "He that taketh the sword shall perish by the sword," which is to be interpreted like Genesis ix, "Whoso sheddeth man's blood," etc. Doubtless Christ refers in these words to that passage and incorporates and confirms it in them. John Baptist teaches the same. When the soldiers asked him what they should do, he answered, "Do injustice or violence to no one, and be content with your wages." If the sword were not divinely appointed he should have commanded them to cease being soldiers, since he was to perfect the people and direct them in a proper Christian way. Hence it is sufficiently clear and certain that it is God's will that the sword and secular law be used for the punishment of the wicked and the protection of the upright.

II. There seems to be a powerful argument on the other side.

Christ says, Matthew v, "Ye have heard that it was said to them of old: An eye for an eye, a tooth for a tooth. But I say unto you, That a man shall not resist evil, but if any one strikes thee upon the right cheek, turn to him the other also; and whoever will go to law with thee to take thy coat, let him have the cloak also, and whoever forces thee a mile, with him go two miles." Likewise Paul, Romans xii, "Dearly beloved, defend not yourselves, but give place to God's wrath, for it is written, Vengeance is mine, I will repay saith the Lord." Likewise Matthew v, "Love your enemies, do good to them that hate you." And I Peter iii, "Let no one repay evil with evil, nor railing with railing," etc. These and the like passages truly would make it appear as though in the New Testament there should be no secular sword among Christians.

Hence the sophists also say that Christ has abolished Moses' law; of such commandments they make counsels for the perfect, and divide Christian teaching and Christians into two classes. One part they call the perfect, and assign to it such counsels. To the other, the imperfect, they assign the commandments. This they do out of sheer perversity and caprice, without any scriptural basis. They do not see that in the same passage Christ lays such stress on His teaching that He is unwilling to have the least word of it set aside, and condemns to hell those who do not love their enemies. Therefore we must interpret these passages differently, so that Christ's words may apply to all alike whether they be "perfect" or "imperfect." For perfection and imperfection consist not in works and do not establish a distinct external order among Christians; but they exist in the heart, in faith and love, so that they who believe and love the most are the perfect ones, whether outwardly they be male or female, prince or peasant, monk or layman. For love and faith produce no sects or outward differences.

III. We must divide all the children of Adam into two classes; the first belong to the kingdom of God, the second to the kingdom of the world. Those belonging to the kingdom of God are all true believers in Christ and are subject to Christ. For Christ is the King and Lord in the Kingdom of God, as the second Psalm and all the Scriptures say. For this reason He came into the world, that He might begin God's kingdom and establish it in the world. Therefore He says before Pilate, "My kingdom is not of the world, but whoever is of the truth hears My voice"; and continually in the Gospel He refers to the kingdom of God and says, "Amend your ways, the kingdom of God is at hand."

Likewise, "Seek first the kingdom of God and His righteousness." He also calls the Gospel, a Gospel of the kingdom, for the reason that it teaches, governs, and contains God's kingdom. Now observe, these people need no secular sword or law. And if all the world were composed of real Christians, that is, true believers, no prince, king, lord, sword, or law would be needed. For what were the use of them, since Christians have in their hearts the Holy Spirit, who instructs them and causes them to wrong no one, to love every one, willingly and cheerfully to suffer injustice and even death from every one. Where every wrong is suffered and every right is done, no quarrel, strife, trial, judge, penalty, law or sword is needed. Therefore, it is not possible for the secular sword and law to find any work to do among Christians, since of themselves they do much more than its laws and doctrines can demand. Just as Paul says in I Timothy i, "The law is not given for the righteous, but for the unrighteous."

Why is this? Because the righteous does of himself all and more than all that all the laws demand. But the unrighteous do nothing that the law demands, therefore they need the law to instruct, constrain, and compel them to do what is good. A good tree does not need any teaching or law to bear good fruit, its nature causes it to bear according to its kind without any law and teaching. A man would be a fool to make a book of laws and statutes telling an apple tree how to bear apples and not thorns, when it is able by its own nature to do this better than man with all his books can define and direct. Just so, by the Spirit and by faith all Christians are throughout inclined to do well and keep the law, much more than any one can teach them with all the laws, and need so far as they are concerned no commandments nor law.

You ask, Why then did God give to all men so many commandments, and why did Christ teach in the Gospel so many things to be done? Concerning this I have written in the Postil [1] and elsewhere. To put it as briefly as possible here, Paul says that the law is given for the sake of the unrighteous, that is, that those who are not Christians may through the law be externally restrained from evil deeds, as we shall hear later. Since, however, no one is by nature Christian or pious, but every one sinful and evil, God places the restraints of the law upon them all, so that they may not dare give rein to their desires and commit outward, wicked deeds. In addition, St. Paul gives the law

[1] A collection of sermons on the Scripture lessons for the Church Year.

another function in Romans vii and Galatians iii. It is to teach
men to recognize sin, that they may be made humble unto grace
and unto faith in Christ. Christ also does this here, when He
teaches in Matthew v that we should not resist evil, and thereby
glorifies the law and teaches how a real Christian ought to be
and must be disposed, as we shall hear further on.

IV. All who are not Christians belong to the kingdom of the
world and are under the law. Since few believe and still fewer
live a Christian life, do not resist the evil, and themselves do no
evil, God has provided for non-Christians a different government
outside the Christian estate and God's kingdom, and has subjected them to the sword, so that, even though they would do so,
they cannot practice their wickedness, and that, if they do,
they may not do it without fear nor in peace and prosperity.
Even so a wild, savage beast is fastened with chains and bands,
so that it cannot bite and tear as is its wont, although it gladly
would do so; whereas a tame and gentle beast does not require
this, but without any chains and bands is nevertheless harmless.
If it were not so, seeing that the whole world is evil and that
among thousands there is scarcely one true Christian, men would
devour one another, and no one could preserve wife and child,
support himself and serve God; and thus the world would be
reduced to chaos. For this reason God has ordained the two
governments; the spiritual, which by the Holy Spirit under
Christ makes Christians and pious people, and the secular, which
restrains the unchristian and wicked so that they must needs
keep the peace outwardly, even against their will. So Paul
interprets the secular sword, Romans xiii, and says it is not a
terror to good works, but to the evil. And Peter says it is for
the punishment of evil doers.

If any one attempted to rule the world by the Gospel, and
put aside all secular law and the secular sword, on the plea
that all are baptised and Christian, and that according to the
Gospel, there is to be among them neither law nor sword, nor
necessity for either, pray, what would happen? He would
loose the bands and chains of the wild and savage beasts, and
let them tear and mangle every one, and at the same time say
they were quite tame and gentle creatures; but I would have
the proof in my wounds. Just so would the wicked under the
name of Christian abuse this freedom of the Gospel, carry on
their knavery, and say that they were Christians subject neither
to law nor sword, as some are already raving and ranting.

To such an one we must say, It is indeed true that Christians so far as they themselves are concerned, are subject to neither law nor sword and need neither; but first take heed and fill the world with real Christians before ruling it in a Christian and evangelical manner. This you will never accomplish; for the world and the masses are and always will be unchristian, although they are all baptised and are nominally Christian. Christians, however, are few and far between, as the saying is. Therefore it is out of the question that there should be a common Christian government over the whole world, nay even over one land or company of people, since the wicked always outnumber the good. Hence a man who would venture to govern an entire country or the world with the Gospel would be like a shepherd who should place in one fold wolves, lions, eagles, and sheep together and let them freely mingle with one another and say, Help yourselves, and be good and peaceful among yourselves; the fold is open, there is plenty of food; have no fear of dogs and clubs. The sheep, forsooth, would keep the peace and would allow themselves to be fed and governed in peace, but they would not live long; nor would any beast keep from molesting another.

For this reason these two kingdoms must be sharply distinguished, and both be permitted to remain; the one to produce piety, the other to bring about external peace and prevent evil deeds; neither is sufficient in the world without the other. For no one can become pious before God by means of the secular government, without Christ's spiritual rule. Hence Christ's rule does not extend over all, but Christians are always in the minority and are in the midst of non-Christians. Where there is only secular rule or law, there, of necessity, is sheer hypocrisy, though the commandments be God's very own. Without the Holy Spirit in the heart no one becomes really pious, he may do as fine works as he will. Where, on the other hand, the spiritual government rules alone over land and people, there evil is given free rein and the door is opened for every kind of knavery; for the natural world cannot receive or comprehend spiritual things.

You see the purpose of Christ's words which we quoted above from Matthew v. They mean that Christians shall not go to law nor use the secular sword among themselves. In reality He says it only to His dear Christians. They alone also accept it and act accordingly, nor do they make counsels of it, as the sophists do, but are so inclined in their heart, through the Spirit, that they do evil to no one and willingly endure evil at every one's hands. If the whole world were Christian, all these words would apply to it and it would keep them. Since, however,

it is unchristian the words do not apply to it, nor does it keep
them, but is under another rule in which those who are not Christians are under external constraint and are forced to keep the
peace and do what is good.

For this reason Christ did not wield the sword nor give it a
place in His kingdom; for He is a King over Christians and rules
by His Holy Spirit alone, without law. And although He acknowledged the sword, He nevertheless did not use it; for it is of no use
in His kingdom, in which are none but the pious. Hence David
of old dared not build the temple, because he had shed much
blood and had borne the sword; not that he had done wrong
thereby, but because he could not be a type of Christ, who without the sword was to have a kingdom of peace. It must be
built by Solomon, whose name means "Frederick" or "peaceful," who had a peaceful kingdom, by which the truly peaceful
kingdom of Christ, the real Frederick and Solomon, could be
represented. In like manner, during the entire building of the
temple not the sound of a tool was heard, as the text says; all
for this reason, that Christ, without constraint and force, without
law and the sword, was to have a people who serve Him freely.

This is what the prophets mean in Psalm cx, "Thy people
shall be willing"; and in Isaiah xi, "They shall not hurt nor
destroy in all my holy mountain"; and in Isaiah ii, "They
shall beat their swords into plowshares and their spears into
pruning hooks, and no one shall lift up the sword against another,
neither shall they busy themselves in war anymore," etc. Whoever would apply these and similar passages wherever Christ's
name is professed, would entirely pervert the Scriptures; for
they are spoken only of true Christians, who really do this among
themselves.

V. But perhaps you will say, Since Christians do not need
the secular sword and the law, why does Paul say to all Christians, in Romans xiii, "Let all souls be subject to power and
authority"? And St. Peter says, "Be subject to every human
ordinance," etc., as quoted above. I answer, as I have said,
that Christians, among themselves and by and for themselves,
need no law or sword, since it is neither necessary nor profitable
for them. Since, however, a true Christian lives and labors on
earth not for himself, but for his neighbor, therefore the whole
spirit of his life impels him to do even that which he need not
do, but which is profitable and necessary for his neighbor. Because the sword is a very great benefit and necessary to the whole
world, to preserve peace, to punish sin and to prevent evil, he

submits most willingly to the rule of the sword, pays tax, honors those in authority, serves, helps, and does all he can to further the government, that it may be sustained and held in honor and fear. Although he needs none of these for himself and it is not necessary for him to do them, yet he considers what is for the good and profit of others, as Paul teaches in Ephesians v.

He serves the State as he performs all other works of love, which he himself does not need. He visits the sick, not that he may be made well; feeds no one because he himself needs food: so he serves the State not because he needs it, but because others need it,—that they may be protected and that the wicked may not become worse. He loses nothing by this, and such service in no way harms him, and yet it is of great profit to the world. If he did not do it, he would be acting not as a Christian but contrary even to love, and would also be setting a bad example to others, who like him would not submit to authority, though they were no Christians. In this way the Gospel would be brought into disrepute, as though it taught rebellion and made self-willed people, unwilling to benefit or serve any one, when in reality it makes a Christian the servant of every one. Thus in Matthew xvii, Christ gave the tribute money that He might not offend them, although He did not need to do it.

Thus you observe in the words of Christ quoted above from Matthew v that He indeed teaches that Christians among themselves should have no secular sword nor law. He does not, however, forbid one to serve and obey those who have the secular sword and the law; much rather, since you have no need of them and are not to have them, are you to serve those who have not progressed so far as you and still need them. Although you do not need to have your enemy punished, your weak neighbor does. You should help him, that he may have peace and that his enemy may be curbed; which is not possible unless power and authority are honored and feared. Christ does not say, "Thou shalt not serve the State or be subject to it," but "Thou shalt not resist evil." As though He said, "Take heed that you bear everything, so that you may not need the State to help and serve you and be of profit to you, but that you may on the other hand, help, serve, and be of profit and use to it. I would have you to be far too exalted and noble to have any need of it, but it should have need of you."

We come now to the main part of this treatise. For as we have learned that there must be temporal authority on earth, and how it is to be employed in a Christian and salutary way, we must now learn how far its arm extends and how far its hand reaches, lest it extend too far and encroach upon God's kingdom and rule. And it is very necessary to know this, since where it is given too wide a scope, intolerable and terrible injury follows; and, on the other hand, it cannot be too much restricted without working injury. In the latter case the punishment is too light; in the former, too severe. It is more tolerable, however, to err on the latter side and punish too little; since it always is better to let a knave live than to kill a good man, for the world will still have knaves, and must have them, but of good men there are few.

In the first place, it must be noted that the two classes of Adam's children, the one in God's kingdom under Christ, the other in the kingdom of the world under the State, have two kinds of laws, as was said above. Every kingdom must have its own laws and regulations, and without law no kingdom or government can exist, as daily experience sufficiently proves. Worldly government has laws which extend no farther than to life and property and what is external upon earth. For over the soul God can and will let no one rule but Himself. Therefore, where temporal power presumes to prescribe laws for the soul, it encroaches upon God's government and only misleads and destroys the souls. We desire to make this so clear that every one shall grasp it, and that our junkers, the princes and bishops, may see what fools they are when they seek to coerce the people with their laws and commandments into believing one thing or another.

When a man-made law is imposed upon the soul, in order to make it believe this or that, as that man prescribes, there is certainly no word of God for it. If there is no word of God for it, it is uncertain whether God will have it so, for we cannot be certain that what He does not command pleases Him. Nay, we are sure that it does not please Him, for He desires that our faith be grounded simply and entirely on His divine Word, as He says in Matthew xvi, "On this rock will I build my church"; and in John x, "My sheep hear my voice and know me; but the voice of strangers they hear not, but flee from them." It follows from this that the secular power forces souls to eternal death with such an outrageous law, for it compels them to believe as right and certainly pleasing to God what is nevertheless uncertain, nay, what is certainly displeasing to Him, since there is no clear word of God for it. For whoever believes that to be right which is wrong or uncertain denies the truth, which is God Himself, and believes in lies and errors and counts that right which is wrong.

Hence it is the height of folly when they command that one shall believe the Church, the fathers, the councils, though there be no word of God for it. The devil's apostles command such things, not the Church ; for the Church commands nothing unless it is sure it is God's Word, as St. Peter says, "If any man speak let him speak as the oracles of God." It will be a very long time, however, before they prove that the statements of the councils are God's Word. Still more foolish is it when they assert that kings and princes and the mass of men believe thus and so. If you please, we are not baptised unto kings, princes, or even unto the mass of men, but unto Christ and unto God himself ; neither are we called kings, princes or common folk, but Christians. No one shall and can command the soul, unless he can show it the way to heaven ; but this no man can do, only God. Therefore in matters which concern the salvation of souls nothing but God's Word shall be taught and accepted.

Again, consummate fools though they are, they must confess that they have no power over souls. For no human being can kill a soul or make it alive, conduct it to heaven or hell. And if they will not believe us in this, Christ indeed will certify strongly enough to it, since He says in Matthew x, "Fear not them which kill the body and after that have power to do naught ; but rather fear Him Who after He has killed the body has power to condemn to hell." I consider that here it is sufficiently clear that the soul is taken out of all human hands and is placed under the power of God alone. Now tell me, how much wit is there in the head of him who imposes commandments where he has no power at all ? Who would not regard one as insane if he commanded the moon to shine when he desired it ? How fitting it would be if the Leipzigers would impose laws on us Wittenbergers, or again, if we in Wittenberg would lay laws on those in Leipzig. They would certainly send the law-makers a thank-offering of hellebore to clear the brain and cure the snuffles. Nevertheless, our emperors and wise princes continue to permit pope, bishops and sophists to lead them on, one blind man leading the other, to command their subjects to believe, without God's Word, whatever they please, and still would be known as Christian princes. God help us !

Besides, we can understand how any authority shall and may act only where it can see, know, judge, change and convert. For what kind of judge would he be who should blindly judge matters which he neither heard nor saw? Tell me, how can a man see, know, judge, condemn and change hearts? This is reserved for God alone, as Psalm vii says, "God trieth the heart and reins"; likewise, "The Lord shall judge the people"; and Acts xv, "God knoweth the hearts"; and, Jeremiah xvii, "Wicked and unsearchable is the human heart; who can know it? I the Lord, who search the heart and reins." A court ought and must be quite certain and clear about everything, if it is to pass sentence. But the thoughts and intents of the heart can be known to no one but God; therefore it is useless and impossible to command or compel any one by force to believe one thing or another. It must be taken hold of in a different way; force cannot accomplish it. And I am surprised at the great fools, since they themselves all say, *De occultis non judicat ecclesia,*—the Church does not judge secret things. If the spiritual rule of the Church governs only public matters, how dare the senseless secular power judge and control such a secret, spiritual, hidden matter as faith?

Furthermore, every man is responsible for his own faith, and he must see to it for himself that he believes rightly. As little as another can go to hell or heaven for me, so little can he believe or disbelieve for me; and as little as he can open or shut heaven or hell for me, so little can he drive me to faith or unbelief. Since, then, belief or unbelief is a matter of every one's conscience, and since this is no lessening of the secular power, the latter should be content and attend to its own affairs and permit men to believe one thing or another, as they are able and willing, and constrain no one by force. For faith is a free work, to which no one can be forced. Nay, it is a divine work, done in the Spirit, certainly not a matter which outward authority should compel or create. Hence arises the well-known saying, found also in Augustine, "No one can or ought be constrained to believe."

Besides, the blind, wretched folk do not see how utterly hopeless and impossible a thing they are attempting. For no matter how much they fret and fume, they cannot do more than make the people obey them by word and deed; the heart they cannot constrain, though they wear themselves out trying. For the proverb is true, "Thoughts are free." Why then would they constrain people to believe from the heart, when they see that it is impossible? In this way they compel weak consciences to lie, to deny, and to say what they do not believe in their hearts, and they load themselves down with dreadful alien sins. For all the lies and false confessions which such weak consciences utter fall back upon him who compels them. It were far better, if their subjects erred, simply to let them err, than that they should constrain them to lie and to say what is not in their hearts; neither is it right to defend evil with what is worse.

Would you like to know why God ordains that the temporal princes must offend so frightfully? I will tell you. God has given them over to a perverse mind and will make an end of them, as well as of the spiritual nobles. For my ungracious lords, the pope and the bishops, should be bishops and preach God's Word; this they leave undone and are become temporal princes, and govern with laws which concern only life and property. How thoroughly they have turned things upside down! Inwardly they ought to be ruling souls by God's Word; hence outwardly they rule castles, cities, land and people and torture souls with unspeakable outrages. Similarly, the temporal lords should rule land and people outwardly; this they do not do. All they can do is to flay and scrape, put tax on tax, tribute on tribute, let loose now a bear, now a wolf. Besides this, there is no justice, fidelity or truth to be found among them; what they do would be beneath robbers and knaves, and their temporal rule has sunk quite as low as that of the spiritual tyrants. Hence God also perverts their minds, that they rush on in their sense-lessness and would establish a spiritual rule over souls, as the others would establish a temporal rule, in order that they may contentedly burden themselves with alien sins, and with God's and all men's hate, until they go under with bishops, priests and monks, one knave with the other. Then they lay all the blame on the Gospel, and instead of doing penance, blaspheme God and say that our preaching has brought about what their perverse wickedness has merited and still unceasingly merits, as the Romans did when they were destroyed. Here then you have God's decree regarding the high and mighty. But they are not to believe it, lest this severe decree of God be hindered by their repentance.

You reply, But Paul said in Romans xiii, "Every soul shall be subject to power and authority," and Peter says, "We should be subject to every ordinance of man." I answer, That is just what I want! These sayings are in my favor. St. Paul speaks of authority and power. Now, you have just heard that no one but God can have authority over souls. Hence Paul cannot be speaking of any obedience except where there can be corresponding authority. From this it follows that he does not speak of faith, and does not say that secular authority should have the right to command faith, but he is speaking of external goods, and that these are to be set in order and controlled on earth.

This his words also clearly indicate, when he prescribes the limits to both authority and obedience, and says, "Render to every one his dues, tribute to whom tribute is due, custom to whom custom; honor to whom honor; fear to whom fear." You see, temporal obedience and power apply only externally to tribute, custom, honor and fear. Likewise when he says, "The power is not a terror to good, but to evil works," he again limits the power, so that it is to have the mastery not over faith or the Word of God, but over evil works.

This is what St. Peter also desires, when he says, "Ordinance of man." Human ordinance cannot possibly extend its authority to heaven and over souls, but belongs only to earth, to the external intercourse of men with each other, where men can see, know, judge, sentence, punish and acquit. Christ Himself made this nice distinction and summed it all up briefly when He said, "Give unto Caesar the things that are Caesar's, and unto God the things that are God's." If, then, imperial power extended to God's kingdom and power, and were not something by itself, He would not thus have made it a separate thing. For, as was said, the soul is not under Caesar's power; he can neither teach nor guide it, neither kill it nor make it alive, neither bind it nor loose it, neither judge it nor condemn it, neither hold it nor release it, which he must do had he power to command it and impose laws upon it; but over life, goods and honor he indeed has this right, for such things are under his authority.

David, too, stated this long ago in one of his short sayings when he says in Psalm cxv, "The heavens hath he given to the Lord of heaven; but the earth hath he given to the children of men." That is, over what is on earth and belongs to the temporal, earthly kingdom, man has authority from God, but that which belongs to the heavenly eternal kingdom is entirely under the heavenly Lord. Nor does Moses forget this when he says in Genesis i, "God said, Let us make man to rule over the beasts of the earth, over the fish in the waters, over the birds in the air." There only external rule is ascribed to men. And, in short, this is the meaning, as St. Peter says, Acts v, "We must obey God rather than men." Thereby he clearly sets a limit to worldly government, for if we had to do all that worldly government demands it would be to no purpose to say, "We must obey God rather than men."

If then your prince or temporal lord commands you to hold with the pope, to believe this or that, or commands you to give up certain books, you should say, It does not befit Lucifer to sit by the side of God. Dear Lord, I owe you obedience with life and goods; command me within the limits of your power on earth, and I will obey. But if you command me to believe, and to put away books, I will not obey; for in this case you are a tyrant and overreach yourself, and command where you have neither right nor power, etc. Should he take your property for this, and punish such disobedience, blessed are you. Thank God, that you are worthy to suffer for the sake of the divine Word, and let him rave, fool that he is. He will meet his judge. For I tell you, if you do not resist him but give him his way, and let him take your faith or your books, you have really denied God.

Let me illustrate. In Meissen, Bavaria, in the Mark, and other places, the tyrants have issued an order that the New Testaments be delivered to the courts everywhere. In this case their subjects ought not deliver a page or a letter, at risk of their salvation. For whoever does so, delivers Christ into Herod's hands, since they act as murderers of Christ, like Herod. But if their houses are ordered searched and books or goods taken by force, they should suffer it to be done. Outrage is not to be resisted, but endured, yet they should not sanction it, nor serve or obey or follow by moving foot or finger. For such tyrants act as worldly princes should act,—"worldly" princes they are; but the world is God's enemy. Therefore they must also do what is opposed to God, and in accord with the world, that they may by no means lose all honor, but remain worldly princes. Hence do not wonder that they rage and mock at the Gospel; they must live up to their name and title.

You must know that from the beginning of the world a wise prince is a rare bird indeed; still more so a pious prince. They are usually the greatest fools or the worst knaves on earth; therefore one must constantly expect the worst from them and look for little good from them, especially in divine matters, which concern the salvation of souls. They are God's jailers and hangmen, and His divine wrath needs them to punish the wicked and preserve outward peace. Our God is a great Lord, and therefore must have such noble, honorable and rich hangmen and beadles, and desires that they shall have riches, honor and fear, in full and plenty, from every one. It pleases His divine will that we call His hangmen gracious lords, fall at their feet and be subject to them in all humility, so long as they do not ply their trade too far and desire to become shepherds instead of hangmen. If a prince becomes wise, pious or a Christian, it is one of the great wonders, and one of the most precious tokens of divine grace upon that land. For the usual course is according to the saying in Isaiah iii, "I will give children to be their princes and babes shall rule over them," and in Hosea xiii, "I will give thee a king in my anger and take him away in my wrath." The world is too wicked, and does not deserve to have many wise and pious princes. Frogs need storks.

Again you say, Temporal power does not force men to believe, but simply prevents them from being misled by false doctrine; otherwise how could heretics be prevented from preaching? I answer, This the bishops should do, to whom, and not to the princes, such duty is entrusted. Heresy can never be prevented by force. That must be taken hold of in a different way, and must be opposed and dealt with otherwise than with the sword. Here God's Word must strive; if that does not accomplish the end it will remain unaccomplished through secular power, though it fill the world with blood. Heresy is a spiritual matter, which no iron can strike, no fire burn, no water drown. God's Word alone avails here, as Paul says, II Corinthians x, "Our weapons are not carnal, but mighty through God to destroy every counsel and high thing that exalteth itself against the knowledge of God, and to bring into captivity every thought to the obedience of Christ."

Moreover, faith and heresy are never so strong as when men oppose them by sheer force, without God's Word. For men count it certain that such force is for a wrong cause and is directed against the right, since it proceeds without God's Word, and does not know how to further its cause except by force, just as the brute beasts do. For even in secular affairs force can be used only after the wrong has been legally condemned. How much less possible is it to act with force, without justice and God's Word, in these high, spiritual matters! See, therefore, what fine, shrewd nobles they are. They would drive out heresy, and set about it in such a way that they only strengthen the opposition, make themselves suspected, and justify the heretics. Friend, would you drive out heresy, then you must find a plan to tear it first of all from the heart and altogether to turn men's wills away from it; force will not accomplish this, but only strengthen the heresy. What avails it to strengthen heresy in the heart and to weaken only its outward expression, and to force the tongue to lie? God's Word, however, enlightens the hearts; and so all heresies and errors perish of themselves from the heart.

Such overpowering of heresy the prophet Isaiah proclaimed in his eleventh chapter when he said, "He shall smite the earth with the rod of His mouth, and slay the wicked with the breath of His lips." You see, if the wicked is to be smitten and converted, it is accomplished by the mouth. In short, such princes and tyrants do not know that to fight against heresy is to fight against the devil, who fills men's hearts with error, as Paul says in Ephesians vi, "We fight not with flesh and blood, but with spiritual wickedness, with the rulers of the darkness of this world." Therefore, as long as the devil is not repelled and driven from the heart, it matters as little to him that I destroy his vessels with fire or sword, as it would if I fought lightning with a straw. Job bore abundant witness to this, when in his forty-first chapter he said that the devil esteemeth iron as straw and fears no power on earth. We learn it also from experience, for although all the Jews and heretics were burned, yet no one has been or will be convinced and converted thereby.

Nevertheless such a world as this deserves such princes, none of whom do their duty. The bishops are to leave the Word of God alone and not rule souls by it, but command the worldly princes to rule them with the sword. The worldly princes, in their turn, are to permit usury, theft, adultery, murder, and other evil works, and themselves do them; and then allow the bishops to punish with the ban. Thus they turn things topsy-turvy, and rule souls with iron and the body with bans, so that worldly princes rule in a spiritual, and spiritual princes in a worldly way. What else does the devil have to do on earth than thus to play the fool and hold carnival with his folk? These are our Christian princes, who defend the faith and devour the Turk. Fine fellows, to be sure, whom we may well trust to accomplish something by such refined wisdom, namely, break their necks and plunge land and people into suffering and want.

I would, however, in all fidelity advise the blinded folk to take heed to the short saying in Psalm cvii, "*Effundit contemptum super principes.*" I swear unto you by God that, if through your fault this little text becomes effective against you, you are lost, though every one of you be as mighty as the Turk; and your snorting and raving will help you nothing. A large part has already come true. For there are very few princes that are not reckoned fools or knaves. That is because they show themselves to be such; the common man is learning to think, and the prince's scourge, which God calls *contemptum*, is gathering force among the mob and with the common man. I fear there is no way to stop it, unless the princes conduct themselves in a princely manner and begin again to rule reasonably and thoroughly. Men ought not, men cannot, men will not suffer your tyranny and presumption much longer. Dear princes and lords, be wise and guide yourselves accordingly. God will no longer tolerate it. The world is no longer what it was when you hunted and drove the people like so much game. Therefore drop your outrage and force, and remember to deal justly and let God's Word have its course, as it will and must and shall, nor will you prevent it. If there is heresy abroad, let it be overcome, as is proper, with God's Word. But if you will keep on brandishing the sword, take heed lest there come one who shall bid you sheath it, and that not in God's name.

But should you ask, Since there is to be no secular sword among Christians, how are they to be ruled outwardly? There certainly must be authority also among Christians. I answer, Among Christians there shall and can be no authority; but all are alike subject to one another, as Paul says in Romans xii, "Each shall count the other his superior," and Peter in I Peter v, "All of you be subject one to another." This is also what Christ means in Luke xiv, "When you are bidden to a wedding sit down in the lowest room." There is no superior among Christians, but Christ Himself and Christ alone. And what kind of authority can there be where all are equal and have the same right, power, possession, and honor, and no one desires to be the other's superior, but each the other's inferior? One could not establish authority where there are such people, even if one would, since their character and nature will not permit them to have superiors, for no one is willing or able to be the superior. But where there are no such people, there are no real Christians.

What, then, are the priests and bishops? I answer, Their government is not one of authority or power, but a service and an office; for they are neither higher nor better than other Christians. Therefore they should not impose any law or decree on others without their will and consent; their rule consists in nothing else than in dealing with God's Word, leading Christians by it and overcoming heresy by its means. For, as was said, Christians can be ruled by nothing but by God's Word. For Christians must be ruled in faith, not by outward works. Faith, however, can come through no word of man, but only through the Word of God, as Paul says in Romans x, "Faith cometh by hearing, and hearing by the Word of God." Those who do not believe are not Christians, do not belong to Christ's kingdom, but to the worldly kingdom, and are constrained and ruled by the sword and by outward rule. Christians do of themselves, without constraint, every good thing, and find God's Word alone sufficient for them. Of this, however, I have written frequently and at length elsewhere.

Now that we know the limits of secular authority, it is time also to inquire how a prince should use it; for the sake of those who fain would be Christian princes and lords, and desire to enter the life beyond, of whom there are very few. For Christ Himself describes the nature of temporal princes in Luke xxii, when he says, "The worldly princes exercise lordship, and they that are chief exercise authority." For if they are born princes or chosen to office, they think only that it is their right to be served and to rule with power. He who would be a Christian prince certainly must lay aside the intention to rule and to use force. For cursed and condemned is every kind of life lived and sought for selfish profit and good; cursed are all works not done in love. But they are done in love when they are directed with all one's heart, not toward selfish pleasure, profit, honor, ease and salvation, but toward the profit, honor and salvation of others.

I will say nothing here of secular affairs and of the laws of government, for that is a large subject and there are too many law-books already; although, if a prince himself is not wiser than his jurists, and does not know more than is in the law-books, he will surely rule according to the saying in Proverbs xxviii, "A prince that wanteth understanding will oppress many with injustice." No matter how good and equitable the laws are, they all make exceptions of cases of necessity, in which they cannot be enforced. Therefore a prince must have the law in hand as firmly as the sword, and decide in his own mind when and where the law must be applied strictly or with moderation, so that reason may always control all law and be the highest law and rule over all laws. A housefather who, although he appoints a definite time and amount of work and food for his servants and children, must yet reserve the power to change or omit such regulations if his servants happen to be sick, imprisoned, detained, deceived, or otherwise hindered, and not deal as severely with the sick as with the well. I say this in order that men may not think it sufficient and an excellent thing if they follow the written law or the legal advisers; more than that is required.

What should a prince do, if he is not sufficiently wise, and must follow the directions of jurists and law books? I answer, For this reason I said that the position of a prince is a perilous one, and if he is not wise enough to master both the law and his advisers, the saying of Solomon is fulfilled, "Woe to the land whose king is a child." Solomon recognized this; therefore he despaired of all law, even of that which Moses, through God, had prescribed for him, and of all his princes and counselors, and turned to God Himself and prayed to Him for a wise heart to rule the people. A prince must follow this example and proceed with fear; he must depend neither upon dead books nor upon living heads, but cling solely to God, pray without ceasing to Him, and ask for a right understanding, above all books and masters, wisely to rule his subjects. Therefore I know of no law to prescribe for a prince, but will simply instruct him what the attitude of his heart and mind ought to be with respect to all laws, counsels, decisions and actions, so that if he govern himself thereby God will surely grant him the power to carry out all laws, counsels, and actions in a proper and godly way.

I. He must consider his subjects and rightly dispose his heart toward them in this matter. He does this if he applies his whole mind to making himself useful and serviceable to them, and does not think, "Land and people are mine; I will do as I please"; but thus, "I belong to land and people; I must do what is profitable and good for them. My concern must be, not how I may rule and be haughty, but how they may be protected and defended by a good peace." And he should picture Christ to himself, and say, "Behold, Christ the chief Ruler came and served me, sought not to have power, profit and honor from me, but only considered my need, and did all He could that I might have power, profit and honor from Him and through Him. I will do the same, not seek mine own advantage in my subjects, but their advantage, and thus serve them by my office, protect them, give them audience and support, that they, and not I, may have the benefit and profit by it. Thus a prince should in his heart empty himself of his power and authority, and interest himself in the need of his subjects, dealing with it as though it were his own need. Thus Christ did unto us; and these are the proper works of Christian love.

You say, Who then would be a prince? For that would make the position of a prince the worst on earth, full of trouble, labor and sorrow. Where would there be room for the princely pleasures, such as dancing, hunting, racing, gaming, and similar worldly enjoyments? I answer, We are not prescribing now how a temporal prince shall live, but how a temporal prince shall be a Christian, in order that he also may reach heaven. Who does not know that a prince is a rare bird in heaven! I do not speak because I have any hope that princes will give heed, but because there might possibly be one of them who would fain be a Christian and would like to know what he ought to do. For I am sure that God's Word will neither turn nor bend to princes; but the princes must bend themselves according to it. It is enough for me to point out that it is not impossible for a prince to be a Christian, though it is a rare thing and surrounded with difficulties. If they would so manage that their dancing, hunting and racing were done without injury to their subjects, and if they would otherwise conduct their office in love toward them, God would not be so hard as to begrudge them their dancing, hunting and racing. But it would follow of itself that, if they served and cared for their subjects as their office requires, full many a fine dance, hunt, race and game would have to be abandoned.

II. He must beware of the high and mighty and of his counselors, and so conduct himself toward them that he despise none, and trust none enough to leave everything to him. For God cannot tolerate either. He once spake by an ass; therefore no man is to be despised, no matter how humble he be. On the other hand, He permitted the highest angel to fall from heaven; therefore no man is to be trusted, no matter how wise, holy and great he is, but one must give a hearing to all and wait to see through which one of them God will speak and act. For the greatest harm done at court is when a prince enslaves his mind to the high and mighty and to the flatterers, and does not look into things himself; since, when a prince fails and plays the fool, not only one person is affected, but land and people must bear the result of such foolishness. Therefore a prince should bestow only so much trust and power upon his rulers that he will still keep the reins of government in his own hand. He must keep his eyes open and give attention, and, like Jehoshaphat, ride through the land and observe everywhere how the government and the law is administered. In this way he will learn for himself that one must not implicitly trust any man. For you have no right to think that another will interest himself in you and in your land so deeply as you yourself, unless he be filled with the Spirit and be a good Christian. The natural man does not do it. Since, however, you do not know whether he is a Christian or how long he will remain one, you cannot safely depend on him.

Beware especially of those who say, "Gracious lord, why does your grace not trust me more? Who is so willing to serve your grace," etc.? Such an one is certainly not guileless, but desires to be lord in the country and make a jackanapes of you. If he were a true and pious Christian he would be quite willing that you should entrust him with nothing, and would praise you for keeping so careful a watch on him; for he acts in accordance with God's will and therefore he is willing, and can bear it, to have his acts brought to the light by you or any one else, as Christ says in John iii, "He that doeth well cometh to the light, that his deeds may be made manifest, for they are wrought in God." The former, however, would blind your eyes, and act under cover of darkness, as Christ also says in the same place, "Every one that doeth evil hateth the light, lest his deeds should be punished." Therefore, beware of him. And if he complain of it, say, "Friend, I do thee no wrong; God is not willing that I trust myself or any other man; find fault with Him, then, because He will have it so, or that He has not made you more than human; although, even if you were an angel, since Lucifer indeed was not to be trusted, I would not trust you completely, for we should trust God alone."

Let no prince think that he shall fare better than David, who is an example to all princes. He had so wise a counselor, named Ahithophel, that the text says, "The counsel which Ahithophel counselled availed as if a man had inquired at the oracle of God." Nevertheless he fell, and sank so low that he sought to betray, kill and destroy David his own lord. Then David had to learn that no man is to be trusted. Why do you suppose God permitted such a horrible example to occur, and to be recorded, if not in order to warn the princes and lords against the most perilous misfortune that may befall them, so that they might trust no one? For it is most deplorable when flatterers reign at court, or when the prince depends on others, puts himself in their hands, and lets every one do as he will.

You say, perchance, If no one is to be trusted, how will one rule land and people? I answer, You should entrust and take the venture, but you should not trust and depend save on God alone. You must certainly entrust the offices to some one and take a chance with him; but you should not trust him otherwise than as one who may fail you and whom you must watch with unfailing vigilance; as a driver has confidence in the horses and wagon he drives, yet does not let them go their own way, but holds reins and lash in his hand and does not sleep. Remember the old proverbs, which are the sure fruits of experience: "A careful master makes a good horse," and "The master's footsteps make a fruitful field,"—that is, if the master does not look after things himself, but depends upon counselors and servants, things never go right. God also will have it so, and causes it to happen, in order that the lords may be driven of necessity to fulfill their office themselves, as everyone must fulfill his calling and every creature do its work; otherwise the lords will become fatted pigs and a worthless lot, of no profit to any one but themselves.

III. He must take heed that he deal justly with evil doers. Here he must be very wise and prudent to mete out punishment without injuring others. I know no better example of this than David again. He had a captain, Joab by name, who played two wicked pranks in that he treacherously murdered two loyal captains, whereby he justly merited death twice over; yet David did not put him to death during his lifetime, but commanded his son Solomon without fail to do so, because he could not punish him without great injury and disturbance. A prince must punish the wicked in such a way that he does not step on the dish while picking up the spoon, and for the sake of one man's head plunge land and people into want and fill the land with widows and orphans. Therefore he must not obey the counselors and fireeaters who incite and provoke him to begin war and say, "What, must we suffer such insults and injustice?" He is a poor Christian indeed who for the sake of a single castle would make an armed camp of the whole land. In brief, here one must hold by the proverb, "He cannot rule who cannot wink at faults." Let this, therefore, be his rule: Where wrong cannot be punished without greater wrong, there let him waive his rights, however just. He must not regard his own injury, but the wrong which others must suffer as a consequence of the penalty he imposes. For what have the many women and children done that they should be made widows and orphans in order that you may avenge yourself on an idle tongue or a wicked hand which has injured you?

You ask, But shall not a prince go to war, nor his subjects follow him into battle? I answer, That is a far-reaching question, but let me answer it very briefly. To act here as a Christian, I say, a prince should not wage war against his overlord—the king, emperor or other liege—but should let him who takes take. For one must not resist the government with force, but only with knowledge of the truth; if it is influenced by it, well; if not, you are innocent, and suffer wrong for God's sake. But if your opponent is your equal, your inferior, or of a foreign government, you should first offer him justice and peace, as Moses taught the children of Israel. If he is unwilling, then use your best strategy and defend yourself by force against force, as Moses well describes it all in Deuteronomy xx. In doing this you must not consider your own interests and how you may remain lord, but your subjects, to whom you owe help and protection, that all may be done in love. For, since your entire land is in peril, you must make the venture, so that with God's help all may not be lost; and if you cannot prevent some from becoming widows and orphans, as a consequence of this, you must nevertheless prevent it that all go to ruin and there be nothing left but widows and orphans.

In this matter subjects are in duty bound to follow and risk life and property for the cause. For in such a case one must risk his property and himself for the sake of the other. And in such a war it is a Christian act and an act of love confidently to kill, rob, and pillage the enemy, and to do everything that can injure him until one has conquered him according to the methods of war. Only, one must beware of sin, not violate wives and virgins, and when victory comes, offer mercy and peace to those who surrender and humble themselves. Therefore in such a case let the saying hold true, "God helps those who help themselves." So Abraham did when he smote the four kings, as Genesis xiv tells us, when he certainly caused great slaughter and showed little mercy until he conquered them. Such happenings must be considered as sent of God, that He may now and then cleanse the land and drive out the knaves.

But when a prince is in the wrong, are his people bound to follow him then too? I answer, No, for it is no one's duty to do wrong; we ought to obey God Who desires the right, rather than men. How is it, when the subjects do not know whether the prince is in the right or not? I answer, As long as they cannot know, nor find out by any possible means, they may obey without peril to their souls. For in such a case one must apply the law of Moses, when he writes in Exodus xxi, that a murderer who has unknowingly and involuntarily killed a man shall be delivered by fleeing to a city of refuge and by the judgment of the congregation. For whichever side is defeated, whether it be in the right or in the wrong, must accept it as a punishment from God; but whichever side wars and wins, in such ignorance, must regard their battle as though one fell from the roof and killed another, and leave the matter to God. For it is the same to God whether He deprives you of goods and life by a just lord or by an unjust. You are His creature, and He can do with you as He will—if only your conscience is clear. God Himself thus excuses Abimelech in Genesis xxi, when he took Abraham's wife, not because he had done right, but because he had not known that she was Abraham's wife.

IV. We come to what really should be foremost, and of which we spoke above. A prince must act also in a Christian way toward his God, that is, he must subject himself to Him in entire confidence and pray for wisdom to rule well, as Solomon did. But of faith and trust in God I have written so much elsewhere that it is not necessary to say more here. Therefore we will close by saying briefly that a prince's duty is fourfold: First, that toward God consists in true confidence and in sincere prayer; second, that toward his subjects consists in love and Christian service; third, that toward his counselors and rulers consists in an open mind and unfettered judgment; fourth, that toward evil doers consists in proper zeal and firmness. Then his state is right, outwardly and inwardly, pleasing to God and to the people. But he must expect much envy and sorrow,—the cross will soon rest on the shoulders of such a ruler. . . .

SELECTED BIBLIOGRAPHY

Sabine, George H., *History of Political Theory*, pp. 354–362.
Cook, Thomas I., *History of Political Philosophy*, pp. 304–326.
Dunning, William A., *Political Theories, from Luther to Montesquieu*, ch. 1, §§ 1, 2.

Lindsay, T. M., "Luther," in *Cambridge Modern History*, Vol. II (1903), ch. 4.
Figgis, John Neville, *Studies in Political Thought from Gerson to Grotius* (Cambridge, 1907), lecture iii.
Allen, J. W., *Political Thought in the Sixteenth Century* (London, 1928), pt. i, chs. 1, 2.
Troeltsch, Ernst, *The Social Teachings of the Christian Church*, translated by Olive Wyon, 2 vols. (London and New York, 1931), Vol. II, pp. 465–576.
Carlyle, R. W. and A. J., *History of Mediæval Political Theory in the West*, Vol. VI (Edinburgh and London, 1936), pp. 271–284.
Smith, Preserved, *The Life and Letters of Martin Luther* (Boston and New York, 1911), chs. 5–8, 14, 19.
Bluntschli, J. K., *Geschichte der neueren Statswissenschaft* (third ed., Munich and Leipsic, 1881), ch. 3.
Bainton, Roland H., "The Development and Consistency of Luther's Attitude to Religious Liberty," in *Harvard Theological Review*, Vol. 22 (1929), pp. 107–149.

Mackinnon, James, *Luther and the Reformation*, 4 vols. (London, 1925–30).
Boehmer, Heinrich, *Luther and the Reformation in the Light of Modern Research*, translated by E. S. G. Potter (London, 1930).

Murray, Robert H., *The Political Consequences of the Reformation* (Boston, 1926).
Pauls, Theodor, *Luthers Auffassung von Staat und Volk* (second ed., Halle, 1927).
Grisar, Hartmann, *Luther*, translated by E. M. Lamond, 6 vols. (London, 1913–17).

CALVIN

XIII. JOHN CALVIN (1509–1564)

INTRODUCTION

Calvin was the most important figure of the Reformation outside of Germany and Scandinavia. He was born in northern France. He prepared first for the priesthood, but turned to legal study when he found himself in disagreement with orthodox doctrines of the Catholic church. When he came more directly under the influence of the novel doctrines spreading from Germany into France, he withdrew from the church and aligned himself definitely with the Reformers. The movement was under attack by the French government, and Calvin found it necessary to leave France. He settled for a while in Basel, where in 1536 he completed the first version of his greatest work — the *Institutes of the Christian Religion* (*Christianae Religionis Institutio*). Passing through Geneva later that year, he was persuaded, by leaders who were trying to fortify the recently established reformist victory in that French-speaking town, to remain and assist them in their work of ecclesiastical and civic reorganization. Discord created by the extreme measures of Calvin and his associates led to his banishment from Geneva in 1538. He settled in Strassburg, center of the Reformation in southwestern Germany. Here he served as pastor of French refugees in that region, assumed leadership in devising a form of church service and organization for the Reformers, lectured on theology, and perfected the doctrine of his *Institutes*. He was recalled to Geneva in 1541 and soon became virtual dictator in both the ecclesiastical and civic life of the community.

Calvin was the only one of the early Reformers who gave any systematic attention to political questions. In the "prefatory address" (to Francis I of France) of the *Institutes*, he declared that one of the objects of the work was to answer the charge that the Reformist doctrine was "new . . . doubtful and uncertain" and that preaching the doctrine had brought in its train "disturbances, tumults, and disputes." It is mainly a work in theology, but it is concerned also with questions of ecclesiastical organization; and a concluding chapter deals with the nature and duties of civil government and the bounds within which obedience is due to it. He rejected, in theory, the union of church and state — such as had been advocated by the Swiss Reformer, Ulrich Zwingli, in Zurich; but the system for which he stood was in effect a theocracy. Although church authorities were to have no dealings with merely secular matters, the care of religion and morality was to be the first duty of civil authorities. The latter could not control belief, but they could enforce outward conformity and impose Christian standards of moral behavior. Calvin followed Luther in the belief that although many civil rulers were wicked and negligent, their punishment should be left to God; both because indiscipline and disorder are worse than oppression, and because God may choose the latter as a means of chastising erring citizens. Calvin went even further than Luther in the advocacy of passive obedience. He conceded that the citizen should not obey a command to do what God explicitly forbids; and he expressed approval of those ancient political systems that had included special offices to restrain the wrong-doings of the chief rulers; but he condemned all rebellious acts by private citizens. Where, however, the Calvinists were, as in France and Scotland, minority groups under governments that were vigorously repressing religious dissent, this doctrine of passive obedience became transformed into the opposite doctrine of the obligation of true Christians to defend their faith even by taking arms against the established authorities.

Calvin put into operation in Geneva a system of stringent regulation of religious doctrine and church services, and of dress, speech, amusements, and other forms of daily conduct. Because Calvin's writings also laid great stress on the "middle-class," "practical," virtues of sobriety, thrift, frugality, and the obligation to glorify God in the diligent discharge of the duties of one's earthly vocation, and because Calvinist sects gained their stronger holds in the newer urban industrial regions, some recent historians have found a close association between Calvinism and the evolution of modern industrial capitalism.[1]

---

[1] See Max Weber, *The Protestant Ethic and the Spirit of Capitalism*, translated by Talcott Parsons (1930).

READINGS FROM THE INSTITUTES OF THE CHRISTIAN RELIGION [1]

1. *The Nature and Function of Civil Government* [2]

1. Having shown above that there is a twofold government in man, and having fully considered the one which, placed in the soul or inward man, relates to eternal life, we are here called to say something of the other, which pertains only to civil institutions and the external regulation of manners. For although this subject seems from its nature to be unconnected with the spiritual doctrine of faith, which I have undertaken to treat, it will appear, as we proceed, that I have properly connected them, nay, that I am under the necessity of doing so, especially while, on the one hand, frantic and barbarous men are furiously endeavoring to overturn the order established by God, and, on the other, the flatterers of princes, extolling their power without measure, hesitate not to oppose it to the government of God. Unless we meet both extremes, the purity of the faith will perish. We may add that it in no small degree concerns us to know how kindly God has here consulted for the human race, that pious zeal may the more strongly urge us to testify our gratitude. And first, before entering on the subject itself, it is necessary to attend to the distinction which we formerly laid down, lest, as often happens to many, we imprudently confound these two things, the nature of which is altogether different. For some, on hearing that liberty is promised in the gospel, a liberty which acknowledges no king and no magistrate among men, but looks to Christ alone, think that they can receive no benefit from their liberty so long as they see any power placed over them. Accordingly, they think that nothing will be safe until the whole world is changed into a new form, when there will be neither courts, nor laws, nor magistrates, nor anything of the kind to interfere, as they suppose, with their liberty. But he who knows to distinguish between the body and the soul, between the present fleeting life and that which is future and eternal, will have no difficulty in understanding that the spiritual kingdom of Christ and civil government are things very widely separated. Seeing, therefore, it is a Jewish vanity to seek and include the kingdom of Christ under the elements of this world, let us, considering, as Scripture clearly

[1] The selections are taken from Vol. III of the translation by Henry Beveridge. Three volumes. Edinburgh, 1845–6. Calvin Translation Society. The passages are from Book IV, ch. xx: *Of Civil Government.*
[2] Bk. IV, ch. xx, §§ 1–4.

teaches, that the blessings which we derive from Christ are
spiritual, remember to confine the liberty which is promised and
offered to us in him within its proper limits. For why is it that
the very same apostle who bids us "stand fast in the liberty
wherewith Christ has made us free, and be not again entangled
with the yoke of bondage " (Gal. v. 1), in another passage forbids slaves to be solicitous about their state (1 Cor. vii. 21),
unless it be that spiritual liberty is perfectly compatible with
civil servitude? In this sense the following passages are to be
understood: "There is neither Jew nor Greek, there is neither
bond nor free, there is neither male nor female" (Gal. iii. 28).
Again: "There is neither Greek nor Jew, circumcision nor uncir-
cumcision, barbarian, Scythian, bond nor free: but Christ is all
and in all " (Col. iii. 11). It is thus intimated, that it matters not
what your condition is among men, nor under what laws you
live, since in them the kingdom of Christ does not at all consist.

2. Still the distinction does not go so far as to justify us in
supposing that the whole scheme of civil government is matter of
pollution, with which Christian men have nothing to do. Fa-
natics, indeed, delighting in unbridled license, insist and vociferate
that, after we are dead by Christ to the elements of this world, and
being translated into the kingdom of God sit among the celestials,
it is unworthy of us, and far beneath our dignity, to be occupied
with those profane and impure cares which relate to matters
alien to a Christian man. To what end, they say, are laws
without courts and tribunals? But what has a Christian man
to do with courts? Nay, if it is unlawful to kill, what have we to
do with laws and courts? But as we lately taught that that kind
of government is distinct from the spiritual and internal kingdom of Christ, so we ought to know that they are not adverse to
each other. The former, in some measure, begins the heavenly
kingdom in us, even now upon earth, and in this mortal and evanes-
cent life commences immortal and incorruptible blessedness,
while to the latter it is assigned, so long as we live among men,
to foster and maintain the external worship of God, to defend
sound doctrine and the condition of the church, to adapt our
conduct to human society, to form our manners to civil justice,
to conciliate us to each other, to cherish common peace and tranquillity. All these I confess to be superfluous, if the kingdom
of God, as it now exists within us, extinguishes the present life.
But if it is the will of God that while we aspire to true piety we
are pilgrims upon the earth, and if such pilgrimage stands in need
of such aids, those who take them away from man rob him of

his humanity. As to their allegation that there ought to be such perfection in the church of God that her guidance should suffice for law, they stupidly imagine her to be such as she never can be found in the community of men. For while the insolence of the wicked is so great, and their iniquity is so stubborn, that it can scarcely be curbed by any severity of laws, what do we expect would be done by hose whom force can scarcely repress from doing ill, were they to see perfect impunity for their wickedness?

3. But we shall have a fitter opportunity of speaking of the use of civil government. All we wish to be understood at present is, that it is perfect barbarism to think of exterminating it, its use among men being not less than that of bread and water, light and air, while its dignity is much more excellent. Its object is not merely, like those things, to enable men to breathe, eat, drink and be warmed (though it includes all these, while it enables them to live together); this, I say, is not its only object, but it is that no idolatry, no blasphemy against the name of God, no calumnies against his truth, nor other offences to religion, break out and be disseminated among the people; that the public quiet be not disturbed, that every man's property be kept secure, that men may carry on innocent commerce with each other, that honesty and modesty be cultivated; in short, that a public form of religion may exist among Christians, and humanity among men. Let no one be surprised that I now attribute the task of constituting religion aright to human polity, though I seem above to have placed it beyond the will of man, since I no more than formerly allow men at pleasure to enact laws concerning religion and the worship of God, when I approve of civil order which is directed to this end, viz., to prevent the true religion, which is contained in the law of God, from being with impunity openly violated and polluted by public blasphemy. But the reader, by the help of a perspicuous arrangement, will better understand what view is to be taken of the whole order of civil government, if we treat of each of its parts separately. Now these are three: The Magistrate, who is president and guardian of the laws; the Laws, according to which he governs; and the People, who are governed by the laws, and obey the magistrate. Let us consider then, first, What is the function of the magistrate? Is it a lawful calling approved by God? What is the nature of his duty? What the extent of his power? Secondly, What are the laws by which Christian polity is to be regulated? And, lastly, What is the use of laws as regards the people? And, What obedience is due to the magistrate?

4. With regard to the functions of magistrates, the Lord has not only declared that he approves and is pleased with it, but, moreover, has strongly recommended it to us by the very honorable titles which he has conferred upon it. . . . Their functions were expressly approved by the Lord. Wherefore no man can doubt that civil authority is, in the sight of God, not only sacred and lawful, but the most sacred, and by far the most honorable, of all stations in mortal life.

2.   The Duties of Magistrates [1]

9. The duty of magistrates, its nature, as described by the word of God, and the things in which it consists, I will here indicate in passing. That it extends to both tables of the law, did Scripture not teach, we might learn from profane writers; for no man has discoursed of the duty of magistrates, the enacting of laws, and the common weal, without beginning with religion and divine worship. Thus all have confessed that no polity can be successfully established unless piety be its first care, and that those laws are absurd which disregard the rights of God, and consult only for men. Seeing then that among philosophers religion holds the first place, and that the same thing has always been observed with the universal consent of nations, Christian princes and magistrates may be ashamed of their heartlessness if they make it not their care. We have already shown that this office is specially assigned them by God, and indeed it is right that they exert themselves in asserting and defending the honor of Him whose vicegerents they are, and by whose favor they rule. Hence in Scripture holy kings are especially praised for restoring the worship of God when corrupted or overthrown, or for taking care that religion flourished under them in purity and safety. On the other hand, the sacred history sets down anarchy among the vices, when it states that there was no king in Israel, and, therefore, every one did as he pleased (Judges xxi. 25). This rebukes the folly of those who would neglect the care of divine things, and devote themselves merely to the administration of justice among men; as if God had appointed rulers in his own name to decide earthly controversies, and omitted what was of far greater moment, his own pure worship as prescribed by his law. Such views are adopted by turbulent men, who, in their eagerness to make all kinds of innovations with impunity, would fain get rid of all the vindicators of violated piety. In

[1] Bk. IV, ch. xx, § 9.

regard to the second table of the law, Jeremiah addresses rulers, "Thus saith the Lord, Execute ye judgments and righteousness, and deliver the spoiled out of the hand of the oppressor: and do no wrong, do no violence to the stranger, the fatherless, nor the widow, neither shed innocent blood " (Jer. xxii. 3). To the same effect is the exhortation in the Psalm, "Defend the poor and fatherless; do justice to the afflicted and needy. Deliver the poor and needy; rid them out of the hand of the wicked " (Psalm lxxxii. 3, 4). Moses also declared to the princes whom he had substituted for himself, "Hear the causes between your brethren, and judge righteously between every man and his brother, and the stranger that is with him. Ye shall not respect persons in judgment; but ye shall hear the small as well as the great: ye shall not be afraid of the face of man, for the judgment is God's " (Deut. i. 16) [1] . . . . But as rulers cannot do this unless they protect the good against the injuries of the bad, and give aid and protection to the oppressed, they are armed with power to curb manifest evil doers and criminals, by whose misconduct the public tranquillity is disturbed or harassed. For we have full experience of the truth of Solon's saying, that all public matters depend on reward and punishment; that where these are wanting, the whole discipline of state totters and falls to pieces. For in the minds of many the love of equity and justice grows cold, if due honor be not paid to virtue, and the licentiousness of the wicked cannot be restrained, without strict discipline and the infliction of punishment. The two things are comprehended by the prophet when he enjoins kings and other rulers to execute "judgment and righteousness " (Jer. xxi. 12; xxii. 3). It is righteousness (justice) to take charge of the innocent, to defend and avenge them, and set them free: it is judgment to withstand the audacity of the wicked, to repress their violence, and punish their faults. [2]

3. The Obedience Due to Civil Rulers [3]

22. The first duty of subjects towards their rulers, is to entertain the most honorable views of their office, recognizing it as a delegated jurisdiction from God, and on that account receiving and reverencing them as the ministers and ambassadors of God. For you will find some who show themselves very obedient to

[1] Other biblical quotations of similar content follow.
[2] Further sections on the duties of magistrates treat of their duty to carry on war and of their right to raise revenue.
[3] Bk. IV, ch. xx, §§ 22–25, 29–32.

magistrates, and would be unwilling that there should be no magistrates to obey, because they know this is expedient for the public good, and yet the opinion which those persons have of magistrates is, that they are a kind of necessary evils. But Peter requires something more of us when he says, "Honor the king" (1 Pet. ii. 17); and Solomon when he says, "My son, fear thou the Lord and the king" (Prov. xxiv. 21). For, under the term honor, the former includes a sincere and candid esteem, and the latter, by joining the king with God, shows that he is invested with a kind of sacred veneration and dignity. We have also the remarkable injunction of Paul, "Be subject not only for wrath, but also for conscience sake" (Rom. xiii. 5). By this he means, that subjects, in submitting to princes and governors, are not to be influenced merely by fear (just as those submit to an armed enemy who see vengeance ready to be executed if they resist), but because the obedience which they yield is rendered to God himself, inasmuch as their power is from God. I speak not of the men as if the mask of dignity could cloak folly, or cowardice, or cruelty of wicked and flagitious manners, and thus acquire for vice the praise of virtue; but I say that the station itself is deserving of honor and reverence, and that those who rule should, in respect of their office, be held by us in esteem and veneration.

23. From this, a second consequence is, that we must with ready minds prove our obedience to them, whether in complying with edicts, or in paying tribute, or in undertaking public offices and burdens which relate to the common defence, or in executing any other orders. "Let every soul," says Paul, "be subject unto the highest powers." "Whosoever, therefore, resisteth the power, resisteth the ordinance of God" (Rom. xiii. 1, 2). Writing to Titus, he says, "Put them in mind to be subject to principalities and powers, to obey magistrates, to be ready to every good work" (Tit. iii. 1).[1] . . . Let no man here deceive himself, since we cannot resist the magistrate without resisting God. For, although an unarmed magistrate may seem to be despised with impunity, yet God is armed, and will signally avenge this contempt. Under this obedience, I comprehend the restraint which private men ought to impose on themselves in public, not interfering with public business, or rashly encroaching on the province of the magistrate, or attempting anything at all of a public nature. If it is proper that anything in a public ordinance should be corrected, let them not act tumultuously, or put their hands to a work where they ought to feel that their hands are tied, but let them

[1] Similar biblical quotations follow.

leave it to the cognizance of the magistrate, whose hand alone here is free. My meaning is, let them not dare to do it without being ordered. For when the command of the magistrate is given, they too are invested with public authority. For as, according to the common saying, the eyes and ears of the prince are his counsellors, so one may not improperly say that those who, by his command, have the charge of managing affairs, are his hands.

24. But as we have hitherto described the magistrate who truly is what he is called, viz., the father of his country, and (as the Poet speaks) the pastor of the people, the guardian of peace, the president of justice, the vindicator of innocence, he is justly to be deemed a madman who disapproves of such authority. And since in almost all ages we see that some princes, careless about all their duties on which they ought to have been intent, live, without solicitude, in luxurious sloth, others, bent on their own interests, venally prostitute all rights, privileges, judgments, and enactments; others pillage poor people of their money, and afterwards squander it in insane largesses; others act as mere robbers pillaging houses, violating matrons, and slaying the innocent; many cannot be persuaded to recognize such persons for princes, whose command, as far as lawful, they are bound to obey. For while in this unworthy conduct, and among atrocities so alien, not only from the duty of the magistrate, but also of the man, they behold no appearance of the image of God, which ought to be conspicuous in the magistrate, while they see not a vestige of that minister of God, who was appointed to be a praise to the good and a terror to the bad, they cannot recognize the ruler whose dignity and authority Scripture recommends to us. And undoubtedly, the natural feeling of the human mind has always been not less to assail tyrants with hatred and execration, than to look up to just kings with love and veneration.

25. But if we have respect to the word of God, it will lead us farther, and make us subject not only to the authority of those princes who honestly and faithfully perform their duty toward us, but all princes, by whatever means they have so become, although there is nothing they less perform than the duty of princes. For though the Lord declares that a ruler to maintain our safety is the highest gift of his beneficence, and prescribes to rulers themselves their proper sphere, he at the same time declares, that of whatever description they may be, they derive their power from none but him. Those, indeed, who rule for the public good, are true examples and specimens of his beneficence, while those who

domineer unjustly and tyrannically are raised up by him to punish the people for their iniquity. Still all alike possess that sacred majesty with which he has invested lawful power. . . . We need not labor to prove that an impious king is a mark of the Lord's anger, since I presume no one will deny it, and that this is not less true of a king than of a robber who plunders your goods, an adulterer who defiles your bed, and an assassin who aims at your life, since all such calamities are classed by Scripture among the curses of God. But let us insist at greater length in proving what does not so easily fall in with the views of men, that even an individual of the worst character, one most unworthy of all honor, if invested with public authority, receives that illustrious divine power which the Lord has by his word devolved on the ministers of his justice and judgment, and that, accordingly, in so far as public obedience is concerned, he is to be held in the same honor and reverence as the best of kings.

29. This feeling of reverence, and even of piety, we owe to the utmost to all our rulers, be their characters what they may. This I repeat the oftener, that we may learn not to consider the individuals themselves, but hold it to be enough that by the will of the Lord they sustain a character on which he has impressed and engraven inviolable majesty. But rulers, you will say, owe mutual duties to those under them. This I have already confessed. But if from this you conclude that obedience is to be returned to none but just governors, you reason absurdly. Husbands are bound by mutual duties to their wives, and parents to their children. Should husbands and parents neglect their duty; should the latter be harsh and severe to the children whom they are enjoined not to provoke to anger, and by their severity harass them beyond measure; should the former treat with the greatest contumely the wives whom they are enjoined to love and to spare as the weaker vessels; would children be less bound in duty to their parents, and wives to their husbands? They are made subject to the froward and undutiful. Nay, since the duty of all is not to look behind them, that is, not to inquire into the duties of one another, but to submit each to his own duty, this ought especially to be exemplified in the case of those who are placed under the power of others. Wherefore, if we are cruelly tormented by a savage, if we are rapaciously pillaged by an avaricious or luxurious, if we are neglected by a sluggish, if, in short, we are persecuted for righteousness' sake by an impious and sacrilegious prince, let us first call up the remembrance of

our faults, which doubtless the Lord is chastising by such scourges. In this way humility will curb our impatience. And let us reflect that it belongs not to us to cure these evils, that all that remains for us is to implore the help of the Lord, in whose hands are the hearts of kings, and inclinations of kingdoms. "God standeth in the congregation of the mighty; he judgeth among the Gods." Before his face shall fall and be crushed all kings and judges of the earth, who have not kissed his anointed, who have enacted unjust laws to oppress the poor in judgment, and do violence to the cause of the humble, to make widows a prey, and plunder the fatherless.

30. Herein is the goodness, power, and providence of God wondrously displayed. At one time he raises up manifest avengers from among his own servants, and gives them his command to punish accursed tyranny, and deliver his people from calamity when they are unjustly oppressed; at another time he employs, for this purpose, the fury of men who have other thoughts and other aims. Thus he rescued his people Israel from the tyranny of Pharaoh by Moses; from the violence of Chusa, king of Syria, by Othniel; and from other bondage by other kings or judges. Thus he tamed the pride of Tyre by the Egyptians; the insolence of the Egyptians by the Assyrians; the ferocity of the Assyrians by the Chaldeans; the confidence of Babylon by the Medes and Persians,—Cyrus having previously subdued the Medes, while the ingratitude of the kings of Judah and Israel, and their impious contumacy after all his kindness, he subdued and punished, —at one time by the Assyrians, at another by the Babylonians. All these things, however, were not done in the same way. The former class of deliverers being brought forward by the lawful call of God to perform such deeds, when they took up arms against kings, did not all violate that majesty with which kings are invested by divine appointment, but armed from heaven, they, by a greater power, curbed a less, just as kings may lawfully punish their own satraps. The latter class, though they were directed by the hand of God, as seemed to him good, and did his work without knowing it, had nought but evil in their thoughts.

31. But whatever may be thought of the acts of the men themselves, the Lord by their means equally executed his own work when he broke the bloody sceptres of insolent kings, and overthrew their intolerable dominations. Let princes hear and be afraid; but let us at the same time guard most carefully against spurning or violating the venerable and majestic authority of rulers, an authority which God has sanctioned by the surest edicts,

although those invested with it should be most unworthy of it, and, as far as in them lies, pollute it by their iniquity. Although the Lord takes vengeance on unbridled domination, let us not therefore suppose that that vengeance is committed to us, to whom no command has been given but to obey and suffer. I speak only of private men.. For when popular magistrates have been appointed to curb the tyranny of kings (as the ephori, who were opposed to kings among the Spartans, or tribunes of the people to consuls among the Romans, or demarchs to the senate among the Athenians; and, perhaps, there is something similar to this in the power exercised in each kingdom by the three orders, when they hold their primary diets). So far am I from forbidding these officially to check the undue license of kings, that if they connive at kings when they tyrannize and insult over the humbler of the people, I affirm that their dissimulation is not free from nefarious perfidy, because they fraudulently betray the liberty of the people, while knowing that, by the ordinance of God, they are its appointed guardians.

32. But in that obedience which we hold to be due to the commands of rulers, we must always make the exception, nay, must be particularly careful that it is not incompatible with obedience to Him to whose will the wishes of all kings should be subject, to whose decrees their commands must yield, to whose majesty their sceptres must bow. And, indeed, how preposterous were it, in pleasing men, to incur the offence of Him for whose sake you obey men! The Lord, therefore, is King of kings. When He opens His sacred mouth, He alone is to be heard, instead of all and above all. We are subject to the men who rule over us, but subject only in the Lord. If they command anything against Him, let us not pay the least regard to it, nor be moved by all the dignity which they possess as magistrates — a dignity to which no injury is done when it is subordinated to the special and truly supreme power of God. On this ground Daniel denies that he had sinned in any respect against the king when he refused to obey his impious decree (Dan. vi. 22), because the king had exceeded his limits, and not only been injurious to men, but, by raising his horn against God, had virtually abrogated his own power. On the other hand, the Israelites are condemned for having too readily obeyed the impious edict of the king. For, when Jeroboam made the golden calf, they forsook the temple of God, and, in submissiveness to him, revolted to new superstitions (1 Kings xii. 28). With the same facility posterity had bowed before the decrees of their kings. For this they are

severely upbraided by the Prophet (Hosea v. 11). So far is the praise of modesty from being due to that pretence by which flattering courtiers cloak themselves, and deceive the simple, when they deny the lawfulness of declining anything imposed by their kings, as if the Lord had resigned his own rights to mortals by appointing them to rule over their fellows, or as if earthly power were diminished when it is subjected to its author, before whom even the principalities of heaven tremble as suppliants. I know the imminent peril to which subjects expose themselves by this firmness kings being most indignant when they are contemned. As Solomon says, "The wrath of a king is as messengers of death" (Prov. xvi. 14). But since Peter, one of heaven's heralds, has published the edict, "We ought to obey God rather than men" (Acts v. 29), let us console ourselves with the thought that we are rendering the obedience which the Lord requires, when we endure anything rather than turn aside from piety. And that our courage may not fail, Paul stimulates us by the additional consideration (1 Cor. vii. 23), that we were redeemed by Christ at the great price which our redemption cost Him, in order that we might not yield a slavish obedience to the depraved wishes of men, far less do homage to their impiety.

SELECTED BIBLIOGRAPHY

Cook, Thomas I., *History of Political Philosophy*, pp. 327–345.
Dunning, William A., *Political Theories, from Luther to Montesquieu* (New York, 1905), ch. 1, §§ 1, 5.
Sabine, George H., *History of Political Theory*, pp. 362–368.

Matthews, W. R., "John Calvin," in F. J. C. Hearnshaw, ed., *Social and Political Ideas of Some Great Thinkers of the Renaissance and the Reformation* (London, 1925), ch. 8.
Allen, J. W., *Political Thought in the Sixteenth Century* (London, 1928), part i, chs. 4–5.
Carlyle, R. W. and A. J., *History of Mediæval Political Theory in the West*, Vol. VI (Edinburgh and London, 1936), pp. 263–270.
Tawney, R. H., *Religion and the Rise of Capitalism* (London, 1926), pp. 102–132.
Smith, Preserved, *The Age of the Reformation* (New York, 1920), chs. 3 and 12.
Hunt, R. N. C., "Calvin's Theory of Church and State," in *Church Quarterly Review*, vol. 108 (1929), pp. 56–71.
Fairbairn, A. M., "Calvin and the Reformed Church," in *Cambridge Modern History* (New York, 1904), Vol. II, ch. 11.
Osgood, Herbert L., "The Political Ideas of the Puritans," in *Political Science Quarterly*, vol. 6 (1891), pp. 1–28.
Weber, Max, *The Protestant Ethic and the Spirit of Capitalism*, translated by Talcott Parsons (London, 1930), pp. 98–127.
Troeltsch, Ernst, *The Social Teaching of the Christian Churches*, translated by Olive Wyon, 2 vols. (London, 1931), Vol. II, pp. 576–656.

Baron, Hans, *Calvins Staatsanschauung und das konfessionelle Zeitalter* (Berlin, 1924).
Haussherr, Hans, *Der Staat in Calvins Gedankenwelt* (Berlin and Halle, 1922).

VINDICIÆ CONTRA TYRANNOS

XIV. THE VINDICIÆ CONTRA TYRANNOS

INTRODUCTION

The doctrine of passive obedience to temporal authority was maintained by Luther, Melanchthon, and Calvin. Calvin particularly, in teaching and practice, stood for a policy of extreme religious intolerance on the part of those in control of government. The first substantial consequence of the Lutheran views appeared to be restraint rather than freedom. On the other hand, the original Lutheran idea of the primary worth that ought to be attributed to individual conscience in matters of religion appeared to have aroused demands for individual freedom in other matters. Moreover, in a very concrete way the religious dissent engendered by the Protestant movement soon came to be productive of advanced political reasoning. In the internal, as well as in the international, wars of the later sixteenth century, differences in religious doctrine were strongly mixed with political rivalries as occasions for armed conflict. In each of three countries—France, England, and Spain—the government, as supporter of a dominant politico-religious faction, dealt oppressively with adherents of the opposing group. These conditions gave origin to many vigorous pamphlets written in defence of resistance to governmental tyranny as it manifested itself in persecution on religious or other grounds. Some of these pamphlets searched deeply and broadly the foundations and limits of political authority and arrived at radical doctrines of governmental responsibility. This is pre-eminently true of the writings of French Huguenots, after the massacre of St. Bartholomew's Day. Democratic ideas are set forth most completely in a tract entitled *Vindiciæ contra Tyrannos*, which appeared in 1579, under the pseudonym "Stephanus Junius Brutus." [1]

[1] Scholars are in dispute as to the authorship of this work. It was at first attributed to Francis Hotoman, a French Protestant refugee, professor of law at the University of Geneva; or to Beza, another French refugee, successor

The discussion in the *Vindiciæ* is presented in the form of answers to four questions, which are as follows: (1) whether subjects are bound to obey a prince who commands what is contrary to the law of God; (2) whether it is lawful to resist a prince who is violating the law of God and devastating the church: if so, who may resist, in what manner, and to what extent; (3) whether and to what extent it is lawful to resist a prince who is oppressing and destroying the state: who may resist, in what manner, and by what right; (4) whether it is the right and duty of princes to give aid to neighboring peoples who are being oppressed on account of adherence to the true religion, or by any other obvious tyranny.

In the answer to the third question the author leads back to the origin of political society. He builds a doctrine of popular sovereignty upon the hypothesis that the original, natural state of mankind was one of complete freedom, and that political organization was everywhere in its beginnings a condition consciously and voluntarily assumed. The author's analysis of the process through which the institution of civil government came about prefigures a doctrine which furnished the foundation, in varying forms, for the systems of eminent political philosophers of the seventeenth and eighteenth centuries. This later doctrine is embodied in the theory of the "social contract." In the *Vindiciæ*, the contract is governmental, rather than social; but the author's conclusions as to the responsibility of government and the right of resistance rest upon his statement of the stipulations of a contract by which the first ruler of any state must be assumed to have been invested with his powers. As with the social-contract theorists, the analysis here of an original contract is partly derived from certain postulates as to the primitive state of mankind. But the author is under mediæval influences, and a primary source of his analysis is the biblical narrative of the setting-up of the first king over the Israelites. His deductions are confirmed by frequent citations of scriptural passages as well as of precedents in legal history and in political history.

to Calvin as head of the clergy in Geneva. Later writers have attributed it to Hubert Languet, a distinguished French diplomat and the author of several pamphlets dealing with religious and political controversies of the time; or to Philippe Duplessis-Mornay. See Ernest Barker, "The Authorship of the *Vindiciæ contra tyrannos*," in *Cambridge Historical Journal*, vol. 3 (1930), pp. 164–181; Paul Janet, *Histoire de la science politique* (fifth ed., 1925), Vol. II, p. 31, note 2; *Encyclopædia Britannica*, under "Languet."

READINGS FROM THE VINDICIÆ CONTRA TYRANNOS[1]

1. *The Institution of the King by the People*

We have shown above that it is God who establishes kings, choosing them and conferring kingdoms upon them. Now we are to show that the people set up kings, commit kingdoms to them, and confirm the selection by their suffrages. Indeed God has willed that it should be done in this manner, in order that kings should acknowledge that whatever authority and power they possess have been received from the people, and that they should, therefore, devote all their thought and efforts to the interests of the people. Nor should kings think that they excel other men through some superiority of nature, as men stand above flocks of sheep or herds of cattle. Let them remember that they are born of the same stuff as other men and have been raised from the ground to their high station by the suffrages and, as it were, upon the shoulders, of the people, in order that henceforth the burden of the commonwealth should rest in great part upon their own shoulders.

Some ages before the people of Israel demanded a king of God, He had ordained the law of royal government, as indicated in the book of Deuteronomy where Moses says : *When thou art come into the land which the Lord thy God giveth thee, and shalt possess it, and shalt dwell therein, and shalt say, I will set a king over me, like as all the nations that are about me, thou shalt in any wise set him king over thee, whom the Lord thy God shall choose.*[2] You see here that the selection (*electio*) of the king is attributed to God, the investment to the people. . . . The elders of Israel, representing the whole body of the people . . . came together at Ramah to meet Samuel; and, wearied of the sons of Samuel, who were unjust judges, and believing that they could by this means wage war more successfully, demanded a king of Samuel. When Samuel asked counsel of the Lord, He made known that he had chosen Saul to rule over the people. Samuel, therefore, anointed Saul. . . . It might perhaps have seemed sufficient if Samuel had presented to the people the king chosen by God, and admonished them to be obedient to him. Nevertheless, in

---

[1] The translations are made from the work as it is printed in a volume entitled : Nicolai Machiavelli Florentini Princeps : ex Sylvestri Tellii Fulginatis Traductione. Adiecta sunt eiusdem argumenti aliorum quorundam contra Machiavellum Scripta, de potestate et officio Principum contra Tyrannos. Hanoviæ, 1595.

The selections are from the third part of the *Vindiciæ*: pp. 73–183.

[2] Deuteronomy xvii. 14–15.

order that the king might know that he was established by the people, Samuel ordered an assemblage of the people at Mizpeh, and there—as if the matter had not already been determined, and the election of Saul not already settled—the lot was cast and fell, first upon the tribe of Benjamin, then upon the family of Matri, and finally upon Saul—the one whom God had chosen. Then by acclamation of all the people Saul was declared the appointed king. Finally—lest he should attribute all these things to chance—after he had given some proof of his valor in relieving Jabesh Gilead from the siege of the Ammonites, he was again in full assembly at Gilgal (a few dissenting to no purpose) confirmed king before God. You see thus that he whom God had chosen and chance had selected from all the rest, was established as king by the suffrages of the people.

In a word, all kings were in the beginning elected. Those who to-day appear to accede to their kingdoms by inheritance were necessarily first established by the people. Although the people of certain countries are accustomed to choose their kings from a particular stock on account of its peculiar merits, nevertheless, it is the stock and not the branch that they choose. Nor do they so choose but that if that stock should degenerate they may select another. Those who are next in line for the kingship are not born kings; they rather become such: they are not deemed kings so much as candidates for the kingship.

2.   The Superiority of the People to the King

Now since kings are established by the people, it seems to follow certainly that the whole body of the people are superior to the king. For it is evident that he who is established by another is accounted less than he that has established him, and that he who receives his authority from another is inferior to him from whom he derives his authority. Potiphar, the Egyptian, thus established Joseph above all his household; Nebuchadnezzar, Daniel over the province of Babylon; Darius, the hundred and twenty governors over his kingdom. Masters are said to establish their servants; kings, their ministers. In like manner the people establish the king as minister of the commonwealth. This name good kings have not disdained, and bad ones have affected it. Wherefore for several generations no Roman emperor (save perhaps some manifest tyrant, as Nero, Domitian, or Caligula) wished to be called lord (*dominus*). Moreover, it is clear that kings were instituted for the benefit of the people. You could not say that for the sake of some hundred men, inferior to most of the rest of the community, the whole community was created; rather that the former were created for the latter. Reason requires that he on whose account another exists should be deemed superior to that other. Thus for the sake of the ship the owner appoints a pilot, who sits at the helm to see that she be not dashed to pieces upon the rocks or follow the wrong course. Relying upon him in that work, the others serve him; even the owner obeys him. Nevertheless, the pilot is but a servant of the ship, differing from the common drudges only in type of work. In the commonwealth the king has the place of pilot, the people that of owner. As long as the king is regardful of the public good the people properly submit to him, yet in such a way that he is esteemed, as he should be, the servant of the commonwealth, in the same capacity as a judge or tribune who differs from the rest of the people only in the respect that he is expected to have greater burdens and expose himself to greater dangers. Wherefore, that which the king acquires through war, as when he occupies territory by right of conquest, or through payments into the fiscus in the administration of justice, he acquires not for himself, but for the kingdom—that is, for the people who have established the kingdom, just as a servant makes acquisitions for his master. Nor can any obligation be contracted with the king save by the authorization of the people.

Moreover, there are many peoples who live without a king; a king without a people, however, you cannot imagine. . . . And why are kings said to have innumerable eyes and ears, long heads, and exceptionally swift feet? Because they are similar to Argus, Gerion, Midas and others represented in legend? Not at all. It is because the people concerned lend to the king their eyes and ears, their strength and their faculties, for the use of the commonwealth. Let the people withdraw from the king, and he who seemed of good sight and hearing, robust and vigorous, will grow blind and deaf, and will suddenly collapse; he who just now triumphed in his magnificence, in one instant becomes most contemptible of all; he who has honors almost divine is compelled to play the schoolmaster at Corinth. . . . Since, therefore, the king exists through, and for the sake of, the people, and without the people cannot stand, who will wonder at our conclusion that the people are greater than the king?

Now what we have said concerning the whole body of the people we wish also to be said concerning those who in every kingdom or city lawfully represent the body of the people, and who are commonly deemed officers of the kingdom and not of the king. For officers of the king are created and discharged by him at his pleasure, and when he is dead they no longer have any authority; they are themselves counted as dead. Officers of the kingdom, on the other hand, receive their authority from the people (at any rate they were formerly accustomed so to do) in public assembly, and can be discharged only by that same power. The former, therefore, depend upon the king, the latter upon the kingdom: the former should be responsible to the supreme officer of the kingdom—to the king; the latter, to the supreme sovereign—the people, upon whom the king himself, and through him his officers, must depend. The function of the former is to guard the king; of the latter, to see that no harm befalls the commonwealth. The former are to aid and serve the king, as domestic servants of a master; the latter are to preserve the rights and privileges of the people and to take diligent care that the king commit or omit nothing to their damage. In fine, the former are ministers, servants, domestics of the king, instituted only to obey him. The latter, as associates of the king in the administration of justice and as partakers of royal authority, are bound, like the king himself, to administer the affairs of the commonwealth; he, as chief among them, holds first place only in degree. As the whole people is superior to the king, so their representatives, though individually inferior to him, should in the aggregate be counted superior to him.

We must now inquire why kings were established in the first instance and what was their principal duty. For a thing is esteemed good only when it fulfils the purpose for which it was instituted. In the first place, it is clear that men by nature free, impatient of servitude, born rather to command than to obey, would not, save for the sake of some great profit, have chosen subjection to another and have renounced their own natural right, so to speak, to submit to the right of another. . . . Nor let us think that kings were chosen to convert to their own uses the goods obtained by the sweat of the many; for every one loves and cherishes his own. Nor were they created that they might squander the public power to their own pleasure; for ordinarily any one hates, or at least envies, his superior. They were established to protect individuals from each other by the administration of justice, and to defend all from dangers from without by repelling force with force. Wherefore Augustine says that those who care for the interests of others are properly said to rule, as the husband rules the wife, or parents their children. Those whose interests are cared for are said to obey; although those who thus rule really serve those whom they are said to command; for, as Augustine also says, they command not for the sake of ruling but because of their duty to care for their charge; not for the glory of domination, but out of pity to guard those committed to their protection. Seneca in his ninety-first epistle says: "In the golden age government was in the hands of the wise. These repressed violence and protected the weak from the strong. They persuaded and dissuaded and pointed out what was useful and what harmful. When anything was needed their wisdom supplied it. Their valor warded off dangers, and increased and enriched the people. Their function was to govern, not to reign. No man tried to see what he could do against them, for each received from them all that he was capable of assimilating." To govern, then, is simply to give counsel. The only end of government is the good of the people. The sole duty of governors and kings is to take care of the people. Royal dignity is, properly speaking, not an honor, but a burden; not a privilege, but a calling; not an immunity, but a duty; not a license, but a public service. Some honor indeed is attached to the office; one would hardly be willing to partake of such troubles unless they were flavored with some relish of honor. The common saying is true that if every one knew with how great annoyances the royal diadem was wreathed no one would pick it up if he found it at his feet along the wayside.

When the words "mine" and "thine" had entered into the world and conflicts arose among citizens concerning ownership of things, and between neighboring peoples over boundaries, it became customary to have recourse to some one who would justly and effectively see that the poor suffered no violence from the rich, or the whole people from their neighbors. When such contests and wars became more violent a permanent choice was made of some one for whose valor and diligence all had high regard. Thus kings were first established to administer justice at home and lead the army abroad. . . . Kings were ordained by God and established by the people for the benefit of the citizens. This benefit consists principally in two things—in the maintenance of justice among individuals and of security against enemies.

We must proceed a little further. Does the king, because he presides in the administration of justice, administer justice according to his own free will? Does the king depend on law, or law on the king? . . . Pausanias the Spartan answers in a word: "Authority pertains to laws as against men, not to men as against laws." [1] . . . We must carry the matter further yet. Since the people were seeking justice through law, if this could be obtained from a single good and just man, they were satisfied with him. But this was hardly possible, and indeed rarely happened. In fact as long as the judgments of kings were received as the equivalent of laws it turned out that certain things were declared as laws at one time and others at another time. It thus became the function of magistrates and other wise men to discover, as it were, laws which could speak with one and the same voice to all men. Kings were then intrusted with the duty of guarding, administering and conserving laws. And because laws were not capable of providing in advance for every contingency, kings might determine certain cases by the same natural equity from which the laws themselves were derived. But lest in these cases the kings should do violence to the law, those superior men (*optimates*), concerning whom we have just spoken, were soon associated with the kings by the people.

Kings themselves should be obedient to law and acknowledge it as their superior. . . . Nor should they consider that they govern any the less because they submit to law. For law is a kind of instrument by means of which human societies are best ruled and directed to a happy end. Wherefore kings were foolish who should think it base to yield to law, just as a geometrician would be who should consider it unbecoming to use the rule and other instruments ordinarily employed by those most expert in making measurements, or as a mariner would be who would prefer to wander recklessly rather than direct the course of his ship by the nautical compass. Who will hestitate to say that it is more expedient and honorable to obey the law rather than a man? Law is the soul of the good king; in it is his inspiration, feeling, and life. The king is the organ of the law, the body through which the law exercises its power, fulfils its function and expresses its meaning. Now it is more reasonable to obey the soul than the body. Law is the concentrated reason and wisdom of many sages. The many are more clear-sighted and far-seeing than the one; it is, therefore, safer to follow the law than a man, however perspicacious he may be. Law is reason or intelligence unperturbed, and free from the influence of anger, cupidity, hate, or prejudice; nor is it deflected by tears or threats. Man, on the other hand, however well endowed with reason, is seized and overcome by wrath, vengeance and other passions; he is so disturbed by these emotions that he is not master of himself; he is compounded

[1] Cicero, *De Officiis*, lib. 2.

of reason and passion, and he cannot always prevent the latter from gaining the upper hand. . . . Law is the coalescence of a multitude of minds; and mind is a parcel of the divine spirit; so that he who obeys the law seems to obey God and to make Him his judge.

3. The Contractual Basis of Royal Authority

We have said that in establishing a king a two-fold pact was entered into: the one, concerning which we have already spoken, between God, on the one hand, and the king and people, on the other; the other, between the king and the people. We must take up the latter now. After Saul was appointed the royal law was delivered to him, according to which he was to govern. David, also, in Hebron made a covenant in the presence of the Lord— that is, God being present as witness—with the elders of Israel, who represented the whole people; after that he was anointed king. . . . Likewise Josias promised to observe the commandments, testimonies and precepts comprised in the book of the covenant; by these words are to be understood the laws, which relate now to piety, now to justice. In all of these passages the covenant is said to have been made with all the people, or with the entire multitude, all the elders, or all the men of Judea: whence we know that not only the chiefs of the tribes but also the captains, centurions and inferior magistrates, were present, representing the towns, so that all might individually covenant with the king.

In this pact it was a matter of creating a king; for the people made the king, not *vice versa*. It cannot be doubted that in this contract the people had the part of stipulator, the king that of promisor. And the part of stipulator is deemed the more advantageous at law. The people, as stipulator, ask the king whether he will govern justly and according to the laws; the king promises that he will. The people then respond that they will faithfully obey him while he governs justly. The king, therefore, promises absolutely, the people conditionally; if the condition is not fulfilled the people are lawfully absolved from every obligation. In the first covenant or contract there is an obligation to piety, in the second, to justice. In the former, the king promises dutifully to obey God, in the latter, that he will rule the people justly; in the one that he will provide for the glory of God, in the other, that he will secure the welfare of the people. In the first contract the condition is—if you observe my law; in the second —if you render to each his due. Failure to fulfil the first pact is duly punished by God; failure to fulfil the second is legitimately punishable by the whole people or by those magistrates whose function it is to protect the people. . . .

Why is it that the king swears first, the people stipulating, unless it is that he thereby accepts a condition, tacitly or expressly? And why is a condition attached to a contract unless it be that if the condition be not fulfilled the contract is by that fact abrogated by law? And if through non-observance of the condition a contract is made null at law, who will call that people perjured who refuse obedience to the king when he disregards the condition which he is obligated and able to fulfil and violates the law to which he has sworn? On the other hand, who would not regard such a perjured and perfidious king as unworthy of his office? The law frees a vassal from his bond of fealty to a lord who has committed a felony upon him, although the lord takes no oath of fealty to the vassal, but only the vassal to the lord; the law of the Twelve Tables holds criminal an advocate who has dealt fraudulently with his client; the civil law permits a freedman to bring an action against his patron for any grievous injury, and under similar circumstances the same law frees a slave from his master, though the obligation be natural, not civil. If all these things are true, is it not even more certain that the people should be absolved from the oath which they have taken to the king, if he, who first swore solemnly to them, as an agent to his principal, has broken his oath?

Even if the formalities of a contract have never taken place, are we not sufficiently taught by Nature herself that kings are established by the people with the condition that they govern well; judges, that they judge justly; military leaders, that they lead forth the army against the enemy? . . .

But, you may ask, what if the people, subdued by force, be compelled by a prince to swear allegiance according to his own terms? I reply, what if a robber, pirate, or tyrant, with whom there is considered to be no bond of justice, should, with uplifted sword, extort a promissory note from any one? Is it not well known that a promise exacted by violence does not bind, especially if anything is promised against good morals or contrary to the law of nature? What is more repugnant to nature than that the people should fasten their own chains and shackles? or that they should promise the king to throw themselves upon the sword or lay violent hands upon themselves? There is, therefore, between king and people a mutual obligation which, whether it be civil or natural, tacit or express, cannot be abrogated by agreement, violated by any law, or rescinded by force. So great is the strength of this obligation that the prince who contumaciously violates it may be truly called a tyrant, and the people who wilfully break it, seditious.

4. The Right of Resistance to Tyrants

Hitherto we have treated of kings. It now remains for us to describe somewhat more accurately the tyrant. We have said that the king is he who rules and governs a kingdom, acceding to his position either through heredity or through election confirmed by the appropriate rites. In contradistinction to this it follows that he is a tyrant who either has seized the government by civil means or, invested therewith in regular manner, rules contrary to right and justice and in violation of the laws and pacts to which he has solemnly bound himself. Both characters of tyrant may inhere in one and the same person. The former is commonly called the tyrant without title (*tyrannus absque titulo*), the latter the tyrant by practice (*tyrannus exercitio*). It may easily come to pass that he who gains a kingdom by violence should rule justly, or that he upon whom a kingdom descends lawfully should rule unjustly. Inasmuch as the kingship is a law-created right rather than inherited property, an office (*functio*) rather than a possession, he would seem more deserving of the name of tyrant who performs his duty badly than he who enters upon his duty in irregular manner. . . .

Now at last we have come by degrees to the principal point of our question. We have seen in what manner kings have been chosen by God and installed by the people; what tasks the king and the officers of the kingdom are under duty to perform; how great power is allowed the king, and how far the function and authority of the officers extend; what and how sacred are the covenants that are made in the installation of the king, and what conditions, tacit or express, are intermixed therewith; finally, who is a tyrant without title, and who a tyrant by practice. Seeing that it is unquestionable that to the lawful king who discharges well his duty to God and the people obedience should be rendered as to God, it remains now for us to determine whether, by whom, and by what means a tyrant may be lawfully resisted. And we must speak first of him who is commonly called a tyrant without title. . . .

In the first place, the law of nature teaches us to preserve and defend our life and our liberty—without which life is hardly worth while, against every violence and wrong. Nature has

implanted this instinct in dogs against wolves, in bulls against
lions, in doves against hawks, in young fowl against kites, and
yet more strongly in man against man himself when a man becomes a wolf to his fellow-man. Therefore, he who questions
whether it is permissible to resist seems to contend with Nature
herself. The law of nations teaches the same: by this dominions
are defined and boundaries established which everyone is obligated to defend against all invaders. It is thus no less lawful
to resist Alexander when, without right and provoked by no
wrong, he invades a country with a powerful fleet, than to resist
Diomedes, the pirate, when he with one vessel renders dangerous
the sea. In such case Alexander surpasses Diomedes not in his
right but only in his security from punishment. It is as proper
to oppose Alexander in ravaging the country as a footpad in
purloining a clock, or a man who would subvert the city by trick-
ery as a robber who would break into a private house.

Furthermore, there is a civil law whereby societies of men are
established under a fixed system, some being governed in one
manner, some in another. Thus some are ruled by one or a few,
others by the people as a whole; some exclude women from the
government, others admit them; some choose their kings from
a single family, others select them promiscuously. If any one
attempts to violate this law by force or fraud we are all bound
to resist him, because he wrongs society, to which he owes everything, and would undermine his country, to which we are devoted
by nature, law, and solemn oath; if we neglect this duty we are
traitors to our country, deserters from human society, contemners
of the law.

As thus the law of nature, the law of nations, and civil law
command us to take arms against tyrants, no other reason can
properly dissuade us. No oath or other pact, public or private,
interposes to prevent us. It is, therefore, permitted to any private
person to eject an intruding tyrant. Nor does the Julian law of
treason which punishes those who rebel against their country
or prince, apply here. For he is no prince who without lawful
title invades the commonwealth or confines of another, nor he a
rebel who defends his country with arms. . . . To as little purpose can the laws of sedition be adduced here. He is seditious who
undertakes to sustain the people in resisting public discipline.
But he who restrains the subverter of the country and of public
discipline does not create sedition; he prevents it. . . .

What we have said has been about the tyrant in the process
of becoming such, when he is devising and laying his plots. But

suppose that after he is possessed of the commonwealth the people, having been overcome, bind themselves to him by oath, or that the commonwealth, having been subdued, transfer authority to him, and the kingdom formally consent to the change of their law; then indeed, inasmuch as he has acquired the title which he lacked before, he seems to be in possession *de jure.* Though the yoke was laid upon the people by compulsion, it is nevertheless just that they submit and acquiesce peacefully in the will of God who at His pleasure transfers kingdoms from one to another. Otherwise there would be no government whose authority might not be questioned. Moreover, it may happen that he, who was before a tyrant without title, having acquired title, should govern lawfully and not practise tyranny. Thus the Jewish people, under the guidance of the king, lawfully resisted Sennacherib, king of the Assyrians, when he invaded Palestine. On the other hand, Zedekiah and all the people were condemned and punished because, after having sworn fealty to Nebuchadnezzar, they revolted, though they had suffered no wrong from him. When faith has once been given there is no longer opportunity for repentance. Though every man in a battle ought to fight with all his valor, yet when he is captured and has taken the oath of loyalty he is bound to keep it. Likewise the people should contend with all vigor to retain their own rights (*jura*); but when they have surrendered, willingly or unwillingly, to the right of another, they should with an even mind endure the government of the victor. . . .

Concerning those who practise tyranny, whether having first acquired their authority lawfully or by force, it is important for us to make careful examination. In the first place, we should consider that all princes are born men and that their reason can as little be made free from passion as the mind can be separated from the body. Therefore, we should not hope to have only perfect princes; we should rather deem ourselves fortunate if we find mediocre ones. If in certain cases the prince does not observe moderation, if now and then he does not yield to reason, if he looks carelessly to the public welfare, if he becomes less diligent in administration of justice or less zealous in warding off war, he must not forthwith be called a tyrant. For he rules not as man over beasts or God over men, but as a man born of the same condition as other men. And as a prince would be considered arrogant who sought to abuse men as if they were beasts, so the people are unjust if they expect a god in a prince or look for divinity in his imperfect nature. But if he deliberately upsets the commonwealth, if he wantonly perverts lawful rights, or has no regard for oaths and covenants, for justice or piety, then indeed he should be adjudged a tyrant—that is, an enemy of God and man. We are thus speaking not of the prince less good, but of the absolutely bad; not of one less wise, but of one who is malicious and treacherous; not of him who is ignorant of the law, but of the contemner of law; not of an unwarlike prince, but of a prince who is enemy of the people and ravager of the kingdom. The weak prince might be disposed to employ the wisdom of the senate, the prætor's knowledge of the law, the tribune's military skill; but the tyrant would be happy if the nobility, the senators and the commanders had only one neck which he might take off with one blow, for no others does he regard with more hatred than these. Although the weak prince might rightly be deposed, nevertheless he can be endured; but the longer the tyrant is tolerated the more insufferable he becomes.

It is not always expedient for the people to do that which they may lawfully do. It often happens that a remedy which is applied is worse than the disease. So it becomes prudent for men to try all means before taking up the sword. If those who represent the people perceive that anything is being done, through force or fraud, against the common weal, they should at once admonish the prince, not waiting until the evil becomes graver and acquires greater strength. For tyranny is like a hectic fever, which, at first easily cured but detected with difficulty, later becomes easily recognizable but almost incurable. Therefore, the representatives should withstand the prince, and not suffer the smallest beginning of tyranny to be made. If the prince persists in his tyrannous course and, though often admonished, does not reform but endeavors to bring matters to the point where he may with impunity do whatever he pleases, then indeed the crime of tyranny is complete, and whatever may be done, through the law or through just resistance, against a tyrant, can be done against him. For tyranny is not a crime merely, but the chiefest, and, as it were, the epitome of all crimes. The tyrant subverts the commonwealth, pillages every one and lays snares for their lives, violates any promise, despising the sanctity of a solemn oath. Therefore, he is as much more vicious than the ordinary bandit, murderer or oath-breaker, as it is more serious to offend against the many or all than against particular individuals. If these private offences are deemed infamous and are punishable by death, is it possible to devise a penalty worthy of a crime so atrocious as tyranny?

Moreover, we have already proved that kings receive their royal dignity from the people, that the whole people are greater than and superior to the king, and that the king or emperor is merely the highest minister and agent of the kingdom or empire. It follows that the tyrant commits a felony against the people— the lord of the fief; he is guilty of treason against the kingdom or empire; he is a rebel. He has thus violated the same laws that the ordinary criminal violates and merits far severer punishment. Therefore, as Bartolus says, he may be either deposed by his superior or punished under the Julian law against public violence. The superior is the whole people, or those who represent them— the electors, palatines, patricians, assembly of estates, etc. If the tyranny has proceeded so far that it cannot be destroyed save by armed force, then it is lawful for the representatives to call the people to arms, enroll an army, and employ not only the valiant strength of the nation, but even strategy and deceit, against the enemy of their country. . . . The officers of the kingdom will not thereby incur the charge of sedition. For in sedition two opposing parties are necessary—one pursuing a just course, the other an unjust course. That party is right which defends the laws, supports the common welfare and preserves the kingdom. That party is wrong which violates laws, or protects violators of law, and defends the destroyers of the country. . . . Whatever tends to the public good is lawful. Wherefore Thomas says that since tyrannical government, established not for the public good but for the private good of him who rules, is unjust, its overthrow does not have the nature of sedition. Nor can the officers of the kingdom be charged with the crime of treason. This crime may, on the one hand, be committed against a legitimate prince. But the prince is simply animate law. Therefore, he who seeks with his utmost power to annihilate law cannot be called by that name, and those who take up arms against him cannot be accused of treason. On the other hand, treason may be committed against the commonwealth. But the commonwealth may be said to exist only so long as the authority of law is maintained and while the private pleasure of the ruler does not absorb the energies of the kingdom. It is, therefore, the tyrant who is guilty of treason against the commonwealth; and those who, relying upon their own authority and sense of duty, assail the tyrant are protectors of the commonwealth. In such case the latter are acting not as individuals, but as the whole people, not as subjects, but as masters demanding from their agent an accounting of his work. . . .

Everywhere there is between prince and people a mutual

and reciprocal obligation: he promises that he will be a good prince; the people promise that if he is such they will obey him. The people are thus obligated to the prince conditionally, he to them absolutely. If the condition be not fulfilled, the people are released, the contract abrogated, the obligation *ipso jure* void. The king is faithless if he governs unjustly; the people, if they neglect to obey him while he rules justly. The people are entirely innocent of the crime of perfidy if they publicly renounce an unjust ruler or endeavor to overpower by force of arms one who without lawful right attempts to hold the kingdom.

It is not merely permissible to the officers of the kingdom to repress a tyrant; it is incumbent upon them as a part of their duty. If they do not discharge this duty they can plead no contract as an excuse. The electors, patricians, peers and other nobles (*optimates*) should not think that they were instituted to exhibit themselves, clothed in their robes of state, at the coronation of the king, according to the ancient custom; as if they were acting in a Greek interlude, or playing the parts of Roland, Oliver, Renaldo and other stage personages representing the knights of King Arthur's table. Nor after the assemblage has been dismissed should they think that they have fulfilled their parts excellently. Such ceremonies are not intended to be executed perfunctorily, or designed for sport—as in children's games when, as Horace describes, they make a king in play. These leaders (*optimates*) should rather know that they are called to a place of work as well as of honor, and that the commonwealth is intrusted to the king as its first and principal guardian and to them as co-guardians. Just as other guardians are appointed to observe the acts of him who holds the place of chief guardian, to demand constant accounting of his administration and watch carefully how he acquits himself of his charge; so likewise officers are appointed to watch the king (who is master only in the sense of having the care of a ward), to see that he does nothing to the detriment of the people. The conduct of the principal guardian is imputed to the co-guardians if, when they ought and can, they do not discover his fault, especially where he neglects to communicate the affairs of administration to them, or executes his guardianship faithlessly, or practises deceit, acts selfishly or ruinously for his ward, or distrains anything from the property of the ward; in fine, they are held to account if he acts stupidly, indifferently or unskilfully. In like manner the chief officers are held responsible for the conduct of the king, if they do not suppress tyranny or prevent its appearance, or supplement his inefficiency by their own vigilance and industry. . . . The commonwealth is intrusted as much to their care as to his; their commission is not only that they serve the public interest through their particular offices, but also that they hold him to his proper function. Both he and they have promised to secure the welfare of the commonwealth. If he violates his oath they are not to imagine that they are thereby absolved from their pledge, any more than are bishops released from their vows if the Pope defends heresy or seeks to destroy the church. The more the king becomes an oath-breaker, the more should the officers consider themselves bound to keep their faith. If they act collusively they are to be accounted prevaricators; if they conspire with him, they are deserters and traitors; if they neglect to deliver the commonwealth from tyranny, they are tyrants themselves. On the other hand, if they undertake to save the commonwealth and defend it with all their powers, they are protectors, guardians, and, in a sense, kings themselves.

SELECTED BIBLIOGRAPHY

Sabine, George, *History of Political Theory*, pp. 376–384.
Dunning, William A., *Political Theories, from Luther to Montesquieu*, ch. 2, §§ 1, 2.
Figgis, John Neville, *Studies of Political Thought from Gerson to Grotius* (Cambridge, 1907), pp. 152–158.
Laski, H. J., "Historical Introduction" to a reprint (London, 1924) of the 1689 translation of the *Vindiciæ* under the title *A Defence of Liberty against Tyrants*.
Barker, Ernest, "The Authorship of the *Vindiciæ contra tyrannos*, in *Cambridge Historical Journal*, Vol. III (1930), pp. 164–181.
Barker, Ernest, "A Huguenot Theory of Politics," in *Essays on Church, State and Study*, (London, 1930), Essay 3.
Carlyle, R. W. and A. J., *A History of Mediæval Political Theory in the West*, Vol. VI (Edinburgh and London, 1936), pp. 338–341.
Armstrong, E., "The Political Theory of the Huguenots," in *American Historical Review*, vol. 4 (1889), pp. 13–40.
Janet, Paul, *Histoire de la science politique*, 2 vols. (fifth ed., Paris, 1925), vol. 2, pp. 31–46.
Weill, Georges, *Les théories sur le pouvoir royal en France sur les guerres de religion* (Paris, 1892), chs. 3–5.
Baudrillart Henri, J. L., *Bodin et son temps. Tableaux des théories politiques et des idées économiques au seizième siècle* (Paris, 1853), pp. 1–110.

BODIN

XV. JEAN BODIN (1530-1596)

INTRODUCTION

Political reasoning in the sixteenth century was, in most instances, closely determined by some current dispute or by an immediate practical problem. Writings on questions of government were generally limited in scope, as the Huguenot pamphlets. A more extended work, like the *Institutes* of Calvin, would include treatment of political subjects only as a subsidiary part of a broader plan. But the century furnishes one great political work, which ranks with Aristotle's *Politics* and Montesquieu's *Spirit of the Laws* in range of topics and wealth of detail. This is the *Six Books Concerning the State*, by the French writer, Jean Bodin. This treatise is comprehensive and systematic. Its principal doctrines, however, reflect contemporary events very truly. One purpose of the author was to discover broad principles of law—principles that would disclose means of deliverance from the religious and political turmoil of his time. He sought also to construct a scheme of state-theory which would be applicable to such a national and territorial sovereignty as was in his lifetime coming steadily and clearly into full strength in France. For the task which Bodin assumed he had training in scholarship and experience. He had been a student of law, and then a lecturer on jurisprudence, at Toulouse. Later he had been a practising advocate in Paris. He was a constant reader in the fields of history, economics, and natural science; he wrote several minor essays on fiscal questions, and an extended and noteworthy essay in the philosophy of history.[1] In public life he was a leading representative of the third estate in the States-General of Blois (which met in 1567), and was counsellor at the courts of Henry III and Henry IV. Though a strong supporter of the monarch's authority in the state, his normal attitude in politics was that of moderate independence; and he advocated toleration in religion. His writing

[1] *Methodus ad facilem Historiarum Cognitionem* (*A Method for the Easy Understanding of History*), published in 1566.

369

is fair in prevailing tone; and the wide range of his historical learning enabled him to give empirical form to his expositions. Bodin's most distinctive contribution to political theory is his doctrine of sovereignty. Perhaps no single conception of a political philosopher has been so influential on subsequent theory as this of Bodin. Sovereignty, according to his definition, is that power, in the state, which is above all limitation by positive law; it is the authority which is the original source of positive law; its presence is the criterion of the statehood of any given community. The selections below, from the *Six Books Concerning the State*, [1] contain the author's discussion of sovereignty, and also his preliminary consideration of the nature and end of the state and the definition of citizenship. Bodin's theory of revolutions and his interpretation of the influence of climate upon government contribute to the importance of his position in the history of political philosophy; but lack of space prevents the inclusion of passages on those topics. The work also comprises, in systematic form, enlightened discussion of numerous minor topics relating to the machinery and functions of government.

READINGS FROM SIX BOOKS CONCERNING THE STATE [2]

1. *The Definition of the State and of Citizenship* [3]

A state is an association of families and their common affairs, governed by a supreme power and by reason. [4] We have placed this definition, omitted by writers on the state, at the beginning of our work, because it is necessary to consider the final stage of inherited enlightenment and accomplishment, before anything else is said; then when the end has been discovered and explored, we may examine the stages through which the goal was reached. For a definition is nothing but the conclusion of a problem that is propounded; [5] and unless it rests upon a firm

---

[1] This work appeared first in French (*Les Six livres de la république*, 1576) and later, with extensive revision, in Latin (*De Republica Libri Sex*, 1586).

[2] The passages are translated from the Frankfort edition, 1641, of the Latin version. Assistance has been derived from the earlier French version, and also from an English translation, by Richard Knolles, 1606, of the French version.

[3] Passages from Bk. I, chs. i and vi.

[4] "Respublica est familiarum rerumque inter ipsas communium, summa potestate ac ratione moderata multitudo."

[5] "Rei propositæ finis."

and stable foundation, whatever you build upon it will collapse in one moment. . . .

We first said that a state should be regulated by reason: for the name of state is sacred; wherefore assemblages of pirates and robbers are to be kept absolutely distinct from the state, which should have no legal or contractual association with such bands. And in all well and wisely constituted societies, whether it be a question of keeping faith and maintaining the public safety, of entering into treaties, making war, regulating the boundaries of the kingdom, or settling controversies between rulers, robbers and pirates are excluded from all social law. Those who govern states according to their own laws and the law of nations have always distinguished their just and lawful enemies from those who strive to overthrow commonwealths and subvert civil order. Wherefore if robbers are not paid the ransom agreed upon for a captive, no fraud is committed, since they do not share the laws of war nor enjoy the rights possessed by lawful enemies, captive or free.[1]

The principles which we have discussed in relation to the household, as a whole and in its individual parts, contain the elements of all political society. And just as the foundations of a house can stand by themselves before any walls have risen above them, so also a household can exist of itself without a state; and the master of a house may exercise supreme power over the members of his household, without depending upon the authority of another; many such households are said to exist in Mauretania and America. But a state without households or a city without walls and buildings can no more exist than terraces or roofs without walls and foundations. When, therefore, the head of a house goes forth from the home, where he holds domestic authority, to join with other family heads for the purpose of transacting their common affairs, he then loses the name of master and lord and becomes an associate and a citizen; in a sense, he leaves his home to enter the body politic, and he transacts public instead of domestic business. Indeed a citizen is no other than a free man who is bound by the supreme power of another.[2] For before any state or commonwealth took form, each *pater familias* had final power of life and death over his children and wives. Afterwards strength and the desire to rule, as well as avarice and the passion of revenge,

---

[1] *De Republica*, pp. 1–2.
[2] "Est autem civis nihil aliud quam liber homo, qui summæ alterius potestati obligatur."

armed one against the other, and the issue of war forced the conquered to serve the pleasure of the more powerful. He who showed himself a valiant leader ruled then not only over his household but also over his enemies and allies—the latter as conquered friends, to each one of whom was given freedom to live as he pleased, the former (his enemies) as slaves. Thus that complete liberty which is derived from nature, was taken away, even from the victors, by him whom the latter had chosen as their leader; at least their liberty was diminished; for each, even in his private capacity, had to recognize the supreme authority of another. Thus we see the origin of slaves and subjects, citizens and foreigners, prince and tyrant. Reason itself teaches us that governments and states were first founded upon force, though we may learn the same thing from history. Books, antiquities and laws are full of testimonies that primitive man held nothing higher than convenience; he would rob, plunder, and kill, or enslave. . . .

In this it seems to me that Aristotle, Demosthenes, and Cicero are wrong; for, following Herodotus (I think) they hold that kings first obtained preferment on account of their reputation for integrity and justice. They have thus pictured to us heroic and golden ages; this I refute elsewhere by positive arguments and evidence. For we see that the earliest communities and kingdoms, before Abraham's time, were full of slaves. Likewise the western islands superabounded in slaves when they were conquered by the Spanish. It is probable that they lost their liberty only through violence and in defiance of the laws of nature. Here is proof of my theory: The people of Gao (in Africa) in the preceding generation had heard of neither kingdoms nor the rule of tyrants, until one of them, in his wandering, saw the majestic power of the king of Timbuctu. Thereupon there came upon him the desire to rule over his people; and, being hard pressed by poverty, he began to plunder the merchants and other rich individuals; finally, having thus obtained wealth and having communicated his design to his friends, he gradually acquired control over the entire region. After him his son, calling himself king, found it necessary to preserve with equity and justice the authority which had originated in robbery. This is the origin of the Gaoian kings who in a short time have advanced so rapidly. Therefore, it may be perceived that the definition of citizen, which we gave above, is true; that is, a citizen is a free man, restrained by the authority of a supreme power. *Free*, I say; for although a slave far more than a free man, is subject to the authority of a supreme power, nevertheless, by common consent it is held that he must be excluded from the roll of citizens. The same cannot be said of the wives and children of citizens; for though they are subject to domestic authority, and their liberty is thereby diminished, they are nevertheless citizens. In the same way something of the natural liberty of all citizens is lost, so that they become subject to the supreme power of another.[1]

It is a more serious fault to say that no one is a citizen who does not participate in public authority, or who has no part in the deliberative or consultative bodies. This is Aristotle's definition, which he himself confesses has place only in a popular state. But a definition which is not general is useless, as appears from the words of Aristotle himself. It is no less illogical when he holds elsewhere that nobles and townspeople are more to be considered citizens than plebeians and peasants, or that youths require to be initiated into citizenship. A definition does not admit of divisions; it contains neither more nor less than the thing which is defined. The description of citizenship which Aristotle has given is not even applicable in a popular state; for in Athens, the most democratic of all communities, the fourth class, containing three-fourths of all the citizens, were excluded altogether from directive and judicial offices; whence those who accept Aristotle's definition must admit that Athenians were, until the time of Pericles, aliens in their own state. . . . It has been more truly said by Plutarch that citizens are those who enjoy the benefits of the laws and privileges of a civil community, varying according to age, sex, rank, and condition, so that, for example, nobles have the rights of nobles, and plebeians the rights of plebeians.[2]

Thus the true and proper distinction between citizen and alien consists in the fact that the former is subject to the local civil authority, whereas the latter can disregard the orders of the prince who is to him an alien. On the other hand, the prince is bound to protect the citizen from injury by enemies or by other citizens, whereas he is not so bound in behalf of the alien unless such protection is solicited and is granted from motives of humanity. Other rights which have relation to the privileges of citizens, such as the right to hold civil or ecclesiastical office, are not comprehended within the definition of citizenship, although almost everywhere aliens are excluded from public functions especially from the priesthood and from the magistracies.[3]

[1] *De Republica*, pp. 71–73.
[2] *Ibid.*, pp. 80–81.   [3] *Ibid.*, p. 96.

2. The Nature and Functions of Sovereignty [1]

Sovereignty is supreme power over citizens and subjects, un-restrained by laws.[2] . . . Since we have already defined the state as the rightful government of a number of families in their common affairs, with a supreme and perpetual power, it should now be explained what is meant by supreme and perpetual power. We say that the power must be perpetual; for supreme power over citizens may be given to some one or several not perpetually, but for a brief period at the expiration of which the authority ceases. Such persons cannot be called sovereign rulers; they are rather custodians of sovereignty until such time as the sovereign prince or people may withdraw the power intrusted, of which they are the true owners and possessors, as those who have lent or pawned their goods to another; just as those who have conferred upon others powers of judgment and command for a certain time, or to be withdrawn at will, do not cease to be masters and possessors of the jurisdiction and authority. So the jurist has said that the prefect of the Roman emperor surrendered his authority upon demand of the magistrate. It makes no difference whether greater or less power is thus conferred; for if the high power conceded by a prince to his lieutenant to be withdrawn at will, be called sovereignty, the power might be used against the prince himself, to whom nothing but an empty title would then remain; so also a servant might command his master, than which nothing more absurd can be imagined. When authority is granted to a magistrate or to a private individual the person of the prince is always excepted. Whatever authority the sovereign gives to another is less than that which he reserves to himself by virtue of his sovereignty; and he is never so divested of his sovereignty that he may not undertake an examination of the affairs committed to his magistrates or officers, by way of prevention, concurrence, or challenge (*evocatione*), or that he may not withdraw power altogether from them. Wherefore, the Roman dictator, the harmosts of the Lacedæmonians, the esymnet of Thessaly, the archons of Malta, or the ancient bailly of Florence (when it had popular government), or those who among us are called regents, or any magistrate or officer to whom is conceded power which though supreme is not perpetual—no such official can be said to have sovereignty.[3]

[1] Passages from Bk. I, chs. viii and x.
[2] "Maiestas est summa in cives ac subditos legibusque soluta potestas."
[3] *De Republica*, pp. 123-4.

But suppose that supreme power, unlimited by laws, and without protest or appeal, be granted by the people to some one or few, shall we say that the latter have sovereignty? For he has sovereignty who, after God, acknowledges no one greater than himself. I hold that sovereignty resides not in such persons, but in the people, at whose pleasure they hold their power, or to whom they must return their authority at the expiration of the period designated. The people cannot be considered as having divested themselves of their power when they intrust supreme authority, unrestrained by laws, to one or a few, if the commitment is for a certain period of time, or at the pleasure of the people; for in either case the holders of the supreme authority must render account of their doings to the prince or people, who, being sovereign, are required to give account to no one, save immortal God. What if supreme power be conferred for a period of ten years; as in Athens one archon, whom they called judge, stood thus preeminent in power in the city? Still the sovereignty of the state did not rest in him; he was rather curator or deputy for the people, and had to render account to them. What if the high power of which I speak be given to one or more for a year, with no requirement that account of their actions be given to any one? So the Cnidians every year chose sixty citizens whom they called *amymones*, that is, men superior to any limitation or censure. Sovereignty, nevertheless, was not in them, since they were compelled, at the expiration of the year, to surrender their authority.[1]

But what if the people have given supreme and perpetual power to any one for life? If the power is given unlimited by laws, and without the name of magistrate, deputy, governor, or guardian, and not at the pleasure of any one, certainly it must be confessed that sovereign rights have been conceded to such a one. The people in such case have despoiled themselves of their authority, in order to give to another all the privileges of sovereignty, without conditions; in like manner as any one might by pure gift surrender to another the ownership and possession of his property; such a perfect donation contains no conditions.[2]

As a prince is bound by no laws of his predecessor, much less is he bound by his own laws. One man may receive a command from another, but no man can command himself. Pomponius says that no obligation can exist if it must receive its sanction from the will of him who makes the promise; this shows conclusively that a prince can in no way be bound by his own laws and orders.

[1] *De Republica*, p. 126. [2] *Ibid.*, p. 128.

As the Pope, according to the jurists, cannot bind his own hands, so the supreme prince, or even the lowest magistrate, or a private person, cannot issue commands to himself. Thus we see at the end of every law, "because it has so pleased us," in order that all may understand that laws, however just in themselves, depend for their force solely upon the will of him who makes the law.

As for the laws of God and of nature, princes and people are equally bound by them, so that no one who attempts to abrogate or weaken them can escape the judgments of divine sovereignty. What we have said as to the freedom of sovereignty from the binding force of law does not have reference to divine or natural law. That Pope who best of all knew the rights of sovereignty and who brought under his sway almost all Christian emperors and princes, said "sovereignty pertains to him who can derogate from ordinary law (*ordinario iuri*)"; the latter expression I interpret to mean the laws of the country (*patriis legibus*). But is a prince bound by the laws of his country if he has sworn to observe them? Here it is necessary to make a distinction. If the prince has sworn to himself, no obligation exists; he is not bound by an oath made to himself; just as private persons are not bound by oaths which they make in mutual contract, if the contract be such as the law does not make binding, however honorably the agreements may have been made. If a prince swears to another ruler not to abrogate the laws made by himself or by his predecessors, he is bound, if the prince to whom he makes the promise has interest in the matter. . . .

Likewise we say that a prince who has made sworn promises to his subjects is bound by them, if the promises are reasonable; but this is true not because he has sworn or because he is bound by his own laws, but because any one is bound by his just covenants, if they are made with another who has any interest, whether the promises be made with or without oath. Moreover, as a private person may be relieved of his obligation if he has been circumvented by fraud, deceit, error, or threat, so a prince may be released not only in those cases which tend to impair his sovereignty, but also where his private convenience and domestic affairs are disturbed.[1]

This, then, I hold: A prince may abrogate, modify, or replace a law made by himself and without the consent of his subjects; such action is fully permissible where justice seems to demand it; the abrogation, modification, or substitution, however, must not

---

[1] *De Republica*, pp. 134–5.

be obscure or ambiguous, but must be set forth in clear detail.
If there is no probable reason for abrogating the law, he is acting
contrary to the duty of a good prince in seeking such abrogation.
However, he is not bound by any obligation assumed by his predecessors, further than what is compatible with his own interest. . . .
We must not confuse laws and contracts. Law depends upon
the will of him who holds supreme power in the state, and who
can bind subjects by his law, but cannot bind himself. A contract
between a prince and his subjects has mutual binding force, so
that it cannot be departed from save with the consent of both
parties; in this the prince seems to have nothing above his subjects, except that the purpose of a law to which he has sworn having ceased to exist, he is no longer bound either by the law or by
the oath which he took with regard to the law. A well-advised
prince will not suffer himself to be bound by oath to observe the
laws, for in such case he does not possess the supreme authority in
the commonwealth.[1]

As to laws concerning the supreme power (*imperii leges*),[2] the
prince cannot abrogate or modify them, since they are attached
to the very sovereignty with which he is clothed; such is the Salic
law, which is the foundation of our monarchy.[3]

The sovereignty of a prince is manifest in the fact that when the
estates and orders of the people, with humble mien, present their
requests to him they are exercising no authority of commanding,
forbidding, or concurring; but the prince by his own judgment
and will directs everything; whatever he desires and orders has
the force of law. The opinion of those who in books scattered
broadcast have written that the king is bound by the popular
command, must be disregarded; such doctrine furnishes seditious
men with material for revolutionary plots, and leads to disturbance in the commonwealth. No reasonable ground can be adduced
why subjects should control princes, or why power should be
attributed to popular assemblies—except in the infancy, madness,
or captivity of the prince, when a guardian or deputy may be
created by the suffrages of the people. If princes were restrained
by laws made by these assemblies or by the commands of the
people, the power of the prince would be worthless and the royal
name a vain thing.[4]

The approval and promulgation of laws, which is commonly

[1] *De Republica*, pp. 136–7.
[2] On the ambiguity of this expression, see Dunning, *Political Theories, from
Luther to Montesquieu*, pp. 100–103.
[3] *De Republica*, p. 139.   [4] *Ibid.*, pp. 139–40.

done in an assembly or senate, does not imply that the sovereignty
of the realm resides in such assembly or senate, but only a species
of authority without which laws issued by the king might be called
in question at his death, or before the senate when it acts judicially.
I hold, therefore, that the sovereignty of the prince is in no degree
diminished by calling together the assemblies or estates, though
indeed a prince grants many things to the assembled people which
he would not so readily grant to individuals; this is because the
voices of individuals are not heard so clearly as the voice of the
multitude; or it is because the prince, accustomed to use the eyes
and ears of others, in the assembly sees and hears the people
directly, and so, impelled by shame, religious fear, or his own good
disposition, he grants their requests. But the highest privilege
of sovereignty consists primarily in giving laws not only to individuals but also to the people as a whole, without their consent.[1]

We may hold that a king who by lawful right assumes the kingship is bound by the contracts and promises of his predecessors, in
so far as such contracts were made for the benefit of the commonwealth. This is especially true if they were made with the judgment and consent of the entire people or of the greater assemblies;
for their good faith is at stake, which it is not only appropriate
but necessary for the king to respect, even though the state may
be harmed thereby. But when a prince has contracted with
strangers or with citizens concerning matters pertaining to the
commonwealth without the consent of the people, if serious injury
would come upon the commonwealth from the performance of the
contracts, his successor is not bound by them, especially if he
obtains his authority through election by the people or the senate;
in such case he has received none of his privileges from his predecessor. It would be otherwise if he had acquired authority by
grant from another; then he would be bound by the latter's promises, unless express exception had been made. But by whatever
right a prince obtains his authority, whether by law, testament,
popular election, or lot, it is just to fulfil those obligations which
were undertaken for the good of the state. Otherwise it would
be permissible for him, through evil practices, contrary to the laws
of nature, to draw profit to himself out of hardships endured by
others. It is of concern to the citizenship to keep the public
faith to the best of its ability, lest when the state is in extreme
danger all means of relief should be cut off. . . .

But why, some one may ask, are the foregoing distinctions necessary, since all princes are bound by the law of nations? For in

[1] *De Republica*, pp. 143–4.

that law compacts and testaments are included. This is not true, if we mean every kind of contract or testament. But admitting it to be true, it does not follow that a prince is more bound by the law of nations than by his own laws, except in so far as the former are in agreement with the laws of nature and of God; to these latter laws all that we have said concerning the obligation of princes must be referred. If certain of the laws of nations are unjust, the prince may abrogate them and forbid his subjects to follow them. This we showed in relation to slavery; this institution was established in many states, by pernicious examples, yet in accord with the law of almost every nation; but through salutary decrees of several princes it has been abolished, in conformity to the laws of nature. What has been said of one thing may be extended to other things of like kind; for a proviso in the whole argumentation is that nothing be sanctioned which is contrary to the laws of God or of nature. For if justice is the end of the law, and law is the command of the prince, and the prince is the image of the almighty God, then the laws of the prince should bear the stamp of divine laws.[1]

The first and principal function of sovereignty is to give laws to the citizens generally and individually, and, it must be added, not necessarily with the consent of superiors, equals, or inferiors. If the consent of superiors is required, then the prince is clearly a subject; if he must have the consent of equals, then others share his authority; if the consent of inferiors—the people or the senate—is necessary, then he lacks supreme authority. . . .

It may be objected that custom does not get its power from the judgment or command of the prince, and yet has almost the force of law, so that it would seem that the prince is master of law, the people of custom. Custom, insensibly, yet with the full compliance of all, passes gradually into the character of men, and acquires force with the lapse of time. Law, on the other hand, comes forth in one moment at the order of him who has the power to command, and often in opposition to the desire and approval of those whom it governs. Wherefore, Chrysostom likens law to a tyrant and custom to a king. Moreover, the power of law is far greater than that of custom, for customs may be superseded by laws, but laws are not supplanted by customs; it is within the power and function of magistrates to restore the operation of laws which by custom are obsolescent. Custom proposes neither rewards nor penalties; laws carry one or the other, unless

[1] *De Republica*, pp. 166–7.

it be a permissive law which nullifies the penalty of some other
law. In short, a custom has compelling force only as long as the
prince, by adding his endorsement and sanction to the custom,
makes it a law.

It is thus clear that laws and customs depend for their force
upon the will of those who hold supreme power in the state. This
first and chief mark of sovereignty is, therefore, of such sort that
it cannot be transferred to subjects, though the prince or people
sometimes confer upon one of the citizens the power to frame laws
(*legum condendarum*), which then have the same force as if they
had been framed by the prince himself. The Lacedæmonians
bestowed such power upon Lycurgus, the Athenians upon Solon;
each stood as deputy for his state, and the fulfilment of his function depended upon the pleasure not of himself but of the people;
his legislation had no force save as the people confirmed it by their
assent. The former composed and wrote the laws, the people
enacted and commanded them.

Under this supreme power of ordaining and abrogating laws, it
is clear that all other functions of sovereignty are included; so
that it may be truly said that supreme authority in the state is
comprised in this one thing—namely, to give laws to all and each
of the citizens, and to receive none from them. For to declare
war or make peace, though seeming to involve what is alien to the
term law, is yet accomplished by law, that is by decree of the
supreme power. It is also the prerogative of sovereignty to
receive appeals from the highest magistrates, to confer authority
upon the greater magistrates and to withdraw it from them, to
allow exemption from taxes, to bestow other immunities, to grant
dispensations from the laws, to exercise power of life and death,
to fix the value, name and form of money, to compel all citizens
to observe their oaths: all of these attributes are derived from the
supreme power of commanding and forbidding—that is, from the
authority to give law to the citizens collectively and individually,
and to receive law from no one save immortal God. A duke,
therefore, who gives laws to all his subjects, but receives law from
the emperor, Pope, or king, or has a co-partner in authority, lacks
sovereignty.[1]

SELECTED BIBLIOGRAPHY

Sabine, George H., *History of Political Theory*, ch. 20.
McIlwain, Charles H., *Growth of Political Thought in the West*, ch. 7.
Cook, Thomas I., *History of Political Philosophy*, ch. 14.
Dunning, William A., *Political Theories, from Luther to Montesquieu*, ch. 3.
Allen, J. W., *History of Political Thought in the Sixteenth Century* (London, 1928), pt. iii, ch. 8.
Hearnshaw, F. J. C., "Bodin and the Genesis of the Doctrine of Sovereignty," in R. W. Seton-Watson, ed. *Tudor Studies* (London, 1924), pp. 109–132.
Shepard, Max A., "Sovereignty at the Crossroads," in *Political Science Quarterly*, vol. 45 (1930), pp. 580–603.
Bluntschli, Johann Kaspar, *Geschichte der neueren Statswissenschaft, allgemeines Statsrecht und Politik* (third ed., Munich and Leipsic, 1881), pp. 26–56.
Chauviré, Roger, *Jean Bodin, auteur de la République* (Paris, 1914).
Hancke, E., *Bodin: eine Studie über den Begriff der Soverainetät*, in *Untersuchen zur Deutschen Staats- und Rechtsgeschichte*, vol. 47 (Breslau, 1894).
Fournol, E., *Bodin, prédécesseur de Montesquieu* (Paris, 1896).
Baudrillart, Henri, *Jean Bodin et son temps* (Paris, 1853).

HOOKER

XVI. RICHARD HOOKER (1553-1600)

INTRODUCTION

The first substantial contribution to political theory written in English is Richard Hooker's *Laws of Ecclesiastical Polity* (published in 1594), which is also the first great theoretical work in English prose literature. English constitutional development had been shaped by men of practical minds and interpreted by lawyers. Political controversies had been usually discussed in terms of English law and custom, not under the categories of political theory. Questions that had been raised by the Protestant movement in the church reached England during the period of the effective absolutism of the Tudors. The movement created religious differences among the people in England as it had elsewhere, and there was some religious persecution; but religious divisions in England were not at that time blended with powerful political factions among the people; and the absolutism of the crown enjoyed the support of strong national sentiment. After the definite adoption of Protestantism by Elizabeth, pamphleteers debated, in somewhat broader terms than formerly, questions concerning the rights of the people or the authority of kings; and they borrowed arguments from continental disputants. Generally, however, neither side presented any such clear and fundamental statement of doctrine as we find in Hooker's work.

Hooker was a learned clergyman of the Anglican church, and his book was the outgrowth of a controversy on church government. He became engaged in a dispute with a Presbyterian clergyman as to the validity of the particular organization that had been the somewhat accidental outcome of the dealings of Tudor monarchs with the ecclesiastical problems produced by the upheaval in the Christian church. He wrote the *Laws of Ecclesiastical Polity* in order to establish a broad basis for refutation of the attacks made by Presbyterians upon the polity and practices of the Anglican church. To the charge that the episcopal organization was unscriptural, Hooker replied that the Scriptures required no fixed

385

polity.   Ecclesiastical laws, he maintained, belong to the type of
laws that must be shaped by the reason of man; they are, therefore, changeable, as distinguished from immutable natural laws.
The basis of the discussion in the *Ecclesiastical Polity* is established
in the first book, which presents a fundamental examination of the
origin, province, and obligation of laws in general.   It is a brief
but comprehensive discussion that presents a striking transition
from medieval to modern political writing.   On the one hand,
Hooker restates not only medieval-scholastic conceptions of the
nature and essential kinds of law, but also older ideas of man's
natural sociability and reasonableness and of the necessity, nevertheless, of coercive political organization because of the imperfect
operation of man's reason.   On the other hand, he derives from
these traditional ideas a theory of government created by the
deliberate action of reasoning men and limited always by some
sort of popular consent expressed chiefly in well-established legal
customs of the community.   His conception of an "original" society, which, although pre-political, is yet controlled generally by
laws of reason, is essentially like the "state of nature" in the theory
of Locke, who acknowledges his indebtedness to the "judicious
Hooker."   Hooker's analysis is a clear philosophic statement of
certain doctrines, with respect to the ground and origin of political
society and the nature and sanction of human laws, which in the
two succeeding centuries were first principles with political theorists
of a democratic tendency.

READINGS FROM LAWS OF ECCLESIASTICAL POLITY [1]

1.   *The Ground and Origin of Political Society* [2]

X.   That which hitherto we have set down is (I hope) sufficient
to shew their brutishness, which imagine that religion and virtue
are only as men will account of them; that we might make as
much account, if we would, of the contrary, without any harm
unto ourselves, and that in nature they are as indifferent one as
the other.   We see then how nature itself teacheth laws and statutes to live by.   The laws which have been hitherto mentioned do
bind men absolutely even as they are men, although they have

---

[1] The selections are taken from *Hooker: Book I of the Laws of Ecclesiastical
Polity*, edited by R. W. Church.   Oxford, 1896.   By permission of the Delegates of the Clarendon Press.
[2] Bk. I, ch. x, §§ 1–4.

never any settled fellowship, never any solemn agreement amongst
themselves what to do or not to do. But forasmuch as we are
not by ourselves sufficient to furnish ourselves with competent
store of things needful for such a life as our nature doth desire, a
life fit for the dignity of man; therefore to supply those defects and
imperfections which are in us living single and solely by ourselves,
we are naturally induced to seek communion and fellowship with
others. This was the cause of men's uniting themselves at the
first in politic societies; which societies could not be without
government, nor government without a distinct kind of law from
that which hath been already declared. Two foundations there
are which bear up public societies; the one, a natural inclination,
whereby all men desire sociable life and fellowship; the other, an
order expressly or secretly agreed upon touching the manner of
their union in living together. The latter is that which we call
the law of a commonweal, the very soul of a politic body, the
parts whereof are by law animated held together, and set
on work in such actions as the common good requireth. Laws
politic, ordained for external order and regiment amongst men,
are never framed as they should be, unless presuming the will of
man to be inwardly obstinate, rebellious, and averse from all
obedience unto the sacred laws of his nature; in a word, unless
presuming man to be in regard of his depraved mind little better
than a wild beast, they do accordingly provide notwithstanding
so to frame his outward actions, that they be no hindrance unto
the common good for which societies are instituted: unless they
do this, they are not perfect. It resteth therefore that we consider how nature findeth out such laws of government as serve to
direct even nature depraved to a right end.

2. All men desire to lead in this world a happy life. That
life is led most happily, wherein all virtue is exercised without
impediment or let. The Apostle,[1] in exhorting men to contentment although they have in this world no more than very bare
food and raiment, giveth us thereby to understand that those are
even the lowest of things necessary; that if we should be stripped of
all those things without which we might possibly be, yet these
must be left; that destitution in these is such an impediment, as
till it be removed suffereth not the mind of man to admit any other
care. For this cause, first God assigned Adam maintenance of
life, and then appointed him a law to observe.[2] For this cause,
after men began to grow to a number, the first thing we read they
gave themselves unto was the tilling of the earth and the feeding of

[1] 1 Tim. vi. 8.　　　　　　　　[2] Gen. i. 29; ii. 17.

cattle.   Having by this mean whereon to live, the principal actions of their life afterward are noted by the exercise of their religion.[1] True it is, that the kingdom of God must be the first thing in our purposes and desires.[2]   But inasmuch as righteous life presupposeth life; inasmuch as to live virtuously it is impossible except we live; therefore the first impediment, which naturally we endeavor to remove, is penury and want of things without which we cannot live.   Unto life many implements are necessary; more, if we seek (as all men naturally do) such a life as hath in it joy, comfort, delight, and pleasure.   To this end we see how quickly sundry arts mechanical were found out, in the very prime of the world.[3]   As things of greatest necessity are always first provided for, so things of greatest dignity are most accounted of by all such as judge rightly.   Although therefore riches be a thing which every man wisheth, yet no man of judgment can esteem it better to be rich, than wise, virtuous and religious.   If we be both or either of these, it is not because we are so born.   For into the world we come as empty of the one as of the other, as naked in mind as we are in body.   Both which necessities of man had at the first no other helps and supplies than only domestical; such as that which the Prophet implieth, saying, *Can a mother forget her child?* [4] such as that which the Apostle mentioneth, saying, *He that careth not for his own is worse than an Infidel:* [5] such as that concerning Abraham, *Abraham will command his sons and his household after him, that they keep the way of the Lord.* [6]

3.   But neither that which we learn of ourselves nor that which others teach us can prevail, where wickedness and malice have taken deep root.   If therefore when there was but as yet one only family in the world, no means of instruction human or divine could prevent effusion of blood;[7] how could it be chosen but that when families were multiplied and increased upon earth, after separation each providing for itself, envy, strife, contention, and violence must grow amongst them?   For hath not nature furnished man with wit and valor, as it were with armor, which may be used as well unto extreme evil as good?   Yea, were they not used by the rest of the world unto evil; unto the contrary only by Seth, Enoch, and those few the rest in that line? [8]   We all make complaint of the iniquity of our times: not unjustly; for the days are evil. But compare them with those times wherein there were no civil societies, with those times wherein there was as yet no manner of

[1] Matt. vi. 33.
[2] Gen. iv. 2, 26.
[3] Gen. iv. 20, 21, 22.
[4] Isa. xlix. 15.
[5] I Tim. v. 8.
[6] Gen. xviii. 19.
[7] Gen. iv. 8.
[8] Gen. vi. 5; Gen. v.

public regiment established, with those times wherein there were not above eight persons righteous living upon the face of the earth;[1] and we have surely good cause to think that God hath blessed us exceedingly, and hath made us behold most happy days.

4. To take away all such mutual grievances, injuries, and wrongs, there was no way but only by growing unto composition and agreement amongst themselves, by ordaining some kind of government public, and by yielding themselves subject thereunto; that unto whom they granted authority to rule and govern, by them the peace, tranquillity, and happy estate of the rest might be procured. Men always knew that when force and injury was offered they might be defenders of themselves; they knew that howsoever men may seek their own commodity, yet if this were done with injury unto others it was not to be suffered, but by all men and by all good means to be withstood; finally they knew that no man might in reason take upon him to determine his own right, and according to his own determination proceed in maintenance thereof, inasmuch as every man is toward himself and them whom he greatly affecteth partial; and therefore that strifes and troubles would be endless, except they gave their common consent all to be ordered by some whom they should agree upon: without which consent there was no reason that one man should take upon him to be lord or judge over another; because, although there be according to the opinion of some very great and judicious men a kind of natural right in the noble, wise, and virtuous, to govern them which are of servile disposition; nevertheless for manifestation of this their right, and men's more peaceable contentment on both sides, the assent of them who are to be governed seemeth necessary.

To fathers within their private families nature hath given a supreme power; for which cause we see throughout the world even from the foundation thereof, all men have ever been taken as lords and lawful kings in their own houses. Howbeit over a whole grand multitude having no such dependency upon any one, and consisting of so many families as every politic society in the world doth, impossible it is that any should have complete lawful power, but by consent of men, or immediate appointment of God; because not having the natural superiority of fathers, their power must needs be either usurped, and then unlawful; or, if lawful, then either granted or consented unto by them over whom they exercise the same, or else given extraordinarily from God, unto whom all the world is subject. It is no improbable opinion therefore

[1] 2 Pet. ii. 5.

which the Arch-philosopher was of, that as the chiefest person in
every household was always as it were a king, so when numbers
of households joined themselves in civil society together, kings
were the first kind of governors amongst them. Which is also
(as it seemeth) the reason why the name of *Father* continued still
in them, who of fathers were made rulers; as also the ancient custom of governors to do as Melchisedec, and being kings to exercise
the office of priests, which fathers did at the first, grew perhaps
by the same occasion.

Howbeit not this the only kind of regiment that hath been
received in the world. The inconveniences of one kind have caused
sundry other to be devised. So that in a word all public regiment
of what kind soever seemeth evidently to have risen from deliberate
advice, consulation, and composition between men, judging it
convenient and behoveful; there being no impossibility in nature
considered by itself, but that men might have lived without any
public regiment. Howbeit, the corruption of our nature being
presupposed, we may not deny but that the law of nature doth
now require of necessity some kind of regiment; so that to bring
things unto the first course they were in, and utterly to take away
all kind of public government in the world, were apparently to
overturn the whole world.

2.   The Nature, Authority, and Kinds of Law [1]

5.   The case of man's nature standing therefore as it doth,
some kind of regiment the law of nature doth require; yet the kinds
thereof being many, nature tieth not to any one, but leaveth
the choice as a thing arbitrary. At the first when some certain
kind of regiment was once approved, it may be that nothing was
then further thought upon for the manner of governing, but all permitted unto their wisdom and discretion which were to rule; till
by experience they found this for all parts very inconvenient, so
as the thing which they had devised for a remedy did indeed but
increase the sore which it should have cured. They saw that to
live by one man's will became the cause of all men's misery. This
constrained them to come unto laws, wherein all men might see
their duties beforehand, and know the penalties of transgressing
them. If things be simply good or evil, and withal universally
so acknowledged, there needs no new law to be made for such
things. The first kind therefore of things appointed by laws
human containeth whatsoever being in itself naturally good or

[1] Bk. I, ch. x, §§ 5–13.

evil, is notwithstanding more secret than that it can be discerned
by every man's present conceit, without some deeper discourse
and judgment. In which discourse because there is difficulty and
possibility many ways to err, unless such things were set down by
laws, many would be ignorant of their duties which now are not,
and many that know what they should do would nevertheless
dissemble it, and to excuse themselves pretend ignorance and
simplicity, which now they cannot.

6. And because the greatest part of men are such as prefer
their own private good before all things, even that good which is
sensual before whatsoever is most divine; and for that the labor
of doing good, together with the pleasure arising from the contrary, doth make men for the most part slower to the one and
proner to the other, than that duty prescribed them by law can
prevail sufficiently with them: therefore unto laws that men do
make for the benefit of men it hath seemed always needful to add
rewards, which may more allure unto good than any hardness
deterreth from it, and punishments, which may more deter from
evil than any sweetness thereto allureth. Wherein as the generality is natural, *Virtue rewardable and vice punishable;* so the particular determination of the reward or punishment belongeth unto
them by whom laws are made. Theft is naturally punishable,
but the kind of punishment is positive, and such lawful as men
shall think with discretion convenient by law to appoint.

7. In laws, that which is natural bindeth universally, that
which is positive not so. To let go those kinds of positive laws
which men impose upon themselves, as by vow unto God, contract
with men, or such like; somewhat it will make unto our purpose,
a little more fully to consider what things are incident into the
making of the positive laws for the government of them that live
united in public society. Laws do not only teach what is good,
but they enjoin it; they have in them a certain constraining force.
And to constrain men unto any thing inconvenient doth seem unreasonable. Most requisite therefore it is that to devise laws which
all men shall be forced to obey none but wise men be admitted.
Laws are matters of principal consequence; men of common
capacity and but ordinary judgment are not able (for how should
they?) to discern what things are fittest for each kind and state
of regiment. We cannot be ignorant how much our obedience
unto laws dependeth upon this point. Let a man though never
so justly oppose himself unto them that are disordered in their
ways, and what one amongst them commonly doth not stomach
at such contradiction, storm at reproof, and hate such as would re-

form them? Notwithstanding even they which brook it worst that men should tell them of their duties, when they are told the same by a law, think very well and reasonably of it. For why? They presume that the law doth speak with all indifferency; that the law hath no side-respect to their persons; that the law is as it were an oracle proceeded from wisdom and understanding.

8. Howbeit laws do not take their constraining force from the quality of such as devise them, but from that power which doth give them the strength of laws. That which we spake before concerning the power of government must here be applied unto the power of making laws whereby to govern; which power God hath over all: and by the natural law, whereunto he hath made all subject, the lawful power of making laws to command whole politic societies of men belongeth so properly unto the same entire societies, that for any prince or potentate of what kind soever upon earth to exercise the same of himself, and not either by express commission immediately and personally received from God, or else by authority derived at the first from their consent upon whose persons they impose laws, it is no better than mere tyranny. Laws they are not therefore which public approbation hath not made so. But approbation not only they give who personally declare their assent by voice, sign, or act, but also when others do it in their names by right originally at the least derived from them. As in parliaments, councils, and the like assemblies, although we be not personally ourselves present, notwithstanding our assent is, by reason of others, agents there in our behalf. And what we do by others, no reason but that it should stand as our deed, no less effectually to bind us than if ourselves had done it in person. In many things assent is given, they that give it not imagining they do so, because the manner of their assenting is not apparent. As for example, when an absolute monarch commandeth his subjects that which seemeth good in his own discretion, hath not his edict the force of a law whether they approve or dislike it? Again, that which hath been received long sithence and is by custom now established, we keep as a law which we may not transgress; yet what consent was ever thereunto sought or required at our hands?

Of this point therefore we are to note, that sith men naturally have no full and perfect power to command whole public multitudes of men, therefore utterly without our consent we would in such sort be at no man's commandment living. And to be commanded we do consent, when that society whereof we are part hath at any time before consented, without revoking the same after by the like universal agreement. Wherefore as any man's deed past is good as long as himself continueth; so the act of a public society of men done five hundred years sithence standeth as theirs who presently are of the same societies, because corporations are immortal; we were then alive in our predecessors, and they in their successors do live still. Laws therefore human of what kind soever, are available by consent.

9. If here it be demanded how it cometh to pass that this being common unto all laws which are made, there should be found even in good laws so great variety as there is; we must note the reason thereof to be the sundry particular ends, whereunto the different disposition of that subject or matter, for which laws are provided, causeth them to have especial respect in making laws. A law there is mentioned amongst the Grecians whereof Pittacus is reported to have been author; and by that law it was agreed, that he which being overcome with drink did then strike any man, should suffer punishment double as much as if he had done the same being sober. No man could ever have thought this reasonable, that had intended thereby only to punish the injury committed according to the gravity of the fact: for who knoweth not that harm advisedly done is naturally less pardonable, and therefore worthy of the sharper punishment? But forasmuch as none did so usually this way offend as men in that case, which they wittingly fell into, even because they would be so much the more freely outrageous; it was for their public good, where such disorder was grown, to frame a positive law for remedy thereof accordingly. To this appertain those known laws of making laws; as that law-makers must have an eye to the place where, and to the men amongst whom: that one kind of laws cannot serve for all kinds of regiment: that where the multitude beareth sway, laws that shall tend unto preservation of that state must make common smaller offices to go by lot, for fear of strife and division likely to arise, by reason that ordinary qualities sufficing for discharge of such offices, they could not but by many be desired, and so with danger contended for, and not missed without grudge and discontentment, whereas at an uncertain lot none can find themselves grieved, on whomsoever it lighteth; contrariwise the greatest, whereof but few are capable, to pass by popular election, that neither the people may envy such as have those honors, inasmuch as themselves bestow them, and that the chiefest may be kindled with desire to exercise all parts of rare and beneficial virtue, knowing they shall not lose their labor by growing in fame and estimation amongst the people:

if the helm of chief government be in the hands of a few of the wealthiest, that then laws providing for continuance thereof must make the punishment of contumely and wrong offered unto any of the common sort sharp and grievous, that so the evil may be prevented whereby the rich are most likely to bring themselves into hatred with the people, who are not wont to take so great an offence when they are excluded from honors and offices, as when their persons are contumeliously trodden upon. In other kinds of regiment the like is observed concerning the difference of positive laws, which to be everywhere the same is impossible and against their nature.

10. Now as the learned in the laws of this land observe, that our statutes sometimes are only the affirmation or ratification of that which by common law was held before; so here it is not to be omitted that generally all laws human, which are made for the ordering of politic societies, be either such as establish some duty whereunto all men by the law of reason did before stand bound; or else such as make that a duty now which before was none. The one sort we may for distinction's sake call *mixedly*, and the other *merely* human. That which plain or necessary reason bindeth men unto may be in sundry considerations expedient to be ratified by human law. For example, if confusion of blood in marriage, the liberty of having many wives at once, or any other the like corrupt and unreasonable custom doth happen to have prevailed far, and to have gotten the upper hand of right reason with the greatest part, so that no way is left to rectify such foul disorder without prescribing by law the same things which reason necessarily *doth* enforce but is not *perceived* that so it doth; or if many be grown unto that which the Apostle did lament in some, concerning whom he writeth, saying, that *Even what things they naturally know, in those very things as beasts void of reason they corrupted themselves*;[1] or if there be no such special accident, yet forasmuch as the common sort are led by the sway of their sensual desires, and therefore do more shun sin for the sensible evils which follow it amongst men, than for any kind of sentence which reason doth pronounce against it; this very thing is cause sufficient why duties belonging unto each kind of virtue, albeit the law of reason teach them, should notwithstanding be prescribed even by human law. Which law in this case we term *mixed*, because the matter whereunto it bindeth is the same which reason necessarily doth require at our hands, and from the law of reason it differeth in the manner of binding only. For whereas

[1] Jude 10.

men before stood bound in conscience to do as the law of reason teacheth, they are now by virtue of human law become constrainable, and if they outwardly transgress, punishable. As for laws which are *merely* human, the matter of them is any thing which reason doth but probably teach to be fit and convenient; so that till such time as law hath passed amongst men about it, of itself it bindeth no man. One example whereof may be this. Lands are by human law in some places after the owner's decease divided unto all his children, in some all descendeth to the eldest son. If the law of reason did necessarily require but the one of these two to be done, they which by law have received the other should be subject to that heavy sentence, which denounceth against all that decree wicked, unjust, and unreasonable things, *woe*.[1] Whereas now whichsoever be received there is no law of reason transgressed; because there is probable reason why either of them may be expedient, and for either of them more than probable reason there is not to be found.

11. Laws whether mixedly or merely human are made by politic societies: some, only as those societies are civilly united; some, as they are spiritually joined and make such a body as we call the church. Of laws human in this later kind we are to speak in the third book following. Let it therefore suffice thus far to have touched the force wherewith almighty God hath graciously endued our nature, and thereby enabled the same to find out both those laws which all men generally are for ever bound to observe, and also such as are most fit for their behoof, who lead their lives in any ordered state of government.

12. Now besides that law which simply concerneth men as men, and that which belongeth unto them as they are men linked with others in some form of politic society, there is a third kind of law which toucheth all such several bodies politic, so far forth as one of them hath public commerce with another. And this third is the *law of nations*. Between men and beasts there is no possibility of sociable communion; because the well-spring of that communion is a natural delight which man hath to transfuse from himself into others, and to receive from others into himself, especially those things wherein the excellency of his kind doth most consist. The chiefest instrument of human communion therefore is speech, because thereby we impart mutually one to another the conceits of our reasonable understanding. And for that cause seeing beasts are not hereof capable, forasmuch as with them we can use no such conference, they being in degree,

[1] Isaiah x. 1.

although above other creatures on earth to whom nature hath
denied sense, yet lower than to be sociable companions of man to
whom nature hath given reason; it is of Adam said that amongst
the beasts *He found not for himself any meet companion.*[1] Civil
society doth more content the nature of man than any private kind
of solitary living, because in society this good of mutual participation is so much larger than otherwise. Herewith notwithstanding
we are not satisfied, but we covet (if it might be) to have a kind of
society and fellowship even with all mankind. Which thing
Socrates intending to signify professed himself a citizen, not of
this or that commonwealth, but of the world. And an effect
of that very natural desire in us (a manifest token that we wish
after a sort a universal fellowship with all men), appeareth
by the wonderful delight men have, some to visit foreign countries,
some to discover nations not heard of in former ages, we all to
know the affairs and dealings of other people, yea to be in league
of amity with them: and this not only for traffic's sake, or to the
end that when many are confederated each may make other the
more strong, but for such cause also as moved the Queen of Saba
to visit Solomon;[2] and in a word, because nature doth presume
that how many men there are in the world, so many Gods as it
were there are, or at leastwise such they would be towards men.

13. Touching laws which are to serve men in this behalf;
even as those laws of reason, which (man retaining his original
integrity) had been sufficient to direct each particular person
in all his affairs and duties, are not sufficient but require the access
of other laws, now that man and his offspring are grown thus
corrupt and sinful; again, as those laws of polity and regiment
which would have served men living in public society together
with that harmless disposition which then they should have had,
are not able now to serve, when men's iniquity is so hardly restrained within any tolerable bounds: in like manner, the national
laws of mutual commerce between societies of that former and
better quality might have been other than now, when nations are
so prone to offer violence, injury, and wrong. Hereupon hath
grown in every of these three kinds that distinction between
Primary and *Secondary* laws; the one grounded upon sincere, the
other built upon depraved nature. Primary laws of nations are
such as concern embassage, such as belong to the courteous
entertainment of foreigners and strangers, such as serve for
commodious traffic, and the like. Secondary laws in the same

---

[1] Gen. ii. 20.
[2] 1 Kings x. 1; 2 Chron. ix. 1; Matt. xii. 42; Luke xi. 31.

kind are such as this present unquiet world is most familiarly acquainted with; I mean laws of arms, which yet are much better known than kept. But what matter the law of nations doth contain I omit to search. The strength and virtue of that law is such that no particular nation can lawfully prejudice the same by any their several laws and ordinances, more than a man by his private resolutions the law of the whole commonwealth or state wherein he liveth. For as civil law, being the act of the whole body politic, doth therefore overrule each several part of the same body; so there is no reason that any one commonwealth of itself should to the prejudice of another annihilate that whereupon the whole world hath agreed. For which cause, the Lacedæmonians forbidding all access of strangers into their coasts are in that respect both by Josephus and Theodoret deservedly blamed, as being enemies to that hospitality which for common humanity's sake all the nations on earth should embrace.

SELECTED BIBLIOGRAPHY

Sabine, George H., *History of Political Theory*, pp. 437–442.
Dunning, William A., *Political Theories, from Luther to Montesquieu*, pp. 208–212.
Sykes, Norman, "Richard Hooker," in F. J. C. Hearnshaw, ed., *Social and Political Ideas of Some Great Thinkers of the Sixteenth and Seventeenth Centuries* (London, 1926), ch. 3.
Allen, J. W., *History of Political Thought in the Sixteenth Century* (London, 1928), pt. ii, ch. 6, and pp. 239–241.
Carlyle, R. W. and A. J., *History of Mediæval Political Theory in the West*, Vol. VI (Edinburgh and London, 1936), pp. 350–357.
Church, R. W., ed., *Hooker: Book I of the Laws of Ecclesiastical Polity* (Oxford, 1873), *Introduction*.
Lee, Sidney, "Richard Hooker," in *Dictionary of National Biography*, Vol. XXVII (London, 1891).

GROTIUS

XVII. HUGO GROTIUS (1583-1645)

INTRODUCTION

So far our readings have been taken from the works of authors whose preoccupation in political reflection was with the internal constitution of the state. The major part of the treatise from which we make the next selection deals with the laws governing intercourse between states. This work is *The Law of War and Peace* (*De jure belli ac pacis*) of the Dutch jurist, Hugo Grotius, who wrote in the early part of the seventeenth century. For several centuries preceding Grotius attempts had been made to reach a rational foundation for the definition of the inter-relations of states. In particular, there had been recognition of the importance of establishing rules to restrict the actions of states during war. In such endeavors mediæval writers had operated with two conceptions inherited from Roman jurisprudence. One of these was the Greek and Roman doctrine of natural law, and a characteristic element of that doctrine was the notion of the applicability of its precepts to all peoples; for natural law was regarded as a dictate of human reason, which was essentially the same among all people. The other conception was that of *jus gentium*, which denoted a body of law constituted of rules discovered to be common to the juristic practice of many different peoples. In developing the relation between these two conceptions, several writers had given some systematic consideration to the rights and duties of political communities.

In the sixteenth century questions of international ethics assumed paramount interest ; this was due to many circumstances of recent history—such as the discovery and colonization of new parts of the world, the relaxation of imperial and papal supervision, the inter-state religious and dynastic wars, the complex inter-relations of the small German principalities. In the solution of such questions Catholic theologians and Protestant jurists devoted special consideration to the formulation of the precepts of natural law. They sought to discover these precepts in the rules of civil or canon law, in the writings of earlier theologians, and also in the practices of Christian nations. In their discussions the idea of a distinct branch of law for international relations appeared, and certain domains of this law were sketched in detail. None of the writers clearly established his formulas either upon universal principles of human reason, or upon precedents in the intercourse of civilized states; but the distinction between the two sources was distinctly recognized by a few—notably, by the Spanish jurist, Suarez.[1]

Grotius utilized and acknowledged the work of these predecessors. The great reputation and influence of his *De jure belli ac pacis*, and his title as founder of a new science, is due in part to the prestige of the author during his lifetime; but it is due chiefly to the qualities of the work itself: the comprehensive scope and systematic form of its analysis, the clear separation of its proper field from the contiguous fields of ethics and jurisprudence, and the general lack of sectarian bias in the discussion.

Grotius was born in Delft, of a family of some local social and political distinction. He was from early youth a student of classical literature and philosophy, and from time to time produced many translations, besides original Latin verses. He was also a lawyer, held important positions in the city of Rotterdam and in the provincial governments of Holland and Zealand, and served on special deputations from the Confederation to France and England. He became involved in the sectarian and political conflict in which Holland was embroiled during his lifetime. Though a strong advocate of religious toleration and a worker for conciliation, he held the "free-will" views of the Arminian party. When the stadtholder, Maurice of Nassau, espoused the cause of the Gomarian (Calvinistic) party (chiefly because that faction would yield stronger support for his political aims) and instituted religious prosecution against adherents of the opposing faction, Grotius was imprisoned. Escaping from prison after a few years, he went to Paris, where he was sustained by a small pension from Louis XII, supplemented by gifts from some friends. Here his *De jure belli ac*

---

[1] For brief sketches of the literature of international law before the time of Grotius, *cf.* C. H. E. Carmichael, "Grotius and the Literary History of the Law of Nations," in *Transactions of the Royal Society of Literature*, Vol. XIV (1884); Thomas E. Holland, *Studies in International Law*, pp. 1–58; Henry Wheaton, *History of the Law of Nations in Europe and America*, pp. 1–67.

pacis was published in 1625.[1] The motive of that work appears in the author's statement in the prolegomena. We appreciate better the significance of that statement of purpose if we recall that Grotius' life had witnessed the following events: the last twenty-five years of the war of the United Provinces against Spain; the continuation of civil war in France, with the assassination of Henry III and IV; the sectarian and political troubles in England and Holland, with the execution of Mary Stuart and the assassination of William of Orange; and the first part of the Thirty Years' War.

For the history of political philosophy our interest, in *The Law of War and Peace*, is centered first in the prolegomena, in which the author lays the foundations of his system in his analysis of the relation of natural law to the "law of nations"; and, secondly, in the preliminary discussion, in the main body of the work, of natural law and of the nature of the state and of sovereignty; it was essential for the author to examine these latter subjects in order to reach a precise determination of what constituted the capacity for possessing international rights and duties.

READINGS FROM DE JURE BELLI AC PACIS [2]

1. The Rational Basis of International Law [3]

1. The civil law,[4] both that of Rome and that of each nation in particular, has been treated of by many, with a view either

---

[1] The *De jure belli ac pacis* is an expansion of an earlier unpublished treatise, *De jure prædæ* (first published in 1868). This earlier work was the outcome of a case in Grotius' legal practice. The question of the case was as to the lawfulness of the capture of a Portuguese prize by a Dutch ship in eastern waters over which Portugal claimed exclusive ownership. This led Grotius to a discussion of the conditions of the lawfulness of war, and of the limits that must be put to claims of dominion over the high seas. A chapter (of the *De jure prædæ*) on the latter topic formed also the basis for another work—the *Mare liberum;* this was published in 1609, when the dispute between the United Provinces and Portugal over the question of the freedom of the seas was at an acute stage.

[2] The translation is made from the text as given in Whewell's edition, Cambridge University Press, 1853. Whewell's abridged translation, which accompanies that text, has been used freely and adopted *verbatim* in many parts; but in many instances it has seemed necessary, in the interest of clearness and correctness, to translate anew.

Grotius' quotations and historical citations are generally omitted.

[3] From the *Prolegomena*.

[4] *Jus* will be uniformly rendered as "law" in the passages from Grotius; and wherever the word "law" appears in this translation it stands for *jus* in the original, save where I indicate otherwise.

to elucidate it, through commentaries, or to present it in a compendious form. But that law which regards the relations between peoples, or between rulers of peoples, whether it proceed from nature or be instituted by divine commands or introduced by custom and tacit agreement, has been touched on by few, and has by no one been treated as a whole and in an orderly manner. And yet that this be done is of concern to the human race.

3. And such a work is the more necessary because of the fact that persons in our own time, as well as in former ages, have held in contempt what has been done in this province of jurisprudence, as if no such thing existed, except as a mere name. Every one is familiar with the saying of Euphemius in Thucydides, that for a king or city who has authority to maintain, nothing is unjust which is useful; and to the same effect is the saying that with good fortune equity is where strength is, and that the commonwealth cannot be administered without doing some wrong. To this we add that the controversies which arise between peoples and between kings commonly have war as their arbiter. But that war has nothing to do with laws is not only the opinion of the ignorant; even wise and learned men often let fall expressions which support such an opinion. For nothing is more common than to place laws and arms in opposition to each other. . . .

5. Since our discussion of law is undertaken in vain if there is no law, it will serve both to commend and fortify our work if we refute briefly this very grave error. And that we may not have to deal with a mob of opponents, let us appoint an advocate to speak for them. And whom can we select fitter than Carneades,[1] who had arrived at the point—the supreme aim of his academic philosophy—where he could use the strength of his eloquence for falsehood as easily as for truth? When he undertook to argue against justice—especially, the justice of which we here treat, he found no argument stronger than this: that men had, as utility prompted, established laws, differing among different peoples as manners differed, and, among the same people, often changing with the change of times; but that there is no natural law, since all men, as well as other animals, are impelled by nature to seek their own advantage; and that either there is no justice, or if it exist, it is the highest folly, since through it one harms oneself in consulting the interests of others.

6. But what this philosopher says, and, following him, the poet—"Nature cannot distinguish the just from the unjust,"[2]

---

[1] A Greek skeptic philosopher of the second century, B. C.
[2] "*Nec natura potest justo secernere iniquum.*" Horat. I. *Sat.* iii. 113.

must by no means be admitted. For though man is indeed an animal, he is an uncommon animal, differing much more from all other animals than they differ from one another; this is evidenced in many actions peculiar to the human species. Among the attributes peculiar to man is the desire for society—that is for communion with his fellow-men, and not for communion simply, but for a tranquil association and one suited to the quality of his intellect; this the Stoics called οἰκείωσιν. Therefore, the statement that by nature every animal is impelled to seek only its own advantage cannot be conceded in this general form.

7. Even in other animals their desires for their own good are tempered by regard for their offspring and for others of their species; this we believe to proceed from some intelligence outside of themselves;[1] for with regard to other acts not at all more difficult than these an equal degree of intelligence does not appear. The same is to be said of infants, in whom, previous to all teaching, there is manifested a certain disposition to do good to others, as is sagaciously remarked by Plutarch; for example, at that age compassion breaks forth spontaneously. A man of full age knows how to act similarly in similar cases, and he has that exceptional craving for society,[2] whose peculiar instrument, language, he alone among all animals possesses; accordingly, he has the faculty of knowing and acting according to general principles; the tendencies which agree with this faculty do not belong to all animals, but are the peculiar properties of human nature.

8. This concern for society,[3] which we have now stated in a rude manner, and which is in agreement with the nature of the human intellect, is the source of law, properly so called, of which we are speaking. It is law that determines the abstention from another's property; the restitution of another's goods which we have in our possession and of any gain we have derived from such possession; the obligation to fulfill promises; the reparation for damage wrongfully done; and the retribution of punishments.

9. From this signification of law there has flowed another larger meaning. For man is superior to other animals not only in the social impulse, of which we have spoken, but also in his judgment in estimating what is pleasant and what is injurious— not only for the present but for the future also, and the things which may lead to good or to ill. We know, therefore, that, in accordance with the quality of the human intellect, it is congruous

---

[1] "Ex principio aliquo intelligente extrinseco."
[2] "Societatis appetitu excellente."
[3] "Societatis custodia."

to human nature to follow, in such matters, a judgment rightly formed and not to be misled by fear or by the enticement of present pleasure, or to be carried away by heedless impulse; and that what is plainly repugnant to such judgment is likewise contrary to natural law, that is, to natural human law.

10. And here comes the question of a wise assignment in bestowing upon each individual and each body of men the things which peculiarly belong to them; this disposition will sometimes prefer the wiser man to the less wise, the neighbor to a stranger, the poor man to the rich man, according as the nature of each act and each matter requires. This question some have made a part of law, strictly and properly so called; though law, properly speaking, has a very different nature; for it consists in this—that each should leave to another what is his and give to him what is his due.

11. What we have said would still be in point even if we should grant, what we cannot without great wickedness, that there is no God, or that He bestows no regard upon human affairs. Since we are assured of the contrary, partly by our reason and partly by constant tradition, confirmed by many arguments and by miracles attested by all ages, it follows that God, as our creator to whom we owe our being and all that we have, is to be obeyed by us without exception, especially since He has in many ways shown himself to be supremely good and supremely powerful. Wherefore, He is able to bestow upon those who obey Him the highest rewards, even eternal rewards, since He himself is eternal; and He must be believed to be willing to do this, particularly if He has promised to do so in plain words; and this we as Christians believe, convinced by the indubitable faith of testimonies.

12. And here we find another origin of law, besides that natural source of which we have spoken; it is the free will of God, to which our reason indisputably tells us we must submit ourselves. But even natural law—whether it be the natural social law, or law in the looser meaning of which we have spoken—may yet be rightfully ascribed to God, though it proceed from the principles of man's inner nature; for it was in accordance with His will that such principles came to exist within us. In this sense Chrysippus and the Stoics said that the origin of law was not to be sought in any other source than Jove himself; and it may be conjectured that the Latins took the word *jus* from the name *Jove*.

13. It may be added that God has made these principles more manifest by the commandments which He has given in order that they might be understood by those whose minds have weaker

powers of reasoning. And He has controlled the aberrations of our impulses, which drive us this way and that, to the injury of ourselves and of others; bridling our more vehement passions, and restraining them within due limits.

15. In the next place, since it is conformable to natural law to observe compacts (for some mode of obliging themselves was necessary among men, and no other natural mode can be imagined) civil rights were derived from that very source. For those who joined any community, or put themselves in subjection to any man or men, either expressly promised or from the nature of the case must have been understood to promise tacitly, that they would conform to that which either the majority of the community, or those to whom power was assigned, should determine.

16. And therefore what Carneades said, and what has been said by others—that utility is the mother of justice and right—is, if we are to speak accurately, not true. For the mother of natural law is human nature itself, which would lead us to desire mutual society even though we were not driven thereto by other wants. The mother of civil law is obligation by compact; and since compacts derive their force from natural law, nature may be said to be the great-grandmother of civil law. But utility supplements (*accedit*) natural law. For the Author of nature ordained that we, as individuals, should be weak and in need of many things for living well, in order that we might be the more impelled to cherish society. But utility furnished the occasion for civil law; for that association or subjection of which we have spoken, was at the first instituted for the sake of some utility. Accordingly, those who prescribe laws for others ordinarily design, or should design, some utility in their laws.

17. But just as the laws of each state regard the utility of that state, so also between all states, or, at least, between most of them, certain laws could be established by consent—and it appears that laws have been established—which regard the utility, not of particular communities but of the great aggregate of communities. And this is what is called the law of nations (*jus gentium*), in so far as we distinguish it from natural law. This part of law is omitted by Carneades, who divides all law into natural law and the civil law of particular peoples; although as he was about to treat of that law which obtains between one people and another (for he subjoins a discussion upon war and acquisitions by war), he was especially called upon to make mention of law of this kind.

18. Moreover, Carneades improperly traduces justice when he calls it folly. For since, as he himself acknowledges, the citizen

is not foolish who in a state obeys the civil law, although in consequence of such respect for the law he may lose some things which
are useful to him, so too a people is not to be deemed foolish which
does not estimate its interests so highly as to disregard the common laws between peoples for the sake of its own advantage.   The
reason is the same in both cases.   For as a citizen who disobeys
the civil law for the sake of present utility destroys that in which
the perpetual utility of himself and his posterity is bound up, so
too a people which violates the laws of nature and of nations breaks
down the bulwark of its own tranquillity for future time.   Even
though no utility were to be looked for from the observation of
law, such a course would be one not of folly but of wisdom, to
which we feel ourselves drawn by nature.

    19.   Wherefore, that saying that we were compelled to estab-
lish laws from fear of wrong,[1] is not universally true; this opinion
is explained by a speaker in Plato's dialogues, who says that laws
were introduced because of the fear of receiving wrong, and that
men are driven to respect justice by a certain compulsion.   But
this applies only to those institutions and statutes which were
devised for the more easy enforcement of law; as when many,
individually weak, fearing oppression by those who were stronger,
combined to establish judicial authorities and to protect them by
their common strength, so that those whom they could not resist
singly, they might, united, control.   Only in this sense may we
properly accept the statement that law is that which pleases the
stronger party: namely, that we are to understand that law does
not attain its external end unless it has force as its servant.   Thus
Solon accomplished great things, as he himself said, *by linking
together force and law.*[2]

    20.   But even law that is unsupported by force is not destitute
of all effect; for justice brings serenity to the conscience, while
injustice brings torments and remorse such as Plato describes as
afflicting the hearts of tyrants.   The common feeling of upright
men approves justice and condemns injustice.   The important
point is that justice has for its friend, God, while injustice has Him
as an enemy; He reserves his judgments for another life, yet in
such manner that He often exhibits their power in this life; we
have many examples of this in history.

    21.   The error which many commit who, while they require
justice in citizens, hold it to be superfluous in a people or the ruler
of a people, is caused primarily by this fact: they are regarding

[1] " *Jura inventa metu injusti fateare necesse est.*" (Horace, I. *Sat.* iii.)
[2] " 'Ομοῦ βίην τε καὶ δίκην συναρμόσας.''

only the utility which arises from the law. This utility is evident in the case of citizens, who individually are too weak to secure their own protection. Great states, on the other hand, which seem to embrace within themselves all that is necessary to support life, do not appear to have need of that virtue which regards extraneous parties and is called justice.

22. But—not to repeat what I have already said, that law is not established for the sake of utility alone—there is no state so strong that it may not at some time need the aid of others external to itself, either in the way of commerce or in order to repel the force of many nations combined against it. Hence we see that alliances are sought even by the most powerful peoples and kings; the force of such alliances is entirely destroyed by those who confine law within the boundaries of a state. It is most true that everything becomes uncertain if we withdraw from law.

28. Since, for the reasons which I have stated, I hold it to be completely proved that there is between nations a common law which is of force with respect to war and in war, I have had many and grave reasons why I should write a work on that subject. For I saw prevailing throughout the Christian world a license in making war of which even barbarous nations would have been ashamed, recourse being had to arms for slight reasons or for no reason; and when arms were once taken up, all reverence for divine and human law was lost, just as if men were henceforth authorized to commit all crimes without restraint.

39. . . . It remains now that I briefly explain with what aids and with what care I have undertaken this work. In the first place, it was my object to refer the truth of the things which belong to natural law to certain notions so certain that no one can deny them without doing violence to his own nature. For the principles of that law, if you attend to them rightly, are of themselves patent and evident, almost in the same way as things which we perceive by our external senses; for these do not deceive us, if the organs are rightly disposed and other necessary things are not wanting. . . .

40. For the demonstration of natural law I have used the testimonies of philosophers, historians, poets, and finally orators. Not that these are to be trusted indiscriminately; for they are ordinarily writing to serve their sect, their argument, or their cause. But when many, writing in different times and places, affirm the same thing as true, their unanimity must be referred to some universal cause, which, in the questions with which we are here con-

cerned, can be no other than either a right deduction proceeding from principles of nature, or some common agreement. The former cause points to the law of nature, the latter to the law of nations; the difference between these two is to be discerned not in the testimonies themselves (for writers everywhere confound the law of nature and the law of nations), but in the quality of the matter. For what can not be deduced from certain principles by unerring reasoning, and yet is seen to be observed everywhere, must have its origin in free consent.

46. Passages of history have a two-fold use in our argument: they supply both examples and judgments. In proportion as examples belong to better times and better nations, they have greater authority; we have therefore preferred the examples from ancient Greece and Rome. Nor are judgments to be despised, especially when many of them agree; for natural law is, as we have said, to be proved by such concord; and the law of nations can be proved in no other manner.

47. The opinions of poets and orators have not so much weight; and these we often use not so much to gain confirmation from them as to give to what we are trying to say some ornamentation from their modes of expression.

48. The books written by men inspired by God, or approved by them, I often use as authority, with a distinction between the Old and the New Testament. . . .

2. The Law of Nature [1]

III. By entitling our treatise, *Concerning the Law of War,* we mean, in the first place, to imply the discussion of the questions whether any war is lawful (*justum*), and what is lawful in war. For *jus* here means simply what is lawful, and that rather in a negative than in a positive sense, so that that comes within the connotation of law, which is not unlawful. That is unlawful which is contrary to the nature of a society of rational creatures. . . .

IV. Law has another signification, derived from the former, and relating to a person. In this sense law, or right,[2] is a moral quality by which a person is competent rightfully to have or do a certain thing. Right in this sense belongs to a person, though sometimes it follows a thing, as easements upon an estate. Such

---

[1] From Bk. I, ch. i, secs. iii–iv, ix–x, xii.

[2] It is necessary in this paragraph to translate *jus* as "right," for *jus* as used here has a meaning that in English is never expressed by "law."

rights are called real rights, in comparison with others which are merely personal; not that they do not pertain to a person, but that they belong only to the person who possesses a certain thing. . . .

IX. Law has a third signification, meaning positive law (*lex*) in its broadest sense, namely, a rule of moral acts obliging to what is right (*rectum*). "Obliging" is essential in this signification; for mere counsel or advice, however good, is not included in the concept of *lex* or *jus*. Permission, moreover, is not an act of law (*lex*), properly speaking, but rather the negation of its action, except in so far as it obliges other persons not to impede him to whom the permission is given. Moreover, we say obliging to what is right, not to what is just; for law in this signification does not include merely justice, but the matter of other virtues also. Yet what is right is sometimes loosely called lawful.

The best distinction of law in this general sense is that made by Aristotle, into natural law and voluntary—that is, positive or enacted—law. . . .

X. Natural law is the dictate of right reason, indicating that any act, from its agreement or disagreement with the rational nature, has in it moral necessity or moral turpitude; and consequently that such act is commanded or forbidden by God, the author of nature.[1]

Acts concerning which there is such a dictate are obligatory or illicit in themselves, and are therefore understood as necessarily commanded or forbidden by God; in this character the law of nature differs, not only from human law, but also from positive divine law; for the latter does not command or forbid acts which are in themselves and by their own nature obligatory or unlawful, but by commanding them makes them obligatory, and by forbidding them makes them unlawful.

In order to understand the law of nature, we must add that some things are said to be according to the law of nature, which are not so properly, but, as the scholastics love to say, reductively, the law of nature not opposing them; as we have said that some things are called just which are merely not unjust. And again by an abuse of expression, some things are said to be according to the law of nature which reason shows to be decent, though not obligatory. . . .

It is to be remarked also that the law of nature deals not only with things which are outside of (*citra*) the human will, but also

[1] "Jus naturale est dictatum rectæ rationis, indicans actui alicui, ex ejus convenientia aut disconvenientia cum ipsa natura rationali ac sociali, inesse moralem turpitudinem, aut necessitatem moralem, ac consequenter ab auctore naturæ Deo talem actum aut vetari, aut præcipi."

with things produced by the act of man. Thus property, as it
now exists, is the result of human will; but being once introduced,
the law of nature itself shows that it is wrong for me to take what
is yours against your will. . . .

The law of nature is so immutable that it cannot be changed
even by God himself. For though the power of God be immense,
there are some things to which it does not extend; because if we
speak of such things being done, our words are mere words and have
no meaning, being self-contradictory. Thus God himself cannot
make twice two not to be four; and in like manner He cannot
make that which, according to reason, is intrinsically bad, not be
bad. For as the essence of things, by virtue of which they exist, does
not depend on anything else, so is it with the properties which follow
necessarily that essence; such a property is the baseness of certain
actions, as compared with the nature of a being enjoying sound
reason. So God himself allows himself to be judged by this rule.

Yet sometimes, in acts directed by the law of nature, there is an
appearance of change, which may mislead the unwary; when in
fact it is not the law of nature which is changed, but the thing
about which that law is concerned. Thus if a creditor gives me
a receipt for my debt, I am no longer bound to pay him; not that
the law of nature has ceased to command me to pay what I owe,
but because I have ceased to owe it. So if God command any one
to be slain or his goods to be taken, this does not make lawful
homicide or theft, which words involve crime; but the act will
no longer be homicide or theft, being authorized by the supreme
Lord of life and of goods.

Furthermore, some things are according to the law of nature,
not simply, but in a certain state of things. Thus community
in the use of things was natural until property was established;
and the right of getting possession of one's own by force existed
before the time of instituted law.

XII. That there is such a thing as the law of nature is commonly proved both *a priori* and *a posteriori*, the former being the
more subtle, the latter, the more popular proof. It is proved
a priori by showing the necessary agreement or disagreement of
anything with rational and social nature. It is proved *a posteriori*
when by certain or very probable accounts we find anything
accepted as natural law among all nations, or at least among the
more civilized nations. For a universal effect requires a universal
cause; now such a universal belief can hardly have any cause
except the common opinion of mankind. . . .

3. The State and Sovereignty [1]

XIII. We have said that there is a second species of law, namely, voluntary or positive law; and this is either human or divine.

XIV. We will take up human law first, as more widely known. This is either civil law, or law in a wider sphere, or law in a narrower sphere. Civil law is that which proceeds from the civil authority. Civil authority is that which governs the state. The state is a perfect association of free men, united for the sake of enjoying the benefits of law and for their common advantage.[2] Law in a narrower sphere, and not derived from civil authority, though subject to it, is various, as paternal precepts, the commands of a master, and the like. Law in a wider sphere is the law of nations—namely, that law which has received an obligatory force from the will of all, or of many, nations. I have added "or of many," because scarce any law, except natural law (which is often also called *jus gentium*), is found common to all nations. Indeed that is often the law of nations in one part of the world which is not so in another part, as we shall show when we come to speak of captivity and *postliminium*. . . .

VII.[3] That power is called sovereign (*summa*) whose acts are not subject to the law of another, so that they can be rendered void by the act of any other human will. When I say "any other," I exclude him who exercises the sovereign authority; for he may change his will, as may likewise his successor, who enjoys the same rights and therefore has the same authority. Let us see then in what this sovereign power resides. That in which a power inheres may be either the general or the special possessor of the power; thus the power of vision is possessed by the body in general, but in the special sense by the eye. In like manner sovereignty inheres in general in the state, which we have before described as the perfect community.

We therefore exclude peoples which have put themselves in subjection to another people, such as were the provinces of the Romans. Such peoples are not by themselves a state, but are the inferior members of a great state, as servants are members of a family. Again, it sometimes happens that several peoples have the same head, though each of these peoples constitutes a perfect

[1] From Bk. I, ch. i, secs. xiii–xiv; ch. iii, secs. vii–xiv, xvi–xviii.
[2] "Est autem civitas cœtus perfectus liberorum hominum, juris fruendi et communis utilitatis causa sociatus."
[3] Ch. iii

community; for though several bodies cannot have one head in the natural person, they may in the moral person, for in the latter the same individual may be separately regarded as the head in his relation to several distinct bodies. Of this thing we have an indication in the fact that when the reigning house becomes extinct the right of government reverts to each people separately. And thus it may happen that several states are combined in a close federal connection and thus make one system (σύστημα), and yet none loses its status as a perfect community.

Therefore, the possessor of sovereignty in general is the state, understood in the way we have described. The possessor in the special sense is a person or group of persons, according to the laws and customs of each particular nation.

VIII. And here we must first reject the opinion of those who say that sovereignty everywhere and without exception belongs to the people, so that the people have authority to coerce and punish kings when they abuse their power. What evil this opinion has caused, and may yet cause, no wise man can fail to see. We refute it with these arguments. A man may by his own act make himself the slave of any one, as appears by the Hebrew and the Roman law. Why then may not a people do the same, so as to transfer the whole right of governing it to one or more persons? And it is not to the purpose to say that we are not to presume such a fact; for the question is not what is to be presumed in cases of doubt, but what may be lawfully done. Nor is it to the purpose to allege the inconveniences which follow or may follow such a course; for whatever form of government you take, you will never escape all inconvenience.

But as there are many ways of living, one better than another, and each man is free to choose which of them he pleases, so each nation may choose what form of government it will; and its right in this matter is not to be measured by the excellence of this or that form, concerning which opinions may be various, but by its choice.

Nor is it difficult to conceive causes why a people may resign the whole power of its own government and transfer it to another; as, for example, if it be in great peril and cannot find a defender on other conditions; or if it be in want and cannot otherwise obtain sustenance. So the Campanians of old, driven by want, submitted themselves to the Romans; and some other peoples which wished to do so were not accepted. What then prevents a people from giving itself up to some very powerful man in the same manner? Or again, it may happen that a large landowner will not allow persons to dwell on his land on any other condition; or if any one have a large body of slaves, he may manumit them on condition of their being his subjects and paying his taxes. . . .

Add to this that, as Aristotle says, some men are by nature slaves, fitted for servitude, so also some nations are more prone to be governed than to govern. So the Cappadocians seemed to have felt when they refused the liberty offered by the Romans and declared that they could not live without a king.[1] . . .

Moreover civil authority, or the right of governing, may be acquired by legitimate war, just as private property may be.

What we have said above applies not only in the case of government by a single ruler, but also where authority is in the hands of a superior few, to the exclusion of the common people. And can any state be found so popular that some are not excluded from public deliberations, as strangers, paupers, women and children?

Some peoples have under them other peoples who are not less subject than if they were under kings. Thus arose the question: Is the Collatine people its own master? And the Campanians, when they had given themselves up to the Romans, are spoken of as not being their own masters. . . . That there are kings who are not subject to the will of the people, even taken as a whole, both sacred and profane history testify.[2] . . .

The arguments that kings are responsible to the people are not difficult to answer. First, the assertion that he who establishes another in authority is superior to the person so established, is only true in that constitution which depends perpetually upon the will of the constituent body, not in that which, though voluntary at first, afterwards becomes compulsory; thus a woman accepts a person as her husband, whom afterwards she is obliged forever to obey. . . . Nor is it true, as is assumed, that all kings are constituted by the people; this we have already shown by the examples of a landowner accepting tenants on condition of their obeying him, and of nations conquered in war.

The other argument is taken from the maxim of the philosophers that all government exists for the sake of the governed, not of the governors; whence they conceive that it follows that, the end being more noble than the means, the governed are superior to him who governs. But it is not universally true that all government exists for the sake of him who is governed. For some kinds of government are for the sake of the governor, as that of a master in his household; for there the advantage of the servant is ex-

---

[1] Par. 5 is omitted.   [2] Pars. 9–12 are omitted.

trinsic and adventitious, as the gain of the physician is extrinsic to the art of medicine. Other kinds of government are for the sake of mutual benefit, as the marital. So some kingly governments may be established for the advantage of the kings, as those which are won by victory; and such are not, therefore, to be called tyrannies, since tyranny, as we now understand it, implies injustice. Some governments, too, may have respect to the utility both of the governor and of the governed, as when a people in distress places over itself a powerful king to protect it.

But I do not deny that in most governments the good of the governed is the object, and that, as Hesiod, Herodotus and Cicero say, kings are constituted for the sake of justice. But it does not follow, as our opponents infer, that peoples are superior to kings; for guardianship is for the sake of the ward, and yet the guardian has authority and power over the ward. And we are not to follow those who urge that, as a guardian who neglects his duty to his ward may be superseded, so a king may be in like case. For this is the case with the guardian because he has a superior; but in political government, because we cannot have an infinite gradation of superiors, we must stop at some person or body whose transgressions, because they have no superior judge, are the peculiar province of God, as He himself declares; He punishes them, if he deem fit to do so, or tolerates them, in order to punish or try the people. . . .

IX. Some assert that there is a mutual subjection, so that the whole people ought to obey the king when he rules rightly, but that when the king rules ill, he is subject to the people. If those who say this mean that those things which are manifestly iniquitous are not to be done, though commanded by the king, they are saying what is true and acknowledged by all good men; but this right to disobey does not include any coercive authority or right of government. If any people intended to share the power of government with the king (on which point we shall have something to say hereafter), such limits ought to be assigned to each of the two authorities as might easily be recognized by distinctions of places, persons, and matters.

But the goodness or badness of an act, which are often matters of great doubt, especially in political matters, are not fit marks to make such distinctions; whence the most extreme confusion must follow if the king and people claim cognizance of the same matter by the allegation of good and evil conduct. Such a disturbed state of things no people, so far as I know, ever thought of introducing.

X.[1] . . . Many think that the distinction between sovereign and subordinate authority is to be found in the difference between transmission of sovereignty by heredity and transmission by election; what comes by succession they hold to be sovereign, not what comes by election. But this is certainly not universally true. For succession is not a title which determines the nature of authority but a continuation of authority already existing. The authority established by the election of a family is continued by succession; whatever the first election bestows, the succession transmits. The Lacedæmonian kings, though inferior in authority to the ephors, were hereditary. On the other hand, the Roman emperor was absolute, though elective.

XI. A second caution is this. We must distinguish between what a thing is and what is the kind of possession of it; this is true as to both corporeal and incorporeal things. A thing is, for example, a piece of land, a road, an act, a right of way. Now such a thing may be held in full right of property (*pleno jure*), or as tenant for life (*jure usufructuario*), or as tenant for a time only (*jure temporario*). Thus the Roman dictator held his authority as temporary tyrant; most kings, both elected and hereditary, by usufructuary right; but some kings, in full right of property, as those who have acquired their authority through legitimate war, or in whose power a people have put itself absolutely in order to escape from some greater hardship.

XII. Some learned men oppose the doctrine that sovereign authority can be held in full right of property, because, they say, free men cannot be held as transferable things. But just as domestic authority is one thing, royal authority another, so personal liberty is one thing, civil liberty another; one is a matter of individuals, the other of groups of individuals (*universorum*). . . . Men may have personal liberty, so as not to be slaves, and yet not have civil liberty, so as to be free citizens. . . . The question here is concerning the liberty not of individuals, but of a people. A people which is under this public, as distinguished from private, subjection, is said to be *non sui juris, non suæ potestatis*. . . .

When a people is transferred from one sovereign to another, it is not the persons, but the right of governing them, which is transferred; so when a freedman was assigned by his patrons to one of his sons, there was no alienation of a free man, but a right attaching to the man was transferred.

Again, some assert that where a king has conquered a people in war, he has won them by the sweat and blood of his citizens,

[1] Pars. 1–4 are omitted.

and, therefore, the acquisition is theirs rather than his. But this objection will not hold. For the king may have supported the army out of his own property or from the royal patrimony. . . . It may therefore happen that a king has authority over a people as a proprietary right, so that he can even alienate that authority to another. . . .

XIII. But in kingdoms where royal authority has been bestowed by the will of the people, it is not to be presumed that it was their will that their king should have the right of alienating that authority. . . .

XIV. That completeness of possession is not a measure of sovereignty is seen not only in the fact that many sovereignties are held not *pleno jure*, but also in the fact that many powers lower than sovereignty are held *pleno jure;* whence it comes about that marquisates and counties are sold and bequeathed more easily than kingdoms.

XVI. The third observation is that the authority does not cease to be sovereign, although he who is to become ruler makes certain promises to his subjects or to God, even concerning matters which relate to the manner of government. I do not now speak of promises to observe natural law, divine law, and the law of nations, to which all kings are bound without promise, but of rules to which they could not be bound without promise. The truth of this appears from the analogy of the master of a family, who, although he should have promised the family to do something which pertains to the government of the family, does not thereby cease to have supreme power in the family, so far as family matters are concerned. Nor does a husband lose his marital authority by making certain promises to his wife.

But still it must be confessed that when this is done, the sovereignty is in some degree limited, whether the obligation respect merely the performance of certain acts, or directly affect the power itself. In the former case an act done against the promise will be unjust because, as we shall later show, a legitimate promise gives a right to the promisee; in the latter case, the act is null by reason of defect of the power of doing it. But it does not follow from this that the person so promising has a superior; for the act is rendered null, in this case not by a superior power, but by natural law.[1] . . .

But suppose the condition be added that if the king violate his promise he should lose his kingdom. Even so his sovereignty

[1] Par. 3 is omitted.

does not cease, but becomes a mode of possession, narrowed by a condition and not unlike temporary sovereignty. . . .

XVII. In the fourth place, it is to be noted that sovereignty, though in itself a unit and indivisible, composed of those parts which we have enumerated, with the addition of irresponsibility, may be divided in possession. Thus the Roman imperial power, though one, was often divided, so that one ruler had the East, another the West; or even into three parts. So too it may happen that a people when it chooses a king may reserve certain acts to itself, and commit others to the king *pleno jure.* This is not the case whenever the king is bound by certain promises, as we have shown above. But it is to be understood to happen when the partition of power is expressly instituted, concerning which we have already spoken; or if a people, hitherto free, lay upon the king some perpetual precept; or if anything be added to the compact, by which it is understood that the king can be compelled or punished. For a precept is the act of a superior, at least in the thing commanded. To compel is not always the act of a superior; for by natural law a creditor has the right of coercing his debtor; but to compel is at variance with the nature of an inferior. Therefore, in the case of such compulsion, a parity of powers, at least, follows, and sovereignty is divided.

Many persons allege many inconveniences against such a two-headed sovereignty. But in political matters nothing is entirely free from inconvenience. And law is to be measured not according to what seems best to this or that person, but by the will of him who is the origin of law. . . . Such engagements as we have been speaking of have been made not only between kings and their peoples, but also among different kings and different peoples, and between kings and neighboring peoples, each giving a guarantee to the other.

XVIII. Those are very much mistaken who consider that there is a division of sovereignty when kings allow certain of their own acts not to be valid except when approved by a senate or some other assembly. For when in such cases acts of the king are rescinded they are to be understood as being rescinded by the authority of the king, who provided such a caution against fallacious representations. Thus Antiochus the Third sent a rescript to the magistrates, that if he commanded anything contrary to the laws, they should not obey him; and Constantine directed that widows and orphans should not be compelled to come to the emperor's court for judgment, though a rescript of the emperor to that effect should be produced.

The case is like that of a testament in which it is added that no subsequent testament shall be valid; for this clause has the effect of making a later testament presumed not to be the real will of the testator. But as such a clause may be rescinded by an express and special signification of the writer, so may the direction of the king.

SELECTED BIBLIOGRAPHY

Cook, Thomas I., *History of Political Philosophy*, pp. 427–442.
Sabine, George H., *History of Political Theory*, pp. 420–429.
Dunning, William A., *Political Theories, from Luther to Montesquieu*, ch. 5.
Gettell, Raymond G., *History of Political Thought*, ch. 10, secs. 3, 4.

Hearnshaw, F. J. C., in his *Social and Political Ideas of Some Great Thinkers of the Sixteenth and Seventeenth Centuries* (London, 1926), ch. 6.
Figgis, John Neville, *Studies of Political Thought from Gerson to Grotius* (Cambridge, 1907), pp. 191–218.
White, Andrew D., *Seven Great Statesmen in the Warfare of Humanity with Unreason* (New York, 1910), pp. 55–110.
Basdevant, Jules, "La vie et des œuvres de Grotius," in *Les fondateurs du droit international: leurs œuvres—leurs doctrines* (Paris, 1904), pp. 125–267.
Franck, Adolphe, *Réformateurs et publicistes de l'Europe: dix-septième siècle* (Paris, 1881), pp. 253–332.
Pradier-Fodéré, M. P., "Essai biographique et historique sur Grotius et sons temps," Vol. I, pp. xiii–lxxvi, of his French translation (Paris, 1867) of the *De jure belli ac pacis*.

Knight, William S. M., *The Life and Works of Hugo Grotius* (London, 1925).
Littlejohn, John M., *The Political Theory of the Schoolmen and Grotius* (New York, 1896).
Vreeland, Hamilton, *Hugo Grotius* (New York, 1917).

MILTON

XVIII. JOHN MILTON (1608–1674)

INTRODUCTION

In the combat between Puritans and Royalists in England in the middle of the seventeenth century, the protagonists of republican ideas founded their doctrines upon general principles of political justice, not upon English law and precedent. In the pamphlets of this era we find that conclusions concerning the rights of the people are derived through arguments similar to those employed by continental pamphleteers of the preceding century. In clear statement of republican doctrine and in specific analysis of the content of the sphere of original human rights, English writers advanced beyond their continental predecessors. The English republican theory was set forth most eloquently and logically in the polemical writings of Milton. Milton's political essays constitute the major part of his literary output between 1640 and 1660. The graceful style and philosophic tone of these essays gave great currency and influence to his views.

Milton was actively identified with the movements which he expounded and defended. He entered first into a controversy concerning church government; in this affair he belonged to the party which advocated complete separation of church and state, the abrogation of the episcopal organization, and the substitution of an order similar to that of the Scotch Presbyterian church. He was a zealous partisan of the Parliamentary party in the civil conflict. In one conspicuous instance, however, he took a strong stand against the action of his party. The "Printing Ordinance," issued by Parliament in 1644, required all publications to be licensed by an official censor. Milton fell under charges of contempt of Parliament for having issued a pamphlet in justification of divorce (following his own divorce) without obtaining a license for the publication. After the charge of contempt was made he published an essay entitled *Areopagitica: a Speech of Mr. John Milton for the Liberty of Unlicensed Printing, to the Parliament of England*. In this essay he broadened his contention against censorship of the press into a defence of liberty in general. The principal element of this discussion is the argument for liberty as an essential feature of the dignity of man and as an indispensable condition for the development of his distinctive faculty of reason. This emphasis upon the relation of man's political rights to his peculiar nature as a rational being constitutes a characteristic quality of Milton's other political writings.

Upon the execution of Charles I Milton immediately aligned himself with the republican group; he expressed his views, in justification of the execution, in a pamphlet on *The Tenure of Kings and Magistrates; proving, that it is lawful and hath been so held through all ages, for any, who have the power, to call to account a Tyrant, or wicked King, and after due conviction, to depose, and put him to death, if the ordinary magistrate have neglected, or denied to do it, and that they, who of late, so much blame deposing are the men that did it themselves.* In ecclesiastical matters Milton had become an upholder of Independency; and in politics he continued consistently to support the dominant party under the Commonwealth and the Protectorate. Throughout this period he held office as "secretary for foreign tongues" in the Council of State; his chief task in this office was that of drafting letters to foreign governments and translating the replies. He rendered particular service to the Commonwealth through his vigorous pamphlets in vindication of the government against charges made by royalist pamphleteers. When the growth of a strong sentiment of dissatisfaction with the Protectorate became manifest, he sought to prevent the movement for the recall of Charles II, by putting forward a plan whereby a republican system might be permanently established. This plan appeared in his pamphlet published in 1660 under the title: *The Ready and Easy Way to Establish a Free Commonwealth, and the Excellence thereof compared with the inconveniences and dangers of readmitting kingship in this nation.* Milton also wrote several widely circulated pamphlets in defense of the policy of the Protectorate: notably the *Eikonoklastes* ("Image-Smasher"), written in reply to the *Eikon Basilike* ("Royal Image"— an anonymous pamphlet believed by many of its numerous royalist readers to have been written by the martyred King himself), and several pamphlets in Latin, addressed to scholars in Britain and on the Continent.

READINGS FROM THE POLITICAL ESSAYS OF MILTON[1]

1. The Origin of Government and the Source and Limits of its Authority [2]

No man, who knows aught, can be so stupid to deny that all men naturally were born free, being the image and resemblance of God himself, and were by privilege above all the creatures, born to command and not to obey. And that they lived so, till from the root of Adam's transgression falling among themselves to do wrong and violence, and foreseeing that such courses must needs tend to the destruction of them all, they agreed by common league to bind each other from mutual injury, and jointly to defend themselves against any that gave disturbance or opposition to such agreement. Hence came cities, towns, and commonwealths. And because no faith in all was found sufficiently binding, they saw it needful to ordain some authority that might restrain by force and punishment what was violated against peace and common right.

This authority and power of self-defence and preservation being originally and naturally in every one of them, and unitedly in them all; for ease, for order, and lest each man should be his own partial judge, they communicated and derived either to one whom for the eminence of his wisdom and integrity they chose above the rest, or to more than one, whom they thought of equal deserving: the first was called a king; the other magistrates: not to be their lords and masters—though afterwards those names in some places were given voluntarily to such as had been authors of inestimable good to the people—but to be their deputies and commissioners, to execute, by virtue of their intrusted power, that justice, which else every man by the bond of nature and of covenant must have executed for himself, and for one another. And to him that shall consider well why among free persons one man by civil right should bear authority and jurisdiction over another, no other end or reason can be imaginable.

These for a while governed well, and with much equity decided all things at their own arbitrament; till the temptation of such a power left absolute in their hands, perverted them at length to injustice and partiality. Then did they who now by trial had found the danger and inconveniences of committing arbitrary power to

[1] The selections are taken from *English Prose Writings of John Milton*, edited by Henry Morley. London, 1889. George Routledge and Sons.
[2] From *The Tenure of Kings and Magistrates* (Morley), pp. 358–362, 364–365, 379–381.

any, invent laws, either framed or consented to by all, that should confine and limit the authority of whom they chose to govern them: that so Man, of whose failing they had proof, might no more rule over them, but Law and Reason, abstracted as much as might be from personal errors and frailties. "While, as the magistrate was set above the people, so the law was set above the magistrate." When this would not serve, but that the law was either not executed, or misapplied, they were constrained from that time, the only remedy left them, to put conditions and take oaths from all kings and magistrates at their first installment, to do impartial justice by law: who, upon these terms and no other, received allegiance from the people, that is to say, bond or covenant to obey them in execution of those laws, which they, the people, had themselves made or assented to. And this ofttimes with express warning, that if the king or magistrate proved unfaithful to his trust, the people would be disengaged. They added also counsellors and parliaments, not to be only at his beck, but, with him or without him, at set times, or at all times, when any danger threatened, to have care of the public safety. Therefore saith Claudius Sesell, a French statesman, "The Parliament was set as a bridle to the king;" which I instance rather, not because our English lawyers have not said the same long before, but because that French monarchy is granted by all to be a far more absolute one than ours. That this and the rest of what hath hitherto been spoken is most true, might be copiously made appear through all stories, heathen and Christian; even of those nations where kings and emperors have sought means to abolish all ancient memory of the people's right by their encroachments and usurpations. But I spare long insertions, appealing to the German, French, Italian, Arragonian, English, and not least the Scottish histories; not forgetting this only by the way, that William the Norman, though a conqueror, and not unsworn at his coronation, was compelled a second time to take oath at St. Alban's ere the people would be brought to yield obedience.

It being thus manifest that the power of Kings and Magistrates is nothing else but what is only derivative, transferred, and committed to them in trust from the People to the common good of them all, in whom the power yet remains fundamentally and cannot be taken from them without a violation of their natural birthright; and seeing that from hence Aristotle and the best of political writers have defined a king, "him who governs to the good and profit of his people, and not for his own ends;" it follows from necessary causes, that the titles of sovereign lord, natural lord and the like are either arrogancies or flatteries, not admitted by emperors and kings of best note, and disliked by the church both of Jews (Isa. xxvi. 13) and ancient Christians, as appears by Tertullian and others. Although generally the people of Asia, and with them the Jews also, especially since the time they chose a king against the advice and counsel of God, are noted by wise authors much inclinable to slavery.

Secondly, that to say, as is usual, the king hath as good right to his crown and dignity as any man to his inheritance, is to make the subject no better than the king's slave, his chattel, or his possession that may be bought and sold: and doubtless, if hereditary title were sufficiently inquired, the best foundation of it would be found but either in courtesy or convenience. But suppose it to be of right hereditary, what can be more just and legal, if a subject for certain crimes be to forfeit by law from himself and posterity all his inheritance to the king, than that a king, for crimes proportional, should forfeit all his title and inheritance to the people? Unless the people must be thought created all for him, he not for them, and they all in one body inferior to him single; which were a kind of treason against the dignity of mankind to affirm.

Thirdly, it follows, that to say kings are accountable to none but God, is the overcoming of all law and government. For if they may refuse to give account, then all covenants made with them at coronation, all oaths are in vain, and mere mockeries; all laws which they swear to keep, made to no purpose: for if the king fear not God—as how many of them do not—we hold then our lives and estates by the tenure of his mere grace and mercy, as from a god, not a mortal magistrate; a position that none but court parasites or men besotted would maintain. Aristotle, therefore, whom we commonly allow for one of the best interpreters of nature and morality, writes in the fourth of his *Politics*, chap. x, that "monarchy unaccountable is the worst sort of tyranny, and least of all to be endured by free-born men."

And surely no Christian prince, not drunk with high mind and prouder than those pagan Cæsars that defied themselves, would arrogate so unreasonably above human condition, or derogate so basely from a whole nation of men, his brethren, as if for him only subsisting and to serve his glory, valuing them in comparison of his own brute will and pleasure no more than so many beasts, or vermin under his feet not to be reasoned with but to be trod on; among whom there might be found so many thousand men for wisdom, virtue, nobleness of mind, and all other respects but the fortune of his dignity, far above him. Yet some would persuade us that this absurd opinion was King David's, because in the 51st Psalm he cries out to God, "Against thee only have I sinned;" as if David had imagined, that to murder Uriah and adulterate his wife had been no sin against his neighbor, whenas that law of Moses was to the king expressly (Deut. xvii) not to think so highly of himself above his brethren. David, therefore, by those words, could mean no other, than either that the depth of his guiltiness was known to God only, or to so few as had not the will and power to question him, or that the sin against God was greater beyond compare than against Uriah. Whatever his meaning were, any wise man will see, that the pathetical words of a psalm can be no certain decision to a point that hath abundantly more certain rules to go by.

How much more rationally spake the heathen king Demophoön, in a tragedy of Euripides, than these interpreters would put upon King David! "I rule not my people by tyranny, as if they were barbarians; but am myself iiable, if I do unjustly, to suffer justly." Not unlike was the speech of Trajan, the worthy emperor, to one whom he made general of his prætorian forces: "Take this drawn sword," saith he, "to use for me if I reign well; if not, to use against me." Thus Dion relates. And not Trajan only, but Theodosius, the younger, a Christian emperor, and one of the best, caused it to be enacted as a rule undeniable and fit to be acknowledged by all kings and emperors, that a prince is bound to the laws; that on the authority of the law the authority of a prince depends, and to the laws ought to submit. Which edict of his remains yet unrepealed in the code of Justinian (1. i. tit. 24), as a sacred constitution to all the succeeding emperors. How can any king in Europe maintain and write himself accountable to none but God, when emperors in their own imperial statutes have written and decreed themselves accountable to law? And indeed where such account is not feared, he that bids a man reign over him above law, may bid as well a savage beast.

It follows, lastly, that since the King or Magistrate holds his authority of the People, both originally and naturally for their good, in the first place, and not his own, then may the people, as oft as they shall judge it for the best, either choose him or reject him, retain him or depose him, though no tyrant, merely by the liberty and right of free-born men to be governed as seems to them best.[1]

Thus far hath been considered chiefly the power of Kings and Magistrates; how it was and is originally the people's, and by them

[1] Pp. 358–362.

conferred in trust only to be employed to the common peace and benefit; with liberty therefore and right remaining in them, to reassume it to themselves, if by kings or magistrates it be abused; or to dispose of it by any alteration, as they shall judge most conducing to the public good.

We may from hence with more ease and force of argument determine what a tyrant is, and what the people may do against him. A tyrant, whether by wrong or by right coming to the crown, is he who, regarding neither law nor the common good, reigns only for himself and his factions: thus St. Basil, among others, defines him. And because his power is great, his will boundless and exorbitant, the fulfilling whereof is for the most part accompanied with innumerable wrongs and oppressions of the people, murders, massacres, rapes, adulteries, desolation, and subversion of cities and whole provinces; look how great a good and happiness a just king is, so great a mischief is a tyrant; as he the public father of his country, so this the common enemy against whom what people lawfully may do, as against a common pest and destroyer of mankind, I suppose no man of clear judgment need go further to be guided than by the very principles of nature in him.[1]

For as to this question in hand, what the people by their just right may do in change of government, or of governor, we see it cleared sufficiently, besides other ample authority, even from the mouths of princes themselves. And surely they that shall boast. as we do, to be a free nation, and not have in themselves the power to remove or to abolish any governor, supreme or subordinate, with the government itself, upon urgent causes, may please their fancy with a ridiculous and painted freedom, fit to cozen babies; but they are indeed under tyranny and servitude, as wanting that power which is the root and source of all liberty, to dispose and economize in the land which God hath given them, as masters of family in their own house and free inheritance. Without which natural and essential power of a free nation, though bearing high their heads, they can in due esteem be thought no better than slaves and vassals born in the tenure and occupation of another inheriting lord, whose government, though not illegal, or intolerable, hangs over them as a lordly scourge, not as a free government; and therefore to be abrogated.

How much more justly then may they fling off tyranny, or tyrants, who being once deposed can be no more than private men, as subject to the reach of justice and arraignment as any other transgressors? And certainly if men, not to speak of heathen

[1] Pp. 364–365.

both wise and religious, have done justice upon tyrants what way they could soonest, how much more mild and humane then is it, to give them fair and open trial; to teach lawless kings, and all who so much adore them, that not mortal man nor his imperious will, but Justice, is the only true sovereign and supreme majesty upon earth? Let men cease therefore, out of faction and hypocrisy, to make outcries and horrid things of things so just and honorable, though perhaps till now no Protestant state or kingdom can be alleged to have openly put to death their king, which lately some have written, and imputed to their great glory; much mistaking the matter. It is not, neither ought it to be, the glory of a Protestant state never to have put their king to death; it is the glory of a Protestant king never to have deserved death. And if the Parliament and military council do what they do without precedent, if it appear their duty, it argues the more wisdom, virtue and magnanimity, that they know themselves able to be a precedent to others; who perhaps in future ages, if they prove not too degenerate, will look up with honor, and aspire toward these exemplary and matchless deeds of their ancestors, as to the highest top of their civil glory and emulation; which heretofore, in the pursuance of fame and foreign dominion, spent itself vaingloriously abroad; but henceforth may learn a better fortitude, to dare execute highest justice on them that shall by force of arms endeavor the oppressing and bereaving of religion and their liberty at home. That no unbridled potentate or tyrant, but to his sorrow, for the future may presume such high and irresponsible licence over mankind, to havoc and turn upside down whole kingdoms of men, as though they were no more in respect of his perverse will than a nation of pismires.[1]

2. Rational Liberty [2]

I conceive, therefore, that when God did enlarge the universal diet of man's body (saving ever the rules of temperance), he then also, as before, left arbitrary the dieting and repasting of our minds; as wherein every mature man might have to exercise his own leading capacity. How great a virtue is temperance, how much of moment through the whole life of man! Yet God commits the managing so great a trust, without particular law or prescription, wholly to the demeanor of every grown man. And therefore when he himself tabled the Jews from heaven, that omer, which was every man's daily portion of manna, is computed to have

[1] Pp. 379–381. [2] From *Areopagitica* (Morley), pp. 322–323, 329–330, 344–347.

been more than might have well sufficed the heartiest feeder thrice as many meals. For those actions which enter into a man rather than issue out of him, and therefore defile not, God uses not to captivate under a perpetual childhood of prescription, but trusts him with the gift of reason to be his own chooser; there were but little work left for preaching, if law and compulsion should grow so fast upon those things which heretofore were governed only by exhortation.[1]

Many there be that complain of divine Providence for suffering Adam to transgress. Foolish tongues! when God gave him reason, he gave him freedom to choose, for reason is but choosing; he had been else a mere artificial Adam, such an Adam as he is in the motions. We ourselves esteem not of that obedience, or love, or gift, which is of force; God therefore left him free, set before him a provoking object ever almost in his eyes; herein consisted his merit, herein the right of his reward, the praise of his abstinence. Wherefore did he create passions within us, pleasures round about us, but that these rightly tempered are the very ingredients of virtue? They are not skilful considerers of human things, who imagine to remove sin by removing the matter of sin; for besides that it is a huge heap increasing under the very act of diminishing, though some part of it may for a time be withdrawn from some persons it cannot from all, in such a universal thing as books are; and when this is done, yet the sin remains entire. Though ye take from a covetous man all his treasure, he has yet one jewel left, ye cannot bereave him of his covetousness. Banish all objects of lust, shut up all youth into the severest discipline that can be exercised in any hermitage, ye cannot make them chaste that came not thither so: such great care and wisdom is required to the right managing of this point.

Suppose we could expel sin by this means; look how much we thus expel of sin, so much we expel of virtue: for the matter of them both is the same: remove that, and ye remove them both alike. This justifies the high providence of God, who, though he commands us temperance, justice, continence, yet pours out before us even to a profuseness all desirable things, and gives us minds that can wander beyond all limit and satiety. Why should we then affect a rigor contrary to the manner of God and of nature, by abridging or scanting those means, which books freely permitted are, both to the trial of virtue and the exercise of truth?

It would be better done, to learn that the law must needs be

[1] Pp. 322–323.

frivolous which goes to restrain things uncertainly and yet equally working to good and to evil. And were I the chooser, a dram of well-doing should be preferred before many times as much the forcible hindrance of evil doing. For God sure esteems the growth and completing of one virtuous person, more than the restraint of ten vicious.[1]

Where there is much desire to learn, there of necessity will be much arguing, much writing, many opinions; for opinion in good men is but knowledge in the making. Under these fantastic terrors of sect and schism, we wrong the earnest and zealous thirst after knowledge and understanding which God hath stirred up in this city. What some lament of, we rather should rejoice at, should rather praise this pious forwardness among men to reassume the ill-deputed care of their religion into their own hands again. A little generous prudence, a little forbearance of one another, and some grain of charity might win all these diligencies to join and unite into one general and brotherly search after truth; could we but forego this prelatical tradition of crowding free consciences and Christian liberties into canons and precepts of men. I doubt not if some great and worthy stranger should come among us, wise to discern the mould and temper of a people and how to govern it, observing the high hopes and aims, the diligent alacrity of our extended thoughts and reasonings in the pursuance of truth and freedom, but that he would cry out as Pyrrhus did, admiring the Roman docility and courage, "If such were my Epirots, I would not despair the greatest design that could be attempted to make a church or kingdom happy."

Yet these are the men cried out against for schismatics and sectaries, as if, while the temple of the Lord was building, some cutting, some squaring the marble, others hewing the cedars, there should be a sort of irrational men, who could not consider there must be many schisms and many dissections made in the quarry and in the timber ere the house of God can be built. And when every stone is laid artfully together, it cannot be united into a continuity, it can but be contiguous in this world. Neither can every piece of the building be of one form; nay, rather the perfection consists in this, that out of many moderate varieties and brotherly dissimilitudes that are not vastly disproportional, arises the goodly and the graceful symmetry that commends the whole pile and structure.

Let us therefore be more considerate builders, more wise in spiritual architecture, when great reformation is expected. For

[1] Pp. 329–330.

now the time seems come, wherein Moses, the great prophet, may sit in heaven rejoicing to see that memorable and glorious wish of his fulfilled, when not only our seventy elders, but all the Lord's people, are become prophets. No marvel then though some men, and some good men too perhaps, but young in goodness, as Joshua then was, envy them. They fret, and out of their own weakness are in agony, lest these divisions and sub-divisions will undo us. The adversary again applauds, and waits the hour: when they have branched themselves out, saith he, small enough into parties and partitions, then will be our time. Fool! he sees not the firm root, out of which we all grow, though into branches; nor will beware, until he see our small divided maniples cutting through at every angle of his ill-united and unwieldy brigade. And that we are to hope better of all these supposed sects and schisms, and that we shall not need that solicitude, honest perhaps though overtimorous, of them that vex in this behalf, but shall laugh in the end at those malicious applauders of our differences, I have these reasons to persuade me.

First, when a city shall be as it were besieged and blocked about, her navigable river infested, inroads and incursions round, defiance and battle oft rumored to be marching up, even to her walls and suburb trenches; that then the people, or the greater part, more than at other times, wholly taken up with the study of highest and most important matters to be reformed, should be disputing, reasoning, reading, inventing, discoursing, even to a rarity and admiration, things not before discussed or written of, argues first a singular good will, contentedness, and confidence in your prudent foresight, and safe government, Lords and Commons; and from thence derives itself to a gallant bravery and well-grounded contempt of their enemies, as if there were no small number of as great spirits among us as his was who, when Rome was nigh besieged by Hannibal, being in the city, bought that piece of ground at no cheap rate whereon Hannibal himself encamped his own regiment.

Next, it is a lively and cheerful presage of our happy success and victory. For as in a body when the blood is fresh, the spirits pure and vigorous, not only to vital but to rational faculties, and those in the acutest and the pertest operations of wit and subtlety, it argues in what good plight and constitution the body is; so when the cheerfulness of the people is so sprightly up, as that it has not only wherewith to guard well its own freedom and safety, but to spare, and to bestow upon the solidest and sublimest points of controversy and new invention, it betokens us not degenerated, nor drooping to a fatal decay, by casting off the old and wrinkled skin of corruption to outlive these pangs and wax young again, entering the glorious ways of truth and prosperous virtue, destined to become great and honorable in these latter ages.

Methinks I see in my mind a noble and puissant nation rousing herself like a strong man after sleep, and shaking her invincible locks. Methinks I see her as an eagle mewing her mighty youth, and kindling her undazzled eyes at the full midday beam; purging and unscaling her long abused sight at the fountain itself of heavenly radiance; while the whole noise of timorous and flocking birds, with those also that love the twilight, flutter about, amazed at what she means, and in their envious gabble would prognosticate a year of sects and schisms.

What should ye do then, should ye suppress all this flowery crop of knowledge and new light sprung up and yet springing daily in this city? Should ye set an oligarchy of twenty engrossers over it, to bring a famine upon our minds again, when we shall know nothing but what is measured to us by their bushel? Believe it, Lords and Commons! they who counsel ye to such a suppressing, do as good as bid ye suppress yourselves; and I will soon show how. If it be desired to know the immediate cause of all this free writing and free speaking, there cannot be assigned a truer than your own mild, and free, and humane government; it is the liberty, Lords and Commons, which your own valorous and happy counsels have purchased us; liberty which is the nurse of all great wits: this is that which hath rarified and enlightened our spirits like the influence of heaven: this is that which hath enfranchised, enlarged, and lifted up our apprehensive degrees above themselves. Ye cannot make us now less capable, less knowing, less eagerly pursuing of the truth, unless ye first make yourselves, that made us so, less the lovers, less the founders of our true liberty. We can grow ignorant again, brutish, formal, and slavish, as ye found us; but you then must first become that which ye cannot be, oppressive, arbitrary and tyrannous, as they were from whom ye have freed us. That our hearts are now more capacious, our thoughts more erected to the search and expectation of greatest and exactest things, is the issue of your own virtue propagated in us; ye cannot suppress that, unless ye reinforce an abrogated and merciless law, that fathers may dispatch at will their own children. And who shall then stick closest to ye and excite others? Not he who takes up arms for coat and conduct, and his four nobles of Danegelt. Although I dispraise not the defence of just immunities, yet love my peace better, if that were all. Give me the liberty to know, to utter, and to argue freely according to conscience, above all liberties.[1]

3. The Character of Free Government [2]

I doubt not but all ingenuous and knowing men will easily agree with me, that a Free Commonwealth without Single Person or House of Lords is by far the best government, if it can be had; but we have all this while, say they, been expecting it, and cannot yet attain it. It is true, indeed, when monarchy was dissolved, the form of a commonwealth should have forthwith been framed, and the practice thereof immediately begun, that the people might have soon been satisfied and delighted with the decent order, ease and benefit thereof. We had been then by this time firmly rooted, past fear of commotions or mutations, and now flourishing; this care of timely settling a new government instead of the old, too much neglected, hath been our mischief. Yet the cause thereof may be ascribed with most reason to the frequent disturbances, interruptions, and dissolutions, which the Parliament hath had, partly from the impatient or disaffected people, partly from some ambitious leader in the army, much contrary, I believe, to the mind and approbation of the army itself, and their other commanders, once undeceived or in their own power.

Now is the opportunity, now the very season, wherein we may obtain a Free Commonwealth, and establish it forever in the land, without difficulty or much delay. Writs are sent out for elections, and, which is worth observing, in the name, not of any king, but of the keepers of our liberty, to summon a free parliament; which then only will indeed be free, and deserve the true honor of that supreme title, if they preserve us a free people. Which never Parliament was more free to do, being now called, not, as heretofore, by the summons of a king, but by the voice of liberty. And if the people, laying aside prejudice and impatience, will seriously and calmly now consider their own good, both religious and civil, their own liberty and the only means thereof as shall be here laid down before them, and will elect their knights and burgesses able men, and according to the just and necessary qualifications—which, for aught I hear, remain yet in force unrepealed, as they were formerly decreed in Parliament—men not addicted to a Single Person or House of Lords, the work is done; at least the foundation firmly laid of a Free Commonwealth, and good part also erected of the main structure.

[1] Pp. 344–347.
[2] From *The Ready and Easy Way to Establish a Free Commonwealth* (Morley), pp. 431–433, 435–437, 441–444.

For the ground and basis of every just and free government—
since men have smarted so oft for committing all to one person—
is a General Council of ablest men, chosen by the People to consult of public affairs from time to time for the common good. In
this Grand Council must the sovereignty, not transferred but delegated only and as it were deposited, reside; with this caution,
they must have the forces by sea and land committed to them for
preservation of the common peace and liberty; must raise and
manage the public revenue, at least with some inspectors deputed
for satisfaction of the people how it is employed; must make or
propose, as more expressly shall be said anon, civil laws; treat of
commerce, peace or war with foreign nations; and, for the carrying
on some particular affairs with more secrecy and expedition, must
elect, as they have already out of their own number and others,
a Council of State.

And, although it may seem strange at first hearing, by reason
that men's minds are prepossessed with the notion of successive
parliaments, I affirm, that the Grand or General Council, being
well chosen, should be perpetual. For so their business is or may
be, and ofttimes urgent; the opportunity of affairs gained or lost
in a moment. The day of Council cannot be set as the day of a
festival, but must be ready always to prevent or answer all occasions. By this continuance they will become every way skil-
fullest, best provided of intelligence from abroad, best acquainted
with the people at home, and the people with them. The ship
of the commonwealth is always under sail; they sit at the stern;
and if they steer well, what need is there to change them, it being
rather dangerous? Add to this, that the Grand Council is both
foundation and main pillar of the whole state; and to move pillars
and foundations, not faulty, cannot be safe for the building.

I see not, therefore, how we can be advantaged by successive
and transitory parliaments; but that they are much likelier continually to unsettle rather than to settle a free government, to
breed commotions, changes, novelties, and uncertainties, to bring
neglect upon present affairs and opportunities, while all minds are
in suspense with expectation of a new assembly, and the assembly,
for a good space, taken up with the new settling of itself. After
which, if they find no great work to do, they will make it, by altering or repealing former acts, or making or multiplying new, that
they may seem to see what their predecessors saw not, and not to
have assembled for nothing; till all law be lost in the multitude
of clashing statutes.[1]

[1] Pp. 431–433.

To make the people fittest to choose, and the chosen fittest to
govern, will be to mend our corrupt and faulty education, to teach
the people faith, not without virtue, temperance, modesty,
sobriety, parsimony, justice; not to admire wealth or honor; to
hate turbulence and ambition; to place everyone his private welfare and happiness in the public peace, liberty and safety. They
shall not then need to be much distrustful of their chosen patriots
in the Grand Council; who will be then rightly called the true
keepers of our liberty, though the most of their business will be
in foreign affairs. But to prevent all mistrust, the people then will
have their several ordinary assemblies (which will henceforth quite
annihilate the odious power and name of committees) in the chief
towns of every county, without the trouble, charge, or time lost
of summoning and assembling from afar in so great a number, and
so long residing from their own houses or removing of their families,
to do as much at home in their several shires, entire or subdivided,
toward the securing of their liberty, as a numerous assembly of
them all formed and convened on purpose with the wariest rotation. Whereof I shall speak more ere the end of this discourse; for
it may be referred to time, so we be still going on by degrees to perfection. The people well weighing and performing these things, I
suppose would have no cause to fear, though the Parliament, abolishing that name, as originally signifying but the parley of our lords
and commons with the Norman king when he pleased to call them,
should, with certain limitations of their power, sit perpetual if
their ends be faithful and for a free commonwealth, under the name
of a Grand or General Council.

Till this be done, I am in doubt whether our state will be ever
certainly and thoroughly settled; never likely till then to see an
end of our troubles and continual changes, or at least never the
true settlement and assurance of our liberty. The Grand Council
being thus firmly constituted to perpetuity, and still, upon the
death or default of any member, supplied and kept in full number,
there can be no cause alleged why peace, justice, plentiful trade,
and all prosperity should not thereupon ensue throughout the whole
land, with as much assurance as can be of human things, that they
shall so continue—if God favor us, and our wilful sins provoke
him not—even to the coming of our true and rightful, and only to
be expected King, only worthy, as he is our only Saviour, the Mes-
siah, the Christ, the only heir of his eternal Father, the only by
him anointed and ordained since the work of our redemption
finished, universal Lord of mankind.

The way propounded is plain, easy, and open before us; without intricacies, without the introducement of new or absolute forms or terms, or exotic models; ideas that would effect nothing but with a number of new injunctions to manacle the native liberty of mankind; turning all virtue into prescription, servitude, and necessity, to the great impairing and frustrating of Christian liberty. I say again, this way lies free and smooth before us; is not tangled with inconveniences; invents no new incumbrances; requires no perilous, no injurious alteration or circumscription of men's lands and properties; secure, that in this commonwealth, temporal and spiritual lords removed, no man or number of men can attain to such wealth or vast possession, as will need the hedge of an agrarian law—never successful, but the cause rather of sedition, save only where it began seasonably with first possession—to confine them from endangering our public liberty.[1]

Having thus far shown with what ease we may now obtain a Free Commonwealth, and by it, with as much ease, all the freedom, peace, justice, plenty, that we can desire; on the other side, the difficulties, troubles, uncertainties, nay, rather impossibilities, to enjoy these things constantly under a monarch; I will now proceed to show more particularly wherein our freedom and flourishing condition will be more ample and secure to us under a free commonwealth, than under kingship.

The whole freedom of man consists either in spiritual or civil liberty. As for spiritual, who can be at rest, who can enjoy anything in this world with contentment, who hath not liberty to serve God and to save his own soul according to the best light which God hath planted in him to that purpose by the reading of his revealed will and the guidance of his Holy Spirit? That this is best pleasing to God, and that the whole Protestant church allows no supreme judge or rule in matters of religion, but the Scriptures, and these to be interpreted by the Scriptures themselves, which necessarily infers liberty of conscience, I have heretofore proved at large in another treatise; and might yet further, by the public declarations, confessions, and admonitions of whole churches and states, obvious in all histories since the Reformation.

This liberty of conscience, which above all other things ought to be to all men dearest and most precious, no government more inclinable not to favor only, but to protect, than a Free Commonwealth; as being most magnanimous, most fearless, and confident of its own fair proceedings. Whereas kingship, though looking big, yet indeed most pusillanimous, full of fears, full of jealousies,

[1] Pp. 435–437.

startled at every umbrage, as it hath been observed of old to have ever suspected most and mistrusted them who were in most esteem for virtue and generosity of mind, so it is now known to have most in doubt and suspicion them who are most reputed to be religious. Queen Elizabeth, though herself accounted so good a Protestant, so moderate, so confident of her subjects' love, would never give way so much as to Presbyterian Reformation in this land, though once and again besought, as Camden relates; but imprisoned and persecuted the very proposers thereof, alleging it as her mind and maxim unalterable, that such Reformation would diminish regal authority.

What liberty of conscience can we then expect of others, far worse principled from the cradle, trained up and governed by Popish and Spanish counsels, and on such depending hitherto for subsistence? Especially what can this last Parliament expect, who having revived lately and published the Covenant, have re-engaged themselves, never to readmit episcopacy? Which no son of Charles returning but will most certainly bring back with him, if he regard the last and strictest charge of his father, "to persevere in, not the doctrine only, but government of the Church of England, not to neglect the speedy and effectual suppressing of errors and schisms;" among which he accounted Presbytery one of the chief.

Or if, notwithstanding that charge of his father, he submit to the Covenant, how will he keep faith to us, with disobedience to him; or regard that faith given, which must be founded on the breach of that last and solemnest paternal charge, and the reluctance, I may say the antipathy, which is in all kings, against Presbyterian and Independent discipline? For they hear the gospel speaking much of liberty; a word which monarchy and her bishops both fear and hate, but a Free Commonwealth both favors and promotes; and not the word only, but the thing itself. But let our governors beware in time, lest their hard measure to liberty of conscience be found the rock whereon they shipwreck themselves, as others have now done before them in the course wherein God was directing their steerage to a Free Commonwealth; and the abandoning of all those whom they call sectaries, for the detected falsehood and ambition of some, be a wilful rejection of their own chief strength and interest in the freedom of all Protestant Religion, under what abusive name soever calumniated.

The other part of our freedom consists in the civil rights and advancements of every person according to his merit: the enjoyment of those never more certain, and the access to these never more open, than in a Free Commonwealth. Both which, in my opinion, may be best and soonest obtained, if every county in the land were made a kind of subordinate commonalty or commonwealth, and one chief town or more, according as the shire is in circuit, made cities, if they be not so called already; where the nobility and chief gentry, from a proportionable compass of territory annexed to each city, may build houses or palaces befitting their quality, may bear part in the government, make their own judicial laws, or use those that are, and execute them by their own elected judicatures and judges without appeal, in all things of civil government between man and man. So they shall have justice in their own hands, law executed fully and finally in their own counties and precincts, long wished and spoken of, but never yet obtained. They shall have none then to blame but themselves, if it be not well administered; and fewer laws to expect or fear from the supreme authority. Or to those that shall be made, of any great concernment to public liberty, they may, without much trouble in these commonalties, or in more general assemblies called to their cities from the whole territory on such occasion, declare and publish their assent or dissent by deputies, within a time limited, sent to the Grand Council; yet so as this their judgment declared shall submit to the greater number of other counties or commonalties, and not avail them to any exemption of themselves, or refusal of agreement with the rest, as it may in any of the United Provinces, being sovereign within itself ofttimes to the great disadvantage of that Union.

In these employments they may, much better than they do now, exercise and fit themselves till their lot fall to be chosen into the Grand Council, according as their worth and merit shall be taken notice of by the people. As for controversies that shall happen between men of several counties, they may repair, as they do now, to the capital city, or any other more commodious, indifferent place, and equal judges. And this I find to have been practised in the old Athenian commonwealth, reputed the first and ancientest place of civility in all Greece, that they had in their several cities a peculiar, in Athens a common government, and their right, as it befell them, to the administration of both.

They should have here also schools and academies at their own choice, wherein their children may be bred up in their own sight to all learning and noble education; not in grammar only, but in all liberal arts and exercises. This would soon spread much more knowledge and civility, yea, religion, through all parts of the land, by communicating the natural heat of government and culture more distributively to all extreme parts, which now lie numb and neglected; would soon make the whole nation more industrious, more ingenious at home, more potent, more honorable abroad. To this a Free Commonwealth will easily assent; nay, the Parliament hath had already some such thing in design; for of all governments a commonwealth aims most to make the people flourishing, virtuous, noble, and high-spirited. Monarchs will never permit; whose aim is to make the people wealthy indeed perhaps, and well fleeced for their own shearing and the supply of regal prodigality, but otherwise softest, basest, viciousest, servilest, easiest to be kept under, and not only in fleece but in mind also sheepishest. And will have all the benches of judicature annexed to the throne, as a gift of royal grace that we have justice done us; whenas nothing can be more essential to the freedom of a people than to have the administration of justice and all public ornaments in their own election, and within their own bounds, without long travelling or depending upon remote places to obtain their right, or any civil accomplishment, so it be not supreme, but subordinate to the general power and union of the whole Republic.

In which happy firmness, as in the particular above mentioned, we shall also far exceed the United Provinces, by having not as they, to the retarding and distracting ofttimes of their counsels on urgentest occasions, many sovereignties united in one commonwealth, but many commonwealths under one united and intrusted sovereignty. And when we have our forces by sea and by land, either of a faithful army or a settled militia, in our own hands, to the firm establishing of a free commonwealth, public accounts under our own inspection, general laws and taxes, with their causes in our own domestic suffrages, judicial laws, offices, and ornaments at home in our own ordering and administration, all distinction of lords and commoners that may any way divide or sever the public interest removed; what can a perpetual senate have then, wherein to grow corrupt, wherein to encroach upon us, or usurp? Or if they do, wherein to be formidable? Yet if all this avail not to remove the fear or envy of a perpetual sitting, it may be easily provided to change a third part of them yearly, or every two or three years, as was above mentioned: or that it be at those times in the people's choice, whether they will change them, or renew their power, as they shall find cause.[1]

[1] Pp. 441–444.

SELECTED BIBLIOGRAPHY

Dunning, William A., *Political Theories, from Luther to Montesquieu*, ch. 7, §§ 1–5.
Sabine, George H., *History of Political Theory*, pp. 508–512.
Saurat, Denis, *Milton, Man and Thinker* (New York, 1925), esp. pp. 181–202.
Gooch, G. P., *English Democratic Ideas in the Seventeenth Century* (new ed. by H. J. Laski, Cambridge, 1927), pp. 150–155, 204–207, 265–270.
Osgood, Herbert L., "The Political Ideas of the Puritans" (II), in *Political Science Quarterly*, vol. 6 (1891), pp. 201–231.
Seeley, J. R., *Lectures and Essays* (London, 1870), ch. 4: "Milton's Political Opinions."
Masson, David, *The Life of John Milton: Narrated in Connexion with the Political, Ecclesiastical and Literary History of His Time*, 7 vols. (Cambridge, 1859–94), Vol. II, pp. 237–268, 356–409; Vol. III, pp. 269–301; Vol. IV, pp. 64–79, 130 ff., 246–267, 580–616; Vol. V, pp. 580–589, 605–615, 644–655, 675–689.

Hardeland, Gertrude, *Miltons Anschauungen von Staat, Kirche, Toleranz* (Halle a. S., 1934).

HOBBES

XIX. THOMAS HOBBES (1588-1679)

INTRODUCTION

The first comprehensive work in political philosophy from the hand of an Englishman was written by a supporter of the royalist cause in the Puritan Revolution. It is the *Leviathan* of Thomas Hobbes. This treatise is not primarily polemical in character; but its doctrine of irresponsible sovereignty is undoubtedly in part a product of the royalist prejudices of the author; and the time of its publication was determined by his desire to put forward a theory of civil government adequate to the political crisis through which the country was passing. In 1637, some years before the completion of the Leviathan, he had published a little pamphlet containing a defence of the royal prerogative with respect to some points of it that were in dispute at that time.

The experiences and associations of Hobbes' life prepared, or at least confirmed, his mind for the construction of a system scientific in plan and conservative in its implications for political practice. A graduate of Oxford, he became in early life tutor in the family of the Earl of Devonshire; the connection with this family continued, with a few interruptions, throughout the remainder of his life; in one of these interruptions he was tutor in mathematics to the Prince of Wales (afterwards Charles II) during the exile of the royal family in France. Hobbes had always been a student of mathematics and philosophy; at Oxford he had been trained according to the methods of scholastic philosophy. In his several sojourns in Europe with his noble pupils he became acquainted with the new school of philosophers and scientists, and fell very much under the influence of their cosmic imagination. The adherents of this school of "mechanical philosophy" were following in various courses Galileo's theory that the laws of motion afford the only true principle whereby the phenomena of physical nature are to be explained. Hobbes set himself the task of evolving a synthetic philosophy. Starting with mathematical principles as

445

applied to the motions of material bodies, this philosophy would comprehend, in its completed form, a unified and logically ordered interpretation of the natural world, man, and society. The third step in the three-fold design just indicated was accomplished before the other two, and is embodied in the work which appeared in 1651 under the title, *Leviathan, or the Matter, Form and Power of a Commonwealth, Ecclesiastical and Civil.*[1] This work includes also, as groundwork for its social philosophy, a treatise on "Man" which constitutes the first part of the *Leviathan;* here Hobbes sets forth his materialistic, deterministic, and hedonistic doctrines of psychology and ethics. Here appears also Hobbes' dark picture of the primitive condition of mankind, which he represents as well nigh intolerable because the dominantly selfish instincts of men engender mutual suspicion and antagonism; the outward result is continual and indiscriminate strife. This unpeaceful stage of society is described as the "state of nature," which Hobbes regards as pre-political in a logical, rather than historical, sense; in other words, it represents the normal state of mankind so far as men are unrestrained by the political order. From this introductory discussion are derived the two great ideas about which group themselves all of the more important conclusions of the second part—"Of Commonwealth." These two leading themes as developed by Hobbes were of important consequence for later political thought; they are his theory of the social contract as the logical starting-point of the state, and his doctrine of the absoluteness of sovereignty, whatever its location.

The third and fourth parts of the *Leviathan* deal with theological and ecclesiastical subjects.

READINGS FROM THE LEVIATHAN [2]

1.   *The State of Nature and the Laws of Nature* [3]

Ch. xiii.   *Of the Natural Condition of Mankind as concerning Felicity and Misery.*

[1] For explanation of the word "Leviathan" see the frontispiece (it is given in the Molesworth edition) illustrating the personation of the state in a giant man made up of men; cf. also the *Introduction.*
[2] *Leviathan* constitutes the third volume of *The English Works of Thomas Hobbes*, edited by Molesworth. It is also available in a volume edited by Henry Morley (third edition, London, 1887).
[3] Part I, chs. xiii–xv. Parts of chs. xiv and xv are omitted.

Nature hath made men so equal, in the faculties of the body and mind, as that though there be found one man sometimes manifestly stronger in body, or of quicker mind than another, yet when all is reckoned together, the difference between man and man is not so considerable, as that one man can thereupon claim to himself any benefit to which another may not pretend, as well as he. For as to the strength of body, the weakest has strength enough to kill the strongest, either by secret machination, or by confederacy with others that are in the same danger with himself.

And as to the faculties of the mind, setting aside the arts grounded upon words, and especially that skill of proceeding upon general and infallible rules, called science; which very few have, and but in few things; as being not a native faculty, born with us; nor attained, as prudence, while we look after somewhat else, I find yet a greater equality amongst men than that of strength. For prudence is but experience; which equal time equally bestows on all men, in those things they equally apply themselves unto. That which may perhaps make such equality incredible is but a vain conceit of one's own wisdom, which almost all men think they have in a greater degree than the vulgar; that is, than all men but themselves, and a few others, whom by fame or for concurring with themselves, they approve. For such is the nature of men, that howsoever they may acknowledge many others to be more witty, or more eloquent, or more learned, yet they will hardly believe there be many so wise as themselves; for they see their own wit at hand, and other men's at a distance. But this proveth rather that men are in that point equal, than unequal. For there is not ordinarily a greater sign of the equal distribution of anything, than that every man is contented with his share.

From this equality of ability ariseth equality of hope in the attaining of our ends. And therefore if any two men desire the same thing, which nevertheless they cannot both enjoy, they become enemies; and in the way to their end, which is principally their own conservation, and sometimes their delectation only, endeavor to destroy or subdue one another. And from hence it comes to pass that where an invader hath no more to fear than another man's single power; if one plant, sow, build, or possess a convenient seat, others may probably be expected to come prepared with forces united, to dispossess and deprive him, not only of the fruit of his labor, but also of his life or liberty. And the invader again is in the like danger of another.

And from this diffidence of one another, there is no way for any man to secure himself so reasonable as anticipation; that is, by force, or wiles, to master the persons of all men he can, so long, till he see no other power great enough to endanger him: and this is no more than his own conservation requireth, and is generally allowed. Also because there be some, that taking pleasure in contemplating their own power in the acts of conquest, which they pursue farther than their security requires; if others, that otherwise would be glad to be at ease within modest bounds, should not by invasion increase their power, they would not be able, long time, by standing only on their defence, to subsist. And by consequence, such augumentation of dominion over men being necessary to a man's conservation, it ought to be allowed him.

Again, men have no pleasure, but on the contrary a great deal of grief, in keeping company, where there is no power able to overawe them all. For every man looketh that his companion should value him, at the same rate he sets upon himself: and upon all signs of contempt, or undervaluing, naturally endeavors, as far as he dares (which amongst them that have no common power to keep them in quiet, is far enough to make them destroy each other), to extort a greater value from his contemners, by damage; and from others, by the example.

So that in the nature of man we find three principal causes of quarrel. First, competition; secondly, diffidence; thirdly, glory. The first maketh men invade for gain; the second, for safety; and the third, for reputation. The first use violence, to make themselves masters of other men's persons, wives, children, and cattle; the second, to defend them; the third, for trifles, as a word, a smile, a different opinion and any other sign of undervalue, either direct in their persons, or by reflection in their kindred, their friends, their nation, their profession, or their name.

Hereby it is manifest that during the time men live without a common power to keep them all in awe, they are in that condition which is called war; and such a war, as is of every man against every man. For war consisteth not in battle only, or the act of fighting; but in a tract of time, wherein the will to contend by battle is sufficiently known: and therefore the notion of time is to be considered in the nature of war, as it is in the nature of weather. For as the nature of foul weather lieth not in a shower or two of rain, but in an inclination thereto of many days together; so the nature of war consisteth not in actual fighting, but in the known disposition thereto during all the time there is no assurance to the contrary. All other time is peace.

Whatsoever therefore is consequent to a time of war, where every man is enemy to every man, the same is consequent to the time wherein men live without other security than what their own strength and their own invention shall furnish them withal. In such condition there is no place for industry, because the fruit thereof is uncertain, and consequently no culture of the earth; no navigation, nor use of the commodities that may be imported by sea; no commodious building; no instruments of moving and removing such things as require much force; no knowledge of the face of the earth; no account of time; no arts; no letters; no society; and, which is worst of all, continual fear and danger of violent death; and the life of man, solitary, poor, nasty, brutish, and short.

It may seem strange to some man, that has not well weighed these things, that nature should thus dissociate, and render men apt to invade and destroy one another; and he may therefore, not trusting to this inference, made from the passions, desire perhaps to have the same confirmed by experience. Let him therefore consider with himself, when taking a journey, he arms himself, and seeks to go well accompanied; when going to sleep, he locks his doors; when even in his house, he locks his chests; and this when he knows there be laws, and public officers, armed, to revenge all injuries shall be done him; what opinion he has of his fellow-subjects, when he rides armed; of his fellow-citizens, when he locks his doors; and of his children and servants, when he locks his chests. Does he not there as much accuse mankind by his actions as I do by my words? But neither of us accuse man's nature in it. The desires and other passions of man are in themselves no sin. No more are the actions that proceed from those passions, till they know a law that forbids them; which till laws be made they cannot know, nor can any law be made till they have agreed upon the person that shall make it.

It may peradventure be thought there was never such a time nor condition of war as this; and I believe it was never generally so, over all the world, but there are many places where they live so now. For the savage people in many places of America, except the government of small families, the concord whereof dependeth on natural lust, have no government at all, and live at this day in that brutish manner, as I said before. Howsoever, it may be perceived what manner of life there would be, where there were no common power to fear, by the manner of life which men that have formerly lived under a peaceful government, use to degenerate into in a civil war.

But though there had never been any time wherein particular men were in a condition of war one against another; yet in all times, kings, and persons of sovereign authority, because of their independency, are in continual jealousies and in the state and posture of gladiators; having their weapons pointing, and their eyes fixed on one another; that is, their forts, garrisons, and guns upon the frontiers of their kingdoms; and continual spies upon their neighbors; which is a posture of war. But because they uphold thereby the industry of their subjects, there does not follow from it that misery which accompanies the liberty of particular men.

To this war of every man, against every man, this also is consequent: that nothing can be unjust. The notions of right and wrong, justice and injustice, have there no place. Where there is no common power, there is no law; where no law, no injustice. Force and fraud are in war the two cardinal virtues. Justice and injustice are none of the faculties neither of the body nor mind. If they were, they might be in a man that were alone in the world, as well as his senses, and passions. They are qualities that relate to men in society, not in solitude. It is consequent also to the same condition, that there be no propriety, no dominion, no "mine" and "thine" distinct; but only that to be every man's that he can get; and for so long as he can keep it. And thus much for the ill condition which man by mere nature is actually placed in; though with a possibility to come out of it, consisting partly in the passions, partly in his reason.

The passions that incline men to peace are fear of death; desire of such things as are necessary to commodious living; and a hope by their industry to obtain them. And reason suggesteth convenient articles of peace, upon which men may be drawn to agreement. These articles are they which otherwise are called the laws of nature: whereof I shall speak more particularly in the two following chapters.

Ch. xiv.   *Of the First and Second Natural Laws, and of Contracts.*
"The right of nature," which writers commonly call *jus naturale,* is the liberty each man hath to use his own power as he will himself, for the preservation of his own nature; that is to say, of his own life; and consequently, of doing anything which in his own judgment and reason he shall conceive to be the aptest means thereunto.

By "liberty," is understood, according to the proper signification of the word, the absence of external impediments: which impediments may oft take away part of a man's power to do what he would; but cannot hinder him from using the power left him, according as his judgment and reason shall dictate to him.

A "law of nature," *lex naturalis,* is a precept or general rule, found out by reason, by which a man is forbidden to do that which is destructive of his life, or taketh away the means of preserving the same; and to omit that by which he thinketh it may be best preserved. For though they that speak of this subject, use to confound *jus* and *lex*, "right" and "law," yet they ought to be distinguished; because "right" consisteth in liberty to do or to forbear; whereas "law" determineth and bindeth to one of them; so that law and right differ as much as obligation and liberty, which in one and the same matter are inconsistent.

And because the condition of man, as hath been declared in the precedent chapter, is a condition of war of every one against every one, in which case every one is governed by his own reason, and there is nothing he can make use of that may not be a help unto him in preserving his life against his enemies, it followeth that in such a condition every man has a right to everything, even to one another's body. And therefore, as long as this natural right of every man to everything endureth, there can be no security to any man, how strong or wise soever he be, of living out the time which nature ordinarily alloweth men to live. And consequently it is a precept, or general rule of reason, "that every man ought to endeavor peace, as far as he has hope of obtaining it; and when he cannot obtain it, that he may seek and use all helps and advantages of war." The first branch of which rule containeth the first and fundamental law of nature; which is, "to seek peace, and follow it." The second, the sum of the right of nature: which is, "by all means we can, to defend ourselves."

From this fundamental law of nature, by which men are commanded to endeavor peace, is derived this second law: "that a man be willing, when others are so too, as far-forth as for peace and defence of himself he shall think it necessary, to lay down this right to all things, and be contented with so much liberty against other men as he would allow other men against himself." For as long as every man holdeth this right of doing anything he liketh, so long are all men in the condition of war. But if other men will not lay down their right, as well as he, then there is no reason for any one to divest himself of his: for that were to expose himself to prey, which no man is bound to, rather than to dispose himself to peace. This is that law of the Gospel: "whatsoever you require that others should do to you, that do ye to them." And that law of all men, *quod tibi fieri non vis, alteri ne feceris.*

To lay down a man's right to anything is to divest himself of the liberty of hindering another of the benefit of his own right to the same. For he that renounceth or passeth away his right, giveth not to any other man a right which he had not before, because there is nothing to which every man had not right by nature, but only standeth out of his way, that he may enjoy his own original right, without hindrance from him; not without hindrance from another. So that the effect which redoundeth to one man, by another man's defect of right, is but so much diminution of impediments to the use of his own right original.

Right is laid aside either by simply renouncing it or by transferring it to another. By simply renouncing, when he cares not to whom the benefit thereof redoundeth. By transferring, when he intendeth the benefit thereof to some certain person or persons. And when a man hath in either manner abandoned or granted away his right, then is he said to be obliged, or bound, not to hinder those to whom such right is granted, or abandoned, from the benefit of it: and that he ought, and it is his duty, not to make void that voluntary act of his own: and that such hindrance is injustice, and injury, as being *sine jure*, the right being before renounced, or transferred. So that injury, or injustice, in the controversies of the world is somewhat like to that which in the disputations of scholars is called absurdity. For as it is there called an absurdity to contradict what one maintained in the beginning: so in the world it is called injustice and injury voluntarily to undo that which from the beginning he had voluntarily done. The way by which a man either simply renounceth or transferreth his right, is a declaration, or signification, by some voluntary and sufficient sign, or signs, that he doth so renounce or transfer, or hath so renounced or transferred the same, to him that accepteth it. And these signs are either words only, or actions only; or, as it happeneth most often, both words and actions. And the same are the bonds by which men are bound, and obliged: bonds that have their strength, not from their own nature, for nothing is more easily broken than a man's word, but from fear of some evil consequence upon the rupture.

Whensoever a man transferreth his right, or renounceth it, it is either in consideration of some right reciprocally transferred to himself, or for some other good he hopeth for thereby. For it is a voluntary act: and of the voluntary acts of every man, the object is some good to himself. And therefore there be some rights which no man can be understood by any words, or other signs, to have abandoned or transferred. As first a man cannot lay down the right of resisting them that assault him by force to take away his life; because he cannot be understood to aim thereby at any good to himself. The same may be said of wounds, and chains, and imprisonment; both because there is no benefit consequent to such patience, as there is to the patience of suffering another to be wounded or imprisoned, as also because a man cannot tell, when he seeth men proceed against him by violence, whether they intend his death or not. And lastly the motive and end for which this renouncing and transferring of right is introduced, is nothing else but the security of a man's person, in his life and in the means of so preserving life, as not to be weary of it. And therefore if a man by words, or other signs, seem to despoil himself of the end for which those signs were intended, he is not to be understood as if he meant it, or that it was his will, but that he was ignorant of how such words and actions were to be interpreted.

The mutual transferring of right is that which men call "contract."

A covenant not to defend myself from force, by force, is always void. For, as I have shown before, no man can transfer or lay down his right to save himself from death, wounds, and imprisonment, the avoiding whereof is the only end of laying down any right; and therefore the promise of not resisting force, in no covenant transferreth any right, nor is obliging. For though a man may covenant thus, "unless I do so, or so, kill me," he cannot covenant thus, "unless I do so, or so, I will not resist you when you come to kill me." For man by nature chooseth the lesser evil, which is danger of death in resisting, rather than the greater, which is certain and present death in not resisting. And this is granted to be true by all men, in that they lead criminals to execution and prison with armed men, notwithstanding that such criminals have consented to the law by which they are condemned. A covenant to accuse oneself, without assurance of pardon, is likewise invalid. For in the condition of nature, where every man is judge, there is no place for accusation: and in the civil state, the accusation is followed with punishment, which being force, a man is not obliged not to resist. The same is also true of the accusation of those by whose condemnation a man falls into misery; as of a father, wife, or benefactor. For the testimony of such an accuser, if it be not willingly given, is presumed to be corrupted by nature, and therefore not to be received: and where a man's testimony is not to be credited, he is not bound to give it. Also accusations upon torture are not to be reputed as testimonies. For torture is to be used but as means of conjecture and light, in the further examination and search of truth; and what is in that case confessed, tendeth to the ease of him that is tortured, not to the informing

of the torturers, and therefore ought not to have the credit of
a sufficient testimony; for whether he deliver himself by true or
false accusation, he does it by the right of preserving his own life.

The force of words being, as I have formerly noted, too weak to
hold men to the performance of their covenants, there are in man's
nature but two imaginable helps to strengthen it. And those are
either a fear of the consequence of breaking their word, or a glory
or pride in appearing not to need to break it. This latter is a
generosity too rarely found to be presumed on, especially in the
pursuers of wealth, command, or sensual pleasure, which are the
greatest part of mankind. The passion to be reckoned upon is
fear, whereof there be two very general objects: one, the power
of spirits invisible; the other, the power of those men they shall
therein offend. Of these two, though the former be the greater
power, yet the fear of the latter is commonly the greater fear. The
fear of the former is in every man his own religion, which hath
place in the nature of man before civil society. The latter hath
not so, at least not place enough to keep men to their promises;
because in the condition of mere nature, the inequality of power
is not discerned, but by the event of battle. So that before the
time of civil society, or in the interruption thereof by war, there is
nothing can strengthen a covenant of peace agreed on, against the
temptations of avarice, ambition, lust, or other strong desire, but
the fear of that invisible power, which they every one worship as
God, and fear as a revenger of their perfidy. All therefore that
can be done between two men not subject to civil power, is to
put one another to swear by the God he feareth, which "swearing,"
or "oath," is "a form of speech added to a promise; by which he
that promiseth, signifieth that unless he perform, he renounceth
the mercy of his God, or calleth to Him for vengeance on himself."
Such was the heathen form, "Let Jupiter kill me else, as I kill
this beast." So is our form, "I shall do thus, and thus, so help
me God." And this, with the rites and ceremonies which every
one useth in his own religion, that the fear of breaking faith might
be the greater.

By this it appears that an oath taken according to any other
form, or rite, than his that sweareth, is in vain, and no oath: and
that there is no swearing by anything which the swearer thinks not
God. For though men have sometimes used to swear by their
kings, for fear, or flattery; yet they would have it thereby understood, they attributed to them divine honor. And that swearing
unnecessarily by God, is but profaning of His name: and swearing
by other things as men do in common discourse, is not swearing,

but an impious custom, gotten by too much vehemence of talking.

It appears also that the oath adds nothing to the obligation. For a covenant, if lawful, binds in the sight of God, without the oath, as much as with it: if unlawful, bindeth not at all; though it be confirmed with an oath.

Ch. xv.   *Of other Laws of Nature.*

From that law of nature, by which we are obliged to transfer to another such rights, as being retained, hinder the peace of mankind, there followeth a third; which is this, "that men perform their covenants made;" without which, covenants are in vain, and but empty words; and the right of all men to all things remaining, we are still in the condition of war.

And in this law of nature consisteth the fountain and original of justice. For where no covenant hath preceded, there hath no right been transferred, and every man has right to everything; and consequently, no action can be unjust. But when a covenant is made, then to break it is unjust: and the definition of injustice is no other than the not performance of covenant. And whatsoever is not unjust is just.

But because covenants of mutual trust, where there is a fear of not performance on either part, as hath been said in the former chapter, are invalid, though the original of justice be the making of covenants, yet injustice actually there can be none, till the cause of such fear be taken away; which while men are in the natural condition of war cannot be done. Therefore before the names of just and unjust can have place, there must be some coercive power to compel men equally to the performance of their covenants, by the terror of some punishment, greater than the benefit they expect by the breach of their covenant; and to make good that propriety, which by mutual contract men acquire, in recompense of the universal right they abandon: and such power there is none before the erection of a commonwealth. And this is also to be gathered out of the ordinary definition of justice in the schools: for they say that justice is the constant will of giving to every man his own. And therefore where there is no "own," that is no propriety, there is no injustice; and where there is no coercive power erected, that is, where there is no commonwealth, there is no propriety, all men having right to all things: therefore where there is no commonwealth, there nothing is unjust. So that the nature of justice consisteth in keeping of valid covenants; but the validity of covenants begins not but with the constitution of a civil power, sufficient to compel men to keep them; and then it is also that propriety begins.

The fool hath said in his heart, there is no such thing as justice; and sometimes also with his tongue; seriously alleging that every man's conservation, and contentment, being committed to his own care, there could be no reason why every man might not do what he thought conduced thereunto: and therefore also to make, or not make, keep, or not keep covenants, was not against reason, when it conduced to one's benefit. He does not therein deny that there be covenants; and that they are sometimes broken, sometimes kept, and that such breach of them may be called injustice, and the observance of them justice; but he questioneth whether injustice, taking away the fear of God, for the same fool hath said in his heart there is no God, may not sometimes stand with that reason which dictateth to every man his own good; and particularly then, when it conduceth to such a benefit as shall put a man in a condition to neglect not only the dispraise, and revilings, but also the power of other men. The kingdom of God is gotten by violence; but what if it could be gotten by unjust violence? were it against reason so to get it, when it is impossible to receive hurt by it? and if it be not against reason, it is not against justice; or else justice is not to be approved for good. From such reasoning as this, successful wickedness hath obtained the name of virtue; and some that in all other things have disallowed the violation of faith, yet have allowed it when it is for the getting of a kingdom. And the heathen that believed that Saturn was deposed by his son Jupiter, believed nevertheless the same Jupiter to be the avenger of injustice; somewhat like to a piece of law in Coke's "Commentaries on Littleton;" where he says, if the right heir of the crown be attainted of treason, yet the crown shall descend to him, and *eo instante* the attainder be void: from which instances a man will be very prone to infer that when the heir apparent of a kingdom shall kill him that is in possession, though his father, you may call it injustice, or by what other name you will; yet it can never be against reason, seeing all the voluntary actions of men tend to the benefit of themselves; and those actions are most reasonable that conduce most to their ends. This specious reasoning is nevertheless false.

For the question is not of promises mutual, where there is no security of performance on either side; as when there is no civil power erected over the parties promising; for such promises are no covenants: but either where one of the parties has performed already, or where there is a power to make him perform, there is the question whether it be against reason, that is, against the benefit of the other to perform or not. And I say it is not against reason. For the manifestation whereof we are to consider; first, that when a man doth a thing, which notwithstanding anything can be foreseen and reckoned on, tendeth to his own destruction, howsoever some accident which he could not expect, arriving may turn it to his benefit, yet such events do not make it reasonably or wisely done. Secondly, that in a condition of war, wherein every man to every man, for want of a common power to keep them all in awe, is an enemy, there is no man who can hope by his own strength, or wit, to defend himself from destruction, without the help of confederates; where every one expects the same defence by the confederation that any one else does: and therefore he which declares he thinks it reason to deceive those that help him, can in reason expect no other means of safety than what can be had from his own single power. He therefore that breaketh his covenant, and consequently declareth that he thinks he may with reason do so, cannot be received into any society that unite themselves for peace and defence, but by the error of them that receive him; nor when he is received, be retained in it, without seeing the danger of their error; which errors a man cannot reasonably reckon upon as the means of his security; and therefore if he be left, or cast out of society, he perisheth; and if he live in society, it is by the errors of other men, which he could not foresee, nor reckon upon; and consequently against the reason of his preservation; and so, as all men that contribute not to his destruction, forbear him only out of ignorance of what is good for themselves.

As for the instance of gaining the secure and perpetual felicity of heaven, by any way, it is frivolous: there being but one way imaginable; and that is not breaking, but keeping of covenant.

And for the other instance of attaining sovereignty by rebellion; it is manifest that though the event follow, yet because it cannot reasonably be expected, but rather the contrary, and because by gaining it so others are taught to gain the same in like manner, the attempt thereof is against reason. Justice therefore, that is to say, keeping of covenant, is a rule of reason, by which we are forbidden to do anything destructive to our life; and consequently a law of nature.

There be some that proceed further; and will not have the law of nature to be those rules which conduce to the preservation of man's life on earth; but to the attaining of an eternal felicity after death; to which they think the breach of government may conduce, and consequently be just and reasonable; such are they that think it a work of merit to kill, or depose, or rebel against the sovereign power constituted over them by their own consent. But because there is no natural knowledge of man's estate after death, much less of the reward that is then to be given to breach of faith, but only a belief grounded upon other men's saying that they know it supernaturally, or that they know those that knew them that knew others that knew it supernaturally, breach of faith cannot be called a precept of reason or nature.

Others, that allow for a law of nature the keeping of faith, do nevertheless make exception of certain persons; as heretics, and such as use not to perform their covenant to others; and this also is against reason. For if any fault of a man be sufficient to discharge our covenant made, the same ought in reason to have been sufficient to have hindered the making of it.

These are the laws of nature, dictating peace, for a means of the conservation of men in multitudes; and which only concern the doctrine of civil society. There be other things tending to the destruction of particular men; as drunkenness, and all other parts of intemperance; which may therefore also be reckoned amongst those things which the law of nature hath forbidden; but are not necessary to be mentioned, nor are pertinent enough to this place.

And though this may seem too subtle a deduction of the laws of nature to be taken notice of by all men, whereof the most part are too busy in getting food, and the rest too negligent to understand, yet to leave all men inexcusable, they have been contracted into one easy sum, intelligible even to the meanest capacity; and that is, "Do not that to another, which thou wouldst not have done to thyself;" which showeth him that he has no more to do in learning the laws of nature, but when weighing the actions of other men with his own, they seem too heavy, he put them into the other part of the balance, and his own into their place, that his own passions and self-love may add nothing to the weight; and then there is none of these laws of nature that will not appear unto him very reasonable.

The laws of nature oblige *in foro interno*—that is to say, they bind to a desire they should take place; but *in foro externo*—that is, to the putting them in act, not always. For he that should be modest, and tractable, and perform all he promises, in such time and place where no man else should do so, should but make himself a prey to others, and procure his own certain ruin, contrary to the ground of all laws of nature, which tend to nature's preservation.

And again, he that having sufficient security that others shall observe the same laws towards him, observes them not himself, seeketh not peace, but war; and consequently the destruction of his nature by violence.

And whatsoever laws bind *in foro interno*, may be broken, not only by a fact contrary to the law, but also by a fact according to it, in case a man think it contrary. For though his action in this case be according to the law, yet his purpose was against the law; which, where the obligation is *in foro interno*, is a breach.

The laws of nature are immutable and eternal; for injustice, ingratitude, arrogance, pride, iniquity, acception of persons, and the rest, can never be made lawful. For it can never be that war shall preserve life, and peace destroy it.

The same laws, because they oblige only to a desire and endeavor, I mean an unfeigned and constant endeavor, are easy to be observed. For in that they require nothing but endeavor, he that endeavoreth their performance, fulfilleth them; and he that fulfilleth the law, is just.

And the science of them is the true and only moral philosophy. For moral philosophy is nothing else but the science of what is good and evil, in the conversation and society of mankind. "Good" and "evil" are names that signify our appetites and aversions; which in different tempers, customs, and doctrines of men, are different: and divers men differ not only in their judgment, on the senses of what is pleasant and unpleasant to the taste, smell, hearing, touch, and sight; but also of what is conformable or disagreeable to reason, in the actions of common life. Nay, the same man, in divers times, differs from himself; and one time praiseth, that is, calleth good, what another time he dispraiseth, and calleth evil: from whence arise disputes, controversies, and at last war. And therefore so long as a man is in the condition of mere nature, which is a condition of war, his private appetite is the measure of good and evil: and consequently all men agree on this, that peace is good, and therefore also the way or means of peace, which, as I have showed before, are "justice," "gratitude," "modesty," "equity," "mercy," and the rest of the laws of nature, are good; that is to say, moral virtues; and their contrary vices, evil. Now the science of virtue and vice is moral philosophy; and therefore the true doctrine of the laws of nature is the true moral philosophy. But the writers of moral philosophy, though they acknowledge the same virtues and vices, yet not seeing wherein consisted their goodness, nor that they come to be praised as the means of peaceable, sociable, and comfortable living, place them in a mediocrity of passions: as if not the cause, but the degree of daring, made fortitude; or not the cause, but the quantity of a gift, made liberality.

These dictates of reason, men used to call by the name of laws, but improperly: for they are but conclusions or theorems concerning what conduceth to the conservation and defence of themselves: whereas law, properly, is the word of him that by right hath command over others. But yet if we consider the same theorems as delivered in the word of God, that by right commandeth all things, then are they properly called laws.

2. The Origin and Nature of the State [1]

Ch. xvii.   *Of the Causes, Generation, and Definition of a Commonwealth.*

The final cause, end, or design of men, who naturally love liberty, and dominion over others, in the introduction of that restraint upon themselves, in which we see them live in commonwealths, is the foresight of their own preservation, and of a more contented life thereby; that is to say, of getting themselves out from that miserable condition of war, which is necessarily consequent, as hath been shown in chapter xiii, to the natural passions of men, when there is no visible power to keep them in awe, and tie them by fear of punishment to the performance of their covenants, and observation of those laws of nature set down in the fourteenth and fifteenth chapters.

For the laws of nature, as "justice," "equity," "modesty," "mercy," and, in sum, "doing to others as we would be done to," of themselves, without the terror of some power to cause them to be observed, are contrary to our natural passions, that carry us to partiality, pride, revenge, and the like. And covenants, without the sword, are but words, and of no strength to secure a man at all. Therefore notwithstanding the laws of nature, which every one hath then kept, when he has the will to keep them, when he can do it safely, if there be no power erected, or not great enough for our security, every man will and may lawfully rely on his own strength and art, for caution against all other men. And in all places where men have lived by small families, to rob and spoil one another has been a trade, and so far from being reputed against the law of nature, that the greater spoils they gained, the greater was their honor; and men observed no other laws therein, but the laws of honor; that is, to abstain from cruelty, leaving to

[1] Part II, ch. xvii.

men their lives, and instruments of husbandry. And as small families did then, so now do cities and kingdoms, which are but greater families, for their own security, enlarge their dominions, upon all pretences of danger, and fear of invasion, or assistance that may be given to invaders, and endeavor as much as they can to subdue or weaken their neighbors, by open force and secret arts, for want of other caution, justly; and are remembered for it in after ages with honor.

Nor is it the joining together of a small number of men that gives them this security; because in small numbers, small additions on the one side or the other make the advantage of strength so great as is sufficient to carry the victory; and therefore gives encouragement to an invasion. The multitude sufficient to confide in for our security is not determined by any certain number, but by comparison with the enemy we fear; and is then sufficient, when the odds of the enemy is not of so visible and conspicuous moment to determine the event of war, as to move him to attempt.

And be there never so great a multitude; yet if their actions be directed according to their particular judgments and particular appetites, they can expect thereby no defence, nor protection. neither against a common enemy, nor against the injuries of one another. For being distracted in opinions concerning the best use and application of their strength, they do not help but hinder one another; and reduce their strength by mutual opposition to nothing: whereby they are easily, not only subdued by a very few that agree together; but also when there is no common enemy, they make war upon each other, for their particular interests. For if we could suppose a great multitude of men to consent in the observation of justice, and other laws of nature, without a common power to keep them all in awe, we might as well suppose all mankind to do the same; and then there neither would be nor need to be any civil government or commonwealth at all; because there would be peace without subjection.

Nor is it enough for the security, which men desire should last all the time of their life, that they be governed and directed by one judgment, for a limited time: as in one battle, or one war. For though they obtain a victory by their unanimous endeavor against a foreign enemy; yet afterwards, when either they have no common enemy, or he that by one part is held for an enemy is by another part held for a friend, they must needs by the difference of their interests dissolve, and fall again into a war amongst themselves.

It is true that certain living creatures, as bees and ants, live sociably one with another, which are therefore by Aristotle numbered amongst political creatures; and yet have no other direction than their particular judgments and appetites; nor speech, whereby one of them can signify to another what he thinks expedient for the common benefit: and therefore some man may perhaps desire to know why mankind cannot do the same.   To which I answer,

First, that men are continually in competition for honor and dignity, which these creatures are not; and consequently amongst men there ariseth on that ground, envy and hatred, and finally war; but amongst these not so.

Secondly, that amongst these creatures, the common good differeth not from the private; and being by nature inclined to their private, they procure thereby the common benefit.   But man, whose joy consisteth in comparing himself with other men, can relish nothing but what is eminent.

Thirdly, that these creatures, having not, as man, the use of reason, do not see, nor think they see any fault in the administration of their common business; whereas amongst men, there are very many that think themselves wiser and abler to govern the public better than the rest; and these strive to reform and innovate, one this way, another that way, and thereby bring it into distraction and civil war.

Fourthly, that these creatures, though they have some use of voice, in making known to one another their desires and other affections; yet they want that art of words by which some men can represent to others that which is good in the likeness of evil, and evil in the likeness of good, and augment or diminish the apparent greatness of good and evil; discontenting men, and troubling their peace at their pleasure.

Fifthly, irrational creatures cannot distinguish between injury and damage; and therefore as long as they be at ease, they are not offended with their fellows: whereas man is then most troublesome when he is most at ease; for then it is that he loves to show his wisdom, and control the actions of them that govern the commonwealth.

Lastly, the agreement of these creatures is natural; that of men is by covenant only, which is artificial: and therefore it is no wonder if there be somewhat else required, besides covenant, to make their agreement constant and lasting; which is a common power, to keep them in awe, and to direct their actions to the common benefit.

The only way to erect such a common power as may be able to defend them from the invasion of foreigners and the injuries of one another, and thereby to secure them in such sort as that by their own industry, and by the fruits of the earth, they may nourish themselves and live contentedly, is to confer all their power and strength upon one man, or upon one assembly of men, that may reduce all their wills, by plurality of voices, unto one will: which is as much as to say, to appoint one man, or assembly of men, to bear their person; and every one to own and acknowledge himself to be author of whatsoever he that so beareth their person shall act, or cause to be acted, in those things which concern the common peace and safety; and therein to submit their wills, every one to his will, and their judgments to his judgment. This is more than consent, or concord; it is a real unity of them all in one and the same person, made by covenant of every man with every man, in such manner as if every man should say to every man, "I authorize and give up my right of governing myself, to this man or to this assembly of men, on this condition, that thou give up thy right to him and authorize all his actions in like manner." This done, the multitude so united in one person is called a "commonwealth," in Latin *civitas*. This is the generation of that great leviathan, or rather, to speak more reverently, of that mortal god, to which we owe under the immortal God, our peace and defence. For by this authority, given him by every particular man in the commonwealth, he hath the use of so much power and strength conferred on him, that by terror thereof, he is enabled to perform the wills of them all, to peace at home, and mutual aid against their enemies abroad. And in him consisteth the essence of the commonwealth; which, to define it, is "one person, of whose acts a great multitude, by mutual covenants one with another, have made themselves every one the author, to the end he may use the strength and means of them all, as he shall think expedient, for their peace and common defence."

And he that carrieth this person is called sovereign, and said to have sovereign power; and every one besides, his subject.

The attaining to this sovereign power is by two ways. One, by natural force; as when a man maketh his children to submit themselves, and their children, to his government, as being able to destroy them if they refuse; or by war subdueth his enemies to his will, giving them their lives on that condition. The other is when men agree amongst themselves to submit to some man, or assembly of men, voluntarily, on confidence to be protected by him against all others. This latter may be called a political commonwealth, or commonwealth by institution; and the former, a commonwealth by acquisition. And first, I shall speak of a commonwealth by institution.

3. Sovereignty [1]

Ch. xviii. *Of the Rights of Sovereignty by Institution.*

A commonwealth is said to be instituted when a multitude of men do agree and covenant, every one with every one, that to whatsoever man or assembly of men shall be given by the major part the right to present the person of them all, that is to say, to be their representative; every one, as well he that voted for it as he that voted against it, shall authorize all the actions and judgments of that man or assembly of men in the same manner as if they were his own, to the end to live peaceably amongst themselves and be protected against other men.

From this institution of a commonwealth are derived all the rights and faculties of him, or them, on whom sovereign power is conferred by the consent of the people assembled.

First, because they covenant, it is to be understood, they are not obliged by former covenant to anything repugnant hereunto. And consequently that they have already instituted a commonwealth, being thereby bound by covenant to own the actions and judgments of one, cannot lawfully make a new covenant amongst themselves to be obedient to any other in any thing whatsoever, without his permission. And therefore, they that are subjects to a monarch, cannot without his leave cast off monarchy, and return to the confusion of a disunited multitude; nor transfer their person from him that beareth it, to another man, or other assembly of men: for they are bound, every man to every man, to own and be reputed author of all that he that already is their sovereign shall do, and judge fit to be done: so that any one man dissenting, all the rest should break their covenant made to that man, which is injustice: and they have also every man given the sovereignty to him that beareth their person; and therefore if they depose him, they take from him that which is his own, and so again it is injustice. Besides, if he that attempteth to depose his sovereign be killed, or punished by him for such attempt, he is author of his own punishment, as being by the institution author of all his sovereign shall do: and because it is injustice for a man to do anything for which he may be punished by his own authority, he is also upon that title unjust. And whereas some men have pretended for their disobedience to their sovereign, a new covenant, made not with men, but with God, this also is unjust: for there is no covenant with God but by mediation of somebody that representeth God's person; which none doth but God's lieutenant, who hath

[1] Part II, ch. xviii.

the sovereignty under God. But this pretence of covenant with God is so evident a lie, even in the pretenders' own consciences, that it is not only an act of an unjust, but also of a vile and unmanly disposition.

Secondly, because the right of bearing the person of them all is given to him they make sovereign, by covenant only of one to another, and not of him to any of them, there can happen no breach of covenant on the part of the sovereign: and consequently none of his subjects, by any pretence of forfeiture, can be freed from his subjection. That he which is made sovereign maketh no covenant with his subjects beforehand, is manifest; because either he must make it with the whole multitude, as one party to the covenant, or he must make a several covenant with every man. With the whole, as one party, it is impossible; because as yet they are not one person; and if he make so many several covenants as there be men, those covenants after he hath the sovereignty are void; because what act soever can be pretended by any one of them for breach thereof, is the act both of himself and of all the rest, because done in the person and by the right of every one of them in particular. Besides, if any one or more of them pretend a breach of the covenant made by the sovereign at his institution; and others, or one other of his subjects, or himself alone, pretend there was no such breach, there is in this case no judge to decide the controversy; it returns therefore to the sword again, and every man recovereth the right of protecting himself by his own strength, contrary to the design they had in the institution. It is therefore in vain to grant sovereignty by way of precedent covenant. The opinion that any monarch receiveth his power by covenant, that is to say, on condition, proceedeth from want of understanding this easy truth, that covenants being but words and breath, have no force to oblige, contain, constrain, or protect any man, but what they have from the public sword; that is, from the united hands of that man or assembly of men that hath the sovereignty, and whose actions are avouched by them all, and performed by the strength of them all, in him united. But when an assembly of men is made sovereign, then no man imagineth any such covenant to have passed in the institution; for no man is so dull as to say, for example, the people of Rome made a covenant with the Romans to hold the sovereignty on such or such conditions; which not performed, the Romans might lawfully depose the Roman people. That men see not the reason to be alike in a monarchy and in a popular government, proceedeth from the ambition of some that are kinder to the government of an assembly, whereof they may hope to participate, than of monarchy, which they despair to enjoy.

Thirdly, because the major part hath by consenting voices declared a sovereign, he that dissented must now consent with the rest, that is, be contented to avow all the actions he shall do, or else justly be destroyed by the rest. For if he voluntarily entered into the congregation of them that were assembled, he sufficiently declared thereby his will, and therefore tacitly covenanted to stand to what the major part should ordain: and therefore if he refuse to stand thereto, or make protestation against any of their decrees, he does contrary to his covenant, and therefore unjustly. And whether he be of the congregation or not, and whether his consent be asked or not, he must either submit to their degrees, or be left in the condition of war he was in before; wherein he might without injustice be destroyed by any man whatsoever.

Fourthly, because every subject is by this institution author of all the actions and judgments of the sovereign instituted, it follows that whatsoever he doth it can be no injury to any of his subjects, nor ought he to be by any of them accused of injustice. For he that doth anything by authority from another doth therein no injury to him by whose authority he acteth: but by this institution of a commonwealth every particular man is author of all the sovereign doth; and consequently, he that complaineth of injury from his sovereign complaineth of that whereof he himself is author, and therefore ought not to accuse any man but himself; no, nor himself of injury, because to do injury to one's self is impossible. It is true that they that have sovereign power may commit iniquity, but not injustice or injury in the proper signification.

Fifthly, and consequently to that which was said last, no man that hath sovereign power can justly be put to death, or otherwise in any manner by his subjects punished. For seeing every subject is author of the actions of his sovereign, he punisheth another for the actions committed by himself.

And because the end of this institution is the peace and defence of them all, and whosoever has right to the end has right to the means, it belongeth of right to whatsoever man or assembly that hath the sovereignty to be judge both of the means of peace and defence, and also of the hindrances and disturbances of the same, and to do whatsoever he shall think necessary to be done, both beforehand, for the preserving of peace and security, by prevention of discord at home and hostility from abroad; and, when peace and security are lost, for the recovery of the same. And therefore,

Sixthly, it is annexed to the sovereignty to be judge of what opinions and doctrines are averse and what conducing to peace; and consequently, on what occasions, how far, and what men are to be trusted withal, in speaking to multitudes of people, and who shall examine the doctrines of all books before they be published. For the actions of men proceed from their opinions, and in the well governing of opinions consisteth the well governing of men's actions, in order to their peace and concord. And though in matter of doctrine nothing ought to be regarded but the truth; yet this is not repugnant to regulating the same by peace. For doctrine repugnant to peace can be no more true than peace and concord can be against the law of nature. It is true that in a commonwealth, where, by the negligence or unskilfulness of governors and teachers, false doctrines are by time generally received, the contrary truths may be generally offensive. Yet the most sudden and rough bursting in of a new truth that can be, does never break the peace, but only sometimes awake the war. For those men that are so remissly governed, that they dare take up arms to defend or introduce an opinion, are still in war; and their condition not peace, but only a cessation of arms for fear of one another; and they live, as it were, in the precincts of battle continually. It belongeth therefore to him that hath the sovereign power to be judge, or constitute all judges, of opinions and doctrines, as a thing necessary to peace, thereby to prevent discord and civil war.

Seventhly, is annexed to the sovereignty, the whole power of prescribing the rules whereby every man may know what goods he may enjoy and what actions he may do, without being molested by any of his fellow-subjects; and this is it men call "propriety." For before constitution of sovereign power, as hath already been shown, all men had right to all things, which necessarily causeth war: and therefore this propriety, being necessary to peace, and depending on sovereign power, is the act of that power, in order to the public peace. These rules of propriety, or *meum* and *tuum*, and of good, evil, lawful, and unlawful in the actions of subjects, are the civil laws; that is to say, the laws of each commonwealth in particular; though the name of civil law be now restrained to the ancient civil laws of the city of Rome, which being the head of a great part of the world, her laws at that time were in these parts the civil law.

Eighthly, is annexed to the sovereignty, the right of judicature, that is to say, of hearing and deciding all controversies which may arise concerning law, either civil or natural, or concerning fact. For without the decision of controversies, there is no pro-

tection of one subject against the injuries of another; the laws
concerning *meum* and *tuum* are in vain, and to every man remaineth, from the natural and necessary appetite of his own conservation, the right of protecting himself by his private strength,
which is the condition of war, and contrary to the end for which
every commonwealth is instituted.

Ninthly, is annexed to the sovereignty, the right of making war
and peace with other nations and commonwealths, that is to say,
of judging when it is for the public good, and how great forces are
to be assembled, armed, and paid for that end, and to levy money
upon the subjects to defray the expenses thereof. For the power
by which the people are to be defended consisteth in their armies,
and the strength of an army, in the union of their strength under
one command, which command the sovereign instituted, therefore
hath; because the command of the "militia," without other
institution, maketh him that hath it sovereign. And therefore
whosoever is made general of an army, he that hath the sovereign
power is always generalissimo.

Tenthly, is annexed to the sovereignty, the choosing of all counsellors, ministers, magistrates, and officers, both in peace and war.
For seeing the sovereign is charged with the end, which is the common peace and defence, he is understood to have power to use
such means as he shall think most fit for his discharge.

Eleventhly, to the sovereign is committed the power of rewarding with riches or honor, and of punishing with corporal or
pecuniary punishment, or with ignominy, every subject according
to the law he hath formerly made; or if there be no law made,
according as he shall judge most to conduce to the encouraging
of men to serve the commonwealth, or deterring of them from doing
disservice to the same.

Lastly, considering what value men are naturally apt to set
upon themselves, what respect they look for from others, and how
little they value other men, from whence continually arise amongst
them, emulation, quarrels, factions, and at last war, to the destroying of one another, and diminution of their strength against a
common enemy, it is necessary that there be laws of honor, and
a public rate of the worth of such men as have deserved or are
able to deserve well of the commonwealth; and that there be
force in the hands of some or other, to put those laws in execution.
But it hath already been shown that not only the whole "militia,"
or forces of the commonwealth, but also the judicature of all controversies, is annexed to the sovereignty. To the sovereign therefore it belongeth also to give titles of honor; and to appoint what

order of place and dignity each man shall hold; and what signs of respect, in public or private meetings, they shall give to one another.

These are the rights which make the essence of sovereignty, and which are the marks whereby a man may discern in what man, or assembly of men, the sovereign power is placed and resideth. For these are incommunicable, and inseparable. The power to coin money, to dispose of the estate and persons of infant heirs, to have preëmption in markets, and all other statute prerogatives, may be transferred by the sovereign, and yet the power to protect his subjects be retained. But if he transfer the "militia," he retains the judicature in vain, for want of execution of the laws: of if he grant away the power of raising money, the "militia" is in vain; or if he give away the government of doctrines, men will be frighted into rebellion with the fear of spirits. And so if we consider any one of the said rights, we shall presently see that the holding of all the rest will produce no effect in the conservation of peace and justice, the end for which all commonwealths are instituted. And this division is it whereof it is said, "a kingdom divided in itself cannot stand:" for unless this division precede, division into opposite armies can never happen. If there had not first been an opinion received of the greatest part of England that these powers were divided between the King, and the Lords, and the House of Commons, the people had never been divided and fallen into this civil war, first between those that disagreed in politics, and after between the dissenters about the liberty of religion; which have so instructed men in this point of sovereign right, that there be few now in England that do not see that these rights are inseparable, and will be so generally acknowledged at the next return of peace, and so continue, till their miseries are forgotten; and no longer, except the vulgar be better taught than they have hitherto been.

And because they are essential and inseparable rights, it follows necessarily that in whatsoever words any of them seem to be granted away, yet if the sovereign power itself be not in direct terms renounced, and the name of sovereign no more given by the grantees to him that grants them, the grant is void: for when he has granted all he can, if we grant back the sovereignty, all is restored, as inseparably annexed thereunto.

This great authority being indivisible and inseparably annexed to the sovereignty, there is little ground for the opinion of them that say of sovereign kings, though they be *singulis majores*, of greater power than every one of their subjects, yet they be *universis minores,* of less power than them all together. For if by "all together" they mean not the collective body as one person, then "all together" and "every one" signify the same; and the speech is absurd. But if by "all together," they understand them as one person, which person the sovereign bears, then the power of all together is the same with the sovereign's power; and so again the speech is absurd: which absurdity they see well enough, when the sovereignty is in an assembly of the people; but in a monarch they see it not; and yet the power of sovereignty is the same in whomsoever it be placed.

And as the power, so also the honor of the sovereign, ought to be greater than that of any or all the subjects. For in the sovereignty is the fountain of honor. The dignities of lord, earl, duke, and prince are his creatures. As in the presence of the master the servants are equal, and without any honor at all; so are the subjects in the presence of the sovereign. And though they shine some more, some less, when they are out of his sight; yet in his presence, they shine no more than the stars in the presence of the sun.

But a man may here object that the condition of subjects is very miserable; as being obnoxious to the lusts, and other irregular passions of him or them that have so unlimited a power in their hands. And commonly they that live under a monarch, think it the fault of monarchy; and they that live under the government of democracy, or other sovereign assembly, attribute all the inconvenience to that form of commonwealth; whereas the power in all forms, if they be perfect enough to protect them, is the same: not considering that the state of man can never be without some incommodity or other; and that the greatest, that in any form of government can possibly happen to the people in general, is scarce sensible, in respect of the miseries and horrible calamities that accompany a civil war, or that dissolute condition of masterless men, without subjection to laws and a coercive power to tie their hands from rapine and revenge: nor considering that the greatest pressure of sovereign governors proceedeth not from any delight or profit they can expect in the damage or weakening of their subjects, in whose vigor consisteth their own strength and glory; but in the restiveness of themselves, that unwillingly contributing to their own defence, make it necessary for their governors to draw from them what they can in time of peace, that they may have means on any emergent occasion, or sudden need, to resist, or take advantage on their enemies. For all men are by nature provided of notable multiplying glasses, that is their passions and self-love, through which every little payment appeareth a great grievance; but are destitute of those prospective glasses, namely, moral and civil science, to see afar off the miseries that hang over them, and cannot without such payments be avoided.

4. The Kinds of State [1]

Ch. xix. *Of the Several Kinds of Commonwealth by Institution, and of Succession to the Sovereign Power.*

The difference of commonwealths consisteth in the difference of the sovereign, or the person representative of all and every one of the multitude. And because the sovereignty is either in one man, or in an assembly of more than one, and into that assembly either every man hath right to enter, or not every one but certain men distinguished from the rest, it is manifest there can be but three kinds of commonwealth. For the representative must needs be one man, or more: and if more, then it is the assembly of all, or but of a part. When the representative is one man, then is the commonwealth a monarchy: when an assembly of all that will come together, then it is a democracy, or popular commonwealth: when an assembly of a part only, then it is called an aristocracy. Other kind of commonwealth there can be none: for either one or more, or all, must have the sovereign power, which I have shown to be indivisible, entire.

There be other names of government in the histories and books of policy, as tyranny, and oligarchy: but they are not the names of other forms of government, but of the same forms misliked. For they that are discontented under monarchy call it tyranny; and they that are displeased with aristocracy call it oligarchy: so also they which find themselves grieved under a democracy, call it anarchy, which signifies want of government; and yet I think no man believes that want of government is any new kind of government; nor by the same reason ought they to believe that the government is of one kind when they like it, and another when they dislike it, or are oppressed by the governors.

It is manifest that men who are in absolute liberty may, if they please, give authority to one man to represent them every one; as well as give such authority to any assembly of men whatsoever; and consequently may subject themselves, if they think good, to a monarch as absolutely as to any other representative. Therefore, where there is already erected a sovereign power, there can be no other representative of the same people, but only to certain

[1] Part II, ch. xix (in part).

particular ends, by the sovereign limited. For that were to erect
two sovereigns; and every man to have his person represented by
two actors, that by opposing one another, must needs divide that
power, which, if men will live in peace, is indivisible, and thereby
reduce the multitude into the condition of war, contrary to the
end for which all sovereignty is instituted. And therefore as it
is absurd to think that a sovereign assembly, inviting the people
of their dominion to send up their deputies, with power to make
known their advice, or desires, should therefore hold such deputies
rather than themselves for the absolute representatives of the
people, so it is absurd also to think the same in a monarchy. And
I know not how this so manifest a truth should of late be so little
observed, that in a monarchy, he that had the sovereignty from
a descent of six hundred years, was alone called sovereign, had
the title of Majesty from every one of his subjects, and was unquestionably taken by them for their king, was notwithstanding never
considered as their representative; the name without contradiction
passing for the title of those men which at his command were
sent up by the people to carry their petitions, and give him, if he
permitted it, their advice. Which may serve as an admonition
for those that are the true and absolute representative of a people,
to instruct men in the nature of that office, and to take heed how
they admit of any other general representation upon any occasion
whatsoever, if they mean to discharge the trust committed to
them.

The difference between these three kinds of commonwealth
consisteth not in the difference of power; but in the difference of
convenience, or aptitude to produce the peace and security of the
people; for which end they were instituted. And to compare
monarchy with the other two, we may observe, first, that whosoever beareth the person of the people, or is one of that assembly
that bears it, beareth also his own natural person. And though he
be careful in his politic person to procure the common interest;
yet he is more or no less careful to procure the private good of
himself, his family, kindred, and friends, and for the most part,
if the public interest chance to cross the private, he prefers the
private: for the passions of men are commonly more potent than
their reason. From whence it follows that where the public
and private interest are most closely united, there is the public
most advanced. Now in monarchy, the private interest is the
same with the public. The riches, power, and honor of a monarch arise only from the riches, strength, and reputation of his
subjects. For no king can be rich, nor glorious, nor secure, whose

subjects are either poor, or contemptible, or too weak through
want or dissension, to maintain a war against their enemies:
whereas in a democracy, or aristocracy, the public prosperity confers not so much to the private fortune of one that is corrupt, or
ambitious, as doth many times a perfidious advice, a treacherous
action, or a civil war.

Secondly, that a monarch receiveth counsel of whom, when,
and where he pleaseth; and consequently may hear the opinion of
men versed in the matter about which he deliberates, of what rank
or quality soever, and as long before the time of action, and with
as much secrecy, as he will. But when a sovereign assembly has
need of counsel, none are admitted but such as have a right thereto
from the beginning: which for the most part are of those who have
been versed more in the acquisition of wealth than of knowledge;
and are to give their advice in long discourses, which may and do
commonly excite men to action, but not govern them in it. For
the understanding is by the flame of the passions never enlightened, but dazzled. Nor is there any place, or time, wherein an
assembly can receive counsel with secrecy, because of their own
multitude.

Thirdly, that the resolutions of a monarch are subject to no
other inconstancy than that of human nature; but in assemblies,
besides that of nature, there ariseth an inconstancy from the
number. For the absence of a few, that would have the resolution
once taken, continue firm, which may happen by security, negligence, or private impediments, or the diligent appearance of a
few of the contrary opinion, undoes to-day all that was concluded
yesterday.

Fourthly, that a monarch cannot disagree with himself, out
of envy or interest; but an assembly may; and that to such a height
as may produce a civil war.

Fifthly, that in monarchy there is this inconvenience: that any
subject, by the power of one man, for the enriching of a favorite
or flatterer, may be deprived of all he possesseth; which I confess
is a great and inevitable inconvenience. But the same may as
well happen where the sovereign power is an assembly: for their
power is the same; and they are as subject to evil counsel, and to be
seduced by orators, as a monarch by flatterers; and becoming one
another's flatterers, serve one another's covetousness and ambition
by turns. And whereas the favorites of monarchs are few, and
they have none else to advance but their own kindred, the favorites of an assembly are many; and the kindred much more numerous than of any monarch. Besides there is no favorite of a

monarch, which cannot as well succor his friends as hurt his
enemies; but orators, that is to say, favorites of sovereign assemblies, though they have great power to hurt, have little to save.
For to accuse requires less eloquence, such is man's nature, than
to excuse; and condemnation, than absolution more resembles
justice.

Sixthly, that it is an inconvenience in monarchy that the
sovereignty may descend upon an infant, or one that cannot discern between good and evil: and consisteth in this, that the use
of his power must be in the hand of another man, or of some
assembly of men, which are to govern by his right and in his name;
as curators and protectors of his person and authority. But to
say there is inconvenience in putting the use of the sovereign
power into the hand of a man, or an assembly of men, is to say
that all government is more inconvenient than confusion and civil
war. And therefore all the danger that can be pretended must
arise from the contention of those that for an office of so great
honor and profit may become competitors. To make it appear
that this inconvenience proceedeth not from that form of government we call monarchy, we are to consider that the precedent
monarch hath appointed who shall have the tuition of his infant
successor, either expressly by testament, or tacitly, by not controlling the custom in that case received: and then such inconvenience,
if it happen, is to be attributed, not to the monarchy, but to the
ambition and injustice of the subjects; which in all kinds of government where the people are not well instructed in their duty and
the rights of sovereignty, is the same. Or else the precedent monarch hath not at all taken order for such tuition; and then the law
of nature hath provided this sufficient rule, that the tuition shall
be in him that hath, by nature, most interest in the preservation
of the authority of the infant, and to whom least benefit can accrue
by his death or diminution. For seeing every man by nature
seeketh his own benefit and promotion, to put an infant into the
power of those that can promote themselves by his destruction,
or damage, is not tuition, but treachery. So that sufficient provision being taken against all just quarrel about the government
under a child, if any contention arise to the disturbance of the
public peace, it is not to be attributed to the form of monarchy,
but to the ambition of subjects, and ignorance of their duty. On
the other side, there is no great commonwealth, the sovereignty
whereof is in a great assembly, which is not, as to consultations
of peace and war, and making of laws, in the same condition as if
the government were in a child. For as a child wants the judg-

ment to dissent from counsel given him, and is thereby necessitated to take the advice of them, or him, to whom he is committed, so an assembly wanteth the liberty to dissent from the counsel of the major part, be it good or bad. And as a child has need of a tutor, or protector, to preserve his person and authority, so also, in great commonwealths, the sovereign assembly, in all great dangers and troubles, have need of *custodes libertatis*, that is of dictators, or protectors of their authority; which are as much as temporary monarchs, to whom for a time they may commit the entire exercise of their power; and have, at the end of that time, been oftener deprived thereof than infant kings, by their protectors, regents, or any other tutors.

5. Liberty [1]

Ch. xxi. *Of the Liberty of Subjects.*

Liberty, or freedom, signifieth, properly, the absence of opposition; by opposition, I mean external impediments of motion; and may be applied no less to irrational and inanimate creatures than to rational. For whatsoever is so tied, or environed, as it cannot move but within a certain space, which space is determined by the opposition of some external body, we say it hath not liberty to go further. And so of all living creatures whilst they are imprisoned, or restrained, with walls or chains; and of the water whilst it is kept in by banks or vessels, that otherwise would spread itself into a larger space, we use to say, they are not at liberty to move in such manner as without those external impediments they would. But when the impediment of motion is in the constitution of the thing itself, we use not to say, it wants the liberty, but the power to move; as when a stone lieth still, or a man is fastened to his bed by sickness.

And according to this proper and generally received meaning of the word, a freeman is he, that in those things, which by his strength and wit he is able to do, is not hindered to do what he has a will to. But when the words "free," and "liberty," are applied to anything but bodies, they are abused; for that which is not subject to motion, is not subject to impediment; and therefore, when it is said for example, the way is free, no liberty of the way is signified, but of those that walk in it without stop. And when we say a gift is free, there is not meant any liberty of the gift, but of the giver, that was not bound by any law or covenant to give it. So when we speak freely, it is not the liberty of

[1] Part II, ch. xxi.

voice, or pronunciation, but of the man, whom no law hath obliged to speak otherwise than he did. Lastly, from the use of the word "free-will," no liberty can be inferred of the will, desire, or inclination, but the liberty of the man; which consisteth in this, that he finds no stop in doing what he has the will, desire, or inclination to do.

Fear and liberty are consistent; as when a man throweth his goods into the sea for fear the ship should sink, he doth it nevertheless very willingly, and may refuse to do it if he will: it is therefore the action of one that was free; so a man sometimes pays his debt, only for fear of imprisonment, which because nobody hindered him from detaining, was the action of a man at liberty. And generally all actions which men do in commonwealths, for fear of the law, are actions which the doers had liberty to omit.

Liberty and necessity are consistent, as in the water that hath not only liberty, but a necessity of descending by the channel; so likewise in the actions which men voluntarily do: which, because they proceed from their will, proceed from liberty; and yet, because every act of man's will, and every desire and inclination proceedeth from some cause, and that from another cause, in a continual chain, whose first link is in the hand of God the first of all causes, proceed from necessity. So that to him that could see the connection of those causes, the necessity of all men's voluntary actions would appear manifest. And therefore God, that seeth and disposeth all things, seeth also that the liberty of man in doing what he will, is accompanied with the necessity of doing that which God will, and no more nor less. For though men may do many things which God does not command, nor is therefore author of them; yet they can have no passion nor appetite to anything, of which appetite God's will is not the cause. And did not His will assure the necessity of man's will, and consequently of all that on man's will dependeth, the liberty of men would be a contradiction and impediment to the omnipotence and liberty of God. And this shall suffice, as to the matter in hand, of that natural liberty, which only is properly called liberty.

But as men, for the attaining of peace, and conservation of themselves thereby, have made an artificial man, which we call a commonwealth; so also have they made artificial chains, called "civil laws," which they themselves, by mutual covenants, have fastened at one end to the lips of that man, or assembly, to whom they have given the sovereign power; and at the other end to their own ears. These bonds, in their own nature but weak, may nevertheless be made to hold, by the danger, though not by the difficulty of breaking them.

In relation to these bonds only it is that I am to speak now of the liberty of subjects. For seeing there is no commonwealth in the world wherein there be rules enough set down for the regulating of all the actions and words of men, as being a thing impossible; it followeth necessarily, that in all kinds of actions by the laws pretermitted, men have the liberty of doing what their own reasons shall suggest, for the most profitable to themselves. For if we take liberty in the proper sense for corporal liberty, that is to say, freedom from chains and prison, it were very absurd for men to clamor as they do for the liberty they so manifestly enjoy. Again, if we take liberty for an exemption from laws, it is no less absurd for men to demand as they do that liberty by which all other men may be masters of their lives. And yet, as absurd as it is, this is it they demand; not knowing that the laws are of no power to protect them, without a sword in the hands of a man, or men, to cause those laws to be put in execution. The liberty of a subject lieth therefore only in those things which in regulating their actions, the sovereign hath pretermitted: such as is the liberty to buy and sell, and otherwise contract with one another; to choose their own abode, their own diet, their own trade of life, and institute their children as they themselves think fit; and the like.

Nevertheless we are not to understand that by such liberty the sovereign power of life and death is either abolished or limited. For it has been already shown that nothing the sovereign representative can do to a subject, on what pretence soever, can properly be called injustice or injury; because every subject is author of every act the sovereign doth; so that he never wanteth right to anything, otherwise than as he himself is the subject of God, and bound thereby to observe the laws of nature. And therefore it may and doth often happen in commonwealths, that a subject may be put to death by the command of the sovereign power; and yet neither do the other wrong: as when Jephtha caused his daughter to be sacrificed; in which, and the like cases, he that so dieth had liberty to do the action, for which he is nevertheless without injury put to death. And the same holdeth also in a sovereign prince that putteth to death an innocent subject. For though the action be against the law of nature, as being contrary to equity, as was the killing of Uriah, by David; yet it was not an injury to Uriah, but to God. Not to Uriah, because the right to do what he pleased was given him by Uriah himself: and

yet to God, because David was God's subject, and prohibited all
iniquity by the law of nature: which distinction, David himself,
when he repented the fact, evidently confirmed, saying, "To thee
only have I sinned." In the same manner the people of Athens,
when they banished the most potent of their commonwealth for
ten years, thought they committed no injustice; and yet they never
questioned what crime he had done, but what hurt he would do:
nay they commanded the banishment of they knew not whom;
and every citizen bringing his oyster-shell into the market-place,
written with the name of him he desired should be banished,
without actually accusing him, sometimes banished an Aristides,
for his reputation of justice; and sometimes a scurrilous jester, as
Hyperbolus, to make a jest of it. And yet a man cannot say, the
sovereign people of Athens wanted right to banish them; or an
Athenian the liberty to jest or to be just.

The liberty whereof there is so frequent and honorable mention
in the histories and philosophy of the ancient Greeks and Romans,
and in the writings and discourse of those that from them have
received all their learning in the politics, is not the liberty of particular men, but the liberty of the commonwealth: which is the
same with that which every man then should have, if there were
no civil laws, nor commonwealth at all. And the effects of it
also be the same. For as amongst masterless men there is perpetual
war, of every man against his neighbor; no inheritance to transmit to the son, nor to expect from the father; no propriety of goods
or lands; no security; but a full and absolute liberty in every particular man: so in states and commonwealths not dependent on
one another, every commonwealth, not every man, has an absolute
liberty to do what it shall judge, that is to say, what that man,
or assembly that representeth it, shall judge most conducing to
their benefit. But withal, they live in the condition of a perpetual
war, and upon the confines of battle, with their frontiers armed,
and cannons planted against their neighbors round about. The
Athenians and Romans were free; that is, free commonwealths:
not that any particular men had the liberty to resist their own
representative; but that their representative had the liberty to
resist, or invade other people. There is written on the turrets of
the city of Lucca, in great characters, at this day, the word "Libertas;" yet no man can thence infer that a particular man has
more liberty, or immunity from the service of the commonwealth
there, than in Constantinople. Whether a commonwealth be
monarchical or popular, the freedom is still the same.

But it is an easy thing for men to be deceived by the specious name of liberty; and for want of judgment to distinguish, mistake that for their private inheritance and birthright, which is the right of the public only. And when the same error is confirmed by the authority of men in reputation for their writings on this subject, it is no wonder if it produce sedition, and change of government. In these western parts of the world, we are made to receive our opinions concerning the institution and rights of commonwealths, from Aristotle, Cicero, and other men, Greeks and Romans, that living under popular states, derived those rights, not from the principles of nature, but transcribed them into their books, out of the practice of their own commonwealths, which were popular; as the grammarians describe the rules of language out of the practice of the time; or the rules of poetry out of the poems of Homer and Virgil. And because the Athenians were taught, to keep them from desire of changing their government, that they were free men, and all that lived under monarchy were slaves; therefore Aristotle put it down in his *Politics* (lib. 6, cap. ii.): "In democracy, 'liberty' is to be supposed: for it is commonly held, that no man is 'free' in any other government." And as Aristotle, so Cicero and other writers have grounded their civil doctrine on the opinions of the Romans, who were taught to hate monarchy, at first, by them that having deposed their sovereign, shared amongst them the sovereignty of Rome; and afterwards by their successors. And by reading of these Greek and Latin authors, men from their childhood have gotten a habit, under a false show of liberty, of favoring tumults, and of licentious controlling the actions of their sovereigns, and again of controlling those controllers; with the effusion of so much blood, as I think I may truly say, there was never anything so dearly bought as these western parts have bought the learning of the Greek and Latin tongues.

To come now to the particulars of the true liberty of a subject; that is to say, what are the things, which though commanded by the sovereign, he may nevertheless, without injustice, refuse to do; we are to consider what rights we pass away when we make a commonwealth; or, which is all one, what liberty we deny ourselves, by owning all the actions, without exception, of the man, or assembly, we make our sovereign. For in the act of our submission, consisteth both our obligation and our liberty; which must therefore be inferred by arguments taken from thence; there being no obligation on any man, which ariseth not from some act of his own; for all men equally are by nature free. And because such arguments must either be drawn from the express words,

"I authorize all his actions," or from the intention of him that submitteth himself to his power, which intention is to be understood by the end for which he so submitteth, the obligation and liberty of the subject is to be derived, either from those words or others equivalent, or else from the end of the institution of sovereignty, namely, the peace of the subjects within themselves, and their defence against a common enemy.

First therefore, seeing sovereignty by institution is by covenant of every one to every one; and sovereignty by acquisition, by covenants of the vanquished to the victor, or child to the parent; it is manifest that every subject has liberty in all those things the right whereof cannot by covenant be transferred. I have shown before in the 14th chapter, that covenants not to defend a man's own body are void. Therefore,

If the sovereign command a man, though justly condemned, to kill, wound, or maim himself; or not to resist those that assault him; or to abstain from the use of food, air, medicine, or any other thing, without which he cannot live; yet hath that man the liberty to disobey.

If a man be interrogated by the sovereign, or his authority, concerning a crime done by himself, he is not bound, without assurance of pardon, to confess it; because no man, as I have shown in the same chapter, can be obliged by convenant to accuse himself.

Again, the consent of a subject to sovereign power is contained in these words, "I authorize, or take upon me, all his actions;" in which there is no restriction at all of his own former natural liberty: for by allowing him to kill me, I am not bound to kill myself when he commands me. It is one thing to say "kill me, or my fellow, if you please;" another thing to say, "I will kill myself, or my fellow." It followeth therefore, that

No man is bound by the words themselves, either to kill himself or any other man; and consequently, that the obligation a man may sometimes have, upon the command of the sovereign to execute any dangerous or dishonorable office, dependeth not on the words of our submission; but on the intention, which is to be understood by the end thereof. When therefore our refusal to obey frustrates the end for which the sovereignty was ordained, then there is no liberty to refuse: otherwise there is.

Upon this ground, a man that is commanded as a soldier to fight against the enemy, though his sovereign have right enough to punish his refusal with death, may nevertheless in many cases refuse, without injustice; as when he substituteth a sufficient soldier in his place: for in this case he deserteth not the service of the commonwealth. And there is allowance to be made for natural timorousness; not only to women, of whom no such dangerous duty is expected, but also to men of feminine courage. When armies fight, there is on one side, or both, a running away; yet when they do it not out of treachery, but fear, they are not esteemed to do it unjustly, but dishonorably. For the same reason, to avoid battle is not injustice, but cowardice. But he that enrolleth himself a soldier, or taketh impressed money, taketh away the excuse of a timorous nature; and is obliged, not only to go to the battle, but also not to run from it, without his captain's leave. And when the defence of the commonwealth requireth at once the help of all that are able to bear arms, every one is obliged; because otherwise the institution of the commonwealth, which they have not the purpose or courage to preserve, was in vain.

To resist the sword of the commonwealth in defence of another man guilty or innocent, no man hath liberty; because such liberty takes away from the sovereign the means of protecting us; and is therefore destructive of the very essence of government. But in case a great many men together have already resisted the sovereign power unjustly, or committed some capital crime for which every one of them expecteth death, whether have they not the liberty then to join together, and assist and defend one another? Certainly they have; for they but defend their lives, which the guilty man may as well do as the innocent. There was indeed injustice in the first breach of their duty; their bearing of arms subsequent to it, though it be to maintain what they have done, is no new unjust act. And if it be only to defend their persons, it it not unjust at all. But the offer of pardon taketh from them to whom it is offered the plea of self-defence, and maketh their perseverance in assisting or defending the rest unlawful.

As for other liberties, they depend on the silence of the law. In cases where the sovereign has prescribed no rule, there the subject hath the liberty to do, or forbear, according to his own discretion. And therefore such liberty is in some places more, and in some less; and in some times more, in other times less, according as they that have the sovereignty shall think most convenient. As for example, there was a time when, in England, a man might enter into his own land, and dispossess such as wrongfully possessed it, by force. But in aftertimes, that liberty of forcible entry was taken away by a statute made by the king in parliament. And in some places of the world men have the liberty of many wives; in other places such liberty is not allowed.

If a subject have a controversy with his sovereign, of debt, or of right of possession of lands or goods, or concerning any service required at his hands, or concerning any penalty, corporal or pecuniary, grounded on a precedent law, he hath the same liberty to sue for his right as if it were against a subject, and before such judges as are appointed by the sovereign. For seeing the sovereign demandeth by force of a former law, and not by virtue of his power, he declareth thereby that he requireth no more than shall appear to be due by that law. The suit therefore is not contrary to the will of the sovereign; and consequently the subject hath the liberty to demand the hearing of his cause, and sentence, according to that law. But if he demand or take anything by pretence of his power there lieth, in that case, no action of law; for all that is done by him in virtue of his power, is done by the authority of every subject, and consequently he that brings an action against the sovereign, brings it against himself.

If a monarch, or sovereign assembly, grant a liberty to all or any of his subjects, which grant standing, he is disabled to provide for their safety, the grant is void, unless he directly renounce or transfer the sovereignty to another. For in that he might openly, if it had been his will, and in plain terms, have renounced or transferred it, and did not; it is to be understood it was not his will, but that the grant proceeded from ignorance of the repugnancy between such a liberty and the sovereign power, and therefore the sovereignty is still retained, and consequently all those powers which are necessary to the exercising thereof; such as are the power of war and peace, of judicature, of appointing officers and councillors, of levying money, and the rest named in the 18th chapter.

The obligation of subjects to the sovereign is understood to last as long, and no longer, than the power lasteth by which he is able to protect them. For the right men have by nature to protect themselves, when none else can protect them, can by no covenant be relinquished. The sovereignty is the soul of the commonwealth, which once departed from the body, the members do no more receive their motion from it. The end of obedience is protection, which, wheresoever a man seeth it, either in his own or in another's sword, nature applieth his obedience to it, and his endeavor to maintain it. And though sovereignty, in the intention of them that make it, be immortal, yet is it in its own nature not only subject to violent death by foreign war, but also, through the ignorance and passions of men, it hath in it, from the very institution, many seeds of a natural mortality, by intestine discord.

If a subject be taken prisoner in war, or his person, or his means of life be within the guards of the enemy, and hath his life and corporal liberty given him on condition to be subject to the victor, he hath liberty to accept the condition; and having accepted it, is the subject of him that took him, because he had no other way to preserve himself. The case is the same if he be detained on the same terms in a foreign country. But if a man be held in prison, or bonds, or is not trusted with the liberty of his body, he cannot be understood to be bound by covenant to subjection; and therefore may, if he can, make his escape by any means whatsoever.

If a monarch shall relinquish the sovereignty, both for himself and his heirs, his subjects return to the absolute liberty of nature; because, though nature may declare who are his sons, and who are the nearest of his kin, yet it dependeth on his own will, as hath been said in the precedent chapter, who shall be his heir. If therefore he will have no heir, there is no sovereignty, nor subjection. The case is the same if he die without known kindred, and without declaration of his heir. For then there can no heir be known, and consequently no subjection be due.

If the sovereign banish his subject, during the banishment he is not subject. But he that is sent on a message, or hath leave to travel, is still subject; but it is by contract between sovereigns, not by virtue of the covenant of subjection. For whosoever entereth into another's dominion is subject to all the laws thereof, unless he have a privilege by the amity of the sovereigns, or by special license.

If a monarch subdued by war render himself subject to the victor, his subjects are delivered from their former obligation, and become obliged to the victor. But if he be held prisoner, or have not the liberty of his own body, he is not understood to have given away the right of sovereignty; and therefore his subjects are obliged to yield obedience to the magistrates formerly placed, governing not in their own name, but in his. For, his right remaining, the question is only of the administration; that is to say, of the magistrates and officers, which, if we have not means to name, he is supposed to approve those which he himself had formerly appointed.

6. Civil Laws [1]

Ch. xxvi. *Of Civil Laws.*

By civil laws, I understand the laws that men are therefore bound to observe, because they are members, not of this or that commonwealth in particular, but of a commonwealth. For the knowledge of particular laws belongeth to them that profess the study of the laws of their several countries; but the knowledge of civil law in general to any man. The ancient law of Rome was called their civil law, from the word *civitas*, which signifies a commonwealth: and those countries which having been under the Roman empire, and governed by that law, retain still such part thereof as they think fit, call that part the civil law, to distinguish it from the rest of their own civil laws. But that is not it I intend to speak of here; my design being not to show what is law here and there; but what is law; as Plato, Aristotle, Cicero, and divers others have done, without taking upon them the profession of the study of the law.

And first it is manifest that the law in general is not counsel, but command; not a command of any man to any man, but only of him whose command is addressed to one formerly obliged to obey him. And as for civil law, it addeth only the name of the person commanding, which is *persona civitatis*, the person of the commonwealth.

Which considered, I define civil law in this manner. "Civil law is to every subject those rules which the commonwealth hath commanded him, by word, writing, or other sufficient sign of the will, to make use of, for the distinction of right and wrong; that is to say, of what is contrary and what is not contrary to the rule."

In which definition, there is nothing that is not at first sight evident. For every man seeth that some laws are addressed to all the subjects in general; some to particular provinces; some to particular vocations; and some to particular men; and are therefore laws to every of those to whom the command is directed, and to none else. As also, that laws are the rules of just and unjust; nothing being reputed unjust that is not contrary to some law. Likewise, that none can make laws but the commonwealth; because our subjection is to the commonwealth only: and that commands are to be signified by sufficient signs; because a man knows not otherwise how to obey them. And therefore, whatsoever can from this definition by necessary consequence be

[1] Part II, ch. xxvi.

deduced, ought to be acknowledged for truth. Now I deduce from it this that followeth.

1. The legislator in all commonwealths is only the sovereign, be he one man, as in a monarchy, or one assembly of men, as in a democracy, or aristocracy. For the legislator is he that maketh the law. And the commonwealth only prescribes and commandeth the observation of those rules which we call law: therefore the commonwealth is the legislator. But the commonwealth is no person, nor has capacity to do anything but by the representative, that is, the sovereign; and therefore the sovereign is the sole legislator. For the same reason, none can abrogate a law made, but the sovereign; because a law is not abrogated but by another law, that forbiddeth it to be put in execution.

2. The sovereign of a commonwealth, be it an assembly or one man, is not subject to the civil laws. For having power to make and repeal laws, he may when he pleaseth free himself from that subjection, by repealing those laws that trouble him and making of new; and consequently he was free before. For he is free that can be free when he will: nor is it possible for any person to be bound to himself; because he that can bind, can release; and therefore he that is bound to himself only, is not bound.

3. When long use obtaineth the authority of a law, it is not the length of time that maketh the authority, but the will of the sovereign signified by his silence, for silence is sometimes an argument of consent; and it is no longer law than the sovereign shall be silent therein. And therefore if the sovereign shall have a question of right grounded, not upon his present will, but upon the laws formerly made, the length of time shall bring no prejudice to his right; but the question shall be judged by equity. For many unjust actions and unjust sentences go uncontrolled a longer time than any man can remember. And our lawyers account no customs law but such as are reasonable, and that evil customs are to be abolished. But the judgment of what is reasonable and of what is to be abolished belongeth to him that maketh the law, which is the sovereign assembly or monarch.

4. The law of nature and the civil law contain each other, and are of equal extent. For the laws of nature, which consist in equity, justice, gratitude, and other moral virtues on these depending, in the condition of mere nature, as I have said before in the end of the fifteenth chapter, are not properly laws, but qualities that dispose men to peace and obedience. When a commonwealth is once settled, then are they actually laws, and

not before; as being then the commands of the commonwealth; and therefore also civil laws: for it is the sovereign power that obliges men to obey them. For in the differences of private men, to declare what is equity, what is justice, and what is moral virtue, and to make them binding, there is need of the ordinances of sovereign power, and punishments to be ordained for such as shall break them; which ordinances are therefore part of the civil law. The law of nature therefore is a part of the civil law in all commonwealths of the world. Reciprocally also, the civil law is a part of the dictates of nature. For justice, that is to say, performance of covenant, and giving to every man his own, is a dictate of the law of nature. But every subject in a commonwealth hath covenanted to obey the civil law; either one with another, as when they assemble to make a common representative, or with the representative itself one by one, when subdued by the sword they promise obedience, that they may receive life; and therefore obedience to the civil law is part also of the law of nature. Civil and natural law are not different kinds, but different parts of law; whereof one part being written, is called civil, the other unwritten, natural. But the right of nature, that is, the natural liberty of man, may by the civil law be abridged and restrained: nay, the end of making laws is no other but such restraint; without the which there cannot possibly be any peace. And law was brought into the world for nothing else but to limit the natural liberty of particular men, in such manner as they might not hurt, but assist one another, and join together against a common enemy.

5. If the sovereign of one commonwealth subdue a people that have lived under other written laws, and afterwards govern them by the same laws by which they were governed before, yet those laws are the civil laws of the victor, and not of the vanquished commonwealth. For the legislator is he, not by whose authority the laws were first made, but by whose authority they now continue to be laws. And therefore where there be divers provinces within the dominion of a commonwealth, and in those provinces diversity of laws, which commonly are called the customs of each several province, we are not to understand that such customs have their force only from length of time; but that they were anciently laws written, or otherwise made known, for the constitutions and statutes of their sovereigns; and are now laws not by virtue of the prescription of time, but by the constitutions of their present sovereigns. But if an unwritten law, in all the provinces of a dominion, shall be generally observed, and no in-

iquity appear in the use thereof, that law can be no other but a law of nature, equally obliging all mankind.

6. Seeing then all laws, written and unwritten, have their authority and force from the will of the commonwealth, that is to say, from the will of the representative, which in a monarchy is a monarch, and in other commonwealths the sovereign assembly, a man may wonder from whence proceed such opinions as are found in the books of lawyers of eminence in several commonwealths, directly or by consequence making the legislative power depend on private men, or subordinate judges. As for example, "that the common law hath no controller but the parliament;" which is true only where a parliament has the sovereign power, and cannot be assembled or dissolved but by their own discretion. For if there be a right in any else to dissolve them, there is a right also to control them, and consequently to control their controllings. And if there be no such right, then the controller of laws is not *parliamentum* but *rex in parliamento*. And where a parliament is sovereign, if it should assemble never so many or so wise men from the countries subject to them, for whatsoever cause, yet there is no man will believe that such an assembly hath thereby acquired to themselves a legislative power. "Item" that the two aims of a commonwealth are force and justice; the first whereof is in the king, the other deposited in the hands of the parliament. As if a commonwealth could consist where the force were in any hand which justice had not the authority to command and govern.

7. That law can never be against reason our lawyers are agreed; and that not the letter that is every construction of it, but that which is according to the intention of the legislator, is the law. And it is true, but the doubt is of whose reason it is that shall be received for law. It is not meant of any private reason, for then there would be as much contradiction in the laws as there is in the schools; nor yet, as Sir Edward Coke makes it, an "artificial perfection of reason, gotten by long study, observation, and experience," as his was. For it is possible long study may increase and confirm erroneous sentences, and where men build on false grounds, the more they build the greater is the ruin: and of those that study and observe with equal time and diligence, the reason and resolutions are, and must remain, discordant, and therefore it is not that *juris prudentia* or wisdom of subordinate judges, but the reason of this our artificial man the commonwealth, and his command that maketh law: and the commonwealth being in their representative but one person, there cannot easily arise

any contradiction in the laws; and when there doth, the same reason is able, by interpretation or alteration, to take it away. In all courts of justice, the sovereign, which is the person of the commonwealth, is he that judgeth; the subordinate judge ought to have regard to the reason which moved his sovereign to make such law that his sentence may be according thereunto, which then is his sovereign's sentence, otherwise it is his own, and an unjust one.

8. From this that the law is a command, and a command consisteth in declaration or manifestation of the will of him that commandeth, by voice, writing, or some other sufficient argument of the same, we may understand that the command of the commonwealth is law only to those that have means to take notice of it. Over natural fools, children, or madmen, there is no law, no more than over brute beasts, nor are they capable of the title of just or unjust; because they had never power to make any covenant, or to understand the consequences thereof, and consequently never took upon them to authorize the actions of any sovereign, as they must do that make to themselves a commonwealth. And as those from whom nature or accident hath taken away the notice of all laws in general; so also every man from whom any accident, not proceeding from his own default, hath taken away the means to take notice of any particular law, is excused if he observe it not, and, to speak properly, that law is no law to him. It is therefore necessary to consider in this place what arguments and signs be sufficient for the knowledge of what is the law, that is to say, what is the will of the sovereign as well in monarchies as in other forms of government.

And first, if it be a law that obliges all the subjects without exception, and is not written, nor otherwise published in such places as they may take notice thereof, it is a law of nature. For whatsoever men are to take knowledge of for law, not upon other men's words, but every one from his own reason, must be such as is agreeable to the reason of all men; which no law can be but the law of nature. The laws of nature therefore need not any publishing, nor proclamation; as being contained in this one sentence, approved by all the world, "Do not that to another, which thou thinkest unreasonable to be done by another to thyself."

Secondly, if it be a law that obliges only some condition of men, or one particular man, and be not written, nor published by word, then also it is a law of nature, and known by the same arguments and signs that distinguish those in such a condition from other subjects. For whatsoever law is not written, or some way published by him that makes it law, can be known no way but by the reason of him that is to obey it; and is therefore also a law not only civil, but natural. For example, if the sovereign employ a public minister, without written instructions what to do, he is obliged to take for instructions the dictates of reason; as if he make a judge, the judge is to take notice that his sentence ought to be according to the reason of his sovereign, which being always understood to be equity, he is bound to it by the law of nature: or if an ambassador, he is, in all things not contained in his written instructions, to take for instruction that which reason dictates to be most conducing to his sovereign's interest; and so of all other ministers of the sovereignty, public and private. All which instructions of natural reason may be comprehended under one name of "fidelity;" which is a branch of natural justice.

The law of nature excepted, it belongeth to the essence of all other laws to be made known to every man that shall be obliged to obey them, either by word, or writing, or some other act, known to proceed from the sovereign authority. For the will of another cannot be understood, but by his own word, or act, or by conjecture taken from his scope and purpose; which in the person of the commonwealth is to be supposed always consonant to equity and reason. And in ancient time, before letters were in common use, the laws were many times put into verse; that the rude people taking pleasure in singing or reciting them, might the more easily retain them in memory. And for the same reason Solomon (Prov. vii. 3) adviseth a man to bind the ten commandments upon his ten fingers. And for the law which Moses gave to the people of Israel at the renewing of the covenant (Deut. xi. 19), he biddeth them to teach it their children, by discoursing of it both at home and upon the way; at going to bed, and at rising from bed; and to write it upon the posts and doors of their houses; and (Deut. xxxi. 12) to assemble the people, man, woman, and child, to hear it read.

Nor is it enough the law be written and published; but also that there be manifest signs that it proceedeth from the will of the sovereign. For private men, when they have, or think they have, force enough to secure their unjust designs, and convoy them safely to their ambitious ends, may publish for laws what they please, without or against the legislative authority. There is therefore requisite, not only a declaration of the law, but also sufficient signs of the author and authority. The author or legislator is supposed in every commonwealth to be evident,

because he is the sovereign, who having been constituted by the
consent of every one, is supposed by every one to be sufficiently
known. And though the ignorance and security of men be such,
for the most part, as that when the memory of the first constitution of their commonwealth is worn out, they do not consider by
whose power they used to be defended against their enemies,
and to have their industry protected, and to be righted when
injury is done them; yet because no man that considers can make
question of it, no excuse can be derived from the ignorance of
where the sovereignty is placed. And it is a dictate of natural
reason, and consequently an evident law of nature, that no man
ought to weaken that power, the protection whereof he hath
himself demanded, or wittingly received against others. Therefore of who is sovereign, no man, but by his own fault (whatsoever
evil men suggest), can make any doubt. The difficulty consisteth
in the evidence of the authority derived from him; the removing
whereof dependeth on the knowledge of the public registers,
public counsels, public ministers, and public seals; by which all
laws are sufficiently verified; verified, I say, not authorized: for
the verification is but the testimony and record, not the authority
of the law; which consisteth in the command of the sovereign
only.

If therefore a man have a question of injury depending on the
law of nature, that is to say, on common equity, the sentence of
the judge that by commission hath authority to take cognizance
of such causes, is a sufficient verification of the law of nature
in that individual case. For though the advice of one that pro-
fesseth the study of the law be useful for the avoiding of
contention, yet it is but advice: it is the judge must tell men what
is law, upon the hearing of the controversy.

But when the question is of injury, or crime, upon a written
law, every man by recourse to the registers, by himself or others,
may, if he will, be sufficiently informed, before he do such injury, or
commit the crime, whether it be an injury or not: nay, he ought to
do so: for when a man doubts whether the act he goeth about be
just or unjust and may inform himself if he will, the doing is
unlawful. In like manner, he that supposeth himself injured
in a case determined by the written law, which he may, by himself or others, see and consider, if he complain before he consults
with the law, he does unjustly, and bewrayeth a disposition
rather to vex other men than to demand his own right.

If the question be of obedience to a public officer, to have seen
his commission with the public seal, and heard it read, or to have

had the means to be informed of it, if a man would, is a sufficient verification of his authority. For every man is obliged to do his best endeavor to inform himself of all written laws that may concern his own future actions.

The legislator known, and the laws, either by writing or by the light of nature, sufficiently published, there wanteth yet another very material circumstance to make them obligatory. For it is not the letter, but the intendment or meaning, that is to say, the authentic interpretation of the law (which is the sense of the legislator), in which the nature of the law consisteth; and therefore the interpretation of all laws dependeth on the authority sovereign; and the interpreters can be none but those which the sovereign, to whom only the subject oweth obedience, shall appoint. For else, by the craft of an interpreter, the law may be made to bear a sense contrary to that of the sovereign, by which means the interpreter becomes the legislator.

All laws, written and unwritten, have need of interpretation. The unwritten law of nature, though it be easy to such as, without partiality and passion, make use of their natural reason, and therefore leave the violators thereof without excuse; yet considering there be very few, perhaps none, that in some cases are not blinded by self-love or some other passion, it is now become of all laws the most obscure, and has consequently the greatest need of able interpreters. The written laws, if they be short, are easily misinterpreted, from the divers significations of a word or two: if long, they be more obscure by the divers significations of many words: insomuch as no written law, delivered in few or many words, can be well understood, without a perfect understanding of the final causes for which the law was made, the knowledge of which final causes is in the legislator. To him therefore there cannot be any knot in the law insoluble; either by finding out the ends, to undo it by; or else by making what ends he will, as Alexander did with his sword in the Gordian knot, by the legislative power, which no other interpreter can do.

The interpretation of the laws of nature in a commonwealth dependeth not on the books of moral philosophy. The authority of writers, without the authority of the commonwealth, maketh not their opinions law, be they never so true. That which I have written in this treatise concerning the moral virtues, and of their necessity for the procuring and maintaining peace, though it be evident truth, is not therefore presently law; but because in all commonwealths in the world it is part of the civil law. For though it be naturally reasonable, yet it is by the sovereign power that it is law: otherwise, it were a great error to call the laws of nature unwritten law; whereof we see so many volumes published, and in them so many contradictions of one another and of themselves.

The interpretation of the law of nature is the sentence of the judge constituted by the sovereign authority, to hear and determine such controversies as depend thereon; and consisteth in the application of the law to the present case. For in the act of judicature, the judge doth no more but consider whether the demand of the party be consonant to natural reason and equity; and the sentence he giveth is therefore the interpretation of the law of nature; which interpretation is authentic, not because it is his private sentence, but because he giveth it by authority of the sovereign, whereby it becomes the sovereign's sentence, which is law for that time, to the parties pleading.

But because there is no judge subordinate nor sovereign but may err in a judgment of equity, if afterward in another like case he find it more consonant to equity to give a contrary sentence, he is obliged to do it. No man's error becomes his own law; nor obliges him to persist in it. Neither, for the same reason, becomes it a law to other judges, though sworn to follow it. For though a wrong sentence given by authority of the sovereign, if he know and allow it, in such laws as are mutable, be a constitution of a new law, in cases in which every little circumstance is the same; yet in laws immutable, such as are the laws of nature, they are no laws to the same or other judges, in the like cases for ever after. Princes succeed one another; and one judge passeth, another cometh; nay, heaven and earth shall pass; but not one tittle of the law of nature shall pass; for it is the eternal law of God. Therefore all the sentences of precedent judges that have ever been cannot altogether make a law contrary to natural equity: nor any examples of former judges can warrant an unreasonable sentence, or discharge the present judge of the trouble of studying what is equity, in the case he is to judge, from the principles of his own natural reason. For example sake, it is against the law of nature to punish the innocent; and innocent is he that acquitteth himself judicially, and is acknowledged for innocent by the judge. Put the case now that a man is accused of a capital crime, and seeing the power and malice of some enemy, and the frequent corruption and partiality of judges, runneth away for fear of the event, and afterwards is taken, and brought to a legal trial, and maketh it sufficiently appear he was not guilty of the crime, and being thereof acquitted, is nevertheless condemned to lose his goods; this is a manifest condemnation of the innocent. I say therefore that there is no place in the world where this can be an interpretation of a law of nature, or be made a law by the sentences of precedent judges that had done the same. For he that judged it first, judged unjustly; and no injustice can be a pattern of judgment to succeeding judges. A written law may forbid innocent men to fly, and they may be punished for flying: but that flying for fear of injury should be taken for presumption of guilt, after a man is already absolved of the crime judicially, is contrary to the nature of a presumption, which hath no place after judgment is given. Yet this is set down by a great lawyer for the common law of England. "If a man," saith he, "that is innocent, be accused of felony, and for fear flyeth for the same, albeit he judicially acquitteth himself of the felony, yet if it be found that he fled for the felony, he shall notwithstanding his innocency, forfeit all his goods, chattels, debts, and duties. For as to the forfeiture of them, the law will admit no proof against the presumption in law, grounded upon his flight." Here you see an innocent man judicially acquitted, notwithstanding his innocency, when no written law forbade him to fly, after his acquittal, upon a presumption in law, condemned to lose all the goods he hath. If the law ground upon his flight a presumption of the fact, which was capital, the sentence ought to have been capital: if the presumption were not of the fact, for what then ought he to lose his goods? This therefore is no law of England; nor is the condemnation grounded upon a presumption of law, but upon the presumption of the judges. It is also against law to say that no proof shall be admitted against a presumption of law. For all judges, sovereign and subordinate, if they refuse to hear proof, refuse to do justice: for though the sentence be just, yet the judges that condemn without hearing the proofs offered, are unjust judges; and their presumption is but prejudice; which no man ought to bring with him to the seat of justice, whatsoever precedent judgments or examples he shall pretend to follow. There be other things of this nature, wherein men's judgments have been perverted by trusting to precedents: but this is enough to show that though the sentence of the judge be a law to the party pleading, yet it is no law to any judge that shall succeed him in that office.

In like manner, when question is of the meaning of written laws, he is not the interpreter of them that writeth a commentary upon them. For commentaries are commonly more subject to cavil than the text, and therefore need other commentaries; and so there will be no end of such interpretation. And therefore unless there be an interpreter authorized by the sovereign, from which the subordinate judges are not to recede, the interpreter can be no other than the ordinary judges, in the same manner as they are in cases of the unwritten law; and their sentences are to be taken by them that plead for laws in that particular case; but not to bind other judges in like cases to give like judgments. For a judge may err in the interpretation even of written laws; but no error of a subordinate judge can change the law, which is the general sentence of the sovereign.

In written laws, men use to make a difference between the letter and the sentence of the law: and when by the letter is meant whatsoever can be gathered by the bare words, it is well distinguished. For the significations of almost all words are either in themselves, or in the metaphorical use of them, ambiguous; and may be drawn in argument, to make many senses; but there is only one sense of the law. But if by the letter be meant the literal sense, then the letter and the sentence or intention of the law, is all one. For the literal sense is that which the legislator intended should by the letter of the law be signified. Now the intention of the legislator is always supposed to be equity: for it were a great contumely for a judge to think otherwise of the sovereign. He ought therefore, if the word of the law do not fully authorize a reasonable sentence, to supply it with the law of nature; or if the case be difficult, to respite judgment till he have received more ample authority. For example, a written law ordaineth that he which is thrust out of his house by force shall be restored by force: it happens that a man by negligence leaves his house empty, and returning is kept out by force, in which case there is no special law ordained. It is evident that this case is contained in the same law: for else there is no remedy for him at all; which is to be supposed against the intention of the legislator. Again, the word of the law commandeth to judge according to the evidence: a man is accused falsely of a fact which the judge himself saw done by another, and not by him that is accused. In this case neither shall the letter of the law be followed to the condemnation of the innocent, nor shall the judge give sentence against the evidence of the witnesses, because the letter of the law is to the contrary, but procure of the sovereign that another be made judge, and himself witness. So that the incommodity that follows the bare words of a written law may lead him to the intention of the law, whereby to interpret the same the better; though no incommodity can warrant a sentence against the law. For every judge of right and wrong is not judge of what is commodious or incommodious to the commonwealth.

The abilities required in a good interpreter of the law, that is to say, in a good judge, are not the same with those of an advocate, namely, the study of the laws. For a judge, as he ought to take notice of the fact from none but the witnesses, so also he ought to take notice of the law from nothing but the statutes and constitutions of the sovereign, alleged in the pleading, or declared to him by some that have authority from the sovereign power to declare them; and need not take care beforehand what he shall judge; for it shall be given him what he shall say concerning the fact, by witnesses; and what he shall say in point of law, from those that shall in their pleadings show it, and by authority interpret it upon the place. The Lords of parliament in England were judges, and most difficult causes have been heard and determined by them; yet few of them were much versed in the study of the laws, and fewer had made profession of them; and though they consulted with lawyers that were appointed to be present there for that purpose, yet they alone had the authority of giving sentence. In like manner, in the ordinary trials of right, twelve men of the common people are the judges, and give sentence, not only of the fact, but of the right; and pronounce simply for the complainant, or for the defendant; that is to say, are judges, not only of the fact, but also of the right: and in a question of crime, not only determine whether done, or not done; but also whether it be murder, homicide, felony, assault, and the like, which are determinations of law: but because they are not supposed to know the law of themselves, there is one that hath authority to inform them of it, in the particular case they are to judge of. But yet if they judge not according to that he tells them, they are not subject thereby to any penalty: unless it be made appear that they did it against their consciences, or had been corrupted by reward.

The things that make a good judge or good interpreter of the laws are, first, a right understanding of that principal law of nature called equity, which depending not on the reading of other men's writings, but on the goodness of a man's own natural reason and meditation, is presumed to be in those most that have had most leisure and had the most inclination to meditate thereon. Secondly, contempt of unnecessary riches and preferments. Thirdly, to be able in judgment to divest himself of all fear, anger, hatred, love, and compassion. Fourthly, and lastly, patience to hear, diligent attention in hearing, and memory to retain, digest and apply what he hath heard.

SELECTED BIBLIOGRAPHY

Sabine, George H., *History of Political Theory*, ch. 23.
Cook, Thomas I., *History of Political Philosophy*, ch. 18.
Dunning, William A., *Political Theories, from Luther to Montesquieu*, ch. 8.
Woodward, E. L., "Thomas Hobbes," in F. J. C. Hearnshaw, ed., *Social and Political Ideas of Some Great Thinkers of the Sixteenth and Seventeenth Centuries* (London, 1926), ch. 7.
Vaughan, C. E., *Studies in the History of Political Philosophy before and after Rousseau*, 2 vols. (Manchester, 1925), Vol. I, ch. 2.
Laird, John, *Hobbes* (London, 1934), chs. 6, 7, 9.
Graham, William, *English Political Philosophy from Hobbes to Maine* (London, 1899), pp. 1–49.
Stephen, Leslie, *Hobbes* (London, 1904), ch. 4.
Bonar, James, *Philosophy and Political Economy in Some of Their Historical Relations* (third ed., London, 1922), bk. ii, ch. 3.
Catlin, George H. C., *Thomas Hobbes as Philosopher, Publicist, and Man of Letters* (Oxford, 1922).
Strauss, Leo, *The Political Philosophy of Hobbes*, translated by Elsa M. Sinclair (Oxford, 1936).
Tönnies, Ferdinand, *Thomas Hobbes, Leben und Lehre* (third ed., Stuttgart, 1925).
Hönigswald, R., *Hobbes und die Staatsphilosophie* (Munich, 1924).
Lubieński, Zbigniew, *Die Grundlagen des ethisch-politischen Systems von Hobbes* (Munich, 1932).

HARRINGTON

HARRINGTON

XX. JAMES HARRINGTON (1611–1677)

INTRODUCTION

Another work written in direct reference to the events of the Puritan Revolution is the *Oceana* of James Harrington. In so far as Harrington shared any association with active politics he took a conciliatory and non-partisan position; and he cannot be definitely classed with the adherents of either royalist or republican factions; his book aroused the suspicions of both parties.

Harrington belonged to an old country family, and was a grand-nephew of the first Lord Harrington. After graduation from Oxford he spent several years in travel through Holland, France, Germany, and Italy; on these journeys his chief interest lay in the observation of political institutions. On his return to England he received appointment to the suite of Charles I, despite the fact that it was known that he entertained republican ideas. After the imprisonment of the king Harrington was dismissed from the royal service by Parliament, under the imputation that he might be willing to aid in the king's escape. Upon the death of the king he set himself the task of designing a model plan of government to be adopted by the English people in place of the monarchy that had been set aside. The result of this undertaking is the *The Commonwealth of Oceana*:[1] the work is a political romance, in which "Oceana" stands for England.

A distinctive feature of the *Oceana* is the doctrine that political supremacy follows naturally superiority in the ownership of property, and that, therefore, political stability can be maintained only where political sovereignty is located in that part of the population which holds the greater amount of property. In most states this would mean, according to the author, that sovereignty follows preponderance in land ownership, since land (in Harrington's time)

---

[1] While first in press this work was seized at Cromwell's order; it was subsequently allowed to be printed, through the intervention of Cromwell's daughter, whose favor Harrington had won. It was published in 1656, dedicated to Cromwell.

was generally the most important form of private property. As a
corollary to this principle Harrington finds indispensable for every
commonwealth, or republic, the device of an "equal agrarian:"
limiting the amount of property in land that may be held by any
one person, and thus preventing the concentration of political
power in the hands of a small class of the people. A further
characteristic feature of the book is the solution offered to the
problem of securing a constitution through which all elements of
the state work toward the common interest of the whole body of
the people. The solution, according to Harrington, is to be found
in the organization of government in conformity to the essential
"principles of authority." One of these is the "psychological"
principle of the supremacy of reason over passion, which makes
the true commonwealth "an empire of laws, and not of man."
Other principles of authority relate to the proper structure of
government and require the provision of such devices as a popular
assembly to ratify measures proposed by more aristocratic bodies,
a secret ballot, and rotation in office.[1]

READINGS FROM THE OCEANA [2]

1. Principles of Political Power: The Material Influences [3]

Janotti, the most excellent describer of the commonwealth
of Venice, divides the whole series of government into two times
or periods: the one ending with the liberty of Rome, which was
the course or empire, as I may call it, of ancient prudence, first
discovered to mankind by God Himself in the fabric of the commonwealth of Israel, and afterwards picked out of His footsteps in nature, and unanimously followed by the Greeks and
Romans; the other beginning with the arms of Cæsar, which,
extinguishing liberty, were the transition of ancient into modern
prudence, introduced by those inundations of Huns, Goths,

---

[1] See David Masson, *Life of John Milton*, Vol. V, pp. 483-4, for the efforts
made by Harrington and his friends to get Parliament to adopt features of his
plan. After the Restoration Harrington was imprisoned by order of Charles
II, on an unfounded charge of conspiracy. He was finally released, but not
until after his health had been permanently impaired by his prison experience.
See the citations of Smith and Dwight (p. 523, *infra*) for study of the influence of Harrington's ideas in America.
[2] The selections are from Henry Morley's edition of the *Oceana*, London,
1887. The passages are selected from the first part—"*The Preliminaries,
showing the Principles of Government*" (Morley, pp. 15-72). In the three other
parts the details of the ideal political organization are presented.
[3] Pp. 15-25.

Vandals, Lombards, Saxons, which, breaking the Roman empire, deformed the whole face of the world with those ill features of government, which at this time are become far worse in these Western parts, except Venice, which, escaping the hands of the Barbarians by virtue of its impregnable situation, has had its eye fixed upon ancient prudence, and is attained to a perfection even beyond the copy.

Relation being had to these two times, government (to define it *de jure*, or according to ancient prudence) is an art whereby a civil society of men is instituted and preserved upon the foundation of common right or interest; or, to follow Aristotle and Livy, it is the empire of laws, and not of men.

And government (to define it *de facto*, or according to modern prudence) is an art whereby some man, or some few men, subject a city or a nation, and rule it according to his or their private interest; which, because the laws in such cases are made according to the interest of a man, or of some few families, may be said to be the empire of men, and not of laws.

The former kind is that which Machiavel (whose books are neglected) is the only politician that has gone about to retrieve; and that Leviathan (who would have his book imposed upon the universities) goes about to destroy. For "it is," says he, "another error of Aristotle's politics that in a well-ordered commonwealth not men should govern, but the laws. What man that has his natural senses, though he can neither write nor read, does not find himself governed by them he fears, and believes can kill or hurt him when he obeys not? Or, who believes that the law can hurt him, which is but words and paper, without the hands and swords of men?" I confess that the magistrate upon his bench is that to the law which a gunner upon his platform is to his cannon. Nevertheless, I should not dare to argue with a man of any ingenuity after this manner. A whole army, though they can neither write nor read, are not afraid of a platform, which they know is but earth or stone; nor of a cannon, which, without a hand to give fire to it, is but cold iron; therefore a whole army is afraid of one man. But of this kind is the ratiocination of Leviathan, as I shall show in divers places that come in my way, throughout his whole politics, or worse; as where he says, of Aristotle and of Cicero, of the Greeks, and of the Romans, who lived under popular states, that they derived those rights not from the principles of nature, but transcribed them into their books out of the practice of their own commonwealths, as grammarians describe the rules of language out of poets. Which is as if a man should tell famous Harvey that he transcribed his circulation of the blood not out of the principles of nature, but out of the anatomy of this or that body.

To go on therefore with his preliminary discourse, I shall divide it, according to the two definitions of government relating to Janotti's two times, in two parts. The first, treating of the principles of government in general, and according to the ancients; the second, treating of the late governments of Oceana in particular, and in that of modern prudence.

Government, according to the ancients, and their learned disciple Machiavel, the only politician of later ages, is of three kinds: the government of one man, or of the better sort, or of the whole people; which, by their more learned names, are called monarchy, aristocracy, and democracy. These they hold, through their proneness to degenerate, to be all evil. For whereas they that govern should govern according to reason, if they govern according to passion they do that which they should not do. Wherefore, as reason and passion are two things, so government by reason is one thing, and the corruption of government by passion is another thing, but not always another government: as a body that is alive is one thing, and a body that is dead is another thing, but not always another creature, though the corruption of one comes at length to be the generation of another. The corruption then of monarchy is called tyranny; that of aristocracy, oligarchy; and that of democracy, anarchy. But legislators, having found these three governments at the best to be naught, have invented another, consisting of a mixture of them all, which only is good. This is the doctrine of the ancients.

But Leviathan is positive that they are all deceived, and that there is no other government in nature than one of the three; as also that the flesh of them cannot stink, the names of their corruptions being but the names of men's fancies, which will be understood when we are shown which of them was *Senatus Populusque Romanus*.

To go my own way, and yet to follow the ancients, the principles of government are twofold: internal, or the goods of the mind; and external, or the goods of fortune. The goods of the mind are natural or acquired virtues, as wisdom, prudence, and courage, etc. The goods of fortune are riches. There be goods also of the body, as health, beauty, strength; but these are not to be brought into account upon this score, because if a man or an army acquires victory or empire, it is more from their discipline, arms, and courage than from their natural health, beauty, or strength, in regard that a people conquered may have more of natural strength, beauty and health, and yet find little remedy. The principles of government then are in the goods of the mind, or in the goods of fortune. To the goods of the mind answers authority; to the goods of fortune, power or empire. Wherefore Leviathan, though he be right where he says that "riches are power," is mistaken where he says that "prudence, or the reputation of prudence, is power;" for the learning or prudence of a man is no more power than the learning or prudence of a book or author, which is properly authority. A learned writer may have authority though he has no power; and a foolish magistrate may have power, though he has otherwise no esteem or authority. The difference of these two is observed by Livy in Evander, of whom he says that he governed rather by the authority of others than by his own power.

To begin with riches, in regard that men are hung upon these, not of choice as upon the other, but of necessity and by the teeth; forasmuch as he who wants bread is his servant that will feed him, if a man thus feeds a whole people, they are under his empire.

Empire is of two kinds, domestic and national, or foreign and provincial.

Domestic empire is founded upon dominion.

Dominion is property, real or personal; that is to say, in lands, or in money and goods.

Lands, or the parts and parcels of a territory, are held by the proprietor or proprietors, lord or lords of it, in some proportion; and such (except it be in a city that has little or no land, and whose revenue is in trade) as is the proportion or balance of dominion or property in land, such is the nature of the empire.

If one man be sole landlord of a territory, or overbalance the people, for example, three parts in four, he is Grand Seignior; for so the Turk is called from his property, and his empire is absolute monarchy.

If the few or a nobility, or a nobility with a clergy, be landlords, or overbalance the people to the like proportion, it makes the Gothic balance (to be shown at large in the second part of this discourse), and the empire is mixed monarchy, as that of Spain, Poland, and late of Oceana.

And if the whole people be landlords, or hold the lands so divided among them that no one man, or number of men, within the compass of the few or aristocracy, overbalance them, the empire (without the interposition of force) is a commonwealth.

If force be interposed in any of these three cases, it must either frame the government to the foundation, or the foundation to the government; or holding the government not according to the balance, it is not natural, but violent; and therefore if it be at the devotion of a prince, it is tyranny; if at the devotion of the few, oligarchy; or if in the power of the people, anarchy. Each of which confusions, the balance standing otherwise, is but of short continuance, because against the nature of the balance, which, not destroyed, destroys that which opposes it.

But there be certain other confusions, which, being rooted in the balance, are of longer continuance, and of worse consequence; as, first, where a nobility holds half the property, or about that proportion, and the people the other half; in which case, without altering the balance there is no remedy but the one must eat out the other, as the people did the nobility in Athens, and the nobility the people in Rome.   Secondly, when a prince holds about half the dominion, and the people the other half (which was the case of the Roman emperors, planted partly upon their military colonies, and partly upon the senate and the people), the government becomes a very shambles, both of the princes and the people. Somewhat of this nature are certain governments at this day, which are said to subsist by confusion.   In this case, to fix the balance, is to entail misery; but in the three former, not to fix it, is to lose the government.   Wherefore it being unlawful in Turkey that any should possess land but the Grand Seignior, the balance is fixed by the law, and that empire firm.   Nor, though the kings often sell, was the throne of Oceana known to shake, until the statute of alienations broke the pillars, by giving way to the nobility to sell their estates.   While Lacedæmon held to the division of land made by Lycurgus, it was immovable; but, breaking that, could stand no longer.   This kind of law fixing the balance in lands is called Agrarian, and was first introduced by God himself, who divided the land of Canaan to His people by lots, and is of such virtue, that wherever it has held that government has not altered, except by consent; as in that unparalleled example of the people of Israel, when being in liberty they would needs choose a king.   But without an agrarian law, government, whether monarchical, aristocratical, or popular, has no long lease.

As for dominion, personal or in money, it may now and then stir up a Melius or a Manlius, which, if the commonwealth be not provided with some kind of dictatorian power, may be dangerous, though it has been seldom or never successful; because to property producing empire, it is required that it should have some certain root or foothold, which, except in land, it cannot have, being otherwise as it were upon the wing.

Nevertheless, in such cities as subsist mostly by trade, and have little or no land, as Holland and Genoa, the balance of treasure may be equal to that of land in the cases mentioned.

But Leviathan, though he seems to skew at antiquity, following his furious master Carneades, has caught hold of the public sword, to which he reduces all manner and matter of government; as, where he affirms this opinion [that any monarch receives his power by covenant, that is to say, upon conditions] "to proceed from the not understanding this easy truth, that covenants being but words and breath, have no power to oblige, contain, constrain, or protect any man, but what they have from the public sword." But as he said of the law, that without this sword it is but paper, so he might have thought of this sword, that without a hand it is but cold iron. The hand which holds this sword is the militia of a nation; and the militia of a nation is either an army in the field, or ready for the field upon occasion. But an army is a beast that has a great belly, and must be fed: wherefore this will come to what pastures you have, and what pastures you have will come to the balance of property, without which the public sword is but a name or mere spitfrog. Wherefore, to set that which Leviathan says of arms and of contracts a little straighter, he that can graze this beast with the great belly, as the Turk does his Timariots, may well deride him that imagines he received his power by covenant, or is obliged to any such toy: it being in this case only that covenants are but words and breath. But if the property of the nobility, stocked with their tenants and retainers, be the pasture of that beast, the ox knows his master's crib; and it is impossible for a king in such a constitution to reign otherwise than by covenant; or if he break it, it is words that come to blows.

"But," says he, "when an assembly of men is made sovereign, then no man imagines any such covenant to have part in the institution." But what was that by Publicola of appeal to the people, or that whereby the people had their tribunes? "Fie," says he, "nobody is so dull as to say that the people of Rome made a covenant with the Romans, to hold the sovereignty on such or such conditions, which, not performed, the Romans might depose the Roman people." In which there be several remarkable things; for he holds the commonwealth of Rome to have consisted of one assembly, whereas it consisted of the

senate and the people; that they were not upon covenant, whereas
every law enacted by them was a covenant between them; that
the one assembly was made sovereign, whereas the people, who
only were sovereign, were such from the beginning, as appears
by the ancient style of their covenants or laws—"The senate has
resolved, the people have decreed;" that a council being made
sovereign, cannot be made such upon conditions, whereas the
Decemvirs being a council that was made sovereign, was made
such upon conditions; that all conditions or covenants making
a sovereign, the sovereign being made, are void; whence it must
follow that, the Decemviri being made, were ever after the
lawful government of Rome, and that it was unlawful for the
commonwealth of Rome to depose the Decemvirs; as also that
Cicero, if he wrote otherwise out of his commonwealth, did not
write out of nature. But to come to others that see more of
this balance.

You have Aristotle full of it in divers places, especially where
he says, that "immoderate wealth, as where one man or the few
have greater possessions than the equality or the frame of the
commonwealth will bear, is an occasion of sedition, which ends
for the greater part in monarchy; and that for this cause the ostracism has been received in divers places, as in Argos and Athens.
But that it were better to prevent the growth in the beginning,
than, when it has got head, to seek the remedy of such an evil."

Machiavel has missed it very narrowly and more dangerously;
for, not fully perceiving that if a commonwealth be galled by the
gentry it is by their overbalance, he speaks of the gentry as
hostile to popular governments, and of popular governments as
hostile to the gentry; and makes us believe that the people in
such are so enraged against them, that where they meet a gentleman they kill him; which can never be proved by any one example,
unless in civil war, seeing that even in Switzerland the gentry
are not only safe, but in honor. But the balance, as I have laid
it down, though unseen by Machiavel, is that which interprets
him, and that which he confirms by his judgment in many others
as well as in this place, where he concludes, "That he who will
go about to make a commonwealth where there be many gentlemen, unless he first destroys them, undertakes an impossibility.
And that he who goes about to introduce monarchy where the
condition of the people is equal, shall never bring it to pass, unless
he cull out such of them as are the most turbulent and ambitious,
and make them gentlemen or noblemen, not in name but in effect;
that is, by enriching them with lands, castles and treasures, that

may gain them power among the rest, and bring in the rest to dependence upon themselves, to the end that, they maintaining their ambition by the prince, the prince may maintain his power by them."

Wherefore, as in this place I agree with Machiavel, that a nobility or gentry, overbalancing a popular government, is the utter bane and destruction of it; so I shall show in another, that a nobility or gentry, in a popular government, not overbalancing it, is the very life and soul of it.

By what has been said, it should seem that we may lay aside further disputes of the public sword, or of the right of the militia; which, be the government what it will, or let it change how it can, is inseparable from the overbalance in dominion: nor, if otherwise stated by the law or custom (as in the commonwealth of Rome, where the people having the sword, the nobility came to have the overbalance), avails it to any other end than destruction. For as a building swaying from the foundation must fall, so it fares with the law swaying from reason, and the militia from the balance of dominion. And thus much for the balance of national or domestic empire, which is in dominion.

The balance of foreign or provincial empire is of a contrary nature. A man may as well say that it is unlawful for him who has made a fair and honest purchase to have tenants, as for a government that has made a just progress and enlargement of itself to have provinces. But how a province may be justly acquired appertains to another place. In this I am to show no more than how or upon what kind of balance it is to be held; in order whereto I shall first show upon what kind of balance it is not to be held. It has been said, that national or independent empire, of what kind soever, is to be exercised by them that have the proper balance of dominion in the nation; wherefore provincial or dependent empire is not to be exercised by them that have the balance of dominion in the province, because that would bring the government from provincial and dependent to national and independent. Absolute monarchy, as that of the Turks, neither plants its people at home nor abroad, otherwise than as tenants for life or at will; wherefore its national and provincial government is all one. But in governments that admit the citizen or subject to dominion in lands, the richest are they that share most of the power at home; whereas the richest among the provincials, though native subjects, or citizens that have been transplanted, are least admitted to the government abroad; for men, like flowers or roots being transplanted,

take after the soil wherein they grow. Wherefore the commonwealth of Rome, by planting colonies of its citizens within the
bounds of Italy, took the best way of propagating itself, and
naturalizing the country; whereas if it had planted such colonies
without the bounds of Italy, it would have alienated the citizens,
and given root to liberty abroad, that might have sprung up
foreign or savage, and hostile to her: wherefore it never made
any such dispersion of itself and its strength, till it was under
the yoke of the Emperors, who, disburdening themselves of the
people, as having less apprehension of what they could do abroad
than at home, took a contrary course.

The Mamalukes (which, till any man show me the contrary, I
shall presume to have been a commonwealth consisting of an
army, whereof the common soldier was the people, the commission officer the senate, and the general the prince) were
foreigners, and by nation Circassians, that governed Egypt,
wherefore these never durst plant themselves upon dominion,
which growing naturally up into the national interest, must have
dissolved the foreign yoke in that province.

The like in some sort may be said of Venice, the government
whereof is usually mistaken; for Venice, though it does not take
in the people, never excluded them. This commonwealth, the
orders whereof are the most democratical or popular of all others,
in regard of the exquisite rotation of the senate, at the first
institution took in the whole people; they that now live under
the government without participation in it, are such as have
since either voluntarily chosen so to do, or were subdued by arms.
Wherefore the subject of Venice is governed by provinces, and the
balance of dominion not standing, as has been said, with provincial government; as the Mamalukes durst not cast their
government upon this balance in their provinces, lest the national
interest should have rooted out the foreign, so neither dare the
Venetians take in their subjects upon this balance, lest the foreign
interest should root out the national (which is that of the three
thousand now governing), and by diffusing the commonwealth
throughout her territories, lose the advantage of her situation,
by which in great part it subsists. And such also is the government of the Spaniard in the Indies, to which he deputes natives
of his own country, not admitting the Creoles to the government
of those provinces, though descended from Spaniards.

But if a prince or a commonwealth may hold a territory that
is foreign in this, it may be asked why he may not hold one
that is native in like manner? To which I answer, because

he can hold a foreign by a native territory, but not a native by a foreign; and as hitherto I have shown what is not the provincial balance, so by this answer it may appear what it is, namely, the overbalance of a native territory to a foreign; for as one country balances itself by the distribution of property according to the proportion of the same, so one country overbalances another by advantage of divers kinds. For example, the commonwealth of Rome overbalanced her provinces by the vigor of a more excellent government opposed to a crazier; or by a more exquisite militia opposed to one inferior in courage or discipline. The like was that of the Mamalukes, being a hardy people, to the Egyptians that were a soft one. And the balance of situation is in this kind of wonderful effect; seeing the king of Denmark, being none of the most potent princes, is able at the Sound to take toll of the greatest; and as this king, by the advantage of the land, can make the sea tributary, so Venice, by the advantage of the sea, in whose arms she is impregnable, can make the land to feed her Gulf. For the colonies in the Indies, they are yet babes that cannot live without sucking the breasts of their mother cities, but such as I mistake if when they come of age they do not wean themselves; which causes me to wonder at princes that delight to be exhausted in that way. And so much for the principles of power, whether national or provincial, domestic or foreign; being such as are external, and founded in the goods of fortune.

2. Principles of Political Authority: The Psychological Influences [1]

I come to the principles of authority, which are internal, and founded upon the goods of the mind. These the legislator that can unite in his government with those of fortune, comes nearest to the work of God, whose government consists of heaven and earth; which was said by Plato, though in different words, as, when princes should be philosophers, or philosophers princes, the world would be happy. And says Solomon: "There is an evil which I have seen under the sun, which proceeds from the ruler [enimvero neque nobilem, neque ingenuum, nec libertinum quidem armis præponere, regia utilitas est]. Folly is set in great dignity, and the rich [either in virtue and wisdom, in the goods of the mind, or those of fortune upon that balance which gives them a sense of the national interest] sit in low places. I have seen servants upon horses, and princes walking as servants upon the earth." Sad complaints, that the principles of power

[1] Pp. 25–29.

and of authority, the goods of the mind and of fortune, do not meet and twine in the wreath or crown of empire! Wherefore, if we have anything of piety or of prudence, let us raise ourselves out of the mire of private interest to the contemplation of virtue, and put a hand to the removal of "this evil from under the sun;" this evil against which no government that is not secured can be good; this evil from which the government that is secure must be perfect. Solomon tells us, that the cause of it is from the ruler, from those principles of power, which, balanced upon earthly trash, exclude the heavenly treasures of virtue, and that influence of it upon government which is authority. We have wandered the earth to find out the balance of power; but to find out that of authority we must ascend, as I said, nearer heaven, or to the image of God, which is the soul of man.

The soul of man (whose life or motion is perpetual contemplation or thought) is the mistress of two potent rivals, the one reason, the other passion, that are in continual suit; and, according as she gives up her will to these or either of them, is the felicity or misery which man partakes in this mortal life.

For, as whatever was passion in the contemplation of a man, being brought forth by his will into action, is vice and the bondage of sin; so whatever was reason in the contemplation of a man, being brought forth by his will into action, is virtue and the freedom of soul.

Again, as those actions of a man that were sin acquire to himself repentance or shame, and affect others with scorn or pity, so those actions of a man that are virtue acquire to himself honor, and upon others authority.

Now government is no other than the soul of a nation or city: wherefore that which was reason in the debate of a commonwealth being brought forth by the result, must be virtue; and forasmuch as the soul of a city or nation is the sovereign power, her virtue must be law. But the government whose law is virtue, and whose virtue is law, is the same whose empire is authority, and whose authority is empire.

Again, if the liberty of a man consists in the empire of his reason, the absence whereof would betray him to the bondage of his passions, then the liberty of a commonwealth consists in the empire of her laws, the absence whereof would betray her to the lust of tyrants. And these I conceive to be the principles upon which Aristotle and Livy (injuriously accused by Leviathan for not writing out of nature) have grounded their assertion, "that a commonwealth is an empire of laws and not of men."

But they must not carry it so. "For," says he, "the liberty, whereof there is so frequent and honorable mention in the histories and philosophy of the ancient Greeks and Romans, and the writings and discourses of those that from them have received all their learning in the politics, is not the liberty of particular men, but the liberty of the commonwealth." He might as well have said that the estates of particular men in a commonwealth are not the riches of particular men, but the riches of the commonwealth; for the equality of estates causes equality of power, and equality of power is the liberty, not only of the commonwealth, but of every man. But sure a man would never be thus irreverent with the greatest authors, and positive against all antiquity, without some certain demonstration of truth—and what is it? Why, "there is written on the turrets of the city of Lucca in great characters at this day the word LIBERTAS; yet no man can thence infer that a particular man has more liberty or immunity from the service of the commonwealth there than in Constantinople. Whether a commonwealth be monarchical or popular, the freedom is the same." The mountain has brought forth, and we have a little equivocation! For to say that a Lucchese has no more liberty or immunity from the laws of Lucca than a Turk has from those of Constantinople; and to say that a Lucchese has no more liberty or immunity by the laws of Lucca, than a Turk has by those of Constantinople, are pretty different speeches. The first may be said of all governments alike; the second scarce of any two; much less of these, seeing it is known that, whereas the greatest Bashaw is a tenant, as well of his head as of his estate, at the will of his lord, the meanest Lucchese that has land is a freeholder of both, and not to be controlled but by the law, and that framed by every private man to no other end (or they may thank themselves) than to protect the liberty of every private man, which by that means comes to be the liberty of the commonwealth.

But seeing they that make the laws in commonwealths are but men, the main question seems to be, how a commonwealth comes to be an empire of laws, and not of men? Or how the debate or result of a commonwealth is so sure to be according to reason; seeing they who debate, and they who resolve, be but men? "And as often as reason is against a man, so often will a man be against reason."

This is thought to be a shrewd saying, but will do no harm; for be it so that reason is nothing but interest, there be divers interests, and so divers reasons.

As first, there is private reason, which is the interest of a private man.

Secondly, there is a reason of state, which is the interest (or error, as was said by Solomon) of the ruler or rulers, that is to say, of the prince, of the nobility, or of the people.

Thirdly, there is that reason, which is the interest of mankind, or of the whole. "Now if we see even in those natural agents that want sense, that as in themselves they have a law which directs them in the means whereby they tend to their own perfection, so likewise that another law there is, which touches them as they are sociable parts united into one body, a law which binds them each to serve to others' good, and all to prefer the good of the whole, before whatsoever their own particular; as when stones, or heavy things, forsake their ordinary wont or centre, and fly upwards, as if they heard themselves commanded to let go the good they privately wish, and to relieve the present distress of nature in common." There is a common right, law of nature, or interest of the whole, which is more excellent, and so acknowledged to be by the agents themselves, than the right or interest of the parts only. "Wherefore, though it may be truly said that the creatures are naturally carried forth to their proper utility or profit, that ought not to be taken in too general a sense; seeing divers of them abstain from their own profit, either in regard of those of the same kind, or at least of their young."

Mankind then must either be less just than the creature, or acknowledge also his common interest to be common right. And if reason be nothing else but interest, and the interest of mankind be the right interest, then the reason of mankind must be right reason. Now compute well; for if the interest of popular government come the nearest to the interest of mankind, then the reason of popular government must come the nearest to right reason.

But it may be said that the difficulty remains yet; for be the interest of popular government right reason, a man does not look upon reason as it is right or wrong in itself, but as it makes for him or against him. Wherefore, unless you can show such orders of a government as, like those of God in nature, shall be able to constrain this or that creature to shake off that inclination which is more peculiar to it, and take up that which regards the common good or interest, all this is to no more end than to persuade every man in a popular government not to carve himself of that which he desires most, but to be mannerly

at the public table, and give the best from himself to decency
and the common interest. But that such orders may be established as may, nay must, give the upper hand in all cases to
common right or interest, notwithstanding the nearness of that
which sticks to every man in private, and this in a way of equal
certainty and facility, is known even to girls, being no other than
those that are of common practice with them in divers cases.
For example, two of them have a cake yet undivided, which
was given between them, that each of them therefore might have
that which is due: "divide," says one to the other, "and I will
choose; or let me divide, and you shall choose." If this be
but once agreed upon, it is enough; for the divident, dividing
unequally, loses, in regard that the other takes the better half;
wherefore she divides equally, and so both have right. "O the
depth of the wisdom of God!" and yet "by the mouths of babes
and sucklings has He set forth His strength;" that which great
philosophers are disputing upon in vain, is brought to light
by two harmless girls, even the whole mystery of a commonwealth,
which lies only in dividing and choosing. Nor has God (if
His works in nature be understood) left so much to mankind
to dispute upon as who shall divide and who choose, but distributed
them for ever into two orders, whereof the one has the natural
right of dividing, and the other of choosing.

3. Principles of Political Authority: The Essential Organs of Government [1]

A commonwealth is but a civil society of men: let us take any
number of men (as twenty) and immediately make a commonwealth. Twenty men (if they be not all idiots, perhaps if they be)
can never come so together but there will be such a difference
in them, that about a third will be wiser, or at least less foolish
than all the rest; these upon acquaintance, though it be but
small, will be discovered, and, as stags that have the largest
heads, lead the herd; for while the six, discoursing and arguing
one with another, show the eminence of their parts, the fourteen
discover things that they never thought on; or are cleared in
divers truths which had formerly perplexed them. Wherefore,
in matter of common concernment, difficulty, or danger, they
hang upon their lips, as children upon their fathers; and the
influence thus acquired by the six, the eminence of whose parts
are found to be a stay and comfort to the fourteen, is the au-

[1] Pp. 29–31, 35–37.

thority of the fathers. Wherefore this can be no other than a natural aristocracy diffused by God throughout the whole body of mankind to this end and purpose; and therefore such as the people have not only a natural but a positive obligation to make use of as their guides; as where the people of Israel are commanded to "take wise men, and understanding, and known among their tribes, to be made rulers over them." The six then approved of, as in the present case, are the senate, not by hereditary right, or in reagrd of the greatness of their estates only, which would tend to such power as might force or draw the people, but by election for their excellent parts, which tends to the advancement of the influence of their virtue or authority that leads the people. Wherefore the office of the senate is not to be commanders, but counsellors of the people; and that which is proper to counsellors is first to debate, and afterward to give advice in the business whereupon they have debated, whence the decrees of the senate are never laws, nor so called; and these being maturely framed, it is their duty to propose in the case to the people. Wherefore the senate is no more than the debate of the commonwealth. But to debate, is to discern or put a difference between things that, being alike, are not the same; or it is separating and weighing this reason against that, and that reason against this, which is dividing.

The senate then having divided, who shall choose? Ask the girls: for if she that divided must have chosen also, it had been little worse for the other in case she had not divided at all, but kept the whole cake to herself, in regard that being to choose too she divided accordingly. Wherefore if the senate have any farther power than to divide, the commonwealth can never be equal. But in a commonwealth consisting of a single council, there is no other to choose than that which divided; whence it is, that such a council fails not to scramble—that is, to be factious, there being no other dividing of the cake in that case but among themselves.

Nor is there any remedy but to have another council to choose. The wisdom of the few may be the light of mankind; but the interest of the few is not the profit of mankind, nor of a commonwealth. Wherefore, seeing we have granted interest to be reason, they must not choose lest it put out their light. But as the council dividing consists of the wisdom of the commonwealth, so the assembly or council choosing should consist of the interest of the commonwealth: as the wisdom of the commonwealth is in the aristocracy, so the interest of the commonwealth is in the whole body of the people. And whereas this, in case the commonwealth consist of a whole nation, is too unwieldy a body to be assembled, this council is to consist of such a representative as may be equal, and so constituted, as can never contract any other interest than that of the whole people; the manner whereof, being such as is best shown by exemplification, I remit to the model. But in the present case, the six dividing, and the fourteen choosing, must of necessity take in the whole interest of the twenty.

Dividing and choosing in the language of a commonwealth is debating and resolving; and whatsoever, upon debate of the senate, is proposed to the people, and resolved by them, is enacted by the authority of the fathers, and by the power of the people, which concurring, make a law.

But the law being made, says Leviathan, "is but words and paper without the hands and swords of men;" wherefore as these two orders of a commonwealth, namely, the senate and the people, are legislative, so of necessity there must be a third to be executive of the laws made, and this is the magistracy: in which order, with the rest being wrought up by art, the commonwealth consists of "the senate proposing, the people resolving, and the magistracy executing;" whereby partaking of the aristocracy as in the senate, of the democracy as in the people, and of monarchy as in the magistracy, it is complete. Now there being no other commonwealth but this in art or nature, it is no wonder if Machiavel has shown us that the ancients held this only to be good; but it seems strange to me that they should hold that there could be any other: for if there be such a thing as pure monarchy, yet that there should be such a one as pure aristocracy, or pure democracy, is not in my understanding. But the magistracy, both in number and function, is different in different commonwealths. Nevertheless there is one condition of it that must be the same in every one, or it dissolves the commonwealth where it is wanting. And this is no less than that, as the hand of the magistrate is the executive power of the law, so the head of the magistrate is answerable to the people, that his execution be according to the law; by which Leviathan may see that the hand or sword that executes the law is in it and not above it.

Athens consisted of the senate of the Bean proposing, of the church or assembly of the people resolving, and too often debating, which was the ruin of it; as also of the senate of the Areopagists, the nine archons, with divers other magistrates, executing.

Lacedæmon consisted of the senate proposing, of the church or congregation of the people resolving only, and never debating, which was the long life of it; and of the two kings, the court of the ephors, with divers other magistrates, executing.

Carthage consisted of the senate proposing and sometimes resolving too, of the people resolving and sometimes debating too, for which fault she was reprehended by Aristotle; and she had her *suffetes*, and her hundred men, with other magistrates, executing.

Rome consisted of the senate proposing, the *concio* or people resolving, and too often debating, which caused her storms; as also of the consuls, censors, ædiles, tribunes, prætors, quæstors and other magistrates, executing.

Venice consists of the senate or *pregati* proposing, and sometimes resolving too, of the great council or assembly of the people, in whom the result is constitutively; as also of the doge, the signory, the censors, the *dieci*, the *quazancies*[1], and other magistrates, executing.

The proceeding of the commonwealths of Switzerland and Holland is of a like nature, though after a more obscure manner; for the sovereignties, whether cantons, provinces, or cities, which are the people, send their deputies, commissioned and instructed by themselves (wherein they reserve the result in their own power), to the provincial or general convention, or senate, where the deputies debate, but have no other power of result than what was conferred upon them by the people, or is further conferred by the same upon further occasion. And for the executive part they have magistrates or judges in every canton, province or city, besides those which are more public, and relate to the league, as for adjusting controversies between one canton, province or city, and another, or the like between such persons as are not of the same canton, province or city.

But that we may observe a little further how the heathen politicians have written, not only out of nature, but as it were out of Scripture: as in the commonwealth of Israel, God is said to have been king, so the commonwealth where the law is king, is said by Aristotle to be "the kingdom of God." And where by the lusts or passions of men a power is set above that of the law deriving from reason, which is the dictate of God, God in that sense is rejected or deposed that He should not reign over them, as He was in Israel. And yet Leviathan will have it, that "by reading of these Greek and Latin (he might as well in this sense have said Hebrew) authors, young men, and all others that are

---

[1] *Dieci*—"the ten "; *quazancies*—"the forty."

unprovided of the antidote of solid reason, receiving a strong and delightful impression of the great exploits of war achieved by the conductors of their armies, receive withal a pleasing idea of all they have done besides, and imagine their great prosperity not to have proceeded from the emulation of particular men, but from the virtue of their popular form of government, not considering the frequent seditions and civil wars produced by the imperfection of their polity." Where, first, the blame he lays to the heathen authors, is in his sense laid to the Scripture; and whereas he holds them to be young men, or men of no antidote that are of like opinions, it should seem that Machiavel, the sole retriever of this ancient prudence, is to his solid reason a beardless boy that has newly read Livy. And how solid his reason is, may appear where he grants the great prosperity of ancient commonwealths, which is to give up the controversy. For such an effect must have some adequate cause, which to evade he insinuates that it was nothing else but the emulation of particular men, as if so great an emulation could have been generated without as great virtue, so great virtue without the best education, and best education without the best law, or the best laws any otherwise than by the excellency of their polity.

But if some of these commonwealths, as being less perfect in their polity than others, have been more seditious, it is not more an argument of the infirmity of this or that commonwealth in particular, than of the excellency of that kind of polity in general, which if they that have not altogether reached, have nevertheless had greater prosperity, what would befall them that should reach?

4. *Principles of Political Authority: Institutions for Safe-guarding the State* [1]

By what has been shown in reason and experience, it may appear, that though commonwealths in general be governments of the senate proposing, the people resolving, and the magistracy executing, yet some are not so good at these orders as others, through some impediment or defect in the frame, balance, or capacity of them, according to which they are of divers kinds.

The first division of them is into such as are single, as Israel, Athens, Lacedæmon, etc.; and such as are by leagues, as those of the Achæans, Ætolians, Lycians, Switz, and Hollanders.

The second (being Machiavel's) is into such as are for pres-

[1] Pp. 39–44.

ervation, as Lacedæmon and Venice, and such as are for increase, as Athens and Rome; in which I can see no more
than that the former takes in no more citizens than are
necessary for defence, and the latter so many as are capable of
increase.

The third division (unseen hitherto) is into equal and unequal,
and this is the main point, especially as to domestic peace and
tranquillity; for to make a commonwealth unequal, is to divide
it into parties, which sets them at perpetual variance, the one
party endeavoring to preserve their eminence and inequality,
and the other to attain to equality; whence the people of Rome
derived their perpetual strife with the nobility and senate. But
in an equal commonwealth there can be no more strife than
there can be overbalance in equal weights; wherefore the commonwealth of Venice, being that which of all others is the most equal
in the constitution, is that wherein there never happened any
strife between the senate and the people.

An equal commonwealth is such a one as is equal both in the
balance or foundation, and in the superstructure; that is to say
in her agrarian law, and in her rotation.

An equal agrarian is a perpetual law, establishing and preserving the balance of dominion by such a distribution, that no
one man or number of men, within the compass of the few or
aristocracy, can come to overpower the whole people by their
possessions in lands.

As the agrarian answers to the foundation, so does rotation
to the superstructures.

Equal rotation is equal vicissitude in government, or succession to magistracy conferred for such convenient terms, enjoying
equal vacations, as take in the whole body by parts, succeeding
others, through the free election or suffrage of the people.

The contrary, whereunto is prolongation of magistracy, which,
trashing the wheel of rotation, destroys the life or natural motion
of a commonwealth.

The election or suffrage of the people is most free where it is
made or given in such a manner that it can neither oblige nor
disoblige another, nor through fear of an enemy, or bashfulness
towards a friend, impair a man's liberty.

Wherefore, says Cicero, the tablet or ballot of the people of
Rome (who gave their votes by throwing tablets or little pieces
of wood secretly into urns marked for the negative or affirmative) was a welcome constitution to the people, as that which,
not impairing the assurance of their brows, increased the free-

dom of their judgment. I have not stood upon a more particular description of this ballot, because that of Venice exemplified in the model is of all others the most perfect.

An equal commonwealth (by that which has been said) is a government established upon an equal agrarian, arising into the superstructures or three orders, the senate debating and proposing, the people resolving, and the magistracy executing, by an equal rotation through the suffrage of the people given by the ballot. For though rotation may be without the ballot, and the ballot without rotation, yet the ballot not only as to the ensuing model includes both, but is by far the most equal way; for which cause under the name of the ballot I shall hereafter understand both that and rotation too.

Now having reasoned the principles of an equal commonwealth, I should come to give an instance of such a one in experience, if I could find it; but if this work be of any value, it lies in that it is the first example of a commonwealth that is perfectly equal. For Venice, though it comes the nearest, yet is a commonwealth for preservation; and such a one, considering the paucity of citizens taken in, and the number not taken in, is externally unequal; and though every commonwealth that holds provinces must in that regard be such, yet not to that degree. Nevertheless, Venice internally, and for her capacity, is by far the most equal, though it has not, in my judgment, arrived at the full perfection of equality; both because her laws supplying the defect of an agrarian, are not so clear nor effectual at the foundation, nor her superstructures, by the virtue of her ballot or rotation, exactly librated; in regard that through the paucity of her citizens her greater magistracies are continually wheeled through a few hands. . . . Wherefore if this in Venice, or that in Lacedæmon, where the kings were hereditary, and the senators (though elected by the people) for life, cause no inequality (which is hard to be conceived) in a commonwealth for preservation, or such a one as consists of a few citizens; yet is it manifest that it would cause a very great one in a commonwealth for increase, or consisting of the many, which, by engrossing the magistracies in a few hands, would be obstructed in their rotation.

But there be who say (and think it a strong objection) that, let a commonwealth be as equal as you can imagine, two or three men when all is done will govern it; and there is that in it which, notwithstanding the pretended sufficiency of a popular state, amounts to a plain confession of the imbecility of that policy, and of the prerogative of monarchy; forasmuch as popular governments in difficult cases have had recourse to dictatorian power, as in Rome.

To which I answer, that as truth is a spark to which objections are like bellows, so in this respect our commonwealth shines; for the eminence acquired by suffrage of the people in a commonwealth, especially if it be popular and equal, can be ascended by no other steps than the universal acknowledgment of virtue: and where men excel in virtue, the commonwealth is stupid and unjust, if accordingly they do not excel in authority. Wherefore this is both the advantage of virtue, which has her due encouragement, and of the commonwealth, which has her due services. These are the philosophers which Plato would have to be princes, the princes which Solomon would have to be mounted, and their steeds are those of authority, not empire; or, if they be buckled to the chariot of empire, as that of the dictatorian power, like the chariot of the sun, it is glorious for terms and vacations or intervals. And as a commonwealth is a government of laws and not of men, so is this the principality of virtue, and not of man; if that fail or set in one, it rises in another who is created his immediate successor. And this takes away that vanity from under the sun, which is an error proceeding more or less from all other rulers under heaven but an equal commonwealth.

These things considered, it will be convenient in this place to speak a word to such as go about to insinuate to the nobility or gentry a fear of the people, or to the people a fear of the nobility or gentry, as if their interests were destructive to each other; when indeed an army may as well consist of soldiers without officers, or of officers without soldiers, as a commonwealth, especially such a one as is capable of greatness, of a people without a gentry, or of a gentry without a people. Wherefore this, though not always so intended, as may appear by Machiavel, who else would be guilty, is a pernicious error. There is something first in the making of a commonwealth, then in the governing of it, and last of all in the leading of its armies, which, though there be great divines, great lawyers, great men in all professions, seems to be peculiar only to the genius of a gentleman. For so it is in the universal series of story, that if any man has founded a commonwealth, he was first a gentleman. Moses had his education by the daughter of Pharaoh; Theseus and Solon, of noble birth, were held by the Athenians worthy to be kings; Lycurgus was of the royal blood; Romulus and Numa princes; Brutus and Publicola patricians; the Gracchi, that lost their

lives for the people of Rome and the restitution of that commonwealth, were the sons of a father adorned with two triumphs,
and of Cornelia the daughter of Scipio, who being demanded
in marriage by King Ptolemy, disdained to become the Queen
of Egypt. And the most renowned Olphaus Megaletor, sole
legislator, as you will see anon, of the commonwealth of Oceana,
was derived from a noble family; nor will it be any occasion of
scruple in this case, that Leviathan affirms the politics to be no
ancienter than his book, *De Cive.* Such also as have got any
fame in the civil government of a commonwealth, or by the leading
of its armies, have been gentlemen; for so in all other respects
were those plebeian magistrates elected by the people of Rome,
being of known descents and of equal virtues, except only that
they were excluded from the name by the usurpation of the
patricians. Holland, through this defect at home, has borrowed
princes for generals, and gentlemen of divers nations for commanders: and the Switzers, if they have any defect in this kind,
rather lend their people to the colors of other princes, than make
that noble use of them at home which should assert the liberty
of mankind. For where there is not a nobility to hearten the
people, they are slothful, regardless of the world, and of the
public interest of liberty, as even those of Rome had been without their gentry: wherefore let the people embrace the gentry
in peace, as the light of their eyes; and in war, as the trophy
of their arms; and if Cornelia disdained to be Queen of Egypt,
if a Roman consul looked down from his tribunal upon the greatest
king, let the nobility love and cherish the people that afford
them a throne so much higher in a commonwealth, in the acknowledgment of their virtue, than the crowns of monarchs.

But if the equality of a commonwealth consist in the equality
first of the agrarian, and next of the rotation, then the inequality
of a commonwealth must consist in the absence or inequality of
the agrarian, or of the rotation, or of both.

Israel and Lacedæmon, which commonwealths (as the people
of this, in Josephus, claims kindred of that) have great resemblance, were each of them equal in their agrarian, and unequal
in their rotation, especially Israel, where the Sanhedrim or
senate, first elected by the people, as appears by the words of
Moses, took upon them ever after, without any precept of God, to
substitute their successors by ordination; which having been
there of civil use, as excommunication, community of goods, and
other customs of the Essenes, who were many of them converted,
came afterward to be introduced into the Christian Church.

And the election of the judge, *suffes*, or dictator, was irregular, both for the occasion, the term, and the vacation of that magistracy; as you find in the book of Judges, where it is often repeated, that in those days there was no king in Israel—that is, no judge; and in the first of Samuel, where Eli judged Israel forty years, and Samuel, all his life. In Lacedæmon the election of the senate being by suffrage of the people, though for life, was not altogether so unequal, yet the hereditary right of kings, were it not for the agrarian, had ruined her.

Athens and Rome were unequal as to their agrarian, that of Athens being infirm, and this of Rome none at all; for if it were more anciently carried it was never observed. Whence, by the time of Tiberius Gracchus, the nobility had almost eaten the people quite out of their lands, which they held in the occupation of tenants and servants, whereupon the remedy being too late, and too vehemently applied, that commonwealth was ruined.

These also were unequal in their rotation, but in a contrary manner. Athens, in regard that the senate (chosen at once by lot, not by suffrage, and changed every year, not in part, but in the whole) consisted not of the natural aristocracy, nor sitting long enough to understand or to be perfect in their office, had no sufficient authority to restrain the people from that perpetual turbulence in the end, which was their ruin, notwithstanding the efforts of Nicias, who did all a man could do to help it. But as Athens, by the headiness of the people, so Rome fell by the ambition of the nobility, through the want of an equal rotation; which, if the people had got into the senate, and timely into the magistracies (whereof the former was always usurped by the patricians, and the latter for the most part) they had both carried and held their agrarian, and that had rendered that commonwealth immovable.

But let a commonwealth be equal or unequal, it must consist, as has been shown by reason and all experience, of the three general orders; that is to say, of the senate debating and proposing, of the people resolving, and of the magistracy executing. Wherefore I can never wonder enough at Leviathan, who, without any reason or example, will have it that a commonwealth consists of a single person, or of a single assembly; nor can I sufficiently pity those "thousand gentlemen, whose minds, which otherwise would have wavered, he has framed [as is affirmed by himself] into a conscientious obedience [for so he is pleased to call it] of such a government."

SELECTED BIBLIOGRAPHY

Sabine, George H., *History of Political Theory*, pp. 496–508.
Cook, Thomas I., *History of Political Philosophy*, pp. 460–467.
Dunning, William A., *Political Theories, from Luther to Montesquieu*, ch. 7, § 6.
Levett, A. E., "James Harrington," in F. J. C. Hearnshaw, ed., *Social and Political Ideas of Some Great Thinkers of the Sixteenth and Seventeenth Centuries* (London, 1926), ch. 8.
Gough, J. W., "Harrington and Contemporary Thought," in *Political Science Quarterly*, vol. 45 (1930), pp. 395–404.
Gooch, G. P., *English Democratic Ideas in the Seventeenth Century* (new ed. by H. J. Laski, Cambridge, 1927), pp. 241–257, 305–307.
Dwight, Theodore, "Harrington and His Influence upon American Political Institutions and Political Thought," in *Political Science Quarterly*, vol. 2 (1887), pp. 1–44.
Smith, H. F. Russell, *Harrington and His Oceana* (Cambridge, 1914).

LOCKE

XXI. JOHN LOCKE (1632-1704)

INTRODUCTION

The three immediately preceding readings were from English authors who wrote during the period of the Puritan Revolution in the middle of the seventeenth century and whose theories bore close relation to the actual political conflicts of that period. The chief political work of John Locke was written in direct reference to the Revolution of 1689. His *Two Treatises of Government* comprise a philosophic defense of the parliamentary party in that conflict; the second treatise contains one of the most thoroughly worked out and influential expositions of the principles of representative government that have been written.

Locke was born and reared in a Puritan family; his father was an attorney and small landholder. He was a student at Oxford at a time when the Independents were in control there; he received his bachelor's degree in 1656, his master's degree a year later, and he became a tutor in Christ Church in 1660. Though dogmatism, formalism and scholasticism were the dominant academic methods at Oxford just then, Locke soon fell under more liberalizing influences which were beginning to be manifest in England. He studied Descartes' writings, pursued some experimental investigation in chemical sciences, and studied and practised medicine for a short period. In the late sixties he became confidential secretary to the Liberal Lord Shaftesbury, great Whig parliamentary leader. This introduced him to a career which broadened his experience and acquaintanceship in such way as profoundly to strengthen the liberalistic tendency of his mind. Through his connection with Lord Shaftesbury he became the associate of many public men and scholars in England and on the Continent. He was in France with Shaftesbury during the latter's exile, from 1675 to 1679; and he resided in Holland from 1685—the year of Shaftesbury's death—until 1689, when he returned to England, after the success of the Revolution. In the latter year he was made Commissioner of Appeals; he was later appointed to the Board of Trade and his counsel was often sought by political leaders.

Locke's greater works were published after 1689. Before leaving England for the first time (in 1675) he had written several essays; and he had begun his great metaphysical work—the *Essay concerning Human Understanding*, which was published in 1690. In 1690 also appeared his *Two Treatises of Government*. In later years he published many important essays on subjects of education, Christianity, and philosophy; chief among these are the *Thoughts on Education* and *The Reasonableness of Christianity*. He also wrote numerous pamphlets in explanation and defense of his characteristic doctrines of empiricism in psychology, toleration in religion, and liberalism in politics.

The first of the *Two Treatises of Government* was written to show the fallacy of the doctrine that any divine prerogatives attach to the office of king; in form it is a systematic refutation of Sir Robert Filmer's *Patriarcha* (written near the middle of the century and first published in 1680), which presented the theory that political sovereignty is derived solely from the original paternal authority given by God to Adam, inherited by Noah, and thenceforth transmitted, under divine auspices, through continuous hereditary succession according to the rule of primogeniture. The second treatise, *Of Civil Government*, contains Locke's positive theory. It is a comprehensive discussion of the origin, character and province of government.

At various points in this second treatise Locke acknowledges his indebtedness to Hooker; and he attributes to Hooker authorship of the idea that men originally lived together without civil government and that political order was instituted by their voluntary and deliberate coöperation. Locke begins, as Hobbes did, with a description of the pre-political "state of nature" and with an analysis of the laws controlling men in that condition; and he also follows with an explanation of the origin of the state through the social contract. But according to Locke's description the laws which, as manifestations of man's natural reason, are controlling in the state of nature, are such as impel men to sociability and generally to voluntary respect for certain primary rights of others. Moreover, Locke formulates the social contract in such way as to establish the ultimate supremacy of the people over the government and to demonstrate that the sphere and powers of government are limited by the terms of the contract.

READINGS FROM BOOK II OF THE TWO TREATISES OF GOVERNMENT [1]

1. The State of Nature.[2]

1. It having been shown in the foregoing discourse :

First. That Adam had not, either by natural right of fatherhood or by positive donation from God, any such authority over his children, or dominion over the world, as is pretended.

Secondly. That if he had, his heirs yet had no right to it.

Thirdly. That if his heirs had, there being no law of nature nor positive law of God that determines which is the right heir in all cases that may arise, the right of succession, and consequently of bearing rule, could not have been certainly determined.

Fourthly. That if even that had been determined, yet the knowledge of which is the eldest line of Adam's posterity being so long since utterly lost, that in the races of mankind and families of the world, there remains not to one above another the least pretense to be the eldest house, and to have the right of inheritance.

All these premises having, as I think, been clearly made out, it is impossible that the rulers now on earth should make any benefit, or derive any the least shadow of authority from that, which is held to be the fountain of all power, "Adam's private dominion and paternal jurisdiction;" so that he that will not give just occasion to think that all government in the world is the product only of force and violence, and that men live together by no other rules but that of beasts, where the strongest carries it, and so lay a foundation for perpetual disorder and mischief, tumult, sedition, and rebellion (things that the followers of that hypothesis so loudly cry out against), must of necessity find out another rise of government, another original of political power, and another way of designing and knowing the persons that have it than what Sir Robert Filmer hath taught us.

2. To this purpose, I think it may not be amiss to set down what I take to be political power; that the power of a magis-

---

[1] The selections are taken from Vol. IV of *The Works of John Locke* (12th edition, London, 1824), with a few corrections from other editions.

[2] Bk. II, chs. i–iii.

trate over a subject may be distinguished from that of a father over his children, a master over his servant, a husband over his wife, and a lord over his slave. All which distinct powers happening sometimes together in the same man, if he be considered under these different relations, it may help us to distinguish these powers one from another, and show the difference betwixt a ruler of a commonwealth, a father of a family, and a captain of a galley.

3. Political power, then, I take to be a right of making laws, with penalties of death, and consequently all less penalties for the regulating and preserving of property, and of employing the force of the community in the execution of such laws, and in the defense of the commonwealth from foreign injury, and all this only for the public good.

Ch. ii.   *Of the State of Nature.*

4. To understand political power right, and derive it from its original, we must consider what state all men are naturally in, and that is a state of perfect freedom to order their actions and dispose of their possessions and persons as they think fit, within the bounds of the law of nature, without asking leave or depending upon the will of any other man.

A state also of equality, wherein all the power and jurisdiction is reciprocal, no one having more than another, there being nothing more evident than that creatures of the same species and rank, promiscuously born to all the same advantages of nature, and the use of the same faculties, should also be equal one amongst another, without subordination or subjection, unless the lord and master of them all should, by any manifest declaration of his will, set one above another, and confer on him, by an evident and clear appointment, an undoubted right to dominion and sovereignty.

6. But though this be a state of liberty, yet it is not a state of license; though man in that state have an uncontrollable liberty to dispose of his person or possessions, yet he has not liberty to destroy himself, or so much as any creature in his possession, but where some nobler use than its bare preservation calls for it. The state of nature has a law of nature to govern it, which obliges every one; and reason, which is that law, teaches all mankind who will but consult it, that being all equal and independent, no one ought to harm another in his life, health, liberty or possessions; for men being all the workmanship of one omnipotent and infinitely wise Maker, all the servants of one sovereign

Master, sent into the world by His order and about His business, they are His property, whose workmanship they are, made to last during His, not one another's pleasure. And, being furnished with like faculties, sharing all in one community of nature, there cannot be supposed any such subordination among us that may authorize us to destroy one another, as if we were made for one another's uses, as the inferior ranks of creatures are for ours. Every one, as he is bound to preserve himself, and not to quit his station willfully, so by the like reason, when his own preservation comes not in competition, ought he as much as he can to preserve the rest of mankind, and may not, unless it be to do justice on an offender, take away, or impair the life, or what tends to the preservation of the life, the liberty, health, limb, or goods of another.

7. And that all men may be restrained from invading others' rights, and from doing hurt to one another, and the law of nature be observed, which willeth the peace and preservation of all mankind, the execution of the law of nature is in that state put into every man's hands, whereby every one has a right to punish the transgressors of that law to such a degree as may hinder its violation. For the law of nature would, as all other laws that concern men in this world, be in vain if there were nobody that in the state of nature had a power to execute that law, and thereby preserve the innocent and restrain offenders; and if any one in the state of nature may punish another for any evil he has done, every one may do so. For in that state of perfect equality, where naturally there is no superiority or jurisdiction of one over another, what any may do in prosecution of that law, every one must needs have a right to do.

8. And thus, in the state of nature, one man comes by a power over another, but yet no absolute or arbitrary power to use a criminal, when he has got him in his hands, according to the passionate heats or boundless extravagancy of his own will, but only to retribute to him so far as calm reason and conscience dictate, what is proportionate to his transgression, which is so much as may serve for reparation and restraint. For these two are the only reasons why one man may lawfully do harm to another, which is that we call punishment. In transgressing the law of nature, the offender declares himself to live by another rule than that of reason and common equity, which is that measure God has set to the actions of men for their mutual security; and so he becomes dangerous to mankind, the tie which is to secure them from injury and violence being slighted and broken by him; which being a trespass against the whole species, and the

peace and safety of it, provided for by the law of nature, every
man upon this score, by the right he hath to preserve mankind
in general, may restrain, or where it is necessary, destroy things
noxious to them, and so may bring such evil on any one who
hath transgressed that law, as may make him repent the doing
of it, and thereby deter him, and by his example others, from
doing the like mischief. And in this case, and upon this ground,
every man hath a right to punish the offender, and be executioner
of the law of nature.

9. I doubt not but this will seem a very strange doctrine to
some men; but before they condemn it, I desire them to resolve
me by what right any prince or state can put to death or punish
any alien for any crime he commits in their country. It is certain
their laws, by virtue of any sanction they receive from the promulgated will of the legislature, reach not a stranger. They speak
not to him, nor, if they did, is he bound to hearken to them. The
legislative authority by which they are in force over the subjects
of that commonwealth hath no power over him. Those who
have the supreme power of making laws in England, France, or
Holland, are, to an Indian, but like the rest of the world—men
without authority. And therefore, if by the law of nature every
man hath not a power to punish offenses against it, as he soberly
judges the case to require, I see not how the magistrates of any
community can punish an alien of another country, since, in
reference to him, they can have no more power than what every
man naturally may have over another.

10. Besides the crime which consists in violating the law,
and varying from the right rule of reason, whereby a man so
far becomes degenerate, and declares himself to quit the principles of human nature and to be a noxious creature, there is
commonly injury done to some person or other, and some other
man receives damage by his transgression; in which case, he who
hath received any damage has (besides the right of punishment
common to him, with other men) a particular right to seek reparation from him that hath done it. And any other person who finds
it just may also join with him that is injured, and assist him in
recovering from the offender so much as may make satisfaction
for the harm he hath suffered.

11. From these two distinct rights (the one of punishing
the crime, for restraint and preventing the like offense, which
right of punishing is in everybody, the other of taking reparation,
which belongs only to the injured party) comes it to pass that
the magistrate, who by being magistrate hath the common right

of punishing put into his hands, can often, where the public good demands not the execution of the law, remit the punishment of criminal offenses by his own authority, but yet cannot remit the satisfaction due to any private man for the damage he has received. That he who hath suffered the damage has a right to demand in his own name, and he alone can remit. The damnified person has this power of appropriating to himself the goods or service of the offender by right of self-preservation, as every man has a power to punish the crime to prevent its being committed again, by the right he has of preserving all mankind, and doing all resonable things he can in order to that end. And thus it is that every man in the state of nature has a power to kill a murderer, both to deter others from doing the like injury (which no reparation can compensate) by the example of the punishment that attends it from everybody, and also to secure men from the attempts of a criminal who, having renounced reason, the common rule and measure God hath given to mankind, hath, by the unjust violence and slaughter he hath committed upon one, declared war against all mankind, and therefore may be destroyed as a lion or a tiger, one of those wild savage beasts with whom men can have no society nor security. And upon this is grounded that great law of nature, "Whoso sheddeth man's blood, by man shall his blood be shed." And Cain was so fully convinced that every one had a right to destroy such a criminal, that, after the murder of his brother, he cries out, "Every one that findeth me shall slay me," so plain was it writ in the hearts of all mankind.

12. By the same reason may a man in the state of nature punish the lesser breaches of that law. It will perhaps be demanded, with death? I answer: Each transgression may be punished to that degree, and with so much severity, as will suffice to make it an ill bargain to the offender, give him cause to repent, and terrify others from doing the like. Every offense that can be committed in the state of nature may, in the state of nature, be also punished equally, and as far forth, as it may, in a commonwealth. For though it would be beside my present purpose to enter here into the particulars of the law of nature, or its measures of punishment, yet it is certain there is such a law, and that too as intelligible and plain to a rational creature and a studier of that law as the positive laws of commonwealths, nay, possibly plainer; as much as reason is easier to be understood than the fancies and intricate contrivances of men, following contrary and hidden interests put into words; for so truly are a great part of the municipal laws of countries, which are only so far right as

they are founded on the law of nature, by which they are to be regulated and interpreted.

13. To this strange doctrine—viz., That in the state of nature every one has the executive power of the law of nature, I doubt not but it will be objected that it is unreasonable for men to be judges in their own cases, that self-love will make men partial to themselves and their friends; and, on the other side, that ill-nature, passion, and revenge will carry them too far in punishing others, and hence nothing but confusion and disorder will follow, and that therefore God hath certainly appointed government to restrain the partiality and violence of men. I easily grant that civil government is the proper remedy for the inconveniences of the state of nature, which must certainly be great where men may be judges in their own case, since it is easy to be imagined that he who was so unjust as to do his brother an injury will scarce be so just as to condemn himself for it. But I shall desire those who make this objection to remember that absolute monarchs are but men; and if government is to be the remedy of those evils which necessarily follow from men being judges in their own cases, and the state of nature is therefore not to be endured, I desire to know what kind of government that is, and how much better it is than the state of nature, where one man commanding a multitude has the liberty to be judge in his own case, and may do to all his subjects whatever he pleases without the least liberty to any one to question or control those who execute his pleasure? and in whatsoever he doth, whether led by reason, mistake, or passion, must be submitted to? Much better it is in the state of nature, wherein men are not bound to submit to the unjust will of another. And if he that judges, judges amiss in his own or any other case, he is answerable for it to the rest of mankind.

14. It is often asked as a mighty objection, where are, or ever were, there any men in such a state of nature? To which it may suffice as an answer at present, that since all princes and rulers of "independent" governments all through the world are in a state of nature, it is plain the world never was, **nor ever will be,** without numbers of men in that state. I have named all governors of "independent" communities, whether they are, or are not, in league with others; for it is not every compact that puts an end to the state of nature between men, but only this one of agreeing together mutually to enter into one community, and make one body politic; other promises and compacts men may make with one another, and yet still be in the state of nature. The promises and bargains for truck, etc., between the two men in

the desert island . . . or between a Swiss and an Indian in the woods of America, are binding to them, though they are perfectly in a state of nature in reference to one another; for truth and keeping of faith belongs to men as men, and not as members of society.

15. To those that say there were never any men in the state of nature, I will not only oppose the authority of the judicious Hooker (Eccl. Pol. lib. i. sect. 10), where he says, "the laws which have been hitherto mentioned"—*i.e.*, the laws of nature—"do bind men absolutely, even as they are men, although they have never any settled fellowship, never any solemn agreement amongst themselves what to do or not to do; but for as much as we are not by ourselves sufficient to furnish ourselves with competent store of things needful for such a life as our nature doth desire, a life fit for the dignity of man, therefore to supply those defects and imperfections which are in us, as living single and solely by ourselves, we are naturally induced to seek communion and fellowship with others; this was the cause of men uniting themselves at first in politic societies." But I, moreover, affirm that all men are naturally in that state, and remain so till, by their own consents, they make themselves members of some politic society, and I doubt not, in the sequel of this discourse, to make it very clear.

Ch. iii. *Of the State of War.*

16. The state of war is a state of enmity and destruction; and therefore declaring by word or action, not a passionate and hasty, but sedate, settled design upon another man's life puts him in a state of war with him against whom he has declared such an intention, and so has exposed his life to the other's power to be taken away by him, or any one that joins with him in his defense, and espouses his quarrel; it being reasonable and just I should have a right to destroy that which threatens me with destruction; for by the fundamental law of nature, man being to be preserved as much as possible, when all cannot be preserved, the safety of the innocent is to be preferred; and one may destroy a man who makes war upon him, or has discovered an enmity to his being, for the same reason that he may kill a wolf or a lion; because such men are not under the ties of the common law of reason, have no other rule but that of force and violence, and so may be treated as beasts of prey, those dangerous and noxious creatures that will be sure to destroy him whenever he falls into their power.

17. And hence it is that he who attempts to get another man
into his absolute power does thereby put himself into a state of
war with him; it being to be understood as a declaration of a design
upon his life. For I have reason to conclude that he who would
get me into his power without my consent would use me as he
pleased when he had got me there, and destroy me too when he
had a fancy to it; for nobody can desire to have me in his absolute
power unless it be to compel me by force to that which is against
the right of my freedom—*i.e.*, make me a slave. To be free
from such force is the only security of my preservation, and
reason bids me look on him as an enemy to my preservation who
would take away that freedom which is the fence to it; so that he
who makes an attempt to enslave me thereby puts himself into
a state of war with me. He that in the state of nature would
take away the freedom that belongs to any one in that state
must necessarily be supposed to have a design to take away
everything else, that freedom being the foundation of all the rest;
as he that in the state of society would take away the freedom
belonging to those of that society or commonwealth must be
supposed to design to take away from them everything else, and
so be looked on as in a state of war.

18. This makes it lawful for a man to kill a thief who has
not in the least hurt him, nor declared any design upon his life,
any farther than by the use of force so to get him in his power
as to take away his money, or what he pleases, from him; because
using force, where he has no right, to get me into his power, let
his pretense be what it will, I have no reason to suppose that he
who would take away my liberty would not, when he had me in
his power, take away everything else. And, therefore, it is
lawful for me to treat him as one who has put himself into a
state of war with me—*i.e.*, kill him if I can; for to that hazard
does he justly expose himself whoever introduces a state of war,
and is aggressor in it.

19. And here we have the plain difference between the state
of nature and the state of war, which however some men have
confounded, are as far distant as a state of peace, goodwill,
mutual assistance, and preservation, and a state of enmity,
malice, violence, and mutual destruction are one from another.
Men living together according to reason, without a common
superior on earth with authority to judge between them, is
properly the state of nature. But force, or a declared design of
force, upon the person of another, where there is no common
superior on earth to appeal to for relief, is the state of war; and

it is the want of such an appeal gives a man the right of war even
against an aggressor, though he be in society and a fellow-subject.
Thus, a thief whom I cannot harm, but by appeal to the law, for
having stolen all that I am worth, I may kill when he sets on me to
rob me but of my horse or coat; because the law, which was made
for my preservation, where it cannot interpose to secure my life
from present force, which if lost is capable of no reparation,
permits me my own defense and the right of war, a liberty to kill
the aggressor, because the aggressor allows not time to appeal to
our common judge, nor the decision of the law, for remedy in a case
where the mischief may be irreparable. Want of a common judge
with authority puts all men in a state of nature; force without right
upon a man's person makes a state of war both where there is, and
is not, a common judge.

21. To avoid this state of war (wherein there is no appeal but
to heaven, and wherein every the least difference is apt to end where
there is no authority to decide between the contenders) is one great
reason of men's putting themselves into society and quitting the
state of nature. For where there is an authority, a power on
earth, from which relief can be had by appeal, there the continuance
of the state of war is excluded, and the controversy is decided by
that power. . . .

2. The Rational Basis of Private Property [1]

Ch. v. *Of Property.*

25. Whether we consider natural reason, which tells us that
men, being once born, have a right to their preservation, and consequently to meat and drink and such other things as nature
affords for their subsistence, or "revelation," which gives us an
account of those grants God made of the world to Adam, and to
Noah and his sons, it is very clear that God, as King David says
(Psalm cxv. 16), "has given the earth to the children of men,"
given it to mankind in common. But, this being supposed, it
seems to some a very great difficulty how any one should ever
come to have a property in anything, I will not content myself to
answer, that, if it be difficult to make out "property" upon a
supposition that God gave the world to Adam and his posterity
in common, it is impossible that any man but one universal
monarch should have any "property" upon a supposition that God

[1] Book II, ch. v.

gave the world to Adam and his heirs in succession, exclusive of all
the rest of his posterity; but I shall endeavour to show how men
might come to have a property in several parts of that which God
gave to mankind in common, and that without any express compact of all the commoners.

26. God, who hath given the world to men in common, hath
also given them reason to make use of it to the best advantage of
life and convenience. The earth and all that is therein is given
to men for the support and comfort of their being. And though
all the fruits it naturally produces, and beasts it feeds, belong to
mankind in common, as they are produced by the spontaneous
hand of nature, and nobody has originally a private dominion
exclusive of the rest of mankind in any of them, as they are thus
in their natural state, yet being given for the use of men, there must
of necessity be a means to appropriate them some way or other
before they can be of any use, or at all beneficial, to any particular
men. The fruit or venison which nourishes the wild Indian, who
knows no enclosure, and is still a tenant in common, must be his,
and so his—i.e., a part of him, that another can no longer have any
right to it before it can do him any good for the support of his life.

27. Though the earth and all inferior creatures be common to all
men, yet every man has a "property" in his own "person." This
nobody has any right to but himself. The "labour" of his body
and the "work" of his hands, we may say, are properly his. Whatsoever, then, he removes out of the state that nature hath provided
and left it in, he hath mixed his labour with it, and joined to it
something that is his own, and thereby makes it his property. It
being by him removed from the common state nature placed it in,
it hath by this labour something annexed to it that excludes the
common right of other men. For this "labour" being the unquestionable property of the labourer, no man but he can have a
right to what that is once joined to, at least where there is enough,
and as good left in common for others.

28. He that is nourished by the acorns he picked up under an
oak, or the apples he gathered from the trees in the wood, has
certainly appropriated them to himself. Nobody can deny but
the nourishment is his. I ask, then, when did they begin to be his?
when he digested? or when he ate? or when he boiled? or when
he brought them home? or when he picked them up? And it is
plain, if the first gathering made them not his, nothing else could.
That labour put a distinction between them and common. That
added something to them more than nature, the common mother
of all, had done, and so they became his private right. And will

any one say he had no right to those acorns or apples he thus appropriated because he had not the consent of all mankind to make them his? Was it a robbery thus to assume to himself what belonged to all in common? If such a consent as that was necessary, man had starved, notwithstanding the plenty God had given him. We see in commons, which remain so by compact, that it is the taking any part of what is common, and removing it out of the state nature leaves it in, which begins the property, without which the common is of no use. And the taking of this or that part does not depend on the express consent of all the commoners. Thus, the grass my horse has bit, the turfs my servant has cut, and the ore I have digged in any place, where I have a right to them in common with others, become my property without the assignation or consent of anybody. The labour that was mine, removing them out of that common state they were in, hath fixed my property in them.

29. By making an explicit consent of every commoner necessary to any one's appropriating to himself any part of what is given in common, children or servants could not cut the meat which their father or master had provided for them in common without assigning to every one his peculiar part. Though the water running in the fountain be every one's, yet who can doubt but that in the pitcher is his only who drew it out? His labour hath taken it out of the hands of nature where it was common, and belonged equally to all her children, and hath thereby appropriated it to himself.

30. Thus this law of reason makes the deer that Indian's who hath killed it; it is allowed to be his goods who hath bestowed his labour upon it, though, before, it was the common right of every one. And amongst those who are counted the civilized part of mankind, who have made and multiplied positive laws to determine property, this original law of nature for the beginning of property, in what was before common, still takes place, and by virtue thereof, what fish any one catches in the ocean, that great and still remaining common of mankind, or what ambergris any one takes up here is by the labour that removes it out of that common state nature left it in, made his property who takes that pains about it. And even amongst us, the hare that any one is hunting is thought his who pursues her during the chase. For being a beast that is still looked upon as common, and no man's private possession, whoever has employed so much labour about any of that kind as to find and pursue her has thereby removed her from the state of nature wherein she was common, and hath began a property.

31. It will, perhaps, be objected to this, that if gathering the acorns or other fruits of the earth, &c., makes a right to them, then any one may engross as much as he will. To which I answer, Not so. The same law of nature that does by this means give us property, does also bound that property too. "God has given us all things richly" (1 Tim. vi. 12) is the voice of reason confirmed by inspiration. But how far has He given it us—"to enjoy?" As much as any one can make use of to any advantage of life before it spoils, so much he may by his labour fix a property in. Whatever is beyond this is more than his share, and belongs to others. Nothing was made by God for man to spoil or destroy. And thus considering the plenty of natural provisions there was a long time in the world, and the few spenders, and to how small a part of that provision the industry of one man could extend itself and engross it to the prejudice of others, especially keeping within the bounds set by reason of what might serve for his use, there could be then little room for quarrels or contentions about property so established.

32. But the chief matter of property being now not the fruits of the earth and the beasts that subsist on it, but the earth itself, as that which takes in and carries with it all the rest; I think it is plain that property in that too is acquired as the former. As much land as a man tills, plants, improves, cultivates, and can use the product of, so much is his property. He by his labour does, as it were, enclose it from the common. Nor will it invalidate his right to say everybody else has an equal title to it, and therefore he cannot appropriate, he cannot enclose, without the consent of all his fellow-commoners, all mankind. God, when He gave the world in common to all mankind, commanded man also to labour, and the penury of his condition required it of him. God and his reason commanded him to subdue the earth—*i.e.*, improve it for the benefit of life and therein lay out something upon it that was his own, his labour. He that, in obedience to this command of God, subdued, tilled, and sowed any part of it, thereby annexed to it something that was his property, which another had no title to, nor could without injury take from him.

33. Nor was this appropriation of any parcel of land, by improving it, any prejudice to any other man, since there was still enough and as good left, and more than the yet unprovided could use. So that, in effect, there was never the less left for others because of his enclosure for himself. For he that leaves as much as another can make use of does as good as take nothing at all. Nobody could think himself injured by the drinking of another man, though he

took a good draught, who had a whole river of the same water left
him to quench his thirst. And the case of land and water, where
there is enough of both, is perfectly the same.

34. God gave the world to men in common, but since He gave
it them for their benefit and the greatest conveniencies of life they
were capable to draw from it, it cannot be supposed he meant it
should always remain common and uncultivated. He gave it to
the use of the industrious and rational (and labour was to be his
title to it) ; not to the fancy or covetousness of the quarrelsome and
contentious. He that had as good left for his improvement as was
already taken up needed not complain, ought not to meddle with
what was already improved by another's labour ; if he did it is
plain he desired the benefit of another's pains, which he had no
right to, and not the ground which God had given him, in common
with others, to labour on, and whereof there was as good left as
that already possessed ; and more than he knew what to do with,
or his industry could reach to.

35. It is true, in land that is common in England or any other
country, where there are plenty of people under government who
have money and commerce, no one can enclose or appropriate any
part without the consent of all his fellow-commoners ; because
this is left common by compact—*i.e.*, by the law of the land, which
is not to be violated. And, though it be common in respect of
some men, it is not so to all mankind, but is the joint property of
this country, or this parish. Besides, the remainder, after such
enclosure, would not be as good to the rest of the commoners as
the whole was, when they could all make use of the whole ; whereas
in the beginning and first peopling of the great common of the
world it was quite otherwise. The law man was under was rather
for appropriating. God commanded, and his wants forced him
to labour. That was his property, which could not be taken from
him wherever he had fixed it. And hence subduing or cultivating
the earth and having dominion, we see, are joined together. The
one gave title to the other. So that God, by commanding to
subdue, gave authority so far to appropriate. And the condition
of human life, which requires labour and materials to work on,
necessarily introduces private possessions.

36. The measure of property nature has well set, by the extent
of men's labour and the conveniency of life. No man's labour
could subdue or appropriate all, nor could his enjoyment consume
more than a small part ; so that it was impossible for any man, this
way, to entrench upon the right of another or acquire to himself
a property, to the prejudice of his neighbour, who would still have

room for as good and as large a possession (after the other had taken
out his) as before it was appropriated. Which measure did confine every man's possession to a very moderate proportion, and
such as he might appropriate to himself without injury to anybody
in the first ages of the world, when men were more in danger to be
lost, by wandering from their company, in the then vast wilderness
of the earth than to be straitened for want of room to plant in.
And the same measure may be allowed still, without prejudice to
anybody, as full as the world seems. For, supposing a man or
family, in the state they were at first peopling of the world by the
children of Adam or Noah, let him plant in some inland vacant
places of America. We shall find that the possessions he could
make himself, upon the measures we have given, would not be
very large, nor, even to this day, prejudice the rest of mankind or
give them reason to complain or think themselves injured by this
man's encroachment, though the race of men have now spread
themselves to all the corners of the world, and do infinitely exceed
the small number was at the beginning. Nay, the extent of
ground is of so little value without labour that I have heard it
affirmed that in Spain itself a man may be permitted to plough,
sow, and reap, without being disturbed, upon land he has no other
title to, but only his making use of it. But, on the contrary, the
inhabitants think themselves beholden to him who, by his industry
on neglected, and consequently waste land, has increased the stock
of corn, which they wanted. But be this as it will, which I lay no
stress on, this I dare boldly affirm, that the same rule of propriety—
viz., that every man should have as much as he could make use of,
would hold still in the world, without straitening anybody, since
there is land enough in the world to suffice double the inhabitants,
had not the invention of money, and the tacit agreement of men
to put a value on it, introduced (by consent) larger possessions and
a right to them; which, how it has done, I shall by-and-by show
more at large.

37. This is certain, that in the beginning, before the desire of
having more than men needed had altered the intrinsic value of
things, which depends only on their usefulness to the life of man,
or had agreed that a little piece of yellow metal, which would
keep without wasting or decay, should be worth a great piece of
flesh or a whole heap of corn, though men had a right to appropriate
by their labour, each one to himself, as much of the things of
nature as he could use, yet this could not be much, nor to the
prejudice of others, where the same plenty was still left, to those
who would use the same industry.

Before the appropriation of land, he who gathered as much of the wild fruit, killed, caught, or tamed as many of the beasts as he could—he that so employed his pains about any of the spontaneous products of nature as any way to alter them from the state nature put them in, by placing any of his labour on them, did thereby acquire a propriety in them; but if they perished in his possession without their due use—if the fruits rotted or the venison putrefied before he could spend it, he offended against the common law of nature, and was liable to be punished: he invaded his neighbour's share, for he had no right farther than his use called for any of them and they might serve to afford him conveniencies of life.

38. The same measures governed the possession of land, too. Whatsoever he tilled and reaped, laid up and made use of before it spoiled, that was his peculiar right; whatsoever he enclosed, and could feed and make use of, the cattle and product was also his. But if either the grass of his enclosure rotted on the ground, or the fruit of his planting perished without gathering and laying up, this part of the earth, notwithstanding his enclosure, was still to be looked on as waste, and might be the possession of any other. Thus, at the beginning, Cain might take as much ground as he could till and make it his own land, and yet leave enough to Abel's sheep to feed on : a few acres would serve for both their possessions. But as families increased and industry enlarged their stocks, their possessions enlarged with the need of them; but yet it was commonly without any fixed property in the ground they made use of till they incorporated, settled themselves together, and built cities, and then, by consent, they came in time to set out the bounds of their distinct territories and agree on limits between them and their neighbours, and by laws within themselves settled the properties of those of the same society. For we see that in that part of the world which was first inhabited, and therefore like to be best peopled, even as low down as Abraham's time, they wandered with their flocks and their herds, which was their substance, freely up and down—and this Abraham did in a country where he was a stranger; whence it is plain that, at least, a great part of the land lay in common, that the inhabitants valued it not, nor claimed property in any more than they made use of; but when there was not room enough in the same place for their herds to feed together, they, by consent, as Abraham and Lot did (Gen. xiii. 5) separated and enlarged their pasture where it best liked them. And for the same reason, Esau went from his father and his brother, and planted in Mount Seir (Gen. xxxvi. 6).

39. And thus, without supposing any private dominion and

property in Adam over all the world, exclusive of all other men, which can no way be proved, nor any one's property be made out from it, but supposing the world, given as it was to the children of men in common, we see how labour could make men distinct titles to several parcels of it for their private uses, wherein there could be no doubt of right, no room for quarrel.

40. Nor is it so strange as, perhaps, before consideration, it may appear, that the property of labour should be able to overbalance the community of land, for it is labour indeed that puts the difference of value on everything; and let any one consider what the difference is between an acre of land planted with tobacco or sugar, sown with wheat or barley, and an acre of the same land lying in common without any husbandry upon it, and he will find that the improvement of labour makes the far greater part of the value. I think it will be but a very modest computation to say, that of the products of the earth useful to the life of man, nine-tenths are the effects of labour. Nay, if we will rightly estimate things as they come to our use, and cast up the several expenses about them—what in them is purely owing to nature and what to labour—we shall find that in most of them ninety-nine hundredths are wholly to be put on the account of labour.

41. There cannot be a clearer demonstration of anything than several nations of the Americans are of this, who are rich in land and poor in all the comforts of life; whom nature, having furnished as liberally as any other people with the materials of plenty—*i.e.*, a fruitful soil, apt to produce in abundance what might serve for food, raiment, and delight; yet, for want of improving it by labour, have not one hundredth part of the conveniences we enjoy, and a king of a large and fruitful territory there feeds, lodges, and is clad worse than a day labourer in England.

42. To make this a little clearer, let us but trace some of the ordinary provisions of life, through their several progresses, before they come to our use, and see how much they receive of their value from human industry. Bread, wine, and cloth are things of daily use and great plenty; yet notwithstanding acorns, water, and leaves, or skins must be our bread, drink and clothing, did not labour furnish us with these more useful commodities. For whatever bread is more worth than acorns, wine than water, and cloth or silk than leaves, skins or moss, that is wholly owing to labour and industry. The one of these being the food and raiment which unassisted nature furnishes us with; the other provisions which our industry and pains prepare for us, which how much they exceed the other in value, when any one hath computed, he will

then see how much labour makes the far greatest part of the value of things we enjoy in this world; and the ground which produces the materials is scarce to be reckoned in as any, or at most, but a very small part of it; so little, that even amongst us, land that is left wholly to nature, that hath no improvement of pasturage, tillage, or planting, is called, as indeed it is, waste; and we shall find the benefit of it amount to little more than nothing.

43. An acre of land that bears here twenty bushels of wheat, and another in America, which, with the same husbandry, would do the like, are, without doubt, of the same natural, intrinsic value. But yet the benefit mankind receives from one in a year is worth £5, and the other possibly not worth a penny; if all the profit an Indian received from it were to be valued and sold here, at least I may truly say, not one thousandth. It is labour, then, which puts the greatest part of value upon land, without which it would scarcely be worth anything; it is to that we owe the greatest part of all its useful products; for all that the straw, bran, bread, of that acre of wheat, is more worth than the product of an acre of as good land which lies waste is all the effect of labour. For it is not barely the ploughman's pains, the reaper's and thresher's toil, and the baker's sweat, is to be counted into the bread we eat; the labour of those who broke the oxen, who digged and wrought the iron and stones, who felled and framed the timber employed about the plough, mill, oven, or any other utensils, which are a vast number, requisite to this corn, from its sowing to its being made bread, must all be charged on the account of labour, and received as an effect of that; nature and the earth furnished only the almost worthless materials as in themselves. It would be a strange catalogue of things that industry provided and made use of about every loaf of bread before it came to our use if we could trace them; iron, wood, leather, bark, timber, stone, bricks, coals, lime, cloth, dyeing-drugs, pitch, tar, masts, ropes, and all the materials made use of in the ship that brought any of the commodities made use of by any of the workmen, to any part of the work, all which it would be almost impossible, at least too long, to reckon up.

44. From all which it is evident, that though the things of nature are given in common, man (by being master of himself, and proprietor of his own person, and the actions or labour of it) had still in himself the great foundation of property; and that which made up the great part of what he applied to the support or comfort of his being, when invention and arts had improved the conveniencies of life, was perfectly his own, and did not belong in common to others.

45. Thus labour, in the beginning, gave a right of property, wherever any one was pleased to employ it, upon what was common, which remained a long while the far greater part, and is yet more than mankind makes use of. Men at first, for the most part, contented themselves with what unassisted nature offered to their necessities; and though afterwards, in some parts of the world, where the increase of people and stock, with the use of money, had made land scarce, and so of some value, the several communities settled the bounds of their distinct territories, and, by laws, within themselves, regulated the properties of the private men of their society, and so, by compact and agreement, settled the property which labour and industry began. And the leagues that have been made between several states and kingdoms, either expressly or tacitly disowning all claim and right to the land in the other's possession, have, by common consent, given up their pretences to their natural common right, which originally they had to those countries; and so have, by positive agreement, settled a property amongst themselves, in distinct parts of the world; yet there are still great tracts of ground to be found, which, the inhabitants thereof not having joined with the rest of mankind in the consent of the use of their common money, lie waste, and are more than the people who dwell on it, do, or can make use of, and so still lie in common; though this can scarce happen amongst that part of mankind that have consented to the use of money.

46. The greatest part of things really useful to the life of man, and such as the necessity of subsisting made the first commoners of the world look after—as it doth the Americans now—are generally things of short duration, such as—if they are not consumed by use—will decay and perish of themselves. Gold, silver, and diamonds are things that fancy or agreement hath put the value on, more than real use and the necessary support of life. Now of those good things which nature hath provided in common, every one hath a right (as hath been said) to as much as he could use, and had a property in all he could effect with his labour; all that his industry could extend to, to alter from the state nature had put it in, was his. He that gathered a hundred bushels of acorns or apples had thereby a property in them; they were his goods as soon as gathered. He was only to look that he used them before they spoiled, else he took more than his share, and robbed others. And, indeed, it was a foolish thing, as well as dishonest, to hoard up more than he could make use of. If he gave away a part to anybody else, so that it perished not uselessly in his possession, these he also made use of. And if he also bartered

away plums that would have rotted in a week, for nuts that would last good for his eating a whole year, he did no injury; he wasted not the common stock; destroyed no part of the portion of goods that belonged to others, so long as nothing perished uselessly in his hands. Again, if he would give his nuts for a piece of metal, pleased with its colour, or exchange his sheep for shells, or wool for a sparkling pebble or a diamond, and keep those by him all his life, he invaded not the right of others; he might heap up as much of these durable things as he pleased; the exceeding of the bounds of his just property not lying in the largeness of his possession, but the perishing of anything uselessly in it.

47. And thus came in the use of money; some lasting thing that men might keep without spoiling, and that, by mutual consent, men would take in exchange for the truly useful but perishable supports of life.

48. And as different degrees of industry were apt to give men possessions in different proportions, so this invention of money gave them the opportunity to continue and enlarge them. For supposing an island, separate from all possible commerce with the rest of the world, wherein there were but a hundred families, but there were sheep, horses, and cows, with other useful animals, wholesome fruits, and land enough for corn for a hundred thousand times as many, but nothing in the island, either because of its commonness or perishableness, fit to supply the place of money. What reason could any one have there to enlarge his possessions beyond the use of his family, and a plentiful supply to its consumption, either in what their own industry produced, or they could barter for like perishable, useful commodities with others? Where there is not something both lasting and scarce, and so valuable to be hoarded up, there men will not be apt to enlarge their possessions of land, were it never so rich, never so free for them to take. For I ask, what would a man value ten thousand or an hundred thousand acres of excellent land, ready cultivated and well stocked, too, with cattle, in the middle of the inland parts of America, where he had no hopes of commerce with other parts of the world, to draw money to him by the sale of the product? It would not be worth the enclosing, and we should see him give up again to the wild common of nature whatever was more than would supply the conveniences of life, to be had there for him and his family.

49. Thus, in the beginning, all the world was America, and more so than that is now; for no such thing as money was anywhere known. Find out something that hath the use and value

of money amongst his neighbours, you shall see the same man will begin presently to enlarge his possessions.

50. But since gold and silver, being little useful to the life of man, in proportion to food, raiment, and carriage, has its value only from the consent of men—whereof labour yet makes in great part the measure—it is plain that the consent of men have agreed to a disproportionate and unequal possession of the earth—I mean out of the bounds of society and compact ; for in governments the laws regulate it ; they having, by consent, found out and agreed in a way how a man may, rightfully and without injury, possess more than he himself can make use of by receiving gold and silver, which may continue long in a man's possession without decaying for the overplus, and agreeing those metals should have a value.

51. And thus, I think, it is very easy to conceive, without any difficulty, how labour could at first begin a title of property in the common things of nature, and how the spending it upon our uses bounded it ; so that there could then be no reason of quarrelling about title, nor any doubt about the largeness of possession it gave. Right and conveniency went together. For as a man had a right to all he could employ his labour upon, so he had no temptation to labour for more than he could make use of. This left no room for controversy about the title, nor for encroachment on the right of others. What portion a man carved to himself was easily seen ; and it was useless, as well as dishonest, to carve himself too much, or take more than he needed.

3. Political Society [1]

Ch. vii. *Of Political or Civil Society.*

77. God, having made man such a creature that, in His own judgment, it was not good for him to be alone, put him under strong obligations of necessity, convenience, and inclination, to drive him into society, as well as fitted him with understanding and language to continue and enjoy it. The first society was between man and wife, which gave beginning to that between parents and children, to which, in time, that between master and servant came to be added. And though all these might, and commonly did, meet together and make up but one family, wherein the master or mistress of it had some sort of rule proper to a family, each of these, or all together, came short of "political society," as we shall see if we consider the different ends, ties, and bounds of each of these.

87. Man being born, as has been proved, with a title to perfect

[1] Book II, chs. vii–viii (in part), ix–x.

freedom and an uncontrolled enjoyment of all the rights and privileges of the law of nature, equally with any other man, or number of men in the world, hath by nature a power not only to preserve his property—that is, his life, liberty, and estate against the injuries and attempts of other men, but to judge of and punish the breaches of that law in others, as he is persuaded the offense deserves, even with death itself, in crimes where the heinousness of the fact, in his opinion, requires it. But because no political society can be, nor subsist, without having in itself the power to preserve the property, and in order thereunto punish the offenses of all those of that society, there, and there only, is political society where every one of the members hath quitted his natural power, resigned it up into the hands of the community in all cases that exclude him not from appealing for protection to the law established by it. And thus all private judgment of every particular member being excluded, the community comes to be umpire by settled standing rules, indifferent and the same to all parties; and by men having authority from the community for the execution of those rules, decides all the differences that may happen between any members of that society concerning any matter of right, and punishes those offenses which any member hath committed against the society with such penalties as the law has established; whereby it is easy to discern who are, and are not, in political society together. Those who are united into one body, and have a common established law and judicature to appeal to, with authority to decide controversies between them and punish offenders, are in civil society one with another; but those who have no such common appeal, I mean on earth, are still in the state of nature, each being where there is no other, judge for himself and executioner; which is, as I have before shown, the perfect state of nature.

88. And thus the commonwealth comes by a power to set down what punishment shall belong to the several transgressions they think worthy of it, committed amongst the members of that society (which is the power of making laws) as well as it has the power to punish any injury done unto any of its members by any one that is not of it (which is the power of war and peace); and all this for the preservation of the property of all the members of that society, as far as is possible. But though every man who has entered into civil society and is become a member of any commonwealth, has thereby quitted his power to punish offenses against the law of nature in prosecution of his own private judgment, yet with the judgment of offences which he has given

up to the legislative, in all cases where he can appeal to the
magistrate, he has given up a right to the commonwealth to employ his force for the execution of the judgments of the commonwealth whenever he shall be called to it, which, indeed, are his
own judgments, they being made by himself or his representative.
And herein we have the original of the legislative and executive
power of civil society, which is to judge by standing laws how far
offences are to be punished when committed within the commonwealth; and also to determine by occasional judgments founded on
the present circumstances of the fact, how far injuries from without are to be vindicated; and in both these to employ all the
force of all the members when there shall be need.

89. Whenever, therefore, any number of men so unite into
one society as to quit every one his executive power of the law
of nature, and to resign it to the public, there and there only is
a political or civil society. And this is done wherever any number
of men in the state of nature, enter into society to make one
people, one body politic, under one supreme government; or else
when any one joins himself to, and incorporates with, any government already made. For hereby he authorizes the society, or
which is all one, the legislative thereof, to make laws for him
as the public good of the society shall require, to the execution
whereof his own assistance (as to his own decrees) is due. And
this puts men out of a state of nature into that of a commonwealth, by setting up a judge on earth with authority to determine
all the controversies and redress the injuries that may happen
to any member of the commonwealth, which judge is the legislative
or magistrate appointed by it. And wherever there are any
number of men, however associated, that have no such decisive
power to appeal to, there they are still in the state of nature.

90. And hence it is evident that absolute monarchy, which
by some men is counted for the only government in the world,
is indeed inconsistent with civil society, and so can be no form
of civil government at all. For the end of civil society being to
avoid and remedy those inconveniences of the state of nature
which necessarily follow from every man's being judge in his own
case, by setting up a known authority to which every one of that
society may appeal upon any injury received, or controversy
that may arise, and which every one of the society ought to obey,
wherever any persons are who have not such an authority to
appeal to for the decision of any difference between them, there
those persons are still in the state of nature; and so is every absolute prince in respect of those who are under his dominion.

91. For he being supposed to have all, both legislative and executive, power in himself alone, there is no judge to be found, no appeal lies open to any one, who may fairly and indifferently, and with authority decide, and from whose decision relief and redress may be expected of any injury or inconveniency that may be suffered from him, or by his order. So that such a man, however entitled, Czar, or Grand Seignior, or how you please, is as much in the state of nature with all under his dominion as he is with the rest of mankind. For wherever any two men are, who have no standing rule and common judge to appeal to on earth for the determination of controversies of right betwixt them, there they are still in the state of nature and under all the inconveniences of it, with only this woeful difference to the subject, or rather slave, of an absolute prince: that whereas in the ordinary state of nature he has a liberty to judge of his right and according to the best of his power to maintain it, now whenever his property is invaded by the will and order of his monarch, he has not only no appeal, as those in society ought to have, but, as if he were degraded from the common state of rational creatures, is denied a liberty to judge of, or defend his right, and so is exposed to all the misery and inconveniences that a man can fear from one, who being in the unrestrained state of nature, is yet corrupted with flattery and armed with power.

Ch. viii. *Of the Beginning of Political Societies.*

95. Men being, as has been said, by nature all free, equal, and independent, no one can be put out of this estate and subjected to the political power of another without his own consent. The only way whereby any one divests himself of his natural liberty and puts on the bonds of civil society, is by agreeing with other men, to join and unite into a community for their comfortable, safe, and peaceable living, one amongst another, in a secure enjoyment of their properties, and a greater security against any that are not of it. This any number of men may do, because it injures not the freedom of the rest; they are left, as they were, in the liberty of the state of nature. When any number of men have so consented to make one community or government, they are thereby presently incorporated, and make one body politic, wherein the majority have a right to act and conclude the rest.

96. For, when any number of men have, by the consent of every individual, made a community, they have thereby made that community one body, with a power to act as one body, which is only by the will and determination of the majority.

For that which acts any community, being only the consent of the individuals of it, and it being necessary to that which is one body to move one way, it is necessary the body should move that way whither the greater force carries it, which is the consent of the majority, or else it is impossible it should act or continue one body, one community, which the consent of every individual that united into it agreed that it should; and so every one is bound by that consent to be concluded by the majority. And therefore we see that in assemblies empowered to act by positive laws where no number is set by that positive law which empowers them, the act of the majority passes for the act of the whole, and of course determines, as having, by the law of nature and reason, the power of the whole.

97. And thus every man, by consenting with others to make one body politic under one government, puts himself under an obligation to every one of that society to submit to the determination of the majority, and to be concluded by it; or else this original compact, whereby he with others incorporates into one society, would signify nothing, and be no compact, if he be left free and under no other ties than he was in before in the state of nature. For what appearance would there be of any compact? What new engagement, if he were no farther tied by any decrees of the society than he himself thought fit and did actually consent to? This would be still as great a liberty as he himself had before his compact, or any one else in the state of nature hath, who may submit himself and consent to any acts of it if he thinks fit.

98. For if the consent of the majority shall not in reason be received as the act of the whole, and conclude every individual, nothing but the consent of every individual can make anything to be the act of the whole; but such a consent is next to impossible ever to be had, if we consider the infirmities of health and avocations of business, which in a number though much less than that of a commonwealth will necessarily keep many away from the public assembly; to which if we add the variety of opinions and contrariety of interests which unavoidably happen in all collections of men, the coming into society upon such terms would be only like Cato's coming into the theater, only to go out again. Such a constitution as this would make the mighty leviathan of a shorter duration than the feeblest creatures, and not let it outlast the day it was born in, which cannot be supposed till we can think that rational creatures should desire and constitute societies only to be dissolved. For

where the majority cannot conclude the rest, there they cannot
act as one body, and consequently will be immediately dissolved
again.

99. Whosoever, therefore, out of a state of nature unite into
a community, must be understood to give up all the power necessary to the ends for which they unite into society to the majority
of the community, unless they expressly agreed in any number
greater than the majority. And this is done by barely agreeing
to unite into one political society, which is all the compact that
is, or needs be, between the individuals that enter into or make up
a commonwealth. And thus, that which begins and actually
constitutes any political society is nothing but the consent of any
number of freemen capable of a majority, to unite and incorporate
into such a society. And this is that, and that only, which did
or could give beginning to any lawful government in the world.

100. To this I find two objections made: 1. That there
are no instances to be found in story of a company of men, independent and equal one amongst another, that met together,
and in this way began and set up a government. 2. It is impossible of right that men should do so, because all men, being
born under government, they are to submit to that, and are not
at liberty to begin a new one.

101. To the first there is this to answer: That it is not at
all to be wondered that history gives us but a very little account
of men that lived together in the state of nature. The inconveniences of that condition, and the love and want of society,
no sooner brought any number of them together, but they presently
united and incorporated, if they designed to continue together.
And if we may not suppose men ever to have been in the state of
nature, because we hear not much of them in such a state, we
may as well suppose the armies of Salmanasser or Xerxes were
never children, because we hear little of them till they were men
and embodied in armies. Government is everywhere antecedent
to records, and letters seldom come in amongst a people till a
long continuation of civil society has, by other more necessary
arts, provided for their safety, ease, and plenty. And then they
begin to look after the history of their founders, and search into
their original when they have outlived the memory of it. For
it is with commonwealths as with particular persons, they are
commonly ignorant of their own births and infancies; and if they
know anything of their original, they are beholden for it to the
accidental records that others have kept of it. And those that
we have of the beginning of any polities in the world, excepting

that of the Jews, where God Himself immediately interposed and which favors not at all paternal dominion, are all either plain instances of such a beginning as I have mentioned, or at least have manifest footsteps of it.

The other objection, I find, urged against the beginning of polities, in the way I have mentioned, is this, viz.:—

113. "That all men being born under government, some or other, it is impossible any of them should ever be free and at liberty to unite together and begin a new one, or ever be able to erect a lawful government." If this argument be good, I ask, How came so many lawful monarchies into the world? For if anybody, upon this supposition, can show me any one man, in any age of the world, free to begin a lawful monarchy, I will be bound to show him ten other free men at liberty, at the same time, to unite and begin a new government under a regal or any other form. It being demonstrated that if any one born under the dominion of another may be so free as to have a right to command others in a new and distinct empire, every one that is born under the dominion of another may be so free too, and may become a ruler or subject of a distinct separate government. And so, by this their own principle, either all men, however born, are free, or else there is but one lawful prince, one lawful government in the world; and then they have nothing to do but barely to show us which that is; which when they have done, I doubt not but all mankind will easily agree to pay obedience to him.

114. Though it be a sufficient answer to their objection to show that it involves them in the same difficulties that it doth those they use it against, yet I shall endeavor to discover the weakness of this argument a little farther.

"All men," say they, "are born under government, and therefore they cannot be at liberty to begin a new one. Every one is born a subject to his father or his prince, and is therefore under the perpetual tie of subjection and allegiance." It is plain mankind never owned nor considered any such natural subjection that they were born in, to one or to the other, that tied them, without their own consents, to a subjection to them and their heirs.

115. For there are no examples so frequent in history, both sacred and profane, as those of men withdrawing themselves and their obedience from the jurisdiction they were born under, and the family or community they were bred up in, and setting up new governments in other places, from whence sprang all that number of petty commonwealths in the beginning of ages, and

which always multiplied as long as there was room enough, till the stronger or more fortunate swallowed the weaker; and those great ones, again breaking to pieces, dissolved into lesser dominions; all which are so many testimonies against paternal sovereignty, and plainly prove that it was not the natural right of the father descending to his heirs that made governments in the beginning; since it was impossible, upon that ground, there should have been so many little kingdoms; all must have been but only one universal monarchy, if men had not been at liberty to separate themselves from their families and the government, be it what it will, that was set up in it, and go and make distinct commonwealths and other governments as they thought fit.

116. This had been the practice of the world from its first beginning to this day; nor is it now any more hindrance to the freedom of mankind, that they are born under constituted and ancient polities that have established laws and set forms of government, than if they were born in the woods amongst the unconfined inhabitants that run loose in them. For those who would persuade us that by being born under any government we are naturally subjects to it, and have no more any title or pretense to the freedom of the state of nature, have no other reason (bating that of paternal power, which we have already answered) to produce for it, but only because our fathers or progenitors passed away their natural liberty, and thereby bound up themselves and their posterity to a perpetual subjection to the government which they themselves submitted to. It is true that whatever engagements or promises any one has made for himself, he is under the obligation of them, but cannot by any compact whatsoever bind his children or posterity. For his son, when a man, being altogether as free as the father, any act of the father can no more give away the liberty of the son than it can of anybody else. He may, indeed, annex such conditions to the land he enjoyed, as a subject of any commonwealth, as may oblige his son to be of that community, if he will enjoy those possessions which were his father's, because that estate being his father's property, he may dispose or settle it as he pleases.

119. Every man being, as has been shown, naturally free, and nothing being able to put him into subjection to any earthly power, but only his own consent, it is to be considered what shall be understood to be a sufficient declaration of a man's consent to make him subject to the laws of any government. There is a common distinction of an express and a tacit consent, which will

concern our present case. Nobody doubts but an express consent
of any man, entering into any society, makes him a perfect
member of that society, a subject of that government. The
difficulty is, what ought to be looked upon as a tacit consent,
and how far it binds—*i.e.*, how far any one shall be looked on to
have consented, and thereby submitted to any government,
where he has made no expressions of it at all. And to this I say,
that every man that hath any possessions, or enjoyment of any
part of the dominions of any government, doth thereby give his
tacit consent, and is as far forth obliged to obedience to the laws
of that government, during such enjoyment, as any one under it,
whether this his possession be of land to him and his heirs for
ever, or a lodging only for a week, or whether it be barely traveling freely on the highway; and, in effect, it reaches as far
as the very being of any one within the territories of that
government.

120. To understand this the better, it is fit to consider that
every man when he at first incorporates himself into any commonwealth, he, by his uniting himself thereunto, annexes also,
and submits to the community, those possessions which he has,
or shall acquire, that do not already belong to any other government. For it would be a direct contradiction for any one to enter
into society with others for the securing and regulating of property,
and yet to suppose his land, whose property is to be regulated
by the laws of the society, should be exempt from the jurisdiction
of that government to which he himself, the proprietor of the
land, is a subject. By the same act, therefore, whereby any one
unites his person, which was before free, to any commonwealth,
by the same he unites his possessions, which were before free,
to it also; and they become, both of them, person and possession,
subject to the government and dominion of that commonwealth
as long as it hath a being. Whoever therefore, from thenceforth,
by inheritance, purchase, permission, or otherwise, enjoys any
part of the land so annexed to, and under the government of that
commonwealth, must take it with the condition it is under—that
is of submitting to the government of the commonwealth, under
whose jurisdiction it is, as far forth as any subject of it.

121. But since the government has a direct jurisdiction only
over the land and reaches the possessor of it (before he has actually
incorporated himself in the society) only as he dwells upon and
enjoys that, the obligation any one is under by virtue of such
enjoyment to submit to the government begins and ends with the
enjoyment; so that whenever the owner, who has given nothing

but such a tacit consent to the government will, by donation, sale or otherwise, quit the said possession, he is at liberty to go and incorporate himself into any other commonwealth, or agree with others to begin a new one *in vacuis locis*, in any part of the world they can find free and unpossessed; whereas he that has once, by actual agreement and any express declaration, given his consent to be of any commonwealth, is perpetually and indispensably obliged to be, and remain unalterably a subject to it, and can never be again in the liberty of the state of nature, unless by any calamity the government he was under comes to be dissolved, or else by some public act cuts him off from being any longer a member of it.

122. But submitting to the laws of any country, living quietly and enjoying privileges and protection under them, makes not a man a member of that society; it is only a local protection and homage due to and from all those who, not being in a state of war, come within the territories belonging to any government, to all parts whereof the force of its law extends. But this no more makes a man a member of that society, a perpetual subject of that commonwealth, than it would make a man a subject to another in whose family he found it convenient to abide for some time, though, whilst he continued in it, he were obliged to comply with the laws and submit to the government he found there. And thus we see that foreigners, by living all their lives under another government, and enjoying the privileges and protection of it, though they are bound, even in conscience, to submit to its administration as far forth as any denizen, yet do not thereby come to be subjects or members of that commonwealth. Nothing can make any man so, but his actually entering into it by positive engagement and express promise and compact. This is that which, I think, concerning the beginning of political societies, and that consent which makes any one a member of any commonwealth.

Ch. ix. *Of the Ends of Political Society and Government.*

123. If man in the state of nature be so free as has been said, if he be absolute lord of his own person and possessions, equal to the greatest and subject to nobody, why will he part with his freedom, why will he give up his empire, and subject himself to the dominion and control of any other power? To which it is obvious to answer, that though in the state of nature he hath such a right, yet the enjoyment of it is very uncertain and constantly exposed to the invasion of others; for all being kings as much as he, every man

his equal, and the greater part no strict observers of equity and
justice, the enjoyment of the property he has in this state is very
unsafe, very insecure. This makes him willing to quit a condition which, however free, is full of fears and continual dangers;
and it is not without reason that he seeks out and is willing to
join in society with others who are already united, or have a mind
to unite for the mutual preservation of their lives, liberties and
estates, which I call by the general name—property.

124. The great and chief end, therefore, of men uniting into
commonwealths, and putting themselves under government, is
the preservation of their property; to which in the state of nature
there are many things wanting.

First: there wants an established, settled, known law, received
and allowed by common consent to be the standard of right and
wrong, and the common measure to decide all controversies
between them. For though the law of nature be plain and intelligible to all rational creatures, yet men, being biased by their
interest, as well as ignorant for want of study of it, are not apt to
allow of it as a law binding to them in the application of it to their
particular cases.

125. Secondly: in the state of nature there wants a known
and indifferent judge, with authority to determine all differences according to the established law. For every one in that
state being both judge and executioner of the law of nature,
men being partial to themselves, passion and revenge is very apt
to carry them too far, and with too much heat in their own cases,
as well as negligence and unconcernedness to make them too remiss in other men's.

126. Thirdly: in the state of nature there often wants power
to back and support the sentence when right, and to give it
due execution. They who by any injustice offend will seldom fail,
where they are able, by force to make good their injustice. Such
resistance many times makes the punishment dangerous, and
frequently destructive to those who attempt it.

127. Thus mankind, notwithstanding all the privileges of
the state of nature, being but in an ill condition while they
remain in it, are quickly driven into society. Hence it comes
to pass, that we seldom find any number of men live any time
together in this state. The inconveniencies that they are therein
exposed to by the irregular and uncertain exercise of the power
every man has of punishing the transgressions of others, make
them take sanctuary under the established laws of government,
and therein seek the preservation of their property. It is this

makes them so willingly give up every one his single power of punishing to be exercised by such alone as shall be appointed to it amongst them, and by such rules as the community, or those authorized by them to that purpose, shall agree on. And in this we have the original right and rise of both the legislative and executive power as well as of the governments and societies themselves.

128. For in the state of nature, to omit the liberty he has of innocent delights, a man has two powers. The first is to do whatsoever he thinks fit for the preservation of himself and others within the permission of the law of nature; by which law, common to them all, he and all the rest of mankind are one community, make up one society distinct from all other creatures; and were it not for the corruption and viciousness of degenerate men, there would be no need of any other, no necessity that men should separate from this great and natural community, and by positive agreements combine into smaller and divided associations. The other power a man has in the state of nature is the power to punish the crimes committed against that law. Both these he gives up when he joins in a private, if I may so call it, or particular political society, and incorporates into any commonwealth separate from the rest of mankind.

129. The first power—viz., of doing whatsoever he thought fit for the preservation of himself and the rest of mankind, he gives up to be regulated by laws made by the society, so far forth as the preservation of himself and the rest of that society shall require; which laws of the society in many things confine the liberty he had by the law of nature.

130. Secondly, the power of punishing he wholly gives up, and engages his natural force (which he might before employ in the execution of the law of nature, by his own single authority, as he thought fit) to assist the executive power of the society as the law thereof shall require. For being now in a new state, wherein he is to enjoy many conveniencies from the labor, assistance, and society of others in the same community, as well as protection from its whole strength, he is to part also with as much of his natural liberty, in providing for himself, as the good, prosperity, and safety of the society shall require, which is not only necessary but just, since the other members of the society do the like.

131. But though men when they enter into society give up the equality, liberty, and executive power they had in the state of nature into the hands of the society, to be so far disposed of

by the legislative as the good of the society shall require, yet it being only with an intention in every one the better to preserve himself, his liberty and property (for no rational creature can be supposed to change his condition with an intention to be worse), the power of the society or legislative constituted by them can never be supposed to extend farther than the common good, but is obliged to secure every one's property by providing against those three defects above mentioned that made the state of nature so unsafe and uneasy. And so, whoever has the legislative or supreme power of any commonwealth, is bound to govern by established standing laws, promulgated and known to the people, and not by extemporary decrees; by indifferent and upright judges, who are to decide controversies by those laws; and to employ the force of the community at home only in the execution of such laws, or abroad to prevent or redress foreign injuries and secure the community from inroads and invasion. And all this to be directed to no other end but the peace, safety, and public good of the people.

4. *Limitations upon Government*[1]

Ch. xi.   *Of the Extent of the Legislative Power.*

134.   The great end of men's entering into society being the enjoyment of their properties in peace and safety, and the great instrument and means of that being the laws established in that society, the first and fundamental positive law of all commonwealths is the establishing of the legislative power; as the first and fundamental natural law, which is to govern even the legislative itself, is the preservation of the society and (as far as will consist with the public good) of every person in it. This legislative is not only the supreme power of the commonwealth, but sacred and unalterable in the hands where the community have once placed it. Nor can any edict of anybody else, in what form soever conceived, or by what power soever backed, have the force and obligation of a law which has not its sanction from that legislative which the public has chosen and appointed; for without this the law could not have that which is absolutely necessary to its being a law, the consent of the society, over whom nobody can have a power to make laws but by their own consent and by authority received from them; and therefore all the obedience, which by the most solemn ties any one can be obliged to pay, ultimately terminates in this supreme power, and is directed by those laws which it enacts. Nor can any oaths

[1] Bk. II, ch. xi.

to any foreign power whatsoever, or any domestic subordinate power, discharge any member of the society from his obedience to the legislative, acting pursuant to their trust, nor oblige him to any obedience contrary to the laws so enacted or farther than they do allow, it being ridiculous to imagine one can be tied ultimately to obey any power in the society which is not the supreme.

135. Though the legislative, whether placed in one or more, whether it be always in being or only by intervals, though it be the supreme power in every commonwealth, yet, first, it is not, nor can possibly be, absolutely arbitrary over the lives and fortunes of the people. For it being but the joint power of every member of the society given up to that person or assembly which is legislator, it can be no more than those persons had in a state of nature before they entered into society, and gave it up to the community. For nobody can transfer to another more power than he has in himself, and nobody has an absolute arbitrary power over himself, or over any other, to destroy his own life, or take away the life or property of another. A man, as has been proved, cannot subject himself to the arbitrary power of another; and having, in the state of nature, no arbitrary power over the life, liberty, or possession of another, but only so much as the law of nature gave him for the preservation of himself and the rest of mankind, this is all he doth, or can give up to the commonwealth, and by it to the legislative power, so that the legislative can have no more than this. Their power in the utmost bounds of it is limited to the public good of the society. It is a power that hath no other end but preservation, and therefore can never have a right to destroy, enslave, or designedly to impoverish the subjects; the obligations of the law of nature cease not in society, but only in many cases are drawn closer, and have, by human laws, known penalties annexed to them to enforce their observation. Thus the law of nature stands as an eternal rule to all men, legislators as well as others. The rules that they make for other men's actions must, as well as their own and other men's actions, be conformable to the law of nature—*i.e.*, to the will of God, of which that is a declaration; and the fundamental law of nature being the preservation of mankind, no human sanction can be good or valid against it.

136. Secondly, the legislative or supreme authority cannot assume to itself a power to rule by extemporary, arbitrary decrees, but is bound to dispense justice and decide the rights of the subject by promulgated standing laws, and known authorized judges. For the law of nature being unwritten, and so nowhere to be

found but in the minds of men, they who, through passion or
interest, shall miscite or misapply it, cannot so easily be convinced
of their mistake where there is no established judge; and so it
serves not, as it ought, to determine the rights and fence the
properties of those that live under it, especially where every one
is judge, interpreter, and executioner of it too, and that in his
own case; and he that has right on his side, having ordinarily
but his own single strength, hath not force enough to defend
himself from injuries or punish delinquents. To avoid these
inconveniencies which disorder men's properties in the state of
nature, men unite into societies that they may have the united
strength of the whole society to secure and defend their properties,
and may have standing rules to bound it, by which every one
may know what is his. To this end it is that men give up all
their natural power to the society they enter into, and the community put the legislative power into such hands as they think
fit; with this trust, that they shall be governed by declared laws,
or else their peace, quiet, and property will still be at the same
uncertainty as it was in the state of nature.

137. Absolute arbitrary power, or governing without settled
standing laws, can neither of them consist with the ends of society
and government, which men would not quit the freedom of the
state of nature for, and tie themselves up under were it not to
preserve their lives, liberties, and fortunes, and by stated rules
of right and property to secure their peace and quiet. It cannot
be supposed that they should intend, had they a power so to do,
to give any one or more an absolute arbitrary power over their
persons and estates, and put a force into the magistrate's hand to
execute his unlimited will arbitrarily upon them; this were to
put themselves into a worse condition than the state of nature
wherein they had a liberty to defend their right against the injuries of others, and were upon equal terms of force to maintain it,
whether invaded by a single man or many in combination. Whereas by supposing they have given up themselves to the absolute
arbitrary power and will of a legislator, they have disarmed themselves, and armed him to make a prey of them when he pleases;
he being in a much worse condition that is exposed to the arbitrary
power of one man who has the command of an hundred thousand
than he that is exposed to the arbitrary power of an hundred
thousand single men, nobody being secure that his will who has
such a command is better than that of other men, though his force
be an hundred thousand times stronger. And, therefore, whatever
form the commonwealth is under, the ruling power ought to govern

by declared and received laws, and not by extemporary dictates and undetermined resolutions; for then mankind will be in a far worse condition than in the state of nature; if they shall have armed one or a few men with the joint power of a multitude, to force them to obey at pleasure the exorbitant and unlimited decrees of their sudden thoughts, or unrestrained, and till that moment, unknown wills, without having any measures set down which may guide and justify their actions. For all the power the government has, being only for the good of the society, as it ought not to be arbitrary and at pleasure, so it ought to be exercised by established and promulgated laws, that both the people may know their duty, and be safe and secure within the limits of the law, and the rulers, too, kept within their bounds, and not be tempted by the power they have in their hands to employ it to such purposes, and by such measures, as they would not have known, and own not willingly.

138. Thirdly, the supreme power cannot take from any man any part of his property without his own consent. For the preservation of property being the end of government, and that for which men enter into society, it necessarily supposes and requires that the people should have property, without which they must be supposed to lose that, by entering into society, which was the end for which they entered into it; too gross an absurdity for any man to own. Men, therefore, in society having property, they have such a right to the goods, which by the law of the community are theirs, that nobody hath a right to take their substance or any part of it from them without their own consent; without this they have no property at all. For I have truly no property in that which another can by right take from me when he pleases against my consent. Hence it is a mistake to think that the supreme or legislative power of any commonwealth can do what it will, and dispose of the estates of the subject arbitrarily, or take any part of them at pleasure. This is not much to be feared in governments where the legislative consists wholly or in part in assemblies which are variable, whose members upon the dissolution of the assembly are subjects under the common laws of their country, equally with the rest. But in governments where the legislative is in one lasting assembly always in being, or in one man as in absolute monarchies, there is danger still that they will think themselves to have a distinct interest from the rest of the community, and so will be apt to increase their own riches and power by taking what they think fit from the people. For a man's property is not at all secure, though there

be good and equitable laws to set the bounds of it between him and his fellow-subjects, if he who commands those subjects have power to take from any private man what part he pleases of his property, and use and dispose of it as he thinks good.

139. But government into whatsoever hands it is put, being as I have before shown, intrusted with this condition, and for this end, that men might have and secure their properties, the prince or senate, however it may have power to make laws for the regulating of property between the subjects one amongst another, yet can never have a power to take to themselves the whole, or any part of the subjects' property, without their own consent; for this would be in effect to leave them no property at all. And to let us see that even absolute power, where it is necessary, is not arbitrary by being absolute, but is still limited by that reason, and confined to those ends, which required it in some cases to be absolute, we need look no farther than the common practice of martial discipline. For the preservation of the army, and in it of the whole commonwealth, requires an absolute obedience to the command of every superior officer, and it is justly death to disobey or dispute the most dangerous or unreasonable of them; but yet we see that neither the sergeant that could command a soldier to march up to the mouth of a cannon, or stand in a breach where he is almost sure to perish, can command that soldier to give him one penny of his money; nor the general that can condemn him to death for deserting his post, or for not obeying the most desperate orders, can yet with all his absolute power of life and death dispose of one farthing of that soldier's estate, or seize one jot of his goods; whom yet he can command anything, and hang for the least disobedience. Because such a blind obedience is necessary to that end for which the commander has his power—viz., the preservation of the rest; but the disposing of his goods has nothing to do with it.

140. It is true governments cannot be supported without great charge, and it is fit every one who enjoys his share of the protection should pay out of his estate his proportion for the maintenance of it. But still it must be with his own consent—*i.e.*, the consent of the majority, giving it either by themselves or their representatives chosen by them; for if any one shall claim a power to lay and levy taxes on the people by his own authority, and without such consent of the people, he thereby invades the fundamental law of property, and subverts the end of government. For what property have I in that which another may by right take when he pleases to himself?

141. Fourthly. The legislative cannot transfer the power of making laws to any other hands, for it being but a delegated power from the people, they who have it cannot pass it over to others. The people alone can appoint the form of the commonwealth, which is by constituting the legislative, and appointing in whose hands that shall be. And when the people have said, "We will submit to rules, and be governed by laws made by such men, and in such forms," nobody else can say other men shall make laws for them; nor can the people be bound by any laws but such as are enacted by those whom they have chosen and authorized to make laws for them. . . .

142. These are the bounds which the trust that is put in them by the society and the law of God and nature have set to the legislative power of every commonwealth, in all forms of government. First: they are to govern by promulgated established laws, not to be varied in particular cases, but to have one rule for rich and poor, for the favorite at court, and the countryman at plow. Secondly: These laws also ought to be designed for no other end ultimately but the good of the people. Thirdly: they must not raise taxes on the property of the people without the consent of the people given by themselves or their deputies. And this properly concerns only such governments where the legislative is always in being, or at least where the people have not reserved any part of the legislative to deputies, to be from time to time chosen by themselves. Fourthly: The legislative neither must nor can transfer the power of making laws to anybody else, or place it anywhere but where the people have.

5. The Separation of Powers in Government[1]

Ch. xii. *Of the Legislative, Executive, and Federative Power of the Commonwealth.*

143. The legislative power is that which has a right to direct how the force of the commonwealth shall be employed for preserving the community and the members of it. But because those laws which are constantly to be executed, and whose force is always to continue, may be made in a little time, therefore there is no need that the legislative should be always in being, not having always business to do. And because it may be too great temptation to human frailty, apt to grasp at power, for the same persons who have the power of making laws to have also in their hands the power to execute them, whereby they may exempt themselves

---

[1] Bk. II, chs. xii–xiii.

from obedience to the laws they make, and suit the law, both in
its making and execution, to their own private advantage, and
thereby come to have a distinct interest from the rest of the community, contrary to the end of society and government,—therefore in well-ordered commonwealths, where the good of the whole
is so considered as it ought, the legislative power is put into the
hands of divers persons who, duly assembled, have by themselves,
or jointly with others, a power to make laws, which when they
have done, being separated again, they are themselves subject
to the laws they have made; which is a new and near tie upon
them to take care that they make them for the public good.

144. But because the laws that are at once and in a short
time made, have a constant and lasting force, and need a perpetual execution, or an attendance thereunto, therefore it is
necessary there should be a power always in being which should
see to the execution of the laws that are made, and remain in
force. And thus the legislative and executive power come often
to be separated.

145. There is another power in every commonwealth which
one may call natural, because it is that which answers to the power
every man naturally had before he entered into society. For
though in a commonwealth the members of it are distinct persons
still, in reference to one another, and, as such, are governed by the
laws of the society, yet, in reference to the rest of mankind, they
make one body, which is, as every member of it before was, still
in the state of nature with the rest of mankind. Hence it is that the
controversies that happen between any man of the society with
those that are out of it are managed by the public, and an injury
done to a member of their body engages the whole in the reparation of it. So that under this consideration the whole community
is one body in the state of nature in respect of all other states or
persons out of its community.

146. This, therefore, contains the power of war and peace,
leagues and alliances, and all the transactions with all persons
and communities without the commonwealth, and may be called
federative if any one pleases. So the thing be understood, I am
indifferent as to the name.

147. These two powers, executive and federative, though they
be really distinct in themselves, yet one comprehending the execution of the municipal laws of the society within itself upon all
that are parts of it, the other the management of the security
and interest of the public without with all those that it may
receive benefit or damage from, yet they are always almost united.

And though this federative power in the well or ill management
of it be of great moment to the commonwealth, yet it is much less
capable to be directed by antecedent, standing, positive laws than
the executive, and so must necessarily be left to the prudence
and wisdom of those whose hands it is in, to be managed for the
public good. For the laws that concern subjects one amongst
another, being to direct their actions, may well enough precede
them. But what is to be done in reference to foreigners depending
much upon their actions, and the variation of designs and interests,
must be left in great part to the prudence of those who have this
power committed to them to be managed by the best of their
skill for the advantage of the commonwealth.

148. Though, as I said, the executive and federative power
of every community be really distinct in themselves, yet they
are hardly to be separated and placed at the same time in the hands
of distinct persons. For both of them requiring the force of the
society for their exercise, it is almost impracticable to place the
force of the commonwealth in distinct and not subordinate hands,
or that the executive and federative power should be placed in
persons that might act separately, whereby the force of the public
would be under different commands, which would be apt some time
or other to cause disorder and ruin.

Ch. xiii. *Of the Subordination of the Powers of the Commonwealth.*

149. Though in a constituted commonwealth standing upon
its own basis and acting according to its own nature—that is,
acting for the preservation of the community, there can be but
one supreme power, which is the legislative, to which all the
rest are and must be subordinate, yet the legislative being only
a fiduciary power to act for certain ends, there remains still in
the people a supreme power to remove or alter the legislative,
when they find the legislative act contrary to the trust reposed
in them. For all power given with trust for the attaining an
end being limited by that end, whenever that end is manifestly
neglected or opposed, the trust must necessarily be forfeited, and
the power devolve into the hands of those that gave it, who may
place it anew where they shall think best for their safety and
security. And thus the community perpetually retains a supreme
power of saving themselves from the attempts and designs of
anybody, even of their legislators, whenever they shall be so
foolish or so wicked as to lay and carry on designs against the
liberties and properties of the subject. For no man or society of

men having a power to deliver up their preservation, or consequently the means of it, to the absolute will and arbitrary dominion of another, whenever any one shall go about to bring them into such a slavish condition, they will always have a right to preserve what they have not a power to part with, and to rid themselves of those who invade this fundamental, sacred, and unalterable law of self-preservation for which they entered into society. And thus the community may be said in this respect to be always the supreme power, but not as considered under any form of government, because this power of the people can never take place till the government be dissolved.

150. In all cases whilst the government subsists, the legislative is the supreme power. For what can give laws to another must needs be superior to him, and since the legislative is no otherwise legislative of the society but by the right it has to make laws for all the parts, and every member of the society, prescribing rules to their actions, and giving power of execution where they are transgressed, the legislative must needs be the supreme, and all other powers in any members or parts of the society derived from and subordinate to it.

151. In some commonwealths where the legislative is not always in being, and the executive is vested in a single person who has also a share in the legislative, there that single person, in a very tolerable sense, may also be called supreme; not that he has in himself all the supreme power, which is that of law-making, but because he has in him the supreme execution, from whom all inferior magistrates derive all their several subordinate powers, or, at least, the greatest part of them; having also no legislative superior to him, there being no law to be made without his consent, which cannot be expected should ever subject him to the other part of the legislative, he is properly enough in this sense supreme. But yet it is to be observed that though oaths of allegiance and fealty are taken to him, it is not to him as supreme legislator, but as supreme executor of the law made by a joint power of him with others, allegiance being nothing but an obedience according to law, which, when he violates, he has no right to obedience, nor can claim it otherwise than as the public person vested with the power of the law, and so is to be considered as the image, phantom, or representative of the commonwealth, acted by the will of the society declared in its laws, and thus he has no will, no power, but that of the law. But when he quits this representation, this public will, and acts by his own private will, he degrades himself, and is but a single private person without

power and without will, that has no right to obedience; the members owing no obedience but to the public will of the society.

152. The executive power, placed anywhere but in a person that has also a share in the legislative, is visibly subordinate and accountable to it, and may be at pleasure changed and displaced; so that it is not the supreme executive power that is exempt from subordination, but the supreme executive power vested in one, who having a share in the legislative, has no distinct superior legislative to be subordinate and accountable to, farther than he himself shall join and consent, so that he is no more subordinate than he himself shall think fit, which one may certainly conclude will be but very little. Of other ministerial and subordinate powers in a commonwealth we need not speak, they being so multiplied with infinite variety in the different customs and constitutions of distinct commonwealths, that it is impossible to give a particular account of them all. Only thus much which is necessary to our present purpose we may take notice of concerning them, that they have no manner of authority, any of them, beyond what is by positive grant and commission delegated to them, and are all of them accountable to some other power in the commonwealth.

153. It is not necessary—no, nor so much as convenient—that the legislative should be always in being; but absolutely necessary that the executive power should, because there is not always need of new laws to be made, but always need of execution of the laws that are made. When the legislative hath put the execution of the laws they make into other hands, they have a power still to resume it out of those hands when they find cause, and to punish for any mal-administration against the laws. The same holds also in regard to the federative power, that and the executive being both ministerial and subordinate to the legislative, which, as has been shown, in a constituted commonwealth is the supreme. The legislative also in this case being supposed to consist of several persons (for if it be a single person it cannot but be always in being, and so will, as supreme, naturally have the supreme executive power, together with the legislative) may assemble and exercise their legislative at the times that either their original constitution or their own adjournment appoints, or when they please, if neither of these hath appointed any time, or there be no other way prescribed to convoke them. For the supreme power being placed in them by the people, it is always in them, and they may exercise it when they please, unless by their original constitution they are limited to certain seasons, or by an act of their supreme power they have adjourned to a

certain time, and when that time comes they have a right to assemble and act again.

154. If the legislative, or any part of it, be made of representatives, chosen for that time by the people, which afterwards return into the ordinary state of subjects, and have no share in the legislature but upon a new choice, this power of choosing must also be exercised by the people, either at certain appointed seasons, or else when they are summoned to it; and, in this latter case, the power of convoking the legislative is ordinarily placed in the executive, and has one of these two limitations in respect of time: —that either the original constitution requires their assembling and acting at certain intervals, and then the executive power does nothing but ministerially issue directions for their electing and assembling according to due forms; or else it is left to his prudence to call them by new elections when the occasions or exigencies of the public require the amendment of old or making of new laws, or the redress or prevention of any inconveniencies that lie on or threaten the people.

155. It may be demanded here, what if the executive power, being possessed of the force of the commonwealth, shall make use of that force to hinder the meeting and acting of the legislative, when the original constitution or the public exigencies require it? I say, using force upon the people, without authority, and contrary to the trust put in him that does so, is a state of war with the people, who have a right to reinstate their legislative in the exercise of their power. For having erected a legislative with an intent they should exercise the power of making laws, either at certain set times, or when there is need of it, when they are hindered by any force from what is so necessary to the society, and wherein the safety and preservation of the people consists, the people have a right to remove it by force. In all states and conditions the true remedy of force without authority is to oppose force to it. The use of force without authority always puts him that uses it into a state of war as the aggressor, and renders him liable to be treated accordingly.

156. The power of assembling and dismissing the legislative, placed in the executive, gives not the executive a superiority over it, but is a fiduciary trust placed in him for the safety of the people in a case where the uncertainty and variableness of human affairs could not bear a steady fixed rule. For it not being possible that the first framers of the government should by any foresight be so much masters of future events as to be able to prefix so just periods of return and duration to the assemblies

of the legislative, in all times to come, that might exactly answer all the exigencies of the commonwealth, the best remedy could be found for this defect was to trust this to the prudence of one who was always to be present, and whose business it was to watch over the public good. Constant, frequent meetings of the legislative, and long continuations of their assemblies, without necessary occasion, could not but be burdensome to the people, and must necessarily in time produce more dangerous inconveniencies, and yet the quick turn of affairs might be sometimes such as to need their present help; any delay of their convening might endanger the public; and sometimes, too, their business might be so great that the limited time of their sitting might be too short for their work, and rob the public of that benefit which could be had only from their mature deliberation. What, then, could be done in this case to prevent the community from being exposed some time or other to imminent hazard on one side or the other, by fixed intervals and periods set to the meeting and acting of the legislative, but to intrust it to the prudence of some who, being present and acquainted with the state of public affairs, might make use of this prerogative for the public good? And where else could this be so well placed as in his hands who was intrusted with the execution of the laws for the same end? Thus, supposing the regulation of times for the assembling and sitting of the legislative not settled by the original constitution, it naturally fell into the hands of the executive; not as an arbitrary power depending on his good pleasure, but with this trust always to have it exercised only for the public weal, as the occurrences of times and change of affairs might require. Whether settled periods of their convening, or a liberty left to the prince for convoking the legislative, or perhaps a mixture of both, hath the least inconvenience attending it, it is not my business here to inquire, but only to show that, though the executive power may have the prerogative of convoking and dissolving such conventions of the legislative, yet it is not thereby superior to it.

157. Things of this world are in so constant a flux that nothing remains long in the same state. Thus people, riches, trade, power, change their stations; flourishing mighty cities come to ruin, and prove in time neglected desolate corners, whilst other unfrequented places grow into populous countries filled with wealth and inhabitants. But things not always changing equally, and private interest often keeping up customs and privileges when the reasons of them are ceased, it often comes to pass that in governments where part of the legislative consists of representa-

tives chosen by the people, that in tract of time, this representation becomes very unequal and disproportionate to the reasons it was at first established upon. To what gross absurdities the following of custom when reason has left it may lead, we may be satisfied when we see the bare name of a town, of which there remains not so much as the ruins, where scarce so much housing as a sheepcote, or more inhabitants than a shepherd is to be found, send as many representatives to the grand assembly of law-makers as a whole county numerous in people and powerful in riches. This strangers stand amazed at, and every one must confess needs a remedy; though most think it hard to find one, because the constitution of the legislative being the original and supreme act of the society, antecedent to all positive laws in it, and depending wholly on the people, no inferior power can alter it. And, therefore, the people when the legislative is once constituted, having in such a government as we have been speaking of, no power to act as long as the government stands, this inconvenience is thought incapable of a remedy.

158. *Salus populi suprema lex* is certainly so just and fundamental a rule, that he who sincerely follows it cannot dangerously err. If, therefore, the executive who has the power of convoking the legislative, observing rather the true proportion than fashion of representation, regulates not by old custom, but true reason, the number of members in all places, that have a right to be distinctly represented, which no part of the people, however incorporated, can pretend to, but in proportion to the assistance which it affords to the public, it cannot be judged to have set up a new legislative, but to have restored the old and true one, and to have rectified the disorders which succession of time had insensibly as well as inevitably introduced; for it being the interest as well as intention of the people to have a fair and equal representative, whoever brings it nearest to that is an undoubted friend to and establisher of the government, and cannot miss the consent and approbation of the community; prerogative being nothing but a power in the hands of the prince to provide for the public good in such cases which, depending upon unforeseen and uncertain occurrences, certain and unalterable laws could not safely direct. Whatsoever shall be done manifestly for the good of the people, and the establishing the government upon its true foundations, is, and always will be, just prerogative. The power of erecting new corporations, and therewith new representatives, carries with it a supposition that in time the measures of representation might vary, and those have a just right to be repre-

sented which before had none ; and by the same reason, those cease to have a right, and be too inconsiderable for such a privilege, which before had it. It is not a change from the present state which, perhaps, corruption or decay has introduced, that makes an inroad upon the government, but the tendency of it to injure or oppress the people, and to set up one part or party with a distinction from and an unequal subjection of the rest. Whatsoever cannot but be acknowledged to be of advantage to the society and people in general, upon just and lasting measures, will always, when done, justify itself; and whenever the people shall choose their representatives upon just and undeniably equal measures, suitable to the original frame of the government, it cannot be doubted to be the will and act of the society, whoever permitted or caused them so to do.

6. The Right of Revolution[1]

Ch. xvii. *Of Usurpation.*

197. As conquest may be called a foreign usurpation, so usurpation is a kind of domestic conquest, with this difference— that an usurper can never have right on his side, it being no usurpation but where one is got into the possession of what another has right to. This, so far as it is usurpation, is a change only of persons, but not of the forms and rules of the government ; for if the usurper extend his power beyond what, of right, belonged to the lawful princes or governors of the commonwealth, it is tyranny added to usurpation.

198. In all lawful governments the designation of the persons who are to bear rule is as natural and necessary a part as the form of the government itself, and is that which had its establishment originally from the people—the anarchy being much alike to have no form of government at all, or to agree that it shall be monarchical, but to appoint no way to design the person that shall have the power, and be the monarch. Hence all commonwealths, with the form of government established, have rules also of appointing those who are to have any share in the public authority and settled methods of conveying the right to them. . . . Whoever gets into the exercise of any part of the power by other ways than what the laws of the community have prescribed hath no right to be obeyed, though the form of the commonwealth be still preserved, since he is not the person the laws have appointed, and consequently, not the person the people have con-

[1] Bk. II, chs. xvii–xviii, xix (in part).

sented to. Nor can such an usurper, or any deriving from him, ever have a title till the people are both at liberty to consent, and have actually consented, to allow and confirm in him the power he hath till then usurped.

Ch. xviii.   *Of Tyranny.*

199. As usurpation is the exercise of power which another hath a right to, so tyranny is the exercise of power beyond right, which nobody can have a right to; and this is making use of the power any one has in his hands, not for the good of those who are under it, but for his own private, separate advantage: when the governor, however entitled, makes not the law, but his will, the rule, and his commands and actions are not directed to the preservation of the properties of his people, but the satisfaction of his own ambition, revenge, covetousness, or any other irregular passion.

200. If one can doubt this to be truth or reason because it comes from the obscure hand of a subject, I hope the authority of a king will make it pass with him. King James, in his speech to the Parliament, 1603, tells them thus: "I will ever prefer the weal of the public and of the whole commonwealth, in making of good laws and constitutions, to any particular and private ends of mine, thinking ever the wealth and weal of the commonwealth to be my greatest weal and worldly felicity—a point wherein a lawful king doth directly differ from a tyrant; for I do acknowledge that the special and greatest point of difference that is between a rightful king and an usurping tyrant is this—that whereas the proud and ambitious tyrant doth think his kingdom and people are only ordained for satisfaction of his desires and unreasonable appetites, the righteous and just king doth, by the contrary, acknowledge himself to be ordained for the procuring of the wealth and property of his people." And again, in his speech to the Parliament, 1609, he hath these words: "The king binds himself, by a double oath, to the observation of the fundamental laws of his kingdom—tacitly, as by being a king, and so bound to protect, as well the people as the laws of his kingdom; and expressly by his oath at his coronation; so as every just king, in a settled kingdom, is bound to observe that paction made to his people, by his laws, in framing his government agreeable thereunto, according to that paction which God made with Noah after the deluge: 'Hereafter, seed-time, and harvest, and cold, and heat, and summer, and winter, and day, and night, shall not cease while the earth remaineth.' And therefore a king, governing in a settled kingdom, leaves to be a king, and degenerates into a tyrant, as soon as he

leaves off to rule according to his laws." And a little after: "Therefore, all kings that are not tyrants, or perjured, will be glad to bound themselves within the limits of their laws, and they that persuade them the contrary are vipers, pests, both against them and the commonwealth." Thus, that learned king, who well understood the notions of things, makes the difference betwixt a king and a tyrant to consist only in this: that one makes the laws the bounds of his power and the good of the public the end of his government; the other makes all give way to his own will and appetite.

201. It is a mistake to think this fault is proper only to monarchies. Other forms of government are liable to it as well as that; for wherever the power that is put in any hands for the government of the people and the preservation of their properties is applied to other ends, and made use of to impoverish, harass, or subdue them to the arbitrary and irregular commands of those that have it, there it presently becomes tyranny, whether those that thus use it are one or many. Thus we read of the thirty tyrants at Athens, as well as one at Syracuse; and the intolerable dominion of the Decemviri at Rome was nothing better.

202. Wherever law ends, tyranny begins, if the law be transgressed to another's harm; and whosoever in authority exceeds the power given him by the law, and makes use of the force he has under his command to compass that upon the subject which the law allows not, ceases in that to be a magistrate, and acting without authority may be opposed, as any other man who by force invades the right of another. This is acknowledged in subordinate magistrates. He that hath authority to seize my person in the street may be opposed as a thief and a robber if he endeavors to break into my house to execute a writ, notwithstanding that I know he has such a warrant and such a legal authority as will empower him to arrest me abroad. And why this should not hold in the highest, as well as in the most inferior magistrate, I would gladly be informed. Is it reasonable that the eldest brother, because he has the greatest part of his father's estate, should thereby have a right to take away any of his younger brother's portions? Or, that a rich man, who possessed a whole country, should from thence have a right to seize, when he pleased, the cottage and garden of his poor neighbor? The being rightfully possessed of great power and riches, exceedingly beyond the greatest part of the sons of Adam, is so far from being an excuse, much less a reason for rapine and oppression, which the endamaging another without authority is, that it is a great aggravation

of it.   For the exceeding the bounds of authority is no more a right
in a great than a petty officer, no more justifiable in a king than
a constable; but is so much the worse in him in that he has more
trust put in him, has already a much greater share than the rest
of his brethren and is supposed, from the advantages of his education, employment and counsellors, to be more knowing in the
measure of right and wrong.

203. May the commands, then, of a prince be opposed?
May he be resisted, as often as any one shall find himself aggrieved,
and but imagine he has not right done him?   This will unhinge
and overturn all polities, and instead of government and order,
leave nothing but anarchy and confusion.

204. To this I answer: That force is to be opposed to nothing
but to unjust and unlawful force.   Whoever makes any opposition in any other case draws on himself a just condemnation,
both from God and man; and so no such danger or confusion will
follow, as is often suggested.   For—

205. First.   As in some countries the person of the prince by
the law is sacred, and so whatever he commands or does, his
person is still free from all question or violence, not liable to force,
or any judicial censure or condemnation.   But yet opposition may
be made to the illegal acts of any inferior officer or other commissioned by him, unless he will, by actually putting himself into a
state of war with his people, dissolve the government, and leave
them to that defense which belongs to every one in the state of
nature.   For of such things, who can tell what the end will be?
And a neighbor kingdom has shown the world an odd example.
In all other cases the sacredness of the person exempts him from
all inconveniencies, whereby he is secure, whilst the government
stands, from all violence and harm whatsoever, than which there
cannot be a wiser constitution.   For the harm he can do in his
own person not being likely to happen often, nor to extend itself
far, nor being able by his single strength to subvert the laws nor
oppress the body of the people, should any prince have so much
weakness and ill-nature as to be willing to do it, the inconveniency of some particular mischiefs that may happen sometimes when a heady prince comes to the throne are well recom-
pensed by the peace of the public and security of the government
in the person of the chief magistrate, thus set out of the reach of
danger; it being safer for the body that some few private men
should be sometimes in danger to suffer than that the head of the
republic should be easily and upon slight occasions exposed.

206. Secondly.   But this privilege, belonging only to the

king's person, hinders not but they may be questioned, opposed, and resisted, who use unjust force, though they pretend a commission from him which the law authorizes not; as is plain in the case of him that has the king's writ to arrest a man, which is a full commission from the king, and yet he that has it cannot break open a man's house to do it, nor execute this command of the king upon certain days nor in certain places, though this commission have no such exception in it; but they are the limitations of the law, which, if any one transgress, the king's commission excuses him not. For the king's authority being given him only by the law, he cannot empower any one to act against the law, or justify him by his commission in so doing. The commission, or command of any magistrate where he has no authority, being as void and insignificant as that of any private man, the difference between the one and the other being that the magistrate has some authority so far and to such ends, and the private man has none at all; for it is not the commission but the authority that gives the right of acting, and against the laws there can be no authority. But notwithstanding such resistance, the king's person and authority are still both secured, and so no danger to governor or government.

207. Thirdly. Supposing a government wherein the person of the chief magistrate is not thus sacred, yet this doctrine of the lawfulness of resisting all unlawful exercises of his power will not, upon every slight occasion, endanger him or embroil the government; for where the injured party may be relieved and his damages repaired by appeal to the law, there can be no pretense for force, which is only to be used where a man is intercepted from appealing to the law. For nothing is to be accounted hostile force but where it leaves not the remedy of such an appeal, and it is such force alone that puts him that uses it into a state of war, and makes it lawful to resist him. A man with a sword in his hand demands my purse in the highway, when perhaps I have not 12*d.* in my pocket. This man I may lawfully kill. To another I deliver £100 to hold only whilst I alight, which he refuses to restore me when I am got up again, but draws his sword to defend the possession of it by force, if I endeavor to retake it. The mischief this man does me is a hundred, or possibly a thousand times more than the other perhaps intended me (whom I killed before he really did me any); and yet I might lawfully kill the one and cannot so much as hurt the other lawfully. The reason whereof is plain; because the one using force which threatened my life, I could not have time to appeal to the law to secure it, and when it was gone it was too late to appeal. The law could

not restore life to my dead carcass. The loss was irreparable; which to prevent the law of nature gave me a right to destroy him who had put himself into a state of war with me and threatened my destruction. But in the other case, my life not being in danger, I might have the benefit of appealing to the law, and have reparation for my £100 that way.

208. Fourthly. But if the unlawful acts done by the magistrate be maintained (by the power he has got), and the remedy, which is due by law, be by the same power obstructed, yet the right of resisting, even in such manifest acts of tyranny, will not suddenly, or on slight occasions, disturb the government. For if it reach no farther than some private men's cases, though they have a right to defend themselves, and to recover by force what by unlawful force is taken from them, yet the right to do so will not easily engage them in a contest wherein they are sure to perish; it being as impossible for one or a few oppressed men to disturb the government, where the body of the people do not think themselves concerned in it, as for a raving madman or heady malcontent to overturn a well-settled state, the people being as little apt to follow the one as the other.

209. But if either these illegal acts have extended to the majority of the people, or if the mischief and oppression has lighted only on some few, but in such cases as the precedent and consequences seem to threaten all, and they are persuaded in their consciences that their laws, and with them, their estates, liberties, and lives are in danger, and perhaps their religion too, how they will be hindered from resisting illegal force used against them I cannot tell. This is an inconvenience, I confess, that attends all governments whatsoever, when the governors have brought it to this pass, to be generally suspected of their people, the most dangerous state they can possibly put themselves in; wherein they are the less to be pitied, because it is so easy to be avoided; it being as impossible for a governor, if he really means the good of his people, and the preservation of them and their laws together, not to make them see and feel it, as it is for the father of a family not to let his children see he loves and takes care of them.

210. But if all the world shall observe pretenses of one kind, and actions of another, arts used to elude the law, and the trust of prerogative (which is an arbitrary power in some things left in the prince's hand to do good, not harm, to the people) employed contrary to the end for which it was given; if the people shall find the ministers and subordinate magistrates chosen, suitable to

such ends, and favored or laid by proportionably as they promote or oppose them; if they see several experiments made of
arbitrary power, and that religion underhand favored, though
publicly proclaimed against, which is readiest to introduce it,
and the operators in it supported as much as may be; and when
that cannot be done, yet approved still, and liked the better,
and a long train of acting show the councils all tending that way,
how can a man any more hinder himself from being persuaded
in his own mind which way things are going, or, from casting
about how to save himself, than he could from believing the captain of a ship he was in was carrying him and the rest of the
company to Algiers, when he found him always steering that
course, though cross winds, leaks in his ship, and want of men
and provisions did often force him to turn his course another
way for some time, which he steadily returned to again as soon
as the wind, weather, and other circumstances would let him?

Ch. xix.   *Of the Dissolution of Governments.*

211. He that will, with any clearness, speak of the dissolution
of government, ought in the first place to distinguish between
the dissolution of the society and the dissolution of the government. That which makes the community, and brings men out
of the loose state of nature into one politic society, is the agreement which every one has with the rest to incorporate and act
as one body, and so be one distinct commonwealth. The usual,
and almost only way whereby this union is dissolved, is the inroad
of foreign force making a conquest upon them. For in that case
(not being able to maintain and support themselves as one entire
and independent body) the union belonging to that body, which
consisted therein, must necessarily cease, and so every one return
to the state he was in before, with a liberty to shift for himself
and provide for his own safety, as he thinks fit, in some other
society. Whenever the society is dissolved, it is certain the
government of that society cannot remain. Thus conquerors'
swords often cut up governments by the roots, and mangle
societies to pieces, separating the subdued or scattered multitude
from the protection of and dependence on that society which
ought to have preserved them from violence. The world is too
well instructed in, and too forward to allow of, this way of dissolving
of governments, to need any more to be said of it; and there wants
not much argument to prove that where the society is dissolved,
the government cannot remain; that being as impossible as for
the frame of a house to subsist when the materials of it are scattered

and displaced by a whirlwind, or jumbled into a confused heap by an earthquake.

212. Besides this overturning from without, governments are dissolved from within :

First, when the legislative is altered. Civil society being a state of peace amongst those who are of it, from whom the state of war is excluded by the umpirage which they have provided in their legislative for the ending all differences that may arise amongst any of them, it is in their legislative that the members of a commonwealth are united and combined together into one coherent living body. This is the soul that gives form, life, and unity to the commonwealth ; from hence the several members have their mutual influence, sympathy, and connection ; and therefore when the legislative is broken, or dissolved, dissolution and death follow. For the essence and union of the society consisting in having one will, the legislative, when once established by the majority, has the declaring and, as it were, keeping of that will. The constitution of the legislative is the first and fundamental act of society, whereby provision is made for the continuation of their union under the direction of persons and bonds of laws, made by persons authorized thereunto, by the consent and appointment of the people, without which no one man, or number of men, amongst them can have authority of making laws that shall be binding to the rest. When any one, or more, shall take upon them to make laws, whom the people have not appointed so to do, they make laws without authority, which the people are not therefore bound to obey; by which means they come again to be out of subjection, and may constitute themselves a new legislative, as they think best, being in full liberty to resist the force of those who, without authority, would impose anything upon them. Every one is at the disposure of his own will, when those who had, by the delegation of the society, the declaring of the public will, are excluded from it, and others usurp the place, who have no such authority or delegation.

213. This being usually brought about by such in the commonwealth, who misuse the power they have, it is hard to consider it aright, and know at whose door to lay it, without knowing the form of government in which it happens. Let us suppose, then, the legislative placed in the concurrence of three distinct persons :—First, a single hereditary person having the constant, supreme, executive power, and with it the power of convoking and dissolving the other two within certain periods of time. Secondly, an assembly of hereditary nobility. Thirdly, an assem-

bly of representatives chosen, *pro tempore*, by the people. Such a form of government supposed, it is evident—

214. First, that when such a single person or prince sets up his own arbitrary will in place of the laws which are the will of the society declared by the legislative, then the legislative is changed. For that being, in effect, the legislative whose rules and laws are put in execution, and required to be obeyed, when other laws are set up, and other rules pretended and enforced than what the legislative, constituted by the society, have enacted, it is plain that the legislative is changed. Whoever introduces new laws, not being thereunto authorized, by the fundamental appointment of the society, or subverts the old, disowns and overturns the power by which they were made, and so sets up a new legislative.

215. Secondly, when the prince hinders the legislative from assembling in its due time, or from acting freely, pursuant to those ends for which it was constituted, the legislative is altered. For it is not a certain number of men—no, nor their meeting, unless they have also freedom of debating and leisure of perfecting what is for the good of the society, wherein the legislative consists; when these are taken away, or altered, so as to deprive the society of the due exercise of their power, the legislative is truly altered. For it is not names that constitute governments, but the use and exercise of those powers that were intended to accompany them; so that he who takes away the freedom or hinders the acting of the legislative in its due seasons, in effect takes away the legislative, and puts an end to the government.

216. Thirdly, when, by the arbitrary power of the prince, the electors or ways of election are altered without the consent and contrary to the common interest of the people, there also the legislative is altered. For if others than those whom the society hath authorized thereunto do choose, or in another way than what the society hath prescribed, those chosen are not the legislative appointed by the people.

217. Fourthly, the delivery also of the people into the subjection of a foreign power, either by the prince or by the legislative, is certainly a change of the legislative, and so a dissolution of the government. For the end why people entered into society being to be preserved one entire, free, independent society, to be governed by its own laws, this is lost whenever they are given up into the power of another.

218. Why, in such a constitution as this, the dissolution of the government in these cases is to be imputed to the prince is evident; because he, having the force, treasure, and offices

of the state to employ, and often persuading himself or being
flattered by others, that, as supreme magistrate, he is incapable
of control; he alone is in a condition to make great advances
towards such changes under pretense of lawful authority, and
has it in his hands to terrify or suppress opposers as factious,
seditious, and enemies to the government; whereas no other part
of the legislative, or people, is capable by themselves to attempt
any alteration of the legislative without open and visible rebellion, apt enough to be taken notice of, which, when it prevails,
produces effects very little different from foreign conquest.
Besides, the prince, in such a form of government, having the
power of dissolving the other parts of the legislative, and thereby
rendering them private persons, they can never, in opposition
to him, or without his concurrence, alter the legislative by a law,
his consent being necessary to give any of their decrees that
sanction. But yet so far as the other parts of the legislative
any way contribute to any attempt upon the government, and do
either promote, or not, what lies in them, hinder such designs,
they are guilty, and partake in this, which is certainly the greatest
crime men can be guilty of one towards another.

219. There is one way more whereby such a government
may be dissolved, and that is, when he who has the supreme
executive power neglects and abandons that charge, so that the
laws already made can no longer be put in execution; this is
demonstratively to reduce all to anarchy, and so effectually to
dissolve the government. For laws not being made for themselves,
but to be, by their execution, the bonds of the society to keep every
part of the body politic in its due place and function, when that
totally ceases, the government visibly ceases, and the people
become a confused multitude without order or connection. Where
there is no longer the administration of justice for the securing of
men's rights, nor any remaining power within the community to
direct the force, or provide for the necessities of the public, there
certainly is no government left. Where the laws cannot be executed it is all one as if there were no laws, and a government without laws is, I suppose, a mystery in politics inconceivable to human
capacity, and inconsistent with human society.

220. In these, and the like cases, when the government is
dissolved, the people are at liberty to provide for themselves
by erecting a new legislative differing from the other by the
change of persons, or form, or both, as they shall find it most
for their safety and good. For the society can never, by the
fault of another, lose the native and original right it has to pre-

serve itself, which can only be done by a settled legislative and a fair and impartial execution of the laws made by it. But the state of mankind is not so miserable that they are not capable of using this remedy till it be too late to look for any. To tell people they may provide for themselves by erecting a new legislative, when, by oppression, artifice, or being delivered over to a foreign power, their old one is gone, is only to tell them they may expect relief when it is too late, and the evil is past cure. This is, in effect, no more than to bid them first be slaves, and then to take care of their liberty, and when their chains are on, tell them they may act like free men. This, if barely so, is rather mockery than relief, and men can never be secure from tyranny if there be no means to escape it till they are perfectly under it; and, therefore, it is that they have not only a right to get out of it, but to prevent it.

221. There is, therefore, secondly, another way whereby governments are dissolved, and that is, when the legislative, or the prince, either of them act contrary to their trust.

First: the legislative acts against the trust reposed in them when they endeavor to invade the property of the subject, and to make themselves, or any part of the community, masters or arbitrary disposers of the lives, liberties, or fortunes of the people.

222. The reason why men enter into society is the preservation of their property; and the end why they choose and authorize a legislative is that there may be laws made, and rules set, as guards and fences to the properties of all the society, to limit the power, and moderate the dominion of every part and member of the society. For since it can never be supposed to be the will of the society that the legislative should have a power to destroy that which every one designs to secure by entering into society, and for which the people submitted themselves to legislators of their own making; whenever the legislators endeavor to take away and destroy the property of the people, or to reduce them to slavery under arbitrary power, they put themselves into a state of war with the people, who are thereupon absolved from any farther obedience, and are left to the common refuge which God hath provided for all men against force and violence. Whensoever, therefore, the legislative shall transgress this fundamental rule of society, and either by ambition, fear, folly, or corruption, endeavor to grasp themselves, or put into the hands of any other, an absolute power over the lives, liberties, and estates of the people, by this breach of trust they forfeit the power the people had put into their hands for quite contrary ends, and it devolves to the

people, who have a right to resume their original liberty, and by
the establishment of a new legislative (such as they shall think
fit), provide for their own safety and security, which is the end
for which they are in society.   What I have said here concerning
the legislative in general holds true also concerning the supreme
executor, who having a double trust put in him, both to have a
part in the legislative and the supreme execution of the law, acts
against both, when he goes about to set up his own arbitrary
will as the law of the society.   He acts also contrary to his trust
when he employs the force, treasure, and offices of the society
to corrupt the representatives, and gain them to his purposes;
when he openly pre-engages the electors, and prescribes, to their
choice, such whom he has, by solicitation, threats, promises, or
otherwise, won to his designs, and employs them to bring in such
who have promised beforehand what to vote and what to enact.
Thus to regulate candidates and electors, and new-model the
ways of election, what is it but to cut up the government by the
roots, and poison the very fountain of public security?   For the
people having reserved to themselves the choice of their representatives as the fence to their properties, could do it for no
other end but that they might always be freely chosen, and so
chosen, freely act and advise as the necessity of the commonwealth
and the public good should, upon examination and mature debate,
be judged to require.   This, those who give their votes before
they hear the debate, and have weighed the reasons on all sides,
are not capable of doing.   To prepare such an assembly as this,
and endeavor to set up the declared abettors of his own will, for the
true representatives of the people, and the lawmakers of the society,
is certainly as great a breach of trust, and as perfect a declaration of
a design to subvert the government, as is possible to be met with.
To which, if one shall add rewards and punishments visibly employed to the same end, and all the arts of perverted law made use
of to take off and destroy all that stand in the way of such a design,
and will not comply and consent to betray the liberties of their
country, it will be past doubt what is doing.   What power they
ought to have in the society who thus employ it contrary to the
trust that went along with it in its first institution, is easy to
determine ; and one cannot but see that he who has once attempted
any such thing as this cannot any longer be trusted.

223.   To this, perhaps, it will be said that the people being
ignorant and always discontented, to lay the foundation of
government in the unsteady opinion and uncertain humor of the
people, is to expose it to certain ruin ; and no government will be

able long to subsist if the people may set up a new legislative whenever they take offense at the old one. To this I answer, quite the contrary. People are not so easily got out of their old forms as some are apt to suggest. They are hardly to be prevailed with to amend the acknowledged faults in the frame they have been accustomed to. And if there be any original defects, or adventitious ones introduced by time or corruption, it is not an easy thing to get them changed, even when all the world sees there is an opportunity for it. This slowness and aversion in the people to quit their old constitutions has in the many revolutions which have been seen in this kingdom, in this and former ages, still kept us to, or after some interval of fruitless attempts, still brought us back again to our old legislative of king, lords and commons; and whatever provocations have made the crown be taken from some of our princes' heads, they never carried the people so far as to place it in another line.

224. But it will be said this hypothesis lays a ferment for frequent rebellion. To which I answer:

First: no more than any other hypothesis. For when the people are made miserable, and find themselves exposed to the ill usage of arbitrary power, cry up their governors as much as you will for sons of Jupiter, let them be sacred and divine, descended or authorized from Heaven, give them out for whom or what you please, the same will happen. The people generally ill treated, and contrary to right, will be ready upon any occasion to ease themselves of a burden that sits heavy upon them. They will wish and seek for the opportunity, which in the change, weakness, and accidents of human affairs, seldom delays long to offer itself. He must have lived but a little while in the world, who has not seen examples of this in his time; and he must have read very little who cannot produce examples of it in all sorts of governments in the world.

225. Secondly: I answer, such revolutions happen not upon every little mismanagement in public affairs. Great mistakes in the ruling part, many wrong and inconvenient laws, and all the slips of human frailty will be borne by the people without mutiny or murmur. But if a long train of abuses, prevarications, and artifices, all tending the same way, make the design visible to the people, and they cannot but feel what they lie under, and see whither they are going, it is not to be wondered that they should then rouse themselves, and endeavor to put the rule into such hands which may secure to them the ends for which government was at first erected, and without which, ancient names and

specious forms are so far from being better, that they are much
worse than the state of nature or pure anarchy; the inconveniencies
being all as great and as near, but the remedy farther off and
more difficult.

226. Thirdly: I answer, that this power in the people of
providing for their safety anew by a new legislative when their
legislators have acted contrary to their trust by invading their
property, is the best fence against rebellion, and the probablest
means to hinder it. For rebellion being an opposition, not to
persons, but authority, which is founded only in the constitutions
and laws of the government; those, whoever they be, who, by
force, break through, and, by force, justify their violation of them,
are truly and properly rebels. For when men, by entering into
society and civil government, have excluded force, and introduced laws for the preservation of property, peace, and unity
amongst themselves, those who set up force again in opposition
to the laws, do *rebellare*—that is, bring back again the state of
war, and are properly rebels; which they who are in power (by
the pretense they have to authority, the temptation of force
they have in their hands, and the flattery of those about them)
being likeliest to do, the properest way to prevent the evil is to
show them the danger and injustice of it who are under the greatest
temptation to run into it.

227. In both the forementioned cases, when either the legislative is changed, or the legislators act contrary to the end for
which they were constituted, those who are guilty are guilty of
rebellion. For if any one by force takes away the established
legislative of any society, and the laws by them made, pursuant
to their trust, he thereby takes away the umpirage which every
one had consented to for a peaceable decision of all their controversies, and a bar to the state of war amongst them. They
who remove or change the legislative take away this decisive
power, which nobody can have but by the appointment and consent of the people, and so destroying the authority which the people
did, and nobody else can set up, and introducing a power which
the people hath not authorized, actually introduce a state of war,
which is that of force without authority; and thus by removing the
legislative established by the society, in whose decisions the people
acquiesced and united as to that of their own will, they untie the
knot, and expose the people anew to the state of war. And if
those, who by force take away the legislative, are rebels, the legislators themselves, as has been shown, can be no less esteemed so,
when they who were set up for the protection and preservation of

the people, their liberties and properties shall by force invade and endeavor to take them away; and so they putting themselves into a state of war with those who made them the protectors and guardians of their peace, are properly, and with the greatest aggravation, *rebellantes*, rebels.

228. But if they who say it lays a foundation for rebellion mean that it may occasion civil wars or intestine broils to tell the people they are absolved from obedience when illegal attempts are made upon their liberties or properties, and may oppose the unlawful violence of those who were their magistrates when they invade their properties, contrary to the trust put in them, and that, therefore, this doctrine is not to be allowed, being so destructive to the peace of the world; they may as well say, upon the same ground, that honest men may not oppose robbers or pirates, because this may occasion disorder or bloodshed. If any mischief come in such cases, it is not to be charged upon him who defends his own right, but on him that invades his neighbor's. If the innocent honest man must quietly quit all he has for peace sake to him who will lay violent hands upon it, I desire it may be considered what a kind of peace there will be in the world which consists only in violence and rapine, and which is to be maintained only for the benefit of robbers and oppressors. Who would not think it an admirable peace betwixt the mighty and the mean, when the lamb, without resistance, yielded his throat to be torn by the imperious wolf? Polyphemus's den gives us a perfect pattern of such a peace and such a government, wherein Ulysses and his companions had nothing to do but quietly to suffer themselves to be devoured. And no doubt Ulysses, who was a prudent man, preached up passive obedience, and exhorted them to a quiet submission by representing to them of what concernment peace was to mankind, and by showing the inconveniencies which might happen if they should offer to resist Polyphemus, who had now the power over them.

229. The end of government is the good of mankind; and which is best for mankind, that the people should be always exposed to the boundless will of tyranny, or that the rulers should be sometimes liable to be opposed when they grow exorbitant in the use of their power, and employ it for the destruction, and not the preservation, of the properties of their people?

230. Nor let any one say that mischief can arise from hence as often as it shall please a busy head or turbulent spirit to desire the alteration of the government. It is true such men may stir whenever they please, but it will be only to their own just ruin

and perdition. For till the mischief be grown general, and the ill designs of the rulers become visible, or their attempts sensible to the greater part, the people, who are more disposed to suffer than right themselves by resistance, are not apt to stir. The examples of particular injustice or oppression of here and there an unfortunate man moves them not. But if they universally have a persuasion grounded upon manifest evidence that designs are carrying on against their liberties, and the general course and tendency of things cannot but give them strong suspicions of the evil intention of their governors, who is to be blamed for it? Who can help it if they, who might avoid it, bring themselves into this suspicion? Are the people to be blamed if they have the sense of rational creatures, and can think of things no otherwise than as they find and feel them? And is it not rather their fault who put things in such a posture that they would not have them thought to be as they are? I grant that the pride, ambition, and turbulency of private men have sometimes caused great disorders in common-wealths, and factions have been fatal to states and kingdoms. But whether the mischief hath oftener begun in the people's wantonness, and a desire to cast off the lawful authority of their rulers, or in the rulers' insolence and endeavors to get and exercise an arbitrary power over their people, whether oppression or disobedience gave the first rise to the disorder, I leave it to impartial history to determine. This I am sure: whoever, either ruler or subject, by force goes about to invade the rights of either prince or people, and lays the foundation for overturning the constitution and frame of any just government, is guilty of the greatest crime I think a man is capable of, being to answer for all those mischiefs of blood, rapine, and desolation, which the breaking to pieces of governments bring on a country; [and he who does it is justly to be esteemed the common enemy and pest of mankind, and is to be treated accordingly.

231. That subjects or foreigners attempting by force on the properties of any people may be resisted with force is agreed on all hands; but that magistrates doing the same thing may be resisted, hath of late been denied; as if those who had the greatest privileges and advantages by the law had thereby a power to break those laws by which alone they were set in a better place than their brethren; whereas their offense is thereby the greater, both as being ungrateful for the greater share they have by the law, and breaking also that trust which is put into their hands by their brethren.

232. Whosoever uses force without right—as every one does

in society who does it without law—puts himself into a state of war with those against whom he so uses it; and in that state all former ties are cancelled, all other rights cease, and every one has a right to defend himself, and to resist the aggressor. . . .

240. Here it is likely the common question will be made, Who shall be judge whether the prince or legislative act contrary to their trust? This, perhaps, ill-affected and factious men may spread amongst the people, when the prince only makes use of his due prerogative. To this I reply, The people shall be judge; for who shall be judge whether his trustee or deputy acts well and according to the trust reposed in him, but he who deputes him and must, by having deputed him, have still a power to discard him when he fails in his trust? If this be reasonable in particular cases of private men, why should it be otherwise in that of the greatest moment, where the welfare of millions is concerned and also where the evil, if not prevented, is greater, and the redress very difficult, dear, and dangerous?

241. But, farther, this question, Who shall be judge? cannot mean that there is no judge at all. For where there is no judicature on earth to decide controversies amongst men, God in heaven is judge. He alone, it is true, is judge of the right. But every man is judge for himself, as in all other cases so in this, whether another hath put himself into a state of war with him, and whether he should appeal to the supreme Judge, as Jephtha did.

242. If a controversy arise betwixt a prince and some of the people in a matter where the law is silent or doubtful, and the thing be of great consequence, I should think the proper umpire in such a case should be the body of the people. For in cases where the prince hath a trust reposed in him, and is dispensed from the common ordinary rules of the law, there, if any men find themselves aggrieved, and think the prince acts contrary to, or beyond that trust, who so proper to judge as the body of the people (who at first lodged that trust in him) how far they meant it should extend? But if the prince, or whoever they be in the administration, decline that way of determination, the appeal then lies nowhere but to Heaven; force between either persons who have no known superior on earth, or which permits no appeal to a judge on earth, being properly a state of war, wherein the appeal lies only to Heaven; and in that state the injured party must judge for himself when he will think fit to make use of that appeal and put himself upon it.

243. To conclude. The power that every individual gave

the society when he entered into it can never revert to the individuals again, as long as the society lasts, but will always
remain in the community; because without this there can be no
community—no commonwealth, which is contrary to the original
agreement; so also when the society hath placed the legislative
in any assembly of men, to continue in them and their successors,
with direction and authority for providing such successors, the
legislative can never revert to the people whilst that government
lasts; because, having provided a legislative with power to continue for ever, they have given up their political power to the
legislative, and cannot resume it. But if they have set limits to
the duration of their legislative, and made this supreme power
in any person or assembly only temporary; or else, when, by the
miscarriages of those in authority, it is forfeited; upon the forfeiture, or at the determination of the time set, it reverts to the
society, and the people have a right to act as supreme, and continue
the legislative in themselves or erect a new form, or under the
old form place it in new hands, as they think good.

SELECTED BIBLIOGRAPHY

Cook, Thomas I., *History of Political Philosophy*, ch. 19.
Dunning, William A., *Political Theories, from Luther to Montesquieu*, ch. 10.
Sabine, George H., *History of Political Theory*, pp. 523–540.

Driver, C. H., "John Locke," in F. J. C. Hearnshaw, ed., *Social and Political
Ideas of Some English Thinkers of the Augustan Age*, A.D. *1650–1750* (Lon-
don, 1928), ch. 4.
Laski, H. J., *Political Thought in England from Locke to Bentham* (London,
1920), ch. 2.
Vaughan, C. E., *Studies in the History of Political Philosophy before and after
Rousseau*, 2 vols. (Manchester, 1925), Vol. I, ch. 4.
Hamilton, Walton H., "Property—According to Locke," in *Yale Law Journal*,
Vol. 41 (1931–32), pp. 864–880.
Bonar, J., *Philosophy and Political Economy in Some of Their Historical Rela-
tions* (third ed., London, 1922), bk. ii, ch. 5.
Pollock, Frederick, *Essays in the Law* (London, 1922), ch. 3 : "Locke's Theory
of the State."
Aaron, R. I., *John Locke* (New York, 1937), pt. iii.
Graham, William, *English Political Philosophy from Hobbes to Maine* (London,
1899), pp. 50–81.
Stephen, Leslie, *History of English Thought in the Eighteenth Century*, 2 vols.
(third ed., New York and London, 1902), Vol. II, pp. 130–152.
Green, Thomas Hill, *Lectures on the Principles of Political Obligation* (London,
1895), pp. 68–79.

Lamprecht, Sterling P., *The Moral and Political Philosophy of John Locke* (New
York, 1918).
Parkin, Paschal, *Property in the Eighteenth Century, with Special Reference to
England and Locke* (Dublin, 1930).
Bastide, Charles, *John Locke: ses théories politiques et leur influence en Angle-
terre* (Paris, 1906).

MONTESQUIEU

XXII. MONTESQUIEU (1689–1755)

INTRODUCTION

The *Spirit of the Laws* (*l'Esprit des lois*) of Montesquieu is concerned primarily with explaining the nature and working of political institutions in general. It is less closely associated with sudden political transformations than were the seventeenth-century English writings. In some measure it reflects contemporary conditions; but its aim is to reform rather than either to vindicate or condemn the existing political and social order. It deals more with questions of governmental efficiency and practical justice than with dogmas as to fundamental rights of citizens or the location and prerogatives of sovereignty. In its comprehensive treatment of these more concrete subjects verification of the various doctrines set forth is sought in examples from history and from contemporary political experience.

Montesquieu was born in Bordeaux of a family of the lesser nobility. He received a legal training, and in early manhood he inherited the presidency of the Parliament of Bordeaux from his uncle. He held the office for about ten years. During this period he read extensively from literature and history, and wrote several papers for the local academy on philosophical, scientific and political topics. In 1721 he published his first major work—the *Persian Letters*, which is a satire (in the form of letters written by two Persians traveling through France) upon the literary, spiritual, political and social customs and traditions of the day in France. This work was exceedingly popular and immediately gave the author a wide reputation. He sold his presidency and moved to Paris, where, shortly, he was elected to the Academy. Soon thereafter he set out upon an extensive journey of observation through Austria and other German states, Hungary, Switzerland, Italy, Holland and, finally, England; he remained about two years in England. Returning then to France he resumed his residence at the family castle at Bordeaux, and soon published his next important work—the *Causes of the Greatness and Decline of the Romans*, which is one of the earliest significant works in the modern philosophy of history.

Montesquieu's greatest work, the *Spirit of the Laws*, was published in 1748, after a long period of preparation. The word "law" in this treatise is employed with a very general and flexible meaning, as appears from the definition of law as "the necessary relations springing from the nature of things." But the work is concerned chiefly with the interpretation of the "spirit" of social laws. In other words, Montesquieu attempts to explain the interrelations among all the elements that make up or surround a political society: physical environment, racial characteristics, social, economic, and religious customs, and civil institutions. A particular object is to show the relations between all these factors, on the one hand, and political and civil liberty, on the other hand. The most influential part of the work is that in which political liberty is defined, and the separation of powers discussed as an indispensable safeguard for the maintenance of political liberty. Here the government of England is analyzed as an exemplification of the dependence of political liberty upon governmental checks and balances.

Montesquieu was relatively moderate and dispassionate in his intellectual style. His position was generally middle-of-the-road, and his ideas have been influential in both "progressive" and "conservative" fields. On the one hand, his condemnation of despotic government and his advocacy of a representative parliament and of constitutional limitations on monarchy were of notable influence on moderate political movements in France, as in the "July Revolution" of 1830. On the other hand, his argument for "checks and balances" and his doctrine that political institutions must be framed in close relation to the physical and social environment as well as to the distinctive "national character" of a people were forces in the conservative reaction against the more doctrinaire democratic groups in France and America during the revolutionary and constitution-making periods of the eighteenth and nineteenth centuries. These two tendencies of his political reflections are not mutually inconsistent. Both fit in logically with his general liberalism and humanitarianism: he urged careful restraint in the definition of political crimes; condemned inhumane and disproportionate penalties in the punishment of ordinary crimes; and held that to maintain political liberty, freedom of speech and association is as important as a free franchise.

READINGS FROM THE SPIRIT OF THE LAWS [1]

1. *The Nature of Laws* [2]

I. *Of the Relation of Laws to Different Beings.*
Laws, in their most general signification, are the necessary
relations arising from the nature of things. In this sense all
beings have their laws: the Deity His laws, the material world its
laws, the intelligences superior to man their laws, the beasts their
laws, man his laws.

They who assert that a blind fatality produced the various
effects we behold in this world talk very absurdly; for can anything
be more unreasonable than to pretend that a blind fatality could
be productive of intelligent beings?

There is, then, a prime reason; and laws are the relations subsisting between it and different beings, and the relations of these
to one another.

God is related to the universe, as Creator and Preserver;
the laws by which He created all things are those by which He
preserves them. He acts according to these rules, because He
knows them; He knows them, because He made them; and He
made them, because they are in relation to His wisdom and power.

Since we observe that the world, though formed by the motion
of matter, and void of understanding, subsists through so long a
succession of ages, its motions must certainly be directed by invariable laws; and could we imagine another world, it must also
have constant rules, or it would inevitably perish.

Thus the creation, which seems an arbitrary act, supposes
laws as invariable as those of the fatality of the Atheists. It would
be absurd to say that the Creator might govern the world without
those rules, since without them it could not subsist.

These rules are a fixed and invariable relation. In bodies
moved, the motion is received, increased, diminished, or lost,
according to the relations of the quantity of matter and velocity;
each diversity is *uniformity*, each change is *constancy*.

Particular intelligent beings may have laws of their own making,
but they have some likewise which they never made. Before
there were intelligent beings, they were possible; they had therefore possible relations, and consequently possible laws. Before
laws were made, there were relations of possible justice. To

[1] The selections are from *The Spirit of the Laws*, translated by Thomas
Nugent. New edition, revised by J. V. Prichard. Two volumes. London,
1878. Bohn's Standard Library. George Bell and Sons.
[2] Book I.

say that there is nothing just or unjust but what is commanded or forbidden by positive laws, is the same as saying that before the describing of a circle all the radii were not equal.

We must therefore acknowledge relations of justice antecedent to the positive law by which they are established: as, for instance, if human societies existed, it would be right to conform to their laws; if there were intelligent beings that had received a benefit of another being, they ought to show their gratitude; if one intelligent being had created another intelligent being, the latter ought to continue in its original state of dependence; if one intelligent being injures another, it deserves a retaliation; and so on.

But the intelligent world is far from being so well governed as the physical. For though the former has also its laws, which of their own nature are invariable, it does not conform to them so exactly as the physical world. This is because, on the one hand, particular intelligent beings are of a finite nature, and consequently liable to error; and on the other, their nature requires them to be free agents. Hence they do not steadily conform to their primitive laws; and even those of their own instituting they frequently infringe.

Whether brutes be governed by the general laws of motion, or by a particular movement, we cannot determine. Be that as it may, they have not a more intimate relation to God than the rest of the material world; and sensation is of no other use to them than in the relation they have either to other particular beings or to themselves.

By the allurement of pleasure they preserve the individual, and by the same allurement they preserve their species. They have natural laws, because they are united by sensation; positive laws they have none, because they are not connected by knowledge. And yet they do not invariably conform to their natural laws; these are better observed by vegetables, that have neither understanding nor sense.

Brutes are deprived of the high advantages which we have; but they have some which we have not. They have not our hopes, but they are without our fears; they are subject like us to death, but without knowing it; even most of them are more attentive than we to self-preservation, and do not make so bad a use of their passions.

Man, as a physical being, is like other bodies governed by invariable laws. As an intelligent being, he incessantly transgresses the laws established by God, and changes those of his own instituting. He is left to his private direction, though a limited being, and subject, like all finite intelligences, to ignorance and error: even his imperfect knowledge he loses; and as a sensible creature, he is hurried away by a thousand impetuous passions. Such a being might every instant forget his Creator; God has therefore reminded him of his duty by the laws of religion. Such a being is liable every moment to forget himself; philosophy has provided against this by the laws of morality. Formed to live in society, he might forget his fellow-creatures; legislators have therefore by political and civil laws confined him to his duty.

2. *Of the Laws of Nature.*

Antecedent to the above-mentioned laws are those of nature, so called, because they derive their force entirely from our frame and existence. In order to have a perfect knowledge of these laws, we must consider man before the establishment of society: the laws received in such a state would be those of nature.

The law which, impressing on our minds the idea of a Creator, inclines us towards Him, is the first in importance, though not in order, of natural laws. Man in a state of nature would have the faculty of knowing, before he had acquired any knowledge. Plain it is that his first ideas would not be of a speculative nature; he would think of the preservation of his being, before he would investigate its origin. Such a man would feel nothing in himself at first but impotency and weakness; his fears and apprehensions would be excessive; as appears from instances (were there any necessity of proving it) of savages found in forests, trembling at the motion of a leaf, and flying from every shadow.

In this state every man, instead of being sensible of his equality, would fancy himself inferior. There would therefore be no danger of their attacking one another; peace would be the first law of nature.

The natural impulse or desire which Hobbes attributes to mankind of subduing one another is far from being well founded. The idea of empire and dominion is so complex, and depends on so many other notions, that it could never be the first which occurred to the human understanding.

Hobbes inquires, *For what reason go men armed, and have locks and keys to fasten their doors, if they be not naturally in a state of war?* But is it not obvious that he attributes to mankind before the establishment of society what can happen but in consequence of this establishment, which furnishes them with motives for hostile attacks and self-defense?

Next to a sense of his weakness man would soon find that of his wants. Hence another law of nature would prompt him to seek for nourishment.

Fear, I have observed, would induce men to shun one another; but the marks of this fear being reciprocal, would soon engage them to associate. Besides, this association would quickly follow from the very pleasure one animal feels at the approach of another of the same species. Again, the attraction arising from the difference of sexes would enhance this pleasure, and the natural inclination they have for each other would form a third law.

Besides the sense or instinct which man possesses in common with brutes, he has the advantage of acquired knowledge; and thence arises a second tie, which brutes have not. Mankind have therefore a new motive of uniting; and a fourth law of nature results from the desire of living in society.

3. *Of Positive Laws.*

As soon as man enters into a state of society he loses the sense of his weakness; equality ceases, and then commences the state of war.

Each particular society begins to feel its strength, whence arises a state of war between different nations. The individuals likewise of each society become sensible of their force; hence the principal advantages of this society they endeavor to convert to their own emolument, which constitutes a state of war between individuals.

These two different kinds of states give rise to human laws. Considered as inhabitants of so great a planet, which necessarily contains a variety of nations, they have laws relating to their mutual intercourse, which is what we call the *law of nations*. As members of a society that must be properly supported, they have laws relating to the governors and the governed, and this we distinguish by the name of *political law*. They have also another sort of laws, as they stand in relation to each other; by which is understood the *civil law*.

The law of nations is naturally founded on this principle, that different nations ought in time of peace to do one another all the good they can, and in time of war as little injury as possible, without prejudicing their real interests.

The object of war is victory; that of victory is conquest; and that of conquest preservation. From this and the preceding principle all those rules are derived which constitute the *law of nations*.

All countries have a law of nations, not excepting the Iroquois themselves, though they devour their prisoners: for they send and receive ambassadors, and understand the rights of war and peace. The mischief is that their law of nations is not founded on true principles.

Besides the law of nations relating to all societies, there is a polity or civil constitution for each particularly considered. No society can subsist without a form of government. *The united strength of individuals*, as Gravina well observes, *constitutes what we call the body politic.*

The general strength may be in the hands of a single person, or of many. Some think that nature having established paternal authority, the most natural government was that of a single person. But the example of paternal authority proves nothing. For if the power of a father relates to a single government, that of brothers after the death of a father, and that of cousin-germans after the decease of brothers, refer to a government of many. The political power necessarily comprehends the union of several families.

Better is it to say, that the government most conformable to nature is that which best agrees with the humor and disposition of the people in whose favor it is established.

The strength of individuals cannot be united without a conjunction of all their wills. *The conjunction of those wills*, as Gravina again very justly observes, *is what we call the civil state.*

Law in general is human reason, inasmuch as it governs all the inhabitants of the earth: the political and civil laws of each nation ought to be only the particular cases in which human reason is applied.

They should be adapted in such a manner to the people for whom they are framed that it should be a great chance if those of one nation suit another.

They should be in relation to the nature and principle of each government; whether they form it, as may be said of political laws; or whether they support it, as in the case of civil institutions.

They should be in relation to the climate of each country, to the quality of its soil, to its situation and extent, to the principal occupation of the natives, whether husbandmen, huntsmen, or shepherds: they should have relation to the degree of liberty which the constitution will bear; to the religion of the inhabitants, to their inclinations, riches, numbers, commerce, manners, and customs. In fine, they have relations to each other, as also to their origin, to the intent of the legislator, and to the order of things on which they are established; in all of which different lights they ought to be considered.

This is what I have undertaken to perform in the following work. These relations I shall examine, since all these together constitute what I call the *spirit of laws*.

I have not separated the political from the civil institutions, as I do not pretend to treat of laws, but of their spirit; and as this spirit consists in the various relations which the laws may bear to different objects, it is not so much my business to follow the natural order of laws as that of these relations and objects.

I shall first examine the relations which laws bear to the nature and principle of each government; and as this principle has a strong influence on laws, I shall make it my study to understand it thoroughly: and if I can but once establish it, the laws will soon appear to flow thence as from their source. I shall proceed afterwards to other and more particular relations.

2.   The Nature of the Forms of Government [1]

1.   *Of the Nature of the Three Different Governments.*

There are three species of government: *republican, monarchical, and despotic.* In order to discover their nature, it is sufficient to recollect the common notion, which supposes three definitions, or rather three facts: that a *republican government is that in which the body, or only a part of the people, is possessed of the supreme power; monarchy, that in which a single person governs by fixed and established laws; a despotic government, that in which a single person directs everything by his own will and caprice.*

This is what I call the nature of each government; we must now inquire into those laws which directly conform to this nature, and consequently are the fundamental institutions.

2.   *Of Republican Government, and the Laws in relation to Democracy.*

When the body of the people is possessed of the supreme power, it is called a *democracy.* When the supreme power is lodged in the hands of a part of the people, it is then an *aristocracy.*

In a democracy the people are in some respects the sovereign, and in others the subject.

There can be no exercise of sovereignty but by their suffrages, which are their own will; now the sovereign's will is the sovereign himself. The laws therefore which establish the right of suffrage

[1] Book II.

are fundamental to this government. And indeed it is as important to regulate in a republic, in what manner, by whom, to whom, and concerning what, suffrages are to be given, as it is in a monarchy to know who is the prince, and after what manner he ought to govern.

Libanius says that at Athens a stranger who intermeddled in the assemblies of the people was punished with death. This is because such a man usurped the rights of sovereignty.

It is an essential point to fix the number of citizens who are to form the public assemblies; otherwise it would be uncertain whether the whole, or only a part of the people, had given their votes. At Sparta the number was fixed at ten thousand. But Rome, designed by Providence to rise from the weakest beginnings to the highest pitch of grandeur; Rome, doomed to experience all the vicissitudes of fortune; Rome, who had sometimes all her inhabitants without her walls, and sometimes all Italy and a considerable part of the world within them; Rome, I say, never fixed the number; and this was one of the principal causes of her ruin.

The people, in whom the supreme power resides, ought to have the management of everything within their reach: that which exceeds their abilities must be conducted by their ministers.

But they cannot properly be said to have their ministers, without the power of nominating them: it is, therefore, a fundamental maxim in this government, that the people should choose their ministers—that is, their magistrates.

They have occasion, as well as monarchs, and even more so, to be directed by a council or senate. But to have a proper confidence in these, they should have the choosing of the members; whether the election be made by themselves, as at Athens, or by some magistrate deputed for that purpose, as on certain occasions was customary at Rome.

The people are extremely well qualified for choosing those whom they are to intrust with part of their authority. They have only to be determined by things to which they cannot be strangers, and by facts that are obvious to sense. They can tell when a person has fought many battles, and been crowned with success; they are, therefore, capable of electing a general. They can tell when a judge is assiduous in his office, gives general satisfaction, and has never been charged with bribery: this is sufficient for choosing a prætor. They are struck with the magnificence or riches of a fellow-citizen; no more is requisite for electing an ædile. These are facts of which they can have better information in a public forum than a monarch in his palace. But are they capable of conducting an intricate affair, of seizing and improving the opportunity and critical moment of action? No; this surpasses their abilities.

Should we doubt the people's natural capacity, in respect to the discernment of merit, we need only cast an eye on the series of surprising elections made by the Athenians and Romans; which no one surely will attribute to hazard.

We know that though the people of Rome assumed the right of raising plebeians to public offices, yet they never would exert this power; and though at Athens the magistrates were allowed, by the law of Aristides, to be elected from all the different classes of inhabitants, there never was a case, says Xenophon, when the common people petitioned for employments which could endanger either their security or their glory.

As most citizens have sufficient ability to choose, though unqualified to be chosen, so the people, though capable of calling others to an account for their administration, are incapable of conducting the administration themselves.

The public business must be carried on with a certain motion, neither too quick nor too slow. But the motion of the people is always either too remiss or too violent. Sometimes with a hundred thousand arms they overturn all before them; and sometimes with a hundred thousand feet they creep like insects.

In a popular state the inhabitants are divided into certain classes. It is in the manner of making this division that great legislators have signalized themselves; and it is on this the duration and prosperity of democracy have ever depended.

Servius Tullius followed the spirit of aristocracy in the distribution of his classes. We find in Livy and in Dionysius Halicarnassus, in what manner he lodged the right of suffrage in the hands of the principal citizens. He had divided the people of Rome into 193 centuries, which formed six classes; and ranking the rich, who were in smaller numbers, in the first centuries, and those in middling circumstances, who were more numerous, in the next, he flung the indigent multitude into the last; and as each century had but one vote, it was property rather than numbers that decided the election.

Solon divided the people of Athens into four classes. In this he was directed by the spirit of democracy, his intention not being to fix those who were to choose, but such as were eligible: there-fore, leaving to every citizen the right of election, he made the. judges eligible from each of those four classes; but the magistrates he ordered to be chosen only out of the first three, consisting of persons of easy fortunes.

As the division of those who have a right of suffrage is a fundamental law in republics, so the manner of giving this suffrage is another fundamental.

The suffrage by *lot* is natural to democracy; as that by *choice* is to aristocracy.

The suffrage by lot is a method of electing that offends no one, but animates each citizen with the pleasing hope of serving his country.

Yet as this method is in itself defective, it has been the endeavor of the most eminent legislators to regulate and amend it.

Solon made a law at Athens, that military employments should be conferred by choice; but that senators and judges should be elected by lot.

The same legislator ordained that civil magistracies attended with great expense should be given by choice, and the others by lot.

In order, however, to amend the suffrage by lot, he made a rule that none but those who presented themselves should be elected; that the person elected should be examined by judges, and that every one should have a right to accuse him if he were unworthy of the office; this participated at the same time of the suffrage by lot, and of that by choice. When the time of their magistracy had expired, they were obliged to submit to another judgment in regard to their conduct. Persons utterly unqualified must have been extremely backward in giving in their names to be drawn by lot.

The law which determines the manner of giving suffrage is likewise fundamental in a democracy. It is a question of some importance whether the suffrages ought to be public or secret. Cicero observes that the laws which rendered them secret towards the close of the republic were the cause of its decline. But as this is differently practised in different republics, I shall offer here my thoughts concerning this subject.

The people's suffrages ought doubtless to be public; and this should be considered as a fundamental law of democracy. The lower class ought to be directed by those of higher rank, and restrained within bounds by the gravity of eminent personages. Hence, by rendering the suffrages secret in the Roman republic, all was lost; it was no longer possible to direct a populace that sought its own destruction. But when the body of the nobles are to vote in an aristocracy, or in a democracy the senate, as the business is then only to prevent intrigues, the suffrages cannot be too secret.

Intriguing in a senate is dangerous; it is dangerous also in a body of nobles; but not so among the people, whose nature is to act through passion. In countries where they have no share in the government, we often see them as much inflamed on account of an actor as ever they could be for the welfare of the state. The misfortune of a republic is when intrigues are at an end; which happens when the people are gained by bribery and corruption: in this case they grow indifferent to public affairs, and avarice becomes their predominant passion. Unconcerned about the government and everything belonging to it, they quietly wait for their hire.

It is likewise a fundamental law in democracies, that the people should have the sole power to enact laws. And yet there are a thousand occasions on which it is necessary the senate should have the power of decreeing; nay, it is frequently proper to make some trial of a law before it is established. The constitutions of Rome and Athens were excellent. The decrees of the senate had the force of laws for the space of a year, but did not become perpetual till they were ratified by the consent of the people.

3. Of the Laws in Relation to the Nature of Aristocracy.

In an aristocracy the supreme power is lodged in the hands of a certain number of persons. These are invested both with the legislative and executive authority; and the rest of the people are, in respect to them, the same as the subjects of a monarchy in regard to the sovereign.

They do not vote here by lot, for this would be productive of inconveniences only. And indeed, in a government where the most mortifying distinctions are already established, though they were to be chosen by lot, still they would not cease to be odious; it is the nobleman they envy, and not the magistrate.

When the nobility are numerous, there must be a senate to regulate the affairs which the body of the nobles are incapable of deciding, and to prepare others for their decision. In this case it may be said that the aristocracy is in some measure in the senate, the democracy in the body of the nobles, and the people are a cipher.

It would be a very happy thing in an aristocracy if the people, in some measure, could be raised from their state of annihilation. Thus at Genoa, the bank of St. George being administered by the people gives them a certain influence in the government, whence their whole prosperity is derived.

The senators ought by no means to have the right of naming their own members; for this would be the only way to perpetuate abuses. At Rome, which in its early years was a kind of aristocracy, the senate did not fill up the vacant places in their own body; the new members were nominated by the censors.

In a republic, the sudden rise of a private citizen to exorbitant power produces monarchy, or something more than monarchy. In the latter the laws have provided for, or in some measure adapted themselves to, the constitution; and the principle of government checks the monarch: but in a republic, where a private citizen has obtained an exorbitant power, the abuse of this power is much greater, because the laws foresaw it not, and consequently made no provision against it.

There is an exception to this rule, when the constitution is such as to have immediate need of a magistrate invested with extraordinary power. Such was Rome with her dictators, such is Venice with her state inquisitors; these are formidable magistrates, who restore, as it were by violence, the state to its liberty. But how comes it that these magistracies are so very different in these two republics? It is because Rome supported the remains of her aristocracy against the people; whereas Venice employs her state inquisitors to maintain her aristocracy against the nobles. The consequence was, that at Rome the dictatorship could be only of short duration, as the people acted through passion and not with design. It was necessary that a magistracy of this kind should be exercised with luster and pomp, the business being to intimidate, and not to punish the multitude. It was also proper that the dictator should be created only for some particular affair, and for this only should have unlimited authority, as he was always created upon some sudden emergency. On the contrary, at Venice they have occasion for a permanent magistracy; for here it is that schemes may be set on foot, continued, suspended, and resumed; that the ambition of a single person becomes that of a family, and the ambition of one family that of many. They have occasion for a secret magistracy, the crimes they punish being hatched in secrecy and silence. This magistracy must have a general inquisition, for their business is not to remedy known disorders, but to prevent the unknown. In a word, the latter is designed to punish suspected crimes; whereas the former used rather menaces than punishment even for crimes that were openly avowed.

In all magistracies, the greatness of the power must be compensated by the brevity of the duration. This most legislators have fixed to a year; a longer space would be dangerous, and a shorter would be contrary to the nature of government. For who is it that in the management even of his domestic affairs would be thus confined? At Ragusa the chief magistrate of the republic is changed every month, the other officers every week, and the governor of the castle every day. But this can take place only in a small republic environed by formidable powers, who might easily corrupt such petty and insignificant magistrates.

The best aristocracy is that in which those who have no share in the legislature are so few and inconsiderable that the governing party have no interest in oppressing them. Thus when Antipater made a law at Athens, that whosoever was not worth two thousand drachms should have no power to vote, he formed by this method the best aristocracy possible, because this was so small a sum as to exclude very few, and not one of any rank or consideration in the city.

Aristocratic families ought therefore, as much as possible, to level themselves in appearance with the people. The more an aristocracy borders on democracy, the nearer it approaches perfection: and, in proportion as it draws towards monarchy, the more is it imperfect.

But the most imperfect of all is that in which the part of the people that obeys is in a state of civil servitude to those who command, as the aristocracy of Poland, where the peasants are slaves to the nobility.

4. *Of the Relation of Laws to the Nature of Monarchical Government.*

The intermediate, subordinate, and dependent powers constitute the nature of monarchical government; I mean of that in which a single person governs by fundamental laws. I said, the *intermediate, subordinate,* and *dependent powers.* And indeed, in monarchies the prince is the source of all power, political and civil. These fundamental laws necessarily suppose the intermediate channels through which the power flows: for if there be only the momentary and capricious will of a single person to govern the state, nothing can be fixed, and of course there is no fundamental law.

The most natural, intermediate, and subordinate power is that of the nobility. This in some measure seems to be essential to a monarchy, whose fundamental maxim is: *no monarch, no nobility; no nobility, no monarch;* but there may be a despotic prince.

There are men who have endeavored in some countries in Europe to suppress the jurisdiction of the nobility, not perceiving that they were driving at the very thing that was done by the parliament of England. Abolish the privileges of the lords, the clergy and cities in a monarchy, and you will soon have a popular state, or else a despotic government.

The courts of a considerable kingdom in Europe have, for many ages, been striking at the patrimonial jurisdiction of the lords and clergy. We do not pretend to censure these sage magistrates; but we leave it to the public to judge how far this may alter the constitution.

Far am I from being prejudiced in favor of the privileges of the clergy; however, I should be glad if their jurisdiction were once fixed. The question is not, whether their jurisdiction was justly established; but whether it be really established; whether it constitutes a part of the laws of the country, and is in every respect in relation to those laws: whether between two powers acknowledged independent, the conditions ought not to be reciprocal; and whether it be not equally the duty of a good subject to defend the prerogative of the prince, and to maintain the limits which from time immemorial have been prescribed to his authority.

Though the ecclesiastic power be so dangerous in a republic, yet it is extremely proper in a monarchy, especially of the absolute kind. What would become of Spain and Portugal, since the subversion of their laws, were it not for this only barrier against the incursions of arbitrary power? A barrier ever useful when there is no other: for since a despotic government is productive of the most dreadful calamities to human nature, the very evil that restrains it is beneficial to the subject.

In the same manner as the ocean, threatening to overflow the whole earth, is stopped by weeds and pebbles that lie scattered along the shore, so monarchs, whose power seems unbounded, are restrained by the smallest obstacles, and suffer their natural pride to be subdued by supplication and prayer.

The English, to favor their liberty, have abolished all the intermediate powers of which their monarchy was composed. They have a great deal of reason to be jealous of this liberty; were they ever to be so unhappy as to lose it, they would be one of the most servile nations upon earth.

Mr. Law, through ignorance both of a republican and monarchical constitution, was one of the greatest promoters of absolute power ever known in Europe. Besides the violent and extraordinary changes owing to his direction, he would fain suppress all the intermediate ranks, and abolish the political communities. He was dissolving the monarchy by his chimerical reimbursements, and seemed as if he even wanted to redeem the constitution.

It is not enough to have intermediate powers in a monarchy; there must be also a depositary of the laws. This depositary can only be the judges of the supreme courts of justice, who promulgate the new laws, and revive the obsolete. The natural ignorance of the nobility, their indolence and contempt of civil government, require that there should be a body invested with the power of reviving and executing the laws, which would be otherwise buried in oblivion. The prince's council are not a proper depositary. They are naturally the depositary of the momentary will of the prince, and not of the fundamental laws. Besides, the prince's council is continually changing; it is neither permanent nor numerous; neither has it a sufficient share of the confidence of the people; consequently it is incapable of setting them right in difficult conjunctures, or in reducing them to proper obedience.

Despotic governments, where there are no fundamental laws, have no such kind of depositary. Hence it is that religion has generally so much influence in those countries, because it forms a kind of permanent depositary; and if this cannot be said of religion, it may of the customs that are respected instead of laws.

5. *Of the Laws in Relation to the Nature of a Despotic Government.*
From the nature of despotic power it follows that the single person invested with this power commits the execution of it also to a single person. A man whom his senses continually inform that he himself is everything and that his subjects are nothing, is naturally lazy, voluptuous, and ignorant. In consequence of this, he neglects the management of public affairs. But were he to commit the administration to many, there would be continual disputes among them; each would form intrigues to be his first slave; and he would be obliged to take the reins into his own hands. It is, therefore, more natural for him to resign it to a vizir, and to invest him with the same power as himself. The creation of a vizir is a fundamental law of this government.

It is related of a pope, that he had started an infinite number of difficulties against his election, from a thorough conviction of his incapacity. At length he was prevailed on to accept the pontificate, and resigned the administration entirely to his nephew. He was soon struck with surprise, and said, *I should never have thought that these things were so easy.* The same may be said of the princes of the East, who, being educated in a prison where eunuchs corrupt their hearts and debase their understandings, and where they are frequently kept ignorant even of their high rank, when drawn forth in order to be placed on the throne, are at first confounded: but as soon as they have chosen a vizir, and abandoned themselves in their seraglio to the most brutal passions, pursuing, in the midst of a prostituted court, every capricious extravagance, they would never have dreamed that they could find matters so easy.

The more extensive the empire, the larger the seraglio; and consequently the more voluptuous the prince. Hence the more nations such a sovereign has to rule, the less he attends to the cares of government; the more important his affairs, the less he makes them the subject of his deliberations.

3. The Principles of the Forms of Government.[1]

1. *Difference between the Nature and Principle of Government.*
Having examined the laws in relation to the nature of each government, we must investigate those which relate to its principle.

There is this difference between the nature and principle of government, that the former is that by which it is constituted, the latter that by which it is made to act. One is its particular structure, and the other the human passions which set it in motion.

Now, laws ought no less to relate to the principle than to the nature of each government. We must, therefore, inquire into this principle, which shall be the subject of this third book.

2. *Of the Principle of different Governments.*
I have already observed that it is the nature of a republican government, that either the collective body of the people, or particular families, should be possessed of the supreme power; of a monarchy, that the prince should have this power, but in the execution of it should be directed by established laws; of a despotic government, that a single person should rule according to his own will and caprice. This enables me to discover their three principles, which are thence naturally derived. I shall begin with a republican government, and in particular with that of democracy.

3. *Of the Principle of Democracy.*
There is no great share of probity necessary to support a monarchical or despotic government. The force of laws in one, and

[1] Book III.

the prince's arm in the other, are sufficient to direct and maintain the whole. But in a popular state, one spring more is necessary, namely, *virtue.*

What I have here advanced is confirmed by the unanimous
testimony of historians, and is extremely agreeable to the nature
of things. For it is clear that in a monarchy, where he who
commands the execution of the laws generally thinks himself
above them, there is less need of virtue than in a popular government, where the person intrusted with the execution of the laws
is sensible of his being subject to their direction.

Clear is it also that a monarch who, through bad advice or
indolence, ceases to enforce the execution of the laws, may easily
repair the evil; he has only to follow other advice; or to shake off
this indolence. But when, in a popular government, there is a
suspension of the laws, as this can proceed only from the corruption of the republic, the state is certainly undone.

A very droll spectacle it was in the last century to behold
the impotent efforts of the English towards the establishment of
democracy. As they who had a share in the direction of public
affairs were void of virtue, as their ambition was inflamed by the
success of the most daring of their members, as the prevailing
parties were successively animated by the spirit of faction, the
government was continually changing: the people, amazed at so
many revolutions, in vain attempted to erect a commonwealth.
At length, when the country had undergone the most violent shocks
they were obliged to have recourse to the very government which
they had so wantonly proscribed.

When Sulla thought of restoring Rome to her liberty, this unhappy city was incapable of receiving that blessing. She had
only the feeble remains of virtue, which were continually diminishing. Instead of being roused from her lethargy by Cæsar, Tiberius, Caius Claudius, Nero, and Domitian, she riveted every day
her chains; if she struck some blows, her aim was at the tyrant,
not at the tyranny.

The politic Greeks, who lived under a popular government,
knew no other support than virtue. The modern inhabitants of
that country are entirely taken up with manufacture, commerce,
finances, opulence, and luxury.

When virtue is banished, ambition invades the minds of those
who are disposed to receive it, and avarice possesses the whole
community. The objects of their desires are changed; what
they were fond of before has become indifferent; they were free
while under the restraint of laws, but they would fain now be

free to act against law; and as each citizen is like a slave who has
run away from his master, that which was a maxim of equity he
calls rigor; that which was a rule of action he styles constraint;
and to precaution he gives the name of fear. Frugality, and not
the thirst of gain, now passes for avarice. Formerly the wealth
of individuals constituted the public treasure; but now this has
become the patrimony of private persons. The members of the
commonwealth riot on the public spoils, and its strength is only
the power of a few, and the license of many.

Athens was possessed of the same number of forces when she
triumphed so gloriously as when with such infamy she was enslaved. She had twenty thousand citizens, when she defended
the Greeks against the Persians, when she contended for empire
with Sparta, and invaded Sicily. She had twenty thousand when
Demetrius Phalereus numbered them, as slaves are told by the
head in a market-place. When Philip attempted to lord it over
Greece, and appeared at the gates of Athens, she had even then
lost nothing but time. We may see in Demosthenes how difficult
it was to awaken her; she dreaded Philip, not as the enemy of her
liberty, but of her pleasures. This famous city, which had withstood so many defeats, and having been so often destroyed had
as often risen out of her ashes, was overthrown at Chæronea, and
at one blow deprived of all hopes of resource. What does it
avail her that Philip sends back her prisoners, if he does not return
her men? It was ever after as easy to triumph over the forces of
Athens as it had been difficult to subdue her virtue.

How was it possible for Carthage to maintain her ground?
When Hannibal, upon his being made prætor, endeavored to
hinder the magistrates from plundering the republic, did not
they complain of him to the Romans? Wretches, who would fain
be citizens without a city, and be beholden for their riches to
their very destroyers! Rome soon insisted upon having three
hundred of their principal citizens as hostages; she obliged them
next to surrender their arms and ships; and then she declared
war. From the desperate efforts of this defenseless city, one may
judge of what she might have performed in her full vigor, and
assisted by virtue.

4. *Of the Principle of Aristocracy.*

As virtue is necessary in a popular government, it is requisite
also in an aristocracy. True it is that in the latter it is not so
absolutely requisite.

The people, who in respect to the nobility are the same as the subjects with regard to a monarch, are restrained by their laws. They have, therefore, less occasion for virtue than the people in a democracy. But how are the nobility to be restrained? They who are to execute the laws against their colleagues will immediately perceive that they are acting against themselves. Virtue is therefore necessary in this body, from the very nature of the constitution.

An aristocratic government has an inherent vigor, unknown to democracy. The nobles form a body, who by their prerogative, and for their own particular interest, restrain the people; it is sufficient that there are laws in being to see them executed.

But easy as it may be for the body of the nobles to restrain the people, it is difficult to restrain themselves. Such is the nature of this constitution, that it seems to subject the very same persons to the power of the laws, and at the same time to exempt them.

Now such a body as this can restrain itself only in two ways: either by a very eminent virtue, which puts the nobility in some measure on a level with the people, and may be the means of forming a great republic; or by an inferior virtue, which puts them at least upon a level with one another, and upon this their preservation depends.

Moderation is therefore the very soul of this government; a moderation, I mean, founded on virtue, not that which proceeds from indolence and pusillanimity.

5. *That Virtue is not the Principle of a Monarchical Government.* In monarchies, policy effects great things with as little virtue as possible. Thus in the nicest machines, art has reduced the number of movements, springs, and wheels.

The state subsists independently of the love of our country, of the thirst of true glory, of self-denial, of the sacrifice of our dearest interests, and of all those heroic virtues which we admire in the ancients, and to us are known only by tradition.

The laws supply here the place of those virtues; they are by no means wanted, and the state dispenses with them: an action performed here in secret is in some measure of no consequence.

Though all crimes be in their own nature public, yet there is a distinction between crimes really public and those that are private, which are so called because they are more injurious to individuals than to the community.

Now in republics private crimes are more public, that is, they attack the constitution more than they do the individuals; and in monarchies, public crimes are more private, that is, they are more prejudicial to private people than to the constitution.

I beg that no one will be offended with what I have been saying: my observations are founded on the unanimous testimony of historians. I am not ignorant that virtuous princes are so very rare; but I venture to affirm that in a monarchy it is extremely difficult for the people to be virtuous.

Let us compare what the historians of all ages have asserted concerning the courts of monarchs; let us recollect the conversations and sentiments of people of all countries, in respect to the wretched character of courtiers, and we shall find that these are not airy speculations, but truths confirmed by a sad and melancholy experience.

Ambition in idleness; meanness mixed with pride; a desire of riches without industry; aversion to truth; flattery, perfidy, violation of engagements, contempt of civil duties, fear of the prince's virtue, hope from his weakness, but, above all, a perpetual ridicule cast upon virtue, are, I think, the characteristics by which most courtiers in all ages and countries have been constantly distinguished. Now, it is exceedingly difficult for the leading men of the nation to be knaves, and the inferior sort to be honest; for the former to be cheats, and the latter to rest satisfied with being only dupes.

But if there should chance to be some unlucky honest man among the people, Cardinal Richelieu, in his political testament, seems to hint that a prince should take care not to employ him. So true is it that virtue is not the spring of this government! It is not indeed excluded, but it is not the spring of government.

6. *In what Manner Virtue is Supplied in a Monarchical Government.*

But it is high time for me to have done with this subject, lest I should be suspected of writing a satire against monarchical government. Far be it from me; if monarchy wants one spring, it is provided with another. Honor, that is, the prejudice of every person and rank, supplies the place of the political virtue of which I have been speaking, and is everywhere her representative: here it is capable of inspiring the most glorious actions, and, joined with the force of laws, may lead us to the end of government as well as virtue itself.

Hence, in well-regulated monarchies, they are almost all good subjects, and very few good men; for to be a good man, a good intention is necessary, and we should love our country, not so much on our own account, as out of regard to the community.

7. *Of the Principle of Monarchy.*

A monarchical government supposes, as we have already observed, preëminences and ranks, as likewise a noble descent. Now since it is the nature of honor to aspire to preferments and titles, it is properly placed in this government.

Ambition is pernicious in a republic. But in a monarchy it has some good effects; it gives life to the government, and is attended with this advantage, that it is in no way dangerous, because it may be continually checked.

It is with this kind of government as with the system of the universe, in which there is a power that constantly repels all bodies from the center, and a power of gravitation that attracts them to it. Honor sets all the parts of the body politic in motion, and by its very action connects them; thus each individual advances the public good, while he only thinks of promoting his own interest.

True it is that philosophically speaking it is a false honor which moves all the parts of the government; but even this false honor is as useful to the public as true honor could possibly be to private persons.

Is it not very exacting to oblige men to perform the most difficult actions, such as require an extraordinary exertion of fortitude and resolution, without other recompense than that of glory and applause?

8. *That Honor is not the Principle of Despotic Government.*

Honor is far from being the principle of despotic government: mankind being here all upon a level, no one person can prefer himself to another; and as on the other hand they are all slaves, they can give themselves no sort of preference.

Besides, as honor has its laws and rules, as it knows not how to submit; as it depends in a great measure on a man's own caprice, and not on that of another person; it can be found only in countries in which the constitution is fixed, and where they are governed by settled laws.

How can despotism abide with honor? The one glories in the contempt of life; and the other is founded on the power of taking it away. How can honor, on the other hand, bear with despotism? The former has its fixed rules, and peculiar caprices; but the latter is directed by no rule, and its own caprices are subversive of all others.

Honor, therefore, a thing unknown in arbitrary governments, some of which have not even a proper word to express it, is the prevailing principle in monarchies; here it gives life to the whole body politic, to the laws, and even to the virtues themselves.

9. *Of the Principle of Despotic Government.*

As virtue is necessary in a republic, and in a monarchy honor, so fear is necessary in a despotic government: with regard to virtue, there is no occasion for it, and honor would be extremely dangerous.

Here the immense power of the prince devolves entirely upon those whom he is pleased to intrust with the administration. Persons capable of setting a value upon themselves would be likely to create disturbances. Fear must therefore depress their spirits, and extinguish even the least sense of ambition.

A moderate government may, whenever it pleases, and without the least danger, relax its springs. It supports itself by the laws, and by its own internal strength. But when a despotic prince ceases for one single moment to uplift his arm, when he cannot instantly demolish those whom he has intrusted with the first employments, all is over: for as fear, the spring of this government, no longer subsists, the people are left without a protector.

It is probably in this sense the Cadis maintained that the Grand Seignior was not obliged to keep his word or oath, when he limited thereby his authority.

It is necessary that the people should be judged by laws, and the great men by the caprice of the prince, that the lives of the lowest subject should be safe, and the pasha's head ever in danger. We cannot mention these monstrous governments without horror. The Sophi of Persia, dethroned in our days by Mahomet, the son of Miriveis,[1] saw the constitution subverted before this resolution, because he had been too sparing of blood.

History informs us that the horrid cruelties of Domitian struck such a terror into the governors, that the people recovered themselves a little during his reign. Thus a torrent overflows one side of a country, and on the other leaves fields untouched, where the eye is refreshed by the prospect of fine meadows.

10. *Difference of Obedience in Moderate and Despotic Governments.*

In despotic states, the nature of government requires the most passive obedience; and when once the prince's will is made known, it ought infallibly to produce its effect.

Here they have no limitations or restrictions, no mediums,

[1] Sufi, Mahmud, Mir Wa'iz are more common forms of these names.

terms, equivalents, or remonstrances; no change to propose: man is a creature that blindly submits to the absolute will of the sovereign.

In a country like this they are no more allowed to represent their apprehensions of a future danger than to impute their miscarriage to the capriciousness of fortune. Man's portion here, like that of beasts, is instinct, compliance, and punishment.

Little does it then avail to plead the sentiments of nature, filial respect, conjugal or parental tenderness, the laws of honor, or want of health; the order is given, and that is sufficient.

In Persia, when the king has condemned a person, it is no longer lawful to mention his name, or to intercede in his favor. Even if the prince were intoxicated, or *non compos*, the decree must be executed; otherwise he would contradict himself, and the law admits of no contradiction. This has been the way of thinking in that country in all ages; as the order which Ahasuerus gave, to exterminate the Jews, could not be revoked, they were allowed the liberty of defending themselves.

One thing, however, may be sometimes opposed to the prince's will, namely, religion. They will abandon, nay they will slay a parent, if the prince so commands; but he cannot oblige them to drink wine. The laws of religion are of a superior nature, because they bind the sovereign as well as the subject. But with respect to the law of nature, it is otherwise; the prince is no longer supposed to be a man.

In monarchical and moderate states, the power is limited by its very spring, I mean by honor, which, like a monarch, reigns over the prince and his people. They will not allege to their sovereign the laws of religion; a courtier would be apprehensive of rendering himself ridiculous. But the laws of honor will be appealed to on all occasions. Hence arise the restrictions necessary to obedience; honor is naturally subject to whims, by which the subject's submission will be ever directed.

Though the manner of obeying be different in these two kinds of government, the power is the same. On which side soever the monarch turns, he inclines the scale, and is obeyed. The whole difference is, that in a monarchy the prince receives instruction, at the same time that his ministers have greater abilities, and are more versed in public affairs, than the ministers of a despotic government.

11. *Reflections on the Preceding Chapters.*

Such are the principles of the three sorts of government: which does not imply that in a particular republic they actually are, but that they ought to be, virtuous; nor does it prove that in a particular monarchy they are actuated by honor, or in a particular despotic government by fear; but that they ought to be directed by these principles, otherwise the government is imperfect.

4. Political Liberty [1]

1. *A General Idea.*
I make a distinction between the laws that establish political liberty, as it relates to the constitution, and those by which it is established, as it relates to the citizen. The former shall be the subject of this book; the latter I shall examine in the next.

2. *Different Significations of the Word Liberty.*
There is no word that admits of more various significations, and has made more varied impressions on the human mind, than that of liberty. Some have taken it as a means of deposing a person on whom they had conferred a tyrannical authority; others for the power of choosing a superior whom they are obliged to obey; others for the right of bearing arms, and of being thereby enabled to use violence; others, in fine, for the privilege of being governed by a native of their own country, or by their own laws. A certain nation for a long time thought liberty consisted in the privilege of wearing a long beard. Some have annexed this name to one form of government exclusive of others: those who had a republican taste applied it to this species of polity; those who liked a monarchical state gave it to monarchy. Thus they have all applied the name of *liberty* to the government most suitable to their own customs and inclinations: and as in republics the people have not so constant and so present a view of the causes of their misery, and as the magistrates seem to act only in conformity to the laws, hence liberty is generally said to reside in republics, and to be banished from monarchies. In fine, as in democracies the people seem to act almost as they please, this sort of government has been deemed the most free, and the power of the people has been confounded with their liberty.

3. *In what Liberty Consists.*
It is true that in democracies the people seem to act as they please; but political liberty does not consist in an unlimited freedom. In governments, that is, in societies directed by laws, liberty can consist only in the power of doing what we ought to will, and in not being constrained to do what we ought not to will.

[1] Book XI, chs. i–vi.

We must have continually present to our minds the difference between independence and liberty. Liberty is a right of doing whatever the laws permit, and if a citizen could do what they forbid he would be no longer possessed of liberty, because all his fellow-citizens would have the same power.

4. *The same Subject Continued.*

Democratic and aristocratic states are not in their own nature free. Political liberty is to be found only in moderate governments; and even in these it is not always found. It is there only when there is no abuse of power. But constant experience shows us that every man invested with power is apt to abuse it, and to carry his authority as far as it will go. Is it not strange, though true, to say that virtue itself has need of limits?

To prevent this abuse, it is necessary from the very nature of things that power should be a check to power. A government may be so constituted as no man shall be compelled to do things to which the law does not oblige him, nor forced to abstain from things which the law permits.

5. *Of the End or View of Different Governments.*

Though all governments have the same general end, which is that of preservation, yet each has another particular object. Increase of dominion was the object of Rome; war, that of Sparta; religion, that of the Jewish laws; commerce, that of Marseilles; public tranquillity, that of the laws of China; navigation, that of the laws of Rhodes; natural liberty, that of the policy of the Savages; in general, the pleasures of the prince, that of despotic states; that of monarchies, the prince's and the kingdom's glory; the independence of individuals is the end aimed at by the laws of Poland, whence results the oppression of the whole.

One nation there is also in the world that has for the direct end of its constitution political liberty. We shall presently examine the principles on which this liberty is founded; if they are sound, liberty will appear in its highest perfection.

To discover political liberty in a constitution, no great labor is requisite. If we are capable of seeing it where it exists, it is soon found, and we need not go far in search of it.

6. *Of the Constitution of England.*

In every government there are three sorts of power: the legislative; the executive in respect to things dependent on the law of nations; and the executive in regard to matters that depend on the civil law.

By virtue of the first, the prince or magistrate enacts temporary or perpetual laws, and amends or abrogates those that have been already enacted. By the second, he makes peace or war, sends or receives embassies, establishes the public security, and provides against invasions. By the third, he punishes criminals, or determines the disputes that arise between individuals. The latter we shall call the judiciary power, and the other simply the executive power of the state.

The political liberty of the subject is a tranquillity of mind arising from the opinion each person has of his safety. In order to have this liberty, it is requisite the government be so constituted as one man need not be afraid of another.

When the legislative and executive powers are united in the same person, or in the same body of magistrates, there can be no liberty; because apprehensions may arise, lest the same monarch or senate should enact tyrannical laws, to execute them in a tyrannical manner.

Again, there is no liberty if the judicial power be not separated from the legislative and executive. Were it joined with the legislative, the life and liberty of the subject would be exposed to arbitrary control; for the judge would be then the legislator. Were it joined to the executive power, the judge might behave with violence and oppression.

There would be an end of everything, were the same man or the same body, whether of the nobles or of the people, to exercise those three powers, that of enacting laws, that of executing the public resolutions, and of trying the causes of individuals.

Most kingdoms in Europe enjoy a moderate government because the prince who is invested with the two first powers leaves the third to his subjects. In Turkey, where these three powers are united in the Sultan's person, the subjects groan under the most dreadful oppression.

In the republics of Italy, where these three powers are united, there is less liberty than in our monarchies. Hence their government is obliged to have recourse to as violent methods for its support as even that of the Turks; witness the state inquisitors, and the lion's mouth into which every informer may at all hours throw his written accusations.

In what a situation must the poor subject be in those republics! The same body of magistrates are possessed, as executors of the laws, of the whole power they have given themselves in quality of legislators. They may plunder the state by their general determinations: and as they have likewise the judiciary power in their hands, every private citizen may be ruined by their particular decisions.

The whole power is here united in one body; and though there is no external pomp that indicates a despotic sway, yet the people feel the effects of it every moment.

Hence it is that many of the princes of Europe, whose aim has been leveled at arbitrary power, have constantly set out with uniting in their own persons all the branches of magistracy, and all the great offices of state.

I allow indeed that the mere hereditary aristocracy of the Italian republics does not exactly answer to the despotic power of the Eastern princes. The number of magistrates sometimes moderates the power of the magistracy; the whole body of the nobles do not always concur in the same design; and different tribunals are erected, that temper each other. Thus at Venice the legislative power is in the *council*, the executive in the *pregadi*, and the judicial in the *quarantia*. But the mischief is, that these different tribunals are composed of magistrates all belonging to the same body; which constitutes almost one and the same power.

The judicial power ought not to be given to a standing senate; it should be exercised by persons taken from the body of the people at certain times of the year, and consistently with a form and manner prescribed by law, in order to erect a tribunal that should last only so long as necessity requires.

By this method the judicial power, so terrible to mankind, not being annexed to any particular state or profession, becomes, as it were, invisible. People have not then the judges continually present to their view; they fear the office, but not the magistrate.

In accusations of a deep and criminal nature, it is proper the person accused should have the privilege of choosing, in some measure, his judges, in concurrence with the law; or at least he should have a right to except against so great a number that the remaining part may be deemed his own choice.

The other two powers may be given rather to magistrates or permanent bodies, because they are not exercised on any private subject; one being no more than the general will of the state, and the other the execution of that general will.

But though the tribunals ought not to be fixed, the judgments ought; and to such a degree as to be ever conformable to the letter of the law. Were they to be the private opinion of the judge, people would then live in society, without exactly knowing the nature of their obligations.

The judges ought likewise to be of the same rank as the accused, or, in other words, his peers; to the end that he may not imagine he is fallen into the hands of persons inclined to treat him with rigor.

If the legislature leaves the executive power in possession of a right to imprison those subjects who can give security for their good behavior, there is an end of liberty; unless they are taken up, in order to answer without delay to a capital crime, in which case they are really free, being subject only to the power of the law.

But should the legislature think itself in danger by some secret conspiracy against the state, or by a correspondence with a foreign enemy, it might authorize the executive power, for a short and limited time, to imprison suspected persons, who in that case would lose their liberty only for a while, to preserve it for ever.

And this is the only reasonable method that can be substituted to the tyrannical magistracy of the *ephori*, and to the state inquisitors of Venice, who are also despotic.

As in a country of liberty, every man who is supposed a free agent ought to be his own governor, the legislative power should reside in the whole body of the people. But since this is impossible in large states, and in small ones is subject to many inconveniences, it is fit the people should transact by their representatives what they cannot transact by themselves.

The inhabitants of a particular town are much better acquainted with its wants and interests than with those of other places; and are better judges of the capacity of their neighbors than of that of the rest of their countrymen. The members, therefore, of the legislature should not be chosen from the general body of the nation; but it is proper that in every considerable place a representative should be elected by the inhabitants.

The great advantage of representatives is their capacity of discussing public affairs. For this the people collectively are extremely unfit, which is one of the chief inconveniences of a democracy.

It is not at all necessary that the representatives who have received a general instruction from their constituents should wait to be directed on each particular affair, as is practised in the diets of Germany. True it is that by this way of proceeding the speeches of the deputies might with greater propriety be called the voice of the nation; but, on the other hand, this would occasion infinite delays, would give each deputy a power of controlling the assembly; and, on the most urgent and pressing occasions, the wheels of government might be stopped by the caprice of a single person.

When the deputies, as Mr. Sidney well observes, represent a body of people, as in Holland, they ought to be accountable to their constituents; but it is a different thing in England, where they are deputed by boroughs.

All the inhabitants of the several districts ought to have a right of voting at the election of a representative, except such as are in so mean a situation as to be deemed to have no will of their own.

One great fault there was in most of the ancient republics, that the people had a right to active resolutions, such as require some execution, a thing of which they are absolutely incapable. They ought to have no share in the government but for the choosing of representatives, which is within their reach. For though few can tell the exact degree of men's capacities, yet there are none but are capable of knowing in general whether the person they choose is better qualified than most of his neighbors.

Neither ought the representative body to be chosen for the executive part of government, for which it is not so fit; but for the enacting of laws, or to see whether the laws in being are duly executed, a thing suited to their abilities, and which none indeed but themselves can properly perform.

In such a state there are always persons distinguished by their birth, riches, or honors: but were they to be confounded with the common people, and to have only the weight of a single vote like the rest, the common liberty would be their slavery, and they would have no interest in supporting it, as most of the popular resolutions would be against them. The share they have, therefore, in the legislature ought to be proportioned to their other advantages in the state; which happens only when they form a body that has a right to check the license of the people, as the people have a right to oppose any encroachment of theirs.

The legislative power is therefore committed to the body of the nobles, and to that which represents the people, each having their assemblies and deliberations apart, each their separate views and interests.

Of the three powers above mentioned, the judiciary is in some measure next to nothing: there remain, therefore, only two; and as these have need of a regulating power to moderate them, the part of the legislative body composed of the nobility is extremely proper for this purpose.

The body of the nobility ought to be hereditary. In the first place it is so in its own nature; and in the next there must be a considerable interest to preserve its privileges—privileges that in themselves are obnoxious to popular envy, and of course in a free state are always in danger.

But as a hereditary power might be tempted to pursue its own particular interests, and forget those of the people, it is proper that where a singular advantage may be gained by corrupting the nobility, as in the laws relating to the supplies, they should have no other share in the legislation than the power of rejecting, and not that of resolving.

By the *power of resolving* I mean the right of ordaining by their own authority, or of amending what has been ordained by others. By the *power of rejecting* I would be understood to mean the right of annulling a resolution taken by another; which was the power of the tribunes at Rome. And though the person possessed of the privilege of rejecting may likewise have the right of approving, yet this approbation passes for no more than a declaration that he intends to make no use of his privilege of rejecting, and is derived from that very privilege.

The executive power ought to be in the hands of a monarch, because this branch of government, having need of dispatch, is better administered by one than by many: on the other hand, whatever depends on the legislative power is oftentimes better regulated by many than by a single person.

But if there were no monarch, and the executive power should be committed to a certain number of persons selected from the legislative body, there would be an end then of liberty; by reason the two powers would be united, as the same persons would sometimes possess, and would be always able to possess, a share in both.

Were the legislative body to be a considerable time without meeting, this would likewise put an end to liberty. For of two things one would naturally follow: either that there would be no longer any legislative resolutions, and then the state would fall into anarchy; or that these resolutions would be taken by the executive power, which would render it absolute.

It would be needless for the legislative body to continue always assembled. This would be troublesome to the representatives, and, moreover, would cut out too much work for the executive power, so as to take off its attention to its office, and oblige it to think only of defending its own prerogatives, and the right it has to execute.

Again, were the legislative body to be always assembled, it might happen to be kept up only by filling the places of the deceased members with new representatives; and in that case, if the legislative body were once corrupted, the evil would be past all remedy. When different legislative bodies succeed one another, the people who have a bad opinion of that which is actually sitting may reasonably entertain some hopes of the next: but were it to be always the same body, the people upon seeing it once corrupted would no longer expect any good from its laws; and of course they would either become desperate or fall into a state of indolence.

The legislative body should not meet of itself. For a body is supposed to have no will but when it is met; and besides, were it not to meet unanimously, it would be impossible to determine which was really the legislative body: the part assembled, or the other. And if it had a right to prorogue itself, it might happen never to be prorogued; which would be extremely dangerous, in case it should ever attempt to encroach on the executive power. Besides, there are seasons, some more proper than others, for assembling the legislative body: it is fit, therefore, that the executive power should regulate the time of meeting, as well as the duration of those assemblies, according to the circumstances and exigencies of a state known to itself.

Were the executive power not to have a right of restraining the encroachments of the legislative body, the latter would become despotic; for as it might arrogate to itself what authority it pleased, it would soon destroy all the other powers.

But it is not proper, on the other hand, that the legislative power should have a right to stay the executive. For as the execution has its natural limits, it is useless to confine it; besides, the executive power is generally employed in momentary operations. The power, therefore, of the Roman tribunes was faulty, as it put a stop not only to the legislation, but likewise to the executive part of government; which was attended with infinite mischief.

But if the legislative power in a free state has no right to stay the executive, it has a right and ought to have the means of examining in what manner its laws have been executed; an advantage which this government has over that of Crete and Sparta, where the *cosmi* and the *ephori* gave no account of their administration.

But whatever may be the issue of that examination, the legislative body ought not to have a power of arraigning the person, nor, of course, the conduct, of him who is intrusted with the executive power. His person should be sacred, because as it is necessary for the good of the state to prevent the legislative body from rendering themselves arbitrary, the moment he is accused or tried there is an end of liberty.

In this case the state would be no longer a monarchy, but a kind of republic, though not a free government. But as the person intrusted with the executive power cannot abuse it without bad counsellors, and such as have the laws as ministers, though the laws protect them as subjects, these men may be examined and punished—an advantage which this government has over that of Gnidus, where the law allowed of no such thing as calling the *amymones* to an account, even after their administration; and therefore the people could never obtain any satisfaction for the injuries done them.

Though, in general, the judicial power ought not to be united with any part of the legislative, yet this is liable to three exceptions, founded on the particular interest of the party accused.

The great are always obnoxious to popular envy; and were they to be judged by the people, they might be in danger from their judges, and would, moreover, be deprived of the privilege which the meanest subject is possessed of in a free state, of being tried by his peers. The nobility, for this reason, ought not to be cited before the ordinary courts of judicature, but before that part of the legislature which is composed of their own body.

It is possible that the law, which is clear-sighted in one sense, and blind in another, might, in some cases, be too severe. But as we have already observed, the national judges are no more than the mouth that pronounces the words of the law, mere passive beings, incapable of moderating either its force or rigor. That part, therefore, of the legislative body, which we have just now observed to be a necessary tribunal on another occasion, is also a necessary tribunal in this; it belongs to its supreme authority to moderate the law in favor of the law itself, by mitigating the sentence.

It might also happen that a subject intrusted with the administration of public affairs may infringe the rights of the people, and be guilty of crimes which the ordinary magistrates either could not or would not punish. But, in general, the legislative power cannot try causes: and much less can it try this particular case, where it represents the party aggrieved, which is the people. It can only, therefore, impeach. But before what court shall it bring its impeachment? Must it go and demean itself before the ordinary tribunals, which are its inferiors, and, being composed, moreover, of men who are chosen from the people as well as itself, will naturally be swayed by the authority of so powerful an accuser?   No: in order to preserve the dignity of the people, and the security of the subject, the legislative part which represents the people must bring in its charge before the legislative part which represents the nobility, who have neither the same interests nor the same passions.

Here is an advantage which this government has over most of the ancient republics, where this abuse prevailed, that the people were at the same time both judge and accuser.

The executive power, pursuant of what has been already said, ought to have a share in the legislature by the power of rejecting, otherwise it would soon be stripped of its prerogative.   But should the legislative power usurp a share of the executive, the latter would be equally undone.

If the prince were to have a part in the legislature by the power of resolving, liberty would be lost.   But as it is necessary he should have a share in the legislature for the support of his own prerogative, this share must consist in the power of rejecting.

The change of government at Rome was owing to this, that neither the senate, who had one part of the executive power, nor the magistrates, who were intrusted with the other, had the right of rejecting, which was entirely lodged in the people.

Here then is the fundamental constitution of the government we are treating of.   The legislative body being composed of two parts, they check one another by the mutual privilege of rejecting.   They are both restrained by the executive power, as the executive is by the legislative.

These three powers should naturally form a state of repose or inaction.   But as there is a necessity for movement in the course of human affairs, they are forced to move, but still in concert.

As the executive power has no other part in the legislative than the privilege of rejecting, it can have no share in the public debates.   It is not even necessary that it should propose, because as it may always disapprove of the resolutions that shall be taken, it may likewise reject the decisions on those proposals which were made against its will.

In some ancient commonwealths, where public debates were carried on by the people in a body, it was natural for the executive power to propose and debate in conjunction with the people; otherwise their resolutions must have been attended with a strange confusion.

Were the executive power to determine the raising of public

money, otherwise than by giving its consent, liberty would be at an end; because it would become legislative in the most important point of legislation.

If the legislative power were to settle the subsidies, not from year to year, but for ever, it would run the risk of losing its liberty, because the executive power would be no longer dependent; and when once it were possessed of such a perpetual right, it would be a matter of indifference whether it held it of itself or of another. The same may be said if it should come to a resolution of intrusting, not an annual, but a perpetual command of the fleets and armies to the executive power.

To prevent the executive power from being able to oppress, it is requisite that the armies with which it is intrusted should consist of the people, and have the same spirit as the people, as was the case at Rome till the time of Marius. To obtain this end, there are only two ways: either the persons employed in the army should have sufficient property to answer for their conduct to their fellow-subjects, and be enlisted only for a year, as was customary at Rome; or if there should be a standing army, composed chiefly of the most despicable part of the nation, the legislative power should have a right to disband them as soon as it pleased; the soldiers should live in common with the rest of the people; and no separate camp, barracks, or fortress should be suffered.

When once an army is established, it ought not to depend immediately on the legislative, but on the executive, power; and this from the very nature of the thing, its business consisting more in action than in deliberation.

It is natural for mankind to set a higher value upon courage than timidity, on activity than prudence, on strength than counsel. Hence the army will ever despise a senate, and respect their own officers. They will naturally slight the orders sent them by a body of men whom they look upon as cowards, and therefore unworthy to command them. So that as soon as the troops depend entirely on the legislative body, it becomes a military government; and if the contrary has ever happened, it has been owing to some extraordinary circumstances. It is because the army was always kept divided; it is because it was composed of several bodies that depended each on a particular province; it is because the capital towns were strong places, defended by their natural situation, and not garrisoned with regular troops. Holland, for instance, is still safer than Venice; she might drown or starve the revolted troops; for as they are not quartered in towns capable of furnishing them with necessary subsistence, this subsistence is of course precarious.

In perusing the admirable treatise of Tacitus, *On the Manners of the Germans*, we find it is from that nation the English have borrowed the idea of their political government. This beautiful system was invented first in the woods.

As all human things have an end, the state we are speaking of will lose its liberty, will perish. Have not Rome, Sparta and Carthage perished? It will perish when the legislative power shall be more corrupt than the executive.

It is not my business to examine whether the English actually enjoy this liberty or not. Sufficient it is for my purpose to observe that it is established by their laws; and I inquire no further.

Neither do I pretend by this to undervalue other governments, nor to say that this extreme political liberty ought to give uneasiness to those who have only a moderate share of it. How should I have any such design, I who think that even the highest refinement of reason is not always desirable, and that mankind generally find their account better in mediums than in extremes?

Harrington, in his *Oceana*, has also inquired into the utmost degree of liberty to which the constitution of a state may be carried. But of him indeed it may be said that for want of knowing the nature of real liberty he busied himself in pursuit of an imaginary one; and that he built a Chalcedon, though he had a Byzantium before his eyes.

SELECTED BIBLIOGRAPHY

Cook, Thomas I., *History of Political Philosophy*, ch. 21.
Dunning, William A., *Political Theories, from Luther to Montesquieu*, ch. 12.
Sabine, George H., *History of Political Theory*, pp. 551–560.

Grant, A. J., "Montesquieu," in F. J. C. Hearnshaw, ed., *The Social and Political Ideas of Some Great French Thinkers of the Age of Reason* (London, 1930), ch. 5.
Martin, Kingsley, *French Liberal Thought in the Eighteenth Century* (London, 1929), Part iii, ch. 6.
Sée, Henri, *L'Évolution de la pensée politique en France au xviiième siècle* (Paris, 1925), pt. ii, ch. 1.
Meinecke, Friedrich, "Montesquieu, Boulainvilliers, Dubos," in *Historische Zeitschrift*, Vol. 145 (1931), pp. 53–68.
Brunetière, Ferdinand, *Études critiques sur l'histoire de la littérature française* (4th series, second ed., Paris, 1894), pp. 243–265.

Carcassonne, Élie, *Montesquieu et le problème de la constitution française au xviii° siècle* (Paris, 1927).
Cattelain, Fernand, *Étude sur l'influence de Montesquieu dans les constitutions américaines* (Besançon, 1927).
Dedieu, Joseph, *Montesquieu* (Paris, 1913).

ROUSSEAU

XXIII. JEAN JACQUES ROUSSEAU (1712–1778)

INTRODUCTION

A great work which in its main doctrines was directed towards the sources of political injustice in France in the eighteenth century, is the *Social Contract* of Rousseau. Although the style of this work is abstract and dogmatic, its practical influence was unmistakable. Its doctrines of the absolute and inalienable sovereignty of the people and of the subordinacy of all governing agencies, hereditary as well as elective, were stated in such clear and eloquent terms as to appeal powerfully to the imagination and emotions of the men of the French Revolution. The close influence of the *Social Contract*, in ideas and terminology, upon the French "Declaration of the Rights of Man" is particularly manifest.

It is impossible to summarize in a few sentences the varied life, singular character and complex work of Rousseau. He was born in Geneva of parents of French Protestant ancestry. He had no stable or practical training of any sort. He ran away from home when sixteen years of age, and thereafter, for twenty years, led a diversified life, residing in many different places, chiefly in France, and trying many pursuits without success. During this period he was without regular occupation, and he spent much of his time in aimless wanderings in the country. In these journeys he took some note of the ideas and feelings of the poorer people with whom he came in contact; and in his sojourns he devoted some attention to the study of philosophy and to practice in writing. In the early forties, through the support of wealthy patrons and the friendship of literary men, he established himself at Paris and did some miscellaneous writing. Diderot accepted him as a contributor to the *Encyclopædia*. He gained a general literary reputation in 1749. In that year the Academy of Dijon announced as the subject for its prize essay: "Has the restoration of the sciences contributed to purify or to corrupt manners?" Rousseau competed, and won the prize. The essay assumes an early state

of society in which all men lived under conditions of simplicity
and innocence; and it traces the present evils of society to the
thirst for knowledge and to the adulation of artificialities introduced
by civilization. In 1754, in a similar competition, he wrote his
second discourse, on "What is the origin of inequality among men,
and is it authorized by natural law?" Here he painted a more
detailed picture of a primitive society of men living happily under
conditions of natural equality and harmony. In 1762 he also
published his *Émile*, a revolutionary treatise on education. This
aroused vigorous opposition from political and ecclesiastical
leaders, not so much because of its revolutionary pedagogical ideas
as for its advocacy of "natural religion" in place of the dogmas
of revealed religion. To escape threatened prosecution he lived
awhile in Switzerland, where he was widely acclaimed for the
democratic ideas of his *Contrat Social*, and later in England. He
was able to return to France in 1767 and spent the last ten years
of his life in retirement, completing his *Confessions*.

In the *Discourse on Inequality*, Rousseau (following Locke)
indicates that political organization was introduced as a means of
conserving rights which originate in the state of nature, and not as
a means of escape from intolerable conditions in that pre-political
life. In the *Contrat Social* he maintains (following both Hobbes
and Locke) that men can be reasonably assumed to have abandoned
the state of nature only if they are also assumed to have done so by
joining into a contract; and the terms of that contract logically
determine the location, scope, and manner of exercising sovereign
political authority. Rousseau's conclusions on these points differ
from both Hobbes' and Locke's conclusions because the terms of
his social contract are different.

Rousseau usually stated his major doctrines as absolute, unvary-
ing truths. However, in certain passages of the *Social Contract*
and in later brief works, he conceded the limitations that actual
conditions place upon the application of these truths in any given
community at any given time in its history. He remained reasonably consistent in his basic ideas : that man is by nature good; that
the arts and institutions of civilization have produced perverted
expressions of his true nature; that good can be restored among
civilized men only through institutions which give the freest possible expression to natural human desires; that organized social

restraint is, therefore, justified only in so far as it rests upon a consent given freely by all normal members of the community.

READINGS FROM THE SOCIAL CONTRACT [1]

1. *The Problem of Political Philosophy* [2]

Introductory Note.

I wish to inquire whether, taking men as they are and laws as they can be made, it is possible to establish some just and certain rule of administration in civil affairs. In this investigation I shall always strive to reconcile what right permits with what interest prescribes, so that justice and utility may not be severed.

I enter upon this inquiry without demonstrating the importance of my subject. I shall be asked whether I am a prince or a legislator that I write on politics. I reply that I am not; and that it is for this very reason that I write on politics. If I were a prince or a legislator, I should not waste my time in saying what ought to be done; I should do it or remain silent.

Having been born a citizen of a free state, and a member of the sovereign body, however feeble an influence my voice may have in public affairs, the right to vote upon them is sufficient to impose on me the duty of informing myself about them; and I feel happy, whenever I meditate on governments, always to discover in my researches new reasons for loving that of my own country.

Ch. i. *Subject of the First Book.*

<u>Man is born free</u>, and everywhere he is in chains. Many a one believes himself the master of others, and yet he is a greater slave than they. How has this change come about? I do not know. What can render it legitimate? I believe that I can settle this question.

If I considered only force and the results that proceed from it, I should say that so long as a people is compelled to obey and does obey, it does well; but that, so soon as it can shake off the yoke and does shake it off, it does better; for, if men recover their freedom by virtue of the same right by which it was taken away, either they are justified in resuming it, or there was no justification for depriving them of it. But the social order is a

---

[1] The selections are from *The Social Contract*, translated by Henry J. Tozer. Third edition. London, 1902. Published by Swan Sonnenschein & Co.

[2] Book I, *Introductory Note*, chs. i–iii, and ch. iv (in part).

sacred right which serves as a foundation for all others. This right, however, does not come from nature. It is therefore based on conventions. The question is to know what these conventions are. Before coming to that, I must establish what I have just laid down.

Ch. ii.   *Primitive Societies.*

The earliest of all societies, and the only natural one, is the family; yet children remain attached to their father only so long as they have need of him for their own preservation. As soon as this need ceases, the natural bond is dissolved. The children being freed from the obedience which they owed to their father, and the father from the cares which he owed to his children, become equally independent. If they remain united, it is no longer naturally but voluntarily; and the family itself is kept together only by convention.

This common liberty is a consequence of man's nature. His first law is to attend to his own preservation, his first cares are those which he owes to himself; and as soon as he comes to years of discretion, being sole judge of the means adapted for his own preservation, he becomes his own master.

The family is, then, if you will, the primitive model of political societies; the chief is the analogue of the father, while the people represent the children; and all, being born free and equal, alienate their liberty only for their own advantage. The whole difference is that in the family the father's love for his children repays him for the care that he bestows upon them; while in the state the pleasure of ruling makes up for the chief's lack of love for his people.

Grotius denies that all human authority is established for the benefit of the governed, and he cites slavery as an instance. His invariable mode of reasoning is to establish right by fact. A juster method might be employed, but none more favorable to tyrants.

It is doubtful, then, according to Grotius, whether the human race belongs to a hundred men, or whether these hundred men belong to the human race; and he appears throughout his book to incline to the former opinion, which is also that of Hobbes. In this way we have mankind divided like herds of cattle, each of which has a master, who looks after it in order to devour it.

Just as a herdsman is superior in nature to his herd, so chiefs, who are the herdsmen of men, are superior in nature to their people. Thus, according to Philo's account, the Emperor Caligula reasoned, inferring truly enough from this analogy that kings are gods, or that men are brutes.

The reasoning of Caligula is tantamount to that of Hobbes and Grotius. Aristotle, before them all, had likewise said that men are not naturally equal, but that some are born for slavery and others for dominion.

Aristotle was right, but he mistook the effect for the cause. Every man born in slavery is born for slavery; nothing is more certain. Slaves lose everything in their bonds, even the desire to escape from them; they love their servitude as the companions of Ulysses loved their brutishness. If, then, there are slaves by nature, it is because there have been slaves contrary to nature. The first slaves were made such by force; their cowardice kept them in bondage.

I have said nothing about King Adam nor about Emperor Noah, the father of three great monarchs who shared the universe, like the children of Saturn with whom they are supposed to be identical. I hope that my moderation will give satisfaction; for, as I am a direct descendant of one of these princes, and perhaps of the eldest branch, how do I know whether, by examination of titles, I might not find myself the lawful king of the human race? Be that as it may, it cannot be denied that Adam was sovereign of the world, as Robinson was of his island, so long as he was its sole inhabitant; and it was an agreeable feature of that empire that the monarch, secure on his throne, had nothing to fear from rebellions, or wars, or conspirators.

Ch. iii.   *The Right of the Strongest.*

The strongest man is never strong enough to be always master, unless he transforms his power into right, and obedience into duty. Hence the right of the strongest—a right apparently assumed in irony, and really established in principle. But will this phrase never be explained to us? Force is a physical power; I do not see what morality can result from its effects. To yield to force is an act of necessity, not of will; it is at most an act of prudence. In what sense can it be a duty?

Let us assume for a moment this pretended right. I say that nothing results from it but inexplicable nonsense; for if force constitutes right, the effect changes with the cause, and any force which overcomes the first succeeds to its rights. As soon as men can disobey with impunity, they may do so legitimately; and since the strongest is always in the right, the only thing is to act in such a way that one may be the strongest. But what sort of a right is it that perishes when force ceases?   If it is necessary to obey by compulsion, there is no need to obey from duty; and if men are no longer forced to obey, obligation is at an end.   We see, then, that this word *right* adds nothing to force; it here means nothing at all.

Obey the powers that be.   If that means, Yield to force, the precept is good but superfluous; I reply that it will never be violated.   All power comes from God, I admit; but every disease comes from him too; does it follow that we are prohibited from calling in a physician?   If a brigand should surprise me in the recesses of a wood, am I bound not only to give up my purse when forced, but am I also morally bound to do so when I might conceal it?   For, in effect, the pistol which he holds is a superior force.

Let us agree, then, that might does not make right, and that we are bound to obey none but lawful authorities.   Thus my original question ever recurs.

Ch. iv.   *Slavery.*

Since no man has any natural authority over his fellow-men, and since force is not the source of right, conventions remain as the basis of all lawful authority among men.

If an individual, says Grotius, can alienate his liberty and become the slave of a master, why should not a whole people be able to alienate theirs, and become subject to a king?   In this there are many equivocal terms requiring explanation; but let us confine ourselves to the word *alienate.*   To alienate is to give or sell.   Now, a man who becomes another's slave does not give himself; he sells himself at the very least for his subsistence. But why does a nation sell itself?   So far from a king supplying his subjects with their subsistence, he draws his from them; and, according to Rabelais, a king does not live on a little.   Do subjects, then, give up their persons on condition that their property also shall be taken?   I do not see what is left for them to keep.

It will be said that the despot secures to his subjects civil peace.   Be it so; but what do they gain by that, if the wars which his ambition brings upon them, together with his insatiable greed and the vexations of his administration, harass them more than their own dissensions would?   What do they gain by it if this tranquillity is itself one of their miseries?   Men live tranquilly also in dungeons; is that enough to make them contented there? The Greeks confined in the cave of the Cyclops lived peacefully until their turn came to be devoured.

To say that a man gives himself for nothing is to say what is absurd and inconceivable; such an act is illegitimate and invalid, for the simple reason that he who performs it is not in his right mind. To say the same thing of the whole nation is to suppose a nation of fools; and madness does not confer rights.

Even if each person could alienate himself, he could not alienate his children; they are born free men; their liberty belongs to them, and no one has a right to dispose of it except themselves. Before they have come to years of discretion, the father can, in their name, stipulate conditions for their preservation and welfare, but not surrender them irrevocably and unconditionally; for such a gift is contrary to the ends of nature, and exceeds the rights of paternity. In order, then, that an arbitrary government might be legitimate, it would be necessary that the people in each generation should have the option of accepting or rejecting it; but in that case such a government would no longer be arbitrary.

To renounce one's liberty is to renounce one's quality as a man, the rights and also the duties of humanity. For him who renounces everything there is no possible compensation. Such a renunciation is incompatible with man's nature, for to take away all freedom from his will is to take away all morality from his actions. In short, a convention which stipulates absolute authority on the one side and unlimited obedience on the other is vain and contradictory. Is it not clear that we are under no obligations whatsoever towards a man from whom we have a right to demand everything? And does not this single condition, without equivalent, without exchange, involve the nullity of the act? For what right would my slave have against me, since all that he has belongs to me? His rights being mine, this right of me against myself is a meaningless phrase.

2. The Social Contract [1]

Ch. v. *That it is Always Necessary to go Back to a First Convention.*

If I should concede all that I have so far refuted, those who favor despotism would be no farther advanced. There will always be a great difference between subduing a multitude and ruling a society. When isolated men, however numerous they may be, are subjected one after another to a single person, this

[1] Bk. I, chs. v and vi.

seems to me only a case of master and slaves, not of a nation and its chief; they form, if you will, an aggregation, but not an association, for they have neither public property nor a body politic. Such a man, had he enslaved half the world, is never anything but an individual; his interest, separated from that of the rest, is never anything but a private interest. If he dies, his empire after him is left disconnected and disunited, as an oak dissolves and becomes a heap of ashes after the fire has consumed it.

A nation, says Grotius, can give itself to a king. According to Grotius, then, a nation is a nation before it gives itself to a king. This gift itself is a civil act, and presupposes a public resolution. Consequently, before examining the act by which a nation elects a king, it would be proper to examine the act by which a nation becomes a nation; for this act, being necessarily anterior to the other, is the real foundation of the society.

In fact, if there were no anterior convention, where, unless the election were unanimous, would be the obligation upon the minority to submit to the decision of the majority? And whence do the hundred who desire a master derive the right to vote on behalf of ten who do not desire one? The law of the plurality of votes is itself established by convention, and presupposes unanimity once at least.

Ch. vi. *The Social Pact.*

I assume that men have reached a point at which the obstacles that endanger their preservation in the state of nature overcome by their resistance the forces which each individual can exert with a view to maintaining himself in that state. Then this primitive condition can no longer subsist, and the human race would perish unless it changed its mode of existence.

Now, as men cannot create any new forces, but only combine and direct those that exist, they have no other means of self-preservation than to form by aggregation a sum of forces which may overcome the resistance, to put them in action by a single motive power, and to make them work in concert.

This sum of forces can be produced only by the combination of many; but the strength and freedom of each man being the chief instruments of his preservation, how can he pledge them without injuring himself, and without neglecting the cares which he owes to himself? This difficulty, applied to my subject, may be expressed in these terms:—

"To find a form of association which may defend and protect

with the whole force of the community the person and property of every associate, and by means of which each, coalescing with all, may nevertheless obey only himself, and remain as free as before." Such is the fundamental problem, of which the social contract furnishes the solution.

The clauses of this contract are so determined by the nature of the act that the slightest modification would render them vain and ineffectual; so that, although they have never perhaps been formally enunciated, they are everywhere the same, everywhere tacitly admitted and recognized, until, the social pact being violated, each man regains his original rights and recovers his natural liberty, while losing the conventional liberty for which he renounced it.

These clauses, rightly understood, are reducible to one only, viz. the total alienation to the whole community of each associate with all his rights; for, in the first place, since each gives himself up entirely, the conditions are equal for all; and, the conditions being equal for all, no one has any interest in making them burdensome to others.

Further, the alienation being made without reserve, the union is as perfect as it can be, and an individual associate can no longer claim anything; for, if any rights were left to individuals, since there would be no common superior who could judge between them and the public, each, being on some point his own judge, would soon claim to be so on all; the state of nature would still subsist, and the association would necessarily become tyrannical or useless.

In short, each giving himself to all, gives himself to nobody; and as there is not one associate over whom we do not acquire the same rights which we concede to him over ourselves, we gain the equivalent of all that we lose, and more power to preserve what we have.

If, then, we set aside what is not of the essence of the social contract, we shall find that it is reducible to the following terms: "Each of us puts in common his person and his whole power under the supreme direction of the general will; and in return we receive every member as an indivisible part of the whole."

Forthwith, instead of the individual personalities of all the contracting parties, this act of the association produces a moral and collective body, which is composed of as many members as the assembly has voices, and which receives from this same act its unity, its common self (*moi*), its life, and its will. This public person, which is thus formed by the union of all the individual members, formerly took the name of *city*, and now takes that of *republic* or *body politic*, which is called by its members *state* when it is passive, *sovereign* when it is active, *power* when it is compared to similar bodies. With regard to the associates, they take collectively the name of *people*, and are called individually *citizens*, as participating in the sovereign power, and *subjects*, as subjected to the laws of the state. But these terms are often confused and are mistaken one for another; it is sufficient to know how to distinguish them when they are used with complete precision.

3. Sovereignty and Law [1]

Ch. vii.   *The Sovereign.*

We see from this formula that the act of association contains a reciprocal engagement between the public and individuals, and that every individual, contracting so to speak with himself, is engaged in a double relation, viz. as a member of the sovereign towards individuals, and as a member of the state towards the sovereign. But we cannot apply here the maxim of civil law that no one is bound by engagements made with himself; for there is a great difference between being bound to oneself and to a whole of which one forms part.

We must further observe that the public resolution which can bind all subjects to the sovereign in consequence of the two different relations under which each of them is regarded cannot, for a contrary reason, bind the sovereign to itself; and that accordingly it is contrary to the nature of the body politic for the sovereign to impose on itself a law which it cannot transgress. As it can only be considered under one and the same relation, it is in the position of an individual contracting with himself; whence we see that there is not, nor can be, any kind of fundamental law binding upon the body of the people, not even the social contract. This does not imply that such a body cannot perfectly well enter into engagements with others in what does not derogate from this contract; for, with regard to foreigners, it becomes a simple being, an individual.

But the body politic or sovereign, deriving its existence only from the sanctity of the contract, can never bind itself, even to others, in anything that derogates from the original act, such as alienation of some portion of itself, or submission to another

[1] Bk. I, ch. vii; Bk. II, chs. i–iv, vi.

sovereign. To violate the act by which it exists would be to annihilate itself; and what is nothing produces nothing.

So soon as the multitude is thus united in one body, it is impossible to injure one of the members without attacking the body, still less to injure the body without the members feeling the effects. Thus duty and interest alike oblige the two contracting parties to give mutual assistance; and the men themselves should seek to combine in this twofold relationship all the advantages which are attendant on it.

Now, the sovereign, being formed only of the individuals that compose it, neither has nor can have any interest contrary to theirs; consequently the sovereign power needs no guarantee towards its subjects, because it is impossible that the body should wish to injure all its members; and we shall see hereafter that it can injure no one as an individual. The sovereign, for the simple reason that it is so, is always everything that it ought to be.

But this is not the case as regards the relation of subjects to the sovereign, which, notwithstanding the common interest, would have no security for the performance of their engagements, unless it found means to insure their fidelity.

Indeed, every individual may, as a man, have a particular will contrary to, or divergent from, the general will which he has as a citizen; his private interest may prompt him quite differently from the common interest; his absolute and naturally independent existence may make him regard what he owes to the common cause as a gratuitous contribution, the loss of which will be less harmful to others than the payment of it will be burdensome to him; and, regarding the moral person that constitutes the state as an imaginary being because it is not a man, he would be willing to enjoy the rights of a citizen without being willing to fulfill the duties of a subject. The progress of such injustice would bring about the ruin of the body politic.

In order, then, that the social pact may not be a vain formulary, it tacitly includes this engagement, which can alone give force to the others,—that whoever refuses to obey the general will shall be constrained to do so by the whole body; which means nothing else than that he shall be forced to be free; for such is the condition which, uniting every citizen to his native land, guarantees him from all personal dependence; a condition that insures the control and working of the political machine, and alone renders legitimate civil engagements, which, without it, would be absurd and tyrannical, and subject to the most enormous abuses.

Book II, ch. i.   *That Sovereignty is Inalienable.*

The first and most important consequence of the principles above established is that the general will alone can direct the forces of the state according to the object of its institution, which is the common good; for if the opposition of private interests has rendered necessary the establishment of societies, the agreement of these same interests has rendered it possible. That which is common to these different interests forms the social bond; and unless there were some point in which all interests agree, no society could exist. Now, it is solely with regard to this common interest that the society should be governed.

I say, then, that sovereignty, being nothing but the exercise of the general will, can never be alienated, and that the sovereign power, which is only a collective being, can be represented by itself alone; power indeed can be transmitted, but not will.

In fact, if it is not impossible that a particular will should agree on some point with the general will, it is at least impossible that this agreement should be lasting and constant; for the particular will naturally tends to preferences, and the general will to equality. It is still more impossible to have a security for this agreement; even though it should always exist, it would not be a result of art, but of chance. The sovereign may indeed say: "I will now what a certain man wills, or at least what he says that he wills;" but he cannot say: "What that man wills to-morrow, I shall also will," since it is absurd that the will should bind itself as regards the future, and since it is not incumbent on any will to consent to anything contrary to the welfare of the being that wills. If, then, the nation simply promises to obey, it dissolves itself by that act and loses its character as a people; the moment there is a master, there is no longer a sovereign, and forthwith the body politic is destroyed.

This does not imply that the orders of the chiefs cannot pass for decisions of the general will, so long as the sovereign, free to oppose them, refrains from doing so. In such a case the consent of the people should be inferred from the universal silence. This will be explained at greater length.

Ch. ii.   *That Sovereignty is Indivisible.*

For the same reason that sovereignty is inalienable it is indivisible; for the will is either general, or it is not; it is either that of the body of the people, or that of only a portion. In the first case, this declared will is an act of sovereignty and constitutes law; in the second case, it is only a particular will, or an act of magistracy—it is at most a decree.

But our publicists, being unable to divide sovereignty in its principle, divide it in its object. They divide it into force and will, into legislative power and executive power; into rights of taxation, of justice, and of war; into internal administration and power of treating with foreigners—sometimes confounding all these departments, and sometimes separating them. They make the sovereign a fantastic being, formed of connected parts; it is as if they composed a man of several bodies, one with eyes, another with arms, another with feet, and nothing else. The Japanese conjurers, it is said, cut up a child before the eyes of the spectators; then, throwing all its limbs into the air, they make the child come down again alive and whole. Such almost are the jugglers' tricks of our publicists; after dismembering the social body by a deception worthy of the fair, they recombine its parts, nobody knows how.

This error arises from their not having formed exact notions about the sovereign authority, and from their taking as parts of this authority what are only emanations from it. Thus, for example, the acts of declaring war and making peace have been regarded as acts of sovereignty, which is not the case, since neither of them is a law, but only an application of the law, a particular act which determines the case of the law, as will be clearly seen when the idea attached to the word *law* is fixed.

By following out the other divisions in the same way, it would be found that, whenever the sovereignty appears divided, we are mistaken in our supposition; and that the rights which are taken as parts of that sovereignty are all subordinate to it, and always suppose supreme wills of which these rights are merely executive.

It would be impossible to describe the great obscurity in which this want of precision has involved the conclusions of writers on the subject of political right when they have endeavored to decide upon the respective rights of kings and peoples on the principles that they had established. Every one can see, in chapters iii and iv of the first book of Grotius, how that learned man and his translator Barbeyrac become entangled and embarrassed in their sophisms, for fear of saying too much or not saying enough according to their views, and so offending the interests that they had to conciliate. Grotius, having taken refuge in France through discontent with his own country, and wishing to pay court to Louis XIII, to whom his book is dedicated, spares no pains to despoil the people of all their rights and, in the most artful manner, bestow them on kings. This also would clearly have been the inclination of Barbeyrac, who dedicated his translation to the king of England, George I. But unfortunately the expulsion of James II, which he calls an abdication, forced him to be reserved and to equivocate and evade, in order not to make William appear a usurper. If these two writers had adopted true principles, all difficulties would have been removed, and they would have been always consistent; but they would have spoken the truth with regret, and would have paid court only to the people. Truth, however, does not lead to fortune, and the people confer neither embassies, nor professorships, nor pensions.

Ch. iii. *Whether the General Will Can Err.*

It follows from what precedes that the general will is always right and always tends to the public advantage; but it does not follow that the resolutions of the people have always the same rectitude. Men always desire their own good, but do not always discern it; the people are never corrupted, though often deceived, and it is only then that they seem to will what is evil.

There is often a great deal of difference between the will of all and the general will; the latter regards only the common interest, while the former has regard to private interests, and is merely a sum of particular wills; but take away from these same wills the pluses and minuses which cancel one another, and the general will remains as the sum of the differences.

If the people came to a resolution when adequately informed and without any communication among the citizens, the general will would always result from the great number of slight differences, and the resolution would always be good. But when factions, partial associations, are formed to the detriment of the whole society, the will of each of these associations becomes general with reference to its members, and particular with reference to the state; it may then be said that there are no longer as many voters as there are men, but only as many voters as there are associations. The differences become less numerous and yield a less general result. Lastly, when one of these associations becomes so great that it predominates over all the rest, you no longer have as the result a sum of small differences, but a single difference; there is then no longer a general will, and the opinion which prevails is only a particular opinion.

It is important, then, in order to have a clear declaration of the general will, that there should be no partial association in the state, and that every citizen should express only his own opinion. Such was the unique and sublime institution of the great Lycurgus. But if there are partial associations, it is necessary to multiply their number and prevent inequality, as Solon, Numa, and Servius did. These are the only proper precautions for insuring that the general will may always be enlightened, and that the people may not be deceived.

Ch. iv.   *The Limits of the Sovereign Power.*

If the state or city is nothing but a moral person, the life of which consists in the union of its members, and if the most important of its cares is that of self-preservation, it needs a universal and compulsive force to move and dispose of every part in the manner most expedient for the whole. As nature gives every man an absolute power over all his limbs, the social pact gives the body politic an absolute power over all its members; and it is this same power which, when directed by the general will, bears, as I said, the name of sovereignty.

But besides the public person, we have to consider the private persons who compose it, and whose life and liberty are naturally independent of it. The question, then, is to distinguish clearly between the respective rights of the citizens and of the sovereign, as well as between the duties which the former have to fulfill in their capacity as subjects and the natural rights which they ought to enjoy in their character as men.

It is admitted that whatever part of his power, property, and liberty each one alienates by the social compact is only that part of the whole of which the use is important to the community; but we must also admit that the sovereign alone is judge of what is important.

All the services that a citizen can render to the state he owes to it as soon as the sovereign demands them; but the sovereign, on its part, cannot impose on its subjects any burden which is useless to the community; it cannot even wish to do so, for, by the law of reason, just as by the law of nature, nothing is done without a cause.

The engagements which bind us to the social body are obligatory only because they are mutual; and their nature is such that in fulfilling them we cannot work for others without also working for ourselves. Why is the general will always right, and why do all invariably desire the prosperity of each, unless it is because there is no one but appropriates to himself this word *each* and thinks of himself in voting on behalf of all? This proves that

equality of rights and the notion of justice that it produces are
derived from the preference which each gives to himself, and
consequently from man's nature; that the general will, to be truly
such, should be so in its object as well as in its essence; that it
ought to proceed from all in order to be applicable to all; and
that it loses its natural rectitude when it tends to some individual
and determinate object, because in that case, judging of what is
unknown to us, we have no true principle of equity to guide us.

Indeed so soon as a particular fact or right is in question with
regard to a point which has not been regulated by an anterior
general convention, the matter becomes contentious; it is a
process in which the private persons interested are one of the
parties and the public the other, but in which I perceive neither
the law which must be followed, nor the judge who should decide.
It would be ridiculous in such a case to wish to refer the matter
for an express decision of the general will, which can be nothing
but the decision of one of the parties, and which, consequently, is
for the other party only a will that is foreign, partial, and inclined
on such an occasion to injustice as well as liable to error. Therefore, just as a particular will cannot represent the general will, the
general will in turn changes its nature when it has a particular
end, and cannot, as general, decide about either a person or a
fact. When the people of Athens, for instance, elected or deposed their chiefs, decreed honors to one, imposed penalties on
another, and by multitudes of particular decrees exercised indiscriminately all the functions of government, the people no longer
had any general will properly so called; they no longer acted as a
sovereign power, but as magistrates. This will appear contrary
to common ideas, but I must be allowed time to expound my
own.

From this we must understand that what generalizes the will is
not so much the number of voices as the common interest which
unites them; for, under this system, each necessarily submits to
the conditions which he imposes on others—an admirable union
of interest and justice, which gives to the deliberations of the
community a spirit of equity that seems to disappear in the discussion of any private affair, for want of a common interest to
unite and identify the ruling principle of the judge with that of
the party.

By whatever path we return to our principle we always arrive
at the same conclusion, viz. that the social compact establishes
among the citizens such an equality that they all pledge themselves under the same conditions and ought all to enjoy the

same rights. Thus, by the nature of the compact, every act of sovereignty, that is, every authentic act of the general will, binds or favors equally all the citizens; so that the sovereign knows only the body of the nation, and distinguishes none of those that compose it.

What, then, is an act of sovereignty properly so called? It is not an agreement between a superior and an inferior, but an agreement of the body with each of its members; a lawful agreement, because it has the social contract as its foundation; equitable, because it is common to all; useful, because it can have no other object than the general welfare; and stable, because it has the public force and the supreme power as a guarantee. So long as the subjects submit only to such conventions, they obey no one, but simply their own will; and to ask how far the respective rights of the sovereign and citizens extend is to ask up to what point the latter can make engagements among themselves, each with all and all with each.

Thus we see that the sovereign power, wholly absolute, wholly sacred, and wholly inviolable as it is, does not, and cannot, pass the limits of general conventions, and that every man can fully dispose of what is left to him of his property and liberty by these conventions; so that the sovereign never has a right to burden one subject more than another, because then the matter becomes particular and his power is no longer competent.

These distinctions once admitted, so untrue is it that in the social contract there is on the part of individuals any real renunciation, that their situation, as a result of this contract, is in reality preferable to what it was before, and that, instead of an alienation, they have only made an advantageous exchange of an uncertain and precarious mode of existence for a better and more assured one, of natural independence for liberty, of the power to injure others for their own safety, and of their strength, which others might overcome, for a right which the social union renders inviolable. Their lives, also, which they have devoted to the state, are continually protected by it; and in exposing their lives for its defense, what do they do but restore what they have received from it? What do they do but what they would do more frequently and with more risk in the state of nature, when, engaging in inevitable struggles, they would defend at the peril of their lives their means of preservation? All have to fight for their country in case of need, it is true; but then no one ever has to fight for himself. Do we not gain, moreover, by incurring, for what insures our safety, a part of the risks that we should have to incur for ourselves individually, as soon as we were deprived of it?

Ch. vi. *The Law.*

By the social compact we have given existence and life to the body politic; the question now is to endow it with movement and will by legislation. For the original act by which this body is formed and consolidated determines nothing in addition as to what it must do for its own preservation.

What is right and conformable to order is such by the nature of things, and independently of human conventions. All justice comes from God, he alone is the source of it; but could we receive it direct from so lofty a source, we should need neither government nor laws. Without doubt there is a universal justice emanating from reason alone; but this justice, in order to be admitted among us, should be reciprocal. Regarding things from a human standpoint, the laws of justice are inoperative among men for want of a natural sanction; they only bring good to the wicked and evil to the just when the latter observe them with every one, and no one observes them in return. Conventions and laws, then, are necessary to couple rights with duties and apply justice to its object. In the state of nature, where everything is in common, I owe nothing to those to whom I have promised nothing; I recognize as belonging to others only what is useless to me. This is not the case in the civil state, in which all rights are determined by law.

But then, finally, what is a law? So long as men are content to attach to this word only metaphysical ideas, they will continue to argue without being understood; and when they have stated what a law of nature is, they will know no better what a law of the state is.

I have already said that there is no general will with reference to a particular object. In fact, this particular object is either in the state or outside of it. If it is outside the state, a will which is foreign to it is not general in relation to it; and if it is within the state, it forms part of it; then there is formed between the whole and its part a relation which makes of it two separate beings, of which the part is one, and the whole, less this same part, is the other. But the whole less one part is not the whole, and so long as the relation subsists, there is no longer any whole, but two unequal parts; whence it follows that the will of the one is no longer general in relation to the other.

But when the whole people decree concerning the whole people,

they consider themselves alone; and if a relation is then constituted, it is between the whole object under one point of view and
the whole object under another point of view, without any division
at all. Then the matter respecting which they decree is general
like the will that decrees. It is this act that I call a law.

When I say that the object of the laws is always general, I
mean that the law considers subjects collectively, and actions as
abstract, never a man as an individual nor a particular action.
Thus the law may indeed decree that there shall be privileges,
but cannot confer them on any person by name; the law can
create several classes of citizens, and even assign the qualifications which shall entitle them to rank in these classes, but it
cannot nominate such and such persons to be admitted to them;
it can establish a royal government and a hereditary succession,
but cannot elect a king or appoint a royal family; in a word, no
function which has reference to an individual object appertains
to the legislative power.

From this standpoint we see immediately that it is no longer
necessary to ask whose office it is to make laws, since they are
acts of the general will; nor whether the prince is above the
laws, since he is a member of the state; nor whether the law can not
be unjust, since no one is unjust to himself; nor how we are free
and yet subject to the laws, since the laws are only registers of
our wills.

We see, further, that since the law combines the universality
of the will with the universality of the object, whatever any man
prescribes on his own authority is not a law; and whatever the
sovereign itself prescribes respecting a particular object is not a
law, but a decree, not an act of sovereignty, but of magistracy.

I therefore call any state a republic which is governed by laws,
under whatever form of administration it may be; for then only
does the public interest predominate and the commonwealth
count for something. Every legitimate government is republican; I will explain hereafter what government is.

Laws are properly only the conditions of civil association.
The people, being subjected to the laws, should be the authors
of them; it concerns only the associates to determine the conditions of association. But how will they be determined? Will
it be by a common agreement, by a sudden inspiration? Has
a body politic an organ for expressing its will? Who will give
it the foresight necessary to frame its acts and publish them
at the outset? Or shall it declare them in the hour of need?
How would a blind multitude, which often knows not what it

wishes because it rarely knows what is good for it, execute of itself an enterprise so great, so difficult, as a system of legislation? Of themselves, the people always desire what is good, but do not always discern it. The general will is always right, but the judgment which guides it is not always enlightened. It must be made to see objects as they are, sometimes as they ought to appear; it must be shown the good path that it is seeking, and guarded from the seduction of private interests; it must be made to observe closely times and places, and to balance the attraction of immediate and palpable advantages against the danger of remote and concealed evils. Individuals see the good which they reject; the public desire the good which they do not see. All alike have need of guides. The former must be compelled to conform their wills to their reason; the people must be taught to know what they require. Then from the public enlightenment results the union of the understanding and the will in the social body; and from that the close coöperation of the parts, and, lastly, the maximum power of the whole. Hence arises the need of a legislator.

4. *Government: Its Nature and Forms* [1]

Before speaking of the different forms of government, let us try to fix the precise meaning of that word, which has not yet been very clearly explained.

Ch. i. *Government in General.*

I warn the reader that this chapter must be read carefully, and that I do not know the art of making myself intelligible to those that will not be attentive.

Every free action has two causes concurring to produce it; the one moral, viz. the will which determines the act; the other physical, viz. the power which executes it. When I walk towards an object, I must first will to go to it; in the second place, my feet must carry me to it. Should a paralytic wish to run, or an active man not wish to do so, both will remain where they are. The body politic has the same motive powers; in it, likewise, force and will are distinguished, the latter under the name of *legislative power*, the former under the name of *executive power*. Nothing is, or ought to be, done in it without their coöperation.

We have seen that the legislative power belongs to the people, and can belong to it alone. On the other hand, it is easy to see from the principles already established, that the executive

---

[1] Bk. III, chs. i–iii.

power cannot belong to the people generally as legislative or sovereign, because that power is exerted only in particular acts, which are not within the province of the law, nor consequently within that of the sovereign, all the acts of which must be laws.

The public force, then, requires a suitable agent to concentrate it and put it in action according to the directions of the general will, to serve as a means of communication between the state and the sovereign, to effect in some manner in the public person what the union of soul and body effects in a man. This is, in the state, the function of the government, improperly confounded with the sovereign of which it is only the minister.

What, then, is the government? An intermediate body established between the subjects and the sovereign for their mutual correspondence, charged with the execution of the laws and with the maintenance of liberty both civil and political.

The members of this body are called magistrates or *kings*, that is, *governors;* and the body as a whole bears the name of *Prince*. Those therefore who maintain that the act by which a people submits to its chiefs is not a contract are quite right. It is absolutely nothing but a commission, an employment, in which, as simple officers of the sovereign, they exercise in its name the power of which it has made them depositaries, and which it can limit, modify, and resume when it pleases. The alienation of such a right, being incompatible with the nature of the social body, is contrary to the object of the association.

Consequently, I give the name *government* or supreme administration to the legitimate exercise of the executive power, and that of Prince or magistrate to the man or body charged with that administration.

It is in the government that are found the intermediate powers, the relations of which constitute the relation of the whole to the whole, or of the sovereign to the state. This last relation can be represented by that of the extremes of a continued proportion, of which the mean proportional is the government. The government receives from the sovereign the commands which it gives to the people; and in order that the state may be in stable equilibrium, it is necessary, everything being balanced, that there should be equality between the product or the power of the government taken by itself, and the product or the power of the citizens, who are sovereign in the one aspect and subjects in the other.

Further, we could not alter any of the three terms without at once destroying the proportion. If the sovereign wishes to govern, or if the magistrate wishes to legislate, or if the subjects refuse to obey, disorder succeeds order, force and will no longer act in concert, and the state being dissolved falls into despotism or anarchy. Lastly, as there is but one mean proportional between each relation, there is only one good government possible in a state; but as a thousand events may change the relations of a people, not only may different governments be good for different peoples, but for the same people at different times.

To try and give an idea of the different relations that may exist between these two extremes, I will take for an example the number of people, as a relation most easy to express.

Let us suppose that the state is composed of ten thousand citizens. The sovereign can only be considered collectively and as a body; but every private person, in his capacity of subject, is considered as an individual; therefore the sovereign is to be the subject as ten thousand is to one, that is, each member of the state has as his share only one ten-thousandth part of the sovereign authority, although he is entirely subjected to it.

If the nation consists of a hundred thousand men, the position of the subjects does not change, and each alike is subjected to the whole authority of the laws, while his vote, reduced to one hundred-thousandth, has ten times less influence in their enactment. The subject, then, always remaining a unit, the proportional power of the sovereign increases in the ratio of the number of the citizens. Whence it follows that the more the state is enlarged, the more does liberty diminish.

When I say that the proportional power increases, I mean that it is farther removed from equality. Therefore, the greater the ratio is in the geometrical sense, the less is the ratio in the common acceptation; in the former, the ratio, considered according to quantity, is measured by the exponent, and in the other, considered according to identity, it is estimated by the similarity.

Now, the less the particular wills correspond with the general will, that is, customs with laws, the more should the repressive power be increased. The government, then, in order to be effective, should be relatively stronger in proportion as the people are more numerous.

On the other hand, as the aggrandizement of the state gives the depositaries of the public authority more temptations and more opportunities to abuse their power, the more force should the government have to restrain the people, and the more should the sovereign have in its turn to restrain the government. I do not speak here of absolute force, but of the relative force of the different parts of the state.

It follows from this double ratio that the continued proportion between the sovereign, the Prince, and the people is not an arbitrary idea, but a necessary consequence of the nature of the body politic. It follows, further, that one of the extremes, viz. the people, as subject, being fixed and represented by unity, whenever the double ratio increases or diminishes, the single ratio increases or diminishes in like manner, and consequently the middle term is changed. This shows that there is no unique and absolute constitution of government, but that there may be as many governments different in nature as there are states different in size.

If, for the sake of turning this system to ridicule, it should be said that, in order to find this mean proportional and form the body of the government, it is, according to me, only necessary to take a square root of the number of the people, I should answer that I take that number here only as an example; that the ratios of which I speak are not measured only by the number of men, but in general by the quantity of action, which results from the combination of multitudes of causes; that, moreover, if for the purpose of expressing myself in fewer words, I borrow for a moment geometrical terms, I am nevertheless aware that geometrical precision has no place in moral quantities.

The government is on a small scale what the body politic which includes it is on a large scale. It is a moral person endowed with certain faculties, active like the sovereign, passive like the state, and it can be resolved into other similar relations; from which arises as a consequence a new proportion, and yet another within this, according to the order of the magistracies, until we come to an indivisible middle term, that is, to a single chief or supreme magistrate, who may be represented, in the middle of this progression, as unity between the series of fractions and that of the whole numbers.

Without embarrassing ourselves with this multiplication of terms, let us be content to consider the government as a new body in the state, distinct from the people and from the sovereign, and intermediate between the two.

There is this essential difference between those two bodies, that the state exists by itself, while the government exists only through the sovereign. Thus the dominant will of the Prince is, or ought to be, only the general will, or the law; its force is only the public force concentrated in itself; so soon as it wishes to perform of itself some absolute and independent act the connection of the whole begins to be relaxed. If, lastly, the Prince should chance to have a particular will more active than that of the sovereign, and if, to enforce obedience to this particular will, it should employ the public force which is in its hands, in such a manner that there would be so to speak two sovereigns, the one *de jure* and the other *de facto*, the social union would immediately disappear, and the body politic would be dissolved.

Further, in order that the body of the government may have an existence, a real life, to distinguish it from the body of the state; in order that all its members may be able to act in concert and fulfill the object for which it is instituted, a particular personality is necessary to it, a feeling common to its members, a force, a will of its own tending to its preservation. This individual existence supposes assemblies, councils, a power of deliberating and resolving, rights, titles, and privileges which belong to the Prince exclusively, and which render the position of the magistrate more honorable in proportion as it is more arduous. The difficulty lies in the method of disposing, within the whole, this subordinate whole, in such a way that it may not weaken the general constitution in strengthening its own; that its particular force, intended for its own preservation, may always be kept distinct from the public force, designed for the preservation of the state; and, in a word, that it may always be ready to sacrifice the government to the people, and not the people to the government.

Moreover, although the artificial body of the government is the work of another artificial body, and has in some respects only a derivative and subordinate existence, that does not prevent it from acting with more or less vigor or celerity, from enjoying, so to speak, more or less robust health. Lastly, without directly departing from the object for which it was instituted, it may deviate from it more or less, according to the manner in which it is constituted.

From all these differences arise the different relations which the government must have with the body of the state, so as to accord with the accidental and particular relations by which the state itself is modified. For often the government that is best in itself will become the most vicious, unless its relations are changed so as to meet the defects of the body politic to which it belongs.

Ch. ii.   *The Principle which Constitutes the Different Forms of Government.*

To explain the general cause of these differences, I must here distinguish the Prince from the government, as I before distinguished the state from the sovereign.

The body of the magistracy may be composed of a greater or

less number of members. We said that the ratio of the sovereign
to the subjects was so much greater as the people were more
numerous; and, by an evident analogy, we can say the same of
the government with regard to the magistrates.

Now, the total force of the government, being always that of the
state, does not vary; whence it follows that the more it employs
this force on its own members, the less remains for operating
upon the whole people.

Consequently, the more numerous the magistrates are, the
weaker is the government. As this maxim is fundamental, let us
endeavor to explain it more clearly.

We can distinguish in the person of the magistrate three wills
essentially different: first, the will peculiar to the individual,
which tends only to his personal advantage; secondly, the common will of the magistrates, which has reference solely to the
advantage of the Prince, and which may be called the corporate
will, being general in relation to the government, and particular
in relation to the state of which the government forms part; in
the third place, the will of the people, or the sovereign will, which
is general both in relation to the state considered as the whole,
and in relation to the government considered as part of the
whole.

In a perfect system of legislation the particular or individual
will should be inoperative; the corporate will proper to the
government quite subordinate; and consequently the general
or sovereign will always dominant, and the sole rule of all the
rest.

On the other hand, according to the natural order, these different wills become more active in proportion as they are concentrated. Thus the general will is always the weakest, the corporate will has the second rank, and the particular will the first
of all; so that in the government each member is, first, himself,
next a magistrate, and then a citizen—a gradation directly
opposed to that which the social order requires.

But suppose that the whole government is in the hands of a
single man, then the particular will and the corporate will are
perfectly united, and consequently the latter is in the highest
possible degree of intensity. Now, as it is on the degree of will
that the exertion of force depends, and as the absolute power of
the government does not vary, it follows that the most active
government is that of a single person.

On the other hand, let us unite the government with the legislative authority; let us make the sovereign the Prince, and all

the citizens magistrates; then the corporate will, confounded with the general will, will have no more activity than the latter, and will leave the particular will in all its force. Thus the government, always with the same absolute force, will be at its minimum of relative force or activity.

These relations are incontestable, and other considerations serve still further to confirm them. We see, for example, that each magistrate is more active in his body than each citizen is in his, and that consequently the particular will has much more influence in the acts of government than in those of the sovereign; for every magistrate is almost always charged with some function of government, whereas each citizen, taken by himself, has no function of sovereignty. Besides, the more a state extends, the more is its real force increased, although it does not increase in proportion to its extent; but, while the state remains the same, it is useless to multiply magistrates, for the government acquires no greater real force, inasmuch as this force is that of the state, the quantity of which is always uniform. Thus the relative force or activity of the government diminishes without its absolute or real force being able to increase.

It is certain, moreover, that the dispatch of business is retarded in proportion as more people are charged with it; that, in laying too much stress on prudence, we leave too little to fortune; that opportunities are allowed to pass by, and that owing to excessive deliberation the fruits of deliberation are often lost.

I have just shown that the government is weakened in proportion to the multiplication of magistrates, and I have before demonstrated that the more numerous the people is, the more ought the repressive force to be increased. Whence it follows that the ratio between the magistrates and the government ought to be inversely as the ratio between the subjects and the sovereign; that is, the more the state is enlarged, the more should the government contract; so that the number of chiefs should diminish in proportion as the number of the people is increased.

But I speak here only of the relative force of the government, and not of its rectitude; for, on the other hand, the more numerous the magistracy is, the more does the corporate will approach the general will; whereas, under a single magistrate, this same corporate will is, as I have said, only a particular will. Thus, what is lost on one side can be gained on the other, and the art of the legislator consists in knowing how to fix the point where the force and will of the government, always in reciprocal proportion, are combined in the ratio most advantageous to the state.

Ch. iii. *Classification of Governments.*

We have seen in the previous chapter why the different kinds or forms of government are distinguished by the number of members that compose them; it remains to be seen in the present chapter how this division is made.

The sovereign may, in the first place, commit the charge of the government to the whole people, or to the greater part of the people, in such a way that there may be more citizens who are magistrates than simple individual citizens. We call this form of government a *democracy.*

Or it may confine the government to a small number, so that there may be more ordinary citizens than magistrates; and this form bears the name of *aristocracy.*

Lastly, it may concentrate the whole government in the hands of a single magistrate from whom all the rest derive their power. This third form is the most common, and is called *monarchy,* or royal government.

We should remark that all these forms, or at least the first two, admit of degrees, and may indeed have a considerable range; for democracy may embrace the whole people, or be limited to a half. Aristocracy, in its turn, may restrict itself from a half of the people to the smallest number indeterminately. Royalty even is susceptible of some division. Sparta by its constitution always had two kings; and in the Roman Empire there were as many as eight Emperors at once without its being possible to say that the Empire was divided. Thus there is a point at which each form of government blends with the next; and we see that, under three denominations only, the government is really susceptible of as many different forms as the state has citizens.

What is more, this same government being in certain respects capable of subdivision into other parts, one administered in one way, another in another, there may result from combinations of these three forms a multitude of mixed forms, each of which can be multiplied by all the simple forms.

In all ages there has been much discussion about the best form of government, without consideration of the fact that each of them is the best in certain cases, and the worst in others.

If, in the different states, the number of the supreme magistrates should be in inverse ratio to that of the citizens, it follows that, in general, democratic government is suitable to small states, aristocracy to those of moderate size, and monarchy to large ones. This rule follows immediately from the principle. But how is it possible to estimate the multitude of circumstances which may furnish exceptions?

5.   The Subordination of Government to Sovereign [1]

Ch. xii.   *How the Sovereign Authority is Maintained.*

The sovereign, having no other force than the legislative power, acts only through the laws; and the laws being nothing but authentic acts of the general will, the sovereign can act only when the people are assembled. The people assembled, it will be said; what a chimera! It is a chimera to-day; but it was not so two thousand years ago. Have men changed their nature?

The limits of the possible in moral things are less narrow than we think; it is our weaknesses, our vices, our prejudices, that contract them. Sordid souls do not believe in great men; vile slaves smile with a mocking air at the word *liberty.*

From what has been done let us consider what can be done. I shall not speak of the ancient republics of Greece; but the Roman Republic was, it seems to me, a great state, and the city of Rome a great city. The last census in Rome showed that there were 400,000 citizens bearing arms, and the last enumeration of the Empire showed more than 4,000,000 citizens, without reckoning subjects, foreigners, women, children, and slaves.

What a difficulty, we might suppose, there would be in assembling frequently the enormous population of the capital and its environs. Yet few weeks passed without the Roman people being assembled, even several times. Not only did they exercise the rights of sovereignty, but a part of the functions of government. They discussed certain affairs and judged certain causes, and in the public assembly the whole people were almost as often magistrates as citizens.

By going back to the early times of nations, we should find that the majority of the ancient governments, even monarchical ones, like those of the Macedonians and the Franks, had similar councils. Be that as it may, this single incontestable fact solves all difficulties; inference from the actual to the possible appears to me sound.

Ch. xiii.   *How the Sovereign Authority is Maintained (Continued).*

It is not sufficient that the assembled people should have once fixed the constitution of the state by giving their sanction to a

[1] Bk. III, chs. xii–xviii.

body of laws; it is not sufficient that they should have established a perpetual government, or that they should have once for all provided for the election of magistrates. Besides the extraordinary assemblies which unforeseen events may require, it is necessary that there should be fixed and periodical ones which nothing can abolish or prorogue; so that, on the appointed day, the people are rightfully convoked by the law, without needing for that purpose any formal summons.

But, excepting these assemblies which are lawful by their date alone, every assembly of the people that has not been convoked by the magistrates appointed for that duty and according to the prescribed forms, ought to be regarded as unlawful and all that is done in it as invalid, because even the order to assemble ought to emanate from the law.

As for the more or less frequent meetings of the lawful assemblies, they depend on so many considerations that no precise rules can be given about them. Only it may be said generally that the more force a government has, the more frequently should the sovereign display itself.

This, I shall be told, may be good for a single city; but what is to be done when the state comprises many cities? Will the sovereign authority be divided? Or must it be concentrated in a single city and render subject all the rest?

I answer that neither alternative is necessary. In the first place, the sovereign authority is simple and undivided, and we cannot divide it without destroying it. In the second place, a city, no more than a nation, can be lawfully subject to another, because the essence of the body politic consists in the union of obedience and liberty, and these words, *subject* and *sovereign*, are correlatives, the notion underlying them being expressed in the one word citizen.

I answer, further, that it is always an evil to combine several towns into a single state, and, in desiring to effect such a union, we must not flatter ourselves that we shall avoid the natural inconveniences of it. The abuses of great states cannot be brought as an objection against a man who only desires small ones. But how can small states be endowed with sufficient force to resist great ones? Just in the same way as when the Greek towns of old resisted the Great King,[1] and as more recently Holland and Switzerland have resisted the House of Austria.

If, however, the state cannot be reduced to proper limits, one resource still remains; it is not to allow any capital, but to make

[1] The Persian king.

the government sit alternately in each town, and also to assemble in them by turns the estates of the country.

People the territory uniformly, extend the same rights everywhere, spread everywhere abundance and life; in this way the state will become at once the strongest and the best governed that may be possible. Remember that the walls of the towns are formed solely of the remains of houses in the country. For every palace that I see rising in the capital, I seem to see a whole rural district laid in ruins.

Ch. xiv. *How the Sovereign Authority is Maintained (Continued)*.

So soon as the people are lawfully assembled as a sovereign body, the whole jurisdiction of the government ceases, the executive power is suspended, and the person of the meanest citizen is as sacred and inviolable as that of the first magistrate, because where the represented are, there is no longer any representative. Most of the tumults that arose in Rome in the *comitia* proceeded from ignorance or neglect of this rule. The consuls were then only presidents of the people and the tribunes simple orators; the senate had no power at all.

These intervals of suspension, in which the Prince recognizes or ought to recognize the presence of a superior, have always been dreaded by that power; and these assemblies of the people, which are the shield of the body politic and the curb of the government, have in all ages been the terror of the chief men; hence such men are never wanting in solicitude, objections, obstacles, and promises, in the endeavor to make the citizens disgusted with the assemblies. When the latter are avaricious, cowardly, pusillanimous, and more desirous of repose than of freedom, they do not long hold out against the repeated efforts of the government; and thus, as the resisting force constantly increases, the sovereign authority at last disappears, and most of the states decay and perish before their time.

But between the sovereign authority and the arbitrary government there is sometimes introduced an intermediate power of which I must speak.

Ch. xv. *Deputies or Representatives*.

So soon as the service of the state ceases to be the principal business of the citizens, and they prefer to render aid with their purses rather than with their persons, the state is already on the brink of ruin. Is it necessary to march to battle, they pay troops and remain at home; is it necessary to go to the council, they elect deputies and remain at home. As a result of indolence and wealth, they at length have soldiers to enslave their country and representatives to sell it.

It is the bustle of commerce and of the arts, it is the greedy pursuit of gain, it is effeminacy and love of comforts, that commute personal services for money. Men sacrifice a portion of their profit in order to increase it at their ease. Give money and soon you will have chains. That word *finance* is a slaves' word; it is unknown among citizens. In a country that is really free, the citizens do everything with their hands and nothing with money; far from paying for exemption from their duties, they would pay to perform them themselves. I am far removed from ordinary ideas; I believe that statute-labor (*les corvées*) is less repugnant to liberty than taxation is.

The better constituted a state is, the more do public affairs outweigh private ones in the minds of the citizens. There is, indeed, a much smaller number of private affairs, because the amount of the general prosperity furnishes a more considerable portion to that of each individual, and less remains to be sought by individual exertions. In a well-conducted city-state every one hastens to the assemblies; while under a bad government no one cares to move a step in order to attend them, because no one takes an interest in the proceedings, since it is foreseen that the general will will not prevail; and so at last private concerns become all-absorbing. Good laws pave the way for better ones; bad laws lead to worse ones. As soon as any one says of the affairs of the state, "Of what importance are they to me?" we must consider that the state is lost.

The decline of patriotism, the active pursuit of private interests, the vast size of states, conquests, and the abuses of government, have suggested the plan of deputies or representatives of the people in the assemblies of the nation. It is this which in certain countries they dare to call the third estate. Thus the private interest of two orders is put in the first and second rank, the public interest only in the third.

Sovereignty cannot be represented for the same reason that it cannot be alienated; it consists essentially in the general will, and the will cannot be represented; it is the same or it is different; there is no medium. The deputies of the people, then, are not and cannot be its representatives; they are only its commissioners and can conclude nothing definitely. Every law which the people in person have not ratified is invalid; it is not a law. The English nation thinks that it is free, but is greatly mistaken, for it is so only during the election of members of

Parliament; as soon as they are elected, it is enslaved and counts for nothing. The use which it makes of the brief moments of freedom renders the loss of liberty well deserved.

The idea of representatives is modern; it comes to us from feudal government, that absurd and iniquitous government, under which mankind is degraded and the name of man dishonored. In the republics, and even in the monarchies, of antiquity, the people never had representatives; they did not know the word. It is very singular that in Rome, where the tribunes were so sacred, it was not even imagined that they could usurp the functions of the people, and in the midst of so great a multitude, they never attempted to pass of their own accord a single *plebiscitum*. We may judge, however, of the embarrassment which the crowd sometimes caused from what occurred in the time of the Gracchi, when a part of the citizens gave their votes on the house-tops. But where right and liberty are all in all, inconveniences are nothing. In that wise nation everything was estimated at a true value; it allowed the lictors to do what the tribunes had not dared to do, and was not afraid that the lictors would want to represent it.

To explain, however, in what manner the tribunes sometimes represented it, it is sufficient to understand how the government represents the sovereign. The law being nothing but the declaration of the general will, it is clear that in their legislative capacity the people cannot be represented; but they can and should be represented in the executive power, which is only force applied to law. This shows that very few nations would, upon careful examination, be found to have laws. Be that as it may, it is certain that the tribunes, having no share in the executive power, could never represent the Roman people by right of their office, but only by encroaching on the rights of the senate.

Among the Greeks, whatever the people had to do, they did themselves; they were constantly assembled in the public place. They lived in a mild climate and they were not avaricious; slaves performed the manual labor; the people's great business was liberty. Not having the same advantages, how are you to preserve the same rights? Your more rigorous climates give you more wants; for six months in a year the public place is untenable, and your hoarse voices cannot be heard in the open air. You care more for gain than for liberty, and you fear slavery far less than you do misery.

What! is liberty maintained only with the help of slavery?

Perhaps; extremes meet. Everything which is not according
to nature has its inconveniences, and civil society more than all
the rest. There are circumstances so unfortunate that people
can preserve their freedom only at the expense of that of others,
and the citizen cannot be completely free except when the slave
is enslaved to the utmost. Such was the position of Sparta. As
for you, modern nations, you have no slaves, but you are slaves;
you pay for their freedom with your own. In vain do you boast
of this preference; I find in it more of cowardice than of humanity.

I do not mean by all this that slaves are necessary and that
the right of slavery is lawful, since I have proved the contrary;
I only mention the reasons why modern nations who believe
themselves free have representatives, and why ancient nations
had none. Be that as it may, as soon as a nation appoints
representatives, it is no longer free; it no longer exists.

After very careful consideration I do not see that it is possible
henceforward for the sovereign to preserve among us the exercise of its rights unless the state is very small. But if it is very
small, will it not be subjugated? No; I shall show hereafter
how the external power of a great nation can be combined with
the convenient polity and good order of a small state.

Ch. xvi.   *That the Institution of the Government is not a Contract.*
The legislative power being once well established, the question
is to establish also the executive power; for this latter, which
operates only by particular acts, not being of the essence of the
other, is naturally separated from it. If it were possible that
the sovereign, considered as such, should have the executive
power, law and fact would be so confounded that it could no
longer be known what is law and what is not; and the body
politic, thus perverted, would soon become a prey to the violence
against which it was instituted.

The citizens being all equal by the social contract, all can
prescribe what all ought to do, while no one has a right to demand that another should do what he will not do himself. Now,
it is properly this right, indispensable to make the body politic
live and move, which the sovereign gives to the Prince in establishing the government.

Several have pretended that the instrument in this establishment is a contract between the people and the chiefs whom
they set over themselves—a contract by which it is stipulated between the two parties on what conditions the one binds itself
to rule, the other to obey. It will be agreed, I am sure, that this

is a strange method of contracting. But let us see whether such a position is tenable.

First, the supreme authority can no more be modified than alienated; to limit it is to destroy it. It is absurd and contradictory that the sovereign should acknowledge a superior; to bind itself to obey a master is to regain full liberty.

Further, it is evident that this contract of the people with such or such persons is a particular act; whence it follows that the contract cannot be a law nor an act of sovereignty, and that consequently it is unlawful.

Moreover, we see that the contracting parties themselves would be under the law of nature alone, and without any security for the performance of their reciprocal engagements, which is in every way repugnant to the civil state. He who possesses the power being always capable of executing it, we might as well give the name contract to the act of a man who should say to another: "I give you all my property, on condition that you restore me what you please."

There is but one contract in the state—that of association; and this of itself excludes any other. No public contract can be conceived which would not be a violation of the first.

Ch. xvii.   *The Institution of the Government.*

Under what general notion, then, must be included the act by which the government is instituted? I shall observe first that this act is complex, or composed of two others, viz. the establishment of the law and the execution of the law.

By the first, the sovereign determines that there shall be a governing body established in such or such a form; and it is clear that this act is a law.

By the second, the people nominate the chiefs who will be intrusted with the government when established. Now, this nomination being a particular act, is not a second law, but only a consequence of the first, and a function of the government.

The difficulty is to understand how there can be an act of government before the government exists, and how the people, who are only sovereign or subjects, can, in certain circumstances, become the Prince or the magistrates.

Here, however, is disclosed one of those astonishing properties of the body politic, by which it reconciles operations apparently contradictory; for this is effected by a sudden conversion of sovereignty into democracy in such a manner that, without any perceptible change, and merely by a new relation of all to all, the citizens, having become magistrates, pass from general acts to particular acts, and from the law to the execution of it.

This change of relation is not a subtlety of speculation without example in practice; it occurs every day in the Parliament of England, in which the Lower House on certain occasions resolves itself into Grand Committee in order to discuss business better, and thus becomes a simple commission instead of the sovereign court that it was the moment before. In this way it afterwards reports to itself, as the House of Commons, what it has just decided in Grand Committee.

Such is the advantage peculiar to a democratic government, that it can be established in fact by a simple act of the general will; and after this, the provisional government remains in power, should that be the form adopted, or establishes in the name of the sovereign the government prescribed by the law; and thus everything is according to rule. It is impossible to institute the government in any other way that is legitimate without renouncing the principles heretofore established.

Ch. xviii. *Means of Preventing Usurpations of the Government.*

From these explanations it follows, in confirmation of chapter xvi, that the act which institutes the government is not a contract, but a law; that the depositaries of the executive power are not the masters of the people, but its officers; that the people can appoint them and dismiss them at pleasure; that for them it is not a question of contracting, but of obeying; and that in undertaking the functions which the state imposes on them, they simply fulfill their duty as citizens, without having in any way a right to discuss the conditions.

When, therefore, it happens that the people institute a hereditary government, whether monarchical in a family or aristocratic in one order of citizens, it is not an engagement that they make, but a provisional form which they give to the administration, until they please to regulate it differently.

It is true that such changes are always dangerous, and that the established government must never be touched except when it becomes incompatible with the public good; but this circumspection is a maxim of policy, not a rule of right; and the state is no more bound to leave the civil authority to its chief men than the military authority to its generals.

Moreover, it is true that in such a case all the formalities requisite to distinguish a regular and lawful act from a seditious tumult, and the will of a whole people from the clamors of a faction, cannot be too carefully observed. It is especially in this case that only such concessions should be made as cannot in strict justice be refused; and from this obligation also the Prince derives a great advantage in preserving its power in spite of the people, without their being able to say that it has usurped the power; for while appearing to exercise nothing but its rights, it may very easily extend them, and, under pretext of maintaining the public peace, obstruct the assemblies designed to reëstablish good order; so that it takes advantage of a silence which it prevents from being broken, or of irregularities which it causes to be committed, so as to assume in its favor the approbation of those whom fear renders silent and punish those that dare to speak. It is in this way that the Decemvirs, having at first been elected for one year, and then kept in office for another year, attempted to retain their power in perpetuity by no longer permitting the *comitia* to assemble; and it is by this easy method that all the governments in the world, when once invested with the public force, usurp sooner or later the sovereign authority.

The periodical assemblies of which I have spoken before are fitted to prevent or postpone this evil, especially when they need no formal convocation; for then the Prince cannot interfere with them, without openly proclaiming itself a violator of the laws and an enemy of the state.

These assemblies, which have as their object the maintenance of the social treaty, ought always to be opened with two propositions, which no one should be able to suppress, and which should pass separately by vote.

The first: "Whether it pleases the sovereign to maintain the present form of government."

The second: "Whether it pleases the people to leave the administration to those at present intrusted with it."

I presuppose here what I believe that I have proved, viz. that there is in the state no fundamental law which cannot be revoked, not even the social compact; for if all the citizens assembled in order to break this compact by a solemn agreement, no one can doubt that it would be quite legitimately broken. Grotius even thinks that each man can renounce the state of which he is a member, and regain his natural freedom and his property by quitting the country. Now it would be absurd if all the citizens combined should be unable to do what each of them can do separately.

SELECTED BIBLIOGRAPHY

Sabine, George H., *History of Political Theory*, ch. 28.
Dunning, William, *Political Theories, from Rousseau to Spencer*, ch. 1.
Cook, Thomas I., *History of Political Philosophy*, ch. 22.

Hearnshaw, F. J. C., *Social and Political Ideas of Some Great French Thinkers of the Age of Reason* (London, 1930), ch. 7.
Martin, Kingsley, *French Liberal Thought in the Eighteenth Century* (London, 1929), part iii, ch. 8.
Bosanquet, Bernard, *The Philosophical Theory of the State* (London, 1899), chs. 4–5.
Ritchie, David G., "Contributions to the History of the Social Contract Theory," in *Political Science Quarterly*, vol. 6 (1891), pp. 656–676.
Sée, Henri, *L'Évolution de la pensée politique en France au xviiième siècle* (Paris, 1925), pt. iii, ch. 1.
Havens, G. R., "La théorie de la bonté naturelle de l'homme chez J.-J. Rousseau," in *Revue d'histoire littéraire de la France*, vol. 31 (1924), pp. 629–642, vol. 32 (1925), pp. 24–37, 212–225.
Lovejoy, A. O., "The Supposed Primitivism of Rousseau's 'Discourse on Inequality,'" in *Modern Philology*, vol. 21 (1923–24), pp. 165–186.
Maritain, Jacques, *Three Reformers: Luther, Descartes, Rousseau* (London, 1928), pp. 93–164.
Schinz, Albert, *La pensée de Jean Jacques Rousseau*, 2 vols. (Smith College, Fiftieth Anniversary Publications, No. ix, Northampton, Mass., 1929), Vol. II, pt. ii, chs. 2, 5, 6.
Wright, Ernest H., *The Meaning of Rousseau* (Oxford, 1929), ch. 3.

Faguet, Émile, *La politique comparée de Montesquieu, Rousseau et Voltaire* (Paris, 1902).
Hubert, R., *Rousseau et l'Encyclopédie: essai sur la formation des idées politiques de Rousseau* (1742–1756) (Paris, 1927).
Babbitt, Irving, *Rousseau and Romanticism* (Boston, 1919).
Champion, Edme, *J. J. Rousseau et la Révolution Française* (Paris, 1909).
Morley, John, *Rousseau*, 2 vols. (third ed., London, 1886).
Moreau-Rendu, S., *L'idée de bonté naturelle chez J.-J. Rousseau* (Paris, 1929).
Rodet, Henri, *Le contrat social et les idées politiques de J. J. Rousseau* (Paris, 1909).

PAINE

XXIV. THOMAS PAINE (1737–1809)

INTRODUCTION

The opposition of the American colonists to the policies of the British government in the eighteenth century brought forth little in the way of original or constructive statement of abstract political theory. However, the controversies upon the eve of the Revolution were the occasion for *Common Sense*, the first important work of the Anglo-American political writer—Thomas Paine. In a later work, *The Rights of Man*, Paine gave a more absolute and intense expression to the doctrine of popular and limited government than had ever before been put forward by an English writer.

Paine was born in a town of Norfolk county, England, in 1737, the son of a Quaker stay-maker. He received no academic training beyong the grammar school, which he left in his fourteenth year. During the following twenty-five years he pursued several occupations with no great success at any one. He attended scientific lectures in London and took part in the debates of the local Whig club in a small town in which he lived for a while. In London also he made the acquaintance of Benjamin Franklin, from whom he brought a letter of introduction when he came to America in 1774.

Paine remained in America for thirteen years and took an active part in political life here. He assisted in the editorship of the "Pennsylvania Magazine," [1] and wrote in defense of woman's rights, in opposition to slavery, and in advocacy of war against England. In 1776 he published *Common Sense:* a pamphlet urging separation of the colonies from England and the setting up of a republic in America. The pamphlet was a clear statement of the practical advantages of prompt action against England and also an incisive argument for the superiority, on grounds both of justice and of utility, of popular to hereditary government. This

[1] Founded in 1775.

671

work as well as other pamphlets written along the same line at irregular intervals during the next few years, under the title of "The Crisis," met with extreme popularity; and they were immediately influential in stimulating and confirming the political passions of the colonists. During the war and the early years of the Confederation he served on several diplomatic missions and in other public positions. At George Washington's suggestion, the Congress of the Confederation voted him a gift of money; and the State of New York granted him an estate, at New Rochelle.

Returning to England in 1787, Paine became involved there in the controversy between radicals and conservatives, and wrote a pamphlet attacking Pitt's war plans against France. In 1791 he published the first part of the *Rights of Man;* this was written as a reply to Burke's *Reflections on the Revolution in France*, which had appeared in the preceding year. The government endeavored to suppress the *Rights of Man;* Paine was indicted for treason, and was tried and convicted in his absence. He had gone to France, where he took part in the Constitutional Convention of 1793. His opposition to the extreme policies of the Jacobins brought him into trouble again. While in prison he completed his *Age of Reason*, which is an exposition of deism; it contains a vigorous criticism of orthodox Christianity and an eloquent plea for a simple morality based on "natural religion." After the fall of Robespierre he was freed, through the intervention of Monroe, Minister from the United States, and he resumed work in the Convention. He returned to the United States in 1802, where he spent the rest of his life. His popularity among the American people had greatly declined: partly because of his unorthodox religious views and partly by reason of a letter in which he disparaged Washington's record both as a military leader and as president.

READINGS FROM COMMON SENSE AND THE RIGHTS OF MAN [1]

1. *The Rights of Man* [2]

The error of those who reason by precedents drawn from antiquity, respecting the rights of man, is that they do not go

---

[1] The selections are taken from *The Writings of Thomas Paine*, collected and edited by Moncure Daniel Conway; four volumes; New York, 1894–5. By courtesy of G. P. Putnam's Sons.

[2] *The Rights of Man* (Conway, Vol. II), pp. 303–307.

far enough into antiquity. They do not go the whole way. They stop in some of the intermediate stages of an hundred or a thousand years, and produce what was then done, as a rule for the present day. This is no authority at all. If we travel still farther into antiquity, we shall find a direct contrary opinion and practice prevailing; and if antiquity is to be authority, a thousand such authorities may be produced, successively contradicting each other; but if we proceed on, we shall at last come out right; we shall come to the time when man came from the hand of his Maker. What was he then? Man. Man was his high and only title, and a higher cannot be given him. But of titles I shall speak hereafter.

We are now got at the origin of man, and at the origin of his rights. As to the manner in which the world has been governed from that day to this, it is no further any concern of ours than to make a proper use of the errors or the improvements which the history of it presents. Those who lived an hundred or a thousand years ago, were then moderns, as we are now. They had *their* ancients, and those ancients had others, and we also shall be ancients in our turn. If the mere name of antiquity is to govern in the affairs of life, the people who are to live an hundred or a thousand years hence, may as well take us for a precedent, as we make a precedent of those who lived an hundred or a thousand years ago. The fact is, that portions of antiquity, by proving everything, establish nothing. It is authority against authority all the way, till we come to the divine origin of the rights of man at the creation. Here our inquiries find a resting-place, and our reason finds a home. If a dispute about the rights of man had arisen at the distance of an hundred years from the creation, it is to this source of authority they must have referred, and it is to this same source of authority that we must now refer.

Though I mean not to touch upon any sectarian principle of religion, yet it may be worth observing, that the genealogy of Christ is traced to Adam. Why then not trace the rights of man to the creation of man? I will answer the question. Because there have been upstart governments, thrusting themselves between, and presumptuously working to *un-make* man.

If any generation of men ever possessed the right of dictating the mode by which the world should be governed forever, it was the first generation that existed; and if that generation did it not, no succeeding generation can show any authority for doing it, nor can set any up. The illuminating and divine principle of the equal rights of man (for it has its origin from the Maker of man) relates, not only to the living individuals, but to generations of men succeeding each other. Every generation is equal in rights to generations which preceded it, by the same rule that every individual is born equal in rights with his contemporary.

Every history of the creation, and every traditionary account, whether from the lettered or unlettered world, however they may vary in their opinion or belief of certain particulars, all agree in establishing one point, *the unity of man;* by which I mean that men are all of *one degree*, and consequently that all men are born equal, and with equal natural right, in the same manner as if posterity had been continued by *creation* instead of *generation*, the latter being the only mode by which the former is carried forward; and consequently every child born into the world must be considered as deriving its existence from God. The world is as new to him as it was to the first man that existed, and his natural right in it is of the same kind.

The Mosaic account of the creation, whether taken as divine authority or merely historical, is full to this point, *the unity or equality of man*. The expression admits of no controversy. "And God said, Let us make man in our own image. In the image of God created he him; male and female created he them." The distinction of sexes is pointed out, but no other distinction is even implied. If this be not divine authority, it is at least historical authority, and shows that the equality of man, so far from being a modern doctrine, is the oldest upon record.

It is also to be observed that all the religions known in the world are founded, so far as they relate to man, on the *unity of man*, as being all of one degree. Whether in heaven or in hell, or in whatever state man may be supposed to exist hereafter, the good and the bad are the only distinctions. Nay, even the laws of governments are obliged to slide into this principle, by making degrees to consist in crimes and not in persons.

It is one of the greatest of all truths, and of the highest advantage to cultivate. By considering man in this light, and by instructing him to consider himself in this light, it places him in a close connection with all his duties, whether to his Creator or to the creation, of which he is a part; and it is only when he forgets his origin, or, to use a more fashionable phrase, his *birth and family*, that he becomes dissolute. It is not among the least of the evils of the present existing governments in all parts of Europe that man, considered as man, is thrown back to a vast distance from his Maker, and the artificial chasm filled up with a succession of barriers, or sort of turnpike gates, through which he has to pass. I will quote Mr. Burke's catalogue of barriers that he has set up between man and his Maker. Putting himself in the character of a herald, he says: "We fear God—we look with *awe* to kings—with affection to Parliaments—with duty to magistrates—with reverence to priests, and with respect to nobility." Mr. Burke has forgotten to put in "*chivalry*." He has also forgotten to put in Peter.

The duty of man is not a wilderness of turnpike gates, through which he is to pass by tickets from one to the other. It is plain and simple, and consists but of two points. His duty to God, which every man must feel; and with respect to his neighbor, to do as he would be done by. If those to whom power is delegated do well, they will be respected: if not, they will be despised; and with regard to those to whom no power is delegated, but who assume it, the rational world can know nothing of them.

Hitherto we have spoken only (and that but in part) of the natural rights of man. We have now to consider the civil rights of man, and to show how the one originates from the other. Man did not enter into society to become *worse* than he was before, nor to have fewer rights than he had before, but to have those rights better secured. His natural rights are the foundation of all his civil rights. But in order to pursue this distinction with more precision, it will be necessary to mark the different qualities of natural and civil rights.

A few words will explain this. Natural rights are those which appertain to man in right of his existence. Of this kind are all the intellectual rights, or rights of the mind, and also all those rights of acting as an individual for his own comfort and happiness, which are not injurious to the natural rights of others. Civil rights are those which appertain to man in right of his being a member of society. Every civil right has for its foundation some natural right preëxisting in the individual, but to the enjoyment of which his individual power is not, in all cases, sufficiently competent. Of this kind are all those which relate to security and protection.

From this short review it will be easy to distinguish between that class of natural rights which man retains after entering into society and those which he throws into the common stock as a member of society.

The natural rights which he retains are all those in which the *power* to execute is as perfect in the individual as the right itself. Among this class, as is before mentioned, are all the intellectual rights, or rights of the mind; consequently religion is one of those rights. The natural rights which are not retained are those in which, though the right is perfect in the individual, the power to execute them is defective. They answer not his purpose. A man, by natural right, has a right to judge in his own cause; and so far as the right of the mind is concerned, he never surrenders it. But what availeth it him to judge, if he has not power to redress? He therefore deposits this right in the common stock of society, and takes the arm of society, of which he is a part, in preference and in addition to his own. Society *grants* him nothing. Every man is a proprietor in society, and draws on the capital as a matter of right.

From these premises two or three certain conclusions will follow:

First. That every civil right grows out of a natural right; or, in other words, is a natural right exchanged.

Secondly. That civil power properly considered as such is made up of the aggregate of that class of the natural rights of man, which becomes defective in the individual in point of power, and answers not his purpose, but when collected to a focus becomes competent to the purpose of every one.

Thirdly. That the power produced from the aggregate of natural rights, imperfect in power in the individual, cannot be applied to invade the natural rights which are retained in the individual, and in which the power to execute is as perfect as the right itself.

2. The Origin and Sphere of Government [1]

Some writers have so confounded society with government, as to leave little or no distinction between them; whereas they are not only different, but have different origins. Society is produced by our wants, and government by our wickedness; the former promotes our happiness *positively* by uniting our affections, the latter *negatively* by restraining our vices. The one encourages intercourse, the other creates distinctions. The first is a patron, the last a punisher.

Society in every state is a blessing, but government, even in its best state, is but a necessary evil; in its worst state an intolerable one: for when we suffer, or are exposed to the same miseries *by a government*, which we might expect in a country *without government*, our calamity is heightened by reflecting that we

[1] *Common Sense* (Conway, Vol. I), pp. 69–71, and *Rights of Man, Part Second* (Conway, Vol. II), pp. 406–409.

furnish the means by which we suffer. Government, like dress, is the badge of lost innocence; the palaces of kings are built upon the ruins of the bowers of paradise. For were the impulses of conscience clear, uniform and irresistibly obeyed, man would need no other lawgiver; but that not being the case, he finds it necessary to surrender up a part of his property to furnish means for the protection of the rest; and this he is induced to do by the same prudence which in every other case advises him, out of two evils to choose the least. Wherefore, security being the true design and end of government, it unanswerably follows that whatever form thereof appears most likely to insure it to us, with the least expense and greatest benefit, is preferable to all others.

In order to gain a clear and just idea of the design and end of government, let us suppose a small number of persons settled in some sequestered part of the earth, unconnected with the rest; they will then represent the first peopling of any country, or of the world. In this state of natural liberty, society will be their first thought. A thousand motives will excite them thereto; the strength of one man is so unequal to his wants, and his mind so unfitted for perpetual solitude, that he is soon obliged to seek assistance and relief of another, who in his turn requires the same. Four or five united would be able to raise a tolerable dwelling in the midst of a wilderness, but one man might labor out the common period of life without accomplishing anything; when he had felled his timber he could not remove it, nor erect it after it was removed; hunger in the meantime would urge him to quit his work, and every different want would call him a different way. Disease, nay even misfortune, would be death; for though neither might be mortal, yet either would disable him from living, and reduce him to a state in which he might rather be said to perish than to die.

Thus necessity, like a gravitating power, would soon form our newly arrived emigrants into society, the reciprocal blessings of which would supersede, and render the obligations of law and government unnecessary while they remained perfectly just to each other; but as nothing but Heaven is impregnable to vice, it will unavoidably happen that in proportion as they surmount the first difficulties of emigration, which bound them together in a common cause, they will begin to relax in their duty and attachment to each other: and this remissness will point out the necessity of establishing some form of government to supply the defect of moral virtue.

Some convenient tree will afford them a State House, under the branches of which the whole colony may assemble to deliberate on public matters. It is more than probable that their first laws will have the title only of Regulations and be enforced by no other penalty than public disesteem. In this first parliament every man by natural right will have a seat.

But as the colony increases, the public concerns will increase likewise, and the distance at which the members may be separated will render it too inconvenient for all of them to meet on every occasion as at first, when their number was small, their habitations near, and the public concerns few and trifling. This will point out the convenience of their consenting to leave the legislative part to be managed by a select number chosen from the whole body, who are supposed to have the same concerns at stake which those have who appointed them, and who will act in the same manner as the whole body would act were they present. If the colony continue increasing, it will become necessary to augment the number of representatives, and that the interest of every part of the colony may be attended to, it will be found best to divide the whole into convenient parts, each part sending its proper number: and that the *elected* might never form to themselves an interest separate from the *electors*, prudence will point out the propriety of having elections often: because as the *elected* might by that means return and mix again with the general body of the *electors* in a few months, their fidelity to the public will be secured by the prudent reflection of not making a rod for themselves. And as this frequent interchange will establish a common interest with every part of the community, they will mutually and naturally support each other, and on this (not on the unmeaning name of king) depends the *strength of government, and the happiness of the governed*.

Here then is the origin and rise of government; namely, a mode rendered necessary by the inability of moral virtue to govern the world; here too is the design and end of government, viz. Freedom and security. And however our eyes may be dazzled with show, or our ears deceived by sound; however prejudice may warp our wills, or interest darken our understanding, the simple voice of nature and reason will say, 'tis right.

Great part of that order which reigns among mankind is not the effect of government. It has its origin in the principles of society and the natural constitution of man. It existed prior to government, and would exist if the formality of government was abolished. The mutual dependence and reciprocal interest which man has upon man, and all the parts of civilized community upon each other, create that great chain of connection which holds it together. The landholder, the farmer, the manufacturer, the merchant, the tradesman, and every occupation, prospers by the aid which each receives from the other, and from the whole. Common interest regulates their concerns, and forms their law; and the laws which common usage ordains have a greater influence than the laws of government. In fine society performs for itself almost everything which is ascribed to government.

To understand the nature and quantity of government proper for man, it is necessary to attend to his character. As Nature created him for social life, she fitted him for the station she intended. In all cases she made his natural wants greater than his individual powers. No one man is capable, without the aid of society, of supplying his own wants; and those wants, acting upon every individual, impel the whole of them into society, as naturally as gravitation acts to a center.

But she has gone further. She has not only forced man into society by a diversity of wants which the reciprocal aid of each other can supply, but she has implanted in him a system of social affections, which, though not necessary to his existence, are essential to his happiness. There is no period in life when this love for society ceases to act. It begins and ends with our being.

If we examine with attention into the composition and constitution of man, the diversity of his wants, and the diversity of talents in different men for reciprocally accommodating the wants of each other, his propensity to society, and consequently to preserve the advantages resulting from it, we shall easily discover that a great part of what is called government is mere imposition.

Government is no further necessary than to supply the few cases to which society and civilization are not conveniently competent; and instances are not wanting to show, that everything which government can usefully add thereto, has been performed by the common consent of society, without government.

For upwards of two years from the commencement of the American War, and to a longer period in several of the American states, there were no established forms of government. The old governments had been abolished, and the country was too much occupied in defense to employ its attention in establishing new governments; yet during this interval order and harmony were preserved as inviolate as in any country in Europe. There is a natural aptness in man, and more so in society, because it embraces a greater variety of abilities and resource, to accommodate itself to whatever situation it is in. The instant formal government is abolished, society begins to act: a general association takes place, and common interest produces common security.

So far is it from being true, as has been pretended, that the abolition of any formal government is the dissolution of society, that it acts by a contrary impulse, and brings the latter the closer together.   All that part of its organization which it has committed to its government devolves again upon itself, and acts through its medium.   When men, as well from natural instinct as from reciprocal benefits, have habituated themselves to social and civilized life, there is always enough of its principles in practice to carry them through any changes they may find necessary or convenient to make in their government.   In short, man is so naturally a creature of society that it is almost impossible to put him out of it.

Formal government makes but a small part of civilized life; and when even the best that human wisdom can devise is established, it is a thing more in name and idea than in fact.   It is to the great and fundamental principles of society and civilization—to the common usage universally consented to, and mutually and reciprocally maintained—to the unceasing circulation of interest, which, passing through its million channels, invigorates the whole mass of civilized man—it is to these things, infinitely more than to anything which even the best instituted government can perform, that the safety and prosperity of the individual and of the whole depend.

The more perfect civilization is, the less occasion has it for government, because the more does it regulate its own affairs, and govern itself; but so contrary is the practice of old governments to the reason of the case, that the expenses of them increase in the proportion they ought to diminish.   It is but few general laws that civilized life requires, and those of such common usefulness, that whether they are enforced by the forms of government or not, the effect will be nearly the same.   If we consider what the principles are that first condense men into society, and what are the motives that regulate their mutual intercourse afterwards, we shall find, by the time we arrive at what is called government, that nearly the whole of the business is performed by the natural operation of the parts upon each other.

Man, with respect to all those matters, is more a creature of consistency than he is aware, or than governments would wish him to believe.   All the great laws of society are laws of nature.

Those of trade and commerce, whether with respect to the inter-course of individuals or of nations, are laws of mutual and recipro-cal interest. They are followed and obeyed, because it is the interest of the parties so to do, and not on account of any formal laws their governments may impose or interpose.

But how often is the natural propensity to society disturbed or destroyed by the operations of government! When the latter, instead of being ingrafted on the principles of the former, assumes to exist for itself, and acts by partialities of favor and oppression, it becomes the cause of the mischiefs it ought to prevent.

3. Republican Government [1]

Reason and Ignorance, the opposites of each other, influence the great bulk of mankind. If either of these can be rendered sufficiently extensive in a country, the machinery of government goes easily on. Reason obeys itself; and Ignorance submits to whatever is dictated to it.

The two modes of the government which prevail in the world are, *first*, government by election and representation: *secondly*, government by hereditary succession. The former is generally known by the name of republic; the latter by that of monarchy and aristocracy.

Those two distinct and opposite forms erect themselves on the two distinct and opposite bases of Reason and Ignorance. As the exercise of government requires talents and abilities, and as talents and abilities cannot have hereditary descent, it is evident that hereditary succession requires a belief from man to which his reason cannot subscribe, and which can only be established upon his ignorance; and the more ignorant any country is, the better it is fitted for this species of government.

On the contrary, government, in a well-constituted republic, requires no belief from man beyond what his reason can give. He sees the *rationale* of the whole system, its origin and its opera-tion; and as it is best supported when best understood, the human faculties act with boldness, and acquire, under this form of government, a gigantic manliness.

As, therefore, each of those forms acts on a different base, the one moving freely by the aid of reason, the other by ignorance, we have next to consider what it is that gives motion to that species of government which is called mixed government, or, as

[1] *Rights of Man* (Conway, Vol. II), pp. 382–383, 385–386, and *Rights of Man, Part Second* (*ibid.*), pp. 421–422.

it is sometimes ludicrously styled, a government of *this*, *that* and *t'other*.

The moving power in this species of government is, of necessity, corruption. However imperfect election and representation may be in mixed governments, they still give exercise to a greater portion of reason than is convenient to the hereditary part; and therefore it becomes necessary to buy the reason up. A mixed government is an imperfect everything, cementing and soldering the discordant parts together by corruption, to act as a whole. Mr. Burke appears highly disgusted that France, since she had resolved on a revolution, did not adopt what he calls "*A British Constitution*"; and the regretful manner in which he expresses himself on this occasion implies a suspicion that the British Constitution needed something to keep its defects in countenance.

In mixed governments there is no responsibility; the parts cover each other till responsibility is lost; and the corruption which moves the machine, contrives at the same time its own escape. When it is laid down as a maxim that *a King can do no wrong*, it places him in a state of similar security with that of ideots and persons insane, and responsibility is out of the question with respect to himself. It then descends upon the Minister, who shelters himself under a majority in Parliament, which, by places, pensions, and corruption, he can always command; and that majority justifies itself by the same authority with which it protects the Minister. In this rotatory motion, responsibility is thrown off from the parts, and from the whole.

What is government more than the management of the affairs of a nation? It is not, and from its nature cannot be, the property of any particular man or family, but of the whole community, at whose expence it is supported; and though by force and contrivance it has been usurped into an inheritance, the usurpation cannot alter the right of things. Sovereignty, as a matter of right, appertains to the nation only, and not to any individual; and a nation has at all times an inherent indefeasible right to abolish any form of government it finds inconvenient, and to establish such as accords with its interest, disposition and happiness. The romantic and barbarous distinction of men into kings and subjects, though it may suit the condition of courtiers, cannot that of citizens; and is exploded by the principle upon which governments are now founded. Every citizen is a member of the sovereignty, and, as such, can acknowledge no personal subjection; and his obedience can be only to the laws.

When men think of what government is, they must necessarily suppose it to possess a knowledge of all the objects and matters upon which its authority is to be exercised. In this view of government, the republican system, as established by America and France, operates to embrace the whole of a nation; and the knowledge necessary to the interest of all the parts is to be found in the center, which the parts by representation form. But the old governments are on a construction that excludes knowledge as well as happiness; government by monks, who knew nothing of the world beyond the walls of a convent, is as consistent as government by kings.

What were formerly called revolutions, were little more than a change of persons, or an alteration of local circumstances. They rose and fell like things of course, and had nothing in their existence or their fate that could influence beyond the spot that produced them. But what we now see in the world, from the revolutions of America and France, are a renovation of the natural order of things, a system of principles as universal as truth and the existence of man, and combining moral with political happiness and national prosperity.

"I. *Men are born, and always continue, free and equal in respect of their rights. Civil distinctions, therefore, can be founded only on public utility.*

"II. *The end of all political associations is the preservation of the natural and imprescriptible rights of man; and these rights are liberty, property, security, and resistance of oppression.*

"III. *The nation is essentially the source of all sovereignty; nor can any* INDIVIDUAL, *or* ANY BODY OF MEN, *be entitled to any authority which is not expressly derived from it.*"

It has always been the political craft of courtiers and court-governments to abuse something which they called republicanism; but what republicanism was, or is, they never attempt to explain. Let us examine a little into this case.

The only forms of government are, the democratical, the aristocratical, the monarchical, and what is now called the representative.

What is called a *republic* is not any *particular form* of government. It is wholly characteristical of the purport, matter or object for which government ought to be instituted, and on which it is to be employed, RES-PUBLICA, the public affairs, or the public good; or, literally translated, the *public thing*. It is a word of a good original, referring to what ought to be the character and business of government; and in this sense it is naturally opposed to the word *monarchy*, which has a base original signification. It means arbitrary power in an individual person; in the exercise of which, *himself*, and not the *res-publica*, is the object.

Every government that does not act on the principle of a *republic*, or, in other words, that does not make the *res-publica* its whole and sole object, is not a good government. Republican government is no other than government established and conducted for the interest of the public, as well individually as collectively. It is not necessarily connected with any particular form, but it most naturally associates with the representative form, as being best calculated to secure the end for which a nation is at the expense of supporting it.

Various forms of government have affected to style themselves a republic. Poland calls itself a republic, which is an hereditary aristocracy, with what is called an elective monarchy. Holland calls itself a republic, which is chiefly aristocratical, with an hereditary stadtholdership. But the government of America, which is wholly on the system of representation, is the only real republic, in character and in practice, that now exists. Its government has no other object than the public business of the nation, and therefore it is properly a republic; and the Americans have taken care that THIS, and no other, shall always be the object of their government, by their rejecting everything hereditary, and establishing governments on the system of representation only. Those who have said that a republic is not a *form* of government calculated for countries of great extent, mistook, in the first place, the *business* of government, for a *form* of government; for the *res-publica* equally appertains to every extent of territory and population. And, in the second place, if they meant anything with respect to *form*, it was the simple democratical form, such as was the mode of government in the ancient democracies, in which there was no representation. The case, therefore, is not that a republic cannot be extensive, but that it cannot be extensive on the simple democratical form; and the question naturally presents itself, *What is the best form of government for conducting the* RES-PUBLICA, *or the* PUBLIC BUSINESS *of a nation, after it becomes too extensive and populous for the simple democratical form?* It cannot be monarchy, because monarchy is subject to an objection of the same amount to which the simple democratical form was subject.

It is possible that an individual may lay down a system of principles, on which government shall be constitutionally established to any extent of territory. This is no more than an operation of the mind, acting by its own powers. But the practice upon those principles, as applying to the various and numerous circumstances of a nation, its agriculture, manufacture, trade, commerce, etc., etc., requires a knowledge of a different kind, and which can be had only from the various parts of society. It is an assemblage of practical knowledge, which no individual can possess; and therefore the monarchical form is as much limited, in useful practice, from the incompetency of knowledge, as was the democratical form from the multiplicity of population. The one degenerates, by extension, into confusion; the other, into ignorance and incapacity, of which all the great monarchies are an evidence. The monarchical form, therefore, could not be a substitute for the democratical, because it has equal inconveniences.

Much less could it when made hereditary. This is the most effectual of all forms to preclude knowledge. Neither could the high democratical mind have voluntarily yielded itself to be governed by children and ideots, and all the motley insignificance of character, which attends such a mere animal system, the disgrace and the reproach of reason and of man.

As to the aristocratical form, it has the same vices and defects with the monarchical, except that the chance of abilities is better from the proportion of numbers, but there is still no security for the right use and application of them.

Referring them to the original simple democracy, it affords the true data from which government on a large scale can begin. It is incapable of extension, not from its principle, but from the inconvenience of its form; and monarchy and aristocracy, from their incapacity. Retaining, then, democracy as the ground, and rejecting the corrupt systems of monarchy and aristocracy, the representative system naturally presents itself; remedying at once the defects of the simple democracy as to form, and the incapacity of the other two with respect to knowledge.

Simple democracy was society governing itself without the aid of secondary means. By ingrafting representation upon democracy, we arrive at a system of government capable of embracing and confederating all the various interests and every extent of territory and population; and that also with advantages as much superior to hereditary government, as the republic of letters is to hereditary literature.

It is on this system that the American government is founded. It is representation ingrafted upon democracy. It has fixed the form by a scale parallel in all cases to the extent of the principle.

What Athens was in miniature America will be in magnitude. The one was the wonder of the ancient world; the other is becoming the admiration of the present. It is the easiest of all the forms of government to be understood and the most eligible in practice; and excludes at once the ignorance and insecurity of the hereditary mode, and the inconvenience of the simple democracy.

It is impossible to conceive a system of government capable of acting over such an extent of territory, and such a circle of interests, as is immediately produced by the operation of representation. France, great and populous as it is, is but a spot in the capaciousness of the system. It is preferable to simple democracy even in small territories. Athens, by representation, would have outrivaled her own democracy.

That which is called government, or rather that which we ought to conceive government to be, is no more than some common center in which all the parts of society unite. This cannot be accomplished by any method so conducive to the various interests of the community, as by the representative system. It concentrates the knowledge necessary to the interest of the parts, and of the whole. It places government in a state of constant maturity. It is, as has already been observed, never young, never old. It is subject neither to nonage nor dotage. It is never in the cradle nor on crutches. It admits not of a separation between knowledge and power, and is superior, as government always ought to be, to all the accidents of individual man, and is therefore superior to what is called monarchy.

SELECTED BIBLIOGRAPHY

Dunning, William A., *Political Theories, from Rousseau to Spencer*, ch. 3, § 5.

Dodd, William E., "Tom Paine," in *American Mercury*, vol. 21 (1930), pp. 477–483.

Sykes, Norman, "Thomas Paine," in F. J. C. Hearnshaw, ed., *The Social and Political Ideas of Some Representative Thinkers of the Revolutionary Era* (London, 1930), ch. 5.

Parrington, V. L., *Main Currents in American Thought*, 3 vols. (New York, 1927–30), Vol. I, pp. 324–341.

Clark, H. H., "Thomas Paine's Relation to Voltaire and Rousseau," in *Revue anglo-américaine*, vol. 9 (1931–32), pp. 305–318, 393–405

Brailsford, H. N., *Shelley, Godwin and Their Circle* (London, 1913), ch. 2.

Tyler, Moses Coit, *The Literary History of the American Revolution*, 2 vols. (New York, 1897), Vol. I, ch. 21; Vol. II, ch. 26.

BENTHAM

XXV. JEREMY BENTHAM (1748–1832)

INTRODUCTION

Bentham's primary interest was less in systematic political theory or comprehensive constitutional change than in revision of governmental practice. His great influence has been within the fields of ethics and jurisprudence, and, on the practical side, in reforms in methods of legislation and administration.

Bentham was the son of a successful London attorney. He was a precocious youth, entering Oxford in his fourteenth year, receiving his bachelor's degree three years later and his master's degree at twenty-one. He engaged in legal practice for a brief period, with very little activity or interest in the work. An inherited fortune relieved him of the necessity of pursuing a regular vocation, and his long life was devoted to study, observation and writing in his favorite fields.

Bentham's great practical aim was to secure the application of ethical and rational principles to governmental action as manifested in the formulation, expression, recording and enforcement of law. His fundamental idea in ethics and jurisprudence is the principle of utility, or of the greatest happiness of the greatest number. He did not originate doctrines in these domains; but he stated and expounded principles in such way as to make almost axiomatic many doctrines which before him enjoyed limited acceptance and understanding. His first book was published anonymously in 1776; the design of this work is indicated in the title—*A Fragment on Government; Being an Examination of what is delivered, on the Subject of Government in General, in the Introduction to Sir William Blackstone's Commentaries; with a Preface in which is given a Critique on the Work at large.* Its attack is directed primarily against the conservative temper and logical fallacies of Blackstone's *Commentaries*. The work in general is a destructive criticism of prevailing ideas in political theory and jurisprudence, particularly the doctrines of natural rights and social contract. But the principle of utility receives positive statement as the all-sufficient foundation of sovereignty and political obligation. The author's numerous subsequent books and pamphlets [1] are the product of his vigorous and broad interest in legal, administrative and fiscal reform, and in the criticism of prevailing tenets in religion and morals.

In 1823 Bentham took part in the foundation of the *Westminster Review*, which became the leading journal of political and religious radicalism. He worked for his various projects through books, pamphlets, magazine articles and an extensive correspondence. In his agitation for immediate changes he was particularly interested in codifying the common law, improving the processes of legislation, removing abuses from judicial procedure, and reforming prison methods.

Bentham's greater influence in political theory comes from his critical discussion, from his logical method, and from his emphasis upon the utilitarian standard for appraising political institutions. His detailed directions for applying the standard to actual legislation and legal administration appear in the *Introduction to the Principles of Morals and Legislation*, printed privately in 1780 and first published in 1789. Bentham also produced one of the most influential statements of the traditional conception of legal sovereignty, in the form in which the conception became a cardinal doctrine of nineteenth-century utilitarian jurists. This statement is a part of his general definition of "political society," in the *Fragment on Government*, which sets forth most succinctly his basic critical and constructive political ideas.

READINGS FROM A FRAGMENT ON GOVERNMENT [2]

1.   *The Distinction between Political and Natural Society* [3]

X.   The idea of a natural society is a *negative* one. The idea of a political society is a *positive* one. 'Tis with the latter, therefore, we should begin.

When a number of persons whom we may style (*subjects*) are

---

[1] For a full list of Bentham's published works, see the Bibliography prepared by C. W. Everett: in Élie Halévy, *Growth of Philosophic Radicalism*, pp. 522–546.

[2] The selections are from *A Fragment on Government*, by Jeremy Bentham. Edited by F. C. Montague. Oxford, 1891. By permission of the Delegates of the Clarendon Press. A few of Bentham's footnotes are reproduced.

[3] Ch. I, pars. x–xvii, xix–xxvii.

supposed to be in the *habit* of paying *obedience* to a person, or an assemblage of persons, of a known and certain description (whom we may call *governor* or *governors*) such persons altogether (*subjects* and *governors*) are said to be in a state of *political* SOCIETY.

XI. The idea of a state of *natural* SOCIETY is, as we have said, a *negative* one. When a number of persons are supposed to be in the habit of *conversing* with each other, at the same time that they are not in any such habit as mentioned above, they are said to be in a state of *natural* SOCIETY.

XII. If we reflect a little, we shall perceive, that, between these two states, there is not that explicit separation which these names, and these definitions might teach one, at first sight, to expect. It is with them as with light and darkness: however distinct the ideas may be, that are, at first mention, suggested by those *names*, the *things* themselves have no determinate bound to separate them. The circumstance that has been spoken of as constituting the difference between these two states, is the presence or absence of an *habit of obedience*. This habit, accordingly, has been spoken of simply as *present* (that is, as being *perfectly* present) or, in other words, we have spoken as if there were a *perfect* habit of obedience, in the *one* case: it has been spoken of simply as *absent* (that is, as being *perfectly* absent) or, in other words, we have spoken as if there were *no* habit of obedience at all, in the *other*. But neither of these manners of speaking, perhaps, is strictly just. Few, in fact, if any, are the instances of this habit being perfectly *absent;* certainly none at all, of its being perfectly *present*. Governments accordingly, in proportion as the habit of obedience is more perfect, recede from, in proportion as it is less perfect, approach to, a state of nature: and instances may present themselves in which it shall be difficult to say whether a habit, perfect, in the degree in which, to constitute a government, it is deemed necessary it *should* be perfect, *does* subsist or *not*.

XIII. On these considerations, the supposition of a *perfect state of nature*, or, as it may be termed, a state of *society perfectly natural*, may, perhaps, be justly pronounced, what our Author for the moment seemed to think it, an extravagant supposition: but then that of a *government* in this sense *perfect*; or, as it may be termed, a state of society *perfectly political*, a state of *perfect political union*, a state of *perfect submission* in the *subject* of *perfect authority* in the *governor*, is no less so.[1]

---

[1] It is true that every person must, for some time, at least, after his birth, necessarily be in a state of subjection with respect to his parents, or those who

XIV. A remark there is, which, for the more thoroughly clearing up of our notions on this subject, it may be proper here to make. To some ears, the phrases, "state of nature," "state of political society," may carry the appearance of being *absolute* in their signification: as if the condition of a man, or a company of men, in one of these states, or in the other, were a matter that depended altogether upon themselves. But this is not the case. To the expression "state of nature," no more than to the expression "state of political society," can any precise meaning be annexed, without reference to a party different from that one who is spoken of as being in the state in question. This will readily be perceived. The difference between the two states lies, as we have observed, in the *habit of obedience*. With respect then to a habit of obedience, it can neither be understood as subsisting in any person, nor as not subsisting in any person, but with reference to some other person. For one party to *obey*, there must be another party that is obeyed. But this party who is obeyed, may at different times be different. Hence may one and the same party be conceived to obey and *not* to obey at the same time, so as it be with respect to different *persons*, or as we may say, to different *objects of obedience*. Hence it is, then, that one and the same party may be said to *be* in a state of nature, and *not* to be in a state of nature, and that at one and the same time, according as it is

---

stand in the place of parents to him; and that a perfect one, or at least as near to being a perfect one, as any that we see. But for all this, the sort of society that is constituted by a state of subjection thus circumstanced, does not come up to the idea that, I believe, is generally entertained by those who speak of a *political* society. To constitute what is meant in general by that phrase, a greater *number* of members is required, or, at least, a *duration* capable of a longer continuance. Indeed, for this purpose nothing less, I take it, than an *indefinite* duration is required. A society, to come within the notion of what is originally meant by a *political* one, must be such as, in its nature, is not incapable of continuing for ever in virtue of the principles which gave it birth. This, it is plain, is not the case with such a family society, of which a parent, or a pair of parents are at the head. In such a society, the only principle of union which is certain and uniform in its operation, is the natural weakness of those of its members that are in a state of subjection; that is, the children; a principle which has but a short and limited continuance. I question whether it be the case even with a family society, subsisting in virtue of *collateral* consanguinity; and that for the like reason. Not but that even in this case a habit of obedience, as perfect as any we see examples of, may subsist for a time; to wit, in virtue of the same *moral* principles which may protract a habit of *filial* obedience beyond the continuance of the *physical* ones which gave birth to it: I mean affection, gratitude, awe, the force of habit, and the like. But it is not long, even in this case, before the bond of connection must either become imperceptible, or lose its influence by being too extended.

These considerations, therefore, it will be proper to bear in mind in applying the definition of political society above given [in par. 10] and in order to reconcile it with what is said further on [in par. 17].

this or *that* party that is taken for the other object of comparison. The case is, that in common speech, when no particular object of comparison is specified, all persons in general are intended: so that when a number of persons are said simply to be in a state of nature, what is understood is, that they are so as well with reference to one another, as to all the world.

XV. In the same manner we may understand how the same man, who is *governor* with respect to one man or set of men, may be *subject* with respect to another: how among governors some may be in a *perfect* state of *nature*, with respect to each other: as the KINGS of FRANCE and SPAIN: others, again, in a state of *perfect subjection*, as the HOSPODARS of WALACHIA and MOLDAVIA with respect to the GRAND SIGNIOR: others, again, in a state of manifest but *imperfect subjection*, as the GERMAN STATES with respect to the EMPEROR: others, again, in such a state in which it may be difficult to determine whether they are in a state of *imperfect subjection* or in a *perfect* state of *nature:* as the KING of NAPLES with respect to the POPE.

XVI. In the same manner, also, it may be conceived, without entering into details, how any single person, born, as all persons are, into a state of perfect subjection to his parents, that is into a state of perfect political society with respect to his parents, may from thence pass into a perfect state of nature; and from thence successively into any number of different states of political society more or less perfect, by passing into different societies.

XVII. In the same manner also it may be conceived how, in any political society, the same man may, with respect to the same individuals, be, at different periods, and on different occasions, alternately, in the state of governor and subject: to-day concurring, perhaps active, in the business of issuing a *general* command for the observance of the whole society, amongst the rest of another man in quality of *Judge:* to-morrow, punished, perhaps, by a *particular* command of that same Judge for not obeying the general command which he himself (I mean the person acting in character of governor) had issued. I need scarce remind the reader how happily this alternate state of *authority* and *submission* is exemplified among ourselves.

XIX. In the same manner, also, it may be conceived, how the same set of men considered *among themselves*, may at one time be in a state of nature, at another time in a state of government. For the habit of obedience, in whatever degree of perfection it be necessary it should subsist in order to constitute a government, may be conceived, it is plain, to suffer interruptions. At different junctures it may take place and cease.

XX. Instances of this state of things appear not to be unfrequent. The sort of society that has been observed to subsist among the AMERICAN INDIANS may afford us one. According to the accounts we have of those people, in most of their tribes, if not in all, the habit we are speaking of appears to be taken up only in time of war. It ceases again in time of peace. The necessity of acting in concert against a common enemy, subjects a whole tribe to the orders of a common chief. On the return of peace each warrior resumes his pristine independence.

XXI. One difficulty there is that still sticks by us. It has been started indeed, but not solved.—This is to find a note of distinction,— a characteristic mark, whereby to distinguish a society in which there *is* a habit of obedience, and that at the degree of perfection which is necessary to constitute a state of government, from a society in which there is *not:* a mark, I mean, which shall have a visible determinate commencement; insomuch that the instant of its first appearance shall be distinguishable from the last at which it has not as yet appeared. 'Tis only by the help of such a mark that we can be in a condition to determine, at any given time, whether any given society is in a state of government, or in a state of nature. I can find no such mark, I must confess, anywhere, unless it be this; the establishment of names of office: the appearance of a certain man, or set of men, with a certain name, serving to mark them out as objects of obedience: such as King, Sachem, Cacique, Senator, Burgomaster, and the like. This, I think, may serve tolerably well to distinguish a set of men in a state of political union among *themselves* from the *same* set of men not yet in such a state.

XXII. But suppose an incontestable political society, and that a large one, formed; and from that a smaller body to break off: by this breach the smaller body ceases to be in a state of political union with respect to the larger: and has thereby placed itself, with respect to that larger body, in a state of nature— What means shall we find of ascertaining the precise juncture at which this change took place? What shall be taken for the *characteristic mark* in this case? The appointment, it may be said, of new governors with new names. But no such appointment, suppose, takes place. The subordinate governors, from whom alone the people at large were in use to receive their commands under the old government, are the same from whom they receive them under the new one. The habit of obedience which these subordinate governors were in with respect to that single person, we will say, who was the supreme governor of the whole, is broken off insensibly and by degrees. The old names by which these subordinate governors were characterized, while they were subordinate, are continued now they are supreme. In this case it seems rather difficult to answer.

XXIII. If an example be required, we may take that of the DUTCH provinces with respect to SPAIN. These provinces were once branches of the Spanish monarchy. They have now, for a long time, been universally spoken of as independent states: independent as well of that of Spain as of every other. They are now in a state of nature with respect to Spain. They were once in a state of political union with respect to Spain: namely, in a state of subjection to a single *governor*, a King, who was King of Spain. At what precise juncture did the dissolution of this political union take place? At what precise time did these provinces cease to be subject to the King of Spain? This, I doubt, will be rather difficult to agree upon.[1]

XXIV. Suppose the defection to have begun, not by entire provinces, as in the instance just mentioned, but by a handful of fugitives, this augmented by the accession of other fugitives, and so, by degrees, to a body of men too strong to be reduced, the difficulty will be increased still farther. At what precise juncture was it that ancient ROME, or that modern VENICE, became an independent state?

XXV. In general then, at what precise juncture is it, that persons subject to a government, become, by disobedience, with respect to that government, in a state of nature? When is it, in short, that a *revolt* shall be deemed to have taken place; and when, again, is it, that that revolt shall be deemed to such a degree successful, as to have settled into *independence*?

XXVI. As it is the obedience of individuals that constitutes a state of submission, so is it their disobedience that must constitute a state of revolt. Is it then every act of disobedience that will do as much? The affirmative, certainly, is what can never be maintained: for then would there be no such thing as government to be found anywhere. Here then a distinction or two obviously presents itself. Disobedience may be distinguished into *conscious* or *unconscious:* and that, with respect as well to the *law* as to the *fact*. Disobedience that is unconscious with

[1] Upon recollection, I have some doubt whether this example would be found historically exact. If not, that of the defection of the Nabobs of Hindostan may answer the purpose. My first choice fell upon the former; supposing it to be rather better known.

respect to either, will readily, I suppose, be acknowledged not to be a revolt. Disobedience again that is conscious with respect to *both*, may be distinguished into *secret* and *open;* or, in other words, into *fraudulent* and *forcible*.[1] Disobedience that is only fraudulent, will likewise, I suppose, be readily acknowledged not to amount to a revolt.

XXVII. The difficulty that will remain will concern such disobedience only as is both *conscious* (and that as well with respect to *law* as *fact*) and *forcible*. This disobedience, it should seem, is to be determined neither by *numbers* altogether (that is, of the persons supposed to be disobedient) nor by *acts*, nor by *intentions:* all three may be fit to be taken into consideration. But having brought the difficulty to this point, at this point I must be content to leave it. To proceed any farther in the endeavor to solve it, would be to enter into a discussion of particular local jurisprudence. It would be entering upon the definition of Treason, as distinguished from Murder, Robbery, Riot, and other such crimes, as, in comparison with Treason, are spoken of as being of a more private nature. Suppose the definition of Treason settled, and the commission of an act of Treason is, as far as regards the person committing it, the characteristic mark we are in search of.

2.   *Criticism of the Social-contract Theory.   The Utilitarian Basis of Political Society* [2]

XXXVI. As to the original contract, by turns embraced and ridiculed by our Author, a few pages, perhaps, may not be ill bestowed in endeavoring to come to a precise notion about its reality and use. The stress laid on it formerly, and still, perhaps, by some, is such as renders it an object not undeserving of attention. I was in hopes, however, till I observed the notice taken of it by our Author, that this chimera had been effectually demolished by Mr. Hume. I think we hear not so much of it now as formerly. The indestructible prerogatives of mankind have no need to be supported upon the sandy foundation of a fiction.

XXXVII. With respect to this, and other fictions, there was

[1] If examples be thought necessary, Theft may serve for an example of *fraudulent* disobedience; Robbery of *forcible*. In Theft, the *person* of the disobedient party, and the *act* of disobedience, are both endeavored to be kept secret. In Robbery, the *act* of disobedience, at least, if not the *person* of him who disobeys, is manifest and avowed.

[2] Ch. I, pars. xxxvi–xlviii.

once a time, perhaps, when they had their use. With instruments of this temper, I will not deny but that some political work may have been done, and that useful work, which, under the then circumstances of things, could hardly have been done with any other. But the season of *Fiction* is now over: insomuch, that what formerly might have been tolerated and countenanced under that name, would, if now attempted to be set on foot, be censured and stigmatized under the harsher appellations of *incroachment* or *imposture*. To attempt to introduce any *new* one, would be *now* a crime: for which reason there is much danger, without any use, in vaunting and propagating such as have been introduced already. In point of political discernment, the universal spread of learning has raised mankind in a manner to a level with each other, in comparison of what they have been in any former time: nor is any man now so far elevated above his fellows, as that he should be indulged in the dangerous license of cheating them for their good.

XXXVIII. As to the fiction now before us, in the character of an *argumentum ad hominem* coming when it did, and managed as it was, it succeeded to admiration.

That compacts, by whomsoever entered into, *ought* to be kept; —that men are *bound* by compacts, are propositions which men, without knowing or inquiring why, were disposed universally to accede to. The observance of promises they had been accustomed to see pretty constantly enforced. They had been accustomed to see kings, as well as others, behave themselves as if bound by them. This proposition, then, "that men are bound by *compacts*;" and this other, "that, if one party performs not his part, the other is released from his," being propositions which no man disputed, were propositions which no man had any call to prove. In theory they were assumed for axioms: and in practice they were observed as rules. If, on any occasion, it was thought proper to make a show of proving them, it was rather for form's sake than for anything else: and that, rather in the way of memento or instruction to acquiescing auditors, than in the way of proof against opponents. On such an occasion the commonplace retinue of phrases was at hand; *Justice, Right Reason* required it the *Law of Nature* commanded it, and so forth; all which are but so many ways of intimating that a man is firmly persuaded of the truth of this or that moral proposition, though he either thinks he *need not*, or finds he *can't*, tell *why*. Men were too obviously and too generally interested in the observance of these rules to entertain doubts concerning the force of any arguments they saw employed in their support.—It is an old observation how Interest smooths the road to Faith.

XXXIX. A compact, then, it was said, was made by the King and people: the terms of it were to this effect. The people, on their part, promised to the King a *general obedience*. The King, on his part, promised to *govern* the people in such a *particular* manner always, as should be *subservient* to their happiness. I insist not on the words: I undertake only for the sense; as far as an imaginary engagement, so loosely and so variously worded by those who have imagined it, is capable of any decided signification. Assuming then, as a general rule, that promises, when made, ought to be observed; and, as a point of fact, that a promise to this effect in particular had been made by the party in question, men were more ready to deem themselves qualified to judge when it was such a promise was *broken*, than to decide directly and avowedly on the delicate question, when it was that a King acted so far in *opposition* to the happiness of his people, that it were better no longer to obey him.

XL. It is manifest, on a very little consideration, that nothing was gained by this maneuver after all: no difficulty removed by it. It was still necessary, and that as much as ever, that the question men studied to avoid should be determined, in order to determine the question they thought to substitute in its room. It was still necessary to determine, whether the King in question had, or had not acted so far in *opposition* to the happiness of his people, that it were better no longer to obey him; in order to determine, whether the promise he was supposed to have made, had, or had not been broken. For what was the supposed purport of this promise? It was no other than what has just been mentioned.

XLI. Let it be said, that part at least of this promise was to govern in *subservience to Law:* that hereby a more precise rule was laid down for his conduct, by means of this supposal of a promise, than that other loose and general rule to govern in subservience to the *happiness of his people:* and that, by this means, it is the letter of the *Law* that forms the tenor of the rule.

Now true it is, that the governing in opposition to Law, is *one* way of governing in opposition to the happiness of the people: the natural effect of such a contempt of the Law being, if not actually to destroy, at least to threaten with destruction, all those rights and privileges that are founded on it: rights and privileges on the enjoyment of which that happiness depends. But still it is not this that can be safely taken for the entire purport of the promise here in question: and that for several reasons. *First,* because the most mischievous, and under certain constitutions the most feasible, method of governing in opposition to the happiness of the people, is, by setting the Law itself in opposition to their happiness. *Secondly,* because it is a case very conceivable, that a King may, to a great degree, impair the happiness of his people without violating the letter of any single Law. *Thirdly,* because extraordinary occasions may now and then occur, in which the happiness of the people may be better promoted by acting, for the moment, in *opposition* to the Law, than in *subservience* to it. *Fourthly,* because it is not any single violation of the Law, as such, that can properly be taken for a breach of his part of the contract, so as to be understood to have released the people from the obligation of performing theirs. For, to quit the fiction, and resume the language of plain truth, it is scarce ever any single violation of the Law that, by being *submitted to,* can produce so much mischief as shall surpass the probable mischief of *resisting* it. If every single instance whatever of such a violation were to be deemed an entire dissolution of the contract, a man who reflects at all would scarce find anywhere, I believe, under the sun, that government which he could allow to subsist for twenty years together. It is plain, therefore, that to pass any sound decision upon the question which the inventors of this fiction substituted instead of the true one, the latter was still necessary to be decided. All they gained by their contrivance was the convenience of deciding it obliquely, as it were, and by a side wind—that is, in a crude and hasty way, without any direct and steady examination.

XLII. But, after all, for what *reason* is it, that men *ought* to keep their promises? The moment any intelligible reason is given, it is this: that it is for the *advantage* of society they should keep them; and if they do not, that, as far as *punishment* will go, they should be *made* to keep them. It is for the advantage of the whole number that the promises of each individual should be kept: and, rather than they should not be kept, that such individuals as fail to keep them should be punished. If it be asked, how this appears? the answer is at hand:—Such is the benefit to gain, and mischief to avoid, by keeping them, as much more than compensates the mischief of so much punishment as is requisite to oblige men to it. Whether the dependence of *benefit* and *mischief* (that is, of *pleasure* and *pain*) upon men's conduct in this behalf, be as here stated, is a question of *fact*, to be decided, in the same manner that all other questions of fact are to be decided, by testimony, observation, and experience.

XLIII. This then, and no other, being the *reason* why men should be made to keep their promises, viz. that it is for the advantage of society that they should, is a reason that may as well be given at once, why *Kings*, on the one hand, in governing, should in general keep within established Laws, and (to speak universally) abstain from all such measures as tend to the unhappiness of their subjects: and, on the other hand, why *subjects* should obey Kings as long as they so conduct themselves, and no longer; why they should obey in short *so long as the probable mischiefs of obedience are less than the probable mischiefs of resistance;* why, in a word, taking the whole body together, it is their *duty* to obey, just so long as it is their *interest,* and no longer. This being the case, what need of saying of the one, that *he* PROMISED so to *govern;* of the other, that they PROMISED so to *obey,* when the fact is otherwise?

XLIV. True it is, that, in this country, according to ancient forms, some sort of vague promise of *good government* is made by Kings at the ceremony of their coronation: and let the acclamations, perhaps given, perhaps not given, by chance persons out of the surrounding multitude, be construed into a promise of *obedience* on the part of the *whole* multitude: that whole multitude itself, a small drop collected together by chance out of the ocean of the state: and let the two promises thus made be deemed to have formed a perfect *compact:*—not that either of them is declared to be the *consideration* of the other.

XLV. Make the most of this concession, one experiment there is, by which every reflecting man may satisfy himself, I think, beyond a doubt, that it is the consideration of *utility,* and no other, that, secretly but unavoidably, has governed his judgment upon all these matters. The experiment is easy and decisive. It is but to reverse, in supposition, in the first place the import of the *particular* promise thus feigned; in the next place, the effect in point of *utility* of the observance of promises *in general.*— Suppose the King to promise that he would govern his subjects *not* according to Law; *not* in the view to promote their happiness: —would this be binding upon *him?* Suppose the people to promise they would obey him *at all events,* let him govern as he will; let him govern to their destruction. Would this be binding upon *them?* Suppose the constant and universal effect of an observance of promises were to produce *mischief,* would it *then* be men's *duty* to observe them? Would it *then* be *right* to make Laws, and apply punishment to *oblige* men to observe them?

XLVI. "No" (it may perhaps be replied); "but for this

reason; among promises, some there are that, as every one allows, are void: now these you have been supposing, are unquestionably of the number. A promise that is in itself *void*, cannot, it is true, create any obligation. But allow the promise to be *valid*, and it is the promise itself that creates the obligation, and nothing else." The fallacy of this argument it is easy to perceive. For what is it then that the promise depends on for its *validity?* what is it that being *present* makes it *valid?* what is it that being *wanting* makes it *void?* To acknowledge that any *one* promise may be void, is to acknowledge that if any *other* is *binding*, it is not merely because it is a promise. That circumstance then, whatever it be, on which the validity of a promise depends, that circumstance, I say, and not the promise itself must, it is plain, be the cause of the obligation on which a promise is apt in general to carry with it.

XLVII. But farther. Allow, for argument sake, what we have disproved: allow that the obligation of a promise is independent of every other: allow that a promise is binding *propriâ vi* —Binding then on whom? On him certainly who makes it. Admit this: for what reason is the same individual promise to be binding on those who *never* made it? The King, *fifty years ago*, promised my *Great-Grandfather* to govern him according to Law: my Great-Grandfather, *fifty years ago*, promised the King to obey him according to Law. The King, *just now*, promised my *neighbor* to govern him according to Law: my neighbor, *just now*, promised the King to obey him according to Law.—Be it so— What are these promises, all or any of them, to *me?* To make answer to this question, some other principle, it is manifest, must be resorted to, than that of the *intrinsic* obligation of promises upon those who make them.

XLVIII. Now this *other* principle that still recurs upon us, what other can it be than the *principle of* UTILITY? The principle which furnishes us with that *reason*, which alone depends not upon any higher reason, but which is itself the sole and all-sufficient reason for every point of practice whatsoever.

8. Criticism of the Theory that Laws of Nature are Limitations upon Sovereignty. The Character of Free Government [1]

XIX. The propriety of this dangerous maxim, so far as the Divine Law is concerned, is what I must refer to a future occasion for more particular consideration. As to the LAW *of Nature*, if (as I trust it will appear) it be nothing but a phrase; if there be no

[1] Ch. IV, pars. xix–xli; ch. V, pars. vii–viii.

other medium for proving any act to be an offense against it, than the mischievous tendency of such act; if there be no other medium for proving a law of the *state* to be contrary to it, than the *inexpediency* of such law, unless the bare unfounded disapprobation of any one who thinks of it be called a proof; if a test for distinguishing such laws as would be *contrary* to the LAW *of Nature* from such as, *without* being contrary to it, are simply *inexpedient*, be that which neither our Author nor any man else so much as pretended ever to give; if, in a word, there be scarce any law whatever but what those who have not liked it have found, on some account or another, to be repugnant to some text of scripture; I see no remedy but that the natural tendency of such doctrine is to impel a man, by the force of conscience, to rise up in arms against any law whatever that he happens not to like. What sort of government it is that can consist with such a disposition, I must leave to our Author to inform us.

XX. It is the principle of *utility*, accurately apprehended and steadily applied, that affords the only clue to guide a man through these straits. It is for that, if any, and for that alone to furnish a decision which neither party shall dare in *theory* to disavow. It is something to reconcile men even in theory. They are at least, *something* nearer to an effectual union, than when at variance as well in respect of theory as of practice.

XXI. In speaking of the supposed contract between King and people, I have already had occasion to give the description, and, as it appears to me, the only *general* description that *can* be given, of that juncture at which, and not before, resistance to government becomes *commendable;* or, in other words, reconcilable to just notions, whether of *legal* or not, at least of *moral*, and, if there be any difference, *religious* duty. What was there said was spoken, at the time, with reference to that particular branch of government which was then in question; the branch that in this country is administered by the King. But if it was just, as applied to *that* branch of government, and in *this* country, it could only be for the same reason that it is so when applied to the *whole* of government, and that in *any* country whatsoever. It is *then*, we may say, and not till then, allowable to, if not incumbent on, every man, as well on the score of *duty* as of *interest*, to enter into measures of resistance; when, according to the best calculation he is able to make, *the probable mischiefs of resistance* (speaking with respect to the community in general) *appear less to him than the probable mischiefs of submission.* This then is to him, that is to each man in particular, the *juncture for resistance*.

XXII. A natural question here is—by what *sign* shall this juncture be known? By what *common* signal alike conspicuous and perceptible to all? A question which is readily enough started, but to which, I hope, it will be almost as readily perceived that it is impossible to find an answer. *Common* sign for such a purpose, I, for my part, know of none: he must be more than a prophet, I think, that can show us one. For that which shall serve a particular person, I have already given one—his own internal persuasion of a balance of *utility* on the side of resistance.

XXIII. Unless such a sign then, which I think impossible, can be shown, the *field*, if one may say so, of the supreme governor's authority, though not *infinite*, must unavoidably, I think, *unless where limited by express convention*, be allowed to be *indefinite*. Nor can I see any narrower, or other bounds to it, under this constitution, or under any other yet *freer* constitution, if there be one, than under the most *despotic*. *Before* the juncture I have been describing were arrived, resistance, even in a country like this, would come too soon: were the juncture arrived *already*, the time for resistance would be come already, under such a government even as any one should call *despotic*.

XXIV. In regard to a government that is *free*, and one that is *despotic*, wherein is it then that the difference consists? Is it that those persons in whose hands that power is lodged which is acknowledged to be supreme, have less power in the one than in the other, when it is from custom that they derive it? By no means. Is it not that the power of one any more than of the other has any certain bounds to it? The distinction turns upon circumstances of a very different complexion:—on the *manner* in which that whole mass of power, which, taken together, is supreme, is, in a free state, *distributed* among the several ranks of persons that are sharers in it:—on the *source* from whence their titles to it are successively derived:—on the frequent and easy *changes* of condition between govern*ors* and govern*ed;* whereby the interests of the one class are more or less indistinguishably blended with those of the other:—on the *responsibility* of the governors; or the right which a subject has of having the reasons publicly assigned and canvassed of every act of power that is exerted over him:— on the *liberty of the press;* or the security with which every man, be he of the one class or the other, may make known his complaints and remonstrances to the whole community:—on the *liberty of public association;* or the security with which malcontents may communicate their sentiments, concert their plans, and practice every mode of opposition short of actual revolt, before the executive power can be legally justified in disturbing them.

XXV. True then, it may be, that, owing to this last circumstance in particular, in a state thus circumstanced, the road to a revolution, if a revolution be necessary, is to appearance shorter; certainly more smooth and easy. More likelihood certainly there is of its being such a revolution as shall be the work of a number; and in which, therefore, the interests of a number are likely to be consulted. Grant then, that by reason of these facilitating circumstances, the juncture itself may arrive sooner, and upon less provocation, under what is called a *free* government, than under what is called an *absolute* one: grant this;—yet till it *be* arrived, resistance is as much too soon under one of them as under the other.

XXVI. Let us avow then, in short, steadily but calmly, what our Author hazards with anxiety and agitation, that the authority of the supreme body cannot, *unless where limited by express convention,* be said to have any assignable, any certain bounds.— That to say there is any act they *cannot* do,—to speak of anything of theirs as being *illegal*,—as being *void;*—to speak of their exceeding their *authority* (whatever be the phrase)—their *power*, their *right*,—is, however common, an abuse of language.

XXVII. The legislature *cannot* do it? The legislature *cannot* make a law to this effect? Why cannot? What is there that should hinder them? Why not this, as well as so many other laws murmured at, perhaps, as inexpedient, yet submitted to without any question of the *right?* With men of the same party, with men whose affections are already lifted against the law in question, anything will go down: any rubbish is good that will add fuel to the flame. But with regard to an impartial bystander, it is plain that it is not denying the right of the legislature, their *authority*, their *power*, or whatever be the word—it is not denying that they *can* do what is in question—it is not that, I say, or any discourse verging that way than can tend to give *him* the smallest satisfaction.

XXVIII. Grant even the proposition in general:—What are we the nearer? Grant that there *are* certain bounds to the *authority* of the legislature:—Of what use is it to say so, when these bounds are what no body has ever attempted to mark out to any useful purpose; that is, in any such manner whereby it might be known beforehand what description a law must be of to fall *within*, and what to fall *beyond* them? Grant that there *are* things which the legislature *cannot* do;—grant that there *are* laws

which exceed the *power* of the legislature to establish. What rule
does this sort of discourse furnish us for determining whether any
one that is in question is, or is not of the number? As far as I
can discover, none. Either the discourse goes on in the confusion
it began; either all rests in vague assertions, and no intelligible
argument at all is offered; or if any, such arguments as are drawn
from the principle of *utility:* arguments which, in whatever variety
of words expressed, come at last to neither more nor less than this;
that the tendency of the law is, to a greater or a less degree,
pernicious. If this then be the result of the argument, why not
come home to it at once? Why turn aside into a wilderness of
sophistry, when the path of plain reason is straight before us?

XXIX. What practical inferences those who maintain this
language mean should be deduced from it, is not altogether clear;
nor, perhaps, does every one mean the same. Some who speak of
a law as being *void* (for to this expression, not to travel through the
whole list, I shall confine myself) would persuade us to look upon
the authors of it as having thereby *forfeited*, as the phrase is, their
whole power: as well that of giving force to the particular law in
question, as to any other. These are they who, had they arrived
at the same practical conclusion through the principle of utility,
would have spoken of the law as being to such a degree pernicious,
as that, were the bulk of the community to see it in its true light,
*the probable mischief of resisting it would be less than the probable
mischief of submitting to it.* These point, in the first instance, at
hostile opposition.

XXX. Those who say nothing about forfeiture are commonly
less violent in their views. These are they who, were they to
ground themselves on the principle of utility, and, to use our
language, would have spoken of the law as being mischievous
indeed, but without speaking of it as being mischievous to the
degree that has been just mentioned. The mode of opposition
which they point to is one which passes under the appellation of
a *legal* one.

XXXI. Admit then the law to be void in their sense, and
mark the consequences. The idea annexed to the epithet *void*
is obtained from those instances in which we see it applied to a
private instrument. The consequence of a *private* instrument's
being void is, that all persons concerned are to act as if no such
instrument had existed. The consequence, accordingly, of a *law's*
being void must be, that people shall act as if there were no such
law about the matter: and therefore that if any person in virtue of
the mandate of the law should do anything in coercion of another

person, which without such law he would be punishable for doing, he would still be punishable; to wit, by appointment of the judicial power. Let the law, for instance, be a law imposing a tax: a man who should go about to levy the tax by force would be punishable as a trespasser: should he chance to be killed in the attempt, the person killing him would *not* be punishable as for murder: should he kill, he himself *would*, perhaps, be punishable as for murder. To whose office does it appertain to do those acts in virtue of which such punishment would be inflicted? To that of the Judges. Applied to practice then, the effect of this language is, by an appeal made to the Judges, to confer on those magistrates a controlling power over the acts of the legislature.

XXXII. By this management a *particular* purpose might perhaps, by chance be answered: and let this be supposed a good one. Still what benefit would, from the *general* tendency of such a doctrine, and such a practice in conformity to it, accrue to the body of the people is more than I can conceive. A Parliament, let it be supposed, is too much under the influence of the Crown: pays too little regard to the sentiments and the interests of the people. Be it so. The people at any rate, if not so great a share as they might and ought to have, have had, at least, *some* share in choosing it. Give to the Judges a power of annulling its acts; and you transfer a portion of the supreme power from an assembly which the people have had *some* share, at least, in choosing, to a set of men in the choice of whom they have not the least imaginable share: to a set of men appointed solely by the Crown: appointed *solely*, and avowedly and *constantly*, by that very magistrate whose partial and occasional influence is the very grievance you seek to remedy.

XXXIII. In the heat of debate, some, perhaps, would be for saying of this management that it was transferring at once the supreme authority from the legislative power to the judicial. But this would be going too far on the other side. There is a wide difference between a *positive* and a *negative* part in legislation. There is a wide difference again between a negative upon *reasons* given, and a negative without any. The power of *repealing* a law even for reasons given is a great power: too great indeed for Judges: but still very distinguishable from, and much inferior to that of *making* one.[1]

[1] Notwithstanding what has been said, it would be in vain to dissemble, but that, upon occasion, an appeal of this sort may very well answer, and has, indeed, in general, a tendency to answer, in some sort, the purposes of those who espouse, or profess to espouse, the interests of the people. A public and authorized debate on the propriety of the law is by this means brought on. The

XXXIV. Let us now go back a little. In denying the existence of any assignable bounds to the supreme power, I added,
"unless where limited by express convention:" for this exception
I could not but subjoin. Our Author indeed, in that passage in
which, short as it is, he is the most explicit, leaves, we may observe,
no room for it. "However they began," says he (speaking of
the several forms of government), "however they began, and by
what right soever they subsist, there is and must be in ALL of
them an authority that is absolute."—To say this, however, of
all governments without exception;—to say that *no* assemblage of
men can subsist in a state of government, without being subject to
some *one* body whose authority stands unlimited so much as by
convention; to say, in short, that not even by convention can any
limitation be made to the power of that body in a state which in
other respects is supreme, would be saying, I take it, rather too
much: it would be saying that there is no such thing as government in the German Empire; nor in the Dutch Provinces; nor in
the Swiss Cantons; nor was of old in the Achæan league.

XXXV. In this mode of limitation I see not what there is that
need surprise us. By what is it that any degree of *power* (meaning
political power) is established? It is neither more nor less, as we
have already had occasion to observe, than a habit of, and disposition to, obedience: *habit*, speaking with respect to *past* acts; *disposition*, with respect to *future*. This disposition it is as easy, or I am
much mistaken, to conceive as being absent with regard to one sort
of acts; as present with regard to other. For a body then, which
is in other respects supreme, to be conceived as being with respect
to a certain sort of acts, limited, all that is necessary is that this
sort of acts be in its description distinguishable from every other.

XXXVI. By means of a convention then we are furnished
with that common signal which, in other cases, we despaired of
finding. A certain act is in the instrument of convention specified,
with respect to which the government is therein precluded from
issuing a law to a certain effect: whether to the effect of commanding the act, of permitting it, or of forbidding it. A law is
issued to that effect notwithstanding. The issuing then of such
a law (the sense of it, and likewise the sense of that part of the
convention which provides against it being supposed clear) is a
fact notorious and visible to all: in the issuing then of such a law

artillery of the tongue is played off against the law, under cover of the law
itself. An opportunity is gained of impressing sentiments unfavorable to it,
upon a numerous and attentive audience. As to any other effects from such an
appeal, let us believe that in the instances in which we have seen it made, it is
the certainty of miscarriage that has been the encouragement to the attempt.

we have a fact which is *capable* of being taken for that common
signal we have been speaking of. These bounds the supreme
body in question has marked out to its authority: of such a de-
marcation then what is the effect? either none at all, or this:
that the disposition to obedience confines itself within these
bounds. Beyond them the disposition is stopped from extending:
beyond them the subject is no more prepared to obey the governing body of his own state than that of any other. What difficulty,
I say, there should be in conceiving a state of things to subsist
in which the supreme authority is thus limited,—what greater
difficulty in conceiving it with this limitation, than without any,
I cannot see. The two states are, I must confess, to me alike
conceivable: whether alike expedient,—alike conducive to the
happiness of the people, is another question.

XXXVII. God forbid, that from anything here said it should
be concluded that in any society any convention is or can be made,
which shall have the effect of setting up an insuperable bar to
that which the parties affected shall deem a reformation:—God
forbid that any disease in the constitution of a state should be
without its remedy. Such might by some be thought to be the
case, where that supreme body ' which in such a convention
was one of the contracting parties, having incorporated itself
with that which was the other, no longer subsists to give any new
modification to the engagement. Many ways might however be
found to make the requisite alteration, without any departure
from the spirit of the engagement. Although that body itself
which contracted the engagement be no more, a *larger body*, from
whence the first is understood to have derived its title, may still
subsist. Let this larger body be consulted. Various are the ways
that might be conceived of doing this, and that without any dis-
paragement to the dignity of the subsisting legislature: of doing
it, I mean to such effect, as that, should the sense of such *larger
body* be favorable to the alteration, it may be made by a law,
which, in this case, neither ought to be, nor probably would be,
regarded by the body of the people as a breach of the convention.[1]

---

[1] In Great Britain, for instance, suppose it were deemed necessary to make an
alteration in the Act of Union. If in an article stipulated in favor of England,
there need be no difficulty; so that there were a majority for the alteration
among the English members, without reckoning the Scotch. The only difficulty would be with respect to an article stipulated in favor of Scotland; on
account, to wit, of the small number of the Scotch members, in comparison
with the English. In such a case, it would be highly expedient, to say no more,
for the sake of preserving the public faith, and to avoid irritating the body of
the nation, to take some method for making the establishment of the new law,
depend upon their sentiments. One such method might be as follows. Let the

XXXVIII. To return for a moment to the language used by those who speak of the supreme power as being limited in its own nature. One thing I would wish to have remembered. What is here said of the impropriety and evil influence of that kind of discourse, is not intended to convey the smallest censure on those who use it, as if intentionally accessory to the ill effects it has a tendency to produce. It is rather a misfortune in the language, than a fault of any person in particular. The original of it is lost in the darkness of antiquity. We inherited it from our fathers, and, mauger all its inconveniencies, are likely, I doubt, to transmit it to our children.

XXXIX. I cannot look upon this as a mere dispute of words. I cannot help persuading myself, that the disputes between contending parties—between the defenders of a law and the opposers of it, would stand a much better chance of being adjusted than at present, were they but explicitly and constantly referred at once to the principle of UTILITY. The footing on which this principle rests every dispute, is that of matter of fact; that is, future fact —the probability of certain future contingencies. Were the debate then conducted under the auspices of this principle, one of two things would happen: either men would come to an agreement concerning that probability, or they would see at length, after due discussion of the real grounds of the dispute, that no agreement was to be hoped for. They would at any rate see clearly and explicitly the point on which the disagreement turned. The discontented party would then take their resolution to resist or to submit, upon just grounds, according as it should appear to them worth their while—according to what should appear to them the importance of the matter in dispute — according to what should appear to them the probability or improbability of success—*according*, in short, *as the mischiefs of submission should appear to bear a less or a greater ratio to the mischiefs of*

new law in question be enacted in the common form. But let its commencement be deferred to a distant period, suppose a year or two: let it then, at the end of that period, be in force, unless petitioned against, by persons of such a description, and in such a number as might be supposed fairly to represent the sentiments of the people in general: persons, for instance, of the description of those who at the time of the Union, constituted the body of electors. To put the validity of the law out of dispute, it would be necessary the fact upon which it was made ultimately to depend, should be in its nature too notorious to be controverted. To determine, therefore, whether the conditions upon which the invalidation of it was made to depend, had been complied with, is what must be left to the simple declaration of some person or persons; for instance the King. I offer this only as a general idea: and as one among many that perhaps might be offered in the same view. It will not be expected that I should here answer objections, or enter into details.

resistance. But the door to reconcilement would be much more open, when they saw that it might be not a mere affair of passion, but a difference of judgment, and that, for anything they could know to the contrary, a sincere one, that was the ground of quarrel.

XL. All else is but womanish scolding and childish altercation, which is sure to irritate, and which never can persuade.—"*I* say, the legislature can*not* do this—*I* say, that it *can*. *I* say, that to do this, *exceeds* the bounds of its *authority*—*I* say, it does *not*."— It is evident, that a pair of disputants setting out in this manner, may go on irritating and perplexing one another for everlasting, without the smallest chance of ever coming to an agreement. It is no more than announcing, and that in an obscure and at the same time, a peremptory and captious manner, their opposite persuasions, or rather affections, on a question of which neither of them sets himself to discuss the grounds. The question of utility, all this while, most probably, is never so much as at all brought upon the carpet: if it be, the language in which it is discussed is sure to be warped and clouded to make it match with the obscure and entangled pattern we have seen.

XLI. On the other hand, had the debate been originally and avowedly instituted on the footing of utility, the parties might at length have come to an agreement; or at least to a visible and explicit issue.—"*I* say, that the mischiefs of the measure in question are to *such* an amount.—*I* say, *not* so, but to a *less*.—*I* say, the benefits of it are only to *such* an amount.—*I* say, *not* so, but to a *greater*."—This, we see, is a ground of controversy very different from the former. The question is now manifestly a question of conjecture concerning so many future contingent matters of fact: to solve it, both parties then are naturally directed to support their respective persuasions by the only evidence the nature of the case admits of;—the evidence of such *past* matters of fact as appear to be analogous to those contingent *future* ones. Now these *past* facts are almost always numerous: so numerous, that till brought into view for the purpose of the debate, a great proportion of them are what may very fairly have escaped the observation of one of the parties: and it is owing, perhaps, to this and nothing else, that that party is of the persuasion which sets it at variance with the other. Here, then, we have a plain and open road, perhaps, to present reconcilement: at the worst to an intelligible and explicit issue,—that is, to such a ground of difference as may, when thoroughly trodden and explored, be found to lead on to reconcilement at the last. Men, let them but once clearly understand one another, will not be long ere they agree. It is the perplexity of ambiguous and sophistical discourse that, while it distracts and eludes the apprehension, stimulates and inflames the passions.

VII.[1] I understand, I think, pretty well, what is meant by the word *duty* (political duty) when applied to myself; and I could not persuade myself, I think, to apply it in the same sense in a regular didactic discourse to those whom I am speaking of as my supreme governors. That is my *duty* to do, which I am liable to be *punished*, according to law, if I do not do: this is the original, ordinary, and proper sense of the word *duty*. Have these supreme governors any such duty? No: for if they are at all liable to punishment according to law, whether it be for *not* doing anything, or for *doing*, they are not, what they are supposed to be, supreme governors: those are the supreme governors, by whose appointment the former are liable to be punished.

VIII. The word duty, then, if applied to persons spoken of as supreme governors, is evidently applied to them in a sense which is figurative and improper: nor therefore are the same conclusions to be drawn from any propositions in which it is used in this sense, as might be drawn from them if it were used in the other sense, which is its proper one.

SELECTED BIBLIOGRAPHY

Dunning, William A., *Political Theories, from Rousseau to Spencer*, ch. 6.
Sabine, George H., *History of Political Theory*, pp. 649–654.
Brinton, Crane, *English Political Thought in the Nineteenth Century* (London, 1933), pp. 14–30.
Wallas, Graham, "Bentham as Political Inventor," in *Contemporary Review*, vol. 129 (1926), pp. 308–319.
Graham, William, *English Political Philosophy from Hobbes to Maine* (London, 1899), pp. 174–270.
Dicey, A. V., *Lectures on the Relation between Law and Public Opinion in England* (second ed., London, 1914), lecture vi.
Halévy, Élie, *The Growth of Philosophic Radicalism*, translated by Mary Morris (New York, 1928), esp. pt. i, chs. 1–3; pt. ii, chs. 1, 3; pt. iii, chs. 2, 3.
Maccunn, John, *Six Radical Thinkers* (London, 1907), ch. 1.
Mill, John Stuart, *Dissertations and Discussions, Political, Philosophical, and Historical*, 4 vols. (New York, 1874), Vol. I, pp. 355–417.
Stephen, Leslie, *The English Utilitarians*, 3 vols. (New York, 1900), Vol. I, chs. 5–6.
Allen, J. W., "Jeremy Bentham," in F. J. C. Hearnshaw, ed., *Social and Political Ideas of Some Representative Thinkers of the Revolutionary Era* (London, 1931), ch. 7.

INDEX

Appointment of officials: Aristotle, 92–4.

Aristocracy: Plato, 35 ff; Aristotle, 73, 79, 82, 84; Polybius, 119–120; Cicero, 140–1; Harrington, 513–4; Montesquieu, 604–6, 611–2.

Aristotle: on the end, nature, and origin of the state, 55–8, 60–1, 71–2; on the family-household, 56, 58; on man "by nature a political animal," 57; on slavery, 58–60; on citizens, 61–3; on the location of supreme power in government, 64 ff; on the nature of a constitution, 71, 80; forms of state compared, 71 ff; on the distinction between democracy and oligarchy, 73–4; on royalty, 74–9; on the rule of law, 76–8; on democracy, 80 ff, 87–9; on polity, 81 ff; on aristocracy, 73, 79, 82, 84; on the relativity of forms of government, 80–1, 83–4; on government by the middle class, 84–7; on liberty, 87–8; on the deliberative organ of government, 89–92; on the appointment of officials, 92–4; on judges, 93–4; on property, 94 ff; on the disadvantages of community of property, 94–8; on limiting the amount of property, 98–101; on the disadvantages of equalizing property, 99 ff; on conditions for the best state, 101 ff; on the proper size for a state, 102–3; on equality and inequality as causes of revolutionary change, 104–5; on other causes of revolution, 105–6; on means of preserving states, 106–9; on education in the spirit of the constitution, 109.

Augustine: on the two cities, 159 ff, 170–2; on the earthly city, 161–2; on justice as an element of the true state, 158, 165–6, 172–4; on slavery, 168–70; on the nature of a People and a Republic, 172–6.

Bentham: the definition of natural and political society, 690–6; criticism of the social-contract theory, 696–9; on utility as the basis of political obligation, 696–701; criticism of the theory of natural law and rights, 701 ff; on "free" and "despotic" government, 703–4; on judicial and other limitations of legislative authority, 704–6; on conventions as limitations on sovereignty, 707–9; on utility as a limitation on sovereignty, 705, 709–11.

Bodin: definition of a state, 370–1; definition of citizen, 371–3; definition of sovereignty, 374–5; on the limits of sovereignty, 375–9; on the function of the sovereign in giving laws, 379–80; on the other functions of sovereignty, 380.

Calvin: on the necessity of civil government, 335–8; on the duty of obedience to civil magistrates, 339–44; on the right of disobedience, 344–5.

Checks and balances: Polybius, 121–5; Harrington, 513–7; Montesquieu, 618–28.

Cicero: on the duty of public service, 130–4; on the nature of a commonwealth, 135; a comparison of forms of government, 135 ff; on democracy, 138–41; on aristocracy, 140–1; on monarchy, 140–1, 144; on mixed government, 137–141; on the cycle of governments, 142 ff; on tyranny, 142, 143–4; on the nature of law, 144 ff; on natural law, 145–51.

Citizenship: Aristotle, 61–3; Marsiglio, 250; Bodin, 371–3.

Civil rights: Milton, 439–41; Paine, 675–6.

Classes in political society: Plato, 18–25.

713